THE COMPLETE
RHYMING
DICTIONARY
AND
POET'S CRAFT BOOK

THE COMPLETE
RHYMING
DICTIONARY
AND
POET'S CRAFT BOOK

Edited by

CLEMENT WOOD

DOUBLEDAY & COMPANY, INC.
Garden City, New York

PRINTED IN THE UNITED STATES OF AMERICA

TO GLORIA GODDARD

ACKNOWLEDGMENTS

ACKNOWLEDGMENT is gratefully made to the following publishers and poets, for the portions of their work used as illustrations herein:

Publisher	Author	Poem Source
Boni & Liveright	Samuel Hoffenstein	Poems in Praise of Practically Nothing
The Century Company	Brander Matthews	En Route
Dodd Mead & Company	Austin Dobson	July; The Ballade of Prose and Rhyme
Dodd Mead & Company	Carolyn Wells	Four Limericks
Doubleday, Doran & Company	Rudyard Kipling	The Sons of Martha
Henry Holt & Company	Walter de la Mare	The Listeners
Henry Holt & Company	Robert Frost	The Death of the Hired Man; The Black Cottage; "Out, Out—"
Henry Holt & Company	Carl Sandburg	Cahoots; Cool Tombs; Fog
Houghton, Mifflin & Company	Guy Wetmore Carryll	How the Helpmate of Bluebeard Made Free with a Door
Alfred A. Knopf, Inc.	John V. A. Weaver	Sonnet
The Macmillan Company	Edwin Arlington Robinson	Merlin; Roman Bartholow
Manas Press	Adelaide Crapsey	Triad
	Samuel Minturn Peck	"Before the Dawn"
The Poets Press	Clement Wood	Canopus; The Flight of the Eagle
Charles Scribner's Sons	Henry Cuyler Bunner	A Pitcher of Mignonette; Behold the Deeds!
Charles Scribner's Sons	William Ernest Henley	Ballade of Dead Actors
Charles Scribner's Sons	Edwin Arlington Robinson	The House on the Hill
Small, Maynard & Company	Charlotte Perkins Gilman	Homes; A Man Must Live
Frederick A. Stokes Company	Alfred Noyes	Marchaunt Adventurers

FOREWORD

THE desire to write poetry, or at least acceptable verse, is almost universal. The achievement of this desire may be gained by anyone, without excessive effort. Almost everyone, at some stage of his or her life, has yielded to the seductive siren, and has done his or her best to write poetry. An adequate craftbook on versification is a necessity, when the urge becomes unconquerable.

When the versifier's problem is narrowed down to rhyme, the need for a convenient and logically arranged rhyming dictionary soon becames self-evident. Rhyme is exclusively a matter of sound: what the scientists call phonetics. The logically arranged rhyming dictionary must be arranged scientifically by sound; arranged phonetically, to use the scientific word. The arrangement of rhyming sounds in the present volume is wholly phonetic.

The introductory study of versification is so complete, that the book will answer almost every question on technique that any would-be poet or versifier desires to have answered. Moreover, it provides models for the most intricate forms of poetry and versification that English-speaking poets use. Following a model is at best finger-exercises. But finger-exercises must precede mastery of the keyboard.

The phonetic devices in the volume are simplified from the leading standard dictionaries, by eliminating in general all phonetic signs except those placed above the accented or rhyming syllable. Once these simple phonetic devices are understood and absorbed, poets and versifiers will begin to think accurately, scientifically and phonetically about rhymes and rhyming. The technique of rhyming will become as automatic as the technique of walking: and the poetic energy will be proportionately released for the more effective creation of poetry.

CLEMENT WOOD.

Bozenkill.

vii

CONTENTS

THE POET'S CRAFT BOOK

POETRY AND VERSIFICATION
Poetry and Verse

THE word *poetry* is often used loosely to mean whatever embodies the products of imagination and fancy, the finer emotions and the sense of ideal beauty. In this lax usage, men speak of "the poetry of motion," the poetry of Rodin or Wagner, the poetry of dahlia-raising. In accurate usage, poetry is a specific fine art, defined as follows:

> Poetry is the expression of thoughts which awake the higher and nobler emotions or their opposites, in words arranged according to some accepted convention.

This definition includes, for instance, Oriental forms of poetry, where the sole convention is the number of syllables to the line. Limiting it to usual Occidental poetry the following definition applies:

> Occidental poetry, in its usual form, is the expression of thoughts which awake the higher and nobler emotions or their opposites, in words whose rhythm tends toward uniformity or regularity, rather than toward variety.

Both prose and poetry have rhythm. But the rhythm of prose tends toward variety; and that of poetry toward regularity. There is no definite dividing line; each poet, each reader and appreciator of poetry, must arrive at his own dividing line. To some, the borderline of poetry includes only the strict regularity of Pope or Dryden, or—

> Baby in the caldron fell,—
> See the grief on mother's brow!
> Mother loved her darling well.
> Darling's quite hard-boiled by now.
>   *Baby,* Harry Graham.

No one can quarrel with this, if it is an honest boundary. To others, the magnificent wilder rhythms of Walt Whitman and

Lincoln's *Gettysburg Address* are definitely poetry. No one can quarrel with this either.

The test as to subject-matter is subjective: does the alleged poem awake in the reader the higher and nobler emotions or their opposites? Each reader, appreciator, or poet is final arbiter in this test, as in the test of technique. The expression of thoughts which fail to register emotionally with a reader as poetry is called *verse*. Thus, divided by technique, there are the two classifications, poetry and prose; divided by subject-matter and its emotional effect, there are the two classifications, poetry and verse.

Poetry in Human Affairs

Poetry preceded prose, as a persisting form of literary expression. Writing was unknown to early man; and poetry was far better adapted to be retained in the mind than its more plodding relative, prose. The conventions of poetry formed memory devices which prose lacked. In the beginning, lyric cries, folk wisdom, tales of tribal heroes, formal odes of jubilation or lamentation, religious teachings, philosophies, pseudo-sciences, histories of men, men-gods, gods and peoples, developed first in the form of poetry.

Insofar as the conventions of poetry were artificial and unnatural, poetry tended constantly to rigidify and petrify. It became artificial and unnatural, whereas prose continued natural. Man learned to write, and to preserve his writing in stone, papyrus, sheepskin, and paper. At first it was the poetry which was so preserved; at length the art patterns were broken, and humbler and more natural prose began to replace poetry. Today, we look to prose for folk wisdom, actual and fictional narratives, religious teachings, philosophies, scientific writings, and histories. Poetry, as the most concentrated and emotional expression of the soul of man, still should have its place in the lyric outbursts, the songs, of man. But poets, bound by fossilized conventions, have become a tepid social group, their words largely unimportant; and in the large prose tends today to replace poetry entirely. Many of the poets today and tomorrow seek and will to restore poetry to something of its original wide popularity, as a natural and unartificial expression of concentrated emotional speech.

Kings, rulers, statesmen, generals, philosophers, scientists, were once of necessity poets: it was their sole socially acceptable form of expression. This is so no longer. Poets were once doers; they are now at best sayers, increasingly unheard. This is one price of man's extreme specialization. The price paid may be more than the human gain, in this particular.

The Poet's Equipment

The poet, like all artists, is one of the race's sensitives: one of those more finely attuned to phrase the past and the present acceptably, and sense and phrase the future. The first necessary equipment is sincerity. This demands that commonplace phrasings must be avoided, in favor of fresh original expression of individual or group concentrated emotions. If the race recognizes these as its own, to that extent the poet will be hailed as poetically great.

Another essential is technical mastery: adeptness in the craft of poetry, skill in handling all the tools of the trade. Familiarity with all the conventions will enable you to break them and make new ones when your fresh subject-matter demands it. Technical mastery is as easy, and no easier, than learning how to raise better peas than your neighbor, or how to build better bridges and skyscrapers than anyone else. Having learned the craft, anyone with an ear for word-music can improvise flawless heroic blank verse or any other form of blank verse by the hour, or improvise elaborately rhymed sonnets with no appreciable hesitation. This is not poetry. But the familiarity with the craft makes the coming of poetry easier, in the rare hours when the poet has a concentrated word that must be said.

Poetic Greatness

One can become great poetically, either in his own sight alone or in the opinions of others, without knowledge of the craft. Homer, Sappho, Villon, Burns, made their own patterns, or poured their burning emotional beauty into ready-made patterns followed without being comprehended. The definitions of patterns were made afterwards, from a scholastic study of poetry widely recognized as great. Such greatness may be achieved by anyone

today—the entirely satisfactory expression of one's soul's yearnings. But the recognition of such greatness today will ordinarily be limited to the poet and his immediate circle of admirers within or without his family.

With a complete technical mastery of the craft of poetry, any poet today can achieve complete greatness in his own sight. Whether he is hailed by others as great, and especially whether or not his name is hailed by his own and subsequent generations as great, depends largely on the extent to which his own concentrated heart-utterances express the desires of the race, in a new, fresh and original form. Given such recognition by the race, and enduring poetic greatness has been achieved. The poet can no more control this than Cnut could act as dictator over the tide.

How Poems Come

Verse upon any theme, and in treatment ranging from the most ponderously serious to the most frivolously flippant, can be manufactured at any time. Its technique is comparatively simple. Its devices, metre, rhyme, alliteration, assonance, consonance, stanza arrangement, may be mastered as easily as multiplication tables.

Poetry comes differently. It is primarily the intellect that manufactures verse; but the intellect plays only a secondary part in creating poetry. The desire that seeks expression, which it finds in the poem, springs from a deeper basic source than thinking. Man, indeed all forms of life, are compact of desires. The fulfilment of one desire causes others to spring hydra-like from its invisible corpse. Psychologists tell us that dreams are likewise expressions of desire, in the form of desires fulfilled: that is, wish-fulfilments. Much thinking is likewise wish-fulfilment; there is truth in Wordsworth's dictum, "The wish is father to the thought." There must be, also, an obstacle to the immediate fulfilment of the wish; otherwise, the poet would proceed to achieve his wish, and have no need for a poem to express it. As one poet has it:

> Singing is sweet; but be sure of this,
> Lips only sing when they cannot kiss.
> *Art,* James Thomson.

Because of the obstacle, a tremendous inner compulsion comes upon the sensitive poet to seek relief by creating his wish-fulfilment in words: and so it is that poems are born. This inner compulsion has, as one of its names, inspiration. Inspiration blows from no outer sky, but from the universe of desires within. The woman's insistent inner compulsion to deliver her child at the appointed hour is hardly more shatteringly imperative than the true poet's insistent inner commandment to write.

At times the whole poem forms itself within the mind, before the first word is written down. At times a couplet, a single line— perhaps the first, but more often the last—or even a phrase or a mood comes first, with the dominant insistence that it be given the intermittent immortality of writing. The wise procedure for the poet is to write down what comes, as it comes, even if only a single line or less is the result. As far as possible, write out the poem without delay, to prevent another visitor from Porlock's silencing part of your poem forever, as Coleridge's *Kubla Khan* was silenced forever.

When the poem or poetic fragment is written down, the critical intellect comes into play. If technical mastery has become habitual, the intellect may have no changes to suggest. The poet who fails to be a critic as well is usually his own self-slayer. More extended poems, of course, require more preparation and slower writing and criticism. In all cases the danger is rather in the overuse of the intellect, than in the use of inspiration.

Originality in Poetry

The easiest way, in poetry, is to rephrase your own emotional reactions in the words and phrases created by the favorite poets of the past: so that a thing is "white as the driven snow," or "red as a June rose." When these similes were first invented, they were creations; their repetition, unless in slightly altered form, is plagiarism or borrowing. Second-rate poets distrust their own vision, which differs in every case from that of every other person in the world; and hence sag into such uncreative repetitions. It is wisest to be true to your own differing vision, and seek to expand the boundaries of poetry by stating your own desires in your own terms.

The weakness of much verse and some poetry of the past is partly traceable to unoriginal teachers of English or versification, who advised their pupils to saturate themselves in this or that poet, and then write. Keats, saturated in Spenser, took a long time to overcome this echoey quality, and emerge into the glorious highland of his *Hyperion.* Many lesser souls never emerge. It is valuable to know the poetry of the past, and love it. But the critical brain should carefully root out every echo, every imitation—unless some alteration in phrasing or meaning makes the altered phrase your own creation.

The present double decade has splendidly altered the technique of versification in poetry, by the addition of freer rhythms, consonance, and other devices in the direction of natural speech. It has altered the themes and subjects of poetry as much, until the *Verboten* sign is unknown to the present generations of poets, as far as themes are concerned. If the speech is natural and conversational; the treatment sincere and original; the craftsmanship matured,—there is no reason in the poet's effort to withhold him from a seat among the immortals.

II

THE TECHNIQUE OF VERSIFICATION: RHYTHM

Accent and Rhythm

RHYTHM is the emphasis structure of successive sounds. It is easy to understand, and not easy to define. In prose and poetry, it means the flow of accented and unaccented syllables. It may be defined as:

The successive rise and fall of sounds, in pitch, stress, or speed; when used of words, depending on accents, pauses, or durational quantities.

In classical Greek and Latin poetry, rhythm was not based on accent, but on the conventionalized time it took to pronounce syllables. Syllables were not accented or unaccented, as in modern poetry, from a standpoint of versification; but were long or short. Since two consonants occurring together made a syllable long, and a short vowel made a syllable short when followed by one consonant, the word *honest* was scanned as short-long: the rhythmic stress occurring on the second syllable, not on the first, as with us. *Honest,* pronounced in the classical Greek or Roman way, would be ta-TUM; with us, it is pronounced rhythmically TUM-ta, the accent falling on the first syllable.

This one example will show why verse written in English according to classical rules of scansion, based upon long and short syllables instead of accent, is unnatural and only slightly pleasing to the ear. It is no more at home among modern poets writing in English than Greek clothing or the Greek language would be.

Modern poetry written in English must be in words whose rhythm, based upon accent, tends toward uniformity, rather than toward variety. Both prose and poetry have rhythm, the stream or flow of accented and unaccented syllables; in prose, the pattern constantly varies, while in poetry it approaches some sort of regularity. This is clearly poetry:

7

Music, when soft voices die,
Vibrates in the memory—
Odours, when sweet violets sicken,
Live within the sense they quicken.

Rose leaves, when the rose is dead,
Are heap'd for the beloved's bed;
And so thy thoughts, when Thou art gone,
Love itself shall slumber on.
"Music, when Soft Voices Die,"
Percy Bysshe Shelley.

It would be no less poetry if it were set up:

Music, when soft voices die, vibrates in the memory. Odours, when sweet violets sicken, live within the sense they quicken. Rose leaves, when the rose is dead, are heap'd for the beloved's bed.

And so thy thoughts, when Thou art gone, Love itself shall slumber on.

It did not take the line-division to make this poetry. Technically, the tendency toward regularity in the rhythm made it definitely verse, and not prose; while its emotional appeal, to most people, makes it poetry. It is equally poetic in either typographic form. Set up the opening of the first chapter of this book in the same line division:

The word poetry is often used
Loosely to mean whatever embodies
The products of imagination
And fancy, the finer emotions

And the sense of ideal beauty.
In this lax usage, men speak of
"The poetry of motion," the poetry
Of Rodin or Wagner, the poetry

This is prose. No magic worked by the line division can bring it any closer to poetry. Only a comparative regularity in the alternation of accented and unaccented syllables can make it acceptable verse; this, plus the proper emotional appeal, alone can make it poetry.

Metre and Metric Feet

Metre is a comparatively regular rhythm in verse or poetry. There are four common metric feet used in English verse. Their names are taken over from classic durational or quantity metres. In the examples below, the accented syllable is marked thus (´), and the unaccented syllables thus (˘). These feet are:

Name of Foot	Scansion	Description	Example	Example scanned	Accent pronunciation
Iamb	˘ /	Unaccent—accent	Delight	De-líght	ta-TUM
Trochee	/ ˘	Accent—unaccent	Going	Gó-ing	TUM-ta
Anapest	˘ ˘ /	Unaccent—unaccent—accent	Appertain	Ap-per-táin	ta-ta-TUM
Dactyl	/ ˘ ˘	Accent—unaccent—unaccent	Merrily	Mér-ri-ly	TUM-ta-ta

The first two feet listed below are occasionally encountered in English verse; the third rarely or never.

Spondee	/ /	Accent—accent	Headlong	Héad-lóng	TUM-TUM
Amphibrach	˘ / ˘	Unaccent—accent—unaccent	Believing	Be-líev-ing	ta-TUM-ta
Pyrrhic	˘ ˘	Unaccent—unaccent	with a	with a	ta-ta

In practice, the spondee may be used as an iamb or as a trochee; in combination, we may have—

Ín héad | -lŏng flíght

in which the word is used as a trochee;

Hĕ plúnged | hĕad-lóng

in which the word is used as an iamb.

In actual verse and poetry, never forget that the actual rhythm of the words, as normally uttered in a conversational tone, differs from the artificial scansion pattern adopted. Take one of the most regular five-foot iambic lines in the language:

The curfew tolls the knell of parting day.
Elegy Written in a Country Churchyard,
Thomas Gray.

Scanned normally, as this would be spoken, we have the following natural scansion:

The cúrfew | tólls | the knéll | of párting | dáy.

Here we have one iamb, two feet consisting of mere accented syllables for which we have no name, and two feet of three syllables each (unaccent—accent—unaccent, or amphibrachs). Yet this is described as an ideal iambic line, because the pattern indubitably is:

ta TUM   ta TUM   ta TUM   ta TUM   ta TUM

To make the actual line fit the planned iambic pattern, we have to divide words as follows:

The cur- | few tólls | the knéll | of párt- | ing dáy.

Absolutely natural iambic lines are rare:

And dwéll | upón | your gráve | when yóu | are déad.
The Comedy of Errors, William Shakespeare.

A repetition of such lines would be monotonous, unnatural and intrinsically unpoetic.

To show a still further group of variations, the opening of Hamlet's most famous soliloquy, commencing "To be or not to be," is theoretically in the same iambic five-foot pattern: three lines, each consisting theoretically of five ta-TUM's. The actual scansion brings in strange and unusual feet, or groups of unaccents with one accent; and shows that these three lines have only four actual feet apiece (a foot being, in English, normally grouped around one accent), where the pattern called for five in each line:

To bé | or nót to bé. | That | is the quéstion.
Whéther | 'tis nóbler | in the mínd | to súffer
The slíngs | and árrows | of outrágeous | fórtune . . .
Hamlet, William Shakespeare.

Here are four feet of two syllables each (two iambs and two trochees); four of three syllables each (three amphibrachs and one anapest); one of one syllable; and three of four syllables each (two of one type, one of another). And only four natural feet to each line.

This is acceptable five-foot iambic verse, in the hands of the world's greatest master. In later plays, his variations became more extreme, until at times his rhythms were less regular than Whitman's typical free verse or polyrhythmic poetry.

What is desired, in metric poetry, is a regular pattern, with restrained freedom and variety in its use. The poet should learn to scan his poetry—that is, to mark the accented and unaccented syllables as above, and then to divide it both into the natural speech rhythm and into the artificial pattern rhythm. There is no need for pride, if the poetry is excessively regular. As a rule, that means that it is strained and unnatural in phrasing, and to that extent falls below true greatness in technique.

In reading poetry aloud or to oneself, avoid most of all an unnatural singsong. Never read the lines from Hamlet as if they had been printed:

> to *BE* or *NOT* to *BE* that *IS* the *QUES*tion.
> whe*THER* 'tis *N O*bler *IN* the *MIND* to *SUF*fer
> the *SLINGS* and *AR*rows *OF* out*RAg*eous *FOR*tune . . .

Instead, read this and all other poetry as naturally as if it were unpatterned prose. The pattern is there, and will make itself felt. Excellence in reading depends upon naturalness in expression.

Iambic Verse

The commonest line-pattern in English verse is based upon the iamb ($\smile\diagup$). Many more words in English are trochees than iambs. Iambic is the preferred pattern, because such trochaic words are normally introduced by a one-syllabled unaccented article, preposition, or the like. Normally lines do not open with the trochee *hoping,* but rather with such a phrase as *in hoping, for hoping, and hoping, this hoping, if hoping,* and so on.

Lines name the metric pattern; and are described by the type of

foot, and the number of feet to the line. Thus a one-foot iambic
line could be written:

> All hail!

A two-foot iambic line would be:

> All hail to you!

A three-foot iambic line would be:

> All hail to you, my friends!

A four-foot iambic line would be:

> All hail to you, my worthy friends!

A five-foot iambic line would be:

> All hail to you, my wholly worthy friends!

Note how naturally trochaic words like *wholly* and *worthy* fit into
this iambic pattern. This line might have been:

> In hailing friendship's wholly worthy sons,

in which case four words (hailing, friendship's, wholly, worthy)
are complete trochees in themselves: yet are transformed into
word-split units in the iambic pattern, by the introductory unaccented word *in* and the concluding accented word *sons*. This is an
entirely legitimate following of the iambic pattern, which can be
most easily remembered as:

> ta TUM   ta TUM   ta TUM   ta TUM   ta TUM.

A word ending on an accented syllable is said to have a *masculine* ending; one ending on an unaccented syllable, a *feminine* ending. The iambic pattern may be used with a feminine ending: that
is, with the addition of an unaccented syllable to the last foot. A
stanza of five lines, successively one-, two-, three-, four-, and five-
foot iambic lines with feminine endings, could be manufactured
easily:

> Good morning,
> Benignant April,
> With all your rainbow blossoms,
> With birds all carolling their rapture,
> With love alive within the hearts of maidens.

The scansion for this would be:

> Gŏod mórn- | ĭng,
> Bĕnig- | nănt Á- | pril,
> With ăll | yŏur rain- | bŏw blŏs- | sŏms,
> With birds | ăll cár- | ŏlling | their ráp- | tŭre,
> With love | ălive | within | the hearts | ŏf maid- | ĕns.

This is often described as if the first line, for instance, were a two-foot line, with one syllable missing: and is called catalectic verse. The reality is that of an iambic foot, followed by a loose or unattached unaccented syllable.

Writing iambic verse is as easy as writing any form of verse. Get the metrical pattern firmly in mind:

> ta TUM   ta TUM   ta TUM   ta TUM

and then proceed to let the words flow into this pattern.

Iambic verse may be altered into trochaic at any time, by *adding* an accented syllable to each line's beginning; or by *removing* the opening unaccented syllable. The process may be reversed as easily, thus changing trochaic verse into iambic. Start with this iambic version:

> And then the little Hiawatha
> Remarked unto the old Nokomis,
> I know that hills are edged with valleys.

By adding an accented syllable at the beginning of each line, this becomes trochaic:

> Now and then the little Hiawatha
> Said aloud unto the old Nokomis,
> Well I know that hills are edged with valleys.

By removing the opening unaccented syllable in each iambic line above, the lines are four-foot trochaic:

> Then the little Hiawatha
> Said unto the old Nokomis,
> All the hills are edged with valleys.

This is the regular metre of Longfellow's *Hiawatha,* and is as easy to write as iambic verse.

Trochaic Verse

Trochaic verse is less usual in English than iambic, because the custom of the language is to introduce most remarks with an unaccented syllable or word. Based upon the trochee ($/\smile$), the pattern is, in the case of four-foot trochees,

TUM-ta   TUM-ta   TUM-ta   TUM-ta

Hiawatha opens upon this pattern:

> Should you ask me, whence these stories,
> Whence these legends and traditions,
> With the odours of the forest,
> With the dew and damp of meadows.
> > *Hiawatha,* Henry Wadsworth Longfellow.

In natural accent, the first three of the lines quoted have only two accents apiece, and not four: so that the natural scansion, as of the third line, is

With the odours | of the forest.

Shakespeare commences a witches' incantation with the abrupt staccato natural accent:

> Round about the cauldron go;
> In the poisoned entrails throw.
> Toad, that under cold stone
> Days and nights has thirty-one
> Sweltered venom sleeping got,
> Boil thou first i' the charmed pot.
> > *Macbeth,* William Shakespeare.

An interesting variation here is the use of *cold* as a dissyllable, as if it were pronounced *có-ŏld*. It may be regarded as the one-syllabled *cold,* followed by a pause consuming the length of time it would take to pronounce an unaccented syllable. In any case, it is an effective variant device.

Trochaic verse might certainly be described with propriety as iambic verse, with the introductory unaccented syllable omitted in each line. The description is unimportant; the important thing is to choose, understand, and use adequately the pattern, whatever it is called.

Again, in the sixth line quoted above from *Macbeth,* there is an extra unaccented syllable, a sort of grace-note, added: making the second foot in reality a dactyl:

Boil thou | first i' the | charmèd | pot.

If preferred, though it is less usual, this could be scanned slightly differently:

Boil thou | first i' | the charmèd | pot,

in which case there is an amphibrach in the third foot; or it might be scanned:

Boil thou | first i' | the char- | mèd pot,

regarding it as two trochees followed by two iambs. But the accepted pattern is trochaic four-foot, and the custom is to prefer the first scansion given. At any time, within reason dictated by the poet's own inner ear and sense of music, the substitution of an anapest or a dactyl for an iamb or a trochee is permitted. Or the substitution of a spondee ($//$), and any of the other feet (iamb, trochee, dactyl or spondee, as well as amphibrach etc.) may be substituted for a foot in anapestic verse. Similar substitutions may take place in dactylic verse. The best poetry contains variety within uniformity.

Notice that in the trochaic lines from *Macbeth* the last unaccented syllable is omitted in every line. This again gives an example of catalectic verse. The name is unimportant: a trochaic line may end on a masculine ending, as easily as an iambic line ends on a feminine ending. A dactylic line may end on a trochee or an accented syllable; an anapestic line may have an extra unaccented syllable, or even two of them, without losing its anapestic character. Variety in uniformity. . . .

Anapestic Verse

The anapest ($\smile \smile /$) is a foot of three syllables, the first two unaccented, the last accented. It may be described as an iamb with an extra unaccented syllable added before it. It may be indicated ta ta TUM, so that a three-foot anapestic pattern would be:

ta ta TUM   ta ta TUM   ta ta TUM.

A typical line following this pattern would be:

> To the end of the world in the dawn.

The English language has more accented syllables than many others, and a succession of two unaccented syllables is comparatively infrequent. Constantly the anapestic pattern is broken by a foot called the *amphimacer* (/ ᵕ /), accent—unaccent—accent, giving us a result such as:

> Let me go anywhere I can find,

scanned as anapestic thus:

> Lĕt mĕ gó | ănywhére | Ĭ căn fínd,

but having a natural scansion consisting of three amphimacers:

> Lét mĕ gó | ánywhĕre | Í căn fínd.

There are so few natural anapests in the language, that this is usual and permitted. The same thing applies to dactylic verse. Even more unusual three-syllabled feet appear, each with two accents: the antibacchius, (/ / ᵕ), the bacchius, (ᵕ / /), the tribrach (ᵕ ᵕ ᵕ), the molossus (/ / /). In anapestic and dactylic verse, a fourth syllable, usually unaccented, again like a gracenote, may appear in any foot. So long as such variations please the inner ear, the inner sense of word music, they are aids.

The natural poet will always make his own patterns, knowing that poetry is self-created, and not devised by rigid rules.

Dactylic Verse

The dactyl (/ ᵕ ᵕ) is a foot of three syllables, the first accented, the next two unaccented. It may be described as a trochee with an extra unaccented syllable added after it. Here is an illustration:

> Cannon to right of them,
> Cannon to left of them,
> Cannon in front of them
> Volleyed and thundered;
> Stormed at with shot and shell,
> Boldly they fought, and well. . . .
> *The Charge of the Light Brigade,* Alfred Tennyson.

Scanned as dactylic verse, this would appear:

Cannon to | right of them,
Cannon to | left of them,
Cannon in | front of them
Volleyed and | thundered;
Stormed at with | shot and shell,
Boldly they | fought, and well.

As a matter of fact, these last two lines would have a different natural scansion, including amphimacers:

Stormed at with | shot and shell,
) Boldly they | fought, and well.

Once the technique of scansion is mastered, the poet must be his own court of last appeal upon it.

Dactylic verse is not wholly at home in English; and amphibrachic verse (using as its norm the amphibrach, ˘ ´ ˘) is as much of an alien. These feet become excessively monotonous in long poems, though they may be used with advantage in brief lyrics.

Variations in Metric Verse

The use of variations in metric verse is widespread. The development of every poet of importance, whose technique did not begin and remain rigid and crystallized, has been in the direction of more and more variety. This is displayed impressively by the development of Shakespeare and of Keats. Little such development is shown in the technique of more rigid minor poets. A few examples must suffice. Shakespeare in his final peak period wrote lines whose natural scansion was as loose as:

A malady
Most in- | cident | to maids; | bold oxlips and
The crown imperial; lilies of all kinds,
The flow- | er-de-luce | being one! | O, these | I lack. . . .

The Winter's Tale, William Shakespeare.

The most unusual usage is the ending of the second line in the extraordinary foot which seems a spondee followed by a pyrrhic, (⁄ ⁄ ⌣ ⌣). The reverse foot opens a line in one of his sonnets,

> Of the wíde wórld | dréamĭng | ŏn thíngs | tŏ cóme.
> *Sonnet CVII*, William Shakespeare.

One of the most praised lines in Keats is:

> Róbs nót | óne líght | séed frŏm | thĕ féath- | ĕr'd gráss.
> *Hyperion*, John Keats.

Here two spondees introduce the rest of the line; the scansion being as if his pattern were—

TUM TUM   TUM TUM   TUM ta   ta TUM   ta TUM

Keats has at least one line, in the same pattern, consisting of five trochees:

> Thĕa! | Thĕa! | Thĕa! | Whĕre ĭs | Satŭrn?
> *Hyperion*, John Keats.

Robert Frost has such masterly lines as the following, in the same five foot iambic pattern:

> And spread her apron to it. She put out her hand. . . .
> *The Death of the Hired Man*, Robert Frost.
> Strange how such innocence gets its own way.
> *The Black Cottage*, Robert Frost.
> And the saw snarled and rattled, snarled and rattled.
> *"Out, Out—"*, Robert Frost.
> So. But the hand was gone already.
> *"Out, Out—"*, Robert Frost.

In this last line the monosyllable *So* is followed by a pause that takes the place of a foot and a half. One of Frost's most triumphant variations is:

> Little —less—nothing! And that ended it.
> *"Out, Out—"*, Robert Frost.

In natural scansion, this would be:

> Líttlĕ— | léss— | nóthĭng! | Ănd thăt éndĕd ĭt

A common variation is an alternation of iamb and anapest, as in this old English ballad:

> Ŏ Ál- | ĭsŏn Gróss, | thăt líves | ĭn yŏn tówer.
> *Alison Gross,* Old English Ballad.

We find the reverse of this order in a Browning lyric,

> Whĕre thĕ cháf- | fĭnch síngs | ŏn thĕ ór- | chărd bóugh. . . .
> *Home-Thoughts, from Abroad,* Robert Browning.

So numerous are the variations to which the metric pattern in English can be adapted, to the greater naturalness of the poetry.

Accent Pattern Instead of Metric

Coleridge, in one poem, abandoned the formal metric foot altogether, in favor of a rediscovered old English method of letting the line pattern consist of a definite number of accents, with any number of unaccented syllables, occurring in any order. Here are the opening lines:

> 'Tĭs thĕ míd- | dlĕ ŏf níght | bў thĕ cás- | tlĕ clóck,
> Ănd thĕ ówls | hăve awák- | ĕnĕd thĕ crów- | ĭng cóck.
> Tú- | whĭt! | Tú- | whóo!
> Ănd hárk, | ăgáin; | thĕ crów- | ĭng cóck
> Hŏw drów- | sĭly | ĭt créw.
> *Christabel,* Samuel Taylor Coleridge.

Thomas Hood uses lines consisting of only three accented syllables,

> Stítch! | Stítch! | Stítch!
> Ĭn póv- | ĕrty, húng- | ĕr ănd dírt. . . .
> *The Song of the Shirt,* Thomas Hood.

This follows the same method of accent versification. Walter de la Mare's most famous poem is built around a pattern of three accents to the line, as the second and fourth line below indicate; he uses unaccented syllables where he pleases:

> But on- | ly a host | of phantom listeners
> That dwelt | in the lone | house then,
> Stood lis- | tening in the qui- | et of the moonlight |
> To that voice | from the world | of men.
> > *The Listeners,* Walter de la Mare.

Other modern poets have done as much, or more. Variety within uniformity. . . .

Blank Verse and Free Verse

Blank verse means simply unrhymed verse. Any line pattern, if unrhymed, is blank verse. *Heroic blank verse* is unrhymed five foot iambic poetry or verse. Most of Shakespeare is written in heroic blank verse. *Heroic couplets,* beloved of Dryden and Pope, are pairs of five foot iambic lines rhymed with each other.

Free verse may be rhymed or unrhymed, although it is usually unrhymed, since rhyming is an even more unnatural convention of poetry than metre; and the poet who has abandoned formal metre will hardly, as a rule, still use the device of rhyming. Free verse is verse without a metric pattern, but with a wider pattern than metre allows. It still tends toward regularity, rather than variety: and the final court of appeals as to whether any example should be classified as poetry or prose from a standpoint of content, or as verse or prose from a standpoint of technique, is the individual poet or reader himself. To many readers, the following are all poetry:

Lord, thou hast been our dwelling-place in all generations. Before the mountains were brought forth, or ever thou hadst formed the earth and the world, even from everlasting to everlasting, thou art God. Thou turnest man to destruction; and sayest, return, ye children of men. . . .   *The Ninetieth Psalm.*

But, in a larger sense, we cannot dedicate—we cannot consecrate—we cannot hallow—this ground. The brave men, living and dead, who struggled here, have consecrated it far above our poor power to add or to detract. The world will little note, nor long remember, what we say here; but it can never forget what they did here. . . .
> *The Gettsburg Address,* Abraham Lincoln.

Out of the cradle endlessly rocking, out of the mockingbird's throat, the musical shuttle, out of the Ninth-month midnight, over the sterile sands, and the fields beyond, where the child leaving his bed wandered alone, bareheaded, barefoot, down from the showered halo, up from the mystic play of shadows twining and twisting as if they were alive. . . .

Out of the Cradle, Endlessly Rocking,
                                        Walt Whitman.

Walt Whitman used the artificial line-division of poetry to present the third of these selections; the King James version of the Bible and Lincoln used the natural line-division so familiar in the printing of prose. Little or nothing is added by the artificial line division:

Out of the cradle endlessly rocking,
Out of the mocking-bird's throat, the musical shuttle,
Out of the Ninth-month midnight,
Over the sterile sands, and the fields beyond, where the
    child leaving his bed wandered alone, bareheaded,
    barefoot,
Down from the showered halo,
Up from the mystic play of shadows twining and
    twisting as if they were alive. . . .

It is poetry, to many, in either form; and the first form is the more natural and readable. Scan the Whitman selection, or any of the others, and the tendency toward regularity of rhythm becomes apparent: a wider regularity, perhaps only an up-rhythm or a down-rhythm; but still inevitably there. This distinguishes free verse from prose, from the technical point of view.

At times writers of free verse let their lines reach surprising lengths, no matter how lovely the music is: thus Sandburg,

Pocahontas' body, lovely as a poplar, sweet as a
    red haw in November or a pawpaw in May,
    did she wonder? does she remember? in the dust,
    in the cool tombs. . . .

Cool Tombs, Carl Sandburg.

Again, the lines can be extremely brief:

It sits looking
over harbor and city

> on silent haunches
> and then moves on.
>> *Fog,* Carl Sandburg.

The free verse writer devises his own line-division pattern. This form, eliminating the devices of metre and rhyme, calls on the poet to avoid the inconsequential and the trivial, and to write down only his important utterances. If rhyme is a shelter for mediocrity, as Shelley wrote in his preface to *The Revolt of Islam,* free verse is a test of the best that the poet has in him.

Line Length in Verse

Oliver Wendell Holmes, himself a doctor, advanced the theory that line length in verse marked physiologically the normal breathing of the poet. In other words, a breath should be taken at the end of each line; and the line should be no longer than the poet's ability to hold his breath. No artificial line division is used in prose, to indicate where a breath should be taken. There is no greater reason for artificial line division in poetry. It still remains true that the long Greek lines, each consisting of six feet, called for huge-breasted warrior-bards to chant them; that the norm of English verse, the five-foot iambic line, indicates a lesser chest-expansion in the typical English poet; and that the briefer modern tendency shows a further deterioration in the chest-expansion of poets.

Where poetry consists in *end-stopped* lines—lines with a natural pause at the end of each line—there is more reason for an artificial line division. Shakespeare began so; many poets never get beyond this, in the main. But when we come to poetry like—

> We are such stuff
> As dreams are made on, and our little life
> Is rounded with a sleep,
>> *The Tempest,* William Shakespeare.

the break comes after *on,* and not after *stuff* or *life;* and the last reason for the artificial line division has vanished.

A sonnet set up in this manner appears:

O bitter moon, O cold and bitter moon, climbing your midnight hillside of bleak sky, the earth, as you, once knew a blazing noon.

Night brings the silver hour when she will die. We shall be cold as you are, and as bitter, icily circling toward a tepid fire, playing at life with our deceitful glitter, past joy, past hope, forever past desire.

Yet still the forest lifts its leafy wings to flutter for a while before the chill. And still the careless heart is gay, and sings in the green temple on the dusty hill. And the gulls tumble, and the homing ships peer for the harbor. . . .

And the sand drips.

The Flight of the Eagle, v, Clement Wood.

In an earlier volume, this had appeared with the usual line-division of poetry as ordinarily printed. Rhyme can occur of course in ordinary prose, although this usage is extremely rare. Where the rhythm of verse is used, as in the sonnet quoted, it is possible for poets to use the line and paragraph division usual to prose, if this is desired.

IMPORTANT CLASSICAL TERMS FOR POETIC DEVICES
VERSES AND GROUPS OF VERSES

Classical Name	*Common Name, or Explanation*
Monometer	A verse containing one metrical foot.
Dimeter	A verse containing two metrical feet.
Dipody	A measure consisting of two metrical feet; a ditrochee.
Trimeter	A verse containing three metrical feet.
Tetrameter	A verse containing four metrical feet.
Pentameter	A verse containing five metrical feet.
Hexameter	A verse containing six metrical feet.
Heptameter	A verse containing seven metrical feet.
Octometer	A verse containing eight metrical feet.
Distich	A strophic verse of two lines, usually called a couplet today.

UNUSUAL METRIC FEET

Tribrach	Three unaccented syllables	⌄ ⌄ ⌄
Molossus	Three accented syllables	/ / /
Amphimacer	Accent, unaccent, accent	/ ⌄ /
Bacchius	Unaccent, accent, accent	⌄ / /
Antibacchius	Accent, accent, unaccent	/ / ⌄

Ditrochee	Two trochees regarded as a compound foot	╱ ⌣ ╱ ⌣
Paeon	Accent, unaccent, unaccent, unaccent	╱ ⌣ ⌣ ⌣
Choriamb	Accent, unaccent, unaccent, accent	╱ ⌣ ⌣ ╱
Epitrite	Three accents and one unaccent: of the 1st, 2nd, 3rd or fourth class, depending on the location of the unaccented syllable	⌣ ╱ ╱ ╱ ╱ ⌣ ╱ ╱ ╱ ╱ ⌣ ╱ ╱ ╱ ╱ ⌣

OTHER TERMS

Classical Name	*Explanation*
Acatalectic Verse	Verse not defective in the last foot; verse complete in its number of syllables.
Arsis	The lighter or unstressed part of a foot, especially in quantitative verse; later, the accented syllable of a foot.
Caesura	A break in a verse caused by the ending of a word within a foot. A *masculine caesura* follows the thesis, or stressed part of a foot. A *feminine caesura* follows the arsis or unstressed part. A *trithemimeral caesura* comes after the third half foot, which means in the second foot; a *penthemimeral caesura,* after the fifth half foot; a *hepthemimeral caesura,* after the seventh half foot; and so on. A *bucolic caesura,* in dactylic hexameter, is a caesura occurring in the fourth foot, especially in pastoral poetry.
Catalectic Verse	Verse lacking a syllable at the beginning, or terminating in an imperfect foot.
Diaeresis, Dieresis	The break caused by the coincidence of the end of a foot with the end of a word. *Bucolic diaeresis,* a diaeresis occurring in the fourth foot, especially in pastoral poetry.
Enjambement	The extension of the sentence beyond the limitations of the distich.
Ictus	Metrical stress.
Thesis	The heavier or stressed part of a foot in classical prosody, especially in quantitative verse; later, the unaccented syllable or syllables of a verse.

III

THE TECHNIQUE OF VERSIFICATION: RHYME

Correct and Incorrect Rhyme

RHYME is as simple to define as rhythm is difficult.

Rhyme is the identity in sound of an accented vowel in a word, usually the last one accented, and of all consonantal and vowel sounds following it; with a difference in the sound of the consonant immediately preceding the accented vowel. Rhyme deals exclusively with sounds, and has nothing to do with spelling. The rhyming dictionary terminating this book is strictly phonetic, and therefore logical and useful.

Correct rhymes may be spelled alike:

ate, plate, mate, abate, syncopate.

They may be spelled differently:

ate, bait, straight, freight.

In this case the spelling is immaterial.

So called "eye rhymes,"—that is, words spelt alike that look alike but are pronounced differently—are not rhymes at all; they slip into versification, if at all, as *consonance,* which will be discussed later. That is, the incorrect rhyme

earth, hearth,

so popular among English versifiers, is no more a rhyme than the following sets of words identically spelled, but pronounced differently:

cow, blow
climber, timber
finger, ginger, singer
cough, enough, plough, though, through.

Identities do not rhyme, no matter what the spelling is; since the preceding consonantal sounds must differ. The following are identities, and not rhymes:

25

> bay, obey
> bare, bear, forbear
> laying, overlaying
> ability, possibility, probability.

Sounds *almost* alike, after the identical accented vowel sounds, do not rhyme. These are properly called assonance, and have not succeeded as a versification device in English. Examples are:

> main, game, reins, lamed
> hate, shape, played
> feed, sleet, creep
> sandwich, orange, lozenge
> childhood, wildwood
> Norfolk, war talk
> anguish, Flatbush
> silver, deliver

You can find examples of incorrect rhymes in poems by many accepted poets, and in a much higher percentage of popular songs and newspaper versification. Two of the above examples were taken directly out of songs nationally popular. Slovenly rhyming is one of the sure signs of mediocrity in versification. Learn correct rhyming first; then, if you wish to break the rule you understand, that is your privilege.

The language's poverty in rhyming has caused the following almost-rhymes to become widely accepted:

> given, Heaven; bosom, blossom; shadow, meadow;
> God, road; war, more; bliss, is; was, grass.

Among widely used "eye rhymes," which are not rhymes at all, but mere identities in spelling, are:

> earth, hearth; bare, are; north, forth; real, steal.

Bosom-blossom, was-grass, are combinations of consonance and assonance; *bliss-is* is assonance; the others in the first list are consonance. The first three pairs in the second set are acceptable consonance; *real, steal* is an attempt to rhyme a two-syllabled word with a one-syllabled one, and has no justification from any standpoint. Use consonance or assonance purposely, if desired; but always know that this is not correct rhyming.

If the poet is tone-deaf as to sounds, it is best to rely upon the

phonetic symbols above each group of rhyming words in the rhyming dictionary that terminates this book, or upon dictionary markings. Many people can not distinguish the obvious difference in sounds between this pair of words, which do not rhyme:

north, forth.

Take away the *th* sound, and many people still hear no difference between this pair of words, which do not rhyme:

nor, fore.

Take away the *r* sound, and some people still hear no difference between this pair of words, which do not rhyme:

gnaw, foe.

Gnaw plus *r* plus *th* can not rhyme with *foe* plus *r* plus *th*. If in doubt as to such off-rhymes, follow the phonetic markings.

A third common error in rhyming comes from such mispronunciations as dropping a terminal -*g*. These do not rhyme:

martin, parting.
herding, burden.

They may be rhymed colloquially, that is, in quoted words, as follows:

martin, partin',
herdin', burden,

the latter being not quite a rhyme, at that. But unless writing colloquially, do not use such incorrect rhymes as those given first above. A similar error comes from ignoring the *r* sounds, which causes such off-rhymes as:

court (pronounced *cou't,* like *coat*), boat
Lord (pronounced *Lawd*), gaud.

Rhymes can be made of two or more words. Here are examples of perfect rhymes:

satin, flat in.
Quentin, went in.
pray tin, hate in.

Such couplings are more appropriate to light and humorous verse than to serious poetry. Rhyming must always give the effect of unobtrusive *naturalness,* or it fails of its proper effect.

Robert Browning is in a class by himself in fantastic many-word rhymings and near-rhymings, often in serious verse:

> The wolf, fox, bear and monkey
> By piping advice in one key. . . .
> *Pacchiarotto, and How He Worked*
> *in Distemper, et cetera,*
>   Robert Browning.

This is not a rhyme, because *monkey* is, phonetically, a rhyme sound for *ŭngki,* or at best *ŭngke;* and *one key* is, phonetically, a rhyme sound for *ŭnkē:* the unguessed *g* sound in the first spoiling it as a rhyme. Again, in the same poem, he uses this fantastic coupling:

> While, treading down rose and ranunculus,
> You *Tommy-make-room-for-your-uncle-us!*

Ranunculus has as its rhyme sound *ungk'ū-lus;* the next line, *ŭngk'ŏŏl-us:* a minor difference, but enough to spoil the rhyme. Much closer is Byron's celebrated couplet:

> O ye lords of ladies inte*llectual,*
> Inform us truly, have they not hen*pecked you all?*
>   *Don Juan,* I, xxii, Lord Byron.

The unaccented last syllable of the first line differs from the unaccented last syllable of the second with the difference of *ă* and *ô.* Barham furnishes many perfect many-worded rhymes, such as:

> Should it even set fire to one's castle and *burn it, you're*
> Amply insured for both building and *furniture.* . . .
>   *Sir Rupert the Fearless,*
>   Richard Harris Barham (Thomas Ingoldsby).

Samuel Hoffenstein furnishes a splendid example:

> You haven't the nerve to take bi*chloride;*
> You lie up nights till you're gaunt and *sore-eyed,*
>   *Poems in Praise of Practically Nothing,*
>   Samuel Hoffenstein.

In using such rhyme combinations, it is wise to put the combination with the inevitable sound first: *bichloride;* following this with the combination of words to rhyme with it. Thus W. S. Gilbert, a master rhymester, uses in this order:

> monotony, got any.
> cerebellum too, tell 'em to.

In light and humorous verse, such rhyming cleverness is a crown; in serious verse, if used sparingly, it is permitted.

Function and Types of Rhyme

In serious verse, since obvious cleverness defeats the appeal to the serious emotions, rhyming should be unobtrusive. To have your rhyme words merely conveniences demanded by your rhyming pattern is one of the chief faults of rhymed verse.

Rhyme is a potent shaper. Once you have written down a line of verse or poetry, and intend to have the next line or the next line but one rhyme with it, your choice of terminal words for the rhyming line is limited by the limited rhyming resources of the language. If a poet commences,

> October is the wildest month,

he has estopped himself from any rhyme; since *month* has no rhyme in English.

Assuming that the first line's rhyming word has certain rhyming mates, the choice of terminal rhyme words for the rhyming line is limited to these; and the direction of the poet's thought and its expression must be deflected into some natural use of one of these rhyming mate words. Rhyming is a brain-stimulant, and may even spur on the poetic imagination. The meaning of the planned poem may have been clear in the mind; but its expression, if rhyme is used, must work in limited fields, and only the master achieves in these that finality of natural utterance which is one of the charms of great poetry.

To the authentic poet, especially the living poet, there is no such thing as *poetic license:* the right to warp and twist the language out of its natural order or grammar, to suit the exigencies of rhyme. Mr. Browning continued his *Tommy-make-room-for-your-uncle-us* couplet with this:

> Quick march! for Xanthippe, my housemaid,
> If once on your pates she a souse made. . . .
> I would not for worlds be your place in,
> Recipient of slops from the basin!

What Browning meant, in the direct natural order, was:

> Quick march! for Xanthippe, my housemaid,
> If once she made a souse on your pates,
> I would not for worlds be in your place,
> Recipient of slops from the basin!

Even this is unnatural; the real order would be, "Quick march!
for if once Xanthippe, my housemaid, made . . ." etc. Let us
suppose that inspiration worked with him in the erratic fashion
quoted above. Then would be the time for the critical sense to
come in, and rigorously to eliminate all such evidences of poetic
license—inversions, ungrammatical constructions, and the like.
Not one has a place in poetry, more than in speech.

This is a rigid rule to lay down. It is not any individual's rule.
It is the rule that Shakespeare followed, when he wrote:

> Tomorrow, and tomorrow, and tomorrow,
> Creeps in this petty pace from day to day
> To the last syllable of recorded time,
> And all our yesterdays have lighted fools
> The way to dusty death. Out, out, brief candle!
> Life's but a walking shadow, a poor player
> That struts and frets his hour upon the stage
> And then is heard no more; it is a tale
> Told by an idiot, full of sound and fury,
> Signifying nothing.
>
> *Macbeth*, William Shakespeare.

This was written some three hundred years ago. There is not an
obsolete or even archaic word in it, not a strained construction,
not an inversion or instance of ungrammatical poetic license. The
quotation given in fragmentary form from Browning, which includes *ranunculus, homunculus, skoramis,* and countless inversions,
was outdated long ago: the words of Shakespeare live. The best
of Burns, of Shelley, of the Keats of *Hyperion,* of the best among
the modern poets, always follows this rule: no inversions, no
archaisms, no poetic license. This is the price of a chance for wide
poetic greatness.

To return to the strict technique of rhyming, one-syllabled
rhymes are called single or masculine rhymes. Examples are:

> we, flee, sea, apostrophe, harmony.
> disk, tamarisk, odalisque.
> fling, sing, carolling.

In the last pair of the first grouping, and the third rhymes in the others, note that only a secondary accent falls on the rhyming syllable. This is enough. A rhyme may be more smothered, if read naturally,—a modern variation in which it may be said that an accented syllable is rhymed with an unaccented one: such as *anguish, wish; ring, wedding.* Used sparingly, this is effective.

Two-syllabled rhymes are called double or feminine rhymes. Examples are:

> ocean, motion, devotion.
> traded, aided, play did.
> see us, flee us.

Three-syllabled rhymes are called triple rhymes. Examples:

> saleable, mailable.
> lyrical, miracle, empirical, satirical.
> going now, blowing now.
> rest of it, best of it, palimpsest of it.

There may be rhymes, especially in light verse, of four or even more syllables. A rhyme like the one last given shows little cleverness, since it is merely "rest, best, palimpsest" with the phrase "of it" added. The lack of cleverness makes it more suitable for serious poetry than for light verse.

End rhyme is used at the end of the lines. Here is an example, the rhyming words being italicized, and the rhyme scheme indicated by the corresponding numerals:

> Gather ye rose-buds while ye *may,*   1
>   Old Time is still *a-flying;*   2
> And this same flower that smiles *today,*   1
>   Tomorrow will be *dying.*   2
>   *Counsel to Girls,* Robert Herrick.

Rhyme 1 is a single or masculine rhyme; rhyme 2 is a double or feminine rhyme.

Internal rhyme is rhyme used within the line, to give added effectiveness by a closer repetition of the rhyming sounds.

"Each day, all day," these poor folk say,
"In the same old *year-long, drear-long* way,
We *weave* in the *mills* and *heave* in the *kilns,*
We *sieve* mine-meshes under the hills,
And *thieve* much gold from the Devil's bank tills,
To *relieve,* O God, what manner of ills?"
                                    The Symphony, Sidney Lanier.

Here *year-long* rhymes internally with *drear-long; weave, heave,
sieve, thieve* and *relieve* are further internal rhymes; and *mills*
is an internal rhyme to *kilns* and the three next end rhymes.

Undesirable Rhymes

Incorrect rhymes, or rhymes constructed by straining the natural expression into inversions and grammatical perversions, ex-
cused on the outworn plea of poetic license, are always undesirable.
Quite as undesirable are rhymes which are hackneyed and over-
worked, such as:
                kiss, bliss.
                yearn, burn; yearning, burning.
                love, dove, above.
                fire, desire.
                trees, breeze.

These are unobjectionable technically. But they have been so used
and overused by other poets, that the only excuse for them today
is use in an entirely new manner.

It is the fact that most rhymes have been comparatively over-
worked that has caused the tendency toward consonance, which
is such a marked feature of modern poetry, from Emily Dickinson
onward.

Alliteration

Alliteration, like rhyme, is a repetition of sounds. But the sound
repeated is only the initial consonant of syllables or words. This
was one of the major devices of Anglo-Saxon poetry, which did
not use rhyme. Langland's *Piers Plowman* opens:

In a *s*ummer *s*eason, when *s*oft was the *s*un,
I *sh*ope me in *sh*roudes, as I a *sh*eep were.
                The Vision of Piers Plowman, William Langland.

Alliteration is used effectively by later poets in connection with rhyme, as this example illustrates:

> Whether *t*empter sent, or whether *t*empest *t*ossed thee here ashore,
> *D*esolate yet all un*d*aunted, on this *d*esert land enchanted,
> In this *h*ome by *H*orror *h*aunted, tell me truly, I implore.
> > *The Raven,* Edgar Allan Poe.

If not overused, this is highly effective. Swinburne was one of the masters of alliteration, tending to overuse it, as in—

> > The *l*ilies and *l*anguors of *v*irtue
> > For the *r*oses and *r*apture of *v*ice.
> > *Dolores,* Algernon Charles Swinburne.

Where there is no sense of unnaturalness in the repetition of alliterative sounds, it may be successfully employed.

Assonance

Assonance, called also *vowel rhyme,* consists in the identity of the final accented vowel sound, with dissimilarity in the subsequent consonantal and vowel sounds. It was used in Provencal and Old French poetry, and is still used in Spanish. George Eliot tried unsuccessfully to introduce it into English, the assonances being italicized:

> > Maiden crowned with glossy *blackness,*
> > Lithe as panther forest-*roaming,*
> > Long-armed naead, when she *dances,*
> > On the stream of ether *floating,*
> > Bright, O bright Fedalma!
> > > *Song of Joan,* in *The Spanish Gipsy,*
> > > > George Eliot.

The repetition here is not sufficiently marked to make this device popular in English versification. Typical groups of assonantal masculine or single-rhymed endings are:

> > grab, crack, had, tan, sham, hang, fat
> > face, shade, hate, pain, claim, male
> > led, wreck, hem, then, set, step
> > bide, kine, fight, pipe, wise, advice

In feminine endings, we would have:

>aiming, faded, scraping, hailing, painter, lateness
>roaming, floated, coping, goader, golden
>coming, dumbness, stubborn, rustle

Unpopular so far, at any time assonance may achieve a popularity in English versification.

Consonance

Consonance, also loosely called *off rhymes, sour rhymes,* and *analyzed rhymes,* consists in an identity of all consonantal and vowel sounds after the accented vowel; and a difference in the accented vowels. An improvised model would be:

>There's a golden willow
>   Underneath a hill,
>By a babbling shallow
>   Brook and waterfall;

>And a mill-wheel turning
>   Under moon and sun,
>As if gently scorning
>   Time and tide and man.

There can be any combination of end and internal consonance with end or internal rhyme in the same poem, according to the best modern practice: the poet himself being the judge of what form is most pleasing to his inner sense of music, and that of his prospective readers.

Edna St. Vincent Millay, in *The Poet and His Book,* uses these pairs of words in consonance:

>worry, bury; withered, gathered; cluttered, spattered;
>   quarrel, laurel; hunters, winter's; valleys, bellies.

She also twice uses assonance:

>cupboard, upward; only, homely.

Elinor Wylie uses such instances of consonance as:

>bloody, body; people, ripple; mourner, corner;
>   primer, dreamer; standard, pondered; noble,
>   trouble; music, physic; Circe, hearsay; Vulcan,

    falcon; languish, distinguish; lost, ghost;
    sword, lord; suns, bronze;

and many more. Emily Dickinson is more lavish in her use of consonance than any of these.

The reason has been hinted before: the limited field of rhymes in the language, in spite of the impressive length of any rhyming dictionary. One advantage of a phonetic rhyming dictionary is that it makes the use of precise and accurate consonance possible. Words are arranged by rhyme, and not by consonance; and yet the phonetic arrangement gives a start toward arriving at accurate consonance. If the following method is used, consonance can be achieved by little more effort than is required for rhyme.

There are five *a* sounds that occur in accented syllables; three *e*'s; two *i*'s; six *o*'s; and three *u*'s, or a total of nineteen vowel sounds appearing in accented syllables. Most of these sets are grouped together: most of the *a*'s; two of the *e*'s (omitting the *e* followed by *r*, which appears only when *er* is reached); both of the *i*'s, and so on. Thus *ĀD* is followed by *ĂD* and this by *ÄD:* so that we may proceed directly from rhyming sounds like *aid* to *sad* and then to *charade*. In double rhymes, *Ō'li, ÔL'i* and *ŎL'i* follow in regular sequence; thus *holy, Macaulay,* and *folly* are near neighbors.

Suppose it is desired to locate all the consonance sounds possible for a line ending with *holy*. Turn under the *a*'s to all the phonetic symbols similar to *Ō'li—Ā'li* (as, *daily*) *ĂL'i* (as, *alley*); under *e,* to *Ē'li* (as, *freely*), *ĔL'i* (as, *jelly*); under *i,* to *Ī'li* (as, *drily*) and *ĬL'i* (as, *hilly*); also under *o* to *ŎOL'i* (as, *woolly*), *OIL'i* (as, *oily*); under *u,* to *Ū'li* (as, *truly*) and *ŬL'i* (as, *dully*). Look up also *OUL'i* and other possible vowel combinations, to make sure there are no rhyme sounds under them. And now the poet has an accurate test to see which words are in precise consonance with *holy*, and which are not.

Thus this most modern of all sound-repetition devices in English versification can be achieved most perfectly through the use of a phonetic rhyming dictionary. The phonetic symbols, of course, must be in precise alphabetical order. Turn, under each of the five vowels (not forgetting that the vowel sounds OI, OO and OU come alphabetically also), to the vowel followed by the

identical consonant and vowel sounds following the accented vowel in the rhymed syllable you wish consonances for; and all consonances that the lists of words affords will be found.

There is small adventure in rhyming, except in the made rhymes of two or more words more common to light verse. Compilers of rhyming dictionaries have completed the adventure, long ago. There is great adventure in the use of consonance, which expands the sound-repetition resources of the language. It is possible to write a poem where not one of the consonance couplets has been used before. The adventurous will not overlook this.

Your Mental Rhyming Dictionary

At times it is inconvenient or impossible to have a rhyming dictionary available. Especially where the poet desires to write such a piece of formal verse as a ballade, requiring fourteen rhymes on one sound, no two of which could be identical, it is advisable to be able to improvise your own temporary rhyming dictionary.

The method is simple. First write down all the single, double and triple consonantal sounds you can remember. It is not necessary to write down all of them, although for your convenience the list on opposite page is approximately complete.

Having jotted down as many of these as you remember, test the rhyme sound desired against this table, and write out the results. Thus, if the rhymes to *aye,* the long *Ā* sound, are desired, the poet would get, to begin with, of the single consonantal sounds:

> aye, bay, day, fay, gay, hay, jay, kay or cay, lay, may, nay or neigh, pay, ray, say, decolleté for the *t* sound, survey for the *v* sound, way, yea.

Be careful, when a one-syllabled rhyme in such an instance is missing, to use ingenuity to find longer words with the desired rhyme, as *decolleté, survey.*

Then, for the double consonantal sound rhymes, the following could be added:

> redoublé for the *bl* sound, bray, dray, flay, fray, gray, clay, McCrae for the *cr* sound, play, pray or prey, shay, risqué

Single (Vowel)	Double	Triple	Rare
B	BL		BW
	BR		
	CH		
—	DR		DW
D			
F	FL		
	FR		
G	GL		GW
	GR		
H			
J			
K (C)	KL (CL)		
	KR (CR)		
L			
M			
N			
P	PL		PW
	PR		
Q (KW)			
R			
S	SH	SHR	
	SK (SC)	SKR (SCR)	
	SL		
	SM		
	SN		
	SP	SPL	
		SPR	
	SQ (SKW)		
	ST	STR	
	SV		
	SW		
T	TH		
	th	thR	
	TR		
	TW		
V			VL
W			
Y			
Z			ZH
			ZL

> for the *sk* sound, slay, dismay perhaps for the *sm* sound,
> stay, sway, they, tray, tway.

In addition, the triple consonantal sounds would give:

> splay, spray, stray.

Altogether, this has furnished thirty-nine rhymes for *aye*: and this is more than enough to satisfy the requirements of any formal verse.

Suppose only four rhymes for the purposes of the rhyming pattern are needed, and the poet decides to use *huge* as one of them. Using the above rhyming dictionary, only a group of *f* rhymes are discovered:—*febrifuge, subterfuge, vermifuge* and so on; and perhaps, if the poet is expert in pronunciation, *gamboge,* which also rhymes with it. But no fourth rhyming sound. The *huge* rhyme-sound would then have to be discarded, and some other sound tried.

Try a double rhyme, *ended.* Using this mental rhyming dictionary, the poet discovers:

> ended, bended, fended or defended, Jen did, Len did, mended
> or amended, depended, rended, tended or attended,
> vended, wended;

and, using double and triple consonantal initial sounds,

> blended, friended and befriended, expended for *sp,* extended
> for *st,* trended, then did, splendid,

and this can be supplemented with *men did* and many other two word rhymes. Here are at least eighteen rhyming mates, which can be used as the 2 rhyme in a ballade, which requires fourteen rhyming mates.

So, even if the rhyming dictionary is left behind, a mental rhyming dictionary can always be improvised, once the mechanism is learned.

IV

STANZA PATTERNS

The Couplet

A SINGLE line of poetry is called, technically, a *verse* of poetry.
A series of lines arranged formally as a part of a poem is called
a *stanza*. Stanza forms may be rigid, with a fixed order of
sequence as to line length, metre, or rhyme; or they may be mere
divisions of a poem, corresponding to the paragraphs of prose.

The simplest stanza is one of two lines, called a couplet. The
word *couplet* is used to mean either a two-line poem, or a two
line stanza—that is, a part of a poem: and this is equally true of
triplets or tercets, quatrains, and so on. It may be rhymed:

> "Where are you going, my pretty maid?"   1
> "I'm going a milking, sir," she said.   1
> > *Mother Goose's Nursery Rhymes.*

Naturally, if our stanza has only two lines, it can be rhymed in
only one way: each line followed immediately by its rhyming
mate. This is called rhyming in couplets, and is indicated by 1, 1.
The second rhyme sound used in the poem would be designated by
2, the third by 3, and so on. Thus a series of couplet stanzas, if
rhymed, would be rhymed 1, 1; 2, 2; 3, 3, and so on. This is called
couplet rhyming,—a term used of any lines rhymed in this
fashion, even when not divided into separate couplet stanzas.

Five-foot iambic lines rhymed couplet fashion are called *heroic
couplets*. This was the favorite measure employed by Dryden and
Pope, who enriched the language with many polished quotations:

> Vice is a monster of so frightful mien   1
> As, to be hated, needs but to be seen;   1
> Yet seen too oft, familiar with her face,   2
> We first endure, then pity, then embrace.   2
> > *An Essay on Man,* Alexander Pope.

39

These pairs of lines are not stanzas, much less complete two-line poems. Thus *couplet* is used with the third meaning of a method of rhyming—the 1, 1; 2, 2 method.

A couplet need not be rhymed: it may be an unrhymed two line poem, or two line stanza. It may be in any rhythm or combination of rhythms.

The Triplet or Tercet

A group of three lines, whether a complete poem or a stanza, is called a triplet, or tercet. This is not as common a form as the couplet or the four-line form, the quatrain. An example is:

A still small voice spake unto me,	1
"Life is so full of misery,	1
Were it not better not to be?"	1

The Two Voices, Alfred Tennyson.

It is clear, that with three lines to work from, the lines in such a group might be rhymed 1, 1, 2, in which the third line rhymes with nothing in the triplet; or 1, 2, 2; or 1, 2, 1. In the case of groups of triplet stanzas, the rhymes may be interlocked:

Make me thy lyre, even as the forest is:	1
What if my leaves are falling like its own!	2
The tumult of thy mighty harmonies	1
Will take from both a deep autumnal tone,	2
Sweet though in sadness. Be thou, Spirit fierce,	3
My spirit! Be thou me, impetuous one!	2
Drive my dead thoughts over the universe	3
Like withered leaves to quicken a new birth!	4
And, by the incantation of this verse,	3
Scatter, as from an unextinguished hearth	4
Ashes and sparks, my words among mankind!	5
Be through my lips to unawakened earth	4
The trumpet of a prophecy! O wind,	5
If Winter comes, can Spring be far behind?	5

Ode to the West Wind, Percy Bysshe Shelley.

This interlocked rhyming, where the unrhymed middle line of one triplet becomes the rhymed first and third lines of the next, the

whole ending with a thirteenth and fourteenth line rhyming with
the unrhymed central line of the preceding triplet, is a special
Italian verse stanza form, called *terza rima*. As Shelley used it, it
might be regarded as an apt variation of the Shakespearean
sonnet. It may be constituted of less or more triplets, always followed by such a concluding couplet.

Notice, in the hands of this master, the rhyming devices. *Is-har-
monies* illustrates rhyming a primary accent with a secondary one:
and the secondary one is an indeterminate sound, more often
rhymed with *seas* than with *is*, which gives it the effect of partial
consonance. *Fierce-universe* is consonance, not rhyme, as is *birth-
hearth-earth*, long defended as an "eye rhyme," but admissible
as consonance. The same is true of *mankind-wind-behind*. It is
incorrect to pronounce the noun *wind* as if it were the verb *to
wind; wind* here rhymed with *thinned*, and is in consonance with
behind.

Triplets may be in any rhythm, including free verse or polyrhythm. And they may be unrhymed:

> I have had playmates, I have had companions,
> In my days of childhood, in my joyful school-days;
> All, all are gone, the old familiar faces.
>
> I have been laughing, I have been carousing,
> Drinking late, sitting late, with my bosom cronies;
> All, all are gone, the old familiar faces.
> > *The Old Familiar Faces,* Charles Lamb.

In this poem Lamb invented his own pattern—unrhymed six foot
trochaic in the main, with seven feet in the fifth line; and with
the terminal line of each triplet a refrain, repeated without
alteration. Any poet may make his own pattern for any poem he
wishes; and, if it finds favor, it may become a standard pattern.

The Quatrain

A quatrain is a stanza or poem of four lines. This is the most
popular brief stanza in English versification, and has a variety
of familiar rhyme schemes. Ordinary *ballad metre* was originally
seven-foot iambic rhymed couplets:

As Robin Hood in the forest strayed, all under the greenwood tree, 1
He was aware of a brave young man, as fine as fine might be.   1
Old English Ballad.

As normally printed today, this becomes a quatrain, with the first
and third lines unrhymed, and only the second and fourth rhyming
—a rhyme scheme that may be used with other metres as well,
and with any number of feet to each line:

> As Robin Hood in the forest strayed,   1
> All under the greenwood tree,   2
> He was aware of a brave young man,   3
> As fine as fine might be.   2

Almost as popular is the quatrain rhymed on alternate lines:

> A violet by a mossy stone   1
> Half-hidden from the eye!   2
> —Fair as a star, when only one   1
> Is shining in the sky.   2
> *The Lost Love,* William Wordsworth.

Quatrains may be rhymed couplet-wise:

> Tiger, tiger, burning bright   1
> In the forests of the night,   1
> What immortal hand or eye   2
> Framed thy fearful symmetry?   2
> *The Tiger,* William Blake.

Note that this is not indented: that is, that line two is set directly
under line one. The purpose of *indentation* is primarily to show
the rhyme scheme: lines rhyming with each other may be normally
set beneath each other, as in the two previous examples. Indentation is used either to show identities of rhyme, or to center
briefer lines in a stanza or poem.

The *In Memoriam* stanza is built upon a four-foot iambic
pattern, rhymed as follows:

> Ring out old shapes of foul disease;   1
> Ring out the narrowing lust of gold;   2
> Ring out the thousand wars of old,   2
> Ring in the thousand years of peace.   1
> *In Memoriam,* Alfred Tennyson.

Edward Fitzgerald's translation or recreation of the quatrains or
Rubaiyat of Omar Khayyam has one of the most famous quatrain
rhyme patterns in the language, using five-foot iambic lines:

> The Moving Finger writes; and, having writ,   1
> Moves on: nor all your Piety nor Wit   1
>   Shall lure it back to cancel half a Line   2
> Nor all your Tears wash out a Word of it.   1
> > *The Rubaiyat of Omar Khayyam,*
> > translated by Edward Fitzgerald.

Other possible quatrain rhyme arrangements are: 1, 1, 1, 1;
1, 1, 1, 2; 2, 2, 2, 2; 1, 2, 1, 1; 1, 2, 3, 1; 1, 1, 2, 3; 1, 2, 3, 3; 1, 2,
2, 3; and no doubt others. Hereafter, no additional rhyming patterns will be listed, since by now it should be understood that none
is forbidden.

As for the number of feet to the line in these quatrains, the
number for the better known patterns is as follows:

> Ballad metre, 4, 3, 4, 3. Called also Long Metre in hymns.
> *In Memoriam,* 4, 4, 4, 4.
> *Rubaiyat,* 5, 5, 5, 5.
> Short metre (in hymns), 3, 3, 4, 3.

This last was popular in the sixteenth century as *Poulter's
measure.* These four are all in iambic lines. Of course, any metric
foot or combination of feet may be employed. It need not be
repeated again that the quatrain, as any other stanza, may be
unrhymed, or may be in polyrhythm.

Stanzas of More Than Four Lines

A five-line stanza or poem is called a cinquain. Adelaide Crapsey
invented one containing 1, 2, 3, 4, and 1 iambic feet respectively
in the lines:

> These be
> Three silent things:
> The falling snow . . . . the hour
> Before the dawn . . . . the mouth of one
> Just dead.
> > *Triad,* by Adelaide Crapsey.

A rhymed cinquain is used in one of Shelley's best known odes:

> Hail to thee, blithe Spirit!   1
> Bird thou never wert,   2
> That from heaven, or near it,   1
> Pourest thy full heart   2
> In profuse strains of unpremeditated art.   2
>> *To a Skylark,* by Percy Bysshe Shelley.

Notice how the indentation centers the briefer lines, as well as indicating, in the first four, rhyming mates. The number of feet here is 3, 3, 3, 3, 6. A terminal six-foot iambic line is called an *Alexandrine;* this was constantly used with iambic five-foot lines as a terminal.

Shelley uses this pattern throughout his poem *To a Skylark.* Poe, another master craftsman, altered his rhyme and metre pattern from stanza to stanza in his greatest lyrics. The familiar love song *To Helen* ("Helen, thy beauty is to me——") has, in his three cinquains or five-line stanzas, these three different rhyme arrangements: 1, 2, 1, 2, 2; 3, 4, 3, 4, 3; 5, 6, 6, 5, 6. To his inner musical ear, these changes were more musical than regularity could have been.

A six-line stanza is called a sextet or sestet. Here is an example:

> Fear no more the heat o' the sun   1
> Nor the furious winter's rages;   2
> Thou thy worldly task hast done,   1
> Home art gone and ta'en thy wages: 2
> Golden lads and girls all must,   3
> As chimney-sweepers, come to dust.   3
>> *Dirge* from *Cymbeline,* William Shakespeare.

The trochaic pattern here is four-foot lines. One of the favorite stanzas of Robert Burns has the iambic pattern of 4, 4, 4, 2, 4, 2; as in his *To a Field-Mouse:*

> Wee, sleekit, cow'rin', tim'rous beastie,   1
> O what a panic's in thy breastie!   1
> Thou need na start awa sae hasty,   1
> Wi' bickering brattle!   2
> I wad be laith to rin and chase thee   1
> Wi' murd'ring pattle!   2
>> *To a Field-Mouse,* Robert Burns.

The consonance, *beastie, breastie, hasty, chase thee* was to be expected, in the hands of a master. A popular pattern (using an unusual trochaic 4, 4, 2, 4, 4, 2 measure) was used by Whittier:

> And if I should live to be   1
> The last leaf upon the tree   1
>   In the spring,   2
> Let them laugh, as I do now,   3
> At the old, forsaken bough   3
>   Where I cling.   2
> *The Last Leaf,* Oliver Wendell Holmes.

This may be used in longer stanzas, with a scheme such as 1, 1, 1, 2, 3, 3, 3, 2, a variant of this being popularized by Tennyson:

> Willows whiten, aspens quiver,   1
> Little breezes dusk and shiver   1
> Through the wave that runs for ever   1
> By the island in the river   1
>   Flowing down to Camelot.   2
> Four gray walls, and four gray towers,   3
> Overlook a space of flowers,   3
> And the silent isle embowers   3
>   The Lady of Shalott.   2
> *The Lady of Shalott,* by Alfred Tennyson.

This stanza is called *tail rhyme* stanza, and is a mere elaboration of the pattern of *The Last Leaf.*

Certain Other Stanzas

It may seem like profanation to some, to subject to the critical scalpel such a masterpiece as Keats's *Ode to a Grecian Urn.* But the poem suffers no loss from the process, for the reader returns to it to find it all uninjured in the end; and no other method will permit an understanding of the technical achievement involved in such lasting beauty. Here are five ten-line stanzas. Each opens with a 1, 2, 1, 2 sequence. Thereafter, there are differences. The first and last have the next six lines 3, 4, 5, 4, 3, 5; the fourth and fifth use instead 3, 4, 5, 3, 4, 5; while the second has 3, 4, 5, 3, 5, 4.

A famous seven-lined stanza is called *Rhyme Royal.* This was

used by James I of Scotland in his *The Kinges Quhair,* and repeatedly by Chaucer and others. Here is a typical use by Chaucer:

To you, my purse, and to none other wight	1
Complain I, for ye be my lady dear.	2
I am full sorry, now that ye be light,	1
For, certes, ye now make me heavy cheer.	2
Me were as lief-y laid upon my bier	2
For which unto your mercy thus I cry,	3
Be heavy again, or elles mote I die.	3

The Complaint to His Empty Purse, Geoffrey Chaucer.

This has a terminal couplet rhyming, 3, 3, which breaks the flow of the narrative somewhat. To avoid this, the *Canopus* stanza points a way out:

The night's mysterious wings pulsed thru the dark,	1
The night's mysterious noises cracked and shivered,	2
And where their fingers met a visible spark	1
Seemed to leap forth at them, and pulsed and quivered	2
Throughout them both. Their thickened tongues were dumb,	3
The pretty words of star-lore undelivered,	2
The pretty words that found no breath would come.	3

Canopus, Clement Wood.

Note here also that the use of some feminine or double rhymes with single or masculine rhymes is effective. This is especially effective in a Shakespearean sonnet.

Ottava Rima is an Italian stanza adopted in English by many poets. It is an eight-line stanza, composed of a sestet rhymed alternately, followed by a terminal rhyming couplet. The Italians use their heroic metre, eleven syllables to the line, in it; the English prefer iambic five-foot measure. Spenser, Milton, and Keats used it, and Byron preferred it, as in his *Don Juan*:

But " why then publish?"—There are no rewards	1
Of fame or profit when the world grows weary.	2
I ask in turn,—Why do you play at cards?	1
Why drink? Why read?—To make some hour less dreary.	2
It occupies me to turn back regards	1
On what I've seen or pondered, sad or cheery;	2
And what I write I cast upon the stream	3
To sink or swim—I have had at least my dream.	3

Don Juan, Lord Byron.

Again note the use of double and single rhymes in the same stanza, quite often effective.

The *Spenserian Stanza* was invented by Edmund Spenser, and has long been used in serious dignified verse. The eight opening five-foot iambic lines are terminated by an Alexandrine, or six-foot iambic line; the pattern may be seen in this opening of Keats's poem, which uses the stanza throughout:

St. Agnes' Eve—ah, bitter chill it was !   1
   The owl, for all his feathers, was acold.   2
The hare limped trembling through the frozen grass,   1
   And silent was the flock in woolly fold.   2
Numb were the Beadsman's fingers while he told   2
   His rosary, and while his frosted breath   3
Like pious incense from a censer old,   2
Seemed taking flight for heaven without a death,   3
Past the sweet Virgin's picture, while his prayer he saith. 3

                    The Eve of St. Agnes, John Keats.

Terza Rima is an iambic rhythm, usually of five feet to the line. It is usually written continuously, and not in stanzas. It consists of groups of three lines, rhymed 1, 2, 1; but the rhyming sound of the middle line, 2, becomes the first and third line of the next group; and so on. The end of the canto or poem is a couplet, tieing up the rhyme sound left loose as the central line terminal sound in the preceding triplet. Thus it is a sort of chain verse, its rhyme scheme proceeding: 1, 2, 1; 2, 3, 2; 3, 4, 3; 4, 5, 4; . . . . . . n-1, n, n-1; n, n. Shelley, in his *Ode to the West Wind,* used this in fourteen line groups, separating the triplets and concluding couplet as if they were separate stanzas.

It is advisable for the poet or versifier to spend some time in the pleasant chore of analyzing the favorite poems of the great poets—the odes of Keats, the sonnets of Shakespeare, the greater lyrics of Poe, and so on. Scansion will indicate the metre employed; and the numeral system 1, 1, 2, 2 will mark for you the rhyming pattern. Let your especial attention be directed to ingenious devices for securing variety within a formal pattern.

The sonnet, which will be reached in the study of lyric poetry, has been used often and successfully as a stanza.

In polyrhythmic or free verse, the stanza division follows the

poet's inner mandate of where each group of lines should end, as if it were a paragraph in prose.

Sapphics and Other Classic Forms

Elegiac verse, according to the classical models, consists of lines alternately dactylic hexameter and dactylic pentameter; and then this difference is explained away by saying that the shorter lines have six accents, but omit the unaccented syllables in the third and sixth feet. Coleridge indicates the method:

> In the hexameter rises the fountain's all-silvery radiance;
> In the pentameter aye falling in melody back.
> *Translation from Schiller,* Samuel Taylor Coleridge.

It is significant that none of the five greatest examples of elegiac poetry—that based upon death, or reflections upon death—in the English language, use this form. These five poems are Milton's *Lycidas,* Shelley's *Adonais,* Tennyson's *In Memoriam,* Gray's famous elegy, and Whitman's *When Lilacs Last in the Dooryards Bloomed,* a tribute to Lincoln.

The Greek *dactylic hexameter,* the classic model as the iambic five-foot line is in English, is far more complicated, according to the prosodists, than it sounds. There are six feet. The first four are dactyls or spondees. The fifth must be a dactyl: otherwise, if a spondee appears here, the verse is called spondaic. The last is a spondee or a trochee. A diagram makes this clearer.

This may be written in English, with an accent basis instead of a quantity basis (that is, long and short syllables).

Hendecasyllabics were 11-syllabled lines composed of a spondee, a dactyl, and trochees. Thus:

This metre has never been successfully naturalized into English.

Alcaics, named from the lyric poet Alcaeus, a contemporary of Sappho, are of several kinds. The first variety has a five-foot line, consisting of a spondee or iamb, an iamb, a long syllable, and two dactyls. Here is the pattern:

$$\text{or} \quad \breve{/}\ \acute{/}\ |\ \smile\ /\ |\ /\ |\ /\ \smile\ \smile\ |\ \smile\ \smile$$

The second variety has two dactyls and two trochees to the line:

$$/\ \smile\ \smile\ |\ /\ \smile\ \smile\ |\ /\ \smile\ |\ /\ \smile$$

And, for the third, the line is composed:

(I) $\smile\ /\ /\ /$			
or			
(II) $/\ \smile\ /\ /$	$/\ \smile\ \smile\ /$	$/\ \smile\ \smile\ /$	
or	(stress on	(stress on	$\smile\ /\ /$
(III) $/\ /\ \smile\ /$	1st or 4th	1st or 4th	(Stress on first
or	syllable)	syllable)	long syllable)
(IV) $/\ /\ /\ \smile$			

What are the names of these feet? The first is an epitrite (first, second, third, or fourth epitrite, depending upon the location of the short syllable); two choriambi or choriambs as above; and a bacchius. This technique does not often produce poetry in English; more often, it produces prosody or verse.

For an *Alcaic ode,* each strophe consists of four lines. The first two are eleven-syllabled Alcaics of the first kind; the third an especial form of iambic two-foot of nine syllables, described as hypercatalectic; and the fourth a ten-syllabled Alcaic of the second kind. Tennyson tried to catch it in:

> O mighty-mouthed inventor of harmonies,
> O skilled to sing of time or eternity,
> God-gifted organ-voice of England,
> Milton, a name to resound for ages.
> > *Milton,* Alfred Tennyson.

Sapphics are named after the poet Sappho, who is said to have used the form with high skill. A sapphic line consists of five equal beats, its central one of three syllables, and the rest of two each. The original Greek sapphic stanza consisted of three of these lines, followed by a shorter line called an *adonic,* the whole following this pattern:

$$/\ \smile\ \Big|\ \begin{matrix}/\ /\\ \text{or}\\ /\ \smile\end{matrix}\ \Big|\ /\ \smile\ \smile\ \Big|\ /\ \smile\ \Big|\ \begin{matrix}/\ /\\ \text{or}\\ /\ \smile\end{matrix}$$

$$/\ \smile\ \Big|\ \begin{matrix}/\ /\\ \text{or}\\ /\ \smile\end{matrix}\ \Big|\ /\ \smile\ \smile\ \Big|\ /\ \smile\ \Big|\ \begin{matrix}/\ /\\ \text{or}\\ /\ \smile\end{matrix}$$

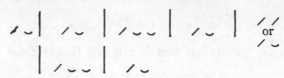

Certain English poets have essayed this metre. In the examples given, the accent sign (́) means a syllable described as long; the other symbol (˘) one described as short. Here is Swinburne's use of the form:

Saw the | white im- | placable | Aphro- | dite,
Saw the | hair un- | bound and the | feet un- | sandalled
Shine as | fire of | sunset on | western | waters;
　　Saw the re- | luctant

Feet, the straining plumes of the doves that drew her,
Looking, always looking with necks reverted,
Back to Lesbos, back to the hills whereunder
　　Shone Mitylene;
　　　　　　Sapphics, Algernon Charles Swinburne.

and so on to the end. A *choriambic line* consists of a spondee, three choriambi, and an iamb. A *galliambic line* is composed of iambs, one of which drops its final syllable: the next foot to the last being an anapest.

Indentation

The purpose of indentation is primarily to indicate the rhyme scheme. Indenting a line means sinking it inward by an increased blank space in the left hand margin. Every paragraph in prose is indented, at its beginning. An early indentation of poetry was similar to this, and consisted in indenting only the first line of each stanza. Where the poet desires to impress the reader with his rhyme scheme, indenting of lines similarly rhymed is proper:

　　　　Yet this inconstancy is such
　　　　　　As you too shall adore;
　　　　I could not love thee, Dear, so much,
　　　　　　Loved I not Honour more.
　　To Lucasta, on Going to the Wars, Richard Lovelace.

The following indentation is improper and essentially illiterate:

> That which her slender waist confined
> Shall now my joyful temples bind:
> No monarch but would give his crown
> His arms might do what this has done.
>   *On a Girdle,* Edmund Waller.

Needless to say, the poet set this up without indentation. The motive for such misindentation seems to be the following foggy thinking on the part of the versifier:

(a) Some poems by great poets are indented.
(b) Therefore I must indent my poem, to make sure it is regarded as great.

Once let the motive for indentation be iearned—to show the similarity of rhyme-sounds terminating lines indented to the same point—and this error will be avoided.

A second purpose of indentation is to center short lines in the central portion of the poem, instead of leaving them dangling off to the left. One of Guy Wetmore Carryll's eight verse poems proceeds:

> A maiden from the Bosphorus,
> With eyes as bright as phosphorus,
> Once wed the wealthy bailiff
> Of the caliph
> Of Kelat.
> Though diligent and zealous, he
> Became a slave to jealousy.
> (Considering her beauty,
> 'Twas his duty
> To be that!)
> *How the Helpmate of Bluebeard Made Free with a Door,*
>   Guy Wetmore.

Here the first, third, fourth, and sixth indentations indicate rhyming changes; the second and fifth are to center briefer rhyming lines. The object is to make the poem appear as presentable as possible, considering rhyme scheme and length of line. Recall the indentation of Shelley's *To a Skylark,* already given.

As to sonnets, there are only two proper ways to present them: indenting for rhyme, and omitting indentation. The Italian and

Shakespearean form would then have the following indentation, if this is used to indicate the rhyme scheme:

Italian Sonnet	Shakespearean Sonnet
1	1
2	2
2	1
1	2
1	3
2	4
2	3
1	4
3	5
4	6
5	5
3	6
4	7
5	7

It is more usual to set up sonnets without indentation. The original method of indenting the Shakespearean sonnet consisted of twelve lines without indentation, and an indentation for the concluding couplet.

All this assumes that the poet wishes to impress on the reader the rhyming scheme, and the poet's fidelity in following it. But this is initiating the reader into the irrelevant laboratory work of the poet, and has its many disadvantages, since the reader primarily wishes to know what the poet has to say,—not the devices by which he increases his effectiveness. The modern tendency is to eliminate indentation in all poems. If poems are printed similar to prose, the indentation will be the same as prose, to indicate paragraph openings, or to inset a quotation.

V

DIVISIONS OF POETRY

Narrative Poetry

POETRY is commonly divided, from the point of view of the poet's presentation of his material, into narrative, dramatic, and lyric poetry. The distinction is simple:

> In *narrative poetry,* the poet tells a story as if he had been a spectator, but not a participant, in the events.
>
> In *dramatic poetry,* the poet lets the characters of the story speak their own words.
>
> In *lyric poetry,* the poet speaks his own moods, thoughts and aspirations.

These, like all definitions, define from the centers, not from the boundaries. A long-winded narrative in the first person, telling the poet's own adventures, might be classed with reason as any of the three: narrative poetry because it tells a story; dramatic, like a long dramatic monologue; and lyric, because the poet himself is speaking. This attitude classification is not of primary importance.

A fourth division, *didactic poetry,* that which teaches or points a moral, was once popular and is still encountered. It is regarded at best as a low flight of poetry.

Epic, Metrical Romance, Tale

An epic is——

> a long narrative poem, dealing with heroic events, usually with supernatural guidance and participation in the action.

Epics are divided into natural or folk epics, and literary epics. There is a suggested theory that folk epics are preceded by and composed of folk ballads. The earliest known epics exhibit little or no trace of any welding or amalgamating process.

The earliest literary remains in Greece are of the epic type, of three varieties. Epics of personal romance and war center around

the semi-mythical blind bard Homer, with his *Iliad*—the story of
the flight of Helen of Sparta with her Trojan lover, Paris; the
war of Greeks against Trojans to avenge this; the anger of Greek
Achilles and its effects; the defeat of Troy—and the *Odyssey,*
telling the world-wanderings of Grecian Odysseus after the sack
of Troy, and of his return to his native Ithaca. Parts of these long
poems are essentially prosy; but they have never been equalled
for long poetic flight in narrative form. Epics dealing with the
mysteries of religion center around the mythical singer Orpheus.
Epics of a didactic nature center around the name of Hesiod.
Scholars state that many lost epics in all three fields preceded the
epics now remaining.

The *Mahabharata* and the *Ramayana* in Sanskrit, the *Shah-
nameh* in Persian, the *Niebelungenlied* in Middle German, *Beo-
wulf* in Anglo-Saxon, the fragmentary *Elder Edda* from Iceland,
the *Poem of the Cid* from Spain, the *Song of Roland* in medieval
France, the *Kalevala* from Finland, are all folk epics. They
originated before the invention of writing, and were transmitted
orally, with inevitable changes and additions from time to time.
Literary epics are a later attempt to catch the charm of the ancient
epics; and as a rule they are a lower flight. Virgil's *Æneid,* Tasso's
Jerusalem Delivered, Ariosto's *Orlando Furioso,* Dante's didactic
Commedia, are the most outstanding among these. The *Lusiads*
of Camoens gave form to the Portuguese language, much as
Dante did to modern Italian, Chaucer to English, and Luther to
German. Spenser's *Faerie Queene* has lost most of its charm for
many modern English readers; even Milton's *Paradise Lost,*
which sought to express English Puritanism as Dante had sought
to express medieval Catholicism, is largely dull to modern readers.

Stories in verse preceded stories in prose. Chaucer's *Canterbury
Tales,* the narrative metrical romances and tales of Scott, Byron,
and others, preceded the novel and the short story in English. But
prose has become the popular medium, as it is the more natural
one: and the long poetic narrative today usually seems artificial.

The Ballad

The ballad, the brief story in verse, alone retains some general
popularity. The name meant first a folk song-and-dance, like the

surviving *London Bridge Is Falling Down* or *Oats, Peas, Beans and Barley Grow*. It came to mean the folksong that tells a brief story—at first to be sung, later to be said or read. The Germanic bards or scalds, the gleemen, harpers, minstrels, troubadours, minnesingers, were a distinguished lot—the oral literature (and music) of races in the pre-bookish age. The chief figures in the ballads at first were noble, since nobles were the patrons of the singers. Later on, the lower classes became vocal—the oppressed Saxons in the Robin Hood ballads, and many early ballads in which a commoner ends by marrying one of noble lineage. The technique at first was simple, often with a simple refrain that the hearers might chorus. In English, the first *ballad metre* was seven-foot iambic lines, rhymed in couplets. A variant of this is the Scottish ballad *Edward, Edward,* with a pause between the invoked names taking the place of a foot in alternate lines:

"Quhy does zour brand sae drop wi' bluid, Edward, Edward?
 Quhy does zour brand sae drop wi' bluid, and quhy sae sad
                                    gang zee, O?"
"O, I hae kill-ed my hauke sae guid, Mither, Mither,
 O, I hae kill-ed my hauke sae guid; and I had nae mair but he, O."

Like the majority of the older ballads, this is a gory thing, full of blood and stark universal passions. If modern poetry gave us more of such red meat instead of caviar canapes, it would hold a wider popularity than it now has.

The rhythm is much freer than centuries of later iambic versification. The modern versifier can learn much of the way to sprinkle anapests in an iambic pattern, and of more important devices in versification, from old English folk ballads, as from that other depository of English folk verse, *Mother Goose*. Folk ballads originate among people largely pre-bookish; certain American mountaineers and certain Negroes still commemorate thrilling events with folk ballads, like the one within our memory on *The Sinking of the Titantic*.

Literary ballads are more successful than literary epics. Ballads by Heine and Housman, Coleridge's *Rime of the Ancient Mariner,* have been taken to the heart of the race. The stanza form is almost invariably simple. Yet it is worth while to study the slight elaborations of the ballad metre that Coleridge employed—with

stanzas ranging from four to nine ballad half-lines. There are many more successful literary ballads.

Dramatic Poetry

Like story-telling, drama is largely a lost field to poetry, purely because of the unnaturalness of poetic drama as usually written. There is a field for drama in natural free verse, which may yet be widely used. Classic drama was divided into *tragedy,* a play ending in death, and *comedy,* a play not ending in death. This division was unworkable, and has been abandoned today.

Thespis, reputed father of Grecian drama, never permitted more than one actor on the stage at one time, with a chorus to interpret the action to the audience. This rigid convention was shattered by Aeschylus, who added a second actor. Sophocles added a third; but classic Greek drama never permitted a fourth. The typical Shakespearean play had five acts, the climax occurring during the third act, the solution at the end. This usually meant a dragging fourth act, which only *Othello* among the great tragedies avoided. Shakespeare and most other English verse dramatists used a five-foot iambic line, most often in blank or unrhymed verse. None of these conventions are more sacred than the one actor convention of Thespis.

The *dramatic monolog* or *dramatic lyric,* sprung from the speeches of Thespis's actor and the unnatural soliloquy of classic and English drama, is the one form of drama in verse which preserves considerable popularity. Robert Browning made this field peculiarly his own, with such magnificent dramatic vignettes as *My Last Duchess, Andrea del Sarto, Caliban upon Setebos,* and so many more. His tremendous *The Ring and the Book* is, within a brief framework, ten immense dramatic monologs: the same group of facts, as seen through the eyes of ten differing personalities. Such dramatic monologs may be in any rhythm, any line length, and with or without rhyme. Success comes in proportion to the naturalness of the speech, the universality and depth of the emotion displayed, and the accuracy in character-drawing.

Lyric Poetry: Ode, Elegy, Pastoral

Perhaps the earliest, and certainly the most enduringly popular type of poetry, is the lyric. As the name indicates, it meant originally poetry to be sung to the lyre,—a dance at first accompanying this.

The *ode,* the most exalted form of lyric poetry, had strict rules in classic times. The Greek Pindaric ode had three movements: a strophe, in which the chorus moved from a given spot toward the right; the antistrophe, following the same versification pattern, and to the same tune, in which the chorus moved correspondingly to the left; and the concluding epode, different in structure, sung to a different tune, and with the chorus standing still. Efforts to revive this form in English have not succeeded. In English, the ode is a dignified lyric on some high theme, with constant progress in its stanzas toward its conclusion. Familiar odes in English include Wordsworth's:

> Our birth is but a sleep and a forgetting;
> The Soul that rises with us, our life's Star,
>   Hath elsewhere its setting
>   And cometh from afar;
>   Not in entire forgetfulness,
>   And not in utter nakedness,
> But trailing clouds of glory do we come
>   From God, who is our home.
> Heaven lies about us in our infancy!
>   *Ode on the Intimations of Immortality from*
>   *Recollections of Early Childhood,*
>   William Wordsworth.

and also the great odes by Shelley and Keats already referred to.

An *elegy* is a formal expression of the poet's grief at death, whether general or centered about the death of an individual. It has no more definite a pattern in English than the ode. Milton, in *Lycidas,* uses an iambic measure, with lines of differing lengths, and a fluidic rhyme scheme. Shelley, in *Adonais,* chose the Spenserian stanza. Tennyson, in *In Memoriam,* selected the quatrain pattern already encountered. Whitman, in his major Lincoln threnody, *When Lilacs Last in the Dooryard Bloomed,* wrote in magnificent polyrhythmic verse. Gray's familiar *Elegy Written in a*

Country Churchyard, alone among these a meditation upon death in general, used alternate-rhymed five-foot iambic lines. There are many familiar short elegies in the language.

The *pastoral* is a reflective lyric upon some aspect of nature, formerly concerned with shepherd life, whence its name. Milton's shapely *L'Allegro* and *Il Penseroso,* and Whittier's *Snowbound,* are examples in this genre. As city living increasingly replaces country living, some form of city lyric may supplant the pastoral, if it does not die without offspring.

The Simple Lyric: The Song

The word *song* is loosely used for any simple lyric, on the theory that it may always be set to music. It is best to reserve the word for a lyric intended to be set to music. This calls for a knowledge, on the part of the poet, of the human voice in music, and the ease or difficulty with which the various sounds are produced. Certain consonants and combinations of consonants are sinagable only with great difficulty. A line like:

The gross-sized much-touched scratch will itch

is not easily singable. The terminal consonants *m, n, l, r* are sung with ease; *s, z, ch, sh,* as terminals, with difficulty. Of the vowels, broad *a,* long *o,* long *a, ou,* are easiest to sing, though no vowel is really difficult. The words chosen should always end, and as far as possible include, only sounds which open the mouth, instead of closing it. Simple words are to be preferred to complicated ones; definite precise words to indefinite abstract ones; emotion-evoking words to intellectualized ones.

The lyric canon in English is one of the glories of its literature. After the dawn-hour lyrics before the Elizabethan age, the golden song of Campion—

> Shall I come, sweet Love, to thee,
>   When the evening beams are set?
> Shall I not excluded be,
>   Will you find no feigned let?
> Let me not, for pity, more
> Tell the long hours at your door;
>   *Shall I Come, Sweet Love?* Thomas Campion.

the equally melodious singable lyrics of Shakespeare and his contemporaries, the lyrics of Shelley, Keats, Byron, Burns, Housman, and so many more in England, and of Poe, Emily Dickinson, Sidney Lanier, and a few later singers, together make up a body of song that the race continues to treasure.

The themes and treatments of the lyric may vary as widely as the desires and visions of the poets. A lyric may have any chosen form of rhythm, with or without rhyme. It is often natural and effective in free verse or polyrhythmic poetry, since in this form the precise emotion-moving thoughts and images may be written down, without the warping often demanded by such devices of versification as rhyme, assonance, consonance, and formal metre and stanza arrangement. Here is an example from the chief American user of the form, in a lyric called *Reconciliation:*

> Word over all, beautiful as the sky,
> Beautiful that war and all its deeds of carnage must
>   in time be utterly lost,
> That the hands of the sisters Death and Night
>   incessantly softly wash again, and ever again,
>   this soil'd world;
> For my enemy is dead, a man divine as myself is dead,
> I look where he lies white-faced and still in the
>   coffin—I draw near,
> Bend down and touch lightly with my lips the white
>   face in the coffin.
>   *Reconciliation,* Walt Whitman.

Modern users of polyrhythmic poetry as a rule use less eloquence than Whitman, and less of the expansive cosmic note; and tend instead toward the tense and gripping emotional appeal usual in rhymed and metric lyrics. Much shorter line-division is also common.

The Sonnet

The sonnet is the most popular fixed form in English. It is a lyric of fourteen iambic five-foot lines, with a defined and definite rhyme scheme. There are two forms of it widely used in English, the Italian or Petrarchian sonnet, and the Shakespearean sonnet.

The rhyme-scheme of the Italian sonnet appears from the following example:

The world is too much with us; late and soon,   1
Getting and spending, we lay waste our powers: 2
Little we see in Nature that is ours;   2
We have given our hearts away, a sordid boon!   1
This sea that bares her bosom to the moon,   1
The winds that will be howling at all hours,   2
And are up-gathered now like sleeping flowers;   2
For this, for everything, we are out of tune;   1
It moves us not.—Great God! I'd rather be   3
A Pagan suckled in a creed outworn;   4
So might I, standing on this pleasant lea,   3
Have glimpses that would make me less forlorn;   4
Have sight of Proteus rising from the sea;   3
Or hear old Triton blow his wreathéd horn.   4

Sonnet, William Wordsworth.

The first eight lines of any sonnet are called the *octave*. In the Italian sonnet, the rhyme-scheme is rigid, and may not be departed from. The octave consists of two quatrains rhymed 1, 2, 2, 1, the *In Memoriam* rhyming pattern made familiar by Tennyson's use of it. The entire octave then rhymes 1, 2, 2, 1; 1, 2, 2, 1. It is not permitted to vary the rhymes in the second half of the octave, by using 1, 2, 2, 1; 3, 2, 2, 3, or a form too commonly encoun-tered, 1, 2, 2, 1; 3, 4, 4, 3.

The concluding six lines of any sonnet are called the sestet. The two permissible rhyme-schemes for the sestet of an Italian sonnet are 3, 4, 3, 4, 3, 4, and 3, 4, 5, 3, 4, 5. It will be noted that the sonnet by Wordsworth, quoted above, uses the proper octave rhyme-scheme and the first of these two sestet arrangements.

As to treatment, the octave must be end-stopped—that is, the eighth line must mark the termination of a sentence. Even the halves of the octave should be end-stopped. The first quatrain should introduce the theme, and develop it in a certain direction; the second should continue this development in the same direction. The sestet introduces a new development in a different direc-tion, with the first tercet carrying this new direction to a definite point; and the final tercet bringing the theme to a conclusion. The actual movement of the strict Italian sonnet may be expressed as a flow in the octave, and an ebb in the sestet—so Theodore Watts-

Dunton phrased it in his sonnet, *The Sonnet's Voice*. This does not mean, of course, that the inspiration or the emotional effect should ebb.

Wordsworth's sonnet, emotionally effective as it is, violates several of these strict rules. The octave movement does not end with the eighth line, but trespasses into the ninth. There is no break in thought between the two tercets that together comprise the sestet. We will find constantly among the masters violations of the rules, at times in the nature of experiments; none of these has as yet established its popularity in English poetry. In his sonnet *On the Extinction of the Venetian Republic,* Wordsworth's octave rhymes 1, 2, 2, 1; 1, 3, 3, 1,—another variation.

One authority examined 6,283 Italian sonnets in English, and found these variations for the terminal sestet rhymes:

3, 4, 5, 3, 4, 5	3, 3, 4, 5, 5, 4
3, 4, 3, 4, 5, 5	3, 4, 5, 5, 3, 4
3, 4, 4, 3, 5, 5	3, 4, 5, 5, 4, 3
3, 4, 5, 4, 3, 5	3, 4, 4, 5, 3, 5
3, 4, 3, 5, 4, 5	3, 4, 5, 4, 5, 3
3, 4, 5, 3, 5, 4	3, 4, 3, 5, 5, 4

Two of these have terminal couplets, the most regrettable variation of the Italian sonnet. Six others include a couplet somewhere within the sestet. In addition to the above, the following two-rhyme variants are found:

3, 4, 3, 4, 3, 4	3, 4, 3, 4, 4, 3
3, 4, 4, 3, 3, 4	3, 4, 3, 3, 4, 4
3, 4, 4, 3, 4, 3	3, 4, 3, 3, 4, 3

Only the first excludes any couplet rhyming. Shelley's poem *Ozymandias* had the rhyme scheme: 1, 2, 1, 2; 1, 3, 4, 3; 5, 4, 5, 6, 5, 6. Milton led the way in failing to separate clearly the octave and sestet, so much so that his type of sonnet is sometimes called the Miltonic—Italian in rhyme-pattern, but without the characteristic Italian flow and ebb of theme, broken after the eighth line.

The Shakespearean sonnet is simpler and more natural in rhyming, and is in wider favor among English-using poets. An example is:

When, in disgrace with fortune and men's eyes,	1
I all alone beweep my outcast state,	2
And trouble deaf heaven with my bootless cries,	1
And look upon myself and curse my fate,	2
Wishing me like to one more rich in hope,	3
Featur'd like him, like him with friends possess'd,	4
Desiring this man's art and that man's scope,	3
With what I most enjoy contented least;	4
Yet in these thoughts myself almost despising,	5
Haply I think on thee, and then my state,	6
Like to the lark at break of day arising	5
From sullen earth, sings hymns at heaven's gate;	6
For thy sweet love remember'd such wealth brings	7
That then I scorn to change my state with kings.	7

Sonnet XXIX, William Shakespeare.

This is the accepted Shakespearean indentation for this form: though it may be indented to show rhyming mates, as the Italian also may be. Both types of the sonnet at times are printed with octave and sestet separated, making a poem of two stanzas; or octave divided into two quatrains, and at times the sestet similarly divided.

The rhyming scheme of the Shakespearean sonnet is three quatrains, 1, 2, 1, 2; 3, 4, 3, 4; 5, 6, 5, 6; with a concluding couplet, 7, 7. A shrewd interspering of double or feminine rhymes aids. Many variations have been tried on this simple rhyming basis. Sir Philip Sidney repeated the rhymes of the first quatrain in the second, giving him a pattern of 1, 2, 1, 2; 1, 2, 1, 2; 3, 4, 3, 4; 5, 5. Spenser, in his hundred and twenty sonnets, used a chain-verse device of interlocking rhymes throughout each sonnet, so that his pattern was: 1, 2, 1, 2,; 2, 3, 2, 3; 3, 4, 3, 4; 5, 5. Keats, in his second sonnet on *Fame,* wedded the Shakespearean octave to the Italian sestet, with his rhyme scheme 1, 2, 1, 2; 3, 4, 3, 4; 5, 6, 5, 7, 7, 6. Rupert Brooke, in the first and fifth of his soldier sonnets, used the Shakespearean octave, and a straight Italian sestet: 5, 6, 7, 5, 6, 7. The third and fourth of the same series also wander from any strict pattern.

The sonnet was invented in Italy in the 13th century, probably by Pier delle Vigne, secretary of state in the Sicilian court of Frederick. His sonnet *Però ch' amore* is the earliest known. His

rhyme form, 1, 2, 1, 2; 1, 2, 1, 2; 3, 4, 5, 3, 4, 5, has never become popular in English. The French sonnet prefers the strict Italian octave, with a sestet of three rhymes commencing with a couplet. This also has not become naturalized in English. There are occasional variations in English poetry, such as 1, 2, 1, 2; 2, 1, 2, 1; 3, 4, 3, 4, 5, 5; Italian sonnets with sestet 3, 4, 3, 4, 5, 5; and so on. Watts-Dunton points out, in his article on the sonnet in the 11th edition of *The Encyclopedia Brittanica,* that the charm of this and other fixed forms comes from familiarity in advance with the rhyme-scheme to be followed; and that this charm is dissipated, when any break in the expected rhyme-scheme occurs. We feel somewhat as if we listened to a limerick with an extra foot or an extra line: a sense of surprise, its pleasure being doubtful. In spite of this, poets continue to vary the rigid forms from time to time, and will continue to do so.

The sonnet, of either form, is used by many poets as a fourteen-line stanza. Many of the Elizabethan sonnet sequences illustrate this; and there are many more recent examples. In writing the sonnet, it will aid to write down the rhyme scheme to the right of the space where your lines are to be written, and thereafter to mark across from each numbered rhyme the initial consonantal sounds used: giving a check against repeating a rhyming sound (that is, identity), which is inexcusable false rhyming. We would then have a notebook page like:

		Rhyme Sounds			
		ŌLD	ĔN	ĪZ	ĔN
Much have I travell'd in the realms of gold	1	G			
And many goodly states and kingdoms seen;	2		S		
Round many western islands have I been	2		B		
Which bards in fealty to Apollo hold.	1	H			
Oft of one wide expanse had I been told	1	T			
That deep-browed Homer ruled as his demesne:	2		M		
Yet never did I breathe its pure serene	2		R		
Till I heard Chapman speak out loud and bold.	1	B			
—Then felt I like some watcher of the skies	3			SK	
When a new planet swims into his ken;	4				K
Or like stout Cortez—when with eagle eyes	3			Vowel	
He stared at the Pacific—and all his men	4				M
Look'd at each other with a wild surmise—	3			M	
Silent, upon a peak in Darien.	4				Vowel

On First Looking into Chapman's Homer, John Keats.

Thus, by this check, it appears that the poet used, for rhyme 1, ŌLD, these consonantal sounds: g, h, t, b; for rhyme 2, ĒN, s, b, m, r; for rhyme 3, ĪZ, sk, the unconsonanted vowel sound, and m; for rhyme 4, ĔN, k, m, and the unconsonanted vowel sound. No identities; rhyme throughout. The sonnet, from a technical rhyming standpoint, has no flaws. When this method is followed during the writing of the sonnet—the first group of columns, that containing the numerals, properly indented, being written down first—this gives a check as the writing of the sonnet proceeds, and saves much rewriting.

VI

THE FRENCH FORMS. LIGHT AND
HUMOROUS VERSE

Into Formal and Light Verse

ANY poetic form may be used either to arouse the great serious emotions, or the lighter and more frivolous ones. Nor is there any reason for holding the serious poet higher than the comic poet. Surely Aristophanes, the great Athenian comic dramatist, ranked as high, and was doubtless more popular and influential, than any of the great serious triad, Aeschylus, Sophocles and Euripides. Shakespeare the comic dramatist, the author of *Merry Wives of Windsor, Midsummer Night's Dream, The Taming of the Shrew,* is as impressive a figure as the Shakespeare who let the melancholy Dane live and die in Elsinore, the Shakespeare who was the chronicler of Othello's jealousy and Lear's senility. Cervantes, who jeered knighthood to death, is greater as a writer than any other Spaniard; Racine, Moliere, Voltaire, Anatole France, were greatest as satirists; and so the roll continues. Serious writers and poets are more popular, and are taken more seriously; but this may be because it is more civilized and difficult to laugh than to weep. Animals can suffer agonies; but they cannot chuckle. And yet the race would not willingly exchange Robert Burn's *Tam o' Shanter* and W. S. Gilbert's *The Bab Ballads* for any number of closet dramas, ponderous versified essays and odes, or a whole trainload of lyrics to spring and young love.

Fixed forms of poetry tend to become outgrown, like a child's shirt too small to close over a man's heart. They then become relegated to minor versifiers, to light verse writers, and to college and high school exercises. Prose ages more quickly than poetry: witness such masterpieces, written for adults, as the world's great fairy stories, Aesop's fables, the *Arabian Nights, Robinson Crusoe, Gulliver's Travels* in the nursery; and the essays and novels of yesterday encountered in school or college. Poetry itself ages:

65

Shakespeare, Milton, Virgil, Horace, are more used in the class-room than in the living room today, and so of the rest of them. In spite of constant insistence that nothing changes under the sun, the nature of man is stretched outward by his expanding environment, and coiled more tensely into molecules and atoms and complexes and other inner things: and the poetry, the concentrated heart's expression, of yesterday cannot forever be the poetry of today. Prose, in the large, must be rephrased every fifty years, or less, to be enjoyable to living men; poetry survives longer, but the hour will come when the most enduring poem of a Shakespeare or a Sappho will seem ancient, and must be restated or recreated by a living poet, to speak again for the maturing soul of man. If this is true of the poetry itself, it is truer of the patterns in which poetry has been uttered, and especially of the fixed forms.

The sonnet, an emigrant from Italy that became naturalized in English literature, still holds its own as a major method of expressing serious poetry, in the eyes of many poets and readers. Even at that, it is now regarded as puerile by the extreme advocates of free verse or polyrhythmic poetry, especially since Whitman and the Imagist movement. Numerous other alien verse forms did not fare so well, and have established themselves primarily as mediums for light and humorous verse. These include the ballade, the rondeau, the villanelle, the triolet, and so on. This may be because of their rigid rules and formal repetitions, which were not acceptable to the living poet. And yet, they started as seriously as Sapphics, heroic blank verse, or polyrhythms. . . .

Of all the forms of verse originating in medieval Provence, among those that failed to acclimatize themselves in English are the *vers, canzo, sirvente, tenso, alba, serena, pastorella, breu-doble,* and the *retroensa.* Only the most elaborate of the lot, the intricate *sestina,* has survived in English. When religious crusades wiped out this culture, the germs of formalized verse took root in northern France, especially under Charles d'Orleans and François Villon. The *ballade* appeared. Spenser used 3,848 of his nine-line Spenserian stanzas in one poem: across the Channel, Eustache Deschamps, a friend of Chaucer's, left no less than 1,175 complete ballades. Froissart the chronicler wrote many. Charles d'Orleans is hailed as the early master of the roundel, as Villon is lauded as the prince of ballade-makers. Jean Passerat gave the

villanelle its present form, in the sixteenth century; Voiture, a
century later, perfected the rondeau. In the seventeenth century,
after the forms had been known for two hundred years in English,
Patrick Carey published a series of dignified religious triolets; and
the over-artificialized forms have repeatedly been revived since.

Rules of the Fixed Verse Forms

In English verse, the rules for the fixed forms are stricter than
in French:

I. No syllable once used as a rhyme can be used again in the
same poem as a rhyme, not even if it be spelled differently;
nor if the whole word is altered by a prefix.

This bars such identities as *Ruth,* a girl's name, and *ruth,* pity;
bear, an animal, *bear,* to support, *bare, forbear,* and so on; *sale*
and *sail; claim, reclaim,* and *disclaim; facility, imbecility;* and,
if this be taken as a single rhyme, not a triple one, it forbids the
use of more than one from this group: *tea, manatee, imbecility,
impossibility, lenity,* and so on.

As to the *refrain,* an important element in many of these forms:

II. The refrain must not be a meaningless repetition of sounds
as in many English ballads; it must aid in the progress of
the thought; come in naturally; and be repeated in all its
sounds, without any change of sound.

Slipshod versifiers alter the refrain by changing the introductory
word, as by using an *and* for a *but,* a *then* for an *if.* This is unfor-
giveable. But the requirement goes no further than the repetition
of all *sounds.* Punctuation may be changed, spelling may be
changed, meaning may be changed: permitting the following—

It's meet, this sale; Its meat, this sail.
Gray day; Grade aye; Grade A.

The Ballade Family

There are two standard forms of the *ballade.* The more usual one
consists of three stanzas of eight lines each; followed by a concluding quatrain, known as the *envoy.* It is thus a poem of twenty-

eight lines, or twice the length of a sonnet. Each stanza, and the envoy, terminate with a line repeated sound by sound, and called the *refrain*. The rhyme scheme is 1, 2, 1, 2, 2, 3, 2, 3R for each stanza, 3R being the refrain; and 2, 3, 2, 3R for the envoy. The rules of the ballade may be stated as follows:

I. The same set of rhyme-sounds used in the first stanza, in the same order, must be used in each stanza; and the last half of this scheme must be used in the envoy.

II. No rhyme-sound once used as a rhyme may be used again for that purpose anywhere in the poem.

III. Each stanza and the envoy must close with the refrain line, repeated without any alteration of sound; though its punctuation, meaning and spelling may be altered.

IV. The sense of the refrain must be supreme throughout the ballade, the culminating refrain line being always brought in without strain or effort as the natural close of the stanza or envoy.

Formerly, the length of the refrain governed the length of the stanza. Thus an eight-syllabled refrain dictated an eight-line stanza, and a ten-syllabled refrain a ten-line stanza. This rule is followed no longer.

V. The stanza should carry an unbroken sense throughout, and not be split in meaning into two quatrains, or any other division. The needful pauses for punctuation are allowed, but the sense is not to be finished midway of the stanza.

VI. The envoy, as used in ballades and the chant royal, was at first addressed to the patron of the poet. It is thus usual to commence it with some such invocation as *Prince! Princess! Sire!* or by some mythical or symbolic person so introduced. This is at times omitted. The envoy is properly both a dedication and a culmination, and should be richer in wording and meaning and more stately in imagery than the preceding lines.

Here is a well-wrought ballade, in four-foot iambic verse. The rhyme-scheme is indicated by the numerals 1, 2, and 3, the refrain line being designated 3R. To the right appear the checking col-

umns for the three rhyming sounds, to make sure that there are no repetitions,—unforgivable, in strict formal verse of this type.

| | | Rhyme Sounds | | |
		AD	Ō	OL
Where are the passions they essayed,	1	S		
And where the tears they made to flow?	2		FL	
Where the wild humours they portrayed	1	TR		
For laughing worlds to see and know?	2		N	
Othello's wrath and Juliet's woe?	2		W	
Sir Peter's whims and Timon's gall?	3			G
And Millamant and Romeo?	2		Vowel	
Into the night go one and all.	3R			Vowel
Where are the braveries, fresh or frayed?	1	FR		
The plumes, the armours—friend and foe?	2		F	
The cloth of gold, the rare brocade,	1	K		
The mantles glittering to and fro?	2		FR	
The pomp, the pride, the royal show?	2		SH	
The cries of youth and festival?	3			V
The youth, the grace, the charm, the glow?	2		GL	
Into the night go one and all.	3R			Vowel
The curtain falls, the play is played:	1	PL		
The Beggar packs beside the Beau;	2		B	
The Monarch troops, and troops the Maid;	1	M		
The Thunder huddles with the Snow.	2		SN	
Where are the revellers high and low?	2		L	
The clashing swords? The lover's call?	3			K
The dancers gleaming row on row?	2		R	
Into the night go one and all.	3R			Vowel

Envoy.

Prince, in one common overthrow	2		THR	
The Hero tumbles with the Thrall;	3			THR
As dust that drives, as straws that blow,	2		BL	
Into the night go one and all.	3R			Vowel

Ballade of Dead Actors, William Ernest Henley.

As to the two requirements about rhyming, a ballade requires six 1 rhymes. Here the six consonantal sounds, as the checking column establishes, are *s, tr, fr, k, pl,* and *m.*

A ballade requires fourteen 2 rhymes. Here the fourteen consonantal sounds, as the checking column establishes, are *fl, n, w,* the unconsonanted vowel, *f, fr, sh, gl, b, sn, l, r, thr,* and *bl.*

A ballade requires five 3 rhymes, one of which reappears three times as the refrain. The five sound used here are *g,* the

unconsonanted vowel, *v, k,* and *thr.* The rhyming is correct throughout.

The refrain line is used without any alteration of any kind throughout, satisfying the third requirement. It is used throughout as a natural climax of each stanza. Each stanza has its own climactic rise to the refrain. The envoy meets the requirements wholly.

This ballade, then may be used as a model.

The meter of a ballade need not be four-foot iambic, as in this example. Andrew Lang's *Ballade of Primitive Man* has a three-foot anapestic movement, with the refrain, " 'Twas the manner of Primitive Man." Dactyls may be used, or anapests. A recent newspaper ballade had only two trochees to the line, its refrain being "Life is gay." Another had merely one iambic foot to each line, with the refrain "I love." No doubt someone has written a ballade with only one syllable to each line.

The most famous of all ballades is François Villon's ballade *Des Dames du Temps Jadis, (Ballade of Bygone Ladies).* There are many familiar translations of this, Rossetti's with the refrain "But where are the snows of yester-year?" John Payne's with "But what is become of last year's snow?" and others. None of these are authentic recreations in living poetry; not even of the refrain *Mais ou sont les neiges d'antan?* (But where are the last year's snows?) In technique, Rossetti has entirely different rhyming sounds in each stanza, and another in the envoy. Payne is accurate, though he repeats some rhyme-sounds, and uses words as unliving as *vade* (that is, *go*), *marish, whilere, dole;* and surely "Virgin debonair" is an unfortunate mistranslation of Villon's stately *Vierge souvraine.* At least, none of this is as archaic as two words in this line of Rossetti's version:

(From love he won such dule and teen!)

Examining the Villon original, we find that he uses the terminal sound -*maine* seven times, and rhymes it with *moyne* and other apparent consonances; rhymes *lis* and *Allis;* and otherwise is as lax as French rules allow, rather than following the strict and at that time unpromulgated English rules. An acceptable version in English may take advantages of the practices in the original; although it will have to be an authentic poetic recreation.

The second standard form of the ballade consists of stanzas of ten lines, usually of ten syllables each, as in the five-foot iambic pattern; followed by an envoy of five lines. The regular rhyme scheme for each stanza is 1, 2, 1, 2, 2, 3, 3, 4, 3, 4R, 4R being the refrain line. For the envoy, the rhyme scheme is 3, 3, 4, 3, 4R. This is much rarer in English than the foregoing.

The *ballade with double refrain* uses two refrains, one occurring at the fourth line of every stanza, and one at the eighth; while, in the envoy, the refrains are the second and fourth lines respectively, the envoy being rhymed couplet-wise. The rhyme scheme for each stanza is 1, 2, 1, 2R; 2, 3, 2, 3R, 2R being the first refrain line, and 3R the second. The rhyme scheme for the envoy is 2, 2R, 3, 3R. The best technique selects two antithetical refrains, and develops each stanza upon the refrain used to close it. Here is an excellent example:

When the roads are heavy with mire and rut,	1
In November fogs, in December snows,	2
When the North Wind howls, and the doors are shut,	1
There is place and enough for the pains of prose;—	2R
But whenever a scent from the whitethorn blows,	2
And the jasmine-stars to the casement climb,	3
And a Rosalind-face at the lattic shows,	3
Then hey!—for the ripple of laughing rhyme!	3R

When the brain gets dry as an empty nut,	
When the reason stands on its squarest toes,	
When the mind (like a beard) has a "formal cut,"	
There is place and enough for the pains of prose;—	2R
But whenever the May-blood stirs and glows,	
And the young year draws to the "golden prime,"—	
And Sir Romeo sticks in his ears a rose,	
Then hey!—for the ripple of laughing rhyme!	3R

In a theme where the thoughts have a pedant strut,	
In a changing quarrel of "Ayes" and "Noes,"	
In a starched procession of "If" and "But",	
There is place and enough for the pains of prose;—	2R
But whenever a soft glance softer glows,	
And the light hours dance to the trysting-time,	
And the secret is told "that no one knows,"	
Then hey!—for the ripple of laughing rhyme!	3R

Envoy

In a work-a-day world,—for its needs and woes,   2
There is place and enough for the pains of prose;   2R
But whenever the May-bells clash and chime, . . .   3
They hey!—for the ripple of laughing rhyme!   3R
   The Ballade of Prose and Rhyme, Austin Dobson.

The position of the two refrains is indicated throughout by 2R and 3R; and the couplet rhyming of the envoy is also indicated.

The *double ballade* consists of six stanzas of eight or ten lines each, rhymed as in the ballades already given. Thus this may be six stanzas rhymed 1, 2, 1, 2, 2, 3, 2, 3R; or 1, 2, 1, 2, 2, 3, 3, 4, 3, 4R. Usually the envoy is omitted. Henley, who liked the form, always used an envoy. His *Double Ballade of the Nothingness of Things* goes beyond these schemes, and has eleven lines to each stanza, rhymed 1, 2, 1, 2, 2, 3, 3, 4, 5, 4, 5R; with an envoy rhymed 3, 3, 4, 5, 4, 5R. And he has stranger varieties. Swinburne's *Ballade of Swimming* has ten lines to the stanza, and seven anapests to each line—a long interval between rhymes.

The *chant royal* is the longest and most dignified offspring of the ballade. It has five stanzas of eleven lines each, usually rhymed 1, 2, 1, 2, 3, 3, 4, 4, 5, 4, 5R. The envoy has five lines, rhymed 4, 4, 5, 4, 5R. Sixty lines, in all. . . . Seven (5) rhymes, ten each of (1), (2), and (3), and eighteen separate rhymes for (4). . . . Here is an amusing example:

I would that all men my hard case might know;
    How grievously I suffer for no sin;
I, Adolphe Culpepper Ferguson, for lo!
I, of my landlady am locked in,
        For being short on this sad Saturday,
        Nor having shekels of silver wherewith to pay;
She has turned and is departed with my key;
Wherefore, not even as other boarders free,
    I sing (as prisoners to their dungeon stones
When for ten days they expiate a spree) :
    Behold the deeds that are done of Mrs. Jones!

One night and one day I have wept my woe;
    Nor wot I when the morrow doth begin,
If I shall have to write to Briggs & Co.,
    To pray them to advance the requisite tin

For ransom of their salesman, that he may
Go forth as other boarders go alway—
As those I hear now flocking from their tea,
Led by the daughter of my landlady
Piano-ward. This day, for all my moans,
Dry bread and water have been servéd me.
Behold the deeds that are done of Mrs. Jones!

Miss Amabel Jones is musical, and so
The heart of the young he-boardér doth win,
Playing "The Maiden's Prayer," *adagio*—
That fetcheth him, as fetcheth the banco skin
The innocent rustic. For my part, I pray:
That Badarjewska maid may wait for aye
Ere she sits with a lover, as did we
Once sit together, Amabel! Can it be
That all that arduous wooing not atones
For Saturday shortness of trade dollars three?
Behold the deeds that are done of Mrs. Jones!

Yea! she forgets the arm was wont to go
Around her waist. She wears a buckle whose pin
Galleth the crook of the young man's elbów;
I forget not, for I that youth have been.
Smith was aforetime the Lothario gay.
Yet once, I mind me, Smith was forced to stay
Close in his room. Not calm, as I, was he:
But his noise brought no pleasaunce, verily.
Small ease he gat of playing on the bones,
Or hammering on the stove-pipe, that I see.
Behold the deeds that are done of Mrs. Jones!

Thou, for whose fear the figurative crow
I eat, accursed be thou and all thy kin!
Thee will I shew up—yea, up will I shew
Thy too thick buckwheats, and thy tea too thin.
Ay! here I dare thee, ready for the fray!
Thou dost *not* "keep a first-class house," I say!
It does not with the advertisements agree.
Thou lodgest a Briton with a puggaree,
And thou hast harboured Jacobses and Cohns,
Also a Mulligan. Thus denounce I thee!
Behold the deeds that are done of Mrs. Jones!

Envoy

Boarders; the worst I have not told to ye:
She hath stolen my trousers, that I may not flee
Privily by the window. Hence these groans,
There is no fleeing in a *robe de nuit.*
Behold the deeds that are done of Mrs. Jones!

> *Behold the Deeds! (Being the Plaint of Adolphe*
> *Culpepper Ferguson, Salesman of Fancy Notions,*
> *held in durance of his Landlady for a failure to*
> *connect on Saturday night,)* Henry Cuyler Bunner.

The stanza rhyme-scheme is 1, 2, 1, 2, 3, 3, 4, 4, 5, 4, 5R, 5R
being the refrain; with the envoy 4, 4, 5, 3, 5R. The rhyming
throughout is accurate, and the result is a perfect chant royal.
The form is intricate, and the method of checking the various
rhyme sounds as they are put down should be followed, to be
sure that no rhyming sound is repeated. A great deal of reworking
is often necessary to perfect such a form as this. In order to
make the envoy the culmination of the verses, it is often necessary
to shift the strongest and most vigorous rhyming sounds to it,
and substitute other words in the earlier stanzas.

It is wise, for rhyme 4, which must be repeated eighteen
times, and similar others repeated constantly in the fixed forms,
to choose a comparatively simple rhyming sound, such as the Ē
here, to prevent a lack of rhyming words.

Chain Verse

We have already noted that form of chain verse used in *terza
rima,* where the triplets rhyme 1. 2, 1; 2, 3, 2; 3, 4, 3; 4, 5, 4,
and so on. Any repetition of a rhyme, word, phrase, line or group
of lines, to tie up a section of the poem with the succeeding section, constitutes chain verse. John Byrom lets line four of each
quatrain become line one of the next:

> My spirit longeth for thee
> Within my troubled breast,
> Although I be unworthy
> Of so divine a Guest.

Of so divine a Guest
Unworthy though I be,
Yet has my heart no rest,
Unless it comes from thee.

Unless it comes from thee,
In vain I look around,
    The Desponding Soul's Wish, John Byrom.

and so on. Chain verse can rise to the elaborateness of a chain of sonnets or more, with the final line in each repeated as the opening line of the next, or even the final word or rhyme-sound so used.

The Kyrielle

The kyrielle, strictly described, consists of quatrains with eight syllables to the line, each stanza terminating with the same line,— a simple use of the refrain. Here is an example from a poem by John Payne:

A little pain, a little pleasure,
A little heaping up of treasure,
Then no more gazing upon the sun.
All things must end that have begun.

Where is the time for hope or doubt?
A puff of the wind, and life is out;
A turn of the wheel, and the rest is won.
All things must end that have begun.

Golden morning and purple night,
Life that fails with the failing light;
Death is the only deathless one.
All things must end that have begun.
    Kyrielle, John Payne.

Here the eight-syllabled pattern is intermittently broken. There is of course no sacredness in any pattern. Such a simple form must compensate by climactic development from stanza to stanza, to justify itself in poetry.

The Pantoum

Ernest Fouinet introduced the Malayan pantoum into French versification, and Victor Hugo popularized it in the *Orientales*. It is written in four-line stanzas; and the second and fourth line of each stanza become the first and third of the succeeding stanza. In the last stanza, the second and fourth lines are the third and first of the first stanza; so that the opening and closing lines of the pantoum are identical. The rhyme scheme would then be: 1, 2, 1, 2; 2, 3, 2, 3; 3, 4, 3, 4; . . . n, 1, n, 1.

Brander Matthews gives an example of one in English:

Here we are riding the rail,
Gliding from out of the station;
Man though I am, I am pale,
Certain of heat and vexation.

Gliding from out of the station,
Out from the city we thrust;
Certain of heat and vexation,
Sure to be covered with dust.

Out from the city we thrust:
Rattling we run o'er the bridges:
Sure to be covered with dust,
Stung by a thousand of midges. . . .
En Route, Brander Matthews.

to the final stanza, ending as the verses began:

Ears are on edge at the rattle,
Man though I am, I am pale,
Sounds like the noise of a battle,
Here we are riding the rail.

The Triolet

The triolet was the first of the rondeau family to appear. The first ones known appeared in the *Cléomadés* of Adenèz-le-Roi, who wrote in the latter part of the thirteenth century. At first, with ten syllables to each line, the triolet dealt with serious subjects. Today the form is usually eight syllables to the line, or even six; and the themes have grown appreciably and constantly lighter.

It has eight lines, with only two rhymes. The first line is repeated as the fourth line; the first two lines reappear as the seventh and eighth. The rhyme scheme is 1R, 2R, 1, 1R, 1, 2, 1R, 2R, the repeated lines appearing as 1R and 2R.

Suppose you decide to write a brief triolet, opening with the couplet:

> Drink deep—the glass
> Is full—and near!

You can at once fill out your fourth, seventh and eighth lines from this, making your pattern now appear as:

Drink deep—the glass	1R
Is full—and near!	2R
————————	1
Drink deep! The glass	1R
————————	1
————————	2
Drink deep—the glass	1R
Is full—and near!	2R

Only three lines, then, remain to be filled in. Once this is done, you have the triolet complete:

> Drink deep—the glass
> Is full—and near!
> Come, lad and lass,
> Drink deep! The glass
> Too soon will pass
> And disappear.
> Drink deep—the glass
> Is full—and near!

At times a more serious mood rules the use of the form. Thus H. C. Bunner wrote:

> A pitcher of mignonette
> In a tenement's highest casement;
> Queer sort of a flower-pot—yet
> That pitcher of mignonette
> Is a garden of heaven set
> To the little sick child in the basement,
> The pitcher of mignonette
> In the tenement's highest casement.
> *Triolet,* Henry Cuyler Bunner.

Here we have no progress in thought in the use of the reiterated refrain or repetend. Worse than that, the refrain line alters from *A pitcher* to *That pitcher* and *The pitcher,* a vital fault in the use of refrains in the French forms.

A transition to the rondeau form is furnished by this eight-line verse by Leigh Hunt:

> Jenny kissed me when we met,
>   Running to the chair I sat in.
> Time, you thief, who love to get
>   Sweets upon your list, put *that* in!
> Say I'm weary, say I'm sad,
>   Say that health and wealth have missed me;
> Say I'm growing old, but add—
>   Jenny kissed me.
>   *"Jenny Kissed Me,"* Leigh Hunt.

The opening half of line one, reappearing as the refrain in line eight, prophesies the rondeau and similar forms. This brilliant little pattern has never become accepted and named.

The Rondel, Rondeau and Roundel Family

The triolet is the seed of the rondeau family. The *rondel* (the word is an old form of the later word *rondeau*) arose in all probability in Provence, and appeared later in the fourteenth century writings of north France, in the verse of Froissart, Deschamps and others. It began as a lyric of two stanzas, each stanza having four or five lines only, and rhyming triolet-wise upon two sounds. . . . Either a triolet, or a ten-line variant of the triolet.

With Charles d'Orleans, the rondel took the distinct form now assigned to it, of fourteen lines on two rhymes. The first two lines reappear as the seventh and eighth, and as the final couplet. —A mere variation of the triolet. This double repetition of the two-lined refrain made the form unwieldy. Later French poets shortened the form to thirteen lines, omitting the second line of the original refrain at the end.

The form as Charles d'Orleans used it appears in this rondel:

Paper, inviolate, white,	1R
Shall it be joy or pain?	2R
Shall I of fate complain,	2
Or shall I laugh tonight?	1
Shall it be hopes that are bright?	1
Shall it be hopes that are vain?	2
Paper, inviolate, white,	1R
Shall it be joy or pain?	2R
'A dear little hand so light,	1
A moment in mine hath lain;	2
Kind was its pressure again—	2
Ah, but it was so slight!	1
Paper, inviolate, white,	1R
Shall it be joy or pain?	2R

To a Blank Sheet of Paper, Cosmo Monkhouse.

The following rondel, by Samuel Minturn Peck, is in the preferred modern pattern:

Before the dawn begins to glow,	1R
A ghostly company I keep;	2R
Across the silent room they creep,	2
The buried forms of friend and foe.	1
Amid the throng that come and go,	1
There are two eyes that make me weep;	2
Before the dawn begins to glow,	1R
A ghostly company I keep.	2R
Two dear dead eyes. I love them so!	1
They shine like starlight on the deep,	2
And often when I am asleep	2
They stoop and kiss me, being low,	1
Before the dawn begins to glow.	1R

"Before the Dawn," Samuel Minturn Peck.

The *rondeau* is, next to the ballade, the French form most popular in English. It is written, like triolet and rondel, on two rhymes throughout: thirteen full-length lines, and two briefer unrhymed refrains. The refrain may consist of the first half of the first line, but may consist merely of the first word. The fifteen lines are

grouped in three stanzas, the first of five lines, the second of three lines and refrain, the third of five lines and refrain. The rhyme scheme then is: 1, 1, 2, 2, 1; 1, 1, 2, R; 1, 1, 2, 2, 1, R. Here is a rondeau that is a poem as well:

A man must live. We justify	1
Low shift and trick to treason high,	1
A little vote for a little gold	2
To a whole senate bought and sold	2
By that self-evident reply.	1
But is it so? Pray tell me why	1
Life at such cost you have to buy?	1
In what religion were you told	2
A man must live?	R
There are times when a man must die.	1
Imagine, for a battle-cry,	1
From soldiers, with a sword to hold,—	2
From soldiers, with the flag unrolled,	2
This coward's whine, this liar's lie,—	1
A man must live!	R

A Man Must Live, Charlotte Perkins Gilman.

The *roundel,* based upon occasional early French variants, is today associated with the name of Swinburne, because of his volume *A Century of Roundels.* As used by Swinburne, the roundel was eleven lines long, two of which were the brief refrain lines. The refrain either consisted of the opening word of line one, or of a portion or a half of that line. If it consisted of more than one word, it usually rhymed with the (2) sound rhyme. The rhyming pattern then would be 1, 2, 1, R; 2, 1, 2; 1, 2, 1, R; or 1, 2, 1, 2R; 2, 1, 2; 1, 2, 1, 2R. Here is an example:

A Roundel is wrought as a ring or a starbright sphere,
With craft of delight and with cunning of sound unsought,
That the heart of the hearer may smile if to pleasure his ear
    A roundel is wrought.

Its jewel of music is carven of all or of aught—
Love, laughter, or mourning—remembrance of rapture or fear—
That fancy may fashion to hang in the ear of thought.

As a bird's quick song runs round, and the hearts in us hear—
Pause answers to pause, and again the same strain caught,
So moves the device whence, round as a pearl or tear,
    A roundel is wrought.
      The Roundel, Algernon Charles Swinburne.

The *rondelet* is a seven-line fixed form, normally of four eight-syllabled lines, and three, the refrain lines, with four syllables each. The rhyme and rhythm scheme is: 1R, 2, 1R, 1, 2, 2, 1R—1R standing for the refrain line, and 1 for the line rhyming with it. Here is an example by May Probyn:

"Which way he went?"	1R
I know not—how should I go spy	2
Which way he went?	1R
I only know him gone. "Relent?"	1
He never will—unless I die!	2
And then, what will it signify	2
Which way he went?	1R

      Rondelet, May Probyn.

The *rondeau redoublé,* a remote relative of the rondeau, is in reality a formalized Theme With Variations treatment. It starts with a quatrain as a theme. This is followed by four additional quatrains, in each of which successively lines one, two, three, and four of the theme quatrain appear as the terminal lines. A concluding stanza has four lines of regular length, and a refrain (the first half of line one of the theme) to terminate.

An example will make this clearer:

My soul is sick of nightingale and rose,	1-a
The perfume and the darkness of the grove;	2-b
I weary of the fevers and the throes,	1-c
And all the enervating dreams of love.	2-d

At morn I love to hear the lark, and rove	2
The meadows, where the simple daisy shows	1
Her guiltless bosom to the skies above—	2
My soul is sick of nightingale and rose.	1-a

The afternoon is sweet, and sweet repose,	1
But let me lie where breeze-blown branches move.	2
I hate the stillness where the sunbeams doze,	1
The perfume and the darkness of the grove.	2-b

I love to hear at eve the gentle dove   2
Contented coo the day's delightful close.   1
  She sings of love and all the calm thereof,—   2
I weary of the fevers and the throes.   1-c

I love the night, who like a mother throws   1
  Her arms round hearts that throbbed and limbs that strove,   2
As kind as Death, that puts an end to woes   1
  And all the enervating dreams of love.   2-d

  Because my soul is sick of fancies wove   2
Of fervid ecstasies and crimson glows;   1
  Because the taste of cinnamon and clove   2
Palls on my palate—let no man suppose   1
      My soul is sick.   R
     Rondeau Redoublé, Cosmo Monkhouse.

As far as strict rhyming goes, *repose—suppose* and *throes—throws* are identities, and not rhymes.

The *glose,* which is superficially a freer variant of the foregoing pattern, derives apparently from a different source, and is found more often in Spanish and Portuguese verse than in French. It begins, like the rondeau redoublé, with a quatrain, here called the *texte,* which may be a quotation. This texte the glose proceeds to develop, in four stanzas of ten lines each, closing each stanza, as in the rondeau redoublé, with the successive four lines of the texte. The concluding stanza and refrain of the preceding form are omitted here. In the rhyme scheme, lines six, nine and the tenth or texte line in each stanza rhyme; the rest of the rhyme scheme differs with different users of the form.

Gleeson White, author of a definitive book on the French forms, was unable to discover at the time he wrote any example of the form in English. There are not many examples available. The texte in the following is from Graham R. Tomson's *Ballade of Asphodel.*

  "Queen Prosperpine, at whose white feet   1-a
    In life my love I may not tell,   2-b
  Wilt give me welcome when we meet   1-c
    Along the mead of Asphodel?"   2-d

Your Majesty, permit me to   3
  Indite, as one would say, this bit   4
Of verse respectfully to you;   3
Of course admitting *entre nous*   3
  You may not really fancy it;   4
Although it will be rather neat.   1
  And yet the dedication 's fit;   4
  I want assistance from your wit: 4
I should permit my heart to beat,   1
Queen Proserpine, at *whose* white feet?   1-a

Remember, Proserpine, I know   5
  That quite discriminatingly   6
You made your mind up long ago;   5
You did not like your Stygian beau;   5
  He smacked a bit of deviltry,—   6
And you were not designed for hell.   2
  This shows you're quite a clever she;   6
  Ergo, you ought to counsel me.   6
I *must* make up my mind, or,—well,   2
In life my love I may not tell.   2-b

Should I ask Venus, she would vote
  (That surely is a goddess' right)
For some dame with "a quivering throat
And bosom of desire"—I quote
  From memory the line tonight.
Minerva would choose some discreet
  Young woman, staid and erudite;
  But only she could give delight
Who would, though life's young roses sweet
Wilt, give me welcome when we meet.   1-c

Come, choose her for me! Let her be
  Stately or dumpy, brown or fair,
If only she'll agree that we
Should learn to dwell in harmony,
  Giving a gay good-bye to care,—
A beatific way to dwell!
  Come, Queen, be gracious to my prayer!
  But, no! Such maidens here are rare;
You'd scarce find such a demoiselle
Along the mead of Asphodel!   2-d
             The Quest, Clement Wood.

Naturally, the rhyming scheme of the texte (which is 1, 2, 1, 2 here), dictates the rhyming of the sixth, ninth and tenth lines of each main stanza. In other examples, the quatrain that forms the texte may have any quatrain rhyming, and so a similar extent dictates similar rhymes in each stanza. It is permissible to use the same rhymes in each stanza, except where the rhyme-sound of the texte line ordains differently. In other words, the four stanzas might be:

1-a, 2-b, 1-c, 2-d
3, 4, 3, 3, 4, 1, 3, 3, 1, 1-a
3, 4, 3, 3, 4, 2, 3, 3, 2, 2-b
3, 4, 3, 3, 4, 1, 3, 3, 1, 1-c
3, 4, 3, 3, 4, 2, 3, 3, 2, 2-d

This is not required by the strict rules.

The Sestina

Arnaut Daniel, a Provençal troubadour, invented the sestina at the end of the thirteenth century. In France it has been slightly popular. Dante and Petrarch liked to use it. Here are the rules, as drawn up by Daniel and his followers in Italy, Spain and Portugal:

1. The sestina has six stanzas, each of six lines, of the same length; and a concluding three-line stanza.
2. The lines of the six stanzas end with the same six words, not rhyming with each other; these end words are chosen exclusively from two-syllabled nouns.
3. The arrangement of these six terminal words follows a regular law, very complex in ancient times, and altered toward simplicity later, as appears hereafter.
4. The closing three-line stanza uses the six terminal words, three at the centers of the lines, three at their ends.

Modern usage permits the variation of allowing the terminating words to rhyme, either on two rhyming sounds, as Swinburne uses it, or on three. In every case, the six terminal words must be repeated, with no change in sound or spelling, through each succeeding stanza. The order for the six terminal words in the six successive stanzas is as follows:

1st	stanza	1, 2, 3, 4, 5, 6
2nd	stanza	6, 1, 5, 2, 4, 3
3rd	stanza	3, 6, 4, 1, 2, 5
4th	stanza	5, 3, 2, 6, 1, 4
5th	stanza	4, 5, 1, 3, 6, 2
6th	stanza	2, 4, 6, 5, 3, 1

The concluding half stanza ends with 2, 4, and 6; and uses 1, 3, and 5 at the beginning—not necessarily as the first word—of the lines; or at the half-line, in rhymes that permit their introduction there.

Here is an example: The numerals refer to terminal words, and not rhyme sounds.

We are the smiling comfortable homes,	1
With happy families enthroned therein,	2
Where baby souls are brought to meet the world,	3
Where women end their duties and desires,	4
For which men labor as the goal of life,	5
That people worship now instead of God.	6

Do we not teach the child to worship God?—	6
Whose soul's young range is bounded by the homes	1
Of those he loves, and where he learns that life	5
Is all constrained to serve the wants therein,	2
Domestic needs and personal desires,—	4
These are the early limits of his world.	3

And are we not the woman's perfect world,	3
Prescribed by nature and ordained of God,	6
Beyond which she can have no right desires,	4
No need for service other than in homes?	1
For doth she not bring up her young therein?	2
And is not rearing young the end of life?	5

And man? What other need hath he in life	5
Than to go forth and labor in the world,	3
And struggle sore with other men therein?	2
Not to serve other men, nor yet his God,	6
But to maintain these comfortable homes,—	1
The end of all a normal man's desires.	4

Shall not the soul's most measureless desires   4
Learn that the very flower and fruit of life   5
Lies all attained in comfortable homes,   1
With which life's purpose is to dot the world   3
And consummate the utmost will of God,   6
By sitting down to eat and drink therein.   2

Yea, in the processes that work therein—   2
Fulfilment of our natural desires—   4
Surely man finds the proof that mighty God   6
For to maintain and reproduce his life   5
Created him and set him in the world;   3
And this high end is best attained in homes.   1

Are we not homes? And is not all therein?   1, 2
Wring dry the world to meet our wide desires!   3, 4
We crown all life! We are the aim of God!   5, 6

Homes, Charlotte Perkins Gilman.

Here the lines end on accented syllables, and by no means on two-syllabled nouns exclusively. There is no sestina in any of the collections in English which follows this convention; it may be dismissed, with the reflection that the French, Spanish and Italian languages have more double rhymes than English.

The movements of each terminal word follow a definite pattern, as a graph of the numbered terminal words will show. The order of position is successively 1, 2, 4, 5, 3, 6, 1, 2, 4, 5, 3, etc. By this means the last word of one stanza terminates the first line of the next; and meanwhile the last line of next has been shifted from third position to last, to terminate line one of the ensuing stanza.

Swinburne uses, as terminal words in one of his rhymed sestinas, *day, night, way, light, may, delight,* as 1, 2, 3, 4, 5, 6; and thereafter achieves alternate rhymes throughout, by creating his own sequence pattern, as follows: 6, 1, 4, 3, 2, 5; 5, 6, 1, 4, 3, 2; 2, 5, 6, 1, 4, 3; 3, 2, 1, 6, 5, 4; 4, 3, 2, 5, 6, 1, with the terminals of the concluding triplet *light, way, delight* (4, 3, 6), and the internal rhymes here *day, night, may* (1, 2, 5). He has worked out even more intricately his rhymed double sestina, *The Complaint of Lisa*—twelve stanzas of twelve lines each, with a concluding sestet, of one hundred and fifty lines in all. Charles W. Coleman, in his sestina *Love's Going,* used three rhyme sounds, *sing, rose, heart, thing, goes, apart;* but he retains the unrhymed sequence

formula, and thus has rhyming couplets in four of his stanzas. Swinburne's variation is to be preferred to this.

Clearly, in writing the sestina, after the first stanza has been completed, the next task is to write down the terminals for all the lines of the next five stanzas, and the terminals and center words of the brief concluding stanza. Then proceed to write. . . . The form is more suitable to clever light verse, than to poetry.

The Villanelle

The villanelle lends itself to seriousness, as well as to frivolity. It consists of nineteen lines: five three-lined stanzas, concluding with a quatrain. The refrain couplet, which terminates the form, consists of lines one and three of the first triplet. Moreover, line one (the first half of the refrain) terminates stanzas two and four, and line three (the other half of the refrain) stanzas three and five. Only two rhyming sounds are used. The following villanelle follows the pattern strictly:

O Singer of Persephone!	1-a
In the dim meadows desolate,	2
Dost thou remember Sicily?	1-b
Still through the ivy flits the bee	1
Where Amaryllis lies in state,	2
O Singer of Persephone!	1-a
Simaetha calls on Hecate,	1
And hears the wild dogs at the gate;	2
Dost thou remember Sicily?	1-b
Still by the light and laughing sea	1
Poor Polypheme bemoans his fate,	2
O Singer of Persephone!	1-a
And still in boyish rivalry	1
Young Daphnis challenges his mate:	2
Dost thou remember Sicily?	1-b
Slim Lacon keeps a goat for thee;	1
For thee the jocund shepherds wait,	2
O Singer of Persephone!	1-a
Dost thou remember Sicily?	1-b

Theocritus, Oscar Wilde.

Edwin Arlington Robinson pours poetry into the form, in a villanelle concluding:

> There is ruin and decay
> In the House on the Hill:
> They are all gone away,
> There is nothing more to say.
>
> *The House on the Hill,* Edwin Arlington Robinson.

The Lai and the Virelai

The ancient French lai was composed of couplets of five-syllabled lines, all on the same rhyme, separated by single lines of two syllables each, which rhymed with one another. The number of lines in each stanzas was not fixed, nor the number of stanzas in the complete poem. An improvised example would be:

Summer heat today	1
In its torrid way,	1
I see,	2
With its awful ray	1
Sears till it must slay	1
Poor me,	2
Tree and grass and clay.	1
It's the bay—the spray	1
And glee!	2

A curious old tradition connected with the form is that the indentation of the shorter lines is forbidden. This detail was called *arbre fourchu,* a forked tree, from the fancied resemblance of the poem on paper to a tree with branches projecting. Where lais have more than one stanza, the two rhymes in each stanza have no reference to the rhymes in any other.

The *virelai* or *virelai ancien* grew out of this, with a sequence of rhymes throughout. Thus, in a twelve-line stanza, the rhymes would be 1, 1, 2, 1, 1, 2, 1, 1, 2, 1, 1, 2. The next stanza would be 2, 2, 3, 2, 2, 3, 2, 2, 3, 2, 2, 3; and so on, until the last stanza appeared as n, n, 1, n, n, 1, n, n, 1, n, n, 1. Thus each rhyme sound would appear once in the longer lines, and once in the shorter. The form is too simple to need illustration.

The *virelai nouveau* is written throughout on two rhymes. Its initial rhymed couplet serves as a refrain for the later stanzas; and

the two lines close each stanza alternately until the last, when they
both appear together, but in inverse order. Here is an example
which begins with the couplet as its first stanza,

Good-bye to the Town!—good-bye!   1 a
Hurrah for the sea and the sky!   1-b
July, Austin Dobson.

The second stanza is rhymed, 1, 1, 1, 2, 1, 1-a. Its third stanza is
1, 2, 1, 2, 1, 2, 2, 1, 1-b. The succeeding stanzas are as irregular,
but each is confined to the two rhymed sounds, and the refrains
occur in the prescribed order. And here is the concluding stanza,
showing the refrain reversed:

So Phyllis, the fawn-footed, hie   1
For a hansom! Ere close of the day 2
Between us a "world" must lie,—   1
Hurrah! for the sea and the sky!   1-b
Good-bye to the Town! GOOD-BYE! 1-a

The *Sicilian octave* at times is used as a fixed form. It consists
in eight iambic five-foot lines, rhymed 1, 2, 1, 2, 1, 2, 1, 2. No
difficulty will be found in writing in this pattern.

The *rispetto* is an Italian form, with inter-rhyming lines ranging from six to ten in number, though not usually exceeding eight.
Used rarely in English, it is usually divided into two stanzas,
rhymed 1, 2, 1, 2; 3, 3, 4, 4.

A brief American fixed form, called the *sonnette,* was originated by Sherman Ripley, and had a vogue for a time. It consisted of seven five-foot iambic lines, rhymed: 1, 2, 2, 1; 3, 2, 3.
It differed only slightly from the *Canopus* stanza, already described, which also used seven five-foot iambic lines, but rhymed
them 1, 2, 1, 2, 3, 2, 3. Both avoid the terminal couplet, and hence
have an uninterrupted flow for narrative verse.

Another recent form is the *Douzet,* its origin unknown. It consists of twelve five-foot iambic lines, rhymed as follows: 1, 2, 2, 1;
3, 4, 4, 3; 1, 2, 3, 4. This introduces a novelty in the repetition of
rhyme not encountered so far elsewhere: the concluding quatrain's
rhyme-scheme amounting to a summary of the rhyme-sounds gone
before.

There is no limit to the patterns that ingenuity in versification

can produce. Only the rare few among these achieve enduring popularity.

The Japanese form, the *hokku,* follows Japanese poetry *(tanka* or *uta)* in having alternate verses of five and seven syllables. The hokku or *haikai* consists of only three lines, of 5, 7, and 5 syllables, or 17 in all. An improvised example is:

> More fleeting than the
> Flash of withered windblown leaf,
> This thing men call life.

The Japanese *tanka* ordinarily has 31 syllables, consisting of five lines, with respectively 5, 7, 5, 7, and 7 syllables. An improvised example is:

> The rippling sea-swell,
> Curling upon the gold sand,
> And, curving over,
> A bough of cherry blossoms,—
> Youth shielding eternal age.

Longer Japanese poems may be constructed in the tanka form, with the invariable alternation of 5 and 7 syllables to the line, and the addition of a terminal 7-syllabled line. The rhythm in Japanese poetry is not regarded. The only convention is the number of syllables to the line.

The Limerick

The limerick is the only fixed form indigenous to the English language. It first appeared in *Songs for the Nursery, or, Mother Goose's Melodies for Children,* published by Elizabeth Goose, (formerly Vertigoose, married to Thomas Fleet, a Boston printer,) in 1719. Moreover, in this collection it appeared in all three of its successive forms. The first stage opened and closed the five-line form with a nonsense line:

> Hickory, dickory, dock!
> The mouse ran up the clock.
> The clock struck one—
> The mouse ran down,
> Hickory, dickory, dock!
> *Nursery Rhymes,* Mother Goose.

The second form, the one used by Edward Lear throughout, ended the first and fifth line with a geographical name, at times these lines being identical:

> As I was going to Bonner,
> Upon my word of honor,
>   I met a pig
>   Without a wig,
> As I was going to Bonner.
>   *Nursery Rhymes,* Mother Goose.

The third and culminating form has a new rhyme sound in the fifth line—as this example:

> There was an old soldier of Bister
> Went walking one day with his sister,
>   When a cow at one poke
>   Tossed her into an oak,
> Before the old gentleman missed her.
>   *Nursery Rhymes,* Mother Goose.

A classic model to follow is the famous limerick—

> There was a young lady from Niger,
> Who smiled as she rode on a tiger.
>   They came back from the ride
>   With the lady inside,
> And the smile on the face of the tiger.
>   *More Limericks,* Cosmo Monkhouse.

The identity instead of rhyme in lines 2 and 5 cannot spoil the charm of this, although the pure pattern would avoid it. This would be—remembering that an extra unaccented syllable can be added either to the 1, 2, 5 rhyme group, or to the 3, 4 group, or to both:

> ta TUM—ta ta TUM—ta ta TUM
> ta TUM—ta ta TUM—ta ta TUM,
>   ta ta TUM—ta ta TUM
>   ta ta TUM—ta ta TUM
> ta ta TUM—ta ta TUM—ta ta TUM.

In other words, an anapestic pattern, 5, 5, 3, 3, 5 feet to the lines respectively, rhymed 1, 1, 2, 2, 1; usually with an iamb opening lines 1 and 2. Any trick rhyming device is permissible, as:

An amorous M. A.
Says that Cupid, that C. D.,
Doesn't cast for his health,
But is rolling in wealth—
He's the John Jaco-B. H.
Anonymous.

This must be read by pronouncing *M. A.* "master of arts," and by rhyming lines two and five properly to it,—"caster of darts" and "Jacob Astor of hearts." Here is one of the tongue-twister variety:

A tutor who tooted the flute
Tried to teach two young tooters to toot.
Said the two to the tutor,
"Is it harder to toot, or
To tutor two tooters to toot?"
Four Limericks, Carolyn Wells.

Among other possible variations is:

There was a young lady of Diss,
Who said, "Now I think skating bliss!"
This no more will she state,
For a wheel off her skate
Made her finish up something like this!
Anonymous.

The writing of limericks at times becomes extremely popular.

Little Willies

Any form may become, almost overnight, a favorite with poets and especially light verse writers. Some college student wrote and published in his college paper a rhyme proceeding approximately like this:

Tobacco is a filthy weed.
I like it.
· It satisfies no normal need.
I like it.
It makes you thin, it makes you lean,
It takes the hair right off your bean;
It's the worst darned stuff I've ever seen.
I like it.
Anonymous.

At once this form was copied by newspaper and other light versifiers the breadth and length of the land, and is still intermittently alive.

Another form assumed wide popularity, arising from one of Col. D. Streamer's (Harry Graham's) *Ruthless Rhymes for Heartless Homes:*

> Billy, in one of his nice new sashes,
> Fell in the fire and was burned to ashes.
> Now, although the room grows chilly,
> I haven't the heart to poke poor Billy.
> *Tender-Heartedness,* Harry Graham.

The quatrain here consists of two couplets, rhymed 1, 1, 2, 2. The metre combines trochees and dactyls; it might be iambs and anapests, of course, or any of the four. Somehow Billy became rechristened Willie, and at least one anonymous volume has appeared since, dealing in this or other simple quatrains with the adventures of Willie and his family. Among famous ones are:

> Willie and two other brats
> Licked up all the Rough-on-Rats.
> Father said, when mother cried,
> "Never mind, they'll die outside."
> Anonymous.

> Father heard his children scream,
> So he threw them in the stream,
> Saying, as he drowned the third,
> "Children should be seen, *not* heard!"
> *The Stern Parent,* Harry Graham.

> Late last night I slew my wife
> Stretched her on the parquet flooring.
> I was loath to take her life,
> But I *had* to stop her snoring.
> *Necessity,* Harry Graham.

> Willie poisoned father's tea;
> Father died in agony.
> Mother looked extremely vexed:
> "Really, Will," she said, "what next?"
> Anonymous.

The model for a Little Willie, with its trick last line and its sadistic content, can be taken from any of these.

Light Verse in English

Light verse, including its elegant form called *vers de société,* demand a technical dexterity greater than that of poetry; for the obviousness and cleverness of the rhyme are a charm here, where they usually interfere with the emotional effect of poetry. The student of versification will benefit by studying Tom Hood, for the use of puns in light verse; *Mother Goose,* for inspired use of rhythm; Edward Lear and Lewis Carroll, for shapely nonsense verse; Charles Stuart Calverley for mastery of every trick of rhyming, and great dexterity in stanza-devising; W. S. Gilbert, for mastery of the whole field. The long finale of his *Iolanthe* is his peak in rhyming, and almost the peak of light verse in English. Split words are a constant device: as in Carroll's—

> Who would not give all else for two p-
> Ennyworth of beautiful soup?
> > *Soup of the Evening,* Lewis Carroll.

or another surprise rhyming sung by Canning:

> Sun, moon, and thou vain world, adieu,
> > That kings and priests are plotting in;
> Here doomed to starve on water-gru-
> -El, never shall I see the U-
> > -Niversity of Gottingen,
> > -Niversity of Gottingen!
> > *Song by Rogero,* George Canning.

Humorous verse need not be clever. A poem like Ernest Lawrence Thayer's *Casey at the Bat* is a perpetual favorite because the theme invokes deep laughter, not because it is trickily versified. Dialect verse is in a class by itself. In writing dialect verse, be careful

(1) To use dialect spelling only where required.

(2) Not to overuse it, or the reader will not understand it. Such an improvised quatrain as—

> Sum niggers iz peculyer,
> I reitteratez agen,
> They mus' come f'um Atlanta
> An' not from Bummin'ham

is full of bad writing. *Sum* is the correct pronunciation of *some*, not a dialect pronunciation; the same is true of *iz, reitteratez,* and *agen.* The same is probably true of *peculyer.* And why *f'um* and *from* in the same poem? This is as inept as using *you* and *thou* (in any form) in the same poem, to refer to the same person. *F'um, mus'* and *an'* are accurate dialect speech.

Among other forms of light verse are *parody,* aping the versifying mannerisms of another; *nonsense verse; whimsical verse* of many kinds; *mosaic* or *composite verse,* each line taken from some other poet; *macaronic verse,* where two or more languages are hashed together; *shaped whimsies,* where the typography pictures the theme, as in the *Song of the Decanter,* on page 96.

Various forms of *typographical oddities* may be devised, in which certain of the lines (as the terminals of each quatrain) represent the way a person walks, sober, or intoxicated, or the way he falls down.

Acrostics are verses where the opening letters of the lines, or the closing letters, or letters arrived at by some other system, name a person, or convey a special message. Here is an example:

> *F*rom your bright sparkling Eyes I was undone;
> *R*ays, you have; more transparent than the Sun,
> *A*midst its glory in the rising Day
> *N*one can you equal in your bright array;
> *C*onstant in your calm and unspotted mind,
> *E*qual to all, but will to none Prove kind,
> *S*o knowing, seldome one so Young, you'll Find,
> *A*h! woe's me, that I should Love and conceal
> *L*ong have I wished, but never dared reveal,
> *E*ven though severely Love's Pains I feel;
> *X*erxes that great, wasn't free from Cupid's Dart,
> *A*nd all the great Heroes, felt the smart.
> *Acrostic,* George Washington.

The words conveyed by the acrostic are revealed by reading downward the first or italicized letters of each line.

The actual writing of light verse calls upon the versifier for every resource and device within the technique of versification. The rhymes should be natural and not rhyme-induced, and the entire treatment natural and adapted to please and amuse.

There was an old decanter
and its mouth was gaping
wide; the rosy wine had
ebbed away and left
its   crystal   side;
and   the   wind
went humming
—humming up
and down: the
wind it flew, and
through the reed-
like hollow neck the
wildest notes it blew.
I placed it in the window,
where the blast was blow-
ing free, and fancied that its
pale   mouth   sang   the   queerest
strains to me. "They tell me—puny
conquerors! the Plague has slain his ten,
and war his hundred thousand of the very
best of men; but I"—'twas thus the Bottle spake—
"but I have conquered more than all your famous
conquerors, so feared and famed of yore. Then come,
ye youths and maidens all, come drink from out my cup,
the beverage that dulls the brain, and burns the spirits up;
that puts to shame your conquerors that slay their scores
below; for this has deluged millions with the lava
tide of woe. Tho' in the path of battle darkest
streams of blood may roll, yet while I killed the
body, I have damned the very soul. The
cholera, the plague, the sword such ruin
never wrought, as I in mirth or
malice on the innocent have
brought. And still I breathe
upon them, and they shrink before
my breath, while year by year my
thousands go my dusty way of death."

Song of the Decanter, Warfield Creath Richardson.

VII

POETRY AND TECHNIQUE

The Vocabulary of Poetry

THE vocabulary used by a poet in his poetry should be the vocabulary that he uses in his living speech. Prose uses this, or else it becomes stilted and affected. If an orator commences,

O Mississippi, Father of Waters, thou wast engendered in the hills of Minnehaha; thou hast meandered through meadows green and valleys dappled for more miles than man computeth,

his hearers feel that there is something strained and unnatural in his words. The same thought occurs, when poetry, especially modern poetry, contain words no longer in the living vocabulary of man, because they have become archaic; or else unknown to the living vocabulary, because they are artificially constructed to meet the exigencies of rhyme or metre: such words as—

Thou, thee, thy, ye, mineself.

Art (verb form), *wast, wert, dost, wilt* (verb form), *hast, hadst, wouldst, shouldst, shalt,* and all verb forms ending in *-est, -st* and the like.

'Tis, 'gainst, 'gin, 'tween, 'neath, e'er, and other contractions not in living speech; as opposed to *it's* and other contractions used in living speech.

Wroth, bethink, reft, reaving, athwart, welkin, rathe, fardel, burthen, murther, nave, chaps, gins, sooth, Norweyan, proof (for *armor*), *composition* (for *terms of peace*), *ronyon,* and all other archaic, obsolescent or obsolete words.

Except for "unless," *memorize* for "make memorable," and other outworn usages of words.

All unnatural and elliptical expressions, improper in living speech, such as *as to* for "as if to," *bethink me* for "recall," *for to that* for "for to that end," and the like.

All inversions and strained expressions improper in living speech, such as *the soldier brave, have I seen, I battles fought,* and the like. These are common, because rhyme-induced.

Poetry that speaks a dead language is dead from its birth; poetry that speaks a warped and distorted language is warped and distorted from its birth. For when real poetry from real poets is encountered, its speech is as direct, forthright and living as:

> Our revels now are ended. These our actors,
> As I foretold you, were all spirits, and
> Are melted into air, into thin air;
> And, like the baseless fabric of this vision,
> The cloud-capp'd towers, the gorgeous palaces,
> The solemn temples, the great globe itself,
> Yea, all which it *inherit,* shall dissolve,
> And, like this insubstantial pageant *faded,*
> Leave not a *rack* behind. We are such stuff
> As dreams are made *on,* and our little life
> Is rounded with a sleep.
>
> > *The Tempest,* William Shakespeare.

The captious might suggest *inherits* for *inherit;* might point out that *faded* is out of place; that "made *of*" is preferable to "made *on*"; we might query the *rack.* At that, *rack* is still used in "rack and ruin," a "cloud-rack," "the rack of a storm": and *rack,* used here in the sense of a vestige, is intelligible and may be regarded as living. And this poetry was written more than three hundred years ago, by William Shakespeare, who knew too much, even then, to stud his verse with *thee's* and *thou's* and their outmoded verb forms, *welkin, athwart, amaranthine,* and so on.

The test for the phrasing of poetry is: could you have said the same thing, or its equivalent, to your maid or your butcher, and not been regarded as eccentric? If your poetry speaks your own living language, its vocabulary is acceptable. If it is marred with word-fossils no longer acceptable in living speech, to that extent it falls below its possible flight.

No word acceptable in acceptable prose is out of place in poetry. Any word may be so ineptly or awkwardly used in poetry, that it becomes a blemish. When Shakespeare wrote:

> It is a tale
> Told by an idiot, full of sound and fury,
> Signifying nothing,
>
> > *Macbeth,* William Shakespeare.

he used *idiot* magnificently and poetically; when Wordsworth
wrote:

> Why bustle thus about your door?
> What means this bustle, Betty Foy?
> Why are you in this mighty fret?
> And why on horseback have you set
> Him whom you love, your Idiot Boy?
> > *The Idiot Boy*, William Wordsworth.

the word *idiot* is as unpoetic as the rest of the passage. The living
speech, the colloquial, can be magical, poetic, as in this sonnet
sestet:

> It is some lie that under a windswept tree,
> > Touching your lips, I touched my vanished youth,
> And found again a young, new ecstasy.
> > It is a lie, I say. This—this is Truth!
> Now—I shall rest. For youth and you are gone.
> Tomorrow I shall put my flannels on.
> > *Sonnet*, John V. A. Weaver.

Edwin Arlington Robinson will be remembered for lines as
colloquially magical as:

> The man who had made other men
> As ordinary as arithmetic . . .

> I'll have to tell you, Brother Bedivere,
> That crowns and orders, and high palaces, . . .
> Will not go rolling down to hell just yet
> Because a pretty woman is a fool.
> > *Merlin*, Edwin Arlington Robinson.

He will have to be forgiven for verse as bookish as:

> Born with a face
> That on a bullfrog would ensure for life
> The lucubrations of a celibate . . .

> Less to remembering an obscure monition
> Than to confessing an assured renascence—
> > *Roman Barthalow,* Edwin Arlington Robinson.

though both of these are not so much archaic as morbidly pedantic.
Frost rarely departs from living speech; he has enriched the

language by phrases immortally and colloquially true, including the familiar:

> The trial by market everything must come to.

Even slang has its place: did not Shakespeare have Hamlet say—

> So I do still, by these pickers and stealers . . .
> > *Hamlet,* William Shakespeare.

Nor is Sandburg more unpoetic, when he writes:

> Play it across the table.
> What if we steal this city blind?
> If they want anything let 'em nail it down.
> > *Cahoots,* Carl Sandburg.

John Livingston Lowes, in *Convention and Revolt in Poetry,* phrases words of gold for poets to remember:

> The very greatest effects of poetry are often produced without the use of a single word which might not be employed in ordinary speech.

Thomas Gray wrote, in one of his letters:

> The language of the age is never the language of poetry. . . . Our poetry . . . has a language peculiar to itself.

This attitude explains the common idea permitting dead speech in verse; it can not resurrect poets following it from the graves their practice of this dug. Such poets live only insofar as they violate this statement.

Wordsworth followed this, when he preluded his *The Force of Prayer* with the double archaism:

> What is good for a bootless bene?

Witty Mary Lamb flashed back, when her brother Charles read this to her, "A shoeless pea," and punned this absurd line into immortality. And there is Rossetti's phrase from his rendition of the Villon ballade,

> From Love he won such dule and teen!

Poetry does not gain by using such mummified speech.

Kipling was more successful than any previous poet so far in using the language of the machine age in poetry:

It is their care, in all the ages, to take the buffet and cushion the
    shock;
It is their care that the gear engages; it is their care that the switches
    lock;
It is their care that the wheels run truly; it is their care to embark
    and entrain,
Tally, transport, and deliver duly the sons of Mary by land and main.
                 The Sons of Martha, Rudyard Kipling.

In a memorandum dealing with the writing of *Leaves of Grass*,
Walt Whitman wrote:

    I had great trouble in leaving out the stock
    "poetical" touches, but succeeded at last.

Even this great plain-speaking master slipped back, as he aged,
into stock poeticisms such as:

    'mid, unrecked, know I, yield we, ye valleys grand.

But in the main he avoided this blemish. And he has made the
task easier for those who followed him.

Sidney Lanier lays stress upon *phonetic syzygy,* that extension
of alliteration which includes all related consonants, as *t, d, th,* and
TH; g, k, ch, and other gutturals, and so on. Other authorities deal
extensively with *onomatopoeia,* the language device in which
words reproduce the sounds they are intended to convey, as in—

    With lisp of leaves and ripple of rain.
  Chorus from Atalanta in Calydon, Algernon Charles Swinburne.

With any inner sense of music, we will avoid lines as awkward,
inept and unsingable as Browning's familiar:

  Irks care the crop-full bird, frets doubt the maw-crammed beast?
             Rabbi Ben Ezra, Robert Browning.

Let your poetic speech be your own living speech at its best, dictated by an innate sense of music, and the result will satisfy.

On Translating Poetry

Poetry can not be translated; it can only be recreated in the
new language. We are dealing with the ingredients of verse, not
of poetry, in this book: a study of the essence of poetry would

not deal with iambs and cinquains and sestinas, it would deal with the stimuli that most deeply affect the human emotions. The emotion-arousing quality in words can not be stated otherwise even in the same language, much less in another one. There is no translation in English for emotion-arousing words such as *home, mother, love,* and so on; not *house* or *domicile,* not *mamma* or *maternal ancestor* or *Moms* or *ma,* not *affection* or *devotion* or *lust* or *rut.* How can *night* be expressed in another word, or *moon* or *sun,* or *May,* or *December?* Each of these words—to some extent each word in the language—has a tone-color, a history, a personality, an effectiveness of its own. With many of the words in the language, each person has strange and personal associations, naturally untranslatable. There are emotions which are not translatable from country to country, but which can only be recreated by some remote equivalent. When Noyes climaxes a poem with the glorious invocation,

> Englande!—Englande!—Englande!—Englande!
> *Marchaunt Adventurers,* Alfred Noyes.

he utters a battle-cry that only an Englishman could thrill to. Its word music is lost the moment it reappears as *Angleterre! Angleterre! Angleterre! Angleterre!* "Finland! Finland! Finland! Finland!" would not thrill similarly, though the rhythm and word tune are the same. A fourfold repetition of *Switzerland,* or *Czechoslovakia,* or, queerly enough, even of *United States,* would not evoke a similar thrill. Moreover, Shelley could have used the same repetition of *England,* in a poem in the bitter mood of *The Masque of Anarchy,* and it would have evoked utter detestation: so intangible are the elements in sounds that uplift or break the heart, that send a Cardigan or a Pickett with a whole brigade of men to death at the monosyllable "Charge!," that spell heaven in a girl's whispered "Yes," and a lifetime's dearth in her even briefer "No."

In Keats's *Ode to a Nightingale* we have two lines of peak magic:

> Charmed magic casements, opening on the foam
> Of perilous seas, in faery lands forlorn.

These two lines can not be said differently in English, without wrecking the magic. Accurately paraphrased, they would give:

> Enchanted supernatural windows, unclosing on the bubbles
> Of dangerous oceans, in unreal romantic countries dejected.

There is no poetry here, now. Translate it with absolute fidelity into another language, and the poetry is as dead. It must be re-created by a poet of like emotional power in the other language, if it is to survive there as poetry.

Fitzgerald did such magic, when he took a literal translation of the poetic *Rubaiyat* of Omar Khayyam, such as these two groups of lines:

> Everywhere that there has been a rose or tulip-bed,
> It has come from the redness of the blood of a king;
> Every violet shoot that grows from the earth
> Is a mole that was once on the cheek of a beauty.
> *Quatrains,* Omar Khayyam.

This is inaccurate botanically, and only whimsically effective as an idea. It is certainly not poetry. Nor is:

> Hell is a spark from my useless worries,
> Paradise is a moment of time when I am tranquil.
> *Quatrains,* Omar Khayyam.

But out of this material Fitzgerald wrought—created, recreated— what thousands hail as poetry:

> I sometimes think that never blows so red
> The Rose, as where some buried Caesar bled;
> That every Hyacinth the Garden wears
> Dropt in her Lap from some once lovely Head. . . .

> Heav'n but the Vision of fulfilled Desire,
> And Hell the Shadow from a Soul on fire,
> Cast on the Darkness into which Ourselves,
> So late emerged from, shall so soon expire.
> *Rubaiyat of Omar Khayyam,* Edward Fitzgerald.

This is no longer Omar Khayyam; it is far more Fitzgerald, inspired by Omar Khayyam. The reflection about the rose is acceptable now; the whimsey about the hyacinth is more pleasing to us than the more fleshly Oriental passion of the mole on the cheek of a beauty. The definitions of heaven and hell no longer resemble the original at all. Oriental impassivity and superiority to things

earthly have been replaced by a viewpoint accurate enough to have
come out of Freud, and acceptable as concentrated truth to many
of us. All of this is expressed with the most effective devices of
versification, a language in which poetry must speak, if it speak at
all.

Something like this must be done, each time you seek to make a
translation. A literal translation can give the idea, but never the
poetry.

For a last example, here is an accurate translation of the first
five verses of the first chapter of *Genesis,* by Fagnani:

> At the beginning of Elohim's forming the heavens and the earth,
> when darkness was upon the face of the abyss, Elohim said, "Let
> there be light," and there was light.
> Elohim saw that the light was excellent.
> And Elohim separated the light from the darkness and he called
> the light Day and the darkness he called Night.
> Evening came, and Morning came.
> > *The Beginning of History, According to the Jews,*
> > Charles Prosper Fagnani.

This is near to poetry, so magnificent is the primitive conception.
But it is not mere familiarity that makes us recognize, from the
hands of greater poets writing in English, the magnificent poetry
of the same verses, as they appear in the King James' Bible:

> In the beginning God created the heavens and the earth.
> And the earth was without form, and void; and darkness was
> upon the face of the deep. And the Spirit of God moved upon the
> face of the waters.
> And God said, Let there be light: and there was light.
> And God saw the light, that it was good; and God divided the
> light from the darkness.
> And God called the light Day, and the darkness he called Night.
> And the evening and the morning were the first day.
> > *Genesis,* King James's Translation.

The most accurate translation of a poem is no more than rude
notes for a poem to be built upon. There is always need for accurate renditions of the poetry of other lands and tongues. But,
unless the English versifier re-issue the product as his own re-cre-
ation, it remains mere verse, a museum curiosity rather than impassioned song.

Exercises in Versification

To give the book its greatest value, the reader, having reached this point, should start over again, and write exercises in each poetic device treated. Practice iambic lines, each number of feet to the line, rhymed and unrhymed. The same with trochaic, anapestic, and dactylic lines. At times seek to pour poetry into these molds; at times find the relief of light verse in them.

Essay the stanzas, from the couplet up to such involved arrangements as the Spencerian stanza and *terza rima*. Work on sonnets of both kinds: aiming at technical mastery, rather than poetic excellence, at first. Get the patterns etched on your mind, and then you can write in them accurately without consciously remembering them. Try the solace of concentrated and poetic free verse. And then, if you care to, go at the fixed forms one after another, preferably in light verse, and among all these attempts you will startle yourself by achieving at times a veritable poem or gem of light verse when you merely intended finger-exercises.

And at all times, when the poetic mood comes, write what comes, from a phrase, a line, a couplet, to an epic fragment: and preserve it, on the chance that, sooner or later, the rest of the poem will come.

VIII

THE COMPLETE RHYMING DICTIONARY

What Rhyme Is

RHYME is the identity in sound of an accented vowel in a word, usually the last one accented, and of all consonantal and vowel sounds following it; with a difference in the sound of the consonant immediately preceding the accented vowel.

Rhyme thus deals exclusively with sound. Sound is indicated in all dictionaries by phonetic markings. In this rhyming dictionary, each group of words that rhyme is preceded by a heading consisting of the accented vowel, marked phonetically, and followed by all the consonantal and vowel sounds following it. The unaccented vowels are not marked phonetically, since they are relatively unimportant: except to distinguish between rhyme sounds like *pasture* (ĂS'tūr) and *faster* (ĂS'tūr).

The one-syllabled rhymes are given first, with the rhyme-sound headings arranged alphabetically, from the first A sound to the last U sound. Then follow the two-syllabled rhymes, similarly arranged; and, last of all, the three-syllabled rhymes.

The Vowel Sounds

In this phonetic arrangement, the vowel sounds used are indicated as follows. After each is given the various ways in which the sound appears in spelling in English.

A

Ā as in ale; heard also in pain, day, break, veil, obey, gaol, gauge, eh.
Â as in care; heard also in there, pear, air, heir, prayer, e'er.
Ă as in add; heard also in plaid, bade.
Ä as in arm, father; heard also in hearth, sergeant, memoir.
Å as in ask. Strictly, authorities say that A should be so pronounced (midway between the A in *father* and the A in *add*) when fol-

lowed by *s, th, f,* or *m* or *n* plus a consonant. In practice, this sound is usually pronounced like the A in *add*. The rule becomes absurd, when we try to pronounce *pan* with the A sound in *add,* and *pans* with a different A sound.

E

Ē as in me; heard also in eve, feet, beam, deceive, people, key, Caesar, machine, field, quay, phoebe.

Ẹ̄ as in here; heard also in fear, dreary, weird.

Ĕ as in end; heard also in heifer, leopard, friends, Aetna, feather, asafoetida, bury, any, Thames, said, says.

I

Ī as in ice; heard also in vie, rye, height, eye, aisle, aye meaning *yes,* sky, buy, choir.

Ĭ as in ill; heard also in sieve, English, pretty, been, breeches, women, busy, build, nymph, hymnal.

O

Ō   as in old; heard also in note, oh, roam, foe, shoulder, grow, owe, sew, yeoman, beau, hautboy, brooch.

Ô   as in or; heard also in all, talk, swarm, haul, caught, law, fought, broad, memoir.

Ŏ   as in odd; heard also in want, wash, shone.

OI   as in oil; heard also in boy.

ŎO   as in foot; heard also in full, wolf, could.

OU   as in out; heard also in cow, sauerkraut.

U

Ū   as in use; heard also in beauty, feud, pew, queue, lieu, view, cue, suit, yule, you, do, rule, true, food, group, drew, fruit, canoe, rheum, maneuvre, blue. (The difference in sound between *dew* and *do* is that *dew* is properly dyŪ, with a consonantal *y* sound preceding the long U. This difference does not affect rhyming, except as it concerns preceding consonants. For the sake of convenience, the yŪ group ordinarily precedes the Ū group.)

Û   as in urn; heard also in fern, err, heard, sir, word, journal, myrrh, colonel.

Ŭ   as in up; heard also in won, one, does, flood, double.

The Consonant Sounds

The consonant sounds used in English, and in most instances spelt phonetically in the headings preceding all groups of words rhyming together, are as follows:

B   as in baby.
CH   as in chair; heard also in match, question, righteous.
D   as in did; heard also in robbed.
F   as in fill; heard also in philosophy, laugh.
G   as in go, anger; heard also in guard, plague, ghost.
GZ   as the sound represented by *x* in exist.
H   as in hat.
HW as the sound represented by *wh* in what.
J   as in joke; heard also in gem, religion, pigeon, soldier, edge.
K   as in keep; heard also in chorus, epoch, cube, pack, conquer, pique.
KS   as the sound represented by *x* in vex.
KW as the sound represented by *qu* in queen.
L   as in late.
M   as in man.
N   as in no.
N   The French nasal sound, not natural in English.
NG   as in sing; heard also in tongue, bank, junction, linger, canker.
P   as in papa.
R   as in red; heard also in rhombus.
S   as in so, this; heard also in cell, scene, hiss.
SH   as in she; heard also in machine, ocean, social, conscious, sure, nauseous, pension, issue, passion, nation.
T   as in time.
TH   as in then.
th   as in thin.
TU   as in nature. This sound is more accurately TY consonantal.
V   as in van.
W   as in want; heard also in persuade, choir.
Y   as in yet; heard also in union.
Z   as in zone; heard also in is, lives, Xenophon.
ZH   as the sound represented by *z* in azure; heard also in glazier, pleasure, vision, abscission, rouge, genre.

A few warnings are important.

C is not a separate sound. Words spelt with *c* appear under K or S

Q is not a separate sound. Words spelt with *qu* or *q* appear under KW.

X is not a separate sound. Words spelt with *x* appear under GZ or KS; initial *x* appears as Z.

NK, in words like *rank,* is properly NGK, and so appears. *Hankow* would appear under ĂN'kow; hanker, under ĂNGK'ur.

To form plurals and other inflections, F, K, P and T are followed by the sound S; the plain vowel, G, D, B, M, N, S, V, J, CH, L, R, KS (X) and Z are followed by the sound Z.

To form past tenses and other inflections, CH, S, F, K and P are followed by the sound T; the plain vowel, G, D, B, M, N, S, V, J, L, R and Z are followed by the sound D.

Sound Does Not Depend on Spelling

Sound does not depend on spelling. "Eye-rhymes," or words matched as rhymes only because they are spelled alike, need not be rhymes at all. For instance, here are five different sounds spelled alike, *ough:*

cough, enough, plough, though, through.

It is as logical to rhyme these together as to rhyme *earth-hearth, bare-are, north-forth, real-steal.*

Again, note that *timber* and *climber* are spelled alike; but the first rhymes with limber (ĬM'bur) and the second with rhymer (ĪM'ur). Three more words spelled alike but rhymed very differently are *ginger*(ĬNJ'ur) ; *singer*(ĬNG'ur) ; and *finger*(ĬNG'gur). Until *cow* rhymes with *blow* it is well to avoid all these words spelled alike but pronounced differently.

This Dictionary Makes Consonance Accurate

Consonance consists in the identity of all consonantal and vowel sounds after the accented vowel; and a difference in the accented vowel. This dictionary, classified according to strict phonetic pronunciation, for the first time makes consonance easy and accurate. Alphabetically arranged by the headings preceding each group of rhyme words, the following three rhyme sounds appear together: Ō'li (wholly), Ô'li (Raleigh), ŎL'i (folly). Naturally these three groups are in consonance with each other.

To get the other groups of rhyming words which may be used in consonance with these three, look up successively Ā'li, ĂL'i, Ē'li, ĔL'i, OIL'i, OŎl'i, OUL'i, Ū'li, ŬL'i; and you have all the possible sounds in consonance with the three sounds given. You may stretch a point and add ÂR'li, ĂR'li, ĒR'li and ÛR'li if you wish, and now nothing conceivable is omitted.

Consonance, always used by the best poets, is growing so increasingly in favor, that this use of the present *Complete Rhyming Dictionary* may become very important.

Why This is Called Complete

This volume contains hundreds of rhyming words omitted from former collections. Many of these omissions are inexplicable, unless by oversight. Others consist of words recently added to the vocabulary, especially in the fields of general science, pure and applied; inventions and popular applications of them, such as moving pictures, aviation, and radio; and the vivid field of recent slang words generally acceptable. The effort has been to include all words that are a proper part of the living vocabulary of man: for it is in this language that living poetry must speak.

Archaic and obsolete words, and many words used only in an artificial solemn or poetic style, have not been omitted. Instead, as a rule these have been italicized. They are still available to the seeker who wishes to use them, each in its proper niche. But this feature both includes them for convenience, and badges them with the suggestion that, since they are not a part of man's living vocabulary, they may well be avoided.

In addition to this, the present volume contains more proper names than were ever listed in a rhyming dictionary before. This includes especially:

The familiar first names of boys and girls, men and women.

The familiar and easily rhymable geographical names.

The more familiar surnames, family names or last names.

In listing proper names, the name is not repeated when it differs only from a common word by the use of a capital. Thus, since *wood* is included, *Wood* is not. Where the spelling differs, the rhyming proper name is usually added. Thus, to *main* is added

Maine. Moreover, unnecessary duplication of words is generally avoided throughout the book. A large number of words ending in -*y* is given as rhymes for the long E sound; but, at the end of this large list, the reader is referred to other words ending in -*y*, to be found in such three-syllabled rhyme groups as the words rhyming with *ability;* which is to be consulted, if the seeker desires more rhymes for long E. Moreover, at the end of the rhyming words listed to rhyme with 'fade,' the reader is referred to the list of words rhyming on the long A sound, to which -*ed* is to be added, to make further rhymes for 'fade'; and this is to be consulted, if the seeker desires more rhymes for 'fade.' There is as little such cross-reference as possible, and it is never perplexing.

The dictionary is not wholly complete, and probably none will ever be. Rare and unusual scientific and geographic terms and names, for instance, as a rule have been omitted. It will add to the value of your copy of the book if you add, at the appropriate place, all omitted words that you discover.

In the lists of words rhyming on the last syllable and on the syllable before the last, certain words are included, which have no rhyming mates. The monosyllables or words accented on the last syllable which appear to be rhymeless are:

aitch, H	lounge	recumb
avenge, revenge	mauve	rouge
avenged, revenged	month	sauce
bilge	morgue	scarce
bourne	mourned, bemourned,	spoilt
bourse	unmourned	swoln
bulb	mouthe	sylph
coif	of, hereof, thereof,	torsk
culm	whereof	twelfth
cusp	peart	plagued, unplagued
doth	porch	warmth
film	pork	wasp
forge	poulp	wharves
fugue	prestige	wolf
gulf, engulf	puss	wolves

In addition to these forty-three rhymeless sounds, there is a group which has no rhyme in the living vocabulary:

amongst	forth, fourth
breadth	ninth
depth	sixth
eighth	tenth
fifth	width

These can all be rhymed by using permissible contractions of archaic or obsolete forms, such as: *clung'st, shed'th, step'th, hate'th, sniff'th, pour'th, pine'th, mix'th, pen'th* and *skid'th*. There is a limited group of words which find their rhyming mates only in proper names, including:

alb (De Kalb)   hemp (Kemp)   oblige (Lije)

There are other words which have no proper rhyming mates, but have words so close in sound that they are used as rhyming mates by many poets:

blague (vague)	en masse (class)
raj (dodge)	basque (mask, masque)
wand (pond)	else (belts)
melange (blanc mange)	grilse (wilts)
swap (top)	Welsh (belch)

THE DICTIONARY
OF RHYMING WORDS

MONOSYLLABLES, AND WORDS ACCENTED ON THE LAST SYLLABLE:

MASCULINE RHYMES; SINGLE RHYMES

A

These words include the following accented vowel sounds:

Ā as in ale; heard also in pain, day, break, veil, obey, gaol, gauge, eh.

Â as in care; heard also in there, pear, air, heir, prayer, e'er.

Ă as in add; heard also in plaid, bade.

Ä as in arm, father; heard also in hearth, sergeant, memoir.

Å as in ask. In practice, this is usually pronounced like the A sound in *add*.

For the vowel sound heard in all, talk, swarm, haul, caught, law, see under Ô.

For the vowel sound heard in want and wash, see under Ŏ.

Ā	astay	belay	Bordelais
affray	astray	bepray	bouquet
agley	au fait	betray	brae
allay	auto-da-fé	*bewray*	bray
alackaday	away	birthday	bridle-way
array	aweigh	Biscay	byway
Ascension-day	*aye*	bobsleigh	cabriolet
assay	bay	bobstay	Calais
assagai	bey	Bombay	caraway

In compound words—words consisting of two or more words united—the parts of the words may be joined without a hyphen, may be joined with a hyphen, or may be written separately. In some words usage is fixed; in others it varies. No standard rule is followed; though the hyphen today is less used than formerly. In this book, the usual practice of the best prose-writers and poets is followed, modified in instances by the editor's own preference. In general, poets and versifiers make such decisions for themselves in each instance.

---

castaway	fairway	interlay	overlay
causeway	fair-play	interplay	overpay
Chevalier	fay	inveigh	overstay
Chevrolet	feather-spray	irongray	papier mâché
Christmas-day	fey	jay	passée
clay	fireclay	judgment-day	Passion-play
Cloisonné	first-day	Kay	pathway
convey	flay	lack-a-day	pay
corvée	footway	Lady-day	payday
coryphée	foray	leaden-gray	play
coupé	forelay	lay	playday
crossway	foresay	leeway	popinjay
dapple-bay	forestay	Leigh	portray
dapple-gray	forlay	Lord's-day	pray
day	fray	mainstay	prepay
dead-pay	gainsay	Malay	prey
decay	gala-day	Mandalay	protegé
defray	galloway	market-day	protegée
dejeuner	gangway	matinée	purvey
delay	gay	May	qua
dey	get-away	mid-day	quarter-day
disarray	good-day	mid-way	railway
dismay	gourmet	Milky Way	raisonné
disobey	gray	mislay	ray
display	grey	missay	relay
distingué	habitué	Monterey	repay
distrait	Haigh	Monterrey	résumé
doomsday	halfway	nay	reveillé
Doré	hay	née	ricochet
dragonné	hearsay	negligêe	Roget
dray	hey	neigh	roturier
Dupré	heyday	noonday	roundelay
Easter-day	*highday*	nosegay	runaway
eh	highway	obey	sachet
émigré	hodden-gray	O'Day	Salomé
employé	hogmanay	Okay	San Jose
employée	holiday	O'Shay	Santa Fé
entremets	Honoré	outlay	Saturday
essay	hooray	outstay	say
estray	horseplay	outré	scray
exposé	inlay	outweigh	settling-day

āle, câre, ădd, ärm, åsk; mē, hẹre, ĕnd; īce, ĭll;

seventh-day	upstay	carnivora	parabola
shay	virelay	chapeau bras	pariah
silver-gray	visé	cholera	pas
slay	water-way	cinema	pasha
sleigh	way	clepsydra	peninsula
sley	waylay	cupola	phantasma-
sobriquet	wedding-day	éclat	goria
soiree	weekday	Egeria	phenomena
soothsay	weigh	ephemera	plethora
soufflé	welladay	et cetera	prolegomena
spay	*wellaway*	fa	Pthah
splay	wey	faux-pas	quadrigesima
spray	whey	formula	quadrumana
stageplay	workaday	genera	quinquagesima
stay	working-day	Golgotha	replica
steerage-way	Wray	gondola	retina
stowaway	yea	grandmamma	septuagesima
strathspey	yesterday	ha	sexagesima
stray		hah	Shah
subway	Ä	ha-ha	silica
survey	Aceldama	Hegira	spa
sway	ah	holla	spatula
thereaway	aha	hurrah	tarantula
they	algebra	huzza	tonic sol-fa
to-day	alumina	hydrophobia	Utopia
Tokay	amphibia	hypochondria	uvula
toupet	anathema	incognita	vertebra
tourniquet	Andromeda	insomnia	viola
tramway	anglophobia	Jah	
tray	animalcula	la	**ĀB**
trey	Apocrypha	ma	Abe
trysting-day	Aquila	mamma	astrolabe
tway	automata	majolica	babe
underlay	baa	mandragora	cosmolabe
underpay	baccarat	nebula	foster-babe
underplay	bacteria	opera	
undersay	bah	orchestra	**ĂB**
unlay	basilica	pa	abb
unpray	blah	padishah	bab
unsay	bourgeois	pah	Babb
uplay	camera	papa	baobab

ōld, ôr, ŏdd, oil. fŏŏt, out; ūse, ûrn, ŭp; THis, thin

bedab	detach	bade	estacade
blab	dispatch	balustrade	estrapade
cab	hatch	barricade	evade
Cantab	latch	bastinade	fade
confab	match	*bejade*	falcade
crab	overmatch	Belgrade	fanfaronade
dab	patch	blade	fire-brigade
drab	percussion-	blockade	flanconnade
frab	match	braid	free-trade
ĝab	*ratch*	brigade	fusillade
grab	*scatch*	brocade	gabionnade
jab	scratch	cade	gallopade
knab	slatch	*camerade*	gambade
lab	*smatch*	*camisade*	gasconade
mab	snatch	cannonade	glade
McNabb	*tache*	carronade	glissade
nab	thatch	cascade	grade
rab	unlatch	cassonade	grass-blade
scab		cavalcade	grenade
shab	**ĂCH**	centigrade	grillade
slab	watch	charade	hade
stab	(see blotch,	co-aid	handmaid
tab	ŎCH)	cockade	harlequinade
taxi-cab		colonnade	harquebusade
	ĂCHT	*corrade*	inlaid
ĂB	hatched	croupade	interlaid
squab	semi-detached	crusade	invade
swab, etc.	attached, etc.	*dade*	jade
(See blob, etc.,		dairy-maid	lade
ŎB)	**ĀD**	Damascus-	laid
	abrade	blade	*lancepesade*
ĀCH	*abraid*	decade	lemonade
aitch	accolade	deep-laid	made
H	Ade	defilade	maid
	Adelaide	degrade	make the grade
ĂCH	afraid	dissuade	marinade
attach	aid	dragonnade	marmalade
batch	alcaide	enfilade	masquerade
brach	*ambassade*	escalade	McDade
catch	ambuscade	escapade	mermaid
cratch	arcade	esplanade	milkmaid

āle,   câre,   ădd,   ärm,   åsk;   mē,   hĕre,   ĕnd;   īce,   ĭll;

new-made	staid	*egad*	couvade
nightshade	stockade	englad	estrade
old-maid	storm-stayed	fad	façade
orangeade	*suade*	footpad	glissade
overlaid	suède	forbade	ha-ha'd
overpaid	tirade	gad	hurrahed
overstayed	trade	glad	*hussa'd*
over-persuade	unafraid	grad	lancepesade
overshade	unarrayed	had	noyade
paid	unassayed	heath-clad	pomade
palisade	unbraid	hebdomad	promenade
panade	underaid	iron-clad	psha'd
parade	underlaid	ivy-clad	roulade
pasquinade	undismayed	lad	wad
passade	unessayed	Leningrad	(see *cod,* etc.)
persuade	unlade	mad	
pervade	unlaid	moss-clad	**ĂDZ**
pesade	unmade	myriad	ads
pistolade	unmaid	Olympiad	adze
plaid	unpaid	pad	scads
plantigrade	unprayed	Petrograd	adds, etc.
pomade	unrepaid	pine-clad	
postpaid	unstaid	plaid	**ĀF**
prepaid	unweighed	*rad*	chafe
promenade	upbraid	sad	enchafe
raid	wade	scad	safe
rayed	(see Ā + ed)	shad	strafe
ready-made		superadd	unsafe
renegade	**ĂD**	tonguepad	vouchsafe
retrograde	ad	Trinidad	waif
rodomontade	add	unclad	
saccade	bad	undergrad	**ĂF**
scalade	bedad	unforbade	actinograph
sea-maid	*begad*	unsad	agraffe
self-made	bade	winter-clad	anagraph
serenade	brad	*yclad*	autograph
serving-maid	cad		behalf
shade	Chad	**ÄD**	belly-laugh
slade	chiliad	baa'd	betterhalf
spade	clad	*chamade*	calf
stade	dad	charade	calligraph

ōld, ôr, ŏdd, oil, fŏŏt, out; ūse, ûrn, ŭp; THis, thin

carafe
cenotaph
chaff
chronograph
cinematograph
cross-staff
cryptograph
diagraph
dictagraph
distaff
draff
eidograph
epigraph
epitaph
flagstaff
gaff
giraffe
graff
hagiograph
half
half-and-half
halfstaff
heliograph
holograph
ideograph
idiograph
laugh
lithograph
monograph
mooncalf
palaeograph
pantograph
paragraph
penny-gaff
phonograph
photograph
polygraph
quaff
quarter-staff
raff
riff-raff

shandy-gaff
staff
stenograph
stereograph
telegraph
tipstaff
whipstaff

ÄF

behalf
belly-laugh
betterhalf
calf
graf
haaf
half
half-and-half
laugh
mooncalf
strafe

ĂFT

abaft
aft
craft
daft
draft
draught
engraft
fellow-craft
graft
haft
handicraft
ingraft
overdraft
priestcraft
raft
river-craft
sea-craft
shaft
waft

witchcraft
chaffed, etc.

ĀG

Hague
plague
Prague
vague

ĂG

bag
battle-flag
brag
Bragg
bullyrag
cag
chew the rag
crag
drag
fag
fishfag
flag
gag
hag
jag
knag
lag
mag
nag
nighthag
quag
rag
ragtag
saddle-bag
sag
scallawag
scrag
shag
shrag
slag
snag

sprag
stag
swag
tag
wag
Wragg
zigzag

ÄG

blague

ĀGD

unplagued

ĂGD

betagged
bagged, etc.

ĀJ

acreage
age
alienage
anchorage
appanage
arbitrage
armitage
assuage
average
baronage
beverage
brigandage
brokerage
cage
cartilage
chaperonage
compage
concubinage
cooperage
discage
disengage
encage

engage	sage	brake	*spake*
enrage	saxifrage	break	stake
equipage	seignorage	cake	steak
espionage	stage	crake	stomachache
flowerage	surplusage	day-break	strake
foliage	swage	drake	sweepstake
foot-page	tutelage	earache	take
fortilage	tutorage	earthquake	toothache
gage	uncage	fake	undertake
gauge	unsage	flake	unmake
harborage	vassalage	*forespake*	upbreak
hemorrhage	verbiage	forsake	uptake
heritage	vicarage	garter-snake	wake
hermitage	vicinage	hake	wapentake
hospitage	*villanage*	hard-bake	water-break
leverage	villenage	heartache	water-crake
lineage	wage	heart-break	water-snake
mage	weather-gauge	jake	wedding-cake
matronage		johnny-cake	
mid-age	**ĂJ**	lake	**ĂK**
mucilage	badge	make	aback
outrage	cadge	mandrake	*alack*
page	fadge	milk-snake	almanac
parentage	hadj	mistake	ammoniac
parsonage		namesake	attack
pastorage	**Ä J**	opaque	bac
pasturage	raj	outbreak	back
patronage	(Cf. badge, ĂJ)	overtake	bareback
peonage		partake	bivouac
personage	**ĀK**	quake	black
pilgrimage	ache	rake	blackjack
pilotage	after-rake	rattlesnake	bootjack
plunderage	*aslake*	robin-wake	*brach*
porterage	awake	sake	bric-a-brac
pre-engage	backache	seed-cake	cardiac
presage	bake	shake	chack
pupilage	barley-brake	sheik	clack
quarterage	bellyache	sheldrake	claque
rage	betake	slake	crack
rampage	blacksnake	snake	cul-de-sac
ramgauge	Blake	snow-flake	demoniac

ōld, ôr, ŏdd, oil, fŏŏt, out; ūse, ûrn, ŭp; THis, thin

dipsomaniac
Dyak
egomaniac
elegiac
Fond du Lac
good-lack
gripsack
hack
Hackensack
hackmatack
haversack
haystack
horseback
huckaback
humpback
hunchback
hypochondriac
jack
jimcrack
kayak
kleptomaniac
knack
knicknack
kodak
lac
lack
ladybrach
lakh
leather-jack
macaque
maniac
monomaniac
natterjack
pack
pickaback
plack
Pontiac
pyromaniac
quack
rack

ransack
rucksack
sac
sack
sacque
sal ammoniac
seawrack
shack
skipjack
slack
slapjack
Slovak
smack
snack
stack
stickleback
symposiac
tack
tamarack
thrack
thunder-crack
thwack
tick-tack
track
umiak
Union-jack
unpack
whack
woolpack
woolsack
wrack
yak
yashmak
yellow-jack
zodiac
zwieback

ĂK

plaque
Sarawak

ĀKS

Jakes
(see ĀK + s)

ĂKS

Analax
anticlimax
Astyanax
ax
battle-ax
flax
Halifax
income-tax
lax
parallax
pax
relax
Sachs
Saxe
slacks
tax
wax
zax
(see ĂK + s.)

ĂKT

abstract
act
attacked
attract
bract
cataract
compact
contract
counteract
detract
diffract
distract
enact
entr' acte
exact

extract
fact
impact
infract
intact
matter-of-fact
overact
pact
protract
react
redact
re-enact
refract
retract
retroact
saddle-backed
subtract
tact
tract
transact
underact
untracked
backed, etc.

ĀL

Abigail
ail
ale
all-hail
assail
avail
aventail
bail
bale
bepale
betail
bewail
blackmail
Bloomingdale
bobtail
brail

āle, câre, ădd, ärm, åsk; mē, hĕre, ĕnd; īce, ĭll;

Braille	*interpale*	vale	apologetical
camail	inveil	veil	apostolical
canaille	jail	wail	arboreal
cocktail	kail	wale	arboricultural
countervail	kale	whale	archeological
curtail	mail	wholesale	architectural
dale	male		arithmetical
dead-pale	martingale	**ĀL**	arsenal
death-pale	monorail	aboriginal	arsenical
derail	nail	academical	ascetical
detail	nightingale	accentual	asthmatical
disentail	outsail	admiral	astrological
dovetail	overveil	aërial	atmospherical
draggle-tail	pail	aesthetical	Babylonical
dwale	pale	affectional	bacchanal
empale	paravail	agricultural	bacchical
engaol	pigtail	Al	bacteriological
engrail	prevail	alchemical	bal
enjail	quail	alchemistical	balsamical
enscale	rail	alexipharmical	banal
entail	regale	alexiterical	barometrical
entrail	retail	algebraical	baronial
exhale	sail	alkalimetrical	basilical
fail	sale	allegorical	beatifical
fairy-tale	scale	allodial	biblical
farthingale	shale	alluvial	bibliographical
flail	sliding-scale	alphabetical	bibliomaniacal
foresail, etc.	snail	amatorial	bibliopolical
frail	spale	analogical	biographical
Gael	stale	analytical	biological
Gail	swale	anarchical	boreal
gale	tael	anatomical	botanical
gaol	tail	angelical	Brahmanical
grail	tale	animal	bureaucratical
grisaille	tenaille	annual	cabal
hail	they'll	antediluvial	cacophonical
hale	trail	anthological	Cal
handrail	travail	antiphonal	Calvinistical
hobnail	*trundle-tail*	antipodal	canal
impale	unveil	antithetical	cannibal
inhale	vail	apochryphal	canonical

capital
caracal
cardinal
carnival
cartographical
casual
casuistical
categorical
catholical
cervical
chaparral
characteristical
chemical
cherubical
chimerical
chronological
circumlocu-
    tional
classical
clerical
climatical
clinical
collateral
colloquial
comical
communal
complexional
conclusional
conditional
confessional
congressional
conical
conjectural
conjugal
connubial
consanguineal
consistorial
constitutional
continual
contradictional
conventical

conventional
conventual
conversational
corporal
corral
cortical
cosmetical
cosmical
coxcombical
criminal
critical
cryptical
cubical
cyclical
cylindrical
cynical
dal
decanal
decimal
deistical
democratical
demoniacal
demonological
denominational
descensional
destinal
devotional
diabolical
diaconal
diacritical
diagonal
diagraphical
dialectical
dialogical
dialogistical
diametrical
diaphonical
dictatorial
didactical
dietetical
digital

digressional
diluvial
diplomatical
dipsomaniacal
discretional
divisional
doctrinal
dogmatical
dolorifical
dominical
dramatical
dropsical
Druidical
dynamical
eccentrical
ecclesiastical
economical
ecstatical
ecumenical
educational
effectual
egoistical
egotistical
electrical
elegiacal
elliptical
emblematical
emotional
emphatical
empirical
empyreal
encomiastical
encyclical
encyclopedical
endemical
energetical
energical
enigmatical
enthusiastical
ephemeral
epical

epidemical
epigrammati-
    cal
Episcopal
episodical
epithetical
equivocal
erotical
esoterical
ethereal
ethical
ethnical
ethnological
etymological
Eucharistical
eulogistical
euphemistical
euphonical
evangelical
eventual
evolutional
exceptional
exegetical
exoterical
exotical
expurgatorial
extemporal
extrinsical
falderal
fanatical
fantastical
farcical
federal
festival
fictional
finical
forensical
fractional
functional
funeral
funereal

---

gal	immaterial	lyrical	notional
galvanical	immechanical	madrigal	numerical
geminal	immemorial	magical	occasional
genealogical	imperial	magnifical	octagonal
general	impersonal	majestical	optical
generical	inaugural	mall	optional
genial	incorporeal	maniacal	oratorical
geographical	individual	mareschal	original
geological	industrial	marginal	pal
geometrical	ineffectual	marital	paradisaical
germinal	infinitesimal	mathematical	parabolical
gradual	infusorial	matinal	parenthetical
grammatical	inimical	matronal	passional
graphical	initial	mechanical	pastoral
habitual	inquisitorial	medical	pathetical
Hal	inspirational	medicinal	pathological
harmonical	institutional	memorial	patrimonial
Hebraical	instructional	mercurial	patronal
heliacal	insurrectional	meridional	patronymical
hemispherical	intellectual	metaphorical	pedagogical
herbal	intentional	metaphysical	pedantical
heretical	intercessional	methodical	pedestal
heroical	interjectional	Methodistical	pedestrial
hexagonal	international	metrical	penological
hierarchical	interval	microscopical	pentagonal
historical	iridal	mineral	perennial
horticultural	ironical	ministerial	periodical
hospital	jesuitical	misanthropical	peripheral
hygienical	jovial	monarchical	periphrastical
hymeneal	juridical	municipal	perpetual
hyperbolical	lachrymal	musical	personal
hypercritical	lackadaisical	mutual	phantasma-
hypochondria-	laical	mystical	gorial
cal	lethargical	mythical	Pharisaical
hypocritical	Levitical	mythological	pharmaceutical
hysterical	liberal	national	phenomenal
identical	literal	natural	philanthropi-
idiotical	littoral	nautical	cal
illogical	liturgical	nectareal	philological
imaginal	logical	nominal	philosophical
imitational	longitudinal	nonsensical	photographical

phrenological
phthisical
physical
physiological
pictorial
pictural
pietistical
piratical
pivotal
platonical
pneumatolog-
  ical
poetical
polemical
political
pontifical
post-prandial
practical
pragmatical
precautional
preternatural
primordial
principal
probational
problematical
processional
prodigal
professional
professorial
progressional
prophetical
proportional
proverbial
provisional
psychiatrical
psychical
psychological
punctual
puritanical
purpureal
pyramidal

pyramidical
pyrotechnical
quadrennial
quadrigesimal
quadrilateral
quadrupedal
quizzical
radical
rational
recessional
reciprocal
remedial
residual
retinal
rhapsodical
rhetorical
rheumatical
rhythmical
ritual
sabbatical
sal
sartorial
satanical
satirical
scenical
skeptical
schismatical
scholastical
scriptural
sculptural
seigneurial
seigniorial
seneschal
sensational
seraphical
several
shall
sideral
sidereal
sociological
Socratical

sophistical
spasmodical
spherical
sporadical
stoical
strategical
supernatural
sybaritical
symbolical
symmetrical
synchronal
synchronical
synodical
synonymal
synonymical
synoptical
synthetical
systematical
tactical
technical
technicological
temporal
terminal
terrestrial
territorial
testimonial
theatrical
theological
theoretical
theosophical
topical
topographical
traditional
tragical
trivial
tropical
typical
typographical
tyrannical
umbilical
uncanonical

usual
uxorial
vatical
vegetal
ventriloquial
vertebral
vertical
vesperal
vicarial
victorial
viminal
virginal
virtual
visional
visual
volitional
vortical
whimsical
zodiacal
zoological

ĂL
kraal
Lasalle
morale

ĂLB
alb
De Kalb

ĂLD
bobtailed
unbewailed
unhaled
unassailed
ailed, etc.

ĂLD
caballed
corralled

āle,   câre,   ădd,   ärm,   ȧsk;   mē,   hẹre,   ĕnd;   īce,   ĭll;

emerald	aflame	ad nauseam	Petersham
palled	aim	am	pram
	ashame	Amsterdam	ram
ĂLF	became	anagram	Rotterdam
Alf	blame	battering-ram	salaam
Ralph	came	Birmingham	Schiedam
	claim	cablegram	scram
ĂLK	counterclaim	cam	sham
catafalque	crème de la	Cham	shram
talc	crème	clam	slam
	dame	cofferdam	stereogram
ĂLKS	declaim	cram	swam
calx	defame	cryptogam	telegram
catafalques	disclaim	cryptogram	tram
	disfame	Cunningham	whim-wham
ĂLP	entame	dam	yam
alp	exclaim	damn	
palp	fame	diagram	**ĂM**
scalp	flame	diaphragm	balm
	frame	dithyramb	becalm
ĂLPS	game	drachm	calm
Alps	hame	dram	embalm
palps, etc.	inflame	epigram	Guam
	lame	flimflam	imam
ĂLT	maim	gam	impalm
shalt	Mame	gram	Islam
	melodrame	ham	ma'am
ĂLV	misname	jam	malm
bivalve	name	jamb	palm
priming-valve	nickname	lam	psalm
safety-valve	overcame	lamb	qualm
salve	proclaim	ma'am	salaam
valve	reclaim	madame	
	same	Mam	**ĂMB**
ĂLZ	self-same	marjoram	dithyramb
Marseilles	shame	McAdam	gamb
Wales	surname	monogram	
(see ĂL + s)	tame	Nizam	**ĂMD**
		Nottingham	unblamed
ĀM	**ĀM**	oriflamme	unclaimed
acclaim	Abraham	parallelogram	unframed

unnamed	**ĀMZ**	champaign	frangipane
unreclaimed	Ames	Champlain	gain
unshamed	James	Charles's Wain	germane
untamed	acclaims, etc.	chatelaine	grain
acclaimed, etc.		chicane	henbane
	ĂMZ	chilblain	humane
ĂMP	alms	chow mein	hurricane
after-damp	balms, etc.	cocaine	hydrophane
camp		Cockaigne	hydroplane
champ	**ĀN**	complain	immane
clamp	abstain	constrain	inane
cramp	aerophane	contain	ingrain
damp	aeroplane	co-ordain	insane
Davy lamp	again	counterpane	interchain
death-damp	Aisne	coxswain	interreign
decamp	allophane	crane	inurbane
encamp	amain	Dane	jain
enstamp	appertain	deign	Jane
firedamp	aquaplane	delaine	Jayne
gamp	arraign	demesne	jean
guimpe	ascertain	deraign	lain
lamp	attain	detain	lane
minedamp	*atwain*	detrain	legerdemain
ramp	bane	diaphane	lithophane
revamp	battering-train	disdain	Lorraine
safety-lamp	Bayne	distrain	main
samp	bearing-rein	domain	Maine
scamp	bestain	drain	maintain
signal-lamp	blain	Duchesne	mane
stamp	boatswain	Duquesne	Mayne
tamp	bower-thane	elecampane	McLain
tramp	brain	enchain	McLean
vamp	bridle-rein	engrain	*mediterrane*
	Cain	entertain	misfeign
ĂMP	Caine	entrain	moraine
swamp	campaign	explain	mortmain
(see ŎMP)	campane	fain	obtain
	cane	fane	ordain
ĂMPT	chain	feign	pain
undamped	chamberlain	fleabane	Paine
camped, etc.	champagne	foreordain	pane

āle,   câre,   ădd,   ärm,   åsk;   mē,   hĕre,   ĕnd;   īce,   ĭll;

Payne	unchain	Batavian	fan
pertain	unrein	Bavarian	firman
plain	uptrain	began	fisherman
plane	urbane	Bezonian	flan
pleasure-train	vain	Bohemian	foo young dan
porcelain	vane	bran	foremast-man
preordain	vein	Briarean	foreran
profane	vervain	Bulgarian	frying-pan
pursuit plane	wain	caducean	fugleman
quatrain	water-crane	Caledonian	Gallican
rain	wane	Cambrian	gargantuan
refrain	weather-vane	can	gentleman
regain		Canadian	hard-pan
reign	**ĂN**	caravan	harridan
rein	Acadian	castellan	Hesperian
remain	African	Catalan	historian
restrain	alabastrian	catamaran	husbandman
retain	Alcoran	charlatan	Indian
sane	Aldebaran	Cimmerian	inspan
scatterbrain	alderman	clan	Isfahan
Seine	Alexandrian	clergyman	Isle of Man
sextain	Algerian	Columbian	Japan
skein	also ran	comedian	journeyman
slain	amatorian	Copernican	juryman
soutane	Amazonian	corban	khan
Spain	American	Corinthian	latitudinarian
sprain	amphibian	cosmopolitan	librarian
stain	an	countryman	lighterman
strain	Anglican	courtesan	liveryman
subterrane	Ann	cran	luggage-van
sugarcane	Anne	custodian	man
sustain	antediluvian	Cyprian	Marianne
suzerain	artisan	Dan	Matapan
swain	Baconian	Delphian	medicine-man
ta'en	ban	diluvian	merchantman
tain	Barbadian	divan	meridian
terrain	barbarian	Dominican	merman
thane	barbican	echinidan	metropolitan
thegn	barracan	Englishman	Mexican
train	bartizan	equestrian	Michigan
twain	basilican	Ethiopian	midshipman

Milan	rattan	wherryman	hot-brained
minute-man	redan	Zoroastrian	interveined
Mohammedan	Republican		maned
Mussulman	Sabbatarian	**ÄN**	muddy-brained
nectarean	Sacramenta-	corban	rattle-brained
nobleman	rian	swan	scatter-brained
octogenarian	sacristan	wan, etc.	self-restrained
Olympian	Samaritan	(see ŎN)	shallow-
oppidan	scan		brained
orang-utan	Sedan	**ANCH**	shatter-brained
ortolan	serving-man	avalanche	travel-stained
ottoman	shandrydan	blanch	unascertained
outran	signal-man	branch	unconstrained
outspan	span	carte-blanche	unplained
overman	spick-and-span	flanch	unprofaned
overran	Stygian	ganch	unreined
pan	subterranean	ranch	unrestrained
Parmesan	suffragan	scranch	unstained
partisan	superman	stanch	unstrained
pavane	talisman		unsustained
pecan	tally-man	**ÄNCH**	untrained
pedestrian	tan	Blanche	abstained, etc.
pelican	than	haunch	
pemmican	Thespian	launch	**AND**
Peruvian	tragedian	manche	*aband*
plan	trepan	paunch	abbey-land
platitudinarian	unman	stanch	ampersand
postmeridan	utilitarian	staunch	and
praetorian	Utopian		band
predestinarian	valerian	**ÄNCHD**	bland
Presbyterian	valetudinarian	unstanched	brand
prison-van	Valkyrian	launched, etc.	bridle-hand
procrustean	van		command
proletarian	Vatican	**ÄND**	contraband
Promethean	vegetarian	bloodstained	countermand
publican	Vesuvian	constrained	demand
puritan	veteran	diaphaned	deodand
quarry-man	veterinarian	disdained	disband
quotidian	vulgarian	feather-	expand
Ramadhan	warming-pan	brained	fairy-land
ran	waterman	hare-brained	fatherland

firebrand	**ĂND**	unpanged	**ĂNGKS**
first-hand	wand	banged, etc.	Manx
four-in-hand	(see ŎND)		(see
full-manned		**ĂNGK**	ĂNGK + s)
gland	**ĂNG**	bank	
grand	bang	Blanc	**ĂNGKT**
hand	bhang	blank	sacrosanct
ill-manned	boomerang	brank	spindle-
imband	clang	chank	shanked
land	fang	clank	unspanked
lotus-land	gang	crank	(see
manned	gobang	dank	ĂNGK + ed)
master-hand	hang	drank	
minute-hand	harangue	embank	**ĂNJ**
multiplicand	meringue	enrank	arrange
overhand	mustang	flank	change
overland	orang-outang	franc	counter-change
rand	overhang	frank	derange
remand	pang	hank	disarrange
reprimand	Penang	lank	enrange
Rio Grande	rang	mountebank	estrange
Samarcand	sang	outflank	exchange
sand	sea-tang	outrank	grange
saraband	serang	plank	interchange
second-hand	shebang	point-blank	mange
self-command	slang	prank	range
stand	slap-bang	rank	rearrange
strand	spang	sank	seachange
underhand	sprang	savings-bank	strange
understand	stang	shank	
unhand	swang	shrank	**ĂNJ**
unland	tang	slank	flange
unmanned	trepang	spank	phalange
unscanned	twang	stank	
upper-hand	uphang	tank	**ĂNS**
washstand	vang	thank	advance
withstand	whang	twank	ambulance
wonderland		water-tank	appurtenance
(see ĂN + ed)	**ĂNGD**	Yank	arrogance
	langued		askance

ōld, ôr, ŏdd, oil, fŏŏt, out; ūse, ûrn, ŭp; THis, thin

bechance	inconsonance	trance	taint
chance	inhabitance	utterance	'taint
circumstance	inheritance	variance	*teint*
complaisance	intemperance	vigilance	unconstraint
concomitance	intolerance	(Cf. ĂNT + s)	unsaint
consonance	irrelevance		
continuance	lance	**ĂNS**	**ĂNT or ÀNT**
conversance	luxuriance	fer-de-lance	abdicant
countenance	manse	insouciance	adamant
country-dance	mischance		adjutant
dance	Nance	**ĀNT**	adulterant
death-dance	ordinance	acquaint	agglutinant
deliverance	penetrance	ain't	*altitonant*
demi-lance	perchance	attaint	*altivolant*
discountenance	petulance	bepaint	ambulant
dissonance	prance	besaint	annuitant
dominance	precipitance	complaint	ant
elance	predominance	constraint	anticipant
elegance	preponderance	*daint*	applicant
enhance	protuberance	depaint	appurtenant
entrance	puissance	distraint	arrogant
expanse	radiance	faint	askant
extravagance	recognizance	feint	aslant
exuberance	reconnaissance	Geraint	aunt
finance	relevance	liver-complaint	brant
France	resonance	mayn't	cant
furtherance	romance	paint	can't
glance	sibilance	plaint	chant
heritance	significance	quaint	combatant
ignorance	stance	restraint	commandant
impuissance	sufferance	saint	communicant
incogitance	suppliance	self-restraint	complaisant
incognisance	tolerance	straint	concomitant

Throughout this rhyming dictionary, sounds as close alike as *ant, chant,* and *abdicant* are listed together as perfect rhymes. Strictly, these three words differ slightly in the pronunciation of the *a* sound: they are properly pronounced as

ănt   chănt   abdicănt

Similarly, words like *age* and *acreage* are listed together as perfect rhymes: for this is the immemorial practice of poets. Their strict pronunciation, as used in conversation or prose, differs: *age* rhyming with *stage,* and *acreage* with *ridge.* The poetic pronunciation might be regarded as an eye-rhyme universally accepted in versification.

confidant	habitant	Protestant	visitant
confidante	hesitant	protuberant	vociferant
congratulant	hierophant	puissant	
consonant	ignorant	pursuivant	**ĂNT**
conversant	illuminant	quant	aunt
cormorant	*imaginant*	rant	can't
corposant	immigrant	recalcitrant	debutante
corroborant	implant	recant	shan't
Corybant	impuissant	recreant	
courant	incogitant	recusant	**ĂNTH**
covenant	incognisant	refrigerant	amaranth
decant	inconsonant	reiterant	amianth
deplant	inhabitant	relevant	tragacanth
descant	insignificant	resonant	
determinant	intolerant	resuscitant	**ĂNTS**
dilettant	intoxicant	reverberant	pants
disenchant	irradiant	ruminant	(see ĂNT + s)
disputant	irrelevant	sacrificant	
dissonant	irritant	scant	**ĀNZ**
dominant	itinerant	scintillant	Raines
elegant	jubilant	sensitive-plant	Raynes
elephant	Kant	shan't	(see ĀN + s)
emigrant	Levant	sibilant	
enchant	litigant	significant	**ĂNZ**
excommunicant	luminant	slant	banns
executant	luxuriant	stimulant	(see ĂN + s)
exorbitant	mendicant	suffragant	
extant	militant	supplant	**ĂNZH**
extravagant	miscreant	suppliant	melange
exuberant	nonchalant	supplicant	
fabricant	occupant	sycophant	**ĀP**
figurant	odorant	*tant*	agape
figurante	pant	termagant	ape
flagellant	penetrant	tintinnabulant	cape
fulminant	petulant	tolerant	chape
gallant	plant	toxicant	crape
gallivant	postulant	transplant	crèpe
Gant	precipitant	undulant	drape
germinant	predominant	variant	escape
grant	preponderant	variant	fire-escape
gratulant	procreant	vigilant	gape

ōld,   ôr,   ŏdd,   oil,   fŏŏt,   out;   ūse,   ûrn,   ŭp;   THis,   thin

grape	heel-tap	Mapes	arrière
jape	Jap	traipse	aware
landscape	knap	apes, etc.	Ayr
Lape	lagniappe		*ayre*
nape	lap	**ĂPS**	backstair
pape	Lapp	apse	bare
rape	map	collapse	bear
red-tape	mayhap	craps	bêche-de-mer
scape	mishap	elapse	bedare
scrape	nap	illapse	beglare
seascape	night-cap	interlapse	beware
shape	overlap	lapse	billionaire
ship-shape	pap	perhaps	blare
tape	percussion-cap	relapse	capillaire
transshape	rap	schnapps	care
trape	rattle-trap	after-claps, etc.	chair
uncape	sap		chare
unshape	scrap	**ĂPT**	chargé
	shoulder-strap	aped	d'affaires
ĂP	slap	(see ĀP + ed)	claire
after-clap	snap		*clare*
agape	stopgap	**ÂPT**	*cockle-stair*
bestrap	strap	adapt	commissionaire
cap	tap	apt	compare
chap	thunder-clap	enrapt	concessionnaire
clap	trap	inapt	dare
claptrap	unlap	moss-capped	debonair
dap	unwrap	rapt	declare
entrap	wapp	snow-capped	Delaware
enwrap	water-tap	wrapt	despair
flap	wishing-cap	bestrapped,	devil-may-care
flip-flap	wrap	etc.	disrepair
foolscap	yap		doctrinaire
forage-cap		**ÂR**	earthenware
frap	**ÂP**	Adair	eclair
gap	gape	affair	e'er
gape	swap	affaire	elsewhcre
genapp	(see ŎP)	air	ensnare
genappe		aire	ere
handicap	**ĂPS**	anywhere	etagère
hap	jackanapes	armchair	everywhere

āle,   câre,   ădd,   ärm,   åsk;   mē,   hĕre,   ĕnd;   īce,   ĭll;

eyre	prayer	vin-ordinaire	debar
fair	prepare	vivandière	deodar
fare	prickly-pear	ware	disbar
flair	proletaire	wear	dissimilar
flare	*quair*	whate'er	embar
forbear	rare	whatsoe'er	evening-star
forswear	repair	whene'er	Excalibar
gare	scare	where	falling-star
glair	sedan-chair	where'er	far
glare	share	wheresoe'er	Farr
Gruyère	Sinclair	yare	feldspar
hair	snare		funicular
hare	solitaire	**ĂR**	gar
heir	somewhere	afar	globular
howe'er	spare	ajar	gnar
impair	square	angular	guitar
jardinière	stair	animalcular	hospodar
lair	stare	annular	hussar
laissez-faire	stere	are	instar
maidenhair	*sware*	avatar	insular
mal de mer	swear	axle-bar	irregular
mare	tare	bar	jaguar
McNair	tear	bazaar	jar
McNare	their	binocular	jaunting-car
mid-air	there	bizarre	jemadar
millionaire	thoroughfare	boulevard	jocular
misfare	threadbare	calendar	jugular
mohair	trouvère	canard	knar
ne'er	tuyère	car	Lascar
otherwhere	unaware	catarrh	lodestar
outdare	*unbeware*	caviar	Loire
outstare	underbear	char	Malabar
outswear	underwear	cigar	mar
outwear	unfair	cinnabar	modular
overbear	unswear	circular	molecular
pair	*unware*	consular	morning-star
pare	upbear	crepuscular	night-jar
parterre	upstare	cymar	north-star
pear	uptear	czar	ocular
Pierre	vair	dar	par
portiere	vare	daystar	parr

ōld, ôr, ŏdd, oil, fōōt, out; ūse, ûrn, ŭp; THis, thin

particular
peninsular
perpendicular
pilot-star
popular
quadrangular
registrar
regular
saddle-bar
scapular
scar
scimitar
sea-star
secular
shackle-bar
shooting-star
similar
singular
somnambular
spar
spectacular
star
stellular
subahdar
tabernacular
tabular
tar
tintamarre
tintinnabular
titular
triangular
tsar
tutelar
unbar
unspar
upbar
uvular
valvular
vehicular
vermicular
vernacular

versicular
vinegar
Zanzibar
zamindar

ÄRB
barb
garb
yarb

ÄRCH
arch
countermarch
dead march
inarch
larch
march
outmarch
overarch
overmarch
parch
starch

ÄRD
Baird
golden-haired
laird
silver-haired
uncared
unheired
unimpaired
unpaired
unprepared
unshared
unspared
aired, etc.

ÄRD
after-guard
avant-garde
bard

Bernard
blackguard
bódy-guard
bombard
boulevard
camelopard
canard
card
chard
closebarred
discard
disregard
dynamitard
enguard
evil-starred
fard
foulard
Girard
guard
hard
interlard
lard
life-guard
milliard
nard
pard
petard
placard
poultry-yard
regard
retard
sard
shard
spikenard
starred
under-sparred
unguard
unmarred
wedding-card
yard
(see ÄR + ed)

ÄRF
'arf and 'arf
larf
scarf

ÄRJ
barge
charge
discharge
embarge
encharge
enlarge
Farge
La Farge
large
litharge
marge
overcharge
sea-marge
sparge
surcharge
targe
uncharge
undercharge

ÄRJD
undischarged
barged, etc.

ÄRK
aardvark
arc
ark
Asiarch
bark
barque
bedark
cark
Clark
Clarke
clerk

āle, câre, ădd, ärm, ăsk; mē, hĕre, ĕnd; īce, ĭll;

dark	ÄRL	unalarmed	ÄRS
debark	Albemarle	alarmed, etc.	farce
disembark	carl		parse
dispark	ensnarl	**ÄRMZ**	sarse
easy mark	gnarl	Armes	sparse
ecclesiarch	harl	assault-at-arms	
embark	imparl	gentleman-at-	**ÄRSH**
endark	jarl	arms	harsh
flood-mark	Karl	king-at-arms	marsh
foot-mark	marl	man-at-arms	
hark	snarl	alarms, etc.	**ÄRT**
hierarch			apart
impark	**ÄRLZ**	**ÄRN**	art
iremarch	Charles	bairn	cart
knark	(see ÄRL + s)	cairn	carte
lark		tairn	chart
marc	**ÄRM**	**ÄRN**	counterpart
mark	alarm	barn	dart
marque	arm	darn	depart
meadow-lark	axle-arm	*imbarn*	dispart
oligarch	barm	incarn	flint-heart
park	becharm	Marne	hart
patriarch	charm	tarn	heart
remark	counter-charm	yarn	impart
sark	decharm		indart
sea-lark	disarm	**ÄRNZ**	lion-heart
shark	disencharm	Barnes	mart
sky-lark	farm	(see ÄRN + s)	part
snark	fire-alarm		quarte
spark	firearm	**ÄRP**	sart
stark	forearm	carp	smart
Starke	gendarme	epicarp	start
water-mark	harm	escarp	sweetheart
	love-charm	harp	tart
ÄRKS	unarm	monocarp	uncart
Marx	uncharm	pericarp	unheart
(see ÄRK + s)	unharm	scarp	upstart
		sharp	water-cart
ÄRKT			
unmarked	**ÄRMD**	**ÄRS**	**ÄRTH**
barked, etc.	forearmed	scarce	Applegarth

ōld, ôr, ŏdd, oil, fŏŏt, out; ūse, ûrn, ŭp; THis, thin

garth | carapace | steeple-chase | kvass
hearth | case | thorough-bass | lass
swarth | chariot-race | Thrace | looking-glass
| chase | trace | mass

ÄRV | commonplace | trysting-place | Michaelmas
carve | dace | ukase | middle-class
larve | debase | unbrace | minute-glass
starve | deface | uncase | morass
| disgrace | underbrace | object-glass

ÄRTS | displace | unlace | overpass
Harz | efface | vase | paillasse
(see ÄRT + s) | embrace | | pass
| encase | **AS** | paterfamilias

ÄRZ | enchase | after-grass | rubasse
backstairs | enlace | alas | sassafras
stairs | erase | All-hallowmas | sparrow-grass
theirs | face | amass | strass
unawares | footpace | ass | surpass
unbewares | footrace | bass | tarantass
unwares | grace | *bonnilass* | tass
airs, etc. | grimace | brass | weather-glass
| hiding-place | Candlemas | working-class

ÄRZ | horse-race | class
Mars | idocrase | crass | **ÄS**
(see ÄR + s) | interlace | crevasse | en masse
| interspace | cuirass

ÄS | lace | declass | **ÄSH**
abase | mace | demi-tasse | crèche
ace | misplace | en masse
aface | outface | first-class | **ÄSH**
anelace | outpace | flint-glass | abash
apace | pace | galloglass | ash
base | place | gas | balderdash
bass | plaice | glass | bash
begrace | populace | grass | bedash
belace | race | Hallowmas | *brache*
birthplace | replace | hippocras | brash
boniface | resting-place | hour-glass | cache
brace | retrace | isinglass | calabash
breathing- | scapegrace | kavass | calash
  space | space | Khyber Pass | calipash

āle, câre, ădd, ärm, ȧsk; mē, hẹre, ĕnd; īce, ĭll;

cash	unlashed	**ÄST**	smock-faced
clash	unthrashed	after-taste	smooth-faced
crash	abashed, etc.	apple-faced	smug-faced
dash		barefaced	snail-paced
fash	**ASK**	baste	strait-laced
flash	antimask	brazen-faced	tallow-faced
gash	ask	chaste	taste
gnash	bask	distaste	thorough-
hash	basque	double-faced	paced
interdash	bemask	dough-faced	two-faced
lâche	Bergamask	fair-faced	traced
lash	cask	foretaste	unbraced
mash	casque	freckle-faced	unchaste
mountain-ash	flask	furrow-faced	undefaced
moustache	*immask*	hard-faced	undisgraced
Nash	mask	haste	ungraced
pash	masque	hatchet-faced	unshamefaced
patache	overtask	horse-faced	untraced
plash	Pasch	impaste	waist
rash	powder-flask	Janus-faced	waste
rehash	task	laced	weasel-faced
sabretache	unmask	lambaste	well-graced
sash	water-cask	leaden-paced	whey-faced
slap-dash	**ÄSKT**	lean-faced	wizen-faced
slash	unasked	lily-faced	abased, etc.
smash	unmasked	mottle-faced	
splash	basked, etc.	pale-faced	**ÄST**
splatter-dash		paper-faced	aghast
squabash	**ÄSP**	paste	avast
thrash	asp	pippin-faced	bast
trash	clasp	platter-faced	blast
unlash	enclasp	plump-faced	bombast
weeping-ash	engrasp	poste-haste	cast
	gasp	pudding-faced	caste
ÄSH	grasp	pug-faced	contrast
quash	hasp	retraced	devast
wash, etc.	rasp	sad-faced	downcast
(see ÕSH)	unclasp	self-abased	ecclesiast
		shame-faced	elegiast
ÄSHT	**ÄSP**	sheep-faced	ember-fast
undashed	wasp	slow-paced	encomiast

enthusiast	abominate	annihilate	bimaculate
fast	abrogate	annotate	binoculate
flabbergast	absinthiate	annulate	cachinnate
forecast	absquatulate	*annumerate*	calculate
ghast	accelerate	annunciate	caliphate
handfast	accentuate	antedate	calumniate
hast	*acclamate*	antepenulti-	campanulate
high-caste	acclimate	mate	camphorate
iconoclast	accommodate	anticipate	cancellate
idoloclast	accumulate	antiquate	candidate
jury-mast	accurate	apostolate	capacitate
last	acidulate	applicate	capitate
mast	actuate	appreciate	capitulate
metaphrast	acuminate	approbate	captivate
metaplast	adequate	appropriate	carbonate
outlast	adjudicate	approximate	cardinalate
overcast	adulate	arbitrate	casemate
paraphrast	adulterate	armour-plate	castigate
past	advocate	arrogate	cate
protoplast	aërate	articulate	celebrate
recast	affectionate	asphyxiate	celibate
repast	affiliate	aspirate	certificate
scholiast	affreight	assassinate	chalybeate
steadfast	agglomerate	asseverate	checkmate
storm-blast	agglutinate	assimilate	chocolate
symposiast	aggravate	*assimulate*	circulate
unfast	aggregate	associate	circumstantiate
unsurpassed	agitate	ate	classmate
vast	alienate	attenuate	coagulate
amassed, etc.	alleviate	*augurate*	cogitate
wast	allocate	aureate	collaborate
	altercate	auspicate	collate
ĀT	alternate	authenticate	collegiate
abalienate	alveolate	aviate	collocate
abate	amalgamate	await	commemorate
abacinate	ambulate	baccalaureate	commensurate
abbreviate	ameliorate	bait	comminate
abdicate	ampliate	bate	commiserate
ablocate	amputate	belate	communicate
abnegate	angulate	berate	compassionate
abnodate	animate	Billingsgate	compensate

āle, câre, ădd, ärm, åsk; mē, hęre, ĕnd; īce, ĭll;

complicate	debate	dilapidate	equate
concatenate	debilitate	dilate	equivocate
concentrate	decapitate	directorate	eradicate
conciliate	decimate	disconsolate	estate
conditionate	decolorate	discriminate	estimate
confabulate	decorate	disintegrate	estivate
confederate	dedicate	dislocate	etiolate
confiscate	degenerate	disseminate	evacuate
conflate	delate	dissimulate	evaluate
conglomerate	delegate	dissipate	evaporate
congratulate	deliberate	dissociate	eventuate
congregate	delicate	doctorate	exacerbate
conjugate	delineate	domesticate	exacinate
consecrate	demonstrate	dominate	exaggerate
considerate	denominate	donate	exasperate
consolidate	denunciate	dunder-pate	excavate
constipate	*deodate*	duplicate	excogitate
consulate	depopulate	educate	excommunicate
consummate	deprecate	effectuate	excoriate
contaminate	depreciate	effeminate	excruciate
contemplate	depredate	efflate	exculpate
co-operate	*depucelate*	eight	execrate
co-ordinate	derivate	ejaculate	exhilarate
copper-plate	derogate	elaborate	exonerate
copulate	desecrate	elate	exorbitate
coronate	desiderate	electorate	expatiate
corporate	designate	electro-plate	expatriate
correlate	desolate	elevate	expectorate
corroborate	desperate	eliminate	expiate
corrugate	deteriorate	elucidate	expostulate
crate	determinate	emaciate	extenuate
create	detonate	emanate	exterminate
cremate	devastate	emancipate	extirpate
crenellate	deviate	emasculate	extortionate
crepitate	devirginate	emigrate	extravagate
criminate	diaconate	emolliate	extricate
culminate	diagnosticate	emulate	fabricate
cultivate	dial-plate	enervate	facilitate
date	dictate	enumerate	fascinate
dead-weight	differentiate	enunciate	fate
death-rate	digitate	episcopate	feather-weight

ōld, ôr, ŏdd, oil, fŏŏt, out; ūse, ûrn, ŭp; THis, thin

federate	illuminate	indeterminate	invalidate
felicitate	illustrate	indevirginate	investigate
fête	imitate	indicate	invertebrate
first-mate	immaculate	indiscriminate	inveterate
first-rate	immarginate	individuate	invigorate
flagellate	*immateriate*	indoctrinate	inviolate
floodgate	immediate	indurate	invocate
fluctuate	*immensurate*	inebriate	irate
foliolate	immigrate	infatuate	irradiate
foreordinate	immoderate	inflate	irrigate
formulate	immolate	infuriate	irritate
fortunate	impassionate	ingerminate	isolate
freight	impersonate	*ingrate*	iterate
fructuate	impetrate	ingratiate	itinerate
frustrate	implicate	ingurgitate	Kate
fulminate	importunate	initiate	lacerate
fumigate	imprecate	innate	lanceolate
funambulate	impropriate	innovate	late
gait	improvisate	inoculate	laureate
gate	inaccurate	inordinate	legislate
gelatinate	inadequate	insatiate	legitimate
generate	inanimate	inseminate	levigate
germinate	inappropriate	insinuate	levirate
gesticulate	inarticulate	instate	liberate
glaciate	inaugurate	instigate	licentiate
graduate	incapacitate	insubordinate	liquidate
granulate	incarcerate	insulate	literate
grate	*incastellate*	integrate	litigate
gratulate	inchoate	intenerate	lixiviate
gravitate	incinerate	intemperate	locate
great	incommensur-	*intercessionate*	lubricate
habilitate	ate	intermediate	lucubrate
habituate	incompassion-	interminate	luxuriate
hate	ate	interpolate	macerate
heavy-weight	inconsiderate	interrogate	machinate
helpmate	incorporate	intimate	magistrate
hesitate	increate	intimidate	magnate
hibernate	incriminate	intonate	manipulate
humiliate	incubate	intoxicate	marinate
hypothecate	inculcate	intricate	marquisate
illiterate	indelicate	inundate	masticate

āle, câre, ădd, ärm, åsk; mē, hęre, ĕnd; īce, ĭll;

mate	participate	promulgate	reprobate
matriculate	passionate	propagate	repudiate
mediate	pastorate	propitiate	restate
meditate	pate	proportionate	resuscitate
mess-mate	patronate	pro-rate	retaliate
migrate	peculate	prostrate	reticulate
militate	penetrate	protectorate	reverberate
mitigate	peninsulate	protuberate	roseate
moderate	pennyweight	provinciate	rotate
modulate	perambulate	proximate	ruminate
motivate	percolate	pulsate	runagate
mutilate	peregrinate	punctuate	rusticate
narrate	perforate	quadruplicate	salivate
Nate	permeate	radiate	sanitate
navigate	perorate	rate	sate
necessitate	perpetrate	ratiocinate	satiate
negociate	perpetuate	rattle-pate	saturate
nickle-plate	personate	rebate	scintillate
nominate	placate	recalcitrate	Sea Gate
novitiate	plait	recapitulate	second-rate
obdurate	plate	reciprocate	secretariate
obligate	playmate	recreate	sedate
obliterate	poet-laureate	recriminate	segregate
obstinate	pontificate	rectorate	separate
obviate	populate	recuperate	shipmate
officiate	postulate	refrigerate	sibilate
operate	potentate	regenerate	silicate
opiate	prate	regrate	silver-plate
orate	precipitate	regulate	simulate
orchestrate	predate	regurgitate	situate
originate	predestinate	rehabilitate	skate
ornate	predicate	reinstate	slate
oscillate	predominate	reiterate	somnambulate
osculate	premeditate	rejuvenate	sophisticate
over-rate	preponderate	relate	spate
overstate	prevaricate	relegate	speculate
overweight	procrastinate	remediate	spifflicate
oxygenate	procreate	remonstrate	spoliate
palliate	professoriate	remunerate	stalemate
palpitate	profligate	renovate	state
paper-weight	prognosticate	repatriate	stearate

ōld, ôr, ŏdd, oil, fŏŏt, out; ūse, ûrn, ŭp; THis, thin

stellulate	uncreate	automat	proletariat
stimulate	underrate	bat	plutocrat
stipulate	understate	bepat	polecat
straight	underweight	brat	rat
strait	undulate	brickbat	requiescat
stridulate	unfortunate	cat	rheostat
stylobate	unstate	caveat	sat
subjugate	vacate	chat	scat
sublimate	vaccinate	civet-cat	secretariat
subordinate	vacillate	commissariat	slat
subrogate	validate	cravat	spat
substantiate	variate	dandiprat	sprat
sufflate	variegate	democrat	Surat
suffocate	vassalate	diplomat	tabby-cat
superannuate	vaticinate	drat	tat
supererogate	vegetate	fallow-chat	that
supplicate	venerate	fat	theocrat
suppurate	ventilate	flat	thereat
syncopate	verberate	frat	thermostat
syndicate	vermiculate	*forgat*	unhat
tabulate	vertebrate	gat	vampire-bat
Tait	vertiginate	gnat	vat
temperate	vicariate	habitat	water-rat
tergiversate	vindicate	hat	whereat
terminate	violate	heliostat	
tête-à-tête	vitiate	hellcat	**ÄT**
third-rate	vituperate	hereat	Kalat
titillate	vizierate	high-hat	Khelat
titivate	vociferate	hydrostat	squat
tolerate	wait	kittycat	what, etc.
trait	water-rate	lariat	yacht
translate	weight	Magnificat	(see ŎT)
transliterate		marrow-fat	
transubstan-	**ÄT**	mat	**ĀTH**
tiate	acrobat	matte	bathe
triangulate	aflat	monocrat	lathe
triturate	Ararat	pat	scathe
triumvirate	aristocrat	pitapat	snathe
ulcerate	assignat	plat	spathe
ultimate	at	Platt	swathe
ululate	autocrat	Platte	unswathe

Āth	ĀV	waive	Hayes
faith	angusticlave	wave	haze
i'faith	architrave		laze
misfaith	behave	ĀV	maize
rathe	belave	have	malaise
Snaith	beslave	Slav	Marseillaise
unfaith	brave		Mays
water-wraith	cave	ĀV	Mayes
wraith	concave	calve	mayonnaise
	crave	enclave	maze
ĀTth	Dave	halve	metaphrase
eighth	deprave	salve	naze
hate'th, etc.	drave	Slav	nowadays
	élève	suave	outblaze
ĂTH	encave	zouave	outgaze
aftermath	enclave		paraphrase
allopath	engrave	ĀZ	phase
Gath	enslave	ablaze	phrase
hath	forgave	adaze	polonaise
homeopath	galley-slave	amaze	praise
math	gave	appraise	raise
osteopath	glaive	baize	rase
philomath	grave	Blaise	raze
physiopath	impave	beacon-blaze	self-praise
psychopath	knave	bepraise	then-a-days
snath	lave	blaze	underpraise
	misbehave	braise	unpraise
ĂTH	misgave	braze	upblaze
bath	nave	chaise	upgaze
bridle-path	outbrave	chrysoprase	upraise
footpath	pave	craze	vase
lath	rave	daze	wonder-maze
path	save	dispraise	(see Ā + s)
rath	shave	emblaze	
wrath	slave	faze	ĂZ
	stave	fraise	as
ĀTS	suave	gaze	has
Bates	they've	glaze	jazz
Cates	thrave	graze	razz
Yates	trave	Haas	whereas
Yeats	ungrave		
(see ĀT + s)			

ōld, ôr, ŏdd. oil, fŏŏt, out; ūse, ûrn, ŭp: THis, thin

ÄZ	ÄZD	entourage	ectoplasm
Shiraz	jazzed	garage	enthusiasm
vase	razzed	menage	iconoclasm
(see Ä + s)		mirage	metaplasm
	ÄZH	persiflage	miasm
ÄZD	cortegé		phantasm
adazed		ÄZM	*phasm*
bemazed	ÄZH	bioplasm	plasm
unamazed	badinage	cataplasm	pleonasm
unpraised	barrage	chasm	protoplasm
amazed, etc.	camouflage	demoniasm	sarcasm
			spasm

E

These words include the following accented vowel sounds:

Ē as in me; heard also in eve, feet, beam, deceive, people, key, Caesar, machine, field, quay, phoebe.

Ḙ as in here; heard also in fear, dreary, weird.

Ĕ as in end; heard also in heifer, leopard, friend, Aetna, feather, asafoetida, bury, any, Thames, said, says.

Ē	appellee	bohea	chickadee
A.B.	appointee	bonhomie	chickeree
abandonee	assignee	bootee	chimpanzee
absentee	avowee	bouilli	Chinee
addressee	axle-tree	bourgeoisie	Christmas-tree
advowee	bailee	bumblebee	coatee
agape	bain-marie	burgee	consignee
Agapemone	banshee	B.V.D.	corroboree
agree	bargee	C.O.D.	coryphee
aknee	bawbee	calipee	Cybele
alee	be	Calliope	D.D.
allottee	bee	calorie	debauchee
anemone	belee	cap-a-pie	debris
Anglice	bel-esprit	catastrophe	decree
antistrophe	Benedicite	Chaldee	dedicatee
apogee	biographee	chariotee	Dee
apostraphe	*blea*	Cherokee	degree

āle, câre, ădd, ärm, åsk; mē, hḙre, ĕnd; īce, ĭll;

devisee	garnishee	McFee	pugaree
devotee	gee	McGee	Q.T.
diablerie	geegee	McKee	quay
disagree	Gethsemane	me	raki
divorcee	ghee	Melpomene	rani
dominie	glee	mestee	rapparee
donee	goatee	mortgagee	rappee
drawee	grandee	mustee	razee
dree	grantee	N.G.	recipe
Dundee	guarantee	nebulae	referee
dungaree	he	Niobe	refugee
Dupree	heart-free	nominee	releasee
eau de vie	honey-bcc	O.G.	remittee
employee	humblebee	obligee	repartee
endorsee	hyperbole	ogee	rhe
nfree	interrogatee	on dit	Rosalie
ennui	jamboree	oversea	rupee
epopee	Japanee	oversee	Sadducee
esprit	jeu d'esprit	Ph.D.	sangaree
etui	jinnee	Parsee	Sault St. Marie
Eugenie	jubilee	*passaree*	scarabee
Eulalie	key	patentee	scree
examinee	killdee	Pawnee	sea
extempore	knee	payee	see
facetiae	langue d'oui	pea	selvagee
facsimile	lea	pedigree	sesame
fäerie	lee	Penelope	settee
fancy-free	legatee	perigee	she
fee	lessee	permittee	si
felo de se	levee	petitionee	simile
fiddle-de-dee	ley	Pharisee	skilligalee
filigree	li	picotee	snee
flea	licensee	plea	snickersnee
flee	litchi	pledgee	spree
fleur-de-lis	M.D.	point-d'appui	stingaree
foresee	manatee	poison-tree	suttee
free	Manichee	pongee	sycee
fricassee	Marie	pontee	synecdoche
fusee	marquee	pot-pourri	systole
Galilee	Marshalsea	presentee	tea
gallows-tree	master-key	promisee	tee

ōld, ôr, ŏdd, oil fŏŏt, out; ūse, ûrn, ŭp; THis, thin

tehee	adversity	ascendancy	Calvary
Tennessee	advisability	asperity	canopy
Terpsichore	affability	assiduity	capability
the	affinity	astrology	capacity
thee	agency	astronomy	captivity
third degree	agility	atrocity	casualty
three	agony	atrophy	catholicity
topee	alacrity	audacity	causticity
toupee	alchemy	augury	cavalry
transferee	allopathy	austerity	cavity
tree	ambiguity	authenticity	celebrity
trustee	amenability	authority	celerity
Tweedledee	amenity	autonomy	century
unforesee	amicability	avidity	certainty
unfree	amity	bakery	changeability
vendee	amnesty	balcony	chancery
vertebrae	analogy	barbarity	charity
vis-a-vis	anarchy	barony	chastity
vouchee	anatomy	barratry	chivalry
warrantee	ancestry	bastardy	Christianity
we	animosity	battery	chronology
wee	anniversary	beggary	civility
weeping-tree	annuity	benignity	clemency
whiffletree	anomaly	bigamy	cogency
whippletree	anonymity	bigotry	colloquy
ye	antipathy	billowy	colony
	antiphony	biography	combustibility
Zuyder Zee	antiquity	biology	comedy
abbacy	anxiety	blasphemy	comity
ability	apathy	blossomy	commodity
absurdity	apology	botany	community
academy	apostasy	bravery	company
acclivity	applicability	brevity	compatability
accompany	archery	bribery	complacency
acerbity	argosy	brilliancy	complexity
acidity	aridity	brutality	complicity
acridity	aristocracy	bryony	complimentary
activity	armory	burglary	comprehensi-
actuality	arrowy	cadency	bility
adaptability	artillery	calamity	compulsory
adultery	artistry	calumny	conformity

connubiality
consanguinity
consistency
conspiracy
constancy
contiguity
contingency
contradictory
contrariety
conveniency
convention-
   ality
convexity
coquetry
courtesy
Coventry
credulity
criminality
crotchety
crudity
cruelty
cupidity
curacy
curiosity
custody
debauchery
debility
decency
declivity
deformity
deity
delivery
democracy
demonry
density
dependency
depravity
deputy
destiny
devilry
deviltry

dexterity
diary
dignity
dimity
diplomacy
directory
discordancy
discourtesy
discovery
discrepancy
dishonesty
disparity
dissatisfactory
dissimilarity
dissuasory
diversity
divinity
docility
domesticity
doxology
drapery
drudgery
dubiety
duplicity
dynasty
ebony
eccentricity
economy
ecstasy
efficiency
effigy
effrontery
elasticity
electricity
elegy
elementary
elusory
embassy
emergency
enemy
energy

enginery
enmity
enormity
entity
Epiphany
epitome
equality
equanimity
equity
errantry
eternity
eulogy
euphony
expectancy
expediency
extremity
facility
factory
faculty
fallacy
falsity
familiarity
family
fantasy
fatality
fatuity
feathery
fecundity
felicity
felony
fernery
ferocity
fertility
fervency
festivity
fidelity
fidgety
fiery
finery
fixity
flagrancy

flattery
flippancy
fluency
flummery
foppery
forestry
forgery
formality
fortuity
fragility
fragrancy
fraternity
frequency
frigidity
frivolity
frugality
futility
futurity
gaiety
galaxy
gallantry
gallery
garrulity
genealogy
generosity
geniality
gentility
geography
geology
geometry
Germany
gluttony
gratuity
gravity
harmony
harvestry
heathery
heraldry
heredity
heresy
hilarity

ōld, ôr, ŏdd, oil, fŏŏt, out; ūse, ûrn, ŭp; THis, thin

history	incongruity	jugglery	mediocrity
homeopathy	inconsistency	juvenility	melody
homily	inconstancy	knavery	memory
honesty	incredulity	knight-errantry	mendacity
hospitality	indignity	laity	mendicity
hostelry	individuality	larceny	merchantry
hostility	industry	laxity	mercury
humanity	inebriety	legacy	mimicry
humility	infallibility	legality	ministry
husbandry	infamy	leniency	minority
hypocrisy	infancy	lenity	misanthropy
identity	infantry	lethargy	misery
idiocy	infelicity	levity	mobility
idiosyncrasy	inferiority	liberality	mockery
idolatry	infertility	liberty	modesty
illiteracy	infidelity	limpidity	monarchy
illusory	infinity	litany	monody
imagery	infirmary	liturgy	monopoly
imbecility	infirmity	livery	monotony
immaturity	ingenuity	Lombardy	monstrosity
immensity	inhumanity	longevity	morality
immodesty	iniquity	loquacity	mortality
immorality	injury	lottery	multiplicity
immortality	insincerity	loyalty	mummery
immunity	insipidity	lubricity	municipality
imparity	insufficiency	lucidity	mutability
impassivity	insularity	lunacy	mutiny
impecuniosity	insurgency	luxuriancy	mystery
impetuosity	integrity	luxury	mythology
impiety	intensity	machinery	nationality
importunity	intestacy	magnanimity	nativity
impropriety	intrepidity	mahogany	necessity
impunity	irony	majesty	neutrality
impurity	Italy	majority	nobility
inability	ivory	malady	non-conformity
inadvertency	jealousy	malignancy	normalcy
incapacity	jeopardy	malignity	Normandy
inclemency	jewelry	masonry	notary
incompatibility	jocundity	mastery	notoriety
incomprehen-	jollity	maternity	novelty
sibility	joviality	maturity	nudity

nullity	piety	propinquity	robbery
nursery	pillory	propriety	rockery
obeisancy	pillowy	prosperity	roguery
obesity	piracy	provinciality	Romany
obliquity	pleasantry	proximity	rosary
obloquy	pliancy	prudery	rosemary
obscurity	poesy	psalmistry	rotundity
oddity	poetry	psalmody	royalty
Odyssey	poignancy	psychiatry	rubicundity
opportunity	policy	publicity	rudimentary
originality	polity	puerility	rusticity
pageantry	polygamy	pugnacity	sagacity
palmary	pomposity	punctuality	salary
panoply	ponderosity	pungency	salinity
papacy	popery	purity	salubrity
parity	popularity	pusillanimity	sanctity
parliamentary	pornography	putridity	sanity
parody	posterity	quackery	satiety
partiality	potency	quality	satisfactory
particularity	poverty	quandary	savagery
paternity	precocity	quantity	scarcity
peculiarity	precursory	quiescency	scenery
pedantry	prelacy	raillery	scrutiny
penalty	priority	rapacity	secrecy
penury	priory	rapidity	security
peppery	privacy	rarity	seigniory
perfidy	privity	rascality	senility
perfumery	probity	reality	sensibility
perfunctory	proclivity	reciprocity	sensuality
perjury	prodigality	recovery	sentimentality
perpetuity	prodigy	rectory	serenity
perplexity	profanity	refractory	servility
personality	professory	regency	severity
perspicuity	proficiency	regeneracy	shadowy
pertinacity	profundity	remedy	shivery
perversity	progeny	revelry	silvery
philanthropy	prolixity	rhapsody	similarity
philosophy	promiscuity	ribaldry	simony
phylactery	propensity	rickety	simplicity
physiognomy	property	rigidity	sincerity
Picardy	prophecy	rivalry	sinewy

ōld, ôr, ŏdd, oil, fŏŏt, out; ūse, ûrn, ŭp; THis, thin

singularity	tenantry	vagrancy	words ending
slavery	tendency	valedictory	in "y")
slippery	tenuity	valiancy	absorbingly
snuggery	testamentary	validity	abusively
sobriety	theocracy	vanity	accordingly
society	theology	vapidity	accurately
solemnity	theory	vapoury	acidly
solidity	theosophy	variety	affectedly
soliloquy	thievery	velocity	aimlessly
solvency	threnody	velvety	airily
sophistry	thundery	venality	alluringly
sorcery	timidity	verbosity	allusively
spontaneity	tonicity	verdancy	ambitiously
stability	topography	verity	amusingly
stagnancy	torpidity	versatility	anciently
sterility	totality	vicinity	appealingly
stolidity	tracery	victory	ardently
strategy	tragedy	villainy	assertively
stupidity	tranquillity	virginity	atrociously
suavity	travesty	viridity	auspiciously
subjectivity	treachery	virility	awfully
sublimity	treasury	virtuality	banefully
subsidy	trickery	virtuosity	becomingly
subtlety	trilogy	viscidity	befittingly
sufficiency	trinity	viscosity	beggarly
sugary	triviality	vivacity	bespottedly
summary	truancy	volatility	bewailingly
superficiality	trumpery	voracity	bitterly
superfluity	tyranny	votary	bloodlessly
superiority	ubiquity	vulgarity	bloomingly
supremacy	unanimity	waggery	bloomlessly
symmetry	uniformity	watery	blushingly
sympathy	unity	whimsicality	blushlessly
symphony	university	willowy	bodily
taciturnity	unsavoury	wintery	bootlessly
tapestry	urbanity	witchery	boundlessly
technicality	urgency	yeomanry	boyishly
telegraphy	usury	zoology	brainlessly
temerity	utility	(see ability, etc.,	breathlessly
tenacity	vacancy	part iii, for	broodingly
tenancy	vacuity	many more	brotherly

āle, câre, ădd, ärm, åsk; mē, hĕre, ĕnd; īce, ĭll;

brutally	divergently	fruitlessly	insensately
bumptiously	divertingly	fulsomely	instantly
carefully	doggedly	giddily	instructively
carelessly	dolefully	girlishly	insultingly
changelessly	doubtfully	gloomily	intermittently
chirpingly	doubtingly	gloriously	inwardly
chokingly	dreamingly	gorgeously	irksomely
churlishly	dreamlessly	gropingly	iridescently
civilly	drippingly	groundlessly	jokingly
clownishly	droopingly	grudgingly	joyfully
complainingly	dustily	gruesomely	joyously
concludingly	easterly	grumblingly	judiciously
condescend-	elusively	grumpily	juicily
ingly	enduringly	guiltily	laughingly
conducively	engagingly	guiltlessly	lavishly
confoundedly	engrossingly	gushingly	legendarily
confusedly	eternally	gustily	lightfootedly
consummately	exclusively	happily	loathingly
convivially	expansively	harmfully	locally
countlessly	exultantly	harmlessly	lonesomely
cousinly	exultingly	heartbrokenly	loungingly
cowardly	fadelessly	heart-rending-	lovelessly
cravingly	fairily	ly	loverly
crouchingly	faithlessly	heavenly	lovingly
crownlessly	fatherly	hereditarily	loyally
cruelly	feelingly	homelessly	lucidly
crushingly	ferociously	hopefully	luckily
cumbrously	fervidly	hopelessly	lucklessly
dastardly	feudally	horridly	luridly
daughterly	flippantly	humanly	luringly
decorously	floridly	hungrily	lustrously
deductively	flurriedly	hurriedly	maidenly
defencelessly	flushingly	illusively	maliciously
deliciously	foolishly	immorally	mannerly
delusively	foppishly	immortally	masterly
devotedly	forebodingly	imploringly	maternally
disapprovingly	foreknowingly	inclusively	matronly
discerningly	forgivingly	indignantly	meltingly
disorderly	formerly	indulgently	merrily
distastefully	forsakenly	infernally	misgivingly
distrustfully	fruitfully	inhumanly	mistrustingly

ōld, ôr, ŏdd, oil, fŏŏt, out; ūse, ûrn, ŭp; THis, thin

modestly	pluckily	scowlingly	stolenly
morally	poetically	secretively	stormfully
morbidly	portentously	secretly	stormily
mortally	prayerfully	seducively	stormlessly
motherly	precociously	seductively	straightfor-
mournfully	prepossess-	seemingly	wardly
mournsomely	ingly	self-accusingly	stubbornly
musingly	pretendingly	self-consciously	studiedly
nakedly	productively	shamefully	stupendously
namelessly	properly	shamelessly	stupidly
necessarily	propitiously	shapelessly	sturdily
neighbourly	provokingly	sharp-wittedly	stylishly
niggardly	publicly	shiftlessly	suddenly
noiselessly	pungently	shrewishly	sultrily
normally	pursuantly	silently	sunnily
northerly	quarterly	sisterly	superhumanly
northwardly	quiescently	sleepily	superstitiously
obnoxiously	rapidly	sleeplessly	surefootedly
obstructively	readily	slouchingly	suspiciously
obtrusively	ready-wittedly	slovenly	swimmingly
officiously	recklessly	sluggishly	swollenly
onwardly	recurrently	smilingly	sylvanly
opposingly	refulgently	smokily	tauntingly
oppressively	rejoicingly	soakingly	tediously
orderly	relentlessly	soberly	thanklessly
outrageously	reluctantly	solemnly	thornily
overtoppingly	remorsefully	solidly	thoroughly
owlishly	remorselessly	sombrely	thumpingly
painfully	responsively	sordidly	tonelessly
painlessly	revengefully	sorrily	tranquilly
pallidly	rippingly	sorrowfully	tremendously
pathetically	ripplingly	soulfully	trippingly
peculiarly	roaringly	soullessly	triumphally
peerlessly	rovingly	soundlessly	triumphantly
peevishly	royally	spirally	troublously
pellucidly	ruefully	splendidly	trustfully
pervertedly	ruffianly	spoonily	trustily
piquantly	ruggedly	sportfully	trustingly
plaintfully	savagely	sportively	truthfully
plaintlessly	scholarly	spotlessly	truthlessly
playfully	scornfully	stirringly	tunefully

āle, câre, ădd, ärm, åsk; mē, hęre, ĕnd; īce, ĭll;

tunelessly
unbecomingly
unbendingly
unbiddenly
unblushingly
unboundedly
unceasingly
unchangingly
uncloudedly
unerringly
unfailingly
unfeelingly
unfeignedly
unflaggingly
unguardedly
unknowingly
unlovingly
unmaidenly
unmannerly
unmotherly
unneighborly
unresistingly
unswervingly
unweariedly
unwittingly
unwontedly
unyieldingly
urgently
usurpingly
utterly
verily
vividly
voluntarily
wantonly
warningly
wastefully
waywardly
wearily
wholesomely
wittingly
wontedly

worthily
worthlessly
yearningly
yeomanly

ĔB

glebe
grebe

ĔB

cobweb
deb
ebb
keb
neb
Seb
web
Webb

ĔBD

ebbed
webbed

ĒBZ

Thebes
(see ĒB + s)

ĔBZ

Debs
ebbs
plebs
webs, etc.

ĒCH

beach
beseech
beech
bleach
breach
breech
each
forereach

forespeech
foreteach
impeach
keech
leach
leech
overreach
peach
preach
queach
reach
screech
sca-reach
sleech
speech
teach
unbreech
unpreach

ĔCH

etch
fetch
fletch
Jack-Ketch
ketch
letch
out-stretch
retch
sketch
stretch
vetch
wretch

ĒCHD

unbleached
unimpeached
beached, etc.

ĔCHD

far-fetched
etched, etc.

ĒD

accede
aniseed
antecede
bead
bleed
brede
breed
cede
centipede
concede
creed
deed
dispeed
Ead
exceed
feed
Ganymede
glede
gleed
god-speed
greed
heed
impede
implead
inbreed
indeed
interbreed
intercede
interplead
invalid
jereed
knead
knock-kneed
lead
mead
Meade
Mede
meed
millipede
misdeed

---

mislead

misread

need

off his feed

outspeed

overfeed

plead

precede

proceed

read

Reade

recede

rede

reed

Reid

retrocede

Runnymede

screed

sea-weed

secede

seed

speed

stampede

steed

succeed

supersede

swede

teed

treed

Tweed

undecreed

unfeed

unpedigreed

upbreed

uplead

velocipede

weed

we'd

(see Ē + d)

ĔD

abed

adread

ahead

arrow-head

bed

bedspread

bedstead

behead

bespread

bestead

billet-head

bled

blunder-head

bread

breviped

chuckle-head

co-ed

copper-head

dead

dead-head

death-bed

death's-head

dread

dunderhead

Ed

embed

feather-head

fed

figure-head

fissiped

fled

foresaid

fountain-head

Fred

full-fed

ginger-bread

go-ahead

head

highbred

homebred

inbred

instead

jolter-head

lead

led

loggerhead

lowlihead

maidenhead

mast-head

misled

Ned

negro-head

niggerhead

outspread

overfed

overhead

overspread

pilot-bread

pled

poppy-head

quadruped

read

red

redd

said

shed

shewbread

shred

sled

sped

spread

stead

surbed

ted

thorough-bred

thread

thunder-head

timber-head

tread

truckle-bed

truebred

trundle-bed

trundle-head

underbred

unhead

unread

unsaid

unsped

unthread

unwed

watershed

wed

well-sped

Winifred

woolly-head

zed

accustomed

anchored

answered

astonished

attributed

balanced

banished

barren-spirited

base-spirited

bediamonded

bewildered

bigoted

blemished

blistered

bold-spirited

bonneted

brandished

breakfasted

burnished

carpeted

clustered

conquered

continued

contributed

covered

coveted

---

crescented
diamonded
diminished
discomforted
discredited
dispirited
disquieted
distributed
dowered
embarrassed
emblazoned
enamored
exhibited
faceted
famished
fine-spirited
flowered
forfeited
furnished
garlanded
gathered
gay-spirited
glimmered
glistened
hearkened
helmeted
heralded
high-spirited
hungered
imprisoned
inhabited
inherited
inspirited
jeoparded
languished
light-spirited
limited
lingered
low-spirited
marvelled
mean-spirited

measured
merited
murmured
overpowered
overtowered
pardoned
patented
perjured
pirated
poor-spirited
prohibited
public-spirited
punished
quieted
ravaged
recovered
relinquished
remembered
ringleted
rivalled
sanctioned
shepherded
shimmered
showered
shuddered
signeted
slumbered
soft-spirited
sorrowed
spirited
suffered
talented
tempered
tenanted
thundered
turreted
unballasted
unbonneted
uninhabited
unlimited
unmerited

unprofited
unrespited
untenanted
visited
wandered
weak-spirited
wearied
winnowed
witnessed
wondered
worshipped

ĔDST

bespread'st
dread'st
fed'st
fled'st
led'st
overspread'st
said'st
thread'st
tread'st
wed'st

ĔDTH

breadth
hairbreadth
bespread'th, etc.

ĒDZ

Eades
Leeds
(see ĒD + s)

ĒF

bas-relief
beef
belief
brief
chief
disbelief

fief
grief
interleaf
leaf
lief
reef
relief
sheaf
shereef
thief
unbelief

ĔF

F
chef
clef
deaf
enfeoff
feoff

ĔFT

aleft
bereft
cleft
deft
eft
enfeoffed
heft
left
reft
theft
unbereft
weft
wheft

ĒG

colleague
enleague
fatigue
intrigue

ōld,   ŏr,   ŏdd,   oil,   fŏŏt,   out;   ūse,   ûrn,   ŭp;   THis,   thin

league

renege

ĔG

beg

beglerbeg

egg

goose-egg

keg

leg

Meg

peg

philabeg

skeg

teg

unpeg

Winnipeg

yegg

ĒGD

overfatigued

fatigued, etc.

ĔGD

spindle-legged

begged, etc.

ĔGZ

dregs

Meggs

sea-legs

begs, etc.

ĒJ

besiege

liege

siege

ĔJ

allege

cledge

dredge

edge

enhedge

fledge

hedge

impledge

interpledge

kedge

ledge

pledge

privilege

sacrilege

sedge

sledge

tedge

unedge

wedge

ĔJD

double-edged

sedged

two-edged

unhedged

dredged, etc.

ĔK

after-peak

aleak

antique

apeak

areek

beak

bespeak

bezique

bleak

bubble and

   squeak

cacique

caique

cheek

Chesapeake

chic

cleek

clinique

clique

comique

creak

creek

critique

eke

forepeak

forespeak

freak

gleek

Greek

hide-and-seck

leak

leek

Martinique

meak

meek

Mozambique

oblique

Passion-week

peak

physique

pique

reek

relique

seek

sheik

shriek

Sikh

sleek

sneak

speak

squeak

streak

teak

tweak

unique

unspeak

upseek

weak

week

wreak

ĔK

beck

bedeck

bewreck

breakneck

by heck

check

cheque

Czech

deck

fleck

henpeck

Kennebec

leatherneck

neck

neck-and-neck

peck

quarter-deck

Quebec

reck

rubberneck

shipwreck

spec

speck

trek

undeck

wreck

ĒKS

breeks

sneaks

beaks, etc.

ĔKS

annex

becks

bedecks
Celotex
circumflex
complex
convex
ex
Exe
flex
inflex
kex
lex
Middlesex
multiplex
perplex
prex
reflex
rex
sex
unsex
vex
(see ĔK + s)

ĔKST
next
pretext
sexed
sext
text
unperplexed
unsexed
unvexed
annexed, etc.

ĔKT
cherry-cheeked
peaked
rosy-cheeked
unwreaked
beaked, etc.

ĔKT
abject
adject
affect
analect
annect
architect
arrect
bisect
circumspect
collect
confect
conject
connect
correct
defect
deflect
deject
detect
dialect
direct
disaffect
disconnect
disinfect
disrespect
dissect
effect
eject
elect
erect
expect
exsect
genuflect
incorrect
indirect
infect
inflect
inject
inspect
intellect
interject

intersect
introspect
misdirect
neglect
non-elect
object
perfect
porrect
prefect
prelect
project
prospect
protect
recollect
refect
reflect
reject
respect
resurrect
retrospect
sect
select
self-respect
subject
suspect
traject
trisect
unchecked
undecked
unsuspect
bedecked, etc.

ĒL
alguazil
all heal
anneal
appeal
automobile
balance-wheel
barleymeal
bastille

Camille
Castile
chenille
cochineal
commonweal
conceal
congeal
creel
deal
deil
deshabille
dial-wheel
difficile
driving-wheel
eel
enseal
feel
fly-wheel
forefeel
genteel
heal
heel
he'll
imbecile
infantile
interdeal
keel
Kiel
kneel
leal
Lille
Lucille
meal
misdeal
Neal
Neil
Neill
ne'er-do-weel
O'Neal
O'Neill
O'Sheel

paddle-wheel
pastille
peal
peel
privy-seal
reel
repeal
reveal
seal
seel
shabby-genteel
sheal
she'll
speel
spiel
squeal
steal
steel
sweal
teal
thunder-peal
tweel
uncongeal
unseal
unseel
vakil
veal
weal
we'll
wheal
wheel
zeal

ĔL

Abarbanel
asphodel
Astrophel
A.W.O.L.
bagatelle
bechamel
befell

bel
bell
belle
bonnibel
brocatel
Canterbury bell
caramel
caravel
carrousel
cell
chanterelle
Chaumontel
citadel
clientele
claribel
cockerel
cockle-shell
compel
cordelle
coronel
Crannell
crenel
damoiselle
damoselle
deathbell
dell
demoiselle
dentelle
dinner-bell
dispel
diving-bell
doggerel
dwell
El
ell
Emmanuel
excel
expel
farewell
fell
foretell

fricandel
gabelle
gazelle
harebell
heather-bell
hell
hotel
hydromel
Immanuel
immortelle
impel
infidel
inshell
intermell
Isabel
jargonelle
jell
Jezebel
kell
knell
lapel
Lionel
love-spell
mackerel
mademoiselle
mangonel
minute-bell
Moselle
muscatel
Nell
nonpareil
pallmall
parallel
Parnell
passing-bell
pell
pell-mell
pennoncelle
personnel
petronel

Philomel
pimpernel
propel
pucelle
Purnell
quadrelle
quell
rebel
refel
repel
rondelle
sacring-bell
sanctus-bell
sea-shell
sell
sentinel
shell
smell
snell
spell
swell
tell
tourelle
undersell
unshell
unspell
upswell
vesper-bell
vielle
villanelle
well
yell
zel
Zell

ĔLCH

belch
squelch
Welch
Welsh

ĒLD
afield
battlefield
Chesterfield
Dangerfield
Delafield
enshield
field
harvest-field
shield
unaneled
unrepealed
weald
wield
yield
annealed, etc.

ĔLD
beheld
eld
geld
held
meld
seld
unbeheld
unknelled
unparalleled
unquelled
upheld
weld
withheld
belled, etc.

ĔLF
delf
elf
Guelph
herself
himself
itself
mantel-shelf

myself
oneself
ourself
pelf
self
shelf
thyself
yourself

ĔLFT
delft

ĔLFTH
twelfth

ĔLK
elk
whelk
yelk

ĔLM
dishelm
elm
helm
overwhelm
realm
unhelm
weather-helm
whelm

ĔLP
help
kelp
self-help
skelp
swelp
whelp
yelp

ĔLPS
Phelps
(see ĔLP + s)

ĔLS
else
(cf. belts, etc.)

ĔLSH
Welsh
(see—leh)

ĔLT
belt
celt
dealt
dwelt
felt
gelt
heart-felt
kelt
knelt
melt
misspelt
pelt
smelt
spelt
svelte
swelt
unbelt
unfelt
veldt
welt

ĔLTH
commonwealth
stealth
health
wealth
dwell'th, etc.

ĔLV
delve
helve

shelve
twelve

ĔLVZ
elves
ourselves
selves
themselves
yourselves
delves, etc.

ĔLZ
Dardanelles
Elles
Lascelles
Seychelles
Welles
Wells
(see ĔL + s)

ĒM
abeam
academe
anatheme
beam
beseem
blaspheme
bream
centime
cream
daydream
deem
disesteem
distream
dream
embeam
enseam
esteem
extreme
fleam
gleam

ice-cream
leam
misdeem
moon-beam
ream
redeem
reem
regime
riem
scheme
scream
seam
seem
self-esteem
steam
stream
supreme
team
teem
theme
unbeseem
unseam
unteam
weather-gleam

ĔM
ad hominem
ahem
anadem
apothegm
bediadem
begem
Bethlehem
Brummagem
clem
condemn
contemn
diadem
em
'em

gem
hem
mem
phlegm
pro tem
requiem
stem
stratagem
them
theorem

ĒMD
undreamed
unredeemed
beamed, etc.

ĔMD
uncondemned
undiademed
begemmed, etc.

ĔMP
hemp
Kemp

ĔMS
temse

ĔMT
adreamt
attempt
contempt
dreamt
exempt
kempt
pre-empt
self-contempt
tempt
undreamt
unkempt

ĒMZ
meseems
beams, etc.

ĔMZ
temse
Thames
gems, etc.

ĒN
advene
Algerine
almandine
alpigene
aniline
anserine
aquamarine
argentine
atropine
atween
Augustine
baleen
bandoline
barkentine
bean
been
Beguine
benzene
benzine
bescreen
between
bombazine
bottine
bowling-green
brigantine
caffeine
canteen
Capuchin
careen
carotene
carrageen

chagrin
chorine
clean
codeine
colleen
come clean
Constantine
contravene
convene
crinoline
cuisine
damascene
dean
demean
demesne
dene
dudeen
duvetyn
ean
e'en
eighteen
Eocene
epicene
Ernestine
Eugene
Evangeline
evergreen
fairy-queen
fascine
fellahin
fifteen
fillipeen
Florentine
foreseen
fourteen
gabardine
galantine
gasoline
gazogene
gelatine
Geraldine

āle, câre, ădd, ärm, åsk; mē, hĕre, ĕnd; īce, ĭll;

Ghibelline	misdemean	sea-green	wolverine
glean	moreen	seen	yean
gleen	nankeen	seine	*yestreen*
go-between	naphthalene	seltzogene	
good-e'en	Nazarene	serene	**ĔN**
gradine	nectarine	serpentine	again
grass-green	Nicene	seventeen	aldermen
green	nicotine	shagreen	amen
guillotine	nineteen	Shean	ben
Hallow-e'en	obscene	shebeen	brevipen
harvest-queen	oleomargarine	sheen	cayenne
heterogene	opaline	sixteen	Cheyenne
impregn	overseen	spalpeen	citizen
incarnadine	overween	spleen	cyclamen
indigene	palanquin	stein	Darien
intervene	Palmyrene	submarine	den
Irene	Pauline	subterrene	denizen
Jean	pean	subvene	equestrienne
Josephine	peen	superterrene	fen
keen	Peregrine	supervene	fountain-pen
kerosene	pistareen	tambourine	glen
lateen	Pleistocene	teen	halogen
lean	Pliocene	terrene	hen
lene	poteen	thirteen	hydrogen
libertine	praying-	tourmaline	impen
lien	machine	trephine	ken
long green	preen	tureen	Magdalen
machine	putting-green	'tween	men
magazine	*quadragene*	ultramarine	nitrogen
Magdalene	quarantine	umfteen	oxygen
margarine	quean	unclean	Parisienne
margravine	queen	unforeseen	pen
marine	quinine	unqueen	prairie-hen
May-queen	ravine	unseen	regimen
mazarine	routine	uplean	Saracen
meadow-queen	St. Augustine	vaseline	sen
mean	sardine	velveteen	sen-sen
mesne	sateen	visne	specimen
mezzanine	scalene	wean	ten
mien	scene	*ween*	then
Miocene	screen	winter-green	tragedienne

unpen
Valenciennes
varsovienne
water-hen
wen
when
wren
yen

ĔNCH

bedrench
bench
blench
clench
drench
flench
French
intrench
monkey-
  wrench
quench
retrench
squench
stench
tench
trench
unclench
wench
wrench

ĔNCHD

unblenched
bedrenched,
  etc.

ĔND

fiend
piend
teind
advened, etc.
cleaned, etc.

ĔND

amend
an-end
append
apprehend
ascend
attend
befriend
bend
blend
commend
comprehend
condescend
contend
defend
depend
descend
distend
dividend
emend
end
expend
extend
fend
forefend
forfend
friend
gable-end
godsend
hornblende
impend
intend
interblend
kenned
lend
mend
minuend
misapprehend
misspend
obtend
offend

Ostend
penned
perpend
pitch-blende
portend
prepend
pretend
recommend
rend
repetend
reprehend
reverend
send
South Bend
spend
subtend
subtrahend
superintend
suspend
tend
transcend
trend
unbend
unfriend
unkenned
unpenned
upend
upsend
vend
vilipend
weather-fend
wend
Zend

ĔNDZ

amends
ascends, etc.

ĔNGK

Schenck

ĔNGKS

Jenkes
Jenks

ĔNGTH

full-length
length
strength

ĔNJ

avenge
revenge
Stonehenge

ĔNJD

unavenged

ĔNS

abstinence
accidence
affluence
beneficence
benevolence
blandiloquence
breviloquence
circumference
coincidence
commence
commonsense
competence
concupiscence
condense
conference
confidence
confluence
consequence
continence
convenience
corpulence
defence
deference

dense
difference
diffidence
diligence
disobedience
dispense
dissidence
eloquence
eminence
equivalence
evidence
excellence
exigence
expedience
expense
experience
fence
flatulence
flocculence
frankincense
fraudulence
grandiloquence
hence
immanence
immense
imminence
impenitence
impertinence
impotence
imprevalence
improvidence
impudence
incense
incidence
incipience
incoincidence
incompetence
incongruence
inconsequence
incontinence
inconvenience

indifference
indigence
indolence
inexpedience
inexperience
inference
influence
innocence
insipience
insolence
intelligence
intense
irreverence
magnificence
magniloquence
maleficence
malevolence
mellifluence
munificence
negligence
nescience
non-residence
obedience
offence
omnipotence
omiscience
opulence
pence
penitence
percipience
permanence
pertinence
pestilence
plenipotence
pre-eminence
preference
prepense
prescience
pretence
prevalence
prominence

propense
providence
prurience
quantivalence
recompense
redolence
reference
residence
resilience
reticence
reverence
salience
sapience
self-confidence
self-defence
sense
somnolence
spence
subservience
subsidence
subtense
succulence
supereminence
suspense
tense
thence
truculence
turbulence
vehemence
violence
virulence
whence
(Cf. ĔNTS)

ĔNST
against
anenst
commenced
condensed
dispensed
evidenced

experienced
fenced
fornenst
'gainst
incensed
inexperienced
influenced
reverenced
sensed

ĔNT
abandonment
abolishment
absent
abstinent
accent
accident
accipient
accompaniment
accomplish-
    ment
accoutrement
acknowledg-
    ment
admeasurement
admonishment
advertisement
affamishment
affluent
affranchise-
    ment
aggrandize-
    ment
aliment
ambient
anent
aperient
apportionment
acquent
arbitrament
argument

ōld, ôr, ŏdd, oil, fŏŏt, out; ūse, ûrn, ŭp; THis, thin

armament
ascent
assent
astonishment
attent
augment
babblement
banishment
battlement
bedevilment
bedizenment
belligerent
beneficent
benevolent
bent
besprent
betterment
bewilderment
blandishment
blazonment
blemishment
blent
botherment
brabblement
brent
cement
cent
chastisement
cherishment
circumambient
circumfluent
circumvent
coincident
comment
competent
complement
compliment
condiment
confident
confluent
congruent

consent
consequent
constituent
content
continent
convenient
corpulent
dazzlement
decipherment
decrement
deferent
dement
demolishment
dent
descent
detent
detriment
development
devilment
different
diffident
diffluent
diligent
diminishment
dimplement
disablement
disarmament
discontent
discourage-
    ment
disfigurement
disfranchise-
    ment
disobedient
disparagement
dispiritment
dissent
dissident
distinguish-
    ment
divertisement

document
element
eloquent
embarrassment
embattlement
embellishment
embezzlement
embitterment
emblazonment
embodiment
eminent
emollient
emolument
empannelment
enablement
encompassment
encouragement
endangerment
endeavorment
enfeeblement
enfranchise-
    ment
enlightenment
ennoblement
enravishment
entanglement
envelopment
environment
envisagement
equivalent
esculent
establishment
esurient
event
evident
excellent
excrement
exigent
expedient
experiment
extent

extinguishment
famishment
fent
ferment
filament
firmament
flocculent
foment
foremeant
forespent
fornent
fosterment
franchisement
fraudulent
frequent
garnishment
gent
Ghent
government
gracilent
gradient
grandiloquent
habiliment
harassment
hereditament
ignipotent
ill-content
immanent
imminent
impediment
impenitent
imperilment
impertinent
implement
impotent
impoverish-
    ment
imprisonment
improvident
impudent
incident

incipient	malevolent	present	subservient
incoincident	management	presentiment	succulent
incompetent	meant	president	supereminent
incongruent	measurement	prevalent	supplement
inconsequent	medicament	prevent	temperament
incontinent	mellifluent	prominent	tenement
inconvenient	merriment	provident	tent
increment	miscontent	prurient	testament
indent	misrepresent	punishment	thereanent
indifferent	misspent	ravishment	torment
indigent	monument	recipient	tournament
indolent	munificent	redolent	tremblement
inexpedient	muniment	refluent	Trent
influent	negligent	regiment	truculent
ingredient	nourishment	relent	turbulent
innocent	nutriment	relinquishment	unbent
insentient	obedient	rent	underwent
insipient	occident	repent	*unkent*
insolent	omnipotent	replenishment	unmeant
instrument	opulent	represent	unsent
integument	orient	resent	unspent
intelligent	ornament	resident	untent
intent	ostent	resilient	vanishment
inveiglement	overspent	reticent	vanquishment
invent	parliament	reverent	vehement
irreverent	pediment	rudiment	vent
Kent	penitent	sacrament	vinolent
lament	pent	salient	violent
languishment	percipient	sapient	virulent
lavishment	permanent	scent	*wanderment*
leant	pertinent	sediment	well-content
lenient	*pesterment*	self-confident	well-meant
lent	pestilent	sent	well-spent
ligament	plenipotent	sentient	went
lineament	portent	sentiment	*wilderment*
liniment	prattlement	settlement	wonderment
luculent	precedent	somnolent	worriment
magnificent	predicament	spent	
magniloquent	pre-eminent	sprent	**ĒNTH**
malcontent	premonishment	stent	greenth
maleficent	prescient	subsequent	thirteenth

fourteenth, etc.
lean'th, etc.

ĔNTH

tenth
pen'th, etc.

ĔNTS

accoutrements
contents
cents, etc.
(Cf. ĔNS)

ĒNZ

Essenes
greens
smithereens
teens
advenes, etc.

ĔNZ

cleanse
ens
flense
gens
lens
Valenciennes
Vincennes
(see ĔN + s)

ĒP

adeep
aheap
asleep
beauty-sleep
beweep
bo-peep
cheap
cheep
clepe
chimney-sweep
chepe

creep
deep
ensweep
estrepe
forweep
heap
keep
leap
neap
outleap
outsleep
outweep
overleap
oversleep
peep
reap
seep
sheep
sleep
steep
sweep
swepe
threap
under-peep
upkeep
weep

ĔP

demi-rep
footstep
hep
overstep
pep
rep
skep
step
steppe

ĒPS

creeps
cheeps, etc.

ĔPS

steps, etc.

ĒPT

beneaped
neaped
unsteeped
upheaped
heaped, etc.

ĔPT

accept
adept
crept
except
inept
intercept
kept
leapt
outslept
overslept
overstepped
pepped
sept
slept
stepped
swept
unkept
unswept
unwept
wept
yclept

EPTH

depth
stepp'th, etc.

ĘR

adhere
äerosphere
affeer

amir
anear
appear
arrear
asmear
atmosphere
auctioneer
austere
bandoleer
bayadere
beer
belvedere
besmear
bevel-gear
bier
blear
bombardier
brevier
brigadier
buccaneer
canceleer
cannoneer
caravaneer
carbineer
career
cashier
cavalier
cere
chandelier
chanticleer
charioteer
cheer
chevalier
chiffonier
chimere
circuiteer
clear
cohere
commandeer
compeer
congé d'élire

āle,　câre,　ădd,　ärm,　ăsk;　mē,　hĘre,　ĕnd;　īce,　ĭll;

crotcheteer	insphere	sheer	adhered, etc.
cuirassier	interfere	sincere	feared, etc.
dear	jeer	skeer	
deer	killdeer	smear	**ĒRS**
disappear	lear	sneer	fierce
domineer	leer	sonneteer	pierce
drear	madrier	souvenir	tierce
ear	meer	spear	transpierce
electioneer	mere	specksioneer	
emir	mir	sphere	**ĒRT**
endear	mountaineer	steer	peart
engineer	muffineer	tabasheer	
ensear	muleteer	targeteer	**ĒRZ**
ensphere	musketeer	tear	Algiers
fakir	mutineer	teer	shears
fallow-deer	near	tier	sheers
fear	overhear	*timberstere*	adheres, etc.
financier	overseer	timoneer	
fineer	pamphleteer	Tyr	**ĒS**
fleer	peer	undersphere	afterpiece
friction-gear	persevere	ungear	ambergris
frontier	petardeer	*unnear*	apiece
fusileer	pier	unsphere	battlepiece
garreteer	pioneer	upcheer	Berenice
gaselier	pistoleer	uprear	Bernice
gazeteer	planisphere	veer	cantatrice
gear	privateer	veneer	caprice
ginger-beer	pulpiteer	vizier	cease
gondolier	queer	volunteer	cerise
gonfalonier	racketeer	weir	chimney-piece
grand-vizier	reappear	year	Clarice
grenadier	rear		coulisse
halberdier	reindeer	**ĒRD**	crease
hear	revere	beard	creese
Heer	scrutineer	flap-eared	decease
hemisphere	sear	lop-eared	decrease
here	seer	*uneared*	esquisse
indear	sere	unfeared	Felice
Indianeer	sermoneer	unfeared	fleece
inhere	severe	unpeered	fowling-piece
insincere	shear	weird	frontispiece

geese	bodiless	fathomless	nevertheless
grease	bottomless	favorless	noblesse
grece	canoness	featureless	numberless
Greece	caress	fess	obsess
increase	cess	fetterless	obsolesce
lease	chess	finesse	odorless
Lucrece	coalesce	flavorless	opalesce
mantel-piece	color!ess	flowerless	oppress
master-piece	comfortless	foreguess	overdress
Maurice	comfortress	fortuneless	pantheress
Nice	compress	frondesce	patroness
niece	confess	full-dress	penniless
obese	conqueress	gala-dress	phosophoresce
peace	conscienceless	*gentilesse*	pitiless
pelisse	convalesce	giantess	pleasureless
piece	cress	governess	poetess
pocket-piece	cultureless	guess	politesse
police	cumberless	harborless	possess
popping–crease	dauphiness	head-dress	powerless
predecease	deaconess	idolatress	power-press
Reese	deliquesce	impress	prepossess
release	demoness	ingress	press
semese	depress	inheritress	prioress
surcease	digress	intumesce	procuress
Therese	dinnerless	jess	profess
valise	dispossess	Kress	progress
verdigris	distress	less	prophetess
	diving-dress	limitless	proprietress
ĔS	dress	marchioness	purposeless
accresce	duress	masterless	pythoness
acquiesce	editress	mayoress	Quakeress
address	effervesce	meaningless	quiesce
aggress	effloresce	measureless	ransomless
ambassadress	effortless	merciless	recess
ancestress	egress	mess	redress
archeress	evanesce	ministress	regress
assess	excess	moneyless	repossess
baroness	executress	monitress	repress
Bess	express	motherless	respiteless
blemishless	fanciless	motionless	retrogress
bless	fatherless	motiveless	rudderless

S.O.S.	agedness	avariciousness	breathlessness
shadowless	aggressiveness	awfulness	brilliantness
shelterless	agileness	awkwardness	brittleness
shepherdess	agreeableness	backhanded-	brokenness
silverless	airiness	ness	brotherliness
slumberless	alimentiveness	backwardness	brushiness
sorceress	alliterativeness	balefulness	brutishness
spiritless	allusiveness	banefulness	bulkiness
stewardess	almightiness	bareheadedness	bumptiousness
stress	amazedness	barrenness	bunchiness
success	ambitiousness	bashfulness	burliness
sultaness	amiableness	beastliness	bushiness
suppress	amicableness	beeriness	buxomness
tailoress	ampleness	beseechingness	candidness
temptationless	ancientness	besottedness	capaciousness
Tess	angelicalness	bitterness	capriciousness
Titaness	angriness	blamelessness	captiousness
transgress	anonymousness	blessedness	carefulness
tress	anticness	blissfulness	carelessness
turgesce	anxiousness	blithesomeness	cautiousness
unbless	apishness	bloatedness	ceaselessness
underdress	apparentness	blockishness	chalkiness
undress	appeasableness	blood-guiltiness	changefulness
unless	appositeness	bloodiness	chariness
valueless	apprehensive-	bloodthirsti-	charmingness
virtueless	ness	ness	chattiness
votaress	approachable-	bloomingness	cheerfulness
water-cress	ness	bluntishness	cheeriness
weaponless	arbitrariness	boastfulness	cheerlessness
yes	ardentness	boisterousness	childishness
abjectedness	arduousness	bonniness	childlessness
abstractedness	aridness	bookishness	chilliness
abusiveness	artfulness	boorishness	chubbiness
accidentalness	articulateness	bootlessness	churlishness
adaptiveness	artificialness	boundlessness	clandestine-
addictedness	artlessness	bounteousness	ness
adhesiveness	assiduousness	boyishness	clannishness
advantageous-	atrociousness	brackishness	cleanliness
ness	attentiveness	brassiness	clearsighted-
affectedness	attractiveness	brawniness	ness
affrontiveness	auspiciousness	brazenness	cleverness

cliquishness
cloddishness
cloudiness
clownishness
clumsiness
coldhearted-
  ness
collectedness
collusiveness
comeliness
commonness
composedness
comprehen-
  siveness
compulsiveness
conceitedness
conclusiveness
conduciveness
confusedness
conjunctive-
  ness
conscientious-
  ness
consciousness
consecutive-
  ness
conspicuous-
  ness
constructive-
  ness
contentedness
contentious-
  ness
contradictious-
  ness
contrariness
contumacious-
  ness
copiousness
cordialness
corrosiveness

costliness
courageousness
courtliness
covertness
covetousness
crabbedness
craftiness
craggedness
cragginess
cravingness
craziness
creaminess
credulousness
crookedness
cruelness
crustiness
cumbrousness
curiousness
curliness
customariness
daintiness
dampishness
daringness
dauntlessness
deadliness
deathfulness
deathiness
debauchedness
deceitfulness
deceptiveness
decisiveness
decorativeness
defectiveness
defenceless-
  ness
defiantness
definiteness
deformedness
degenerateness
dejectedness
deliciousness

delightfulness
delightsome-
  ness
deliriousness
delusiveness
dementedness
depressiveness
derisiveness
desirousness
despitefulness
destructiveness
desultoriness
detersiveness
detractiveness
devotedness
dewiness
diffusedness
diffusiveness
dilatoriness
dilutedness
dinginess
direfulness
disastrousness
discontented-
  ness
discursiveness
disdainfulness
disinterested-
  ness
dismalness
disposedness
disputatious-
  ness
distastefulness
distinctiveness
dizziness
doggedness
dolefulness
doubtfulness
doughtiness
downiness

dreadfulness
dreaminess
dreariness
droughtiness
drowsiness
drunkenness
dumpishness
duskiness
dustiness
dwarfishness
eagerness
earliness
earnestness
earthiness
earthliness
earthly-
  mindedness
easefulness
easiness
eeriness
effectiveness
efficaciousness
effusiveness
egregiousness
elatedness
emotiveness
emptiness
endearedness
endlessness
enduringness
engagingness
enormousness
entertaining-
  ness
equalness
essentialness
estrangedness
evasiveness
everlastingness
exaltedness
exceptiousness

excessiveness	flakiness	frugalness	graphicness
exclusiveness	flashiness	fruitfulness	grassiness
excursiveness	fleshiness	fruitlessness	gratefulness
expansiveness	fleshliness	frumpishness	greasiness
expeditiousness	flexibleness	fugaciousness	greediness
expensiveness	flightiness	fulsomeness	greenishness
explicitness	flimsiness	fumishness	grievousness
expressiveness	flippantness	fundamental-	griminess
exquisiteness	floridness	ness	grittiness
extensiveness	floweriness	furiousness	grogginess
facetiousness	fluentness	fussiness	groundlessness
factiousness	fogginess	fustiness	guardedness
faithfulness	foolhardiness	gaddishness	guidelessness
faithlessness	foolishness	gallantness	guilefulness
fallaciousness	foppishness	gamesomeness	guiltiness
false-hearted-	forcedness	garishness	guiltlessness
ness	foreignness	garrulousness	gustfulness
far-sightedness	forgetfulness	gashliness	hairiness
fastidiousness	formlessness	gaudiness	handiness
fatefulness	forwardness	generousness	handsomeness
fatherliness	fractiousness	genialness	haplessness
faultlessness	fragileness	gentleness	happiness
favoredness	frankhearted-	ghastliness	hard-hearted-
fearfulness	ness	ghostliness	ness
fearlessness	francticness	giddiness	hardiness
feeble-	fraudlessness	giftedness	harmfulness
mindedness	freakishness	girlishness	harmlessness
feebleness	freckledness	gladfulness	harmonious-
feignedness	freehearted-	gladsomeness	ness
ferociousness	ness	glariness	hastiness
fervidness	fretfulness	glassiness	hatefulness
fickleness	friendlessness	gloominess	haughtiness
fictiousness	friendliness	gloriousness	haziness
fiendishness	frightfulness	glossiness	headiness
fieriness	frigidness	godlessness	healthfulness
filminess	friskiness	godliness	healthiness
fishiness	frivolousness	goodliness	healthlessness
fitfulness	frostiness	gorgeousness	heartedness
fixedness	frothiness	gracefulness	heartiness
flabbiness	frowardness	gracelessness	heartlessness
flaccidness	frozenness	graciousness	heathenness

---

heavenliness
heavenly-
   mindedness
heaviness
heedfulness
heedlessness
heinousness
hellishness
helpfulness
helplessness
heterogeneous-
   ness
hiddenness
hideousness
highminded-
   ness
hilliness
hoariness
hoggishness
holiness
hollowness
homelessness
homeliness
hopefulness
hopelessness
horridness
huffishness
humbleness
humidness
humorousness
hurtfulness
huskiness
iciness
idleness
ignobleness
illicitness
illiterateness
ill-naturedness
illusiveness
illustriousness

imaginative-
   ness
imitativeness
immaculate-
   ness
impartialness
impassiveness
imperfectness
imperiousness
imperviousness
impetuousness
impiousness
implicitness
imponderous-
   ness
imposingness
impressiveness
impulsiveness
inattentiveness
inauspicious-
   ness
incapaciousness
incautiousness
incidentalness
incoherentness
incomprehen-
   siveness
inconclusive-
   ness
incongruous-
   ness
inconsistent-
   ness
inconspicuous-
   ness
indebtedness
indecisiveness
indecorous-
   ness
inefficacious-
   ness

infectiousness
ingeniousness
ingenuousness
injuriousness
inkiness
innoxiousness
inobtrusive-
   ness
inoffensiveness
insidiousness
insipidness
instructiveness
intensiveness
intrusiveness
inventiveness
invidiousness
invincibleness
involuntariness
inwardness
irefulness
irksomeness
jaggedness
jauntiness
jealousness
jettiness
Jewishness
jolliness
jovialness
joyfulness
joylessness
joyousness
judiciousness
juiciness
jumpiness
kind-hearted-
   ness
kindliness
kingliness
knavishness
knightliness
knottiness

languidness
large-hearted-
   ness
lasciviousness
lawfulness
lawlessness
laziness
leafiness
leaflessness
leaviness
lengthiness
licentiousness
lifelessness
light-hearted-
   ness
lightsomeness
likeableness
likeliness
limberness
limpidness
liquidness
lissomeness
listlessness
literalness
litigiousness
littleness
liveliness
lividness
livingness
loathliness
loathsomeness
loftiness
loneliness
lonesomeness
longsomeness
loquaciousness
lordliness
loutishness
love-in-idleness
loveliness
lovingness

---

lowliness
loyalness
lucidness
luckiness
lugubriousness
luminousness
lumpishness
lusciousness
lustfulness
lustiness
maidenliness
maliciousness
manfulness
manliness
mannerliness
mannishness
many-sidedness
marshiness
massiness
massiveness
matchlessness
mawkishness
maziness
meagreness
mealiness
meatiness
meditativeness
mellowness
meltingness
meretorious-
    ness
meretricious-
    ness
merriness
mightiness
milkiness
mindfulness
miraculousness
miriness
mirthfulness
mirthlessness

miscellaneous-
    ness
mischievous-
    ness
misshapenness
missishness
mistiness
modernness
modishness
momentous-
    ness
monkishness
monotonous-
    ness
monstrousness
moodiness
mopishness
morbidness
mortalness
mossiness
motherliness
mouldiness
mournfulness
mulishness
multifarious-
    ness
mumpishness
murkiness
muskiness
mustiness
mutinousness
mysteriousness
mysticalness
nakedness
namelessness
narrow-mind-
    edness
narrowness
nastiness
nationalness
nativeness

nattiness
naturalness
naughtiness
near-sighted-
    ness
nebulousness
necessariness
necessitious-
    ness
nectareousness
needfulness
neediness
needlessness
nefariousness
neglectedness
neglectfulness
neighborliness
nervousness
niggardliness
nimbleness
nobleness
noiselessness
noisiness
noisomeness
notableness
notedness
notelessness
nothingness
notoriousness
noxiousness
numerousness
nutritiousness
objectiveness
obligatoriness
obligingness
obliviousness
obsequiousness
observableness
obstreperous-
    ness
obtrusiveness

obviousness
odiousness
odoriferous-
    ness
odorousness
offensiveness
officiousness
oiliness
oleaginousness
openhanded-
    ness
openhearted-
    ness
openness
oppressiveness
opprobrious-
    ness
orderliness
ostentatious-
    ness
outlandishness
outrageousness
outwardness
painfulness
painlessness
pallidness
paltriness
parlousness
parsimonious-
    ness
passiveness
pawkiness
peaceableness
peacefulness
pearliness
peerlessness
peevishness
pellucidness
penetrative-
    ness
pennilessness

ōld, ôr, ŏdd, oil, foŏt, out; ūse, ûrn, ŭp; THis, thin

pensileness
pensiveness
penuriousness
peremptoriness
perfectness
perfidiousness
perfunctoriness
perilousness
perniciousness
perplexedness
perplexiveness
perspicacious-
  ness
perspicuous-
  ness
persuasiveness
pertinacious-
  ness
pervicacious-
  ness
perviousness
pestilential-
  ness
pettiness
pettishness
piercingness
pig-headedness
pitchiness
piteousness
pithiness
pitiableness
pitilessness
placableness
placidness
plaintiveness
playfulness
playsomeness
pleasantness
pleasingness
plenteousness
pliantness

poachiness
pointedness
pompousness
ponderous-
  ness
poorliness
porousness
portliness
positiveness
powerfulness
powerlessness
practicalness
praiseworthi-
  ness
prayerfulness
prayerlessness
precariousness
preciousness
precipitous-
  ness
precociousness
prejudicialness
preposterous-
  ness
presumptu-
  ousness
pretentious-
  ness
prettiness
previousness
prickliness
pridefulness
priestliness
priggishness
primitiveness
princeliness
prodigiousness
productive-
  ness
progressive-
  ness

properness
propitiousness
prosiness
prospective-
  ness
protectiveness
prudishness
public-minded-
  ness
puffiness
pugnacious-
  ness
pulpiness
pulpousness
pulselessness
punctiliousness
puniness
pursiness
pusillanimous-
  ness
putridness
quakiness
qualmishness
queasiness
queenliness
quenchlessness
querulousness
quick-sighted-
  ness
quick-witted-
  ness
quietness
rabidness
raciness
raggedness
raininess
rakishness
rancidness
rapaciousness
rapidness
ravenousness

readiness
rebelliousness
recentness
receptiveness
recklessness
reddishness
reflectiveness
refractiveness
refractoriness
regardlessness
relativeness
relentlessness
remorsefulness
remorseless-
  ness
reproachful-
  ness
repulsiveness
resistlessness
resoluteness
respectfulness
responsiveness
restfulness
restiveness
restlessness
restrictiveness
retentiveness
revengefulness
rightfulness
right-handed-
  ness
right-minded-
  ness
rigidness
rigorousness
riotousness
robustiousness
rockiness
roguishness
rompishness
roominess

ropiness
rosiness
rottenness
ruddiness
ruefulness
ruggedness
ruthlessness
sacredness
sacrilegious-
    ness
sagaciousness
saintliness
salaciousness
sallowness
salutariness
sanctimonious-
    ness
sandiness
sanguineness
sappiness
satisfactoriness
sauciness
savageness
savingness
savoriness
scaliness
scantiness
scorchingness
scornfulness
scragginess
scurviness
sea-worthiness
secondariness
secretiveness
secretness
sedentariness
seditiousness
seediness
seemingness
seemliness
seldomness

self-conceited-
    ness
self-conscious-
    ness
selfishness
self-righteous-
    ness
senselessness
sensitiveness
sensuousness
sententious-
    ness
seriousness
shabbiness
shadiness
shadowiness
shagginess
shakiness
shallowness
shamefulness
shamelessness
shapelessness
shapeliness
sheepishness
shieldlessness
shiftiness
shiftlessness
shiningness
shoaliness
short-sighted-
    ness
showeriness
showiness
shrewishness
shrubbiness
sickliness
sightlessness
silentness
silkiness
silliness

simplemind-
    edness
simpleness
simultaneous-
    ness
sinfulness
singleness
sinlessness
sketchiness
skilfulness
skittishness
slabbiness
slatiness
slavishness
sleaziness
sleepiness
sleeplessness
sleetiness
slenderness
sliminess
slipperiness
slothfulness
sluggishness
smilingness
smokiness
snappishness
sneakiness
snobbishness
sober-minded-
    ness
soberness
sociableness
soft-hearted-
    ness
solidness
solitariness
solubleness
sombreness
sombrousness
sonorousness
sordidness

sorriness
sorrowfulness
sottishness
spaciousness
sparklingness
speciousness
speckledness
speculativeness
speechlessness
speediness
spiciness
spitefulness
splendidness
sponginess
spontaneous-
    ness
sportiveness
spotlessness
spottedness
spottiness
springiness
spriteliness
spuminess
spuriousness
squeamishness
starchiness
starriness
stateliness
steadfastness
steadiness
stealthfulness
stealthiness
steeliness
steepiness
stickiness
stinginess
stintedness
stolidness
stoniness
storminess

straightfor-
wardness
strenuousness
stringentness
stringiness
stubbiness
stubbornness
studiousness
stuffiness
stuntedness
stupendousness
stupidness
sturdiness
stylishness
subjectiveness
submissiveness
subordinate-
ness
substantialness
subtleness
successfulness
suddenness
sugariness
suggestiveness
suitableness
sulkiness
sulleness
sultriness
sumptuousness
sunniness
supercilious-
ness
superstitious-
ness
suppleness
suppliantness
surliness
surprisingness
susceptiveness
suspectedness
suspiciousness

swarthiness
sweatiness
sweetishness
talkativeness
tamelessness
tardiness
tastefulness
tastelessness
tawdriness
tawniness
tediousness
tempestuous-
ness
temporariness
temptingness
tenaciousness
tender-hearted-
ness
tepidness
testiness
thankfulness
thievishness
thirstiness
thoroughness
thoughtfulness
thoughtless-
ness
threadiness
thriftiness
thriftlessness
thrivingness
ticklishness
tidiness
timeliness
timidness
timorousness
tipsiness
tiresomeness
toilsomeness
toothsomeness
torpidness

torridness
tortuousness
totalness
touchiness
toyishness
tracklessness
traitorousness
tranquilness
transcendent-
ness
transientness
transitiveness
transitoriness
transparent-
ness
trashiness
treacherous-
ness
tremendous-
ness
tremulousness
tributariness
trickiness
trickishness
tricksiness
true-hearted-
ness
trustfulness
trustiness
trustlessness
trustworthi-
ness
truthfulness
truthlessness
tunefulness
turfiness
turgidness
ugliness
umbrageous-
ness

unanimous-
ness
unbendingness
unblessedness
unbounded-
ness
uncleanliness
uncloudedness
uncourtliness
undauntedness
uneasiness
unexpected-
ness
unfeignedness
unfriendliness
ungainliness
ungentleness
ungodliness
ungrounded-
ness
unholiness
universalness
unkindliness
unlikeliness
unloveliness
unmanliness
unprepared-
ness
unquietness
unreadiness
unrighteous-
ness
unruliness
unseaworthi-
ness
unseemliness
unsightliness
unstableness
untowardness
untrustiness
unwieldiness

āle, câre, ădd, ārm, ȧsk; mē, hȩre, ĕnd; īce, ĭll;

unwillingness
unwontedness
unworldliness
unworthiness
uppishness
usefulness
uselessness
uxoriousness
vacuousness
vagrantness
valetudinari-
   ness
valiantness
validness
vapidness
vexatiousness
viciousness
victoriousness
vigorousness
vindictiveness
viridness
virtuousness
viscousness
visionariness
vitreousness
vivaciousness
vividness
vociferousness
voluminous-
   ness
voluntariness
voluptuousness
voraciousness
vulgarness
waggishness
wakefulness
wantonness
warefulness
wariness
warm-hearted-
   ness

washiness
waspishness
wastefulness
watchfulness
waveringness
waviness
waxiness
waywardness
wealthiness
weariness
wearisomeness
weightiness
welcomeness
whimsicalness
whitishness
wholesome-
   ness
wickedness
wilderness
wilfulness
wiliness
willingness
winsomeness
wiriness
wishfulness
wistfulness
witheredness
witlessness
wittiness
woefulness
womanliness
wondrousness
wontedness
woodiness
woolliness
wordiness
wordishness
worldliness
worldy-mind-
   edness
worshipfulness

worthiness
worthlessness
wrathfulness
wretchedness
wretchlessness
wrongfulness
wrongheaded-
   ness
yeastiness
yellowishness
yellowness
yieldingness
youthfulness
zealousness

ĒSH

affiche
leash
McLeish
McNeish
schottische
unleash

ĔSH

afresh
crèche
enmesh
flesh
fresh
mesh
nesh
refresh
secesh
thresh

ĔSK

arabesque
barbaresque
burlesque
chivalresque
Dantesque

desk
gardensque
gigantesque
grotesque
Moresque
naturalesque
picaresque
picturesque
plateresque
reading-desk
Romanesque
sculpturesque
soldatesque
statuesque

ĔST

archpriest
artiste
batiste
beast
deceased
east
feast
harvest-feast
least
modiste
priest
queest
triste
underpoliced
unpriest
wedding-feast
yeast
pieced, etc.
ceased, etc.
fleeced, etc.

ĔST

abreast
acquest
alkahest

ōld, ôr, ŏdd, oil, fŏŏt, out; ūse, ûrn, ŭp; THis, thin

anapest	molest	*attributest*	dreamiest
arrest	nest	*banishest*	dreariest
attest	north-west	beamiest	drowsiest
behest	obsessed	beguilingest	dustiest
bequest	obtest	bleariest	earliest
best	over-dressed	blestfullest	easiest
blest	palimpsest	*blisterest*	eeriest
breast	pest	blithefulest	effectedest
Brest	predigest	blithesomest	*emblazonest*
Bucharest	protest	*blunderest*	emptiest
Budapest	quest	breeziest	*enviest*
cest	recessed	brilliantest	evenest
chest	request	briniest	*exhibitest*
congest	rest	burliest	filmiest
contest	second-best	cheerfullest	filthiest
crest	self-possessed	cheeriest	fleeciest
depressed	suggest	cheerliest	flimsiest
detest	test	chilliest	flightiest
devest	tressed	chokiest	flintiest
digest	Trieste	cleanliest	*flowerest*
distressed	unblest	*clusterest*	foamiest
divest	unbreast	*conquerest*	forcefullest
dressed	under-crest	*continuest*	*forfeitest*
Everest	underdressed	cosiest	*freshenest*
funest	undressed	costliest	friendliest
gest	unexpressed	courtliest	funniest
golden-tressed	unguessed	*coverest*	fussiest
guest	unprepossessed	creamiest	*gatherest*
hard-pressed	unpressed	creepiest	genialest
hest	unredressed	cruellest	giddiest
imprest	unrest	crustiest	*glimmerest*
increst	untressed	curliest	*glistenest*
infest	vest	daintiest	gloomiest
ingest	west	decisivest	glossiest
interest	wrest	derisivest	*glowerest*
invest	yessed	*determinest*	goutiest
jessed	zest	dingiest	grimiest
jest	(see ĔS + ed)	dizziest	guilefulest
Key West	*answerest*	doughtiest	guiltiest
lest	*astonishest*	dowdiest	gustiest
manifest	attentivest	*dowerest*	happiest

haughtiest	mellowest	ruggedest	*sufferest*
healthiest	*meritest*	rustiest	*sunderest*
hearkenest	merriest	sacredest	sunniest
heartiest	mightiest	sedgiest	surliest
heaviest	moistiest	seemliest	tearfullest
holiest	morbidest	*severest*	*temperest*
homeliest	mossiest	*shimmerest*	thirstiest
hopefullest	mouldiest	shiniest	thriftiest
horridest	mournfullest	shoddiest	*thunderest*
huffiest	*murmurest*	showiest	timidest
hungerest	muskiest	*shudderest*	trustiest
hungriest	mustiest	sightliest	ugliest
huskiest	*narrowest*	silentest	unholiest
iciest	noisiest	silliest	unreadiest
incumberest	*nourishest*	sketchiest	veriest
inheritest	*offerest*	skilfullest	vindictivest
inkiest	*pardonest*	skinniest	vulgarest
inliest	patentest	sleepiest	*wanderest*
inspiritest	pearliest	slimiest	wealthiest
jolliest	pensivest	*slumberest*	weariest
juiciest	pleasantest	smokiest	wheeziest
kindliest	*pleasurest*	snuffiest	windiest
kingliest	portliest	soapiest	wilfulest
knightliest	preciousest	solidest	*winnowest*
labourest	*predestinest*	*sorrowest*	winsomest
languishest	princeliest	spiciest	wintriest
libellest	prosiest	spikiest	*witnessest*
likeliest	*punishest*	*spiritest*	*wonderest*
lingerest	*quarrellest*	splendidest	*worriest*
lissomest	*questionest*	spongiest	yeastiest
listenest	quietest	spooniest	
lithesomest	*recoverest*	springiest	**ĒT**
liveliest	*relinquishest*	spriteliest	accrete
livenest	*rememberest*	steadiest	afreet
loftiest	*rescuest*	stealthiest	athlete
loneliest	restfulest	stilliest	balance-sheet
loveliest	rightfulest	stingiest	beat
lowerest	*rivallest*	stormiest	beet
lowliest	rosiest	stuffiest	bitter-sweet
loyalest	rowdiest	stupidest	bleat
marvellest	royalest	sturdiest	carte-de-visite

ōld,   ôr,   ŏdd,   oil.   fŏŏt,   out;   ūse,   ûrn,   ŭp;   THis,   thin

cheat	leet	wheat	calumet
cheet	lorikeet	winding-sheet	canzonet
cleat	maltreat		carcanet
cleet	marguerite	ĔT	cassolette
compete	meadow-sweet	abet	castanet
complete	meat	aigrette	cellaret
conceit	meet	ailette	chansonette
concrete	mercy-seat	alette	chemisette
country-seat	mete	allumette	cigarette
county-seat	neat	all wet	clarinet
Crete	obsolete	alphabet	coquette
dead-beat	overeat	amourette	coronet
dead-heat	parrakeet	amulet	corvette
dead-meat	peat	anchoret	coverlet
deceit	pleat	angelet	croquette
defeat	*preconceit*	anisette	crossette
delete	receipt	Annette	crystal set
deplete	repeat	Antoinette	curvet
discreet	replete	backset	dancette
Dutch treat	retreat	baguette	dead-set
eat	sea-beat	banneret	debt
effete	seat	banquette	duet
elite	secrete	barbette	epaulet
entreat	self-conceit	Barnett	epithet
escheat	self-deceit	baronet	estafette
estreat	sheet	bassinet	etiquette
facete	skeet	bayonet	facette
feat	sleet	beget	falconet
feet	street	benet	farmerette
fleet	suite	beset	flageolet
geat	sunny-sweet	bet	flet
greet	sweet	bewet	floweret
heat	teat	blanquette	forget
help-meet	terete	bobbinet	formeret
honey-sweet	treat	Brett	fossette
ill-treat	unmeet	brevet	fourchette
incomplete	unseat	brochette	fret
indiscreet	unsweet	brunette	frett
judgment-seat	vegete	Burnett	fumette
Lafitte	weet	cabinet	gazette
ĩeat		cadet	genet

āle,   câre,   ădd,   ärm,   åsk;   mē,   hęre,   ĕnd;   īce,   ĭll;

get
Gillette
globulet
grisette
Harriet
historiette
illset
inset
interset
jet
Jeanette
Joliet
judgment-debt
Juliet
Juliette
landaulet
leaderette
let
Lett
leveret
lorgnette
Lucette
luncheonette
lunette
Margaret
marionette
marmoset
martinet
medalet
met
mignonette
minaret
minionette
minuet
misbeget
motet
musette
Nanette
net
noisette
novelette

octet
off-set
Olivet
omelet
oubliette
overset
parapet
parroket
parquet
pet
pianette
pillaret
pipette
piquet
piquette
pirouette
planchette
poussette
quartet
quintet
regret
ret
revet
ricochet
rivulet
rosette
roulette
sarcenet
septet
serviette
sestet
set
sett
sextet
sharp-set
silhouette
somerset
soubrette
statuette
stet
suffragette

sunset
sweat
tabaret
tabinet
taboret
Thibet
thickset
threat
Tibet
toilette
tournette
tourniquet
tret
underset
unfret
unget
upset
vedette
vet
vignette
villanette
vinaigrette
violet
wagonette
well-met
wet
whet
yet
zonulet

ĒTH

bequeath
breathe
ensheath
enwreathe
inbreathe
insheathe
interwreathe
inwreathe
seethe
sheathe

sneathe
teethe
unsheathe
unwreathe
upbreathe
wreathe

Ēth

beneath
heath
Keith
Leith
'neath
sheath
sneath
teeth
underneath
wreath

Ĕth

Ashtoreth
breath
death
Elizabeth
Macbeth
saith
'sdeath
Seth
shibboleth
twentieth
thirtieth, etc.
answereth
astonisheth
attributeth
banisheth
blemisheth
blistereth
blundereth
busieth
clustereth
conquereth

ōld, ôr, ŏdd, oil, fŏŏt, out; ūse, ûrn, ŭp; THis, thin

continueth	relinquisheth	aggrieve	shire-reeve
covereth	remembereth	beeve	shrieve
determineth	rescueth	believe	sleave
dowereth	rivalleth	bereave	sleeve
emblazoneth	severeth	breve	steeve
enspiriteth	shimmereth	Christmas-eve	Steve
envieth	showereth	cleave	thieve
exhibiteth	shuddereth	conceive	undeceive
flowereth	silvereth	deceive	unreave
forfeiteth	slumbereth	deev	unreeve
gathereth	sorroweth	disbelieve	unweave
glisteneth	spiriteth	eave	upheave
glowereth	suffereth	engrieve	vive
hearkeneth	sundereth	eve	weave
hungereth	tempereth	greave	we've
incumbereth	thundereth	grieve	yester-eve
inheriteth	ventureth	heave	
inspiriteth	wandereth	interleave	ĒVD
laboureth	wearieth	interweave	self-deceived
languisheth	whispereth	inweave	unbelieved
libelleth	winnoweth	keeve	unperceived
lingereth	witnesseth	khedive	unrelieved
listeneth	wondereth	leave	achieved, etc.
liveneth	worrieth	lieve	
lowereth	worshippeth	make-believe	ĒVZ
marvelleth		misconceive	eaves
measureth	ĒTHD	naive	achieves, etc.
meriteth	unbreathed	New Year's	
murmureth	bequeathed,	eve	ĒZ
nourisheth	etc.	perceive	aborigines
offereth		preconceive	analyses
overpowereth	ĔTZ	qui vive	Annamese
overtowereth	Keats	reave	antipodes
pardoneth	beats, etc.	receive	antitheses
pleasureth		recitative	appease
predestineth	ĔTZ	reeve	Arakanese
punisheth	Metz	relieve	Aragonese
quarrelleth	bets, etc.	reprieve	Assamese
questioneth		retrieve	bee's knees
quieteth	ĒV	seave	Belize
recovereth	achieve	sheave	Bengalese

āle, câre, ădd, ärm, ȧsk; mē, hĕre, ĕnd; īce, ĭll;

bise	frieze	obsequies	Tyrolese
Bolognese	Genevese	parentheses	unease
breeze	grease	pease	unfreeze
Burmese	Havanese	periphrases	valise
B.V.D.s	heart's-ease	Pierides	Veronese
Carlylese	heeze	please	Viennese
Caryatides	Hesperides	Pleiades	vortices
cerise	hypotheses	*Polonese*	wheeze
Ceylonese	imprese	Portuguese	(see Ē + s)
cheese	indices	Pyrenees	
chemise	isosceles	rabies	**ĔZ**
chersonese	Japanese	remise	cortez
cheval-de-frise	Javanese	sea-breeze	fez
Chinese	Johnsonese	seize	says
congeries	journalese	Siamese	
D.T.'s	lees	Singhalese	**ĒZH**
Diogenes	Leonese	sneeze	prestige
disease	Louise	squeeze	tige
displease	Maltese	syntheses	
ease	Milanese	tease	**ĔZH**
enfreeze	mease	these	barège
Eumenides	Navarrese	trapeze	cortège
feaze	Nepaulese	tweeze	manège
freeze			

I

These words include the following accented vowel sounds:

Ī as in ice; heard also in vie, rye, height, eye, aisle, aye meaning *yes,* sky, buy, choir.

Ĭ as in ill; heard also in sieve, English, pretty, been, breeches, women, busy, build, nymph, hymnal.

Ī	alkalify	apply	bedye
acidify	ally	awry	belie
adry	amplify	ay	bespy
alacrify	angelify	aye	black eye
alibi	Anglify	beatify	brutify
alkali	apple-pie	beautify	butterfly

ōld, ôr, ŏdd, oil, fŏŏt, out; ūse, ûrn, ŭp; THis, thin

buy	falsify	lye	rye
by	fie	magnify	saccharify
bye	firefly	magpie	sanctify
bye-bye	fly	modify	satisfy
by-and-by	forby	mollify	scarify
by the by	fortify	mortify	scorify
candify	fossilify	multiply	scye
certify	Frenchify	my	sea-pie
clarify	fructify	my eye	sheep's-eye
classify	fry	mystify	shy
cockneyfy	gasify	nigh	sigh
codify	genii	notify	signify
comply	glorify	nullify	simplify
countrify	go-by	nye	sky
crucify	good-bye	occupy	Skye
cry	gratify	ossify	sky-high
damnify	gri	outcry	sly
dandify	guy	outfly	sny
decry	heigh	outvie	solidify
defy	hereby	pacify	specify
deify	hie	passer-by	spry
demi	high	personify	spy
demy	horrify	petrify	stander-by
deny	humanify	pi	stellify
descry	humble-pie	pie	stultify
die	hushaby	ply	stupefy
dignify	identify	preachify	sty
disqualify	imply	preoccupy	supply
dissatisfy	incubi	prophesy	tabefy
diversify	indemnify	pry	termini
dragon-fly	*ineye*	purify	terrify
dry	intensify	putrefy	testify
dye	July	qualify	thereby
edify	justify	quantify	thigh
electrify	labefy	ramify	*thy*
emulsify	lazuli	rarefy	tie
ensky	lenify	ratify	torpify
espy	lie	rectify	torrefy
eternify	lignify	rely	transmogrify
exemplify	liquefy	reply	try
eye	lullaby	revivify	typify

āle,   câre,   ădd,   ärm,   åsk;   mē,   hẹre,   ĕnd;   īce,   ĭll;

umble-pie
under-buy
underlie
unify
unshy
untie
verbify
verify
versify
vie
vilify
vitrify
vivify
weather-eye
weather-spy
well-nigh
whereby
why
wry
wye

ĬB

ascribe
bribe
circumscribe
describe
diatribe
gibe
imbibe
inscribe
interscribe
jibe
kibe
prescribe
proscribe
scribe
subscribe
superscribe
transcribe
tribe

ĬB

ad lib
bib
Bibb
crib
dib
drib
fib
gib
Gibb
glib
jib
nib
quib
rib
sib
squib

ĬBD

uninscribed
ascribed, etc.

ĬBD

rock-ribbed
cribbed, etc.

ĬBZ

dibs
Gibbs
his nibs
cribs, etc.

ĬCH

bewitch
bitch
Cesarewitch
chich
czarevitch
ditch
enrich
fitch

flitch
Gabrilowitsch
hitch
itch
lich
miche
niche
pitch
quitch
rich
scritch
stitch
switch
twitch
which
witch

ĬCHT

unbewitched
unhitched
unwitched
bewitched, etc.

ĪD

abide
Allhallow-tide
alongside
Argus-eyed
aside
astride
backslide
barmecide
Bartholomew-
    tide
bedside
beside
bestride
betide
bide
bonafide
bride

broadside
bromide
chide
Christmas-tide
Clyde
cockeyed
coincide
collide
confide
countrified
countryside
decide
deicide
deride
dignified
dissatisfied
diversified
divide
double-dyed
dove-eyed
dull-eyed
eagle-eyed
Eastertide
ebb-tide
elide
Ember-tide
eventide
evil-eyed
excide
fireside
flood-tide
foreside
fortified
fratricide
full-eyed
glide
goggle-eyed
green-eyed
gride
guide
Hallowtide

ōld, ôr, ŏdd, oil, fŏŏt, out; ūse, ûrn, ŭp; THis, thin

hawk-eyed
herpicide
hide
high-tide
hillside
homicide
Hyde
I'd
infanticide
insecticide
inside
iodide
justified
Lammas-tide
landslide
lapicide
lee-tide
liberticide
lynx-eyed
matricide
meek-eyed
misallied
misguide
morning-tide
nation-wide
nide
noontide
open-eyed
outride
outside
outstride
override
owl-eyed
ox-eyed
pale-eyed
parenticide
parricide
Passion-tide
patricide
pied
pie-eyed

pop-eyed
preside
pride
provide
purified
qualified
regicide
reside
ride
riverside
sea-side
self-pride
self-satisfied
Shrove-tide
side
slide
snide
soft-eyed
sororicide
spring-tide
squint-eyed
state-wide
stillicide
stride
subdivide
subside
suicide
sulphide
tide
tyrannicide
unapplied
unbetide
underside
undertide
undescried
undignified
undried
unespied
ungratified
unpurified
unqualified

unsanctified
unsatisfied
unspied
untried
uxoricide
vaticide
vermicide
vitrified
vulpicide
wall-eyed
water-side
wayside
weather-side
weather-tide
Whitsuntide
wide
Yule-tide
(see Ī + ed)

ĪD

amid
bid
chid
Cid
did
fid
forbid
fordid
gid
grid
hid
invalid
katydid
kid
lid
Madrid
mid
outbid
outdid
overbid
overdid

pyramid
quid
rid
skid
slid
squid
thrid
unbid
underbid
undid
unforbid

ĪDST

amidst
bid'st
chid'st
did'st
forbid'st
hid'st
kid'st
midst
rid'st
slid'st

ĪDTH

width
bid'th, etc.

ĪDZ

besides
ides
abides, etc.

ĪF

after-life
bowie-knife
fife
fishwife
goodwife
housewife
knife

life
rife
still-life
strife
wife

ĬF
biff
cliff
diff
glyph
griff
handkerchief
hieroglyph
hippogriff
if
jiff
miff
neckerchief
skiff
sniff
stiff
Tenerife
Teneriffe
tiff
undercliff
whiff
wiff

ĬFT
adrift
drift
forelift
gift
lift
rift
shift
shrift
sift
snow-drift
spendthrift

spiffed
spindrift
swift
thrift
tift
topping-lift
unthrift
uplift
miffed, etc.

ĬFTH
fifth
miff'th, etc.

ĬG
big
brig
cig
dig
fig
gig
grig
guinea-pig
infra-dig
jig
nig
periwig
pig
prig
renege
rig
snig
sprig
swig
thimblerig
thingumajig
trig
twig
unrig
Whig

whirligig
wig

ĬGD
bewigged
full-rigged
jury-rigged
square-rigged
digged, etc.

ĬGZ
Biggs
Briggs
Higgs
Riggs
(see ĬG + s)

ĪJ
Lije
oblige

ĬJ
abridge
bridge
enridge
midge
nidge
ridge
upridge
(see also ĀJ)

ĬJD
unabridged
unbridged
abridged, etc.

.

ĪK
Alibi Ike
alike
assassin-like
belike

bike
boarding-pike
brotherlike
dislike
dyke
fairy-like
fyke
ghostlike
hike
kike
like
maidenlike
manlike
marlinspike
mike
mislike
oblique
peasantlike
pike
shrike
spike
starlike
strike
tyke
unlike
Vandyck
Vandyke
Van Wyck
womanlike
workmanlike
Wyke

ĬK
arithmetic
arsenic
bailiwick
Benedick
bestick
bishopric
brick   .
candlestick

candlewick | tick | Trix | strict
Catholic | trick | (see ĬK + s) | unlicked
chick | turmeric | | unpicked
chivalric | walking stick | **ĬKST** | bricked, etc.
choleric | wick | atwixt |
click | | betwixt | **ĪL**
crick | **ĬKS** | *click'st* | aisle
Dick | Dykes | *kick'st* | Anglophile
double-quick | Rikes | *lick'st* | awhile
fiddle-stick | Sykes | *pick'st* | beguile
flick | (see ĪK + s) | *prick'st* | bibliophile
heart-sick | | *stick'st* | bile
heretic | **ĬKS** | *trick'st* | camomile
hick | admix | 'twixt | chyle
impolitic | affix | unfixed | compile
kick | Beatrix | unmixed | crocodile
kinnikinnick | cicatrix | admixed, etc. | defile
lick | commix | | diastyle
limerick | crucifix | **ĬKSTH** | enisle
love-sick | Dix | sixth | ensile
lunatic | executrix | *mix'th,* etc. | *erewhile*
maverick | fiddlesticks | | *erstwhile*
mick | fix | **ĬKT** | file
nick | Hicks | addict | Francophile,
pick | Hix | afflict | etc.
plethoric | immix | astrict | guile
pogo-stick | inheritrix | benedict | infantile
politic | intermix | conflict | isle
prick | mix | constrict | juvenile
quick | nix | contradict | Kabyle
rhetoric | Pnyx | convict | lisle
rick | politics | delict | Lyle
sic | prefix | depict | meanwhile
sick | prolix | derelict | mercantile
single-stick | pyx | evict | mile
slick | Ricks | inflict | Nile
snick | Rix | interdict | otherwhile
stich | six | Pict | paper-file
stick | Styx | predict | pentastyle
thick | transfix | relict | peristyle
tic | | restrict | pile

---

puerile
reconcile
resile
revile
rile
smile
somewhile
spile
stile
style
therewhile
tile
up-pile
versatile
vibratile
vile
voltaic pile
while
wile

ĬL
Amityville
Anglophile
befrill
bestill
bibliophile
bill
Bozenkill
Brazil
brill
chill
chlorophyle
chrysophyll
Cobleskill
codicil
daffodil
dill
distil
domicile
downhill
drill

enthrill
Evansville
espadrille
fill
Francophile,
    etc.
freewill
frill
fulfil
gill
good-will
grill
grille
hill
ill
ill-will
imbecile
infantile
instil
jill
juvenile
kill
kiln
Louisville
mercantile
mill
nil
pill
powder-mill
prill
puerile
quadrille
quill
rill
self-will
Seville
shrill
sill
skill
spadille
spill

squill
still
stock-still
swill
thill
thrill
till
trill
twill
'twill
until
unwill
uphill
versatile
vibratile
vill
volatile
water-mill
whip-poor-will
will

ĬLCH
filch
milch
pilch
Zilch

ĬLD
child
childe
enfiled
foster-child
love-child
mild
self-styled
unbeguiled
unchild
unmild
unreconciled
unwild
wild

Wilde
beguiled, etc.
aisled

ĪLD
befrilled
begild
build
gild
guild
rebuild
self-willed
unbuild
unchilled
unfulfilled
unskilled
untilled
unwilled
chilled, etc.

ĬLF
sylph

ĬLJ
bilge

ĬLK
bilk
ilk
milk
silk
spun-silk

ĬLKS
Wilkes
(see ĬLK + s)

ĬLM
film

ĬLN
kiln
Milne

ōld, ôr, ŏdd, oil, fŏŏt, out; ūse, ûrn, ŭp; THis, thin

ĬLS
grilse
(cf.—lts)

ĬLST
beguil'st
defil'st
whilst
whils't, etc.

ĬLT
atilt
basket-hilt
begilt
built
clinker-built
clipper-built
frigate-built
gilt
guilt
hilt
jilt
kilt
lilt
milt
quilt
rebuilt
silt
spilt
stilt
tilt
unbuilt
ungilt
Vanderbilt
wilt

ĬLTH
filth
spilth
tilth
till'th, etc.

ĬLTS
kilts
[cf. grilse]
basket-hilts,
   etc.

ĬLZ
Giles
Miles
otherwhiles
whiles
wiles
beguiles, etc.

ĪM
aftertime
bedtime
begrime
belime
berhyme
beslime
birdlime
breathing-time
chime
chyme
climb
clime
crime
daytime
dime
eaning-time
grime
Guggenheim
haying-time
I'm
lifetime
lime
Lyme
maritime
meantime
mime

overtime
pairing-time
pantomime
prime
quicklime
rhyme
Rosenheim
rime
seed-time
slime
sometime
spring-time
sublime
summer-time
thyme
time
upclimb

ĬM
antonym
bedim
betrim
brim
cherubim
dim
enlimn
gim
glim
grim
gym
him
hymn
interim
Jim
Kim
Klim
limb
limn
maritime
Nym
prelim

prim
pseudonym
rim
Sanhedrim
seraphim
shim
skim
slim
swim
synonym
Tim
trim
vim
whim
zimb

ĪMD
well-timed
begrimed, etc.

ĬMD
brimmed
untrimmed
bedimmed, etc.

ĬMF
lymph
nymph
sea-nymph

ĬMP
blimp
crimp
gimp
imp
jimp
limp
pimp
primp
scrimp
shrimp

simp	brine	Evangeline	pine
skimp	Byzantine	*eyne*	porcupine
tymp	caballine	Fescennine	powder-mine
	caffeine	fine	Proserpine
ĬMPS	calcine	Florentine	recline
glimpse	canine	Ghibelline	refine
crimps, etc.	Capitoline	Goldstein	repine
	carabine	Hoffenstein	resign
ĬMZ	Caroline	hyaline	resupine
betimes	celandine	incarnadine	Rhine
oftentimes	Celestine	incline	Rubinstein
ofttimes	chine	infantine	saline
sometimes	Clementine	interline	sapphirine
begrimes, etc.	Clyne	intermine	saturnine
	columbine	intertwine	serpentine
ĬMZ	combine	Jacqueline	shine
Simms	concubine	kine	shrine
(see ĬM + s)	condign	Klein	sibylline
	confine	Kline	sign
ĬN	consign	*langsyne*	sine
Adaline	Constantine	leonine	snow-line
Adeline	coraline	libertine	spine
adulterine	countermine	Liechtenstein	spline
agatine	countersign	life-line	star-shine
align	crystalline	line	stein
alkaline	decline	load-line	subdivine
aniline	define	Madeline	*subsign*
anodyne	design	malign	sunshine
anserine	dine	matutine	superfine
Apennine	disincline	mine	supine
apple-wine	divine	moonshine	swine
aquiline	dyne	nine	sycamine
argentine	eglantine	opaline	*syne*
ashine	Esquiline	opine	*thine*
asinine	enshrine	outshine	tine
assign	ensign	overtwine	trephine
Beckstein	entwine	Palatine	trine
benign	Epstein	pavonine	Turn Verein
beshine	Esenwein	peregrine	turpentine
bine	Esquiline	petaline	twine
brigantine	Evaline	Philistine	Tyne

ōld, ôr, ŏdd, oil, fŏŏt, out; ūse, ûrn, ŭp; THis, thin

unbenign	Berlin	herein	sin
underline	bin	heroine	skin
undermine	Boleyn	hyaline	spin
undersign	bulletin	in	sycamine
unline	Byzantine	incarnadine	take-in
untwine	caballine	infantine	tambourin
Ursuline	caffeine	inn	therein
valentine	cannikin	Jacobin	thick-and-thin
vespertine	Capuchin	javelin	thin
vine	carabine	jessamine	tigerkin
viperine	carotin	jinn	tiger-skin
vulturine	Catherine	Katherine	tin
water-line	Celestine	kilderkin	tourmaline
Weinstein	chagrin	kin	twin
whine	chin	libertine	underpin
wine	chinquapin	lin	Ursuline
wolverine	clavecin	Lynn	unpin
woodbine	codeine	mandarin	unsin
Zollverein	coraline	mandolin	vaseline
	crinoline	manikin	vespertine
IN	crystalline	masculine	violin
adulterine	culverin	mezzanine	viperine
agatine	din	minikin	vulturine
agrin	discipline	moccasin	wherein
akin	Evangeline	nectarine	whin
alizarin	feminine	nicotine	whipper-in
alkaline	Fescennine	opaline	win
all in	fin	origin	within
almandine	finikin	paladin	Zeppelin
aniline	Finn	pavonine	
anserine	Florentine	peregrine	**INCH**
aquiline	francolin	petaline	bepinch
argentine	gelatin	Philistine	cinch
aspirin	genuine	pin	chinch
atropine	Ghibelline	Quinn	clinch
baldachin	gin	saccharine	fallow-finch
bandoline	Glyn	sapphirine	finch
bearskin	Glynn	seal-skin	flinch
been	grin	shin	inch
begin	gyn	sibylline	linch
belaying-pin	harlequin	side-spin	lynch

āle, câre, ădd, ärm, ásk; mē, hẹre, ĕnd; īce, ĭll;

pinch	upbind	fling	altering
unclinch	upwind	full-swing	angering
winch	vined	heart-string	answering
	wind	king	apparelling
IND	womankind	lifespring	arguing
behind	combined, etc.	ling	armouring
bind		Ming	astonishing
blind	**IND**	outwing	attributing
color-blind	abscind	ping	auctioning
crined	disciplined	ring	auditing
disinclined	exscind	sea-king	auguring
find	lind	seal-ring	awakening
gavelkind	Lynd	sea-wing	badgering
grind	rescind	shuffle-wing	balancing
hind	Rosalind	signet-ring	ballasting
humankind	storm-wind	sing	bandying
inbind	tamarind	sling	banishing
interwind	thick-skinned	spring	bantering
intertwined	thin-skinned	starveling	barbering
kind	undisciplined	sting	bargaining
mankind	wind	string	barracking
master-mind	grinned, etc.	swing	barrelling
mind		Synge	bartering
overtwined	**ING**	thing	battering
purblind	anything	ting	bedeviling
remind	atheling	underling	beflattering
rind	besing	underwing	beggaring
rynd	bewing	unking	belaboring
snow-blind	bing	unsling	beleaguering
storm-wind	bring	unstring	belecturing
unbind	chitterling	wedding-ring	bellowing
unblind	cling	weeping-spring	bepattering
unconfined	daughterling	wing	bepowdering
undefined	dayspring	wring	bepummelling
underbind	ding	abandoning	bescattering
undersigned	driving-spring	accomplishing	beslabbering
undesigned	easterling	accrediting	bespattering
unkind	enring	accustoming	betokening
unrefined	evening	actioning	bevelling
unshrined	everything	admonishing	bewildering
unwind	fairy-king	afforesting	bickering

blackening	chastening	dishonoring	filtering
blandishing	chattering	disparaging	fingering
blanketing	chiselling	dispiriting	finicking
blarneying	christening	displeasuring	finishing
blathering	Christmasing	disquieting	flattering
blazoning	ciphering	dissevering	flavoring
blemishing	clambering	distinguishing	flickering
blistering	clamoring	distributing	flittering
blossoming	clattering	dowering	flourishing
blubbering	clustering	drivelling	flowering
blundering	cockering	duelling	flurrying
blustering	coloring	embarrassing	flustering
bolstering	compassioning	embellishing	fluttering
bonneting	conjecturing	emblazoning	focussing
brandishing	conquering	embodying	following
breakfasting	considering	emboldening	foregathering
broadening	continuing	embosoming	foreshadowing
buffeting	contributing	empitying	foretokening
bullying	conveyancing	enameling	forfeiting
burdening	covering	enamoring	forwarding
burnishing	coveting	encouraging	freshening
burying	cowering	encumbering	furnishing
busying	crediting	enharboring	furthering
butchering	cudgelling	enheartening	galloping
buttressing	cumbering	enravishing	gambolling
cancelling	dallying	entering	gammoning
candying	damaging	entrammelling	gardening
cankering	darkening	envisaging	garlanding
cannoning	deadening	envying	garnishing
cantering	deciphering	establishing	gathering
canvassing	destining	examining	gesturing
capering	determining	exhibiting	gladdening
capturing	devilling	faltering	glimmering
carolling	dickering	famishing	glittering
carpeting	dieting	fancying	glowering
carrying	diminishing	farrowing	gravelling
cautioning	discouraging	fashioning	grovelling
cavilling	discrediting	fathoming	hallowing
challenging	disestablishing	favoring	hammering
channelling	disfavoring	feathering	hampering
chartering	dishallowing	festering	hankering

 āle,   câre,   ădd,   ärm,   ȧsk;   mē,   hẹre,   ĕnd;   īce,   ĭll;

happening	littering	overmastering	pilfering
harassing	livening	overpowering	pillaging
harboring	lobbying	overshadowing	placarding
hardening	long-suffering	overtowering	plastering
harrowing	lowering	paltering	pleasuring
harrying	lumbering	pampering	plundering
harvesting	maddening	polishing	racketing
hastening	managing	pommelling	rallying
hazarding	manufacturing	pondering	ransoming
hearkening	marketing	pottering	rapturing
heartening	marrying	powdering	ravaging
heralding	marshalling	practising	ravening
hovering	martyring	predestining	ravishing
humoring	marvelling	prohibiting	reasoning
hungering	meandering	promising	reckoning
imagining	measuring	prospering	recovering
imprisoning	menacing	publishing	remembering
incumbering	mentioning	punishing	rendering
indenturing	meriting	purposing	rescuing
inhabiting	mirroring	quarrelling	revelling
inheriting	modelling	quarrying	rivalling
inspiriting	monkeying	quartering	riveting
issuing	mothering	quavering	roystering
jabbering	motoring	querying	rubbering
jeoparding	murdering	questioning	rubbishing
jollying	murmuring	quieting	saddening
junketing	mustering	quivering	sallying
labelling	muttering	pandering	sanctioning
laboring	narrowing	panelling	sauntering
lacquering	neighboring	pardoning	savaging
languishing	nourishing	parrying	savoring
lathering	numbering	passioning	scaffolding
lavishing	offering	patenting	scampering
lazying	omening	pattering	scattering
lecturing	opening	pedalling	scavenging
lessening	ordering	pencilling	seasoning
levelling	outbalancing	pensioning	severing
libelling	outnumbering	peppering	shadowing
limiting	outrivalling	perishing	shattering
lingering	overbalancing	perjuring	shepherding
listening	overburdening	pestering	shimmering

ōld, ôr, ŏdd, oil, fŏŏt, out; ūse, ûrn, ŭp; THis, thin

shivering	tittering	watering	ink
shouldering	toadying	wavering	interlink
showering	tottering	weakening	jink
shuddering	towelling	wearying	kink
sickening	towering	weathering	link
silvering	trafficing	westering	meadow-pink
simmering	travelling	whimpering	mink
simpering	tunnelling	whinneying	pink
sistering	undervaluing	whispering	prink
slackening	unfaltering	winnowing	rink
slandering	unflattering	wintering	shrink
slaughtering	unmeriting	witnessing	sink
slobbering	unmurmuring	wondering	skink
slumbering	unperishing	worrying	slink
smartening	unpitying	worshipping	snow-blink
smattering	unpromising		stink
smouldering	unravelling	**INGD**	think
snivelling	unreasoning	bewinged	tiddlywink
sorrowing	unremember-	dinged	tink
spattering	ing	eagle-winged	trink
spiralling	unslumbering	ringed	twink
spiriting	unwandering	stringed	unlink
spluttering	unwavering	winged, etc.	unthink
stammering	upholstering		wink
stationing	uttering	**INGK**	zinc
stencilling	valuing	bethink	
stuttering	vanishing	blink	**INGKS**
suffering	vanquishing	bobolink	jinx
sugaring	vaporing	brink	lynx
summering	varnishing	chink	methinks
sundering	velveting	cinque	minx
sweetening	venturing	clink	sphinx
tallying	visioning	counter-sink	tiddledywinks
tampering	visiting	drink	tiddlywinks
tapering	volleying	enlink	clinks, etc.
tarnishing	voyaging	Finck	
tarrying	wakening	Fink	**INGKT**
tasselling	walloping	*forethink*	blinked
tempering	wandering	gink	distinct
thundering	wantoning	hoodwink	extinct
tinselling	wassailling	Humperdinck	indistinct

instinct
procinct
succinct
tinct
clinked, etc.

ÍNGZ

awakenings
leading-strings
besings, etc.

ÍNJ

befringe
binge
constringe
cringe
dinge
fringe
hinge
impinge
infringe
perstringe
scringe
singe
springe
swinge
tinge
twinge
unhinge

ÍNJD

unhinged
unsinged
befringed, etc.

ÍNS

convince
evince
merchant-
    prince
mince

prince
quince
rinse
since
unprince
Vince
wince
(cf. flints,
    chintz)

ÍNSK

Dvinsk
Minsk
Pinsk

ÍNT

ahint
behint
pint

ÍNT

asquint
calamint
dint
flint
footprint
glint
hint
imprint
lint
mezzotint
mint
misprint
peppermint
print
quint
reprint
septuagint
sodamint
spearmint
splint

sprint
squint
stint
tint
vint

ÍNTH

ninth
pine'th, etc.

ÍNTH

colocynth
hyacinth
labyrinth
plinth
terebinth

ÍNTS

Heintz
pints

ÍNTS

aquatints
chintz
flints, etc.
(cf. convince,
    etc.)

ÍNZ

Appenines
Tynes
dines, etc.

ÍNZ

ods-bodikins
winze
withershins
(see ÍN + s)

ÍP

antitype
archetype

autotype
bagpipe
blowpipe
daguerreotype
dead-ripe
electrotype
graphotype
gripe
gutter-snipe
heliotype
hornpipe
hype
kipe
linotype
logotype
monotype
overripe
pipe
pitchpipe
prototype
ripe
snipe
stereotype
stipe
stripe
swipe
teletype
tintype
tripe
type
unripe
windpipe
wipe

ÍP

apple-pip
atrip
battleship
chip
clip
dip

drip
equip
flip
grip
grippe
gyp
hip
horsewhip
hyp
kip
landslip
lip
nip
outstrip
overtrip
pip
pleasure-trip
quip
rip
scrip
ship
sip
skip
slip
snip
strip
tip
training-ship
tranship
trip
underlip
unrip
unship
warship
weather-strip
whip
zip
acquaintance-
  ship
administra-
  torship

agentship
aldemanship
apprentice-
  ship
archonship
babyship
bachelorship
cardinalsip
censorship
chairmanship
championship
chancellorship
chaplainship
chieftainship
churchman-
  ship
churchmem-
  bership
citizenship
collectorship
commander-
  ship
companion-
  ship
consortship
consulship
controllership
co-partner-
  ship
cousinship
craftsmanship
creatorship
deaconship
demonship
draughtsman-
  ship
eldership
electorship
emperorship
ensignship
farmership

fathership
fellowship
generalship
good-fellow-
  ship
governorship
guardianship
horsemanship
huntsmanship
impostorship
inspectorship
jockeyship
justiceship
leadership
lectureship
legislatorship
librarianship
lordship
marksmanship
marshalship
mastership
membership
Messiahship
neighborship
noviceship
ownership
paintership
partnership
pastorship
penmanship
praetorship
preachership
prelateship
probationship
professorship
proprietorship
questorship
rajahship
rangership
readership
recordership

rectorship
regentship
relationship
scholarship
seamanship
secretaryship
senatorship
sextonship
sheriffship
sizarship
speakership
spectatorship
sponsorship
sportsmanship
statesmanship
stewardship
studentship
sultanship
suretyship
survivorship
swordsman-
  ship
treasurership
umpireship
viceroyship
virtuosoship
wardenship
workmanship
wranglership

ĪPS

pipes, etc.

ĬPS

Apocalypse
chips
eclipse
ellipse
Phipps
apple-pips

acquaintance-
   ships, etc.

ĬPST

chip'st
clip'st
dip'st
eclipsed
equip'st
grip'st
rip'st
ship'st
sip'st
skip'st
slip'st
strip'st
tip'st
trip'st
uneclipsed
whip'st

ĬPT

hunger-griped
prison-striped
griped, etc.

ĬPT

apocalypt
crypt
frost-nipped
hipped
manuscript
script
subscript
superscript
tipt
chipped, etc.

ĪR

acquire
admire

afire
aspire
attire
beacon-fire
bemire
byre
choir
conspire
death-fire
desire
dire
enquire
entire
esquire
expire
fire
flat tire
galley-fire
grandsire
gyre
hell-fire
hire
inquire
inspire
ire
lyre
McIntyre
Meyer
mire
Molly Maguire
perspire
pyre
quire
require
respire
retire
shire
signal-fire
sire
spitfire
squire

spire
suspire
swire
tire
transpire
Tyre
unsquire
Untermyer
vire
wildfire
wire
(cf. crier, high-
   er, prior, fri-
   ar, etc.)

ĪRD

overtired
spired
unacquired
undesired
unexpired
uninspired
acquired, etc.

ĪS

advice
bespice
bice
concise
device
dice
entice
gneiss
grice
ice
lice
mice
nice
overnice
Paradise
precise

price
rice
sacrifice
self-sacrifice
sice
slice
spice
splice
suffice
syce
thrice
trice
twice
vice
vise
Weiss
Zeiss

ĬS

abiogenesis
abyss
acropolis
ambergris
amiss
anabasis
analysis
antithesis
apheresis
aphesis
armistice
artifice
avarice
Beatrice
benefice
biogenesis
bis
bliss
chrysalis
cicatrice
clematis
cockatrice

cowardice
cuisse
dehisce
dentifrice
diæresis
dialysis
diathesis
Dis
dismiss
edifice
ectogenesis
elephantiasis
emphasis
fortalice
genesis
hiss
hypostasis
hypothesis
kiss
liquorice
Liss
metabasis
metamorphosis
metastasis
metathesis
metropolis
miss
M'liss
necropolis
nemesis
orifice
paralysis
parenthesis
periphrasis
precipice
prejudice
remiss
Salamis
sis
siss
sui generis

Swiss
synthesis
this
verdigris
vis
wis
y-wis

ĬSH

cnish
dish
fish
gibberish
impoverish
McNish
pilot-fish
pish
slish
squish
swish
Tish
unwish
wish
babyish
bitterish
cleverish
Cockneyish
devilish
dowdyish
feverish
heathenish
kittenish
lickerish
mammonish
ogreish
quakerish
tigerish
vaporish
viperish
vixenish
vulturish

waterish
willowish
womanish
yellowish, etc.

ĬSK

asterisk
basilisk
bisque
brisk
disc
disk
fisc
Fiske
frisk
obelisk
odalisque
risk
tamarisk
whisk

ĬSP

crisp
encrisp
lisp
whisp
wisp

ĪST

antichrist
Christ
emparadised
enticed
tryst
bespiced, etc.

ĬST

agist
amethyst
assist
atwist

bekissed
bemist
beneficed
cist
coexist
consist
cyst
desist
dismissed
enlist
entwist
exist
fist
frist
gist
glist
grist
hissed
hist
insist
intertwist
kissed
list
missed
mist
persist
pre-exist
prejudiced
resist
schist
sissed
sist
subsist
trist
tryst
twist
unkissed
unmissed
untwist
unwist
whist

āle,   câre,   ădd,   ärm,   åsk;   mē,   hęre,   ĕnd;   īce,   ĭll;

wist
wrist
xyst
abolitionist
absolutist
academist
accompanist
aerologist
agamist
agonist
agricolist
agriculturalist
agriculturist
alchemist
allegorist
allopathist
amorist
anagrammatist
analogist
analyst
anarchist
anatomist
animalculist
animist
annalist
annualist
antagonist
anthropologist
antinomist
antipathist
apathist
aphorist
apiarist
apologist
Arabist
arboriculturist
arborist
archaeologist
artillerist
atheist
atomist

augurist
balladist
biblicist
bibliophilist
bibliopolist
bicyclist
bigamist
bimetallist
biologist
Bolshevist
botanist
Bourbonist
Brahmanist
cabalist
Calvinist
campanologist
canonist
capitalist
casuist
catechist
centralist
chirographist
chiropodist
choralist
chronologist
circumlocu-
    tionist
classicalist
classicist
coalitionist
colloquist
colonist
colorist
communist
conchologist
Confucionist
congregation-
    alist
constitutional-
    ist
constitutionist

constructionist
contortionist
controversialist
conversationist
corruptionist
cremationist
culturist
dactylist
Darwinist
degenerationist
demonist
demonologist
despotist
destinist
destructionist
deuterogamist
devotionalist
devotionist
dialist
dialogist
diplomatist
dogmatist
dramatist
dualist
duellist
ecclesiologist
economist
educationalist
educationist
egoist
egotist
electro-
    biologist
elegist
elocutionist
empiricist
enamelist
enigmatist
entomologist
epigrammatist
epitomist

equilibrist
essayist
eternalist
ethicist
etymologist
Eucharist
eudemonist
eulogist
euphuist
evangelist
evolutionist
excursionist
exorcist
experimental-
    ist
externalist
fabulist
fatalist
federalist
feudalist
fictionist
financialist
floriculturist
formalist
fossilist
fossilogist
funambulist
futilist
galvanist
genealogist
geologist
glacialist
gymnosophist
harmonist
Hebraist
hedonist
Hellenist
herbalist
horticulturist
humanist
humorist

hyperbolist	misanthropist	philologist	revivalist
hypnotist	miscellanist	philosophist	revolutionist
idealist	misogamist	phlebotomist	rhapodist
illusionist	misogynist	photographist	rigorist
imitationist	modernist	phrenologist	ritualist
immaterialist	monogamist	philatelist	Romanist
immersionist	monopolist	physicist	romanticist
immortalist	moralist	physiognomist	royalist
imperialist	motorist	physiologist	ruralist
inspirationist	mythologist	pianist	satanist
instrumentalist	Napoleonist	pietist	satirist
insurrectionist	nationalist	plagiarist	schematist
intellectualist	naturalist	platonist	scientist
internationalist	necrologist	pleasurist	sciolist
journalist	neologist	pluralist	scripturalist
Judaist	Neoplatonist	pneumatologist	scripturist
Latinist	nepotist	polygamist	secessionist
legitimist	nihilist	positivist	secularist
liberalist	nominalist	posturist	seismologist
literalist	novelist	pragmatist	sensationalist
lithologist	obstructionist	precisianist	sensualist
lobbyist	oculist	prelatist	sentimentalist
loyalist	ontologist	progressionist	sexualist
magnetist	opinionist	prohibitionist	sibyllist
malthusianist	oppositionist	protagonist	socialist
mammonist	optimist	protectionist	sociologist
mannerist	organist	proverbialist	soloist
martyrologist	Orientalist	provincialist	somnambulist
materialist	ornithologist	psalmodist	Sorbonist
mechanist	pacifist	psychologist	specialist
medallist	passionist	publicist	spiritualist
melodist	pathologist	pugilist	steganograph-
melodramatist	penologist	pythonist	ist
memorialist	perfectionist	quietist	stenographist
Menshevist	pessimist	rabbinist	strategist
mesmerist	petrologist	rapturist	subjectivist
metalist	pharmacist	rationalist	suffragist
meteorologist	pharmacologist	realist	symbolist
methodist	phenomenist	religionist	sympathist
mineralogist	philanthropist	repudiationist	syncopist
ministerialist	Philhellenist	resurrectionist	syncretist

---

synodist	zoophilist	cosmopolite ·	indite
synonymist	zootomist	crystallite	invite
synthesist		daylight	Ishmaelite
tautologist	IT	dead-light	Islamite
technicist	Aaronite	delight	Israelite
technologist	acolyte	despite	Jacobite
telegraphist	aconite	*dight*	kite
teleologist	actinolite	disunite	knight
telephonist	Adamite	dolomite	light
terrorist	Adullamite	downright	malachite
textualist	aerolite	dynamite	mammonite
theologist	affright	Ebionite	Maronite
theophilan-	alight	ebonite	McKnight
thropist	aluminite	Elamite	meteorite
theorist	Ammonite	electrolyte	midnight
theosophist	anchorite	entomolite	midshipmite
threnodist	*anight*	enwrite	might
tobacconist	anthracite	eremite	mite
topographist	appetite	erudite	Moabite
toxicologist	aright	excite	moonlight
trades-unionist	Baalite	expedite	Mormonite
traditionalist	Babylonite	Fahrenheit	Muscovite
traditionist	*bedight*	fight	Nazarite
transcenden-	bedlamite	Fite	neophyte
talist	*behight*	flight	night
unionist	beknight	foresight	outright
universalist	belemnite	forthright	*overdight*
vaccinist	benight	fright	overnight
vacuist	Bethlehemite	good-night	oversight
vaticanist	bight	Gothamite	parasite
ventriloquist	bipartite	grapholite	plebiscite
verbalist	bite	harbor-light	plight
violist	blatherskite	headlight	polite
visionist	blight	height	pre-Adamite
vitalist	bright	heteroclite	pre-Raphaelite
vocabulist	Canaanite	*hight*	proselyte
vocalist	Carmelite	ichnolite	Puseyite
volumist	chrysolite	ignite	quite
votarist	cite	impolite	recite
zealotist	contrite	incite	recondite
zoologist	copyright	indict	requite

reunite
right
rite
satellite
sea-fight
sea-light
second-sight
siderolite
sight
signal-light
site
sleight
slight
smite
snow-white
spite
sprite
starlight
sunlight
sybarite
theodolite
tight
to-night
toxophilite
tripartite
trite
troglodyte
troth-plight
twilight
underwrite
undight
unite
unright
unsight
unwrite
upright
vulcanite
water-sprite
water-tight
white
wight

wright
write
yesternight
zoolite
zoophyte

ĬT

acquit
admit
after-wit
apposite
befit
beknit
benefit
bit
bitt
chit
cit
commit
counterfeit
definite
demit
DeWitt
emit
exquisite
favorite
fit
flit
frit
grit
hit
hypocrite
immit
indefinite
infinite
inknit
interknit
intermit
intromit
it
Jesuit

kit
knit
lit
manumit
McNitt
misfit
mitt
moon-lit
mother-wit
nit
omit
opposite
outfit
outsit
outwit
permit
perquisite
pit
Pitt
plebiscite
pretermit
preterite
prerequisite
quit
recommit
refit
remit
requisite
rifle-pit
Schmidt
sit
slit
smit
spit
split
sprit
submit
tit
tom-tit
to-wit
transmit

twit
unbit
unfit
unknit
unwit
whit
wit
Witt
writ

ĬTH

blithe
lithe
scythe
Smythe
tithe
withe
writhe

Ĭth

myth
stythe

ĪTH

forthwith
herewith
therewith
wherewith
with
withe

Ĭth

acrolith
aerolith
Arrowsmith
frith
kith
Ladysmith
lith
monolith
myth

palaeolith	rive	compulsative	laudative
pith	shive	confirmative	lenitive
sith	shrive	consecutive	lucrative
smith	skive	conservative	nominative
withe	stive	contemplative	nutritive
forthwith	strive	contributive	premonitive
herewith	survive	correlative	preparative
therewith	thrive	curative	prerogative
wherewith	unhive	declarative	preservative
with	wive	definitive	primitive
		demonstrative	prohibitive
ĬTS	**ĬV**	derivative	provocative
anights	forgive	derogative	pulsative
footlights	fugitive	desiccative	punitive
tights	give	diminutive	putative
acolytes, etc.	live	dispensative	quantitive
	misgive	disputative	recitative
ĬTS	narrative	distributive	reformative
Fritz	negative	evocative	reparative
quits	outlive	exclamative	representative
Schlitz	overlive	executive	restorative
acquits, etc.	positive	expletive	retributive
	relative	figurative	sanative
ĪV	sieve	formative	sedative
alive	ablative	fugitive	semblative
arrive	accusative	genitive	sensitive
chive	acquisitive	illustrative	siccative
Clive	admonitive	impeditive	substantive
connive	affirmative	imperative	superlative
contrive	alternative	imputative	talkative
deprive	amative	incarnative	tentative
derive	argumentative	inchoative	transitive
dive	causative	incrassative	vibrative
drive	coercitive	indicative	vocative
five	combative	infinitive	
gyve	comparative	informative	**ĪVD**
hive	compellative	inquisitive	long-lived
I've	compensative	insensitive	short-lived
live	competitive	intensative	unshrived
power dive	complimenta-	interrogative	unwived
revive	tive	intuitive	arrived, etc.

ōld, ôr, ŏdd, oil, fŏŏt, out; ūse, ûrn, ŭp; THis, thin

ĬVD
long-lived
negatived
outlived
short-lived
unlived

ĪVZ
fives
knives
lives
arrives, etc.

ĪZ
acclimatize
achromatize
actualize
adonize
advertise
advise
Africanize
after-wise
agatize
aggrandize
agonize
agrarianize
albumenize
alchemize
alcoholize
alkalize
allegorize
alphabetize
amalgamize
ambrosialize
Americanize
analyze
anathematize
anatomize
angelize
Anglicize
animalize

annalize
antagonize
anywise
aphorize
apologize
apostatize
apostrophize
apotheosize
appetize
apprise
arise
aromatize
artificialize
assize
astrologize
astronomize
atheize
atomize
atticize
attitudinize
augurize
authorize
balladize
baptize
barbarize
battologize
botanize
bowdlerize
brutalize
canonize
capitalize
capsize
catechize
cauterize
centralize
characterize
chastise
chimerize
Christianize
circularize
civilize

climatize
cognize
colonize
comprize
compromise
constitution-
  alize
contrariwise
conventionalize
corner-wise
crescent-wise
criticise
crystallize
dandyize
dastardize
decimalize
decolorize
dehumanize
demagnetize
demise
democratize
demonetize
demoralize
denarcotize
denaturalize
deodorize
deputize
despise
detonize
devilize
devise
devitalize
diabolize
dialogize
dialyze
disguise
disillusionize
disorganize
dogmatize
doxologize
dramatize

ebonize
economize
ecstasize
Edenize
effeminize
electrolyze
emblematicize
emblematize
emblemize
emphasize
emprize
energize
enigmatize
enterprise
epigrammatize
epitomize
equalize
eternalize
etherealize
etherize
etymologize
eulogize
euphemize
euphonize
euphuize
Europeanize
evangelize
excise
excursionize
exercise
exorcise
experimental-
  ize
extemporize
fabulize
familiarize
fanaticize
federalize
fertilize
feudalize
fluidize

āle, câre, ădd, ärm, åsk; mē, hĕre, ĕnd; īce, ĭll;

focalize	italicize	Mohammedan-	Platonize
formalize	jeopardize	ize	plebeianize
formulize	journalize	monetize	pluralize
fossilize	Judaize	monopolize	poetize
fraternize	Latinize	moonrise	polarize
galvanize	legalize	moralize	pollenize
gelatinize	legitimatize	mythologize	polygamize
genealogize	lethargize	narcotize	popularize
generalize	liberalize	nasalize	prelatize
gentilize	likewise	nationalize	remise
geologize	lionize	naturalize	revise
geometrize	liquidize	neutralize	prize
gluttonize	literalize	novelize	proselytize
gorgonize	Lize	organize	Protestantize
gormandize	localize	ostracize	proverbialize
gospelize	Londonize	*otherguise*	provincialize
guise	macadamize	otherwise	psalmodize
gutteralize	magnetize	overwise	pulverize
harmonize	Mahomedanize	oxidize	Puritanize
heathenize	mammonize	oxygenize	rapturize
Hebraicize	manumize	paganize	rationalize
Hebraize	martialize	panegyrize	realize
Hellenize	martyrize	parallelize	recognize
Hibernicize	materialize	paralyze	rejuvenize
histrionize	matronize	particularize	remise
humanize	mechanize	patronize	remonetise
hyperbolize	mediatize	pauperize	reprise
hypnotize	memorialize	pavonize	republicanize
hypothesize	memorize	peculiarize	resurrectionize
idealize	mercerize	pedestrianize	revise
idiotize	merchandise	penalize	revolutionize
idolatrize	mesmerize	penny-wise	rhapsodize
idolize	methodize	personalize	rhetorize
immortalize	mineralize	personize	rise
impatronize	minimize	pessimize	Romanize
imperialize	misanthropize	philologize	royalize
improvise	misprize	philosophize	ruralize
incise	mobilize	physiognomize	saccharize
individualize	modelize	pilgrimize	sacrifice
internationalize	modernize	plagiarize	satirize
Italianize		platitudinize	scandalize

ōld, ôr, ŏdd, oil, fŏŏt, out; ūse, ûrn, ŭp; THis, thin

scepticize
schismatize
Scotticize
scrupulize
scrutinize
sectarianize
secularize
seigniorize
seniorize
sensualize
sentimentalize
sepulchralize
sermonize
sexualize
sice
signalize
silverize
singularize
size
soberize
socialize
Socinianize
solarize
solemnize
soliloquize
sonnetize
specialize
spiritualize
sterilize
stigmatize
subsidize
subtilize
summarize
sunrise
supervise
surmise
surprise
syllogize
symbolize
sympathize
symphonize

synchronize
syncopize
synonymize
synthesize
synthetize
systematize
systemize
tabularize
tantalize
tautologize
temporize
terrorize
Teutonize
theologize
theorize
theosophize
timonize
totalize
tranquillize
tyrannize
underprize
universalize
unwise
uprise
utilize
vagabondize
vaporize
ventriloquize
verbalize
victimize
villianize
visualize
vitalize
vocalize
volatilize
vulcanize
vulgarize
wantonize
weather-wise
wise
(see Ī + s)

ĬZ
Ariz.
befriz
biz
Cadiz
fizz
friz
his
is
Liz
phiz
quiz
riz
sizz
'tis
viz
whiz

ĬZD
ill-advised
unadvised
unapprised
unauthorized
unbaptized
uncanonized
uncivilized
undersized
undespised
undisguised
unprized
unsurmised
acclimatized,
etc.

ĬZM
abolitionism
absolutism
abysm
academism
accidentalism
achromatism

actinism
aestheticism
Africanism
agnosticism
agonism
agrarianism
agriculturism
alcoholism
alienism
altruism
Americanism
anachronism
anarchism
anathematism
anatomism
aneurism
Anglicanism
Anglicism
Anglo-
    Saxonism
animalism
animism
anomalism
antagonism
antiquarianism
anti-Semitism
aphorism
archaism
asceticism
Asiaticism
asteism
asterism
astigmatism
atavism
atheism
atomism
Baalism
babyism
bacchanalian-
    ism
bachelorism

āle, câre, ădd, ārm, ăsk; mē, hĕre, ĕnd; īce, ĭll;

barbarism	constitutional-	evangelism	Ibsenism
behaviorism	ism	exorcism	idealism
biblicism	cosmopolitan-	exoticism	ism
bibliophilism	ism	exquisitism	idiotism
bibliopolism	cretinism	fairyism	immaterialism
bi-metallism	criticism	fanaticism	imperialism
bloomerism	cynicism	fantasticism	individualism
bluestocking-	dandyism	fatalism	industrialism
ism	Darwinism	federalism	intellectualism
bogeyism	demoniacism	Fenianism	international-
Bohemianism	demonianism	fetishism	ism
Bolshevism	demonism	feudalism	Irishism
boobyism	denomina-	flunkeyism	Islamism
Bourbonism	tionalism	fogeyism	Italianism
braggardism	despotism	foreignism	Italicism
Brahmanism	determinism	formalism	Jesuitism
brutalism	devilism	fossilism	jockeyism
Buchmanism	diabolism	Fourierism	journalism
cabalism	dialogism	frivolism	Judaism
Calvinism	diamagnetism	Gallicism	laconicism
cataclysm	diplomatism	galvanism	laconism
catechism	dogmatism	gentilism	ladyism
Catholicism	dualism	Germanism	Latinism
centralism	ecclesiasticism	Ghandiism	latitudinarian-
characterism	eclecticism	heathenism	ism
Chauvinism	egoism	Hebraism	legitimism
chloralism	egotism	hedonism	Leninism
chrism	electicism	Hellenism	liberalism
classicalism	embolism	heroism	libertinism
classicism	emotionalism	Hibernianism	literalism
clericalism	empiricism	Hibernicism	localism
Cockneyism	epicureanism	Hinduism	Lollardism
colloquialism	equestrianism	histrionicism	Londonism
colonialism	Erastianism	histrionism	loyalism
communalism	esotericism	Hitlerism	lyricism
communism	etherealism	humanism	magnetism
Confucianism	etherism	hyperbolism	Mahometan-
congregational-	eudemonism	hypercriticism	ism
ism	euphemism	hypnotism	mammonism
conservatism	euphonism	hypochondriac-	mannerism
	euphuism	ism	materialism

mechanism
mediaevalism
Menshevism
mesmerism
metacism
methodism
modernism
Mohammedan-
  ism
monarchism
monasticism
monkeyism
Montanism
moralism
Mormonism
mysticism
nativism
naturalism
necessarianism
neologism
Neoplatonism
nepotism
nihilism
nominalism
occultism
ogreism
optimism
organism
orientalism
ostracism
pacifism
paganism
pantheism
parallelism
paroxysm
patricianism
patriotism
pauperism
peanism
pedantism
pedestrianism

peonism
peripateticism
personalism
pessimism
phalansterism
phenomenalism
phenomenism
philanthropic-
  ism
Philhellenism
Philistinism
philosophism
physicism
pietism
plagiarism
Platonism
plebeianism
pluralism
positivism
pragmatism
precisianism
predestinarian-
  ism
prelatism
pre-Raphaelism
Presbyterian-
  ism
prism
proletarianism
protectionism
Protestantism
proverbialism
provincialism
pugilism
puppyism
Puritanism
Puseyism
pythonism
Quakerism
quietism
Quixotism

rabbinism
radicalism
realism
religionism
Republicanism
rationalism
revivalism
rheumatism
rigorism
ritualism
Romanism
romanticism
royalism
ruffianism
ruralism
sabbatarianism
sacerdotalism
satanism
savagism
Saxonism
scepticism
schism
scholasticism
sciolism
Scotticism
scoundrelism
scripturalism
secessionism
sectarianism
secularism
Semitism
sensationalism
sensualism
sentimentalism
shamanism
Shavianism
Shintoism
socialism
Socinianism
solecism

somnambulism
somnolism
sovietism
Stalinism
stoicism
subjectivism
subtilism
supernatural-
  ism
syllogism
symbolism
synchronism
syncretism
Syrianism
terrorism
Teutonicism
theosophism
tigerism
Toryism
totemism
trades-union-
  ism
traditionalism
transcendental-
  ism
tribalism
unionism
Unitarianism
universalism
utilitarianism
Utopianism
valetudinarian-
  ism
vampirism
vandalism
Vaticanism
vegetarianism
ventriloquism
verbalism
vitalism

āle,   câre,   ădd,   ärm,   åsk;   mē,   hĕre,   ĕnd;   īce,   ĭll;

| vocalism | vulpinism | Wesleyanism | Yankeeism |
| vulgarism | vulturism | witticism | zanyism |

O

These words include the following accented vowel sounds:

Ō   as in old; heard also in note, oh, roam, foe, shoulder, grow, owe, sew, yeoman, beau, hautboy, brooch.

Ô   as in or; heard also in all, talk, swarm, haul, caught, law, fought, broad, memoir.

Ŏ   as in odd; heard also in wan͠t, wash, shone.

OI as in oil; heard also in boy.

O͞O as in foot; heard also in full, wolf, could.

OU as in out; heard also in cow, sauerkraut.

For the vowel sound heard in *do,* see under Ū.

For the vowel sound heard in *one, flood,* see under Ŭ

Ō	bravissimo	domino	furbelow
adagio	buffalo	dough	gazabo
aglow	bummalo	duodecimo	generalissimo
ago	bungalow	eau	gigolo
alow	bureau	*embow*	glow
although	cachalot	embroglio	go
apropos	calico	embryo	grow
archipelago	cameo	entrepot	half-a-mo
arow	chapeau	escrow	haricot
banjo	chateau	Eskimo	heigh-ho
bateau	Co.	ex-officio	ho
beau	comme il faut	Flo	hoe
below	crow	floe	how-so
besnow	curaçoa	flow	hullo
bestow	death-blow	foe	ice-flow
blow	death-throe	folio	imbroglio
bo	depot	forego	impresario
bon-mot	de trop	foreknow	incognito
Bordeaux	Diderot	foreshow	indigo
bow	do	fortissimo	inflow
braggadocio	doe	fro	in statu quo

ōld, ôr, ŏdd, oil, fo͞ot, out; ūse, ûrn, ŭp; THis, thin

intaglio
jabot
Jo
Joe
know
little-go
lo
long-ago
long-bow
Lothario
low
Lowe
magnifico
malapropos
manito
Mexico
mistletoe
morceau
mot
mow
mustachio
no
nuncio
O
oboe
oh
olio
oratorio
outflow
outgo
outgrow
overcrow
overflow
overgrow
overthrow
owe
Papilio
pianissimo
pistachio
plateau
Po

Poe
portfolio
portico
portmanteau
pro
proximo
punctilio
quid-pro-quo
rainbow
raree-show
ratio
roe
rondeau
rouleau
Rousseau
row
Rowe
sabot
saddle-bow
seraglio
sew
shew
show
sloe
slow
snow
so
so-and-so
soho
sow
stow
strow
studio
tableau
tally ho
though
throe
throw
timber-toe
tiptoe
to-and-fro

toe
Tokio
touch-and-go
tow
tremolo
trousseau
trow
ultimo
undergo
under-tow
unknow
upgrow
upthrow
vertigo
Westward ho
woe

Ô

Arkansas
awe
begnaw
braw
brother-in-law
caw
chaw
claw
craw
daughter-in-
 law
dauw
daw
dawe
draw
father-in-law
faugh
flaw
foresaw
gnaw
guffaw
haw
heehaw

jackdaw
jaw
landau
law
macaw
maw
McGraw
mother-in-law
overawe
overdraw
oversaw
papaw
paw
pilau
pshaw
raw
saw
scaw
see-saw
Shaw
sister-in-law
slaw
son-in-law
spa
squaw
straw
tau
taw
thaw
thraw
underjaw
undraw
unlaw
usquebaugh
withdraw
yaw

ŌB

conglobe
disrobe
enrobe

globe	**ŎBZ**	notch	rode
Job	Dobbs	outwatch	spode
lobe	Hobbes	Scotch	strode
Loeb	Hobbs	splotch	toad
probe	ods-bobs	swatch	unbestowed
robe	scobs	watch	unload
unrobe	blobs, etc.		unowed
		ŌCHD	woad
ŌB	**ŌCH**	unapproached	(see Ō + ed)
bedaub	abroach	unbroached	
daub	approach	approached,	**ŌD**
nawab	broach	etc.	abroad
	brooch		applaud
ŎB	coach	**ŌD**	bawd
athrob	cockroach	abode	belaud
blob	croche	a la mode	broad
bob	encoach	antipode	Claude
cabob	encroach	*arrode*	defraud
cob	loach	bestrode	fraud
Cobb	poach	bode	gaud
corncob	reproach	bridle-road	lantern-jawed
fob	roach	Clode	laud
gob	self-reproach	code	maraud
hob	slowcoach	commode	maud
hob-and-nob		corrode	overawed
hobnob	**ŎCH**	discommode	unawed
job	debauch	episode	whopper-jawed
knob	nautch	erode	awed, etc.
lob		explode	
mob	**ŎCH**	forebode	**ŎD**
nob	anchor-watch	goad	Aaron's-rod
quab	blotch	incommode	*begod*
rob	botch	load	clod
slob	crotch	lode	cod
snob	death-watch	lycopode	Codd
sob	gotch	mode	demi-god
squab	harbour-watch	node	divining-rod
stob	hotch	ode	Dodd
swab	hopscotch	overload	dry-shod
thingumbob	hotch-potch	pigeon-toed	Eisteddfod
throb	larboard-watch	road	God

golden-rod
hod
lycopod
nod
od
odd
piston-rod
platypod
plod
pod
prod
quad
quod
river-god
rod
rough-shod
sea-god
shod
slipshod
sod
squad
tod
trod
ungod
unshod
untrod
wad

ŎDZ

Rhoades
Rhodes
(see ŎD + s)

ŎDZ

emerods
odds
clods, etc.

ŌF

goaf
loaf

oaf
quartern-loaf

ŎF

cloff
cough
doff
golf
koff
long-field-off
off
pairing-off
philosophe
prof
scoff
shroff
sign off
soph
toff
toph
trough

ŎFT

aloft
croft
loft
oft
soft
toft
undercroft
doffed, etc.

ŎG

apologue
astrologue
brogue
collogue
embogue
Hogue
pirogue
prorogue

rogue
togue
trogue
vogue

ŎG

agog
analogue
apologue
befog
bog
bulldog
catalogue
clog
cog
Dannebrog
decalogue
demagogue
dialogue
dog
egg-nog
embog
epilogue
flog
fog
frog
Gog
grog
hedgehog
Herzog
hog
hot dog
incog
jog
log
monologue
mystagogue
nog
Patchogue
pedagogue
pettifog

philologue
Pokogue
polliwog
prairie-dog
prog
Quogue
scrog
shog
slog
synagogue
theologue
travelog
unclog

ŎGD

frogged
water-logged
befogged, etc.

ŎGZ

togs
befogs, etc.

OI

ahoy
alloy
annoy
boy
buoy
charity-boy
cloy
convoy
corduroy
coy
decoy
deploy
destroy
employ
enjoy
foy
goy

hobbledehoy
hoy
Illinois
joy
loblolly-boy
Loy
overjoy
paduasoy
Pomeroy
saveloy
Savoy
sepoy
soy
teapoy
toy
troy
viceroy
yellow-boy

OID

actinoid
albuminoid
alkaloid
aneroid
anthropoid
asteroid
avoid
"boid"
celluloid
coralloid
crystalloid
deltoid
dendroid
devoid
helicoid
hyaloid
metalloid
mongoloid
negroid
overjoyed
ovoid

pachyderma-
    toid
paraboloid
petaloid
pyramidoid
tabloid
trapezoid
unalloyed
unbuoyed
unemployed
varioloid
void
alloyed, etc.

OIDZ

Lloyd's
avoids, etc.

OIF

coif

OIL

aboil
assoil
boil
Boyle
broil
coil
counterfoil
Coyle
despoil
disembroil
Doyle
embroil
entoil
estoile
foil
langue d'oil
moil
noil
oil

overtoil
parboil
quatrefoil
recoil
roil
soil
spoil
toil
turmoil
uncoil
upcoil

OILD

hard boiled
unsoiled
unspoiled
boiled, etc.

OILT

spoilt

OILZ

noils
boils, etc.

OIN

adjoin
almoign
Boyne
coign
coin
conjoin
Des Moines
disjoin
eloign
enjoin
foin
frankalmoigne
groin
interjoin
join

loin
purloin
quoin
rejoin
sejoin
sirloin
subjoin
tenderloin

OIND

dead poind
poind
uncoined
adjoined, etc.

OINT

adjoint
anoint
appoint
aroint
conjoint
counterpoint
coverpoint
disappoint
disjoint
dowel-joint
dry-point
joint
point
reappoint
repoint

OIS

Boyce
choice
invoice
Joyce
outvoice
rejoice
voice

OIST
foist
hoist
joist
loud-voiced
moist
shrill-voiced
unrejoiced
unvoiced
voiced, etc.

OIT
adroit
dacoit
Detroit
doit
droit
exploit
maladroit
quoit
Voight

OIZ
avoirdupois
counterpoise
equipoise
erminois
froise
noise
Noyes
poise
(see OI + s)

ŎJ
doge
gamboge
horologe

ŎJ
dislodge
dodge

hodge
hodge-podge
horologe
lodge
splodge
stodge
unlodge

ŌK
artichoke
asoak
awoke
baroque
besmoke
bespoke
bloke
broke
choke
cloak
coak
coke
convoke
counterstroke
croak
death-stroke
equivoque
evoke
folk
forespoke
forspoke
gentlefolk
invoke
joke
Larocque
loke
master-stroke
moke
oak
outbroke
poke
provoke

revoke
scrub-oak
sloke
smoke
soak
spoke
stoke
stroke
thunder-stroke
toke
toque
unbroke
uncloak
understroke
unyoke
up-broke
woke
yoke
yolk

ÔK
auk
awk
balk
cakewalk
calk
chalk
dawk
Falk
gawk
hawk
mawk
Mohawk
outwalk
pawk
sidewalk
sparrow-hawk
squawk
stalk
talk

tomahawk
walk

ŎK
acock
alpenstock
amok
Antioch
Bach
Bankok
baroque
bedrock
belock
bemock
billycock
Bloch
block
bock
brock
chock
chockablock
clock
cock
crock
dead-lock
dock
fetlock
firelock
flintlock
flock
forelock
frock
half-cock
havelock
hoc
hock
hollyhock
interlock
jock
knock
lady's-smock

āle, câre, ădd, ärm, ȧsk; mē, hẹre, ĕnd; īce, ĭll;

langue d'oc	**ŌKS**	**ŎKT**	feme-sole
laughing-	coax	concoct	foal
stock	hoax	decoct	foliole
Little Rock	Nokes	recoct	fumarole
loch	Oakes	unfrocked	furole
lock	Stokes	blocked, etc.	fusarole
love-lock	Vokes		girandole
Medoc	artichokes,	**ŌL**	girasole
mock	etc.	augur-hole	gloriole
Mohock		aureole	gloryhole
padlock	**ŎKS**	banderole	goal
Painted Rock	ballot-box	barcarolle	heart-whole
peacock	bandbox	bibliopole	hole
penstock	box	blowhole	inscroll
percussion-	chickenpox	bole	jowl
lock	Christmas-	boll	knoll
plock	box	borecole	kohl
pock	Cox	bowl	log-roll
poppycock	equinox	bunghole	loophole
Ragnarock	fox	buttonhole	Maypole
roc	hatbox	cajole	mole
rock	heterodox	camisole	oriole
shock	mailbox	capriole	parole
shuttle-cock	orthodox	caracole	patrol
smock	ox	carambole	peephole
soc	paddlebox	cariole	petiole
sock	paradox	carmagnole	pigeon-hole
spatch-cock	phlox	casserole	pinhole
stock	pillar-box	coal	pinole
stumbling-	powder-box	cole	pistole
block	signal-box	comptrol	pole
turkey-cock	smallpox	condole	poll
turncock	vox	console	porthole
understock	alpenstocks,	control	rantipole
undock	etc.	curtainpole	rigmarole
unfrock		dhole	role
unlock	**ŎKT**	dole	roll
weathercock	unprovoked	droll	scroll
weepingrock	water-soaked	enbowl	scupper-hole
woodcock	evoked, etc.	enroll	segol
		extoll	self-control

ōld, ôr, ŏdd, oil, fŏŏt, out; ūse, ûrn, ŭp; THis, thin

			ŌLD
Seminole	caterwaul	spall	**ŌLD**
shoal	caul	spawl	acold
shole	crawl	sprawl	afterhold
sole	disenthrall	spurgall	ahold
soul	drawl	squall	anchor-hold
stole	dwal	stall	behold
stroll	enthrall	tall	blindfold
tadpole	evenfall	therewithal	bold
thole	fall	thrall	bullet-mould
toll	fireball	trawl	clay-cold
tophole	football	trumpet-call	coaled
troll	footfall	wall	cold
unroll	forestall	waterfall	copyhold
unsoul	gall	wherewithal	enfold
unwhole	Gaul	windfall	fold
uproll	hall	withal	foothold
vacuole	haul	yawl	foretold
variole	install		fourfold
virole	judgment-hall	**ŎL**	freehold
vole	kraal	alcohol	gold
wassail-bowl	landfall	atoll	half-soled
whole	mall	baby doll	high-souled
	maul	capitol	hold
ŎL	McCall	consol	household
all	miscall	doll	ice-cold
all-in-all	nightfall	entresol	infold
appal	overfall	extol	interfold
awl	overhaul	folderol	leaf-mold
ball	pall	girasol	leasehold
banquet-hall	Paul	gun moll	Leopold
baseball	pawl	loll	manifold
basketball	pitfall	moll	marigold
bawl	rainfall	parasol	mold
befall	recall	poll	multifold
bemawl	Saul	protocol	old
Bengal	scall	Sol	overbold
bethrall	scrawl	vitriol	refold
blackball	sea-wall		retold
boxstall	shawl	**ŎLCH**	sable-stoled
brawl	small	Balch	scold
call	snowball	Walch	sold

---

spun-gold	holt	devolve	Jerome
stone-cold	jolt	dissolve	loam
stronghold	lavolt	evolve	metallochrome
thousandfold	molt	*exolve*	metronome
told	poult	intervolve	microsome
twice-told	revolt	involve	monochrome
twofold, etc.	shackle-bolt	resolve	nobody home
uncontrolled	smolt	revolve	no'm
unfold	thunderbolt	solve	Nome
unsold	unbolt		ohm
untold	volt	**ŌLVD**	palindrome
uphold		undissolved	polychrome
withhold	**ŌLT**	unresolved	pome
wold	assault	unsolved	roam
cajoled, etc.	basalt	absolved, etc.	Rome
	cobalt		Salome
ŌLD	default	**ŌM**	sea-foam
Archibald	envault	aerodrome	sea-holm
auld	exalt	afoam	sloam
blackballed	fault	befoam	tome
bald	gault	brome	
scald	halt	catacomb	**ŎM**
so called	malt	chrome	haum
unappalled	salt	chromosome	imaum
uncalled	seasalt	clomb	maum
unenthralled	smalt	comb	shawm
ungalled	somersault	currycomb	
unrecalled	spalt	dome	**ŎM**
appalled, etc.	vault	endome	aplomb
		foam	axiom
ŌLN	**ŌLTS**	Frome	bomb
swoln	false	gastronome	dom
	salts	*gloam*	from
ŎLSH	valse	gnome	hecatomb
Walsh	waltz	harvest-home	om
	assaults, etc.	heliochrome	pogrom
ŌLT		hippodrome	pompom
bolt	**ŌLV**	holm	rhomb
colt	absolve	home	swom
demi-volt	circumvolve	honey-comb	therefrom
dolt	convolve		

ŎMP

comp
pomp
romp
swamp
trompe

ŎMPT

imprompt
prompt
romped, etc.

ŎMZ

Holmes
(see ŎM + s)

ŎN

alone
antiphone
Athlone
atone
audiphone
backbone
baritone
begroan
bemoan
bestrown
blown
bone
Boulogne
brimstone
chaperone
cicerone
clingstone
Cologne
condone
cone
corner-stone
crone
curbstone
depone

dethrone
dictaphone
disown
dispone
Dordogne
drone
eau-de-cologne
electrophone
enthrone
enzone
flagstone
flown
foreknown
foreshown
foundation-
  stone
fresh-blown
full-blown
full-grown
gramophone
graphophone
grass-grown
grindlestone
grindstone
groan
grown
hailstone
headstone
hearthstone
high-flown
holy stone
hone
impone
imposing-stone
interpone
intone
Joan
keystone
known
knucklebone
ladrone

limestone
loadstone
loan
lone
macrotone
marrow-bone
megaphone
microphone
milestone
millstone
moan
monotone
moonstone
moss-grown
mown
ochone
outblown
overgrown
overthrown
own
phone
pone
postpone
prone
propone
radiophone
Rhone
roan
saxophone
semitone
sewn
shewn
shown
soapstone
sown
stone
strown
telephone
throne
thrown
tone

trombone
unbeknown
unblown
undertone
unforeknown
ungrown
unknown
unsewn
unsown
unthrone
vitaphone
weather-blown
whalebone
whetstone
xylophone
zone

ŎN

awn
"bawn"
brawn
"cawn"
dawn
drawn
faun
fawn
impawn
indrawn
lawn
pawn
prawn
sawn
spawn
undrawn
withdrawn
yawn

ŎN

agone
amazon
anon

antiphon	mastodon	haunch	**ŎNG**
automaton	Micklejohn	launch	all-along
Babylon	myrmidon	paunch	along
begone	Oberon		battlesong
Bellerophon	octagon	**ŎND**	belong
benison	on	high-toned	daylong
bonbon	Oregon	unatoned	ding dong
bonne	outshone	unmoaned	drinking-song
celadon	pantechnicon	unowned	dugong
Ceylon	paragon	unzoned	erelong
chiffon	Parthenon	zoned	evensong
colophon	pentagon	atoned, etc.	flong
con	phaeton		gong
cretonne	phenomenon	**ŎND**	headlong
decagon	polygon	beau monde	headstrong
demijohn	prolegomenon	demi-monde	Hong Kong
dies non	put upon	Fronde	lifelong
don	Rubicon	Gironde	livelong
Donne	Saskatchewan	monde	long
echelon	shone		mah-jongg
encephalon	silicon	**ŎND**	night-long
enchiridion	sine quâ non	abscond	overlong
encomion	stereopticon	beau monde	pingpong
Euroclydon	swan	beyond	prolong
glyptodon	tarragon	blond	prong
gone	thereon	bond	scuppernong
gonfalon	thereupon	correspond	sing-song
hanger-on	undergone	demi-monde	song
Helicon	upon	despond	souchong
hereon	wan	fond	strong
hereupon	whereon	frond	thong
hexagon	whereupon	overfond	throng
hoot mon	woebegone	plafond	tong
Hyperion	*yon*	monde	undersong
iguanodon	(cf. accordion,	pond	wong
irenicon	etc., under	respond	wrong
Jeanne	ŬN)	unparagoned	
John	Yvonne	vagabond	**ŎNGD**
lexicon		wand	unwronged
long-field-on	**ŎNCH**	*yond*	belonged, etc.
Luzon	craunch	donned, etc.	

ōld, ôr, ŏdd, oil, fŏŏt, out; ūse, ûrn, ŭp; THis, thin

ŎNGK

conch
conk
honk
honky-tonk

ŎNGKS

Bronx
conchs, etc.

ŎNGST

alongst
belong'st
long'st
prolong'st
throng'st
wrong'st

ŎNGZ

tongs
belongs, etc.

ŎNS

ensconce
nonce
response
sconce

ŎNT

don't
won't

ÔNT

aflaunt
a-taunt
avaunt
daunt
flaunt
gaunt
haunt
jaunt

romaunt
taunt
vaunt
want

ŎNT

Dupont
font
Hellespont
want

ŎNTS

fonts
wants
(cf. nonce)

ŎNZ

Davy Jones
Jones
nones
atones, etc.

ŎNZ

bonze
bronze
by-gones
Johns
pons
(see ŎN+s)

OŎD

could
dead-wood
firewood
good
hood
misunderstood
plastic wood
purple-wood
sandal-wood
should

stood
understood
Underwood
unhood
wildwood
withstood
wood
would
angelhood
babyhood
brotherhood
deaconhood
fatherhood
foolhardihood
gentlemanhood
hardihood
kinglihood
kittenhood
ladyhood
likelihood
livelihood
lustihood
maidenhood
manhood
matronhood
monk's-hood
motherhood
neighbourhood
orphanhood
parenthood
sisterhood
spinsterhood
unlikelihood
widowerhood
widowhood
womanhood

OŎK

betook
book
brook

Chinook
cook
crook
forsook
hook
ingle-nook
look
minute-book
mistook
nook
outlook
overlook
overtook
partook
pastry-cook
pocket-book
rook
shook
took
unhook
undertook
uplook

OŎKS

Crookes
snooks
tenterhooks
crooks, etc.

OŌL

abb-wool
bull
cock-and-bull
full
lamb's-wool
pull
wool
beautiful
bountiful
dutiful
fanciful

āle, câre, ădd, ārm, ȧsk; mē, hĕre, ĕnd; īce, ĭll;

masterful	illegible	insensible	ratable
merciful	immovable	insoluble	redeemable
pitiful	immutable	insupportable	reliable
plentiful	impalpable	insupposable	reprehensible
powerful	impassable	insuppressible	respectable
sorrowful	impeccable	insurmountable	responsible
thimbleful	imperturbable	intangible	sensible
unmerciful	implacable	intelligible	susceptible
weariful	impossible	interchange-	syllable
wonderful	impregnable	able	tangible
worshipful	improbable	intractible	tenable
acceptable	improvable	invaluable	terrible
accessible	inaccessible	invincible	tractable
accountable	inadmissible	irascible	unimpeachable
adorable	inaudible	irrepressible	unmatchable
affable	incapable	irreproachable	unquenchable
amenable	incomparable	irresistible	visible
amiable	incompatible	irresponsible	voluble
attainable	incomprehen-	irretrievable	
audible	sible	justifiable	**ŎŎLF**
available	inconceivable	laudable	wolf
avoidable	incontestable	legible	
believable	incontrovert-	Mehitable	**ŎŎLVZ**
capable	ible	mutable	wolves
changeable	incorruptible	notable	
combustible	incredible	ostensible	**ŎŎS**
commendable	incurable	palpable	puss
compatible	indelible	passable	
constable	indescribable	perceptible	**ŎŎSH**
contemptible	indestructible	permissible	bramble-bush
corruptible	indispensable	placable	bush
crucible	ineffable	plausible	push
culpable	ineffaceable	portable	
damnable	inexcusable	possible	**ŎŎSK**
delectable	inexhaustible	praisable	brusque
deplorable	inexpressible	presentable	
desirable	infallible	principle	**ŎŎT**
detestable	inflammable	probable	afoot
flexible	inflexible	procurable	foot
forcible	infrangible	producible	forefoot
horrible	inscrutable	pronounceable	pussyfoot

put
underfoot

ŎP

agrope
antelope
anti-pope
aslope
astroscope
baroscope
bioscope
cantaloupe
Cape of Good
  Hope
cope
dispope
dope
electroscope
elope
envelope
foot-rope
galvanoscope
grope
gyroscope
helioscope
heliotrope
hope
horoscope
hydroscope
interlope
kaleidoscope
lope
microscope
misanthrope
mope
ope
polariscope
pope
rope
scope
seismoscope

slope
soap
spectroscope
stereoscope
stethoscope
stope
telescope
thermoscope
tope
trope
unpope

ŎP

gaup
scaup
whaup
yawp

ŎP

after-crop
atop
bedrop
chop
co-op
cop
crop
drop
eavesdrop
estop
flipflop
flippity-flop
flop
fop
foretop
galop
ginger-pop
hop
knop
lollipop
lop

overtop
mizzen top
mop
overtop
plop
pop
prop
shop
slop
snowdrop
soda pop
sop
stop
strop
swap
tiptop
top
underprop
unstop
whop
wop
workshop

ŎPS

copse
drops, etc.

ŎPT

unhoped
unsoaped
eloped, etc.

ŎPT

adopt
copped
Copt
outcropped
uncropped
unstopped
dropped, etc.

ŌR

adore
afore
albacore
ashore
back-door
Baltimore
battledore
before
boar
Boer
bore
chore
commodore
core
corps
crore
death's-door
deplore
door
encore
evermore
explore
first-floor
floor
folklore
foot-sore
forbore
fore
foreshore
forswore
four
fourscore
frore
furthermore
galore
gore
heartsore
heretofore
hoar
ignore

implore	upsoar	inheritor	visitor
inshore	weather-shore	inquisitor	war
Lahore	whore	interior	
lore	wore	interlocutor	**ŌRB**
matador	yore	janitor	absorb
mirador		Labrador	corb
more	**ŌR**	legator	orb
nevermore	abhor	lessor	reabsorb
oar	ambassador	lor	resorb
o'er	ancestor	louis d'or	
ore	anterior	man-of-war	**ŌRBD**
outpour	apparitor	matador	full-orbed
outroar	assignor	metaphor	absorbed, etc.
outsoar	auditor	meteor	
Parramore	bachelor	minotaur	**ŌRCH**
picador	chancellor	mirador	porch
pinafore	competitor	monitor	
pore	compositor	mortgagor	**ŌRCH**
pour	conqueror	nominor	bortsch
restore	conspirator	nor	scorch
roar	contributor	or	torch
sagamore	corridor	orator	
score	councillor	posterior	**ŌRD**
sea-shore	counsellor	primogenitor	aboard
semaphore	creditor	progenitor	afford
shore	depositor	proprietor	beaverboard
Singapore	dinosaur	Salvador	board
snore	dor	scaur	broadsword
soar	Dukhobor	senator	ford
sophomore	Ecuador	senor	gourd
sore	editor	servitor	hoard
spore	emperor	solicitor	horde
stevedore	excelsior	superior	ironing-board
store	executor	therefor	oared
swore	expositor	Thor	seaboard
sycamore	exterior	tor	shuffle-board
Theodore	for	toreador	surfboard
tore	governor	troubadour	sword
troubadour	guarantor	ulterior	undeplored
underscore	ichthyosaur	verderor	unexplored
uproar	inferior	vice-chancellor	ungored

ōld, ôr, ŏdd, oil, fŏŏt, oᴜt; ūse, ûrn, ŭp; THis, thin

unhoard	**ŌRJ**	deiform	borne
unimplored	forge	dendriform	bourn
unrestored		diversiform	foot-worn
weather-board	**ŌRJ**	floriform	forborne
adored, etc.	disgorge	form	forsworn
	engorge	inform	mourn
ŌRD	George	misform	outworn
accord	gorge	misinform	overborne
award	regorge	multiform	sea-worn
belord	**ŌRK**	norm	shorn
bord		perform	sworn
chord	pork	reform	toil-worn
concord	**ŌRK**	snow-storm	torn
cord	cork	stelliform	unshorn
disaccord	fork	storm	unsworn
fiord	New York	sunny-warm	water-worn
fjord	"orch"	swarm	wave-worn
harpsichord	stork	thunder-storm	way-worn
landlord	torque	transform	weather-worn
lord	uncork	uniform	worn
lyrichord	weeding-fork	unwarm	(cf. adorn, etc.)
master-chord	York	upswarm	
McCord		vermiform	**ŌRN**
misericord	**ŌRKD**	warm	adorn
Orde	storked		alpen-horn
overlord	corked, etc.	**ŌRMD**	barleycorn
polychord		unformed	bescorn
record	**ŌRL**	uninformed	blackthorn
reward	orle	unperformed	born
sward	schorl	unreformed	buckthorn
unlord	whorl	unstormed	Cape Horn
ward		well-informed	Capricorn
abhorred, etc.	**ŌRM**	bestormed, etc.	cloudborn
	aeriform		corn
ŌRF	aquiform	**ŌRMTH**	disadorn
corf	bestorm	warmth	dishorn
dwarf	chloroform	*storm'th,* etc.	drinking-horn
wharf	conform		first-born
	cruciform	**ŌRN**	fog-horn
ŌRG	cuneiform	bemourn	forewarn
morgue	deform	betorn	forlorn

French-horn	**ŌRND**	remorse	**ŌRT**
greenhorn	unadorned	retrorse	abort
hawthorn	unforewarned	sea-horse	amort
heaven-born	adorned, etc.	stalking-horse	assort
high-born		torse	athwart
horn	**ŌRP**	unhorse	bort
Horne	dorp		cavort
hunting-horn	thorp	**ŌRSK**	consort
inborn	warp	torsk	contort
Langhorne			*detort*
longicorn	**ŌRPS**	**ŌRST**	distort
lorn	corpse	addorsed	escort
love-lorn	warps, etc.	endorsed	exhort
Matterhorn		horsed	extort
morn	**ŌRS**	Horst	mort
night-born	coarse	unhorsed	*ort*
Norn	course		quart
peppercorn	discourse	**ŌRT**	resort
popcorn	divorce	comport	retort
powder-horn	enforce	county court	short
priming-horn	force	court	snort
readorn	hoarse	davenport	sort
scorn	intercourse	*decourt*	*swart*
sea-born	perforce	deport	thwart
self-scorn	recourse	disport	tort
sky-born	reinforce	export	wart
still-born	resource	fort	(cf. court, etc.)
suborn	source	forte	
thorn	water-course	import	**ŌRTH**
tricorn		misreport	forth
trueborn	**ŌRS**	passport	fourth
unborn	corse	port	henceforth
unicorn	deadhorse	Porte	setter-forth
warn	dextrorse	rapport	thenceforth
yestermorn	*dorse*	report	*pour'th*, etc.
	endorse	sally-port	
	gorse	seaport	**ŌRTH**
ŌRND	hobby-horse	sport	north
bemourned	horse	support	Orth
mourned	Morse	transport	swarth
unmourned	Norse	(cf. ŌRT)	*abhorr'th*, etc.

ōld, ôr, ŏdd, oil, fŏŏt, out; ūse, ûrn, ŭp; THis, thin

ÔRTS

quartz
Schwartz
shorts
Swarz
aborts, etc.

ÔRVZ

wharves

ÔRZ

all-fours
Azores
indoors
outdoors
adores, etc.

ÔRZ

Louis-
   Quatorze
quatorze
(see ÔR + s)

ŎS

actuose
adipose
aggerose
albuminose
animose
annulose
bellicose
cellulose
close
comatose
cose
diagnose
dose
engross
floccose
foliose
gibbose

globose
glucose
grandiose
gross
jocose
metempsy-
   chose
morose
nodose
otiose
overdose
underdose
verbose

ŎS

applesauce
sauce

ŎS

across
albatross
Bos
boss
coloss
cross
doss
double cross
dross
emboss
fiery-cross
floss
fosse
gloss
joss
lacrosse
loss
moss
recross
rhinoceros
rosy-cross
sea-moss

Setebos
toss
weeping-cross

ŎSH

Foch
gauche
guilloche

ŎSH

awash
bellywash
bewash
bosch
bosh
debosh
frosh
galosh
gosh
hogwash
kibosh
josh
mackintosh
McIntosh
musquash
quash
slosh
squash
swash
splosh
tosh
wash

ŎSHT

caboshed
great unwashed
unwashed
squashed, etc.

ŎSK

bosk

imbosk
kiosk
mosque

ŎSP

wasp

ŎST

aftermost
bettermost
boast
bottommost
coast
dosed
engrossed
finger-post
foremost
furthermost
ghost
hindermost
hithermost
host
innermost
lowermost
most
nethermost
northernmost
oast
outermost
post
riposte
roast
sea-coast
southernmost
toast
undermost
uppermost
uttermost
westernmost
whipping-post

āle, câre, ădd, ärm, àsk; mē, hĕre, ĕnd; īce, ĭll;

ŎST	denote	vote	thought
exhaust	devote	wrote	unbesought
holocaust	dote	Witenagemot	unbought
	float	wrote	unfraught
ŎST	folkmote		unfought
accost	footnote	ŎT	untaught
adossed	garrote	aeronaut	unthought
betossed	gloat	after-thought	unwrought
cabossed	goat	argonaut	upbrought
cost	groat	*astraught*	upcaught
double crossed	life-boat	aught	wrought
embossed	*lote*	besought	
enmossed	misquote	*bestraught*	ŎT
frost	moat	bethought	aliquot
geognost	mote	*bewrought*	allot
hoar-frost	note	bought	apricot
Lacoste	oat	brought	asquat
lost	outvote	caught	beauty-spot
Pentecost	overcoat	dear-bought	begot
sea-tossed	petticoat	distraught	bergamot
tempest-tost	pilot-boat	dreadnought	besot
uncrossed	promote	forethought	blot
unlost	quote	fought	bott
wast	redevote	fraught	cachalot
crossed, etc.	redingote	freethought	calotte
	remote	ghât	Camelot
ŎT	river-boat	hard-fought	capot
afloat	rote	inwrought	clot
anecdote	scote	Juggernaut	compatriot
antidote	sea-boat	maut	cocotte
asymptote	shote	merry-thought	cot
bedote	slote	*methought*	counterplot
bequote	smote	naught	dogtrot
bloat	stoat	nought	dot
boat	table d'hote	onslaught	dry-rot
capote	telephote	ought	eschalot
coat	throat	overwrought	fiery-hot
commote	tote	selftaught	first-begot
connote	troat	sought	forget-me-not
cote	underwrote	taught	forgot
creosote	unsmote	taut	gallipot

ōld, ôr, ŏdd, oil, fŏŏt, out; ūse, ûrn, ŭp; THis, thin

garrote	swat	**Ŏth**	*enow*
gavotte	tot	Ashtaroth	Foochow
got	tommyrot	barley-broth	frau
grape-shot	trot	behemoth	frow
grass-plot	*unbegot*	broadcloth	Hankow
grot	underplot	broth	hoosegow
hard-got	undershot	cloth	how
hot	unforgot	Coth	Howe
Hottentot	ungot	froth	kow-tow
Huguenot	unknot	Goth	Kwangchow
ill-got	*wat*	moth	landau
ink-pot	watt	Ostrogoth	mow
jogtrot	what	pilot-cloth	now
jot	witenagemot	saddle-cloth	overbrow
knot	*wot*	troth	plough
kumquat	yacht	Visigoth	plow
lot		wroth	powwow
love-knot	**ŌTH**		prow
misbegot	clothe	**ŌTS**	row
not	loathe	Coates	scow
overshot		Oates	slough
patriot	**Ŏth**	boats, etc.	snow-plough
plague-spot	aftergrowth		somehow
plot	behemoth	**ŎTS**	Soochow
polyglot	betroth	Potts	sow
pot	both	(see ŎT + s)	Swatow
quot	growth		*thou*
rot	loath	**OU**	upplow
sans-culotte	oath	allow	vow
Scot	overgrowth	anyhow	Wenchow
Scott	*quoth*	avow	wow
shallot	sloth	bough	
shot	Thoth	bow	**OUCH**
shoulder-knot	troth	bow-wow	avouch
sighting-shot	undergrowth	brow	couch
slot		chow	crouch
somewhat	**Ŏth**	cow	grouch
sot	swath	dhow	ouch
spot	wrath	disallow	pouch
squat	wroth	disavow	scaramouch
Stott		endow	

āle, câre, ădd, ärm, åsk; mē, hĕre, ĕnd; īce, ĭll;

slouch
vouch

OUD

aloud
becloud
beetle-browed
beshroud
cloud
crowd
disendowed
disenshroud
encloud
enshroud
intercloud
loud
overcloud
overcrowd
proud
shroud
thunder-cloud
unbowed
uncloud
unshroud
allowed, etc.

OUJ

gouge
scrouge

OUL

afoul
befoul
behowl
cowl
dowl
foul
fowl
growl
guinea-fowl

howl
jowl
owl
peafowl
prowl
scowl
screech-owl
sea-fowl
water-fowl

OULD

uncowled
befouled, etc.

OUN

adown
brown
clown
crown
decrown
discrown
down
downtown
drown
eider-down
embrown
frown
godown
gown
hand-me-down
noun
nut-brown
reach-me-down
renown
town
tumble-down
uncrown
ungown
upside-down
uptown

OUND

abound
aground
around
astound
back-ground
bloodhound
bound
boozehound
compound
confound
dumfound
expound
flower-crowned
found
ground
hell-bound
hidebound
home-bound
hound
icebound
impound
inbound
iron-bound
Mahound
merry-go-round
middle-ground
mound
outbound
outward-bound
pine-crowned
pleasure-
    ground
pound
profound
propound
rebound
redound
renowned
resound
round

smuthound
sound
spell-bound
superabound
surround
triple-crowned
unbound
underground
unground
unsound
vantage-ground
wound
browned, etc.

OUNDZ

zounds
abounds, etc.

OUNJ

lounge

OUNS

announce
bounce
denounce
enounce
flounce
frounce
ounce
pounce
pronounce
renounce
rounce
trounce
(cf. accounts,
    etc.)

OUNT

account
amount
catamount

ōld, ôr, ŏdd, oil, fŏŏt, out; ūse, ûrn, ŭp; THis, thin

count	customhouse	diner-out	whereout
discount	doghouse	doubt	without
dismount	douse	drinking-bout	
fount	flindermouse	drought	**OUTH**
miscount	flittermouse	flout	mouthe
mount	Gnauss	gadabout	
paramount	grouse	gout	**OUth**
recount	house	grout	bemouth
remount	Kraus	hereabout	drouth
surmount	louse	*hereout*	mouth
tantamount	madhouse	holing-out	south
	Mickey Mouse	knockabout	*allow'th,* etc.
OUNTS	mouse	knockout	
accounts, etc.	nous	knout	**OUTS**
(cf. announce,	outhouse	kraut	hereabouts
etc.)	penthouse	look-out	outs
	pleasure-house	lout	thereabouts
OUR	poorhouse	mahout	whereabouts
bescour	prison-house	out	bouts, etc.
besour	public-house	out-and-out	
deflour	slaughterhouse	pout	**OUZ**
devour	souse	redoubt	arouse
flour	storehouse	right-about	blouse
hour	warehouse	roundabout	blowze
our	whorehouse	roustabout	bouse
scour	workhouse	rout	browse
sour		sauerkraut	carouse
sustaining hour	**OUST**	scout	drowse
(cf. OU'ur.)	browst	shout	espouse
	oust	snout	house
OURD	roust	spout	rouse
unsoured	unhoused	sprout	souse
bescoured, etc.	choused, etc.	stirabout	spouse
		stout	touse
OUS	**OUT**	thereabout	unhouse
backhouse	about	thereout	uprouse
blouse	beshout	throughout	(see OU + s)
chapterhouse	bespout	tout	
charnelhouse	bout	trout	**ŌV**
charterhouse	clout	water-spout	clove
chouse	devout	whereabout	cove

āle, câre, ădd, ärm, åsk: mē, hĕre, ĕnd; īce, ĭll;

dove	close	presuppose	taws
drove	clothes	propose	vase
grove	compose	prose	yaws
hove	couleur-de-rose	recompose	(see Ō + s)
interwove	damask-rose	repose	
inwove	decompose	rose	**ŎZ**
Jove	depose	superpose	Boz
mauve	disclose	suppose	Oz
rove	discompose	those	was
shrove	dispose	transpose	
stove	doze	tuberose	**ŌZD**
strove	enclose	unclose	dozed
throve	expose	unfroze	ill-disposed
treasure-trove	foreclose	(see Ō + s)	indisposed
wove	froze		juxtaposed
	gloze	**ÔZ**	predisposed
ŎV	hose	applause	unopposed
hereof	impose	because	well-disposed
of	inclose	cause	closed, etc.
thereof	indispose	clause	
whereof	*interclose*	Dawes	**ŌZH**
	interpose	gauze	eloge
ŌZ	moss-rose	Hawes	loge
arose	nose	hawse	
bramble-rose	oppose	lantern-jaws	**ŎZM**
brose	pose	menopause	macrocosm
chose	predispose	pause	microcosm

ōld, ôr, ŏdd, oil, fŏŏt, out; ūse, ûrn, ŭp; THis, thin

U

These words include the following accented vowels sounds :

Ū as in use; heard also in beauty, feud, pew, queue, lieu, view, cue, suit, yule, you, do, rule, true, food, group, drew, fruit, canoe, rheum, maneuvre, blue. The difference between *dew* and *do* is that *dew* is properly dyŪ, with a consonantal *y* sound preceding the long U; while *do* is merely dŪ.

Û as in urn; heard also in fern, err, heard, sir, word, journal, myrrh, colonel.

Ŭ as in up; heard also in won, one, does, flood, double.

For the vowel sound in *full,* see under ŎO.

Ū	brew	derring-do	Gentoo
acajou	bugaboo	dew	glue
accrue	cachou	do	gillaroo
adieu	canoe	drew	gnu
ado	caribou	due	googoo
anew	cashew	Elihu	grew
aperçu	catechu	emu	halloo
askew	chandoo	endew	haut-gout
avenue	chew	endue	hereinto
baboo	clew	ensue	hereto
ballyhoo	clue	entre nous	hereunto
bamboo	cockatoo	eschew	hew
barbecue	construe	ewe	Hindu
barley-broo	coo	feu	hitherto
battue	corkscrew	feverfew	honeydew
bayou	coup	few	hoodoo
bedew	crew	fichu	hue
beshrew	cuckoo	firenew	Hugh
bestrew	cue	Fitzhugh	hullabaloo
billet-doux	curlew	flew	igloo
blew	Daibutsu	flu	imbrue
blue	Daikoku	flue	imbue
boo	debut	*fordo*	immew
boohoo	Depew	foreknew	impromptu

āle, câre, ădd, ärm, åsk; mē, hĕre, ĕnd; īce, ĭll;

indue	pursue	tew	yahoo
ingenue	queue	thereinto	yew
interview	ragout	thereto	yoohoo
in transitu	rendezvous	thereunto	you
I.O.U	renew	thew	zoo
Jew	residue	thitherto	Zulu
Kalamazoo	retinue	threw	
kangaroo	revenue	through	ŬB
karroo	review	Timbuktu	boob
Kew	rough hew	to	cube
kinkajou	roux	to-do	Rube
knew	rue	too	tube
lieu	screw	toodle-oo	
loo	sea-mew	to-whit-towhoo	ŬB
Manitou	set-to	true	battle-club
meadow-rue	shampoo	trueblue	Beelzebub
mew	shoe	two	blub
misconstrue	shoo	unclew	bub
misdo	shrew	underdo	chub
moo	Sioux	undo	Chubb
mountain-dew	skew	undue	club
napoo	skidoo	unglue	Clubb
new	sky-blue	unmew	cub
night-dew	slew	unscrew	drub
outdo	sloo	untrue	dub
overdo	slough	view	fub
overdue	slue	view-halloo	grub
overstrew	smew	virtu	hub
overthrew	sou	voodoo	hubbub
parvenu	spew	wahoo	nub
passe-partout	sprue	wallaroo	pub
peekaboo	stew	wanderoo	rub
perdu	strew	well-to-do	rub-a-dub
Peru	subdue	whew	scrub
pew	sue	whereinto	shrub
phew	sundew	whereto	sillabub
pooh	surtout	whereunto	slub
preview	*surview*	who	snub
prie-dieu	taboo	withdrew	stub
Pugh	tattoo	woo	sub
Purdue			tub

ŬCH

brooch
cooch
hooch
hoochy-cooch
mooch
pooch

ŬCH

clutch
crutch
cutch
Dutch
for-as-much
hutch
in-as-much
in-so-much
master-touch
much
mutch
overmuch
retouch
scutch
smutch
such
touch

ŬCHD

untouched
clutched, etc.

ŪD

abrood
abstrude
acerbitude
acritude
allude
altitude
amaritude
amplitude

aptitude
assuetude
attitude
beatitude
brood
certitude
claritude
collude
conclude
consuetude
crassitude
crude
decrepitude
definitude
delude
denude
desuetude
detrude
disquietude
dude
elude
exactitude
exclude
extrude
exude
feud
finitude
food
fortitude
gratitude
habitude
hebetude
home-brewed
illude
inaptitude
incertitude
include
ineptitude
infinitude
ingratitude

inquietude
insuetude
interclude
interlude
intrude
Jude
lassitude
latitude
lenitude
lewd
longitude
magnitude
mansuetude
mollitude
mood
multitude
necessitude
nude
obtrude
occlude
parvitude
platitude
plenitude
pood
preclude
prelude
promptitude
protrude
prude
pulchritude
quietude
rainbow-hued
reclude
rectitude
retrude
rood
rude
seclude
senectitude
serenitude

servitude
shrewd
similitude
slewed
snood
solicitude
solitude
stude
subnude
subtrude
thewed
torpitude
transude
turpitude
unglued
unpursued
unrenewed
unrude
unrued
unstrewed
unsubdued
unwooed
(see Ū+ed)
vastitude
verisimilitude
vicissitude
you'd

ŪD

bestud
blood
bud
Budd
cud
dud
flood
fud
Judd
life-blood
lud
mud

rudd   breadstuff   bepuffed, etc.   subterfuge
'sblood   buff   (cf. scuft)   vermifuge
scud   chough
spud   chuff   ŬG   ŬJ
stud   clough   fugue   adjudge
thud   counterbuff   begrudge
                cuff   ŬG   budge
ŬDZ   duff   bug   drudge
duds   enough   bunnyhug   forejudge
suds   fluff   doodlebug   fudge
buds, etc.   garden-stuff   drug   grudge
                gruff   dug   judge
ŬF   huff   fug   misjudge
aloof   luff   hug   nudge
behoof   muff   jug   prejudge
bullet-proof   powder-puff   lug   rejudge
disproof   puff   mug   Rudge
fire-proof   rebuff   plug   sludge
foolproof   rough   pug   smudge
gable-roof   ruff   rug   trudge
goof   scruff   shrug
hoof   scuff   slug   ŬJD
loof   slough   smug   ill-judged
opera-bouffe   snuff   snug   unjudged
proot   sough   thug   adjudged, etc.
reproof   stuff   trug
roof   tough   tug   ŬK
shadoof   tuff   archduke
spoof   ŬGZ   bashi-bazouk
Tartuffe   ŬFS   go bugs   beduke
unroof   fisticuffs   drugs, etc.   chibouk
virtue-proof   bepuffs, etc.   Chinook
waterproof   ŬJ   duke
weather-proof   ŬFT   demonifuge   fluke
woof   clovenhoofed   febrifuge   Heptateuch
                hoofed   gamboge   Hexateuch
ŬF   roofed, etc.   huge   juke
bepuff   insectifuge   Luke
besnuff   ŬFT   Scrooge   mameluke
blindman's-buff candytuft   scrouge   Marmaduke
bluff   tuft   stooge   Pentateuch

ōld, ôr, ŏdd, oil, fŏŏt, out; ūse, ûrn, ŭp; THis, thin

peruke
puke
rebuke
snook
spook
stook

ŬK

amuck
awestruck
beduck
buck
Canuck
chuck
cluck
Donald Duck
duck
horror-struck
ill-luck
Kalmuck
lame duck
laverock
luck
misluck
muck
pluck
pot-luck
puck
roebuck
ruck
rukh
shuck
struck
stuck
suck
terror-struck
thunder-struck
truck
tuck
waterbuck

woodchuck
wonderstruck

ŬKS

crux
dux
flux
lux
shucks
(see ŬK + s)

ŬKT

abduct
aqueduct
conduct
construct
deduct
duct
educt
eruct
good-plucked
induct
instruct
misconduct
misconstruct
obstruct
oviduct
product
reduct
reluct
subduct
substruct
superstruct
unplucked
usufruct
viaduct
beducked, etc.

ŪL

April-fool
befool

buhl
charity-school
cool
drool
ducking-stool
fool
footstool
ghoul
Istambul
Liverpool
mewl
misrule
molecule
mule
O'Toole
overrule
pool
pule
reticule
ridicule
rule
school
spool
stool
Sunday School
toadstool
tool
Toole
tulle
vermicule
vestibule
whirpool
who'll
you'll
Yule

ŬL

ahull
annul
barnacle

chronicle
cull
disannul
dull
gull
hull
lull
miracle
Mogul
monocle
mull
null
numskull
obstacle
pinnacle
scull
sea-gull
skull
spectacle
stull
trull
vehicle
versicle

ŬLB

bulb

ŬLCH

gulch
mulch

ŪLD

unruled
unschooled
(see UL + d)

ŬLD

mulled
thick-skulled
annulled, etc.

āle,　câre,　ădd,　ärm.　ăsk;　mē,　hẹre,　ĕnd;　īce,　ĭll;

ŬLF	pulse	diningroom	unplume
engulf	repulse	drawing-room	tomb
gulf	(cf. adult + s)	dressing-room	untomb
		elbow-room	whom
ŬLJ	**ŬLT**	embloom	womb
bulge	adult	engloom	
divulge	catapult	entomb	**ŬM**
effulge	consult	enwomb	ad libitum
indulge	cult	exhume	adventuresome
promulge	difficult	flume	adytum
	exult	foredoom	aquarium
ŬLK	incult	fume	auditorium
bulk	indult	gloom	become
hulk	insult	groom	benumb
skulk	occult	grume	bum
sulk	result	heirloom	Bumbledom
		illume	burdensome
ŬLKT	**ŪLZ**	inhume	cardamom
bulked	gules	jibboom	Christendom
mulct	(see ŪL + s)	Khartoum	chrysanthe-
hulked, etc.		legume	mum
	ŪM	livingroom	chum
ŬLM	abloom	loom	Cockneydom
culm	*addoom*	lumber-room	come
	anteroom	perfume	compendium
ŪLP	assume	plume	cranium
poulp	begloom	power-loom	crematorium
	beplume	predoom	crum
ŬLP	bloom	presume	crumb
gulp	boom	reading-room	cumbersome
pulp	bridegroom	reassume	curriculum
sculp	broom	relume	delirium
	brougham	resume	drearisome
ŬLS	brume	rheum	drum
appulse	consume	room	dumb
bulse	coom	sea-room	emporium
convulse	coomb	simoom	encomium
dulse	costume	spoom	epithalamium
expulse	disentomb	spume	equilibrium
impulse	displume	subsume	exordium
mulse	doom		fee-fi-fo-fum

flunkeydom
frolicsome
geranium
glum
grum
gum
gymnasium
halidom
heathendom
hum
humdrum
humorsome
intermeddle-
    some
kettle-drum
laudanum
Lum
martyrdom
maximum
meddlesome
medium
mettlesome
millennium
minimum
misbecome
modicum
moratorium
mum
natatorium
numb
odium
opium
opprobrium
overcome
pabulum
palladium
pandemonium
pelargonium
pendulum
pericardium
petroleum

platinum
plum
plumb
premium
prud'homme
quarrelsome
quietsome
radium
rascaldom
rebeldom
recumb
residuum
rhumb
rum
sanatorium
Saxondom
scrum
scum
sensorium
slum
some
speculum
strum
stum
succumb
sugar-plum
sum
swum
symposium
tedium
thrum
thumb
troublesome
tum
tum-tum
tweedledum
tympanum
unplumb
vacuum
venturesome
viaticum

wearisome
worrisome
wranglesome

ŪMD

assumed, etc.
full-bloomed
implumed
unfumed
ungloomed
unillumed
addoomed, etc.

ŬMD

begummed
bethumbed
unplumbed
benumbed, etc.

ŬMP

bethump
bump
chump
clump
crump
dump
frump
hump
jump
lump
mugwump
mump
plump
pump
rump
slump
stump
sump
thump
trump

tump
ump

ŬMPS

mumps
bethumps, etc.

ŪN

afternoon
aswoon
attune
baboon
balloon
barracoon
bassoon
batoon
bestrewn
boon
bridoon
Broun
buffoon
Calhoun
cartoon
cocoon
Colquoun
commune
coon
croon
Doon
doubloon
dragoon
dune
eftsoon
entune
excommune
expugn
festoon
forenoon
frigatoon
gadroon
galloon

ăle, câre, ădd, ārm, ăsk; mē, hĕre, ĕnd; īce, ĭll;

gambroon	quintroon	Chesterton	Parthenon
gazon	racoon	done	pentagon
gossoon	Rangoon	dun	percussion-gun
harpoon	ratoon	Dunn	phenomenon
harvest-moon	rigadoon	foredone	polygon
hewn	rough-hewn	forerun	prolegomenon
honey-moon	rune	foster-son	pun
immune	saloon	fun	quaternion
inopportune	Schroon	galleon	run
importune	seroon	Galveston	sally lunn
impugn	shalloon	ganglion	shun
intercommune	*shoon*	garrison	simpleton
jejune	simoon	gonfalon	singleton
June	soon	gun	skeleton
lacune	spadroon	halcyon	son
lagoon	spittoon	hard-run	spun
lampoon	spontoon	hard-won	stun
loon	spoon	Helicon	sun
lune	strewn	homespun	sunn
macaroon	swoon	hon	ton
Mahoun	tune	Hun	tun
maroon	Tycoon	jettison	unbegun
mid-noon	typhoon	Middleton	underrun
monsoon	untune	minute-gun	undone
moon	walloon	mon	unison
musketoon		myrmidon	unnun
noon	**ŬN**	none	venison
octoroon	A 1	nun	Whitsun
opportune	accordion	Number one	won
oppugn	Albion	Oberon	
oversoon	amazon	oblivion	**ŬNCH**
overstrewn	begun	octagon	brunch
pantaloon	benison	one	bunch
patroon	bun	orison	clunch
picaroon	Bunn	outdone	crunch
picayune	cardamon	outrun	hunch
platoon	caparison	orison	lunch
poltroon	cinnamon	overdone	munch
pontoon	colophon	overrun	punch
prune	comparison	pantechnicon	punch
quadroon		paragon	scrunch

ōld, ôr, ŏdd, oil, fŏŏt, out; ūse, ûrn, ŭp; THis, thin

ŬND

disattuned
unattuned
untuned
wound
attuned, etc.
crooned, etc.

ŬND

bund
cummerbund
dunned
fund
immund
moribund
obrotund
orotund
punned
refund
retund
Rosamond
rotund
rubicund
shunned
stunned
unparagoned
unsunned
verecund
(cf. ŬN+ed)

ŬNG

among
behung
betongue
bung
clung
dung
flung
high-strung
hung
lung

mother-tongue
overhung
pung
rung
slung
sprung
strung
stung
sung
swung
tongue
underhung
Ung
unhung
unstrung
unsung
unwrung
upsprung
wither-wrung
wrung
young

ŬNGD

bunged
double-tongued
honey-tongued
leather-lunged
loud-lunged
pleasant-
    tongued
shrill-tongued
silver-tongued
tongued
trumpet-
    tongued

ŬNGK

bunk
chunk
drunk

flunk
funk
hunk
junk
monk
plunk
punk
quidnunc
shrunk
skunk
slunk
spunk
stunk
sunk
trunk
unk
wunk

ŬNGKT

bunked
compunct
conjunct
defunct
disjunct
funked
trunked

ŬNGST

amongst
clung'st, etc.

ŬNJ

allonge
blunge
dispunge
expunge
lunge
muskellunge
plunge
sponge

ŬNS

dunce
once
(cf.affront+s)

ŬNT

affront
afront
blunt
brunt
bunt
confront
exeunt
forefront
front
grunt
hunt
Lunt
punt
runt
shunt
sprunt
stunt
wont

ŬNTH

month
run'th, etc.

ŬNZ

Cameroons
eftsoons
croons, etc.

ŬP

adroop
aggroup
apple-scoop
cantaloupe

āle,   câre,   ădd,   ärm,   ȧsk;   mē,   hẹre,   ĕnd;   īce,   ĭll;

cock-a-hoop
coop
croup
droop
drupe
dupe
Guadeloupe
group
hoop
jupe
liripoop
loop
nincompoop
poop
recoup
roup
scoop
scroop
sloop
soup
stoop
stoup
supe
swoop
troop
troupe
unhoop
whoop

ŬP
blowing-up
buttercup
crup
cup
fed up
grace-cup
gup
hard-up
keyed-up
loving-cup
make-up

pup
scup
setter-up
slap-up
stirrup-cup
sup
tup
up
up-and-up
wassail-cup

ŬPT
abrupt
corrupt
cupped
disrupt
erupt
incorrupt
interrupt
supped

ŪR
abature
abbreviature
abjure
adjure
allure
amateur
amour
aperture
armature
assure
blackamoor
boor
breviature
brochure
calenture
candidature
caricature
cocksure
colure

comfiture
conjure
connoisseur
contour
coverture
cure
curvature
cynosure
demure
detour
discomfiture
divestiture
dure
endure
ensure
entablature
epicure
expenditure
forfeiture
furniture
garmenture
garniture
guipure
immature
immure
impure
insecure
insure
intermure
inure
investiture
judicature
Kohinoor
ligature
liqueur
literature
lure
manicure
manure
mature
miniature

moor
obscure
Ostermoor
overture
paramour
pedicure
perdure
perendure
poor
portraiture
premature
primogeniture
procure
pure
quadrature
reassure
reinsure
secure
sepulture
signature
sinecure
spoor
sure
tablature
temperature
tour
troubadour
unmoor
unsure
vestiture
water-cure
your
you're
(cf. Ū+er)

ŬR
aberr
astir
aver
befur

bestir	coeur	batterer	demolisher
blur	colporteur	bibliographer	determiner
burr	connoisseur	bickerer	diameter
chirr	farceur	biographer	diaper
concur	franc-tireur	blandisher	discoverer
confer	friseur	blazoner	disparager
cur	frondeur	blunderer	distributer
defer	hauteur	blusterer	dowager
demur	litterateur	borrower	driveller
deter	mitrailleur	botherer	embellisher
disinter	persifleur	brandisher	emblazoner
err	restaurateur	broiderer	enameler
fir	trouveur	burdener	encourager
fur	voltigeur	burnisher	endeavourer
her	voyageur	calender	engenderer
incur		caliper	enlightener
infer	administer	canister	enlivener
inter	admonisher	carpenter	establisher
Kerr	adulterer	caterer	examiner
knur	adventurer	cellarer	Excalibur
liqueur	affiancer	chafferer	executioner
myrrh	almoner	challenger	fashioner
occur	amphitheatre	character	favorer
per	answerer	chatterer	flatterer
prefer	arbiter	cherisher	flutterer
purr	archiater	chorister	forager
recur	armiger	chronicler	foreigner
refer	armourer	cofferer	forester
shirr	artificer	comforter	forfeiter
sir	astrologer	commissioner	furtherer
slur	astronomer	commoner	galloper
spur	autobiographer	confectioner	gardener
stir	baluster	conjurer	gatherer
transfer	banisher	coroner	gossamer
were	banister	cottager	gossiper
whir	banqueter	coverer	harbinger
	banterer	cricketer	harborer
accoucheur	bargainer	customer	harvester
amateur	barometer	cylinder	hexameter
chasseur	barrister	decipherer	idolater
chauffeur	barterer	deliverer	imprisoner

āle, câre, ădd, ärm, åsk; mē, hęre, ĕnd; īce, ĭll;

interpreter	pepperer	saunterer	victualer
islander	perjurer	scavenger	villager
jabberer	pesterer	scimiter	vintager
juniper	petitioner	sepulchre	visiter
Jupiter	pewterer	sinister	voyager
languisher	philologer	skirmisher	wagerer
lavender	philosopher	slanderer	wagoner
lavisher	phonographer	slaughterer	wanderer
lecturer	photographer	slumberer	wassailer
leveller	pilferer	smatterer	waverer
libeller	pillager	sophister	whimperer
lingerer	pitier	sorcerer	whisperer
lithographer	plasterer	splutterer	widower
loiterer	plunderer	squanderer	wonderer
Londoner	polisher	stenographer	worshipper
Lowlander	porringer	stutterer	
lucifer	posturer	succorer	blearier
malingerer	poulterer	sufferer	breezier
manager	practitioner	swaggerer	brinier
manufacturer	presbyter	tamperer	burlier
mariner	prisoner	terrier	cheerfuller
marshaller	probationer	tetrameter, etc.	cheerier
massacre	profferer	theatre	cheerlier
measurer	provender	thermometer	chillier
messenger	publisher	thunderer	cleanlier
milliner	punisher	topographer	cosier
minister	purchaser	torturer	costlier
miniver	quarreller	totterer	creamier
modeller	quaverer	traveller	creepier
murderer	questioner	treasurer	crueller
murmurer	ransomer	trespasser	curlier
mutterer	ravager	trumpeter	dingier
nourisher	ravisher	typographer	dizzier
officer	reasoner	upholsterer	doughtier
palaverer	register	usurer	dowdier
parishioner	relinquisher	utterer	drearier
passenger	reveller	valuer	drowsier
pasturer	reversioner	vanquisher	dustier
patterer	rioter	vaporer	earlier
pensioner	riveter	venturer	easier
pentameter	roisterer	verderer	eerier

ōld, ôr, ŏdd, oil, fŏŏt, out; ūse, ûrn, ŭp; THis, thin

emptier	lovelier	stingier	**ŬRCH**
evener	lowlier	stormier	besmirch
filmier	loyaler	stuffier	birch
filthier	merrier	stupider	church
fleecier	mightier	sturdier	lurch
flightier	moldier	sunnier	perch
flimsier	mossier	surlier	research
foamier	mournfuller	thirstier	search
friendlier	muskier	thriftier	smirch
funnier	mustier	timider	weeping-birch
fussier	narrower	trustier	
giddier	noisier	vivider	**ŬRCHT**
gloomier	pearlier	wealthier	unsmirched
glossier	pleasanter	wearier	birched, etc.
goutier	portlier	wheezier	
grimier	princelier	windier	**ŬRD**
guiltier	prosier	winsomer	gourd
happier	rosier	wintrier	reassured
healthier	rowdier	(cf. ambassador	self-assured
heavier	ruggeder	and other ŎR	unassured
hillier	seemlier	words)	uninsured
holier	shinier		unmatured
homelier	shoddier	**ŬRB**	abjured, etc.
horrider	showier	acerb	ensured, etc.
huffier	sightlier	blurb	
hungrier	silenter	curb	**ŬRD**
huskier	sillier	disturb	absurd
icier	skilfuller	gerb	begird
inkier	skinnier	herb	bird
jollier	sleepier	perturb	Cape Verde
juicier	slimier	Serb	curd
kindlier	soapier	suburb	engird
kinglier	solider	superb	frigate-bird
knightlier	spicier	verb	gallows-bird
likelier	spikier		gird
lissomer	spongier	**ŬRBD**	heard
lithesomer	spoonier	imperturbed	hedge-bird
livelier	springier	uncurbed	herd
loftier	spritelier	undisturbed	humming-bird
lonelier	steadier	unperturbed	Kurd
lonesomer	stealthier	curbed, etc.	

---

lady-bird	dramaturge	smirk	whirl
lovebird	emerge	stirk	whorl
mocking-bird	gurge	Turk	
night-bird	immerge	underwork	**ÛRLD**
overheard	merge	water-work	impearled
pilot-bird	purge	wonderwork	new-world
sea-bird	scourge	work	old-world
sherd	serge	yerk	pearled
shirred	splurge		uncurled
snow-bird	Spurge	**ÛRKT**	underworld
song-bird	submerge	overworked	world
storm-bird	surge	irked, etc.	becurled, etc.
surd	thaumaturge		
third	urge	**ÛRL**	**ÛRM**
undergird	verge	becurl	affirm
ungird		bepearl	berm
unsepulchred	**ÛRJD**	burl	confirm
verd	unurged	charity-girl	derm
word	converged, etc.	churl	disaffirm
(see ÛR + ed)		curl	firm
	ÛRK	earl	germ
ÛRF	O'Rourke	furl	infirm
scurf		girl	isotherm
serf	**ÛRK**	hurl	misterm
surf	Burke	impearl	pachyderm
turf	cirque	knurl	reaffirm
	clerk	merle	sperm
ÛRG	dirk	mother-of-pearl	squirm
berg	fancy-work	pearl	term
burg	frostwork	pirl	worm
exergue	handiwork	purl	
Goldberg	irk	querl	**ÛRMD**
Heidelberg	jerk	seed-pearl	unconfirmed
iceberg	jerque	skirl	affirmed, etc.
	kirk	swirl	
ÛRJ	lurk	thurl	**ÛRN**
converge	master-work	twirl	bourn
demiurge	murk	uncurl	
deterge	perk	unfurl	**ÛRN**
dirge	quirk	upcurl	adjourn
diverge	shirk	upwhirl	astern

attorn	urn	**ŬRS**	verse
Berne	yearn	accurse	worse
burn		adverse	
Byrne	**ŬRND**	amerce	**ŬRST**
churn	hard-earned	asperse	accurst
concern	unconcerned	averse	athirst
Dern	undiscerned	becurse	becurst
durn	unlearned	birse	burst
discern	unturned	burse	curst
earn	adjourned, etc.	coerce	double-first
erne		converse	durst
eterne	**ŬRNT**	curse	*erst*
externe	burnt	cutpurse	first
fern	earnt	disburse	Hearst
Hearn	learnt	disperse	Hurst
Hearne	unburnt	diverse	outburst
hern	unlearnt	Erse	thirst
intern	weren't	excurse	uncursed
interne		foster-nurse	unversed
inurn	**ŬRNZ**	hearse	versed
kern	Burns	herse	verst
learn	Kearns	imburse	worst
lucern	(see ŬRN + s)	immerse	accursed, etc.
lucerne		inhearse	
O'Byrne	**ŬRP**	intersperse	**ŬRT**
overturn	blurp	inverse	Adelbert
pirn	burp	nurse	advert
quern	chirp	perverse	alert
return	discerp	precurse	animadvert
secern	*extirp*	purse	assert
sojourn	twirp	rehearse	avert
spurn	usurp	reimburse	begirt
stern		reverse	Bert
subaltern	**ŬRPT**	sesterce	blurt
taciturn	chirped	submerse	cert
tern	excerpt	subverse	chert
turn	usurped	terce	concert
unconcern		terse	controvert
unlearn	**ŬRS**	transverse	convert
upturn	bourse	traverse	curt
		universe	desert

āle, câre, ădd, ärm, åsk; mē, hẹre, ĕnd; īce, ĭll;

dessert
dirt
disconcert
divert
engirt
Englebert
Ethelbert
evert
exert
expert
exsert
extrovert
flirt
girt
gurt
hurt
indesert
inert
inexpert
insert
intersert
intervert
introvert
invert
liverwort
malapert
obvert
pert
pervert
preconcert
retrovert
revert
sea-girt
shirt
skirt
spirt
spurt
squirt
subvert
syrt
transvert

ungirt
unhurt
vert
wert
Wirt
wort

ÛRTH

berth
birth
dearth
earth
firth
fuller's-earth
girth
inearth
mirth
penny-worth
Perth
unearth
unworth
worth

ÛRTZ

Wurtz
(see ÛRT + s)

ÛRV

conserve
curve
deserve
disserve
incurve
nerve
observe
outcurve
preserve
reserve
serve
subserve
swerve

unnerve
verve

ÛRVD

ill-deserved
undeserved
well-preserved
conserved, etc.

ÛRVZ

turves
conserves, etc.

ÛRZ

Tours
yours
amours, etc.

ÛRZ

furze
(see ÛR + s)

ŪS

abstruse
abuse
adduce
Bruce
burnoose
caboose
calaboose
Charlotte-russe
conduce
cruse
deduce
deuce
diffuse
disuse
douce
Druce
educe

excuse
flower-de-luce
goose
hypotenuse
induce
introduce
juice
loose
luce
misuse
moose
noose
nous
pappoose
obtuse
occluse
pertuse
produce
profuse
puce
recluse
reduce
reproduce
retuse
Roos
Russ
seduce
sluice
spruce
superinduce
Syracuse
Toulouse
traduce
transluce
truce
unloose
unsluice
use
vamoose
Zeus

ŬS

abaculus
abacus
acephalus
angelus
animus
blunderbuss
bus
buss
caduceus
Cerberus
convolvulus
cumulus
cuss
denarius
discuss
Erebus
esophagus
excuss
fuss
harquebus
Hesperus
hippopotamus
humerus
hydrocephalus
ignis fatuus
impetus
incubus
incuss
Leviticus
minimus
muss
nautilus
nonplus
nucleus
octopus
omnibus
overplus
Pegasus
percuss
phosphorus

platypus
plus
polypus
pus
radius
ranunculus
repercuss
rhus
Russ
sarcophagus
Sirius
stimulus
succubus
syllabus
tantalus
Tartarus
terminus
thus
truss
untruss
us

abstemious
acclivitous
acephalous
acidulous
adulterous
adventurous
agricolous
albuminous
aliferous
aligerous
alimonious
alkalous
alluvious
aluminous
amatorious
Americus
amorous
ambiguous
amphibolous

amphibious
analogous
androgenous
androphagous
anemophilous
anfractuous
angulous
anomalous
anonymous
anserous
antipathous
aqueous
arborous
arduous
armigerous
assiduous
augurous
balsamiferous
barbarous
beauteous
bibulous
bicephalous
bigamous
bipetalous
bituminous
blasphemous
blusterous
boisterous
bounteous
bulbiferous
burdenous
burglarious
cadaverous
calamitous
calcareous
calumnious
cancerous
cankerous
cantankerous
carboniferous
carnivorous

cautelous
cavernous
censorious
ceremonious
chivalrous
cinereous
circuitous
clamorous
commodious
congruous
compendious
consanguin-
  eous
conspicuous
contempora-
  neous
contemptuous
conterminous
contiguous
continuous
contrarious
contumelious
copious
courteous
covetous
crapulous
credulous
crepusculous
Cretaceous
criminous
curious
dangerous
deciduous
deleterious
delirious
devious
dexterous
diaphanous
diatomous
discourteous
disingenuous

---

doloriferous	gratuitous	inharmonious	multivious
dolorous	gregarious	iniquitous	murderous
dubious	harmonious	injurious	murmurous
dulcifluous	hazardous	innocuous	mutinous
duteous	herbaceous	inodorous	mysterious
emulous	heterogeneous	inquisitorious	nauseous
endogenous	hideous	insensuous	nebulous
envious	hilarious	insidious	necessitous
eponymous	homogeneous	instantaneous	nectareous
equilibrious	homologous	invidious	nefarious
erroneous	humorous	jeopardous	notorious
ethereous	idolatrous	laborious	numerous
exiduous	igneous	languorous	oblivious
expurgatorious	ignominious	lascivious	obsequious
extempora-	illustrious	lecherous	obstreperous
neous	*imaginous*	leguminous	obvious
extraneous	*immeritous*	libellous	odious
fabulous	impecunious	libidinous	odoriferous
farinaceous	imperious	ligneous	odorous
fastidious	impervious	litigious	oleaginous
fatuitous	impetuous	ludicrous	ominous
fatuous	impious	lugubrious	omnivorous
felicitous	imponderous	luminous	onerous
felonious	imposturous	luxurious	opprobrious
terruginous	incendious	magnanimous	oviparous
fluminous	incestuous	marvelous	pachyderma-
fortitudinous	incommodious	mellifluous	tous
fortuitous	incongruous	melodious	parsimonious
fossiliferous	inconspicuous	membranous	pendulous
frivolous	incredulous	meretorious	penurious
fuliginous	incurious	metalliferous	perfidious
furious	indecorous	meticulous	periculous
garrulous	indigenous	miraculous	perilous
gelatinous	indubious	miscellaneous	perjurous
generous	industrious	mischievous	perspicuous
globulous	inebrious	monogamous	pervious
glorious	infamous	monotonous	pesterous
glutenous	infelicitous	mountainous	pestiferous
glutinous	ingenious	mucilaginous	petalous
gluttonous	ingenuous	multifarious	piteous
graminivorous	inglorious	multitudinous	platinous

ŏld, ôr, ŏdd, oil, fŏŏt, out; ūse, ûrn, ŭp; THis, thin

platitudinous

plenteous

poisonous

polygamous

ponderous

populous

posthumous

precarious

precipitous

predaceous

preposterous

presumptuous

previous

promiscuous

prosperous

pseudony-

  mous

punctilious

pusillanimous

quarrelous

querulous

rancorous

rapturous

ravenous

rebellious

resinous

ridiculous

rigorous

riotous

roisterous

ruinous

sacchariferous

salacious

salubrious

sanctimonious

sanguineous

saponaceous

savorous

scandalous

scintillous

scrofulous

scrupulous

scrutinous

scurrilous

sedulous

sensuous

serious

setaceous

sibilous

simultaneous

sinuous

slanderous

slumberous

solicitous

somniferous

spontaneous

spurious

stentorious

strenuous

stridulous

studious

subterraneous

sulphurous

sumptuous

supercilious

superfluous

synchronous

synonymous

tautologous

tedious

temerarious

tempestuous

tenebrous

tenuous

thunderous

timidous

timorous

tintinnabulous

tortuous

torturous

traitorous

treacherous

treasonous

tremulous

tuberculous

tumultuous

tyrannous

ubiquitous

unanimous

unchivalrous

undulous

unscrupulous

uproarious

ungenerous

usurious

uxorious

vacuous

vagarious

vainglorious

valetudinarious

valetudinous

valorous

vaporous

various

vegetous

velutinous

venomous

ventriculous

venturous

verdurous

verisimilous

verminous

vernaculous

vertiginous

vicarious

vicissitudinous

victorious

vigorous

villainous

viperous

virtuous

vitreous

viviparous

vociferous

voluminous

voluptuous

voraginous

vortiginous

vulturous

zoophagous

ŬSH

barouche

bonne-bouche

bouche

cartouche

debouch

douche

gobemouche

Hindu Kush

Joosh

mouche

ruche

Scaramouch

ŬSH

blush

brush

crush

flush

gush

hush

lush

missel-thrush

mush

outblush

outrush

plush

rush

slush

thrush

tush

underbrush

uprush

āle,   câre,   ădd,   ärm,   åsk;   mē,   hẹre,   ĕnd;   īce,   ĭll;

ŬSK

adusk
brusque
busk
dehusk
dusk
fusc
husk
Lusk
musk
rusk
subfusk
tusk

ŬSP

cusp

ŬST

adduced
unproduced
deduced, etc.

boost
browst
joust
loosed
noosed
roost
spruced
unloosed
roust
vamoosed

ŬST

adjust
adust
angust
august
bedust
betrust
bust

coadjust
combust
crust
disgust
distrust
dost
dust
encrust
entrust
fust
gust
just
lust
mistrust
must
non-plussed
robust
rust
self-distrust
stardust
thrust
trust
unjust
untrussed
(see ŬS + ed)

ŪT

absolute
acute
argute
arrowroot
astute
attribute
baldicoot
beaut
birthday suit
boot
bruit
brute
Butte
cahoot

cheroot
chute
comminute
commute
compute
confute
constitute
coot
cornute
cute
deaf-mute
depute
destitute
dilute
dispute
disrepute
dissolute
electrocute
emeute
enroot
en route
execute
first-fruit
flute
forbidden-fruit
fruit
galoot
hirsute
hoot
imbrute
immute
impute
institute
involute
irresolute
jute
loot
lute
marabout
meute
minute

moot
mute
newt
outshoot
overshoot
parachute
permute
persecute
Piute
pollute
prosecute
prostitut/
pursuit
Rajput
recruit
refute
repute
resolute
root
route
salute
scoot
scute
shoot
snoot
solute
soot
subacute
substitute
suit
suppute
toot
transmute
unboot
unroot
uproot
upshoot
Ute
versute
volute

ŬT
abut
astrut
besmut
betel-nut
but
butt
catgut
clear-cut
coconut
crut
cut
glut
gut
halibut
hut
jut
Lilliput
McNutt
mutt
nut
occiput
outshut
peanut
putt
rebut
rut
scut
scuttle-butt
shut
slut
smut
strut
surrebut
tut
uncut
waterbutt
woodcut

ŬTH
besmooth

booth
polling-booth
smooth
soothe

Ūth
booth
Duluth
forsooth
insooth
ruth
sleuth
sooth
tooth
truth
uncouth
untooth
untruth
youth

Ŭth
doth

ŪTHD
unsoothed
smoothed, etc.

ŪTS
cahoots
boots, etc.

ŬTS
smuts
(see ŬT + s)

ŪV
amove
approve
behoove
disapprove
disprove

groove
improve
ingroove
move
prove
remove
reprove
you've

ŬV
above
belove
dove
foxglove
glove
lady-love
light-o'-love
love
mourning-dove
self-love
shove
true-love
turtle-dove
unglove

ŪVD
unimproved
unmoved
unproved
unreproved
approved, etc.

ŬVD
unbeloved
unloved
beloved, etc.

ŪZ
abuse
accuse
amuse

bemuse
Betelgeuse
blues
booze
bruise
choose
circumfuse
confuse
contuse
cruise
cruse
diffuse
disabuse
disuse
effuse
enthuse
excuse
fuse
guze
Hughes
incuse
infuse
interfuse
lose
mews
misuse
muse
news
noose
ooze
percussion-fuse
perfuse
peruse
refuse
ruse
Santa Cruz
sea-ooze
snooze
suffuse
superinfuse

āle, câre, ădd, ärm, åsk; mē, hęre, ĕnd; īce, ĭll;

the blues	**ŬZ**	does	ill-used
transfuse	Chartreuse	doz.	misused
trews		fuzz	self-accused
use	**ŬZ**	Luz	abused, etc.
Vera Cruz		Uz	
who's	abuzz		**ŪZH**
whose	buzz	**ŪZD**	rouge
(see Ū + s)	coz	fused	Bruges

ōld, ôr, ŏdd, oil, fŏŏt, out; ūse, ûrn, ŭp; THis, thiŋ

WORDS ACCENTED ON THE SYLLABLE BEFORE THE LAST: PENULTS; FEMININE RHYMES; DOUBLE RHYMES

A

For a discussion of words included under the accented vowels following, see the beginning of A rhymes in Section I.

Ā'ad
naiad

Ā'al
Baal
betrayal
defrayal
portrayal
surveyal

Ā'an
Biscayan

Ā'ans
abeyance
conveyance
purveyance
surveyance

Ā'ant
abeyant

Ā'ba
copaiba
Faba

Ä'ba
Kaaba

Ā'ban
Laban

ĂB'ard
(see ĂB'urd)

ĂB'as
Barabbas

ĂB'ath
Sabbath

Ä'be
Rabe

ĂB'er etc.
(see ĂB'ur, etc.)

ĂB'es
abbess

ĂB'est
blabbest
dabbest
drabbest
gabbest
grabbest

jabbest
stabbest

ĂB'eth
blabbeth
dabbeth
gabbeth
grabbeth
jabbeth
stabbeth

Ā'bez
Jabez
tabes
(cf. Ā'bi + s)

Ā'bi
Abey
baby
maybe

ĂB'i
abbey
Abbie
babby
cabby
crabby
dabby

drabby
flabby
gabby
grabby
rabbi
scabby
shabby
slabby
tabby

Ä'bi
kohl-rabi
tabi
Wahabi

ĂB'id
rabid
tabid

ĂB'ij
cabbage

ĂB'ik
decasyllabic
dissyllabic
hendecasylla-
  bic
imparisyllabic

āle, câre, ădd, ärm, ăsk; mē, hẹre, ĕnd; īce, ĭll;

monosyllabic	able	*dabblest*	re-establish
multisyllabic	Abe'll	*drabblest*	*stablish*
octosyllabic	Babel	*gabblest*	**Ā'blur**
parisyllabic	cable	*scrabblest*	abler
polysyllabic	disable		disabler
quadrisyllabic	enable	**ĂB'let**	enabler
syllabic	fable	tablet	fabler
trisyllabic	*flabel*		stabler
	gable	**ĂB'leth**	tabler
ĀB'ĭl	label	*cableth,* etc.	
labile	Mabel		**ĂB'lur**
(cf. ĀB'l)	sable	**ĂB'leth**	babbler
	stable	*babbleth*	bedrabbler
Ā'bin	table	*bedabbleth*	brabbler
Sabine	unable	*brabbleth*	cabbler
	unstable	*dabbleth*	dabbler
ĂB'ing		*drabbleth*	drabbler
blabbing	**ĂB"l**	*gabbleth*	gabbler
cabbing	babble	*grabbeth*	grabbler
confabbing	bedabble	*scrabbleth*	scabbler
dabbing	bedrabble		scrabbler
gabbing	brabble	**ĂB'li**	
jabbing	cabble	babbly	**Ā'bob**
nabbing	dabble	dabbly	nabob
slabbing	drabble	drably	
stabbing	gabble		**ĂB'ot**
taxicabbing	gibble-gabble	**ĂB'ling**	abbot
	grabble	babbling	Abbott
ĂB'it	rabble	bedabbling	Cabot
cohabit	ribble-rabble	bedrabbling	sabot
grab it	scabble	brabbling	
habit	scrabble	cabbling	**Ă'bra**
inhabit		dabbling	candelabra
rabbet	**Ā'blest**	drabbling	
rabbit	ablest	gabbling	**Ā'brak**
riding-habit	*cablest,* etc.	grabbling	day-break
		scrabbling	
ĂB'jekt	**ĂB'lest**		**ĂB'sens**
abject	*babblest*	**ĂB'lish**	absence
	bedabblest	disestablish	
Ăb'l	*bedabblest*	establish	**ĂB'sent**
Abel	*brabblest*		absent

Ă'bur	**ĂCH'est**	hatches	hatchment
beggar-my-	*attachest*	latches	*ratchment*
neighbor	*catchest*	matches	
belabor	*detachest*	Natchez	**ĂCH'up**
caber	*dispatchest*	patches	catchup
Gheber	*hatchest*	scratches	
labor	*latchest*	snatches	**ĂCH'ur**
neighbor	*matchest*	thatches	attacher
saber	*patchest*	unlatches	back-scratcher
tabor	*scratchest*		body-snatcher
	snatchest	**ĂCH'i**	catcher
ĂB'ur	*thatchest*	catchy	cony-catcher
beslabber	*unlatchest*	patchy	detacher
blabber		snatchy	dispatcher
bonny-clabber	**ĂCH'et**		fly-catcher
dabber	Bob Cratchet	**ĂCH'ing**	hatcher
grabber	hatchet	attaching	matcher
jabber	latchet	batching	patcher
knabber	ratchet	catching	scratcher
nabber		detaching	snatcher
slabber	**ĂCH'eth**	dispatching	Thacher
stabber	*attacheth*	hatching	thatcher
	batcheth	latching	unlatcher
ĀB'urd	*catcheth*	matching	
unlabored	*detacheth*	patching	**ĂCH'wa**
belabored, etc.	*dispatcheth*	scratching	hatchway
	hatcheth	snatching	
ĂB'urd	*latcheth*	thatching	**ĂCH'wurk**
beslabbered	*matcheth*	unlatching	catchwork
jabbered	*patcheth*		patchwork
scabbard	*scratcheth*	**ĂCH'les**	
slabbered	*snatcheth*	matchless	**Ā'dā**
tabard	*thatcheth*	patchless	hey-day
	unlatched	scratchless	lay-day
ĂCH'el		thatchless	May-day
Rachel	**ĂCH'ez**		pay-day
Vachel	attaches	**ĂCH'ment**	play-day
	batches	attachment	
ĂCH'el	catches	catchment	**Ā'dā**
hatchel	detaches	detachment	Ada
satchel	dispatches	dispatchment	armada

āle,   câre,   ădd,   ärm,   ȧsk;   mē,   hẽre,   ĕnd;   īce,   ĭll;

cicada	aided	heavy-laden	*madest*
Grenada	ambuscaded	laden	*over-persuadest*
Maida	barricaded	maiden	*persuadest*
Veda	bejaded	menhaden	*pervadest*
Zayda	blockaded	mermaiden	staidest
	braided	milkmaiden	*tradest*
ĂD'a	brocaded	overladen	*upbraidest*
dada	cannonaded	sea-maiden	*wadest*
	degraded	serving-maiden	
ĂD'a	dissuaded	underladen	**ĂD'est**
armada	evaded	unladen	*addest*
cicada	faded		baddest
Dada	graded	**ĂD'en**	*gaddest*
Granada	invaded	engladden	gladdest
Grenada	jaded	gladden	maddest
haggada	masqueraded	McFadden	*paddest*
Nevada	persuaded	madden	saddest
posada	pervaded	Macfadden	
Sierra Nevada	raided	sadden	**ĂD'eth**
	serenaded		*aideth*
ĂD'am	shaded	**ĂD'en**	*bejadeth*
Adam	traded	Aden	*braideth*
madam	unaided		*degradeth*
McAdam	unbraided	**ĂD'ens**	*dissuadeth*
	unfaded	cadence	*evadeth*
ĂD'ans, ĂD'ens	unshaded	(see ĂD'ans)	*fadeth*
aidance	upbraided		*invadeth*
cadence	waded	**ĂD'ent**	*madeth*
decadence		cadent	*over-per-*
	ĂD'ed	(see ĂD'ant)	*suadeth*
ĂD'ant, ĂD'ent	added		*persuadeth*
abradant	padded	**ĂD'est**	*pervadeth*
aidant	plaided	*abradest*	*raideth*
cadent	superadded	*aidest*	*serenadeth*
decadent		*bejadest*	*spadeth*
	ĂD'en	*braidest*	*tradeth*
ĂD'kap	Aden	*degradest*	*upbraideth*
madcap	Aidenn	*dissuadest*	*wadeth*
	bower-maiden	*evadest*	
ĂD'ed	dairy-maiden	*fadest*	**ĂD'eth**
abraded	handmaiden	*invadest*	*addeth*

ōld, ôr, ŏdd, oil, fŏŏt, out; ūse, ûrn, ŭp; THis, thin

gladdeth   Mahdi   lading   faddish
paddeth   wadi   masquerading   gladdish
                                  overlading   maddish
ĂD'ez   ĂD'ij   over-persuad-   radish
Hades   adage   ing   saddish
(cf. ĂD'its)   parading
                  ĂD'ik   persuading   ĂD'it
ĂD'ful   decadic   pervading   adit
gladful   dyadic   raiding
madful   faradic   retrograding   ĀD'iz
sadful, etc.   haggadic   serenading   ladies, etc.
                  monadic   shading
Ā'di   nomadic   spading   ĂD'iz
belady   Sotadic   trading   caddies, etc.
Brady   sporadic   unbraiding
braidy   tetradic   underaiding   ĂD'jet
cadi   triadic   unlading   gadget
cascady   vanadic   upbraiding   Padgett
fady   wading
glady   AD'ing   ĀD"l
Grady   abrading   ĂD'ing   cradle
lady   aiding   adding   encradle
landlady   ambuscading   gadding   ladle
Maidie   barricading   gladding
O'Grady   bejading   madding   ĂD"l
shady   blockading   padding   addle
                  braiding   superadding   astraddle
ĂD'i   brocading   bestraddle
caddie   cascading   ĂD'is   daddle
caddy   co-aiding   Addis   faddle
daddy   crusading   caddis   fiddle-faddle
faddy   degrading   paddle
finnan haddie   dissuading   ĂD'ish   raddle
laddie   enfilading   maidish   saddle
paddy   evading   mermaidish   skedaddle
plaidie   fading   oldmaidish   spraddle
sugar daddy   free-trading   staidish   staddle
                  gasconading   straddle
Ă'di   grading   ĂD'ish   unsaddle
cadi   invading   baddish
irade   jading   caddish   ĀD'les
                                                   aidless

barricadeless
bladeless
braidless
brigadeless
brocadeless
fadeless
gradeless
maidless
paradeless
serenadeless
shadeless
spadeless
tradeless

ĂD'li

gradely
retrogradely
staidly

ĂD'li

badly
Bradley
gladly
madly
sadly

ĂD'ling

cradling
encradling
ladling

ĂD'ling

addling
daddling
faddling
fiddle-faddling
paddling
raddling
saddling
skedaddling
straddling

spraddling
unsaddling

ĂD'lok

padlock

ĂD'lur

addler
daddler
faddler
fiddle-faddler
paddler
raddler
saddler
skedaddler
straddler

ĂD'man

Cadman

ĂD'mus

Cadmus

ĂD'ne

Ariadne

ĂD'nes

staidness
unstaidness

ĂD'nes

badness
gladness
madness
plaidness
sadness

Ā'do

ambuscado
barricado
bastinado

camisado
carbonado
crusado
dado
desperado
fumado
gambado
grenado
muscovado
renegado
scalado
stoccado
strappado
tornado

ĂD'o

foreshadow
overshadow
shadow

Ă'do

amontillado
amorado
avocado
bravado
Colorado
dado
desperado
El Dorado
imbrocado
Mikado
passado
pintado
stoccado
strappado
travado

ĂD'od

foreshadowed
overshadowed

shadowed
unshadowed

ĂD'ok

haddock
paddock
raddocke
shaddock

ĂD'on

Abaddon

ĂD'os

extrados
intrados

ĂD'pol

tadpole

ĂD'som

gladsome
madsome

ĂD'ur

aider
barricader
blockader
braider
crusader
degrader
dissuader
evader
free-trader
gasconader
grader
harquebusader
invader
nadir
over-persuader
parader
persuader

promenader	delayest	betrayeth	Ā'far
raider	dismayest	bewrayeth	Mayfair
serenader	disobeyest	brayeth	Playfair
trader	displayest	conveyeth	
unbraider	essayest	decayeth	Ā'feld
upbraider	flayest	defrayeth	Mayfield
wader	frayest	delayeth	Rayfield
	gainsayest	dismayeth	
ĂD'ur	gayest	disobeyeth	ĂF'est
adder	grayest	displayeth	chafest
bladder	greyest	essayeth	safest
gadder	inlayest	frayeth	vouchafest
gladder	inveighest	gainsayeth	
ladder	layest	inlayeth	ĂF'eth
madder	mislayest	inveigheth	chafeth
padder	missayest	layeth	Japheth
sadder	obeyest	mislayeth	vouchsafeth
step-ladder	overpayest	missayeth	
	overstayest	obeyeth	ĂF'gan
Ă'dur	payest	overpayeth	Afghan
cadre	playest	overstayeth	
	portrayest	payeth	ĂF'i
ĂD'us	prayest	playeth	baffy
gradus	preyest	portrayeth	chaffy
	purveyest	prayeth	daffy
ĂD'vent	repayest	preyeth	draffy
advent	sayest	purveyeth	taffy
	slayest	repayeth	
ĂD'vurb	sprayest	sayeth	ĂF'ik
adverb	stayest	slayeth	anaglypto-
	surveyest	stayeth	graphic
Ā'est	swayest	strayeth	autobiographic
allayest	underpayest	surveyeth	autographic
arrayest	uplayest	swayeth	bibliographic
assayest	waylayest	underpayeth	biographic
bayest	weighest	uplayeth	cacographic
betrayest		waylayeth	calligraphic
bewrayest	Ā'eth	weigheth	cartographic
brayest	allayeth		cinemato-
conveyest	arrayeth	ĂF'a	graphic
defrayest	assayeth	café	chirographic

āle, câre, ădd, ärm, ăsk; mē, hẽre, ĕnd; īce, ĭll;

choregraphic
chorographic
clinographic
cosmographic
cryptographic
crystallo-
  graphic
diagraphic
epigraphic
epitaphic
ethnographic
galvanographic
geographic
glyptographic
graphic
heliographic
heterographic
hierographic
historiographic
holographic
homolographic
horologio-
  graphic
hydrographic
hyetographic
ichnographic
ideographic
idiographic
lexicographic
lexigraphic
lichenographic
lithographic
logographic
maffick
monographic
orographic
orthographic
paleographic
pantographic
paragraphic
pasigraphic

petrographic
phonographic
photographic
polygraphic
pornographic
Sapphic
scenographic
sciagraphic
seismographic
selenographic
seraphic
siderographic
sphenographic
stenographic
stereographic
stratigraphic
stratographic
stylographic
tachygraphic
telegraphic
topographic
traffic
uranographic
xylographic
zincographic
zoographic

ĂF'ing
chafing
enchafing
vouchsafing

ĂF'ing
chaffing
gaffing
graffing
heliographing
lithographing
paragraphing
photographing

stenographing
telegraphing

ĂF'ing
laughing
quaffing
strafing

ĂF'ir
sapphire

ĂF'ish
raffish

ĂF'l
baffle
gaffle
haffle
raffle
scraffle
snaffle
yaffle

ĀF'li
safely
unsafely

ĂF'ling
baffling
haffling
raffling
scraffling
snaffling

ĂF'lur
baffler
haffler
raffler
scraffler

ĂF'ne
Daphne

ĂF'old
Saffold
scaffold
(cf. baffled,
    etc.)

ĂF'ral
taffrail

ĂF'rik
Afric

ĂF'ron
saffron

ĂF'som
laughsome

ĂF'ted
upwafted
wafted

ĂF'ted
drafted
engrafted
grafted
ingrafted
rafted
shafted
wafted

ĂF'test
daftest
draughtest
graftest
waftest

ĂF'teth
draughteth
grafteth
wafteth

ōld, ôr, ŏdd, oil, fŏŏt, out; ūse, ûrn, ŭp; THis, thin

ĂFT'hors
draft-horse
shaft-horse

ĂF'tĭ
safety

ĂF'tĭ
crafty
drafty
grafty

ĂF'tĭj
waftage

ĂF'ting
engrafting
drafting
grafting
hafting
rafting
shafting
wafting

ĂFT'les
craftless
draftless
graftless
raftless
shaftless

ĂF'ton
Afton
Grafton

ĂFTS'man
craftsman
draftsman
handicraftsman
raftsman

ĂF'tūr
wafture

ĂF'tūr
after
dafter
drafter
grafter
hafter
hereafter
hereinafter
laughter
rafter
thereafter
wafter

Ā'ful
playful
trayful

Ā'fur
chafer
cockchafer
safer
wafer

ĂF'ur
Kaffir
zaffer

ĂF'ur
chaffer
gaffer
graffer
laugher
quaffer

ĂF'urd
Safford
Stafford
Trafford

ĂG'a
plaga
rutabaga
saga

ĂG'a
aga
quagga

Ä'ga
aga
saga

ĂG'al
plagal
vagal

ĂG'an
Hagan
pagan
O'Hagan
Regan

ĂG'ard
haggard
laggard
staggard
staggered
swaggered

ĂG'art
braggart
Taggart

ĂG'at
agate
moss-agate
(cf. faggot,
  etc.)

ĂG'ed
cragged

jagged
ragged
scragged

ĂG'end
fag-end
lagend

ĂG'est
plaguest
vaguest

ĂG'est
braggest
draggest
faggest
flaggest
gaggest
laggest
naggest
waggest

ĂG'eth
braggeth
draggeth
faggeth
flaggeth
gaggeth
laggeth
naggeth
raggeth
waggeth

ĂG'i
Aggie
baggy
braggy
craggy
faggy
flaggy
gaggy

jaggy	naggish	flagman	Ā'go
knaggy	waggish	ragman	farrago
laggy			Chicago
Maggie	**ĂG'l**	**ĂG'ment**	Santiago
naggy	*bedaggle*	fragment	
quaggy	bedraggle		**ĂG'on**
raggy	daggle	**ĂG'mir**	dragon
saggy	draggle	quagmire	flagon
scraggy	gaggle		pendragon
shaggy	haggle	**ĂG'mit**	snap-dragon
slaggy	raggle	stalagmite	wagon
snaggy	raggle-taggle		
swaggy	straggle	**ĂG'nant**	**ĂG'ot**
taggy	waggel	stagnant	fagot
waggy	waggle		maggot
		ĂG'nat	magot
ĂG'ij	**ĂG'ling**	agnate	(cf. agate)
baggage	*bedaggling*	magnate	
	bedraggling	stagnate	**ĂG'pi**
ĂG'ing	daggling		magpie
bagging	draggling	**ĂG'nes**	
bragging	gaggling	Agnes	**ĂG'pip**
dragging	haggling		bagpipe
fagging	raggling	**ĂG'net**	
flagging	straggling	magnet	**ĂG'rans**
gagging	waggling		flagrance
lagging		**ĂG'num**	fragrance
magging	**ĂG'lur**	magnum	(cf. vagrants)
nagging	bedraggler		
ragging	daggler	**Ā'go**	**ĂG'rant**
sagging	draggler	farrago	flagrant
tagging	haggler	imago	fragrant
unflagging	straggler	lumbago	infragrant
wagging	waggler	plumbago	vagrant
		sago	
ĂG'is	**ĂG'mag**	San Diego	**ĂG'rik**
haggis	cagmag	Terra del	chiragric
		Fuego	podagric
ĂG'ish	**ĂG'man**	Tobago	
haggish	bagman	virago	**Ā'gu**
laggish	dragman	vorago	ague

ĀG′ur

maigre
plaguer
vaguer

ĀG′ur

bagger
bragger
carpet-bagger
dagger
dragger
fagger
flagger
four-bagger
gagger
jagger
lagger
magger
nagger
one-bagger
ragger
sagger
stagger
swagger
tagger
three-bagger
two-bagger
wagger

Ā′gus

archimagus
choragus
magus

ĀGZ′man

cragsman
dragsman

Ā′hoo

wahoo
yahoo

Ā′i

clayey
sprayey
wheyey

Ä′ib

sahib

Ä′ij

drayage
weighage

Ä′ik

alcaic
algebraic
alhambraic
altaic
ante-Mosaic
Aramaic
archaic
Brahmaic
Chaldaic
Cyrenaic
deltaic
Eddaic
Hebraic
Jagataic
Judaic
laic
mosaic
paradisaic
pharisaic
prosaic
Ptolemaic
Passaic
Romaic
saddusaic
Sinaic
sodaic
spondaic
stanzaic

tesseraic
trochaic
voltaic

Ā′ing

allaying
amaying
arraying
assaying
baying
belaying
betraying
bewraying
braying
claying
conveying
decaying
defraying
delaying
disarraying
dismaying
disobeying
displaying
essaying
flaying
foresaying
fraying
gainsaying
haying
horseplaying
hurraying
inlaying
interlaying
interplaying
inveighing
laying
maying
mislaying
missaying
neighing
obeying

outlaying
outstaying
outweighing
overlaying
overpaying
overstaying
paying
playing
portraying
praying
prepaying
preying
purveying
relaying
repaying
saying
slaying
soothsaying
spraying
staying
surveying
swaying
undecaying
underpaying
underplaying
unsaying
unweighing
waylaying
weighing

Ā′is

dais
Lais

Ā′ish

clayish
gayish
grayish
greyish
silver-grayish

Ā'ist
algebraist
archaist
prosaist
Ptolemaist

Ā'izm
Chaldaism
Laism
Mosaism
prosaism

Ā'ja
maharajah
rajah

ĀJ'ant
pageant

ĀJ'ed
aged

Ā'jent
agent
reagent

ĀJ'est
agest
assuagest
engagest
enragest
gagest
gaugest
outragest
presagest
ragest
sagest
stagest
swagest
wagest

ĀJ'eth
ageth
assuageth
engageth
enrageth
gageth
gaugeth
outrageth
presageth
rageth
wageth

ĀJ'ez
ages
assuages
cages
disengages
encages
engages
enrages
gages
gauges
greengages
outrages
pages
pre-engages
presages
rages
sages
stages
wages
weather-gages

Ā'ji
cagey
ragy
sagy
stagy

ĀJ'i
cadgy

hadji
howadji

ĀJ'ik
archipelagic
ellagic
hemorrhagic
magic
omophagic
pelagic
tragic

ĀJ'il
agile
fragile

ĀJ'in
imagine

ĀJ'ind
imagined
unimagined

ĀJ'ing
aging
assuaging
caging
engaging
enraging
gaging
gauging
paging
presaging
raging
staging

ĀJ'ing
badging
cadging

ĀJ'les
ageless

cageless
gageless
gaugeless
pageless
rageless
sageless
stageless
wageless

ĀJ'li
sagely

ĀJ'ling
cageling

ĀJ'ment
assuagement
encagement
engagement
enragement
pre-engagement
presagement

ĀJ'nes
sageness

ĀJ'ur
assuager
cager
disengager
engager
enrager
gager
gauger
major
old-stager
pager
presager
sager
stager

ōld, ôr, ŏdd, oil, fŏŏt, out; ūse, ûrn, ŭp; THis, thin

trumpet-major
wager

ĀJ'ur
agger
badger
cadger

ĀJ'us
advantageous
ambagious
contagious
courageous
disadvanta-
  geous
oragious
outrageous
rampageous
umbrageous

Ă'ka
raca
Jamaica

ĂK'a
alpaca
Malacca
polacca

Ă'ka
jararaca

ĂK'al
jackal
pack-all

ĂK'ard
placard

ĂK'at
baccate

placate
saccate

ĂK'brand
crack-brained
slack-brained

ĂK'but
hackbut
sackbut

ĂK'daw
jackdaw

ĂK'doun
breakdown
shakedown

ĂK'ed
naked
(see ĂK + ed)

ĂK'en
awaken
bacon
forsaken
Jamaican
kraken
mistaken
overtaken
shaken
taken
undertaken
uptaken
waken
wind-shaken

ĂK'en
blacken
bracken
slacken

Ă'ken
kraken

ĂK'end
unawakened
awakened, etc.

ĂK'est
achest
awakest
bakest
betakest
breakest
fakest
forsakest
makest
mistakest
opaquest
overtakest
partakest
quakest
rakest
shakest
spakest
stakest
takest
undertakest
wakest

ĂK'est
attackest
backest
blackest
clackest
crackest
hackest
lackest
packest
quackest
rackest
ransackest

sackest
slackest
smackest
tackest
trackest
unpackest
whackest

ĂK'et
bracket
flacket
Hackett
jacket
packet
placket
racket
tacket

ĀK'eth
acheth
awaketh
baketh
betaketh
breaketh
faketh
forsaketh
maketh
mistaketh
overtaketh
partaketh
quaketh
raketh
shaketh
staketh
taketh
undertaketh
waketh

ĂK'eth
attacketh
backeth

blacketh
clacketh
cracketh
hacketh
lacketh
packeth
quacketh
racketh
ransacketh
sacketh
slacketh
smacketh
tacketh
tracketh
unpacketh
whacketh

ĂK′ful
wakeful

ĂK′i
achey
braky
caky
faky
flaky
quaky
shaky
snaky

ĂK′i
blackey
cracky
knacky
lackey

Ä′ki, Ā′ki
sake
saki

ĂK′ij
breakage

ĂK′ij
package
sackage
stackage
trackage
wrackage

ĂK′ĭk
bacchic
stomachic

ĂK′sen
vaccine

ĂK′ing
aching
awaking
baking
betaking
braking
breaking
caking
faking
flaking
forsaking
heartbreaking
making
mistaking
overtaking
partaking
quaking
raking
shaking
slaking
spaking
staking
taking
undertaking
unmaking
upbreaking

uptaking
waking

ĂK′ing
attacking
backing
bivouacing
blacking
clacking
cracking
hacking
knacking
lacking
packing
quacking
racking
ransacking
sacking
slacking
smacking
tacking
thwacking
tracking
unpacking

ĂK′ish
rakish
snakish

ĂK′ish
blackish
brackish
knackish
quackish

ĂK′kloth
packcloth
sackcloth

ĂK″l
cackle

crackle
grackle
hackle
macle
quackle
ramshackle
shackle
tackle

ĂK″ld
unshackled
cackled, etc.

ĂK′les
knackless
sackless
trackless

ĂK′let
lakelet

ĂK′li
blackly
cackly
crackly
shackly
tackly

ĂK′ling
cackling
crackling
hackling
shackling
tackling

ĂK′log
backlog
hacklog

ĂK′lur
cackler

crackler	Ā'kob	arefaction	subtraction
hackler	Jacob	*assuefaction*	tabefaction
shackler		attraction	taction
tackler	ĂK'on	benefaction	tepefaction
	bacon	calefaction	torrefaction
ĂK'man	Lacon	coaction	traction
blackman	Macon	compaction	transaction
jackman	(see ĂK'en)	contaction	tumefaction
packman		contraction	
	Ā'korn	counteraction	ĂK'shus
ĂK'me	acorn	counter-	factious
acme		attraction	fractious
	ĂP'pot	detraction	
ĂK'nes	crackpot	dissatisfaction	ĂK'sez
blackness	jackpot	distraction	axes
slackness		exaction	battle-axes
	ĂK'red	extraction	relaxes
ĂK'ne	sacred	faction	taxes
acne		fraction	waxes
hackney	ĂK'rid	inaction	Maxie's
	acrid	infraction	
ĂK'ning		interaction	ĂK'si
wakening	ĂK'ring	labefaction	biotaxy
	sacring	liquefaction	braxy
Ā'ko		lubrifaction	Cotopaxi
Saco	ĂK'rist	madefaction	flaxy
Waco	sacrist	malefaction	heterotaxy
		paction	homotaxy
ĂK'o	ĂK'rum	petrifaction	taxi
goracco	sacrum	protraction	waxy
shako	simulacrum	putrefaction	
Sacco		rarefaction	
tobacco	ĂK'sent	reaction	ĂK'sid
	accent	redaction	flaccid
Ä'ko		refraction	
guaco	ĂK'ses	retraction	ĂK'sim
guanaco	access	retroaction	maxim
Gran Chaco		rubefaction	
	ĂK'shun	satisfaction	ĂK'sis
ĂK'of	abstraction	stupefaction	axis
take-off	action	subaction	praxis

āle, câre, ădd, ärm, åsk; mē, hĕre, ĕnd; īce, ĭll;

synaxis
taxis

ĂK"sl
axle

ĂK'sman
cracksman
tacksman

ĂK'son
Anglo-Saxon
caxon
flaxen
Jackson
klaxon
Saxon
waxen

ĂK'sta
backstay
jack-stay

ĂK'ston
Braxton
Caxton
Claxton

ĂK'swell
Maxwell

ĂK'tat
ablactate
lactate
tractate

ĂK'ted
abstracted
acted
attracted
compacted

contracted
counteracted
detracted
distracted
enacted
exacted
extracted
overacted
protracted
reacted
refracted
retracted
subtracted
transacted
unacted
underacted

ĂK'test
abstractest
actest
attractest
contractest
counteractest
detractest
distractest
enactest
exactest
extractest
protractest
reactest
retractest
subtractest
transactest

ĂK'teth
abstracteth
acteth
attracteth
contracteth
counteracteth
detracteth

distracteth
enacteth
exacteth
extracteth
protracteth
reacteth
retracteth
subtracteth
transacteth

ĂKT'ful
tactful

ĂK'tik
catallactic
didactic
emphractic
eupractic
galactic
lactic
parallactic
prophylactic
protactic
stalactic
syntactic
tactic

ĂK'tiks
catallactics
tactics

ĂK'til
attractile
contractile
dactyl
didactyl
heterodactyl
leptodactyl
pachydactyl
protractile
pterodactyl

retractile
tactile
tractile

ĂK'ting
abstracting
acting
attracting
contracting
counteracting
detracting
distracting
double-acting
enacting
exacting
infracting
overacting
protracting
reacting
refracting
retracting
retroacting
self-acting
subtracting
transacting
underacting

ĂK'tis
practice

ĂK'tit
stalactite

ĂK'tiv
abstractive
active
attractive
calefactive
coactive
contractive
counteractive

counter-
  attractive
detractive
diffractive
distractive
enactive
extractive
inactive
liquefactive
olfactive
petrifactive
protractive
putrefactive
radioactive
rarefactive
reactive
refractive
retractive
retroactive
satisfactive
stupefactive
subtractive
tractive

ĂKT'les

actless
bractless
factless
tactless
tractless

ĂKT'li

compactly
exactly
matter-of-factly

ĂKT'ment

enactment
extractment
reenactment

ĂKT'nes

compactness
exactness
intactness

ĂK'to

de facto
ex post facto

ĂK'tres

actress
benefactress
contractress
detractress
exactress
factress
malefactress

ĂK'tūr

facture
fracture
manufacture
vitrifacture

ĂK'tūr

abstracter
actor
attracter
benefactor
climacter
compacter
contractor
detractor
distracter
enactor
exacter
extractor
factor
infractor
malefactor
olfactor

phylacter
protractor
refractor
retractor
subtracter
tractor
transactor

ĂK'tus

cactus

ĂK'up

break-up
make-up
wake-up

ĀK'ur

acre
awaker
baker
ballad-maker
bookmaker
breaker
dressmaker
faker
fakir
forsaker
God's-acre
heart-breaker
image-breaker
maker
match-maker
mischief-maker
mistaker
nacre
painstaker
partəker
peacemaker
Quaker
raker

Sabbath-
  breaker
shaker
taker
truce-breaker
undertaker
watchmaker

ĂK'ur

attacker
backer
blacker
bushwhacker
clacker
cracker
hacker
hijacker
knacker
lacker
lacquer
nut-cracker
packer
racker
ransacker
sacker
slacker
smacker
tacker
tracker
unpacker
whacker

ĂK'urz

breakers
awakers, etc.

ĂK'us

Bacchus
Flaccus
jacchus

āle, câre, ădd, ärm, ásk; mē, hĕre, ĕnd; īce, ĭll;

ĂK'wa
backway
pack-way
trackway

Ā'kwen
fay-queen
May-queen

ĂK'woodz
backwoods

Ā'la
gala
shillalah

ĂL'a
Allah
calla
galla
mashallah
Valhalla

Ä'la
gala

ĂL'ad
ballad
salad

ĂL'ans
balance
counter-
   balance
outbalance
overbalance
valance

ĂL'anst
balanced
outbalanced

overbalanced
unbalanced

ĀL'ant
assailant
exhalent
inhalent
intranscalent
transcalent

Ā'lanks
phalanx

ĂL'ard
Allard
Ballard
Callard
mallard

ĂL'as
balas
Dallas
palace
Pallas
(cf. chalice)

ĂL'ast
ballast

ĂL'bum
album

ĂL'burd
jailbird

ĂL'burt
Albert

ĂL'dik
heraldic

ĂL'din
Aldine

Ä'le
finale
kali
pastorale

Ā'leb
Caleb

ĂL'ek
Aleck
Halleck
smart Aleck
Talleck

ĂL'en
Alan
Allen

ĂL'enj
challenge

ĂL'enjd
challenged
unchallenged

ĂL'ens
valence

ĂL'ent
gallant
talent
ungallant

Ā'les
clayless
dayless
hayless
payless

playless
preyless
rayless
sprayless
wayless

ĀL'est
ailest
assailest
availest
bailest
balest
bewailest
curtailest
derailest
detailest
engaolest
entailest
exhalest
failest
frailest
hailest
halest
impalest
inhalest
mailest
nailest
outsailest
palest
prevailest
quailest
railest
regalest
retailest
sailest
scalest
trailest
unveilest
wailest

ĂL'et	Ā'lez or Ă'lez	Aunt Sally	ĀL'ik
gallet	or Ä'lez	bally	Gaelic
mallet	Gonzales	dally	malic
palate		dilly-dally	Salic
palette	ĂL'fa	galley	
pallet	alfalfa	Hallie	ĂL'ik
sallet	alpha	kali	acrocephalic
valet		Lallie	bimetallic
	ĂL'fred	O'Malley	brachisto-
ĂL'eth	Alfred	rally	cephalic
aileth	ĂL'ful	Sallie	brachycephalic
assaileth	baleful	sally	cephalic
availeth	pailful	shilly-shally	dolichocephalic
baileth	wailful	tally	encephalic
baleth		tomalley	eurycephalic
bewaileth	ĂL'gam	valley	Gallic
curtaileth	amalgam	(see estatically,	grallic
deraileth		and all other	italic
detaileth	Ā'li	-ally adjec-	macrencephalic
engaoleth	Bailey	tives, ĂL +	macrocephalic
entaileth	bailie	i)	malic
exhaleth	Braley		medallic
haileth	capercaillie	ĂL'id	mesocephalic
impaleth	daily	dallied	metallic
inhaleth	Daly	dilly-dallied	microcephalic
naileth	gaily	impallid	monometallic
outsaileth	Haley	invalid	oxalic
paleth	kali	pallid	phallic
prevaileth	Mailly	rallied	platycephalic
quaileth	Maley	sallied	salic
raileth	rationale	shilly-shallied	thallic
regaleth	shaly	tallied	Uralic
retaileth	shillaly	valid	Vandalic
saileth	ukelele		vocalic
scaleth	vale	ĂL'if	
traileth	(cf. palely,	bailiff	ĂL'ik
unveileth	etc.)	Caliph	pashalik
veileth	ĂL'i	ĂL'ij	ĂL'iks
waileth	alley	bailage	calyx
	Allie	curtailage	Salix
		retailage	

āle, câre, ădd, ärm, ȧsk; mē, hẽre, ĕnd; īce, ĭll;

ĂL'in or ÄL'in

Stalin

ĀL'ing

ailing
assailing
availing
bailing
baling
bewailing
blackmailing
countervailing
curtailing
derailing
detailing
empaling
entailing
exhaling
grayling
Greyling
hailing
haling
impaling
inhaling
jailing
mailing
nailing
outsailing
paling
prevailing
quailing
railing
regaling
retailing
sailing
scaling
Schmeling
tailing
trailing
unveiling

veiling
wailing
whaling
wholesaling

ĂL'ing

caballing
palling

ĂL'is

Alice
allice
chalice
Challis
malice
(cf. palace)

ĂL'is

Cornwallis

ĂL'ish

palish
shalish
stalish

ĂL'ji

cephalalgy
neuralgy
nostalgy
odontalgy

ĂL'jik

antalgic
cephalalgic
neuralgic
nostalgic
odontalgic

ĂL'kar

mailcar
railcar

ĂL'kat

defalcate
falcate

ĂL'kin

grimalkin

ĂL'ker

valkyr

ĂL'li

frailly
halely
palely
stalely
(cf. ĀL'i)

ĂL'ma

Alma
Thalma

ĂL'mat

palmate

ĂL'ment

ailment
assailment
availment
bailment
bewailment
curtailment
derailment
entailment
impalement
inhalement
prevailment
regalement
retailment

ĂL'mud

Talmud

ĂL'muk

Kalmuck

ĂL'nes

frailness
haleness
paleness
staleness

Ā'lo

halo

ĂL'o

All-hallow
aloe
callow
dishallow
fallow
hallow
mallow
marshmallow
sallow
shallow
summer-fallow
tallow
unhallow

ĂL'o

swallow
wallow
(see Ŏ'lo)

ĂL'on

gallon
talon

ĂL'on

salon

ĂL'op

gallop

ōld, ôr, ŏdd, oil, fŏŏt, out; ūse, ûrn, ŭp; THis, thin

jalap
scallop
shallop

ÅL'ot
ballot

ÅL'oz
gallows
hallows, etc.

ÅL'pin
Alpine
cisalpine
transalpine

ÅL'ping
scalping

ÅL'spin
tailspin

ÅL'ti
frailty

ÅL'to
alto
contralto

ÅL'to
rialto

ÅL'u
undervalue
value

ÅL'um
alum

ĀL'ūr
failure

ĀL'ŭr
assailer
bailer
baler
bewailer
curtailer
derailer
detailer
entailer
failer
frailer
gaoler
haler
impaler
inhaler
jailer
nailer
paler
prevailer
quailer
railer
regaler
retailer
sailer
sailor
Sayler
scaler
squalor
staler
tailor
Taylor
trailer
unveiler
wailer
whaler

ÅL'ur
caballer
pallor
valor

ÅL'us
callous
gallus

ÅL'va
Alva
Alvah
Halveh

ÅL'vij
salvage

ÅL'vin
Alvin
Calvin

ÅL'vo
salvo

ÅL'vur
quack-salver
salver
salvor

ÅL'vurt
Calvert

ÅL'win
Alwin

ÅL'ya
Bacchanalia
castalia
dahlia
mammalia
marginalia
paraphernalia
penetralia
regalia
saturnalia

terminalia
(cf. azalea)

ÅL'ya
dahlia

ÅL'ya
dahlia

ĀL'yan
alien
Australian
bacchanalian
Dædalian
episcopalian
Idalian
mammalian
marsupialian
Messalian
paralian
phantasmalian
Phigalian
Pygmalion
regalian
saturnalian
sesquipedalian
tenaillon
tobaccanalian
universalian

ÅL'yant
valiant

ÅL'yard
gaolyard
kailyard

ÅL'yo
intaglio
seraglio

āle, câre, ădd, ärm, åsk; mē, hēre, ĕnd; īce, ĭll;

ĂL'yon	panorama	**ĂM'bent**	*scramblest*
battalion	pajama	lambent	*shamblest*
Italian	pyjama		
medallion	Rama	**ĂM'bi**	**ĂM'bleth**
rapscallion	Teshu Lama	namby-pamby	*ambleth*
rascallion	Yama		*gambleth*
scallion	Yokohama	**ĂM'bik**	*rambleth*
stallion		choliambic	*scrambleth*
	Ā'man	choriambic	*shambleth*
ĀLZ'man	cayman	dithyrambic	
dalesman	dayman	elegiambic	**ĂM'b'lz**
salesman	drayman	galliambic	ambles
talesman	highwayman	iambic	gambles
whalesman	layman		rambles
		ĂM'bist	scrambles
ĂM'a	**ĂM'ant**	cambist	shambles
Bahama	claimant	gambist	
krama	(cf. raiment,		**ĂM'bling**
	etc.)	**ĂM'bit**	ambling
ĂM'a		ambit	brambling
Alabama	**ĂM'ant**	gambit	gambling
digamma	clamant		rambling
mamma		**ĂM'kin**	scambling
	ĂM'as	lambkin	scrambling
ĂM'a	Lammas		shambling
Bahama		**ĂM'b'l**	
Brahma	**ĂM'ask**	amble	**ĂM'blur**
cyclorama	damask	bramble	ambler
cosmorama		gamble	gambler
Dalai Lama	**Ā'mat**	preamble	rambler
diorama	day-mate	ramble	scambler
drama	desquamate	scamble	scrambler
Fujiyama	hamate	scramble	shambler
georama	playmate	shamble	
kaama		skimble-	**ĂM'bo**
Kama	**ĂM'az**	skamble	ambo
lama	cat's pajamas		crambo
llama	Brahmas, etc.	**ĂM'blest**	flambeau
mamma		*amblest*	sambo
melodrama	**ĂM'ba**	*gamblest*	zambo
neorama	gamba	*ramblest*	

ōld, ôr, ŏdd, oil, fŏŏt, out · ūse, ûrn, ŭp; THis, thin

ĂM'bol
gambol

ĂM'brik
cambric

ĂM'bur
ante-chamber
chamber

ĂM'būr
tambour

ĂM'bur
amber
camber
clamber

ĂM'bus
dithyrambus
iambus

ĂM'bush
ambush

ĂM'el
camel
Campbell
enamel
entrammel
Hamal
mammal
trammel

ĂM'eld
enamelled
untrammelled

Ā'men
amen
Bremen

examen
flamen
foramen
gravamen
Haman
Lehmann
stamen

Ă'men
amen

Ā'ment
allayment
betrayment
defrayment
payment
prepayment
raiment
(cf. claimant)

ĀM'est
acclaimest
aimest
blamest
claimest
declaimest
defamest
disclaimest
exclaimest
flamest
framest
gamest
inflamest
lamest
maimest
namest
proclaimest
reclaimest
shamest
tamest

ĂM'est
crammest
dammest
damnest
rammest
shammest
slammest

ĂM'est
calmest
embalmest
salaamest

ĀM'eth
acclaimeth
aimeth
blameth
claimeth
declaimeth
defameth
disclaimeth
exclaimeth
flameth
foreshameth
frameth
inflameth
lameth
maimeth
nameth
overcameth
proclaimeth
reclaimeth
shameth
tameth

ĂM'eth
crammeth
dammeth
damneth
rammeth

shammeth
slammeth

ĂM'eth
calmeth
embalmeth
salaameth

ĂM'fir
samphire

ĂM'flet
pamphlet

ĂM'for
camphor

ĂM'ful
blameful
flameful
shameful

ĂM'i
Amy
gamy
flamy
Mamie

ĂM'i
chamois
clammy
gammy
mammy
rammy
shammy
tammy

ĂM'i
balmy
calmy
Miami

āle, câre, ădd, ärm, ȧsk; mē, hẹre, ĕnd; īce, ĭll;

palmy
pastrami
qualmy
salmi
swami

ĂM'ij
damage

ĂM'ik
Abrahamic
Adamic
adynamic
agamic
autodynamic
balsamic
biodynamic
ceramic
cinnamic
cosmoramic
cryptogamic
cycloramic
dioramic
dynamic
electro-
  dynamic
epithalamic
gamic
hydrodynamic
hyperdynamic
Islamic
isodynamic
keramic
monogamic
monogrammic
panoramic
parallelogram-
  mic
phanerogamic
polygamic
potamic

preadamic
telegrammic
trigrammic

ĂM'il
amyl
Tamil

ĂM'in
examine
famine
gamin

ĀM'ing
acclaiming
aiming
blaming
claiming
declaiming
defaming
disclaiming
exclaiming
flaming
framing
gaming
inflaming
laming
maiming
misnaming
naming
nicknaming
proclaiming
reclaiming
shaming
surnaming
taming

ĀM'ing
cramming
damming
damning

lambing
lamming
ramming
shamming
slamming
tramming

ĂM'ing
becalming
calming
embalming
qualming
salaaming

ĂM'is
amice
chlamys
tamis

ĀM'ish
lamish
tamish

ĂM'ish
affamish
enfamish
famish
Hamish
rammish

ĂM'ish
calmish
qualmish

ĂM'ist
embalmist
palmist
psalmist

ĂM'it
samite

ĀM'les
aimless
blameless
claimless
fameless
flameless
frameless
gameless
nameless
shameless
tameless

ĂM'les
balmless
palmless
psalmless
qualmless

ĂM'let
camlet
hamlet
samlet

ĀM'li
gamely
lamely
namely
tamely

ĂM'li
calmly

ĂM'ling
lambling

ĂM'ment
becalmment
embalmment

ĀM'nes
gameness

---

lameness	ĂM'paz	decamping	ĂMP'ment
sameness	pampas	encamping	decampment
tameness		lamping	encampment
	ĂM'pen	ramping	
ĂM'nes	dampen	scamping	ĂMP'nes
calmness		stamping	dampness
	ĂM'per	tamping	
ĂM'ok	ampere	tramping	ĂM'pri
hammock		vamping	lamprey
mammock	ĂM'pest		
	campest	ĂM'pir	ĂMP'son
ĂM'on	*crampest*	vampire	Lampson
Ammon	dampest		Sampson
backgammon	*decampest*	ĂM'pish	(cf. Samson)
daman	*encampest*	dampish	
gammon	*rampest*	scampish	ĂMP'ton
mammon	*scampest*		Crampton
salmon	*stampest*	ĂM'p'l	Hampton
shaman	*trampest*	ample	
	vampest	*ensample*	ĂM'pur
Ā'mond		example	camper
Raymond	ĂM'peth	sample	champer
	campeth	trample	clamper
ĂM'ond	*crampeth*		cramper
Hammond	*dampeth*	ĂM'p'ld	damper
	decampeth	untrampled	hamper
Ā'mos	*encampeth*	sampled, etc.	pamper
Amos	*rampeth*		scamper
Shaemas	*scampeth*	ĂMP'li	stamper
	stampeth	damply	tamper
ĂM'oth	*trampeth*		tramper
mammoth	*vampeth*	ĂMP'ling	vamper
		ensampling	ĂM'purd
ĂM'pan	ĂM'pi	sampling	hampered
jampan	crampy	trampling	pampered
sampan			tampered
tampan	ĂM'ping	ĂMP'lur	unhampered
	camping	ampler	
	clamping	exampler	ĂM'pus
ĂM'part	cramping	sampler	campus
rampart	damping	trampler	grampus

ĂM′rod	dammer	**ĂM′zon**	Susanna
ramrod	damner	damson	Susquehanna
	enamor		sultana
ĂM′rok	gammer	**Ā′na**	Texarkana
shamrock	glamor	Americana, etc	Tia Juana
	grammar	ana	Urbana
ĂM′stur	hammer	anana	
gamester	ninnyhammer	arcana	**Ăn′a**
	rammer	campana	Americana, etc.
ĂM′ond	shammer	Cartagena	acqua tofana
almond	slammer	Curtana	anana
bitter-almond	sledge-hammer	fistiana	banana
	stammer	Nicotiana	Curtana
ĂM′ur	yammer	poinciana	Fata Morgana
acclaimer	yellow-hammer	scena	fistiana
aimer		vox-humana	Guiana
blamer	**ĂM′ur**		iguana
claimer	Balmer	**ĂN′a**	kerana
declaimer	calmer	Americana, etc.	liana
defamer	embalmer	anna	Messana
disclaimer	palmer	bandana	Nirvana
disfamer		Christiana	purana
exclaimer	**ĂM′wa**	Diana	sultana
framer	tramway	fistiana	thana
gamer		Georgiana	zenana
inflamer	**ĂM′us**	Hanna	
Kramer	biramous	Hannah	**Ā′nal**
lamer	famous	Havana	anal
maimer	hamous	hosanna	
misnamer	ignoramus	Indiana	**ĂN′al**
namer	mandamus	ipecacuanha	annal
nicknamer	squamous	Joanna	cannel
proclaimer	**ĂM′ut**	Juliana	channel
reclaimer	gamut	Louisiana	empanel
shamer		manna	flannel
tamer	**ĂM′zel**	Montana	impanel
testamur	amsel	Pollyanna	panel
	damsel	Roxana	pannel
ĂM′ur		savanna	scrannel
clamor	**ĂM′zi**	Savannah	stannel
crammer	Malmsey	Stephana	unpanel

ĂN'alz
annals
flannels, etc.

ĂN'ant
complainant

ĂN'at
impanate
lanate

ĂN'at
khanate
pomegranate
tannate

ĂN'at
khanate

ĂN'bo
rainbow

ĂN'chest
launchest
stanchest

ĂN'chest
blanchest
scranchest

ĂN'chet
manchet
planchet

ĂN'cheth
launcheth
stancheth

ĂN'cheth
blancheth
scrancheth

ĂN'chez
launches
paunches
stanches

ĂN'chez
avalanches
blanches
branches
ranches

ĂN'chi
paunchy

ĂN'chi
branchy

ĂN'ching
launching
stanching

ĂN'ching
blanching
branching
ranching

ĂN'chiz
affranchise
disfranchise
enfranchise
franchise

ĂNCH'les
launchless
paunchless

ANCH'les
branchless
ranchless
stanchless

ĂN'chur
launcher
stancher

ĂN'chur
brancher
rancher

ĂN'da
Amanda
jacaranda
Miranda
memoranda
propaganda
veranda

ĂN' dal
Randall
(cf. Randle)

ĂN'dant
commandant
demandant
mandant

ĂN'dat
mandate

ĂND'bag
handbag
sand-bag

ĂND'bal
hand-ball
sand-ball

ĂND'boi
band-boy
sand-boy

ĂND'boks
bandbox
sand-box

ĂND'child
grand-child

ĂN'de
Rio Grande

ĂN'ded or
ĂN'ded
backhanded
banded
blackhanded
branded
candid
clean-handed
close-handed
commanded
contrabanded
countermanded
demanded
deodanded
disbanded
empty-handed
even-handed
expanded
first-handed
forehanded
fourhanded
freehanded
full-handed
handed
hard-handed
heavy-handed
high-handed
landed
left-handed
light-handed
lily-handed
neat-handed
open-handed
over-handed
red-handed

āle, câre, ădd, arm, åsk; mē, hęre, ĕnd; īce, ĭll;

remanded	*disbandeth*	**ĂN'dij**	**ĂN'd'l**
reprimanded	*expandeth*	bandage	candle
right-handed	*handeth*	glandage	dandle
short-handed	*landeth*	standage	handle
single-handed	*remandeth*		sandal
stranded	*reprimandeth*	**ĂN'ding** or	scandal
swift-handed	*standeth*	**ĂN'ding**	vandal
two-handed	*withstandeth*	ampersanding	
unbranded		banding	**ĂND'les** or
underhanded	**ĂN'dez**	branding	**ĂND'les**
unhanded	Andes	commanding	bandless
unlanded	Hernandez	countermand-	brandless
		ing	commandless
ĂN'dent	**ĂND'fast**	demanding	glandless
candent	handfast	disbanding	handless
scandent	**ĂN'di**	expanding	landless
ĂN'der	Andy	handing	sandless
reindeer	bandy	landing	strandless
	brandy	notwithstand-	
ĂN'dest or	candy	ing	**ĂND'ling**
ĂN'dest	dandy	outstanding	brandling
bandest	handy	remanding	handling
brandest	jaborandi	reprimanding	
commandest	jackadandy	sanding	**ĂND'lur**
demandest	Jim Dandy	standing	Candler
disbandest	Mandy	stranding	chandler
expandest	pandy	understanding	dandler
grandest	randy	withstanding	handler
handest	Rio Grande	**ĂN'dish**	tallow-chandler
landest	sandy	blandish	
remandest	sugar-candy	brandish	**ĂND'lord**
reprimandest	unhandy	grandish	landlord
standest	**ĂN'did**	outlandish	
withstandest	bandied		**ĂND'li**
ĂN'deth or	brandied	**ĂN'dist**	blandly
ĂN'deth	candid	contrabandist	grandly
bandeth	candied	propagandist	
brandeth	uncandid		**ĂND'mad**
commandeth	(cf. banded,	**ĂN'dit**	hand-made
demandeth	p. 328)	bandit	handmaid

ĂND'mark
landmark

ĂND'ment or
  ĂND'ment
commandment
disbandment
remandment

ĂND'nes
blandness
grandness

ĂN'do or
  ĂN'do
commando
Ferdinando
Fernando
grando
Hernando
lentando
Orlando

ĂN'don
abandon
Landon
Shandon

ĂND'out
handout

ĂN'dra or
  ĂN'dra
Alessandra
Alexandra
Cassandra

ĂN'drel
spandrel

ĂN'dres
pandress

ĂN'dres
laundress

ĂN'drik
polyandric
theandric

ĂN'dril
mandril

ĂN'drin
Alexandrine
salamandrine

ĂN'dri or
  ĂN'dri
chandry
commandry
meandry
polyandry
shandry

ĂN'dri
laundry

ĂN'drus
meandrous
polyandrous

ĂND'sir
grandsire

ĂND'skap
landscape

ĂND'son
grandson

ĂND'stand
band-stand
grand-stand

ĂN'dum
ad captandum
avizandum
mandom
memorandum
random
tandem

ĂN'dur
attainder
remainder

ĂN'dūr
grandeur

ĂN'dur or
  ĂN'dur
Africander
Alexander
back-hander
blander
bystander
brander
candor
commander
coriander
dander
demander
disbander
dittander
expander
gander
gerrymander
glander
goosey-gander
grander
hander
lander
Leander
meander
Menander

oleander
pander
philander
Pomander
remander
reprimander
right-hander
salamander
sander
slander
stander
understander
withstander

ĂN'dur
launder

ĂN'durd or
  ĂN'durd
meandered
pandered
philandered
slandered
standard

ĂN'durz
Sanders
Saunders

ĂNDZ'man
bandsman
landsman

Ā'nes
gayness
greyness

ĀN'est
abstainest
appertainest

āle,   câre,   ădd,   ärm,   åsk;   mē,   hĕre,   ĕnd;   īce,   ĭll;

arraignest
ascertainest
attainest
canest
chainest
complainest
constrainest
containest
cranest
deignest
detainest
disdainest
enchainest
entertainest
explainest
feignest
humanest
inanest
maintainest
obtainest
ordainest
painest
plainest
profanest
rainest
refrainest
regainest
reignest
remainest
restrainest
retainest
sanest
stainest
strainest
sustainest
trainest
unchainest
urbanest
vainest
wanest

ĂN'est
bannest
fannest
mannest
plannest
scannest
spannest
tannest

ĂN'et
gannet
granite
Janet
planet
quannet
(cf. pomegran-
ate)

ĂN'eth
abstaineth
appertaineth
arraigneth
ascertaineth
attaineth
caneth
chaineth
complaineth
constraineth
containeth
craneth
deigneth
detaineth
disdaineth
draineth
enchaineth
entertaineth
explaineth
feigneth
foreordaineth
gaineth
maintaineth

obtaineth
ordaineth
paineth
profaneth
raineth
refraineth
regaineth
reigneth
remaineth
restraineth
retaineth
staineth
straineth
sustaineth
traineth
unchaineth
waneth

ĂN'eth
banneth
fanneth
manneth
planneth
scanneth
spanneth
tanneth

ĂN'far
fanfare

ĂN'feld
Canfield

ĂN'ful
baneful
complainful
disdainful
painful

ĂN'gang
chain-gang
train-gang

ĂNG'gar
hangar

ĂNG'gor
languor

ĂNG'gur
anger
angor
clangor

ĂNG'gwid
languid

ĂNG'gwij
language

ĂNG'gwin
anguine
ensanguine
sanguine

ĂNG'gwish
anguish
languish

ĂNG'i
clangy
fangy
slangy

ĂNG'ing
banging
clanging
hanging
haranguing
overhanging
paper-hanging
slanging
slangwhanging
twanging

ōld, ôr, ŏdd, oil, fŏŏt, out; ūse, ûrn, ŭp; THis, thin

ĂNG′kest

blankest
clankest
dankest
embankest
flankest
frankest
lankest
outflankest
rankest
thankest
sankest
spankest

ĂNG′ket

banket
blanket

ĂNG′keth

clanketh
embanketh
flanketh
franketh
outflanketh
ranketh
sanketh
thanketh

ĂNGK′ful

prankful
thankful

ĂNG′ki

cranky
hanky
hanky-panky
lanky
planky
pranky
Yankee

ĂNG′king

banking
clanking
embanking
flanking
franking
outflanking
outranking
planking
ranking
spanking
thanking
yanking

ĂNG′kish

dankish
frankish
lankish
prankish

ĂNGK″l

ankle
crankle
hankle
rankle

ĂNGK′les

bankless
clankless
crankless
flankless
plankless
prankless
rankless
shankless
spankless
thankless

ĂNGK′let

anklet

ĂNGK′li

blankly
dankly
frankly
lankly
rankly

ĂNGK′ling

hankling
rankling

ĂNGK′ment

bankment
embankment
outflankment

ĂNGK′nes

blankness
crankness
dankness
frankness
lankness
rankness

ĂNG′ko

banco
calamanco

ĂNGK′shun

sanction

ĂNGK′shus

anxious

ĂNGK′tum

sanctum

ĂNGK′wet

banquet

ĂNGK′wil

tranquil

ĂNGK′wish

vanquish

ĂNG′kur

anchor
banker
blanker
canker
clanker
danker
encanker
flanker
franker
hanker
outflanker
planker
pranker
rancor
ranker
sheet-anchor
spanker
tanker
thanker
unanchor

ĂNG′kurd

brancard
cankered
tankard
unanchored
anchored, etc.

ĂNG″l

angle
bangle
bemangle
bespangle
brangle
dangle
disentangle
embrangle

entangle	**ĂNG'o**	**ĂN'i**	galvanic
interjangle	contango	Annie	Germanic
intertangle	fandango	branny	hydrocyanic
jangle	mango	canny	Indo-Germanic
mangle	Pago Pago	cranny	interoceanic
mingle-mangle	tango	Fannie	lexiphanic
phalangal		granny	Magellanic
quadrangle	**ĂNG'gri**	mannie	mechanic
sea-tangle	angry	Nannie	Messianic
spangle		uncanny	montanic
strangle	**ĂN'grov**		Mussulmanic
tangle	mangrove	**ĂN'i**	oceanic
triangle		frangipani	organic
twangle	**ĂNG'stur**	Galvani	Ossianic
untangle	gangster	Hindustani	paganic
Wrangel		rani	panic
wrangle	**ĂNG'ur**	soprani	Puranic
	banger		Puritanic
ĂNG"ld	clangor	**ĂN'id**	quercitannic
new-fangled	ganger	crannied	rhodanic
star-spangled	hangar		Romanic
angled, etc.	hanger	**ĂN'ij**	satanic
	haranguer	cranage	stannic
ĂNG'les	paper-hanger	drainage	sultanic
fangless	slang-whanger		talismanic
pangless	straphanger	**ĂN'ij**	tannic
		manage	tetanic
ĂNG'li	**ĂN'hood**	pannage	Theophanic
spangly	manhood	tannage	titanic
tangly			tympanic
	ĂN'i	**ĂN'ik**	tyrannic
ĂNG'ling	Allegheny	Alcoranic	Uranic
angling	brainy	aldermanic	valerianic
dangling, etc.	Cheyney	Alemannic	volcanic
	Delaney	Aristophanic	vulcanic
ĂNG'lur	Eugenie	botanic	
angler	grainy	Brahmanic	**ĂN'iks**
dangler, etc.	Rainey	Britannic	humanics
	rainy	charlatanic	mechanics
ĂNG'man	veiny	diaphanic	panics
hangman	zany	ferricyanic	

ōld, ôr, ŏdd, oil, fŏŏt, out; ūse, ûrn, ŭp; THis, thin

ĂN'ĭl
anil

ĀN'ĭl
anile

Ā'nim
paynim

ĀN'ing
abstaining
airplaning
appertaining
arraigning
ascertaining
attaining
bestaining
braining
campaigning
caning
chaining
complaining
constraining
containing
craning
deigning
deraigning
detaining
disdaining
draining
enchaining
entertaining
entraining
explaining
feigning
foreordaining
gaining
graining
hydroplaning
ingraining
maintaining

obtaining
ordaining
paining
pertaining
plaining
planing
preordaining
profaning
raining
refraining
regaining
reigning
reining
remaining
restraining
retaining
spraining
staining
straining
sustaining
training
unchaining
uncomplaining
unfeigning
uptraining
veining
waning

ĂN'ing
banning
canning
fanning
flanning
inspanning
japanning
manning
outspanning
panning
planning
scanning
spanning

tanning
trepanning
unmanning

ĂN'is
anise

ĀN'ish
Danish
sanish
urbanish
vainish

ĂN'ish
Alcoranish
banish
clannish
evanish
fannish
mannish
Mussulmanish
planish
Spanish
vanish

ĂN'ist
Alcoranist
pianist
tanist

ĂN'jel
angel

ĂN'jel
evangel

ĂN'jent
frangent
plangent
tangent

ĀN'jest
arrangest
changest
derangest
disarrangest
estrangest
exchangest
rangest
strangest

ĀN'jeth
arrangeth
changeth
derangeth
disarrangeth
estrangeth
exchangeth
interchangeth
rangeth

ĀN'jez
arranges
changes
deranges
disarranges
enranges
estranges
exchanges
granges
interchanges
ranges

ĂN'jez
flanges
Ganges
phalanges

ĂN'ji
mangy
rangy

ĀN'jing
arranging
changing
counter-
    changing
deranging
disarranging
estranging
exchanging
interchanging
ranging
unchanging

ĀNJ'ling
changling

ĀNJ'les
changeless
rangeless

ĀNJ'li
strangely

ĀNJ'ment
arrangement
derangement
disarrangement
estrangement
exchangement
interchange-
    ment

ĀNJ'nes
strangeness

ĀN'jur
arranger
bushranger
changer
danger
deranger

disarranger
endanger
estranger
exchanger
granger
interchanger
manger
money-changer
ranger
stranger

ĂN'ka or
    ĂN'ka
Bianca

ĂN'kin
Hankin
Rankin

ĂN'king
Nanking

ĂN'kinz
Hankins
Rankins

ĂN'kok
Hancock

ĀN'land
mainland

ĀN'les
brainless
caneless
chainless
craneless
domainless
drainless
gainless
grainless
maneless

painless
rainless
stainless
swainless
vaneless

ĂN'les
banless
clanless
fanless
manless
planless
spanless
tanless

ĂN'li
gainly
humanely
inanely
insanely
mainly
plainly
profanely
sanely
vainly

ĂN'li
Danley
Manley
manly
spick-and-
    spanly
Stanley
unmanly

ĂN'ling
manling
tanling

ĀN'ment
arraignment

ascertainment
attainment
obtainment
ordainment

ĀN'nes
humaneness
inaneness
insaneness
plainness
profaneness
saneness

Ā'no
volcano

ĂN'o
piano
Hanno
soprano

Ä'no
guano
Montesano
piano
soprano

ĂN'ok
bannock
jannock

ĂN'on
Balleyshannon
cannon
canon
fanon
Shannon

ĂN'sa
gainsay

ōld, ôr. ŏdd, oil, fŏŏt, out: ūse, ûrn, ŭp; THis, thin

ĂN'sal
mainsail

ĂN'sel
cancel
chancel
handsel

ĂN'sest
advancest
chancest
dancest
enhancest
entrancest
glancest
prancest
romancest

ĂN'set
lancet

ĂN'seth
advanceth
chanceth
danceth
enhanceth
entranceth
glanceth
pranceth
romanceth

ĂN'sez
advances
chances
dances
enhances
entrances
expanses
finances
glances
lances

mischances
prances
romances
trances

ĂNS'fur
transfer

ĂN'shal
circumstantial
financial
substantial
supersubstan-
   tial

ĂN'she
banshee

ĂN'shent
ancient

ĂN'shent
transient

ĂN'shun
expansion
mansion
scansion
stanchion

ĂN'si
aeromancy
aldermancy
alectoromancy
alectryomancy
aleuromancy
alphitomancy
anthropomancy
astragalo-
   mancy
austromancy

axinomancy
belomancy
bibliomancy
botanomancy
capnomancy
catoptromancy
ceromancy
chancy
chiromancy
cleromancy
consonancy
coscinomancy
crithomancy
crystallomancy
dactyliomancy
dancy
Delancey
enoptromancy
exorbitancy
extravagancy
exuberancy
fancy
gastromancy
geomancy
gyromancy
halomancy
hesitancy
hieromancy
hydromancy
ichthyomancy
lecanomancy
lithomancy
mendicancy
meteoromancy
mischancy
Miss Nancy
militancy
myomancy
Nancy
necromancy
occupancy

œnomancy
oneiromancy
onomancy
onychomancy
ophiomancy
ornithomancy
pedomancy
petulancy
precipitancy
pyromancy
psephomancy
psychomancy
sciomancy
sibilancy
sideromancy
significancy
spodomancy
stichomancy
supplicancy
sycophancy
tephramancy
termagancy
unchancy

ĂN'sid
fancied
rancid

ĂN'sing
advancing
chancing
dancing
enhancing
entrancing
fiancing
glancing
lancing
Lansing
necromancing
prancing
romancing

ĂN'sis
glancer
Frances
lancer
Francis
merganser
necromancer
ĂN'sist
prancer
romancist
romancer

ĂN'siv
ĂN'tā
advancive
infante
expansive

ĂN'ta
ĂNS'ment
anta
advancement
Atalanta
enhancement
Atlanta
entrancement
infanta
Santa
ĂN'som
Vedanta
handsome
sainted
hansom
ĂN'ta
ransom
Vedanta
transom
unhandsome

ĂN'tal
ĂN'son
consonantal
gigantal
Anson
quadrantal
Hanson

ĂN'sta
ĂN'tam
main-stay
bantam
phantom
ĂN'sur
ĂN'tans
advancer
Anser
acquaintance
answer
ĂN'tazm
cancer
phantasm
chancer
chiromancer
ĂN'te
dancer
enhancer
ante
entrancer
Dante
geomancer
dilettante

pococurante
zante
ĂN'te
andante
Dante
(cf. chianti)
ĀN'ted
acquainted
attainted
bepainted
besainted
depainted
fainted
feinted
painted
sainted
tainted
unacquainted
unattainted
unsainted
untainted
ĂN'ted, ĂN'ted
canted
chanted
decanted
enchanted
granted
implanted
panted
planted
ranted
recanted
slanted
supplanted
ĂN'test
acquaintest
faintest

feintest
paintest
quaintest
taintest
ĂN'test,
ĂN'test
cantest
chantest
decantest
enchantest
grantest
implantest
pantest
plantest
rantest
recantest
scantest
supplantest
ĂN'teth
acquainteth
feinteth
painteth
tainteth
ĂN'teth,
ĂN'teth
canteth
chanteth
decanteth
enchanteth
granteth
implanteth
panteth
planteth
recanteth
supplanteth
ĂN'tez
atlantes

---

corybantes
(cf. ĂN'ti + s)

ĂN'them
anthem

ĂNT'hood
sainthood

ĂN'thik
œnanthic
xanthic

ĂN'thin
acanthine
amaranthine
anthine
Rhadamanthine
tragacanthin
xanthin

ĂN'thur
anther
panther

ĂN'thus
acanthous
acanthus
Agapanthus
ailanthus
amianthus
anacanthous
ananthous
canthus
Chimonanthus
dianthus
epanthous
Galanthus
Hæmanthus
hysteranthous

polyanthus
synanthous

ĂN'ti
dainty

ĂN'ti
bacchante
canty
panty
scanty
shanty

ĂN'ti
aunty

ĂN'tif
plaintiff

ĂN'tij
advantage
disadvantage
plantage
vantage

ĂN'tik
antic
Atlantic
chiromantic
consonantic
corybantic
frantic
geomantic
gigantic
hierophantic
hydromantic
mantic
necromantic
onomantic
pedantic
pyromantic

romantic
spodomantic
sycophantic
transatlantic

ĂN'tik
Vedantic

ĂN'tin
adamantine
Brabantine
Byzantine
chrysele-
　phantine
Diophantine
elephantine
gigantine
Levantine

ĂN'ting
acquainting
attainting
fainting
feinting
painting
tainting
word-painting

ĂN'ting,
　ĂN'ting
Banting
canting
chanting
decanting
descanting
disenchanting
enchanting
granting
hanting
implanting

panting
planting
ranting
recanting
slanting
supplanting
transplanting

ĂN'tist
ignorantist
Kantist

ĂN'tist
Vedantist

ĂN'tiv
constraintive
plaintive

ĂN'tizm
dilettantism
ignorantism
Kantism
obscurantism
pococurantism
rantism

ĂN't'l
cantle
dismantle
immantle
mantel
mantle
scantle

ĂN't'ld
dismantled
ivy-mantled
mantled

ĂNT'let
cantlet

mantelet	ĂN'to or ĀN'to	ĂN'tur or	disdainer
plantlet	canto	ĀN'tur	drainer
ĂNT'let	coranto	banter	enchainer
	portmanteau	canter	entertainer
gauntlet	pro tanto	chanter	explainer
ĂNT'let	quo warranto	decanter	feigner
		descanter	gainer
gantlet	ĂN'tom	enchanter	grainer
ĂNT'li	(see ĂN'tam)	granter	inaner
		implanter	maintainer
quaintly	ĂN'ton	instanter	nonabstainer
saintly	Canton	Levanter	obtainer
unsaintly	Clanton	panter	ordainer
ĂNT'li	Danton	planter	plainer
	Scranton	ranter	profaner
aslantly	Stanton	recanter	refrainer
scantly		supplanter	regainer
ĂNT'lik	ĂN'tor	transplanter	restrainer
	cantor	trochanter	retainer
saintlike	grantor		saner
ĂNT'ling		ĀN'tur	stainer
bantling	ĀN'tres	chanter	strainer
mantling	chantress	disenchanter	sustainer
scantling	enchantress	enchanter	trainer
			unchainer
ĂNT'lur	ĂN'tri	ĂN'turn	uptrainer
antler	pantry	lantern	vainer
dismantler	ĂN'tri	ĂN'ur	ĀN'ur
mantler	chantry	abstainer	banner
pantler		appertainer	canner
ĂNT'ment	ĂN'tu	arraigner	fanner
disenchantment	Bantu	ascertainer	japanner
enchantment		attainer	lanner
	ĂN'tur	bestainer	manner
ĂNT'nes	acquainter	campaigner	manor
faintness	fainter	complainer	planner
quaintness	painter	constrainer	scanner
	quainter	container	spanner
ĂNT'nes	tainter	cordwainer	tanner
scantness	word-painter	detainer	

ōld, ôr, ŏdd, oil, fŏŏt, out; ūse, ûrn, ŭp; THis, thin

trepanner	Nathaniel	ĂP'en	*enwrappeth*
vanner	spaniel	happen	*flappeth*
ĂN'urd	staniel		*lappeth*
	water-spaniel	ĂP'est	*mappeth*
bannered		*apest*	*nappeth*
ill-mannered	**ĂN'yur**	*drapest*	*rappeth*
mannered	pannier	*escapest*	*sappeth*
unmannered		*gapest*	*slappeth*
well-mannered	**ĂN'za**	*rapest*	*snappeth*
ĂN'us	bonanza	*scrapest*	*trappeth*
	extravaganza	*shapest*	*wrappeth*
heinous	ganza		
incanous	stanza	ĂP'est	**ĂP'got**
Janus		*clappest*	scape-goat
Silvanus	**ĂNZ'feld**	*enwrappest*	
veinous	Mansfield	*flappest*	**ĂP'gras**
ĂN'vas		*lappest*	scape-grace
	ĂN'zi	*mappest*	
canvas	chimpanzeee	*nappest*	**ĂP'i**
canvass	pansy	*rappest*	
ĂN'vil	tansy	*sappest*	crapy
		slappest	gapy
anvil	**ĂN'zvil**	*snappest*	red-tapy
Danville	Janesville	*trappest*	scrapy
Granville	Zanesville	*wrappest*	
ĂN'wurk			**ĂP'i**
	Ā'o	ĂP'ĕt	chappy
brainwork	cacao	lappet	gappy
chainwork	tetrao	tappet	gapy
plain-work			happy
ĂN'yan	**Ā'on**	ĂP'eth	knappy
banyan	crayon	*apeth*	nappy
canyon		*drapeth*	pappy
companion	**Ā'on**	*escapeth*	sappy
	gaon	*gapeth*	scrappy
ĂN'yard		*rapeth*	snappy
lanyard	**Ā'os**	*scrapeth*	
Spaniard	chaos	*shapeth*	**ĂP'id**
			rapid
ĂN'yel	**Ā'oth**	ĂP'eth	sapid
Daniel	Sabaoth	*clappeth*	vapid

āle,   câre,   ădd,   ärm,   ăsk;   mē,   hĕre,   ĕnd;   īce,   ĭll;

ĂP'ik
jalapic
Lappic

ĂP'in
rapine

ĀP'ing
aping
draping
escaping
gaping
raping
scraping
shaping

ĂP'ing
capping
clapping
dapping
entrapping
enwrapping
flapping
gaping
handicapping
lapping
mapping
napping
overlapping
rapping
sapping
scrapping
slapping
snapping
strapping
tapping
trapping
understrapping
unwrapping
wrapping
yapping

AP'is
apis
lapis
Serapis
tapis

ĂP'is
lapis
tapis

ĂP'ish
apish
papish

ĂP'ish
knappish
snappish

ĂP'ist
lanscapist
papist
redtapist

ĂP'izm
papism
red-tapism

ĂP"l
anti-papal
capel
maple
papal
staple
wool-staple

ĂP"l
ante-chapel
apple
chapel

dapple
grapple
knapple
love-apple
rappel
scapple
scrapple
thrapple

ĂP'les
apeless
capeless
crapeless
escapeless
grapeless
napeless
scrapeless
shapeless
tapeless

ĂP'les
capless
hapless
napless
sapless

ĂP'let
chaplet

ĂP'li
shapely

ĂP'li
haply

ĂP'lin
chaplain
Chaplin

ĂP'ling
dappling

grappling
lapling
sapling

ĂP'l'z
Naples
Staples

ĂP'man
Capman
Chapman
Knapman

ĂP'nel
grapnel
shrapnel

ĂP'on
capon
misshapen
tapen
unshapen

ĂP'ril
April

ĂP'shun
caption
collapsion
contraption
elapsion
recaption

ĂP'shus
captious

ĂP'sing
collapsing
lapsing
relapsing

ĂP'stan
capstan

ĂP'stur
tapster

ĂP'ted
adapted

ĂP'test
adaptest
aptest
inaptest
raptest

ĂP'tin
captain

ĂP'tiv
adaptive
captive

ĂP'tizm
anabaptism
baptism

ĂPT'li
aptly
inaptly
raptly

ĂPT'nes
aptness
inaptness
raptness
unaptness

ĂP'trap
clap-trap

ĂP'tŭr
capture

enrapture
rapture
recapture

ĂP'tŭr
adapter
apter
captor
chapter
rapter
recaptor

ĀP'ur
aper
caper
draper
escaper
gaper
landscaper
paper
raper
sapor
scraper
shaper
sky-scraper
taper
tapir
undraper
vapor

ĂP'ur
capper
clapper
dapper
entrapper
enwrapper
flapper
fly-flapper
gaper
handicapper
lapper

mapper
napper
overlapper
rapper
sapper
slapper
snapper
snippersnapper
strapper
tapper
trapper
understrapper
unwrapper
whipper-
    snapper
wrapper
yapper

ĂP'urz
walking-papers
capers, etc.

ĂP'us
pappus
trappous

ĂP'wing
lapwing

Ā'ra
cordillera
dulcamara
Marah
Sara
Sarah

'ĂR'a
Sahara
tiara

Ă'ra
Bara
Clara

Ä'ra
caracara
Ferrara
Gemara
Sahara
solfatara
tiara

ĂR'ab
Arab
scarab

ĂR'ak
arrack
barrack
carrack

Ā'rans
abearance
forbearance
(cf. apparence)

Ā'rant
declarant
forbearant
(cf. parent,
    etc.)

ĂR'ant
arrant

ĂR'ant
warrant
(see ŎR'ent)

ĂR'as
arras

debarrass
disembarrass
embarrass
harass

ÄR'bel
harebell
prayer-bell

ÄR'bi
Darby
Derby

ÄR'bij
garbage

ÄR'b'l
barbel
emmarble
garbel
garble
marble

ÄR'blur
garbler
marbler

ÄR'bling
garbling
marbling

ÄR'bord
larboard
starboard

ÄR'boil
parboil

ÄR'bon
carbon
charbon

ÄR'bur
arbor
barber
Barbour
enharbor
harbor
unharbor

ÄR'chest
archest
enarchest
marchest
parchest
starchest

ÄR'cheth
archeth
enarcheth
marcheth
parcheth
starcheth

ÄR'chez
arches
counter-
 marches
larches
marches
outmarches
overarches
parches
starches

ÄR'chi
archy
larchy
starchy

ÄR'ching
arching
counter-
 marching

marching
outmarching
overarching
overmarching
parching
starching

ÄRCH'ment
archment
emparchment
parchment

ÄRCH'nes
archness

ÄR'chur
archer
clear-starcher
Larcher
marcher
starcher

ÄRCH'wa
archway

ÄR'dant
gardant
regardant
(cf. ardent)

ÄRD'arm
yard-arm

ÄR'ded
bombarded
carded
discarded
disregarded
guarded
larded
regarded

retarded
sharded
unguarded
unregarded
unretarded

ÄR'del
fardel

**ÄR'den,
 ÄR'don**
beergarden
bombardon
caseharden
enharden
garden
harden
pardon

**ÄR'dend,
 ÄR'dond**
case-hardened
hardened
pardoned
weather-
 hardened

ÄR'dĕnt
ardent
(cf., ÄR'dant)

ÄR'dest
bombardest
discardest
disregardest
guardest
hardest
lardest
regardest
retardest

ōld, ôr, ŏdd, oil, fŏŏt, out; ūse, ûrn, ŭp; THis, thin

ÄR'deth	unguarding	**ÄRD'ship**	**ÄR'en**
discardeth	wool-carding	guardship	Karen
disregardeth		hardship	McLaren
guardeth	**ÄR'd'l**		
lardeth	Bardle	**ÄRDZ'man**	**ÄR'ens**
regardeth	McArdle	guardsman	apparence
retardeth			Clarence
	ÄRD'les	**ÄR'dur**	transparence
ÄRD'ful	cardless	ardor	(cf. forbear-
disregardful	guardless	bombarder	ance)
guardful	regardless	carder	
regardful		discarder	**ÄR'ent**
	ÄRD'li	disregarder	apparent
ÄR'di	hardly	guarder	celarent
foolhardy		harder	parent
hardy	**ÄRD'ment**	larder	transparent
tardy	bombardment	regarder	(cf. declarant,
	retardment	retarder	etc.)
ÄRD'ik			
anacardic	**ÄRD'nes**	**ÄR'e**	**ÄR'es**
bardic	hardness	shikaree	heiress
bezoardic		(cf. ÄR'i)	
Lombardic	**ÄRD'ning**		**ÄR'est**
pericardic	gardening	**ÄR'el**	*airest*
	hardening	apparel	*barest*
ÄR'din	pardoning	barrel	*bearest*
nardine		carol	*carest*
sardine	**ÄRD'nur**	Carroll	*comparest*
	gardener	disapparel	*darest*
ÄR'ding	hardener	Farrell	*declarest*
bombarding	pardner	Harrell	*despairest*
carding	pardoner	parrel	*ensnarest*
discarding		pork barrel	*fairest*
disregarding	**ÄR'do**		*farest*
guarding	bocardo	**ÄR'eld**	*forbearest*
Harding	bombardo	apparelled	*glarest*
larding		carolled	*impairest*
placarding	**ÄR'dom**	double-	*outdarest*
regarding	backstairdom	barrelled	*pairest*
retarding	heirdom	**ÄR'em**	*parest*
		harem	*preparest*

ăle,   câre,   ădd,   ärm,   åsk;   mē,   hẹre,   ĕnd;   īce,   ĭll;

rarest	*fareth*	**ÄR′for**	**ÄR′i**
repairest	*flareth*	wherefore	ablutionary
sharest	*forbeareth*	(cf. therefore,	accessary
snarest	*forsweareth*	ÛR′for).	accidentiary
sparest	*glareth*		accustomary
squarest	*impaireth*	**ÄR′ful**	actuary
starest	*outdareth*	careful	additionary
swearest	*paireth*	prayerful	adminculary
tearest	*pareth*	uncareful	adversary
unfairest	*prepareth*		airy
wearest	*repaireth*	**ÄR′gan**	ancillary
	shareth	Dargan	antiquary
ÄR′est	*snareth*		apothecary
barrest	*spareth*	**ÄR′gēt**	arbitrary
debarrest	*squareth*	target	Ave Mary
jarrest	*stareth*		beneficiary
marrest	*sweareth*	**ÄR′gin**	bicentenary
scarrest	*teareth*	bargain	canary
sparrest	*wearth*		capillary
starrest		**ÄR′g′l**	Carey
tarrest	**ÄR′eth**	argle-bargle	cassowary
	barreth	gargle	cautionary
ÄR′et	*debarreth*		centenary
carat	*marreth*	**ÄR′go**	chary
carrot	*scarreth*	Argo	commentary
claret	*sparreth*	argot	commissary
garret	*starreth*	botargo	confectionary
Garrett	*tarreth*	cargo	constabulary
parrot		Dargo	contemporary
	ÄR′ez	embargo	contrary
ÄR′eth	Benares	Fargo	contributary
aireth	Buenos Ayres	largo	corollary
bareth		Spargo	culinary
beareth	**ÄR′fasd**	supercargo	customary
careth	barefaced		dairy
compareth	fair-faced	**ÄR′gon**	depositary
dareth		argon	dictionary
declareth	**ÄR′fish**	jargon	dietary
despaireth	garfish		dignitary
ensnareth	starfish	**ÄR′gu**	disciplinary
		argue	discretionary

ōld, ôr, ŏdd, oil, fŏŏt, out; ūse, ûrn, ŭp; THis, thin

dromedary
eleemosynary
elocutionary
epistolary
estuary
evolutionary
extraordinary
fairy
February
fiduciary
formulary
fragmentary
functionary
ganglionary
glairy
hairy
hebdomadary
hereditary
honorary
imaginary
incendiary
insurrectionary
intermediary
janissary
January
legendary
legionary
literary
luminary
Mary
maxillary
mercenary
military
millenary
missionary
momentary
monetary
mortuary
necessary
obituary
ordinary

passionary
pecuniary
pensionary
petitionary
planetary
prairie
prebendary
processionary
prolegomenary
proprietary
prothonotary
provisionary
pulmonary
quandary
questionary
questuary
reactionary
reliquary
residuary
reversionary
revolutionary
rosemary
salivary
salutary
sanctuary
sanguinary
sanitary
scapulary
scary
secondary
secretary
sedentary
seditionary
seminary
snary
solitary
stationary
statuary
stipendiary
sublunary
subsidiary

sumptuary
supernumerary
temporary
tertiary
Tipperary
titulary
traditionary
tributary
tuitionary
tumulary
tumultuary
tutelary
ubiquitary
unchary
unwary
vagary
valetudinary
vairy
vary
veterinary
vicissitudinary
visionary
vocabulary
voluntary
voluptuary
vulnerary
wary
(cf. ẸR'ĭ)

ĂR'ĭ

Barrie
Carrie
carry
charivari
harri-karri
harry
intermarry
Larry
marry
miscarry

parry
tarry

ĂR'ĭ

araçari
barry
carbonari
charry
scarry
sparry
starry
tarry
(cf. shikaree)

ĂR'ĭd

varied

ĂR'ĭd

arid
carried
harried
intermarried
married
miscarried
parried
tarried

ĂR'ĭf, ĂR'ĭf

hairif

ĂR'ĭf

harif
tariff

ĂR'ĭj

carriage
disparage
intermarriage
marriage
miscarriage

railway-   flaring   sparring   *enlargest*
   carriage   forbearing   starring   largest
water-carriage   forswearing   tarring   *overchargest*
                        glaring   unbarring
ÄR'ik   impairing   **ÄR'jet**
agaric   outdaring   **ÄR'ingks**   garget
Amharic   outstaring   larynx   parget
Balearic   outswearing   pharynx
barbaric   outwearing   **ÄR'jeth**
baric   overbearing   **ÄR'is**   *chargeth*
Bulgaric   pairing   Farris   *dischargeth*
cinnabaric   paring   Harris   *enlargeth*
Garrick   preparing   Paris   *overchargeth*
isobaric   repairing   phalaris
Megaric   scaring   polaris   **ÄR'jez**
pimaric   sea-faring   barges
Pindaric   sharing   **ÄR'ish**   charges
polaric   snaring   bearish   discharges
saccharic   sparing   debonairish   enlarges
stearic   squaring   fairish   marges
tartaric   staring   garish   targes
                        swearing   marish
ÄR'ik   tale-bearing   squarish   **ÄR'jik**
Amharic   tearing   tarish   lethargic
                        unbearing
ÄR'ing   underbearing   **ÄR'ish**   **ÄR'jin**
airing   unsparing   marish   margin
baring   upbearing   parish
bearing   upstaring   **ÄR'jing**
blaring   uptearing   **ÄR'izm**   barging
caring   wayfaring   proletairism   charging
chairing   wearing   Voltairism   discharging
charing   enlarging
cheese-paring   **ÄR'ing**   overcharging
comparing   barring   **ÄR'jent**
daring   charring   argent
declaring   debarring   sergeant   **ÄRJ'li**
despairing   disbarring   largely
ensnaring   jarring   **ÄR'jest**
fairing   marring   *chargest*   **ÄRJ'ment**
faring   scarring   *dischargest*   enlargement

ÄRJ'ur	*marketh*	ÄR'kist	ÄR'kur
barger	*remarketh*	heptarchist	barker
charger		oligarchist, etc.	darker
discharger	ÄR'ki		embarker
enlarger	barky	ÄR'kivs	harker
larger	darky	archives	larker
sparger	heterarchy	ÄR'k'l	marcor
surcharger	hierarchy		marker
undercharger	larky	darkle	parker
	oligarchy	sparkle	sharker
ÄR'kal	patriarchy	ÄRK'let	sparker
anarchal		parklet	starker
hierarchal	ÄR'kik	sparklet	
monarchal	anarchic		ÄRK'wis
oligarchal	antianarchic	ÄRK'li	marquis
patriarchal	climatarchic	clarkly	
squirearchal	heptarchic	darkly	ÄR'land
	hierarchic	starkly	engarland
ÄR'kazm	monarchic		Farland
sarcasm	oligarchic	ÄRK'ling	garland
	patriarchic	darkling	
ÄR'ken		sparkling	ÂR'les
bedarken	ÄR'kin		airless
darken	Larkin	ÄRK'nes	careless
endarken		darkness	hairless
hearken	ÄR'king		heirless
	barking	ÄRK'nur	pairless
ÄR'kest	carking	darkener	prayerless
barkest	disembarking	hearkener	snareless
darkest	embarking		tareless
embarkest	harking	ÄR'kol	
markest	larking	charcoal	ÄR'les
remarkest	marking	ÄRK'som	scarless
starkest	parking	darksome	starless, etc.
	remarking		
ÄR'ket	sky-larking	ÄRK'spur	ÄR'let
market		larkspur	carlet
	ÄR'kish		scarlet
ÄR'keth	darkish	ÄRK'tik	starlet
barketh	larkish	Antarctic	varlet
embarketh	sparkish	Arctic	(cf. harlot)

ÄR'li
barely
fairly
rarely
unfairly
yarely

ÄR'li
Arleigh
barley
Charley
Farley
gnarly
Harley
marli
McCarley
parley

ÄR'līk
starlike, etc.

ÄR'lĭk
garlic
pilgarlick
sarlyk

ÄR'lin
air-line
hair-line

ÄR'lind
carelined
hair-lined

ÄR'ling
darling
Harling
snarling
sparling
starling

ÄR'līt
starlight

ÄR'lĭt
far-lit
starlit

ÄR'lok
charlock
harlock
(cf. Harlech)

ÄR'lot
Charlotte
harlot
(cf. scarlet)

ÄR'lum
heirloom

ÄR'lur
gnarler
parlor
snarler

ÄR'lus
parlous

ÄR'mad
barmaid

ÄR'man
chairman

ÄR'men
carmen

ÄR'ment
debarment
disbarment
garment
sarment

ÄR'mest
alarmest
armest
charmest
disarmest
farmest
harmest

ÄR'met
armet

ÄR'meth
alarmeth
armeth
charmeth
disarmeth
farmeth
harmeth

ÄRM'ful
armful
charmful
harmful
unharmful

ÄR'mi
army
barmy

ÄR'mik
alexipharmic
lexipharmic
ptarmic

ÄR'min
carmine
harmine

ÄR'ming
alarming
arming

baby-farming
charming
disarming
farming
forearming
harming
unalarming
unarming
uncharming
unharming

ÄRM'les
armless
charmless
harmless

ÄRM'let
armlet
charmlet

ÄR'mot
carmot
marmot

ÄR'mur
alarmer
armor
baby-farmer
charmer
disarmer
farmer
harmer
plate-armor
serpent-
  charmer

ÄR'nal
carnal
carnel
charnel
darnel
uncharnel

ōld, ôr, ŏdd, oil, fŏŏt, out; ūse, ûrn, ŭp; THis, thin

ÄR'nard	tarnished	claro	**ÄR'pur**
Barnard	ungarnished	taro	carper
	untarnished		harper
ÄR'nat	unvarnished	**ÄR'on**	sharper
incarnate	varnished	Aaron	
		Charon	**ÄR'sal**
ÄR'nes	**ÄR'nold**		metatarsal
bareness	Arnold	**ÄR'old**	tarsal
debonairness		Harold	varsal
fairness	**ÄRN'li**	carolled, etc.	
rareness	Darnley		**ÄR'sel**
spareness		**ÄR'on**	parcel
squareness	**ÄR'nur**	baron	*sarcel*
threadbare-	darner	barren	
ness	garner		**ÄR'sez**
unfairness	yarner	**ÄR'pest**	farces
whereness		*carpest*	parses
	ÄR'o	*harpest*	sarses
ÄR'nes	pharaoh	sharpest	
farness	Rio de Janeiro		**ÄR'shal**
harness		**ÄR'pet**	earl-marshal
	ÄR'o	carpet	field-marshal
ÄRN'ham	bolero		*immartial*
Farnham	caballero	**ÄR'peth**	impartial
(cf. Farnum,	faro	*carpeth*	marshal
Barnum)	llanero	*harpeth*	Marshall
	sombrero		martial
ÄR'ni	vaquero	**ÄR'pi**	partial
blarney		carpy	unmartial
carney	**ÄR'o**	harpy	
Killarney	arrow		**ÄRS'li**
	barrow	**ÄR'ping**	scarcely
ÄR'nij	farrow	carping	
carnage	harrow	harping	**ÄRS'ness**
	marrow	sharping	scarceness
ÄR'nish	narrow		
garnish	sparrow	**ÄR'pist**	**ÄR'son**
tarnish	yarrow	harpist	arson
varnish			Carson
ÄR'nisht	**ÄR'o**	**ÄRP'nes**	Larsen
garnished	carbonaro	sharpness	

āle, câre, ădd, ärm, ȧsk; mē, hẹre, ĕnd; īce, ĭll;

Larson	leaden-hearted	**ÄR'test**	**ÄR'ti**
parson	light-hearted	*cartest*	Astarte
	lion-hearted	*dartest*	charter-party
ÄR'sur	marble-hearted	*departest*	ex parte
parser	open-hearted	*impartest*	hearty
sparser	pale-hearted	*partest*	McCarty
	parted	smartest	party
ÄR'tan	pigeon-hearted	*startest*	
Spartan	proud-hearted	*upstartest*	**ÄR'tin**
tartan	public-hearted		martin
(cf. marten)	right-hearted	**ÄR'teth**	
	sad-hearted	*carteth*	**ÄR'ting**
ÄR'ted	shallow-hearted	*darteth*	carting
broken-hearted	simple-hearted	*departeth*	darting
carted	single-hearted	*imparteth*	departing
charted	smarted	*parteth*	hearting
chicken-hearted	soft-hearted	*smarteth*	imparting
cold-hearted	started	*starteth*	smarting
darted	stony-hearted	*upstarteth*	starting
departed	stout-hearted		sweet-hearting
double-hearted	tender-hearted	**ÄRT'ful**	uncarting
down-hearted	traitor-hearted	artful	upstarting
faint-hearted	triparted		
false-hearted	truehearted	**ÄR'tha**	**ÄR'tist**
flint-hearted	unhearted	Martha	artist
frank-hearted	unimparted		Chartist
free-hearted	upstarted	**ÄR'thest**	
full-hearted	warm-hearted	farthest	**ÄR'tit**
gentle-hearted	weak-hearted		bipartite
great-hearted	wise-hearted	**ÄR'thi**	
half-hearted		McCarthy	**ÄR't'l**
hard-hearted	**ÄR'ten, Är'ton**		dartle
hare-hearted	barton	**ÄR'thing**	startle
hearted	carton	farthing	
hen-hearted	dishearten		**ÄRT'les**
high-hearted	enhearten	**ÄR'THur**	artless
imparted	hearten	farther	chartless
iron-hearted	kindergarten		heartless
kind-hearted	marten	**ÄR'thur**	**ÄRT'let**
large-hearted	smarten	Arthur	heartlet

ōld, ôr, ŏdd, oil, fŏŏt, out; ūse, ûrn, ŭp; THis, thin

martlet	smarter	rarer	ÄR'vest
tartlet	starter	repairer	harvest
	tartar	sea-farer	*starvest*
ÄRT'li	tarter	sharer	
partly	unmartyr	snarer	ÄR'vi
smartly	upstarter	sparer	Garvey
tartly		squarer	Harvey
	ÄR'um	standard-	
ÄRT'ling	arum	bearer	ÄR'ving
startling	carrom	starer	carving
	harum-scarum	swearer	starving
ÄRT'ment	*larum*	sword-bearer	
apartment	marum	tale-bearer	ÄRV'ling
compartment		tankard-bearer	marvelling
department	ÄR'um	tearer	starveling
impartment	*alarum*	train-bearer	
		upbearer	ÄR'vur
ÄRT'nes	ÄR'ur	way-farer	carver
smartness	airer	wearer	marver
tartness	armor-bearer		starver
	barer	ÄR'ur	
ÄRT'rij	bearer	barrer	ÄR'wavs
cartridge	blarer	bizarrer	air-waves
partridge	comparer	debarrer	
	darer	marrer	ÄR'wel
ÄRT'wa	declarer	sparrer	farewell
cartway	despairer	tarrer	
part-way	ensnarer		ÄR'whil
	fairer	ÄR'val	erewhile
ÄR'tur	flarer	larval	
barter	forbearer		ÄR'worn
bemartyr	forswearer	ÄR'vel	careworn
carter	glarer	carvel	prayerworn
charter	impairer	marvel	
darter	mace-bearer		ÄS'a
departer	outdarer	ÄR'veld	Amasa
garter	outstarer	marvelled	Asa
imparter	overbearer		ÄS'a
martyr	parer	ÄR'ven	Hadasseh
parter	preparer	carven	Manasseh
protomartyr			

Ā'sal	*bracest*	**ĀS'eth**	braces
basal	*chasest*	*abaseth*	breathing-
casal	*debasest*	*baseth*	spaces
	defacest	*begraceth*	cases
ĀS'at	*disgracest*	*belaceth*	chariot-traces
cassate	*displacest*	*braceth*	chases
incrassate	*effacest*	*chaseth*	commonplaces
	embracest	*debaseth*	debases
Ā'sens, Ā'sans	*enlacest*	*defaceth*	defaces
abaisance	*erasest*	*disgraceth*	disgraces
adjacence	*facest*	*displaceth*	displaces
complacence	*gracest*	*effaceth*	effaces
connascence	*interlacest*	*embraceth*	embraces
interjacence	*lacest*	*enlaceth*	enlaces
obeisance	*outpacest*	*eraseth*	faces
renascence	*pacest*	*faceth*	footpaces
	placest	*graceth*	footraces
Ā'sent, Ā'sant	*racest*	*interlaceth*	graces
adjacent	*replacest*	*laceth*	grimaces
circumjacent	*retracest*	*outpaceth*	hiding-places
complacent	*spacest*	*paceth*	horse-races
connascent	*tracest*	*placeth*	interlaces
"daycent"	*unlacest*	*raceth*	interspaces
enascent		*replaceth*	laces
indurascent	**ĀS'est**	*retraceth*	maces
interjacent	*amassest*	*spaceth*	misplaces
jacent	*classest*	*traceth*	outfaces
naissant	crassest	*unlaceth*	outpaces
nascent	*massest*		paces
renaissant	*passest*	**ĀS'eth**	placcs
renascent	*surpassest*	*amasseth*	races
"raycent"		*classeth*	replaces
subjacent	**ĀS'et**	*masseth*	resting-places
superjacent	asset	*passeth*	retraces
	basset	*surpasseth*	spaces
ĀS'ēst	brasset		steeple-chases
abasest	facet	**ĀS'ez**	traces
basest	fascet	aces	trysting-places
begracest	placet	bases	ukases
belacest	(cf. tacit)	begraces	uncases
		belaces	

ōld, ôr, ŏdd, oil, fŏŏt, out; ūse, ûrn, ŭp; THis, thin

unlaces	ĂSH'bord	ĂSH'ez	balderdashing
vases	dashboard	abashes	cashing
	splashboard	ashes	clashing
ĂS'ez		caches	crashing
amasses	Ā'shens	cashes	dashing
asses	patience	clashes	fashing
brasses		crashes	flashing
classes	Ā'shent	dashes	gashing
gases	impatient	flashes	gnashing
glasses	patient	gashes	hashing
grasses		gnashes	lashing
lasses	ĂSH'est	hashes	mashing
masses	cashest	lashes	plashing
molasses	clashest	mashes	slashing
morasses	crashest	mustaches	smashing
passes	dashest	rashes	splashing
surpasses	flashest	rehashes	thrashing
ĀS'ful	gashest	sashes	unlashing
disgraceful	gnashest	slashes	
graceful	lashest	smashes	ĂSH'li
ungraceful	mashest	splashes	Ashley
	slashest	unlashes	flashly
ĂSH'a	smashest		gashly
attaché	splashest	ĂSH'ful	
cachet	thrashest	bashful	ĂSH'man
sachet		gashful	ashman
	ĂSH'eth	rashful	"flashman"
Ā'shal	casheth	unbashful	
abbatial	clasheth		Ā'sho
craniofacial	crasheth	ĂSH'i	Horatio
facial	dasheth	ashy	
glacial	flasheth	flashy	Ā'shun
palatial	gasheth	hashy	abalienation
prelatial	gnasheth	mashie	abacination
racial	lasheth	mashy	abbreviation
spatial	masheth	plashy	abdication
unifacial	slasheth	slashy	aberration
(cf. basial)	smasheth	splashy	abjudication
	splasheth	trashy	abjuration
Ā'shan	thrasheth		ablactation
(cf. Ā'shun)		ĂSH'ing	ablation
		abashing	

āle, câre, ădd, ärm, ȧsk; mē, hẹre, ĕnd; īce, ĭll;

abnegation
abomination
abrogation
absentation
acceleration
acceptation
acclamation
acclimatation
acclimation
acclimatization
accommodation
accreditation
accrimination
accubation
accumulation
accusation
acervation
acidification
activation
actualization
actuation
acumination
acupunctuation
adaptation
adequation
adhortation
adjudication
adjuration
administration
admiration
adoration
adornation
adulation
adulteration
adumbration
adversation
advocation
aëration
aërostation
affectation
affiliation

affirmation
afflation
afforestation
aggeration
agglomeration
agglutination
aggrandization
aggravation
aggregation
agitation
agnation
agnomination
alcoholization
alienation
alimentation
alkalization
allegation
allegorization
alleviation
alligation
alliteration
allocation
alteration
altercation
alternation
amalgamation
ambulation
amelioration
Americaniza-
   tion
ampliation
amplification
amputation
analysation
anathematiza-
   tion
anglicization
Anglification
angulation
animalization
animation

annexation
annihilation
annomination
annotation
annulation
annumeration
annunciation
anticipation
antilibration
appellation
application
appreciation
approbation
appropriation
approximation
aration
arbitration
arcuation
argentation
argumentation
aromatization
arrestation
arrogation
articulation
Asian
asphyxiation
aspiration
assassination
assentation
asseveration
assignation
assimilation
assimulation
association
atomization
attenuation
attestation
attrectation
augmentation
auguration
auscultation

authentication
authorization
averruncation
aviation
avocation
backwardation
basification
beatification
beautification
bifurcation
blood-relation
blusteration
bombilation
botheration
brutalization
brutification
cachinnation
calcification
calcination
calculation
calorification
calumniation
cameration
canalization
cancellation
canonization
cantillation
capitalization
capitation
capitulation
caprification
captivation
carbonization
carbunculation
carnation
cassation
castellation
castigation
castrametation
catechization
causation

ōld, ôr, ŏdd, oil, fŏŏt, out; ūse, ûrn, ŭp; THis, thin

cauterization	commendation	consolidation	debilitation
celebration	commensura-	constellation	decalcification
cementation	tion	consternation	decantation
centralisation	communication	consubstantia-	decapitation
cerebration	commination	tion	decentraliza-
certification	commiseration	consultation	tion
cessation	communication	consummation	decimation
cetacean	commutation	contamination	declamation
chain station	compellation	contemplation	declaration
characteriza-	compensation	continuation	declination
tion	compilation	contravallation	decollation
chrismation	complication	conversation	deconsecration
Christian-	compotation	convocation	decoration
ization	compurgation	co-operation	decortication
cineration	computation	co-optation	decrepitation
circulation	concentration	co-ordination	decubation
circumgyration	concertation	copulation	decussation
circumnaviga-	conciliation	cornification	dedication
tion	condemnation	coronation	defalcation
circumnutation	condensation	corporation	defamation
circumvallation	condonation	correlation	defecation
circumvolation	confabulation	corroboration	deflagration
citation	confederation	corrugation	defloration
civilization	configuration	coruscation	deformation
clarification	confirmation	creation	defraudation
classification	confiscation	cremation	degeneration
coagulation	conflagration	crenellation	degradation
coaxation	conformation	crepitation	degustation
codification	confrontation	crimination	dehortation
cogitation	confutation	crustacean	deification
cognation	congelation	crustation	delation
cohabitation	conglomeration	crystallization	delectation
collation	congratulation	*cubation*	delegation
colligation	congregation	culmination	deliberation
collocation	conjugation	cultivation	delimitation
colonization	conjuration	cupellation	delineation
coloration	connotation	curvation	deliration
columniation	consecration	Dalmatian	deltafication
combination	conservation	damnation	demarcation
commemora-	consideration	damnification	dementation
tion	consolation	debarkation	demonetization

āle, câre, ădd, ärm, ăsk; mē, hẹre, ĕnd; īce, ĭll;

demonstration
demoralization
denationaliza-
   tion
denization
denomination
denotation
dentation
denticulation
dentilation
denudation
denunciation
deodorization
deoppilation
deosculation
deoxidation
deoxygenation
depilation
deploration
depopulation
deportation
depositation
depravation
deprecation
depreciation
depredation
deprivation
depuration
deputation
derivation
derogation
desecration
desiccation
desideration
designation
desolation
desperation
despoliation
desquamation
destination
deterioration

determination
deterration
detestation
detonization
detruncation
devastation
deviation
devirgination
dictation
diffarreation
differentiation
digitation
dilapidation
dilatation
dilation
dimidiation
disapprobation
discoloration
discontinuation
discrimination
disculpation
disfiguration
disinclination
disintegration
dislocation
dispensation
disputation
disqualification
dissemination
dissentation
dissertation
disseveration
dissimulation
dissipation
dissociation
distillation
divagation
divarication
diversification
divination
divulgation

documentation
domestication
domiciliation
domination
donation
dotation
dulcification
duplication
duration
economization
edification
education
edulcoration
effectuation
effemination
effeminization
efflation
effoliation
ejaculation
ejulation
elaboration
elation
electrification
electrization
electrolyzation
elevation
elimination
elixation
elucidation
emaciation
emanation
emancipation
emasculation
embrocation
emendation
emigration
emulation
endenization
enervation
enthronization
enucleation

enumeration
enunciation
equalization
equation
equilibration
equitation
equivocation
eradication
eructation
estimation
estivation
eternization
etherealization
etiolation
evacuation
evangelization
evaporation
even**tu**ation
evisceration
evocation
evolation
exacerbation
exaggeration
exaltation
examination
exasperation
excavation
excitation
exclamation
excogitation
excommuni-
   cation
excoriation
excruciation
exculpation
execration
exemplification
exercitation
exfoliation
exhalation
exhilaration

exhortation
exhumation
exoneration
expatiation
expatriation
expectation
expectoration
experimen-
  tation
expiation
expiration
explanation
explication
exploitation
exploration
expoliation
exportation
expostulation
expropriation
expugnation
expurgation
exsiccation
exsufflation
extemporiza-
  tion
extenuation
extermination
externalization
extirpation
extravasation
extrication
exudation
exultation
fabrication
facilitation
falcation
falsification
familiarization
fasciation
fascination
fecundation

federation
felicitation
feneration
fenestration
fermentation
ferrumination
fertilization
feudalization
fibrination
figuration
filiation
filtration
fissiparation
fixation
flagellation
flagitation
flirtation
floccillation
florification
flossification
flotation
fluctuation
flusteration
fluxation
foliation
fomentation
forcipation
foreordination
formation
formulization
fortification
fossilification
fossilization
foundation
fraternation
fraternization
frequentation
friation
frication
frondation
fructification

frumentation
frustration
fulguration
fulmination
fumigation
furcation
furfuration
galvanization
gasification
gelatination
gelatinization
gemination
gemmation
generalisation
generation
generification
geniculation
germination ·
gestation
gesticulation
glaciation
glandulation
glomeration
gloriation
glorification
glutination
gradation
graduation
granitification
granulation
graticulation
gratification
gratulation
gravidation
gravitation
gunation
gustation
gyration
habilitation
habitation
habituation

hallucination
hariolation
harmonization
hebetation
hellenization
hepatization
hesitation
hibernation
Hibernization
homologation
horrification
hortation
humanization
humectation
humiliation
hybridization
hydration
hypothecation
idealization
ideation
identification
illaqueation
illation
illustration
imagination
imbrication
imitation
immaculation
immanation
immigration
immoderation
immolation
immortalization
impanation
impersonation
implication
imploration
importation
imprecation
impregnation
improvisation

āle, câre, ădd, ärm, ăsk; mē, hĕre, ĕnd; īce, ĭll;

impugnation
imputation
inadequation
inaffectation
inanimation
inapplication
inappreciation
inarticulation
inauguration
inauration
incameration
incantation
incapacitation
incarceration
incarnation
incarnification
inchoation
incineration
incitation
incivilization
inclination
incommodation
inconsideration
incorporation
incrassation
incremation
incrustation
incubation
inculcation
inculpation
incultivation
incurvation
indemnification
indentation
indetermination
indication
indigitation
indignation
indiscrimina-
tion

individualiza-
tion
individuation
indoctrination
induration
inebriation
inequation
infatuation
infestation
infeudation
infiltration
inflammation
inflation
information
ingemination
ingratiation
ingravidation
ingurgitation
inhabitation
inhalation
inhumation
initiation
innervation
innovation
inoculation
inordination
inosculation
insinuation
inspiration
inspissation
installation
instauration
instigation
instillation
instrumentation
insubordination
insufflation
insulation
insultation
integration

integumenta-
tion
inteneration
intensation
intensification
intercalation
intercolumni-
ation
intercommu-
nication
interdigitation
interlineation
interlocation
intermediation
intermigration
intermutation
interpellation
interpenetra-
tion
interpolation
interpretation
interrelation
interrogation
interstratifi-
cation
intimation
intimidation
intoleration
intonation
intoxication
intrication
inundation
invalidation
investigation
invigoration
invitation
invocation
irradiation
irrigation
irritation
isolation

iteration
jactitation
jaculation
jobation
jollification
jubilation
Judaization
justification
laceration
lachrymation
lactation
lallation
lamentation
lamination
lancination
laniation
lapidation
lapidification
Latinization
laudation
laureation
lavation
laxation
legalization
legation
legislation
legitimation
levation
levigation
levitation
libation
liberation
libration
licentiation
lignification
limitation
lineation
liquation
liquidation
literalization
litigation

ōld, ôr, ŏdd, oil, fŏŏt, out; ūse, ûrn, ŭp; THis, thin

lixiviation
localization
location
lubrication
lucubration
lunation
lustration
luxation
luxuriation
macadam-
  ization
maceration
machicolation
machination
maculation
magnetization
magnification
maladmin-
  istration
maleficiation
malformation
malleation
malversation
manifestation
manipulation
marmoration
martyrization
mastication
materialization
materiation
matriculation
maturation
maximization
mediation
mediatization
medication
meditation
melioration
mellification
mendication
mensuration

mesmerization
metallization
methodization
migration
ministration
miscegenation
mitigation
mobilization
moderation
modernization
modification
modulation
molestation
mollification
monetization
monstration
moralization
mortification
multiplication
mummification
mundification
murmuration
mutation
mutilation
mutuation
mystification
narration
nasalization
natation
nation
naturalization
navigation
necessitation
negation
negotiation
neologization
nervation
neutralization
nictation
nictitation
nidification

nidulation
nigrification
nitrification
nobilitation
noctambulation
noctivagation
nodation
nomination
normalization
notation
notification
Novatian
novation
nudation
nudification
nugation
nullification
numeration
obfuscation
objurgation
oblation
oblatration
obligation
obliteration
obnubilation
obscuration
obsecration
observation
obstination
obviation
occultation
occupation
oneration
operation
oppugnation
oration
orbiculation
orchestration
ordination
organization
orientation

origination
ornamentation
oscillation
oscitation
osculation
ossification
ostentation
otiation
ovation
oxidation
oxygenation
ozonation
ozonification
ozonization
pacation
pacification
pagination
palification
palliation
palpation
palpitation
pandiculation
panification
paralysation
participation
patronization
pauperization
pausation
pectination
peculation
penetration
perambulation
percolation
peregrination
perfectation
perfectionation
perforation
perlustration
permeation
permutation
pernoctation

---

peroration	preservation	racemation	relocation
perpetration	prestidigitation	radiation	remanation
perpetuation	prevarication	*radication*	remonetization
perscrutation	privation	ramification	remonstration
personation	probation	ratification	remuneration
personification	proclamation	ratiocination	renegation
perspiration	procrastination	ration	renovation
perturbation	procreation	realization	renunciation
pestillation	procuration	recalcitration	reparation
petrification	profanation	recantation	repatriation
philosophation	profligation	recapitulation	replication
phonation	prognosticion	recidivation	representatiⱷ
phonetization	prolation	reciprocation	reprobation
piscation	prolification	recitation	reptation
placation	prolongation	reclamation	repudiation
plantation	promulgation	recognization	reputation
plebification	pronation	recommenda-	reservation
plication	pronunciation	tion	resignation
pluralization	propagation	reconciliation	resinification
polarization	*propination*	recordation	respiration
police-station	propitiation	recreation	restoration
pollicitation	propugnation	recrimination	resupination
pollination	prorogation	rectification	resuscitation
polling-station	prostration	*recubation*	retaliation
population	protestation	recuperation	retardation
porphyrization	protuberation	recurvation	reticulation
postillation	provocation	recusation	retractation
postulation	publication	redintegration	retrogradation
potation	pullulation	reformation	revelation
precipitation	pulsation	refrigeration	reverberation
predacean	pulverization	refutation	revibration
predation	punctuation	regelation	revivification
predestination	purgation	regeneration	revocation
predication	purification	registration	*rhetorication*
predomination	quadruplica-	regulation	roboration
premeditation	tion	rehabilitation	rogation
pre-occupation	qualification	reiteration	rose-carnation
preparation	quantification	rejuvenation	rotation
preponderation	quartation	relation	rubification
presensation	quassation	relaxation	ruination
presentation	quotation	relegation	rumination

rustication
saburration
sacrification
salification
salination
salivation
saltation
salutation
salvation
sanctification
sanguification
sanitation
saponification
satiation
sation
saturation
scarification
scintillation
sciscitation
scorification
scrutation
secularization
secundation
sedimentation
segmentation
segregation
self-centration
self-
   preservation
self-
   renunciation
semination
sensation
sensualization
separation
sequestration
serration
serrulation
sibilation
siccation
sideration

signation
signification
silicification
simplification
simulation
sinuation
situation
solarization
solemnization
solicitation
solidification
somnambula-
   tion
sophistication
specialization
specification
speculation
speechification
spiflication
spiritualization
spoliation
sputation
stagnation
starvation
station
stellation
sternutation
stigmatization
stimulation
stipulation
strangulation
stratification
striation
stridulation
stultification
stupration
subarrhation
subjugation
sublation
sublevation
subligation

sublimation
sublimification
sublimitation
sublineation
subordination
subornation
subrogation
substantiation
subtilization
succussation
sudation
sufflation
suffocation
suggilation
sulcation
sulphuration
summation
superannuation
supererogation
supination
supplantation
supplementa-
   tion
supplication
supportation
suppuration
surrogation
suspensation
suspiration
sustentation
susurration
syllabication
syllogization
symbolization
synchroniza-
   tion
syncopation
systematiza-
   tion
tabularization
tabulation

tantalization
tarnation
tartarization
taxation
temeration
temporization
temptation
terebration
tergiversation
termination
tessellation
testacean
testamentation
testation
testification
theorization
Thracian
thurification
tintinnabula-
   tion
titillation
titration
titteration
titubation
toleration
trabeation
tractation
tractoration
tralation
tranquillization
transanimation
transcolation
transfiguration
transformation
translation
transliteration
translocation
transmigration
transmogrifica-
   tion
transmutation

transpiration
transplantation
transportation
transubstantia-
    tion
transudation
tremulation
trepidation
triangulation
tribulation
triplication
tripudiation
trituration
trucidation
trullization
truncation
tubulation
tumultuation
turbination
typification
ulceration
ultimation
ululation
undulation
unification
ustulation
usurpation
utilization
vacation
vaccination
vacillation
vacuolation
validation
valuation
vaporation
vaporization
vapulation
variation
variegation
vaticination
vegetation

vellication
venation
venenation
veneration
ventilation
verbalization
verberation
verification
vermiculation
vernation
versification
vesication
vexation
vexillation
vibration
vigesimation
vilification
vindemiation
vindication
violation
visitation
vitalization
vitiation
vitrification
vitriolation
vitriolization
vituperation
vivification
vocalization
vocation
vociferation
volatilization
volcanization
vulcanization
(cf. ĂSH'i-an)
    words

**ĂSH'en,
ĂSH'un**
ashen
compassion

fashion
impassion
master-passion
passion
(cf. Circassian,
    and ĂSH'i-
    an words)

ĂSH'und
dispassioned
fashioned
impassioned
old-fashioned
passioned
unfashioned
unimpassioned
unpassioned

ĂSH'ur
Asher
baggage-
    smasher
Brasher
casher
clasher
crasher
dasher
flasher
gasher
haberdasher
lasher
masher
rasher
slasher
smasher
splasher
thrasher
unlasher

Ā'shus
audacious

bibacious
capacious
contumacious
disgracious
disputatious
edacious
efficacious
execratious
fallacious
feracious
flirtatious
fugacious
fumacious
gracious
incapacious
inefficacious
linguacious
loquacious
mendacious
minacious
misgracious
mordacious
ostentatious
palacious
perspicacious
pertinacious
pervicacious
predacious
procacious
pugnacious
rampacious
rapacious
sagacious
salacious
sequacious
spacious
tenacious
ungracious
veracious
vexatious

ōld, ôr, ŏdd, oil, fŏŏt, out; ūse, ûrn, ŭp; THis, thin

vivacious
voracious

acanaceous
acanthaceous
alliaceous
amylaceous
arenaceous
bulbaceous
cactaceous
camphoraceous
capillaceous
carbonaceous
cetaceous
corallaceous
coriaceous
cretaceous
crustaceous
cylindraceous
erinaceous
fabaceous
farinaceous
ferulaceous
filaceous
foliaceous
frumentaceous
fungaceous
furfuraceous
gallinaceous
gemmaceous
herbaceous
lappaceous
lardaceous
liliaceous
marlaceous
micaceous
olivaceous
orchidaceous
palmaceous
pectinaceous
perdaceous

perlaceous
piperaceous
pomaceous
porraceous
psittaceous
pulveraceous
ranunculaceous
resinaceous
rosaceous
rutaceous
sabaceous
salicaceous
saponaceous
sarmentaceous
saxifragaceous
schorlaceous
scoriaceous
sebaceous
setaceous
stercoraceous
testaceous
tophaceous
torfaceous
truttaceous
turbinaceous
vinaceous
violaceous

ĂSH'vil

Ashville
Nashville

ĂS'i

Gracie
Lacey
lacy
précis
racy

ĂS'i

brassie

brassy
classy
gassy
glassy
grassy
lassie
Malagasy
massy
morassy
sassy
Tallahasseē

Ā'sid

bayside
braeside
wayside

ĂS'id

acid
placid

ĂS'ij

brassage
passage

ĂS'ik

aphasic
basic
bibasic
dibasic
quadribasic
tribasic

ĂS'ik

boracic
classic
Jurassic
Liassic
potassic
sebacic

thoracic
Triassic

ĂS'il

facile
gracile

ĂS'in

basin
(cf. ĀS'n)

ĂS'in

assassin

ĂS'in

spadassin

ĂS'ing

abasing
basing
begracing
belacing
bracing
casing
chasing
debasing
defacing
disgracing
displacing
effacing
embracing
enlacing
erasing
facing
foot-racing
gracing
horse-racing
interlacing
interspacing
lacing
misplacing

āle, câre, ădd, ärm, ăsk; mē, hẹre, ĕnd; īce, ĭll;

outfacing
outpacing
pacing
placing
racing
replacing
retracing
self-abasing
spacing
steeple-chasing
tight-lacing
tracing
uncasing
underbracing
unlacing

ĂS'ing

amassing
classing
gassing
massing
overpassing
passing
surpassing
underclassing

ĂS'is

basis
crasis
glacis
oasis
phasis

ĂS'is

chassis

ĂS'it

tacit
(cf. ĂS'et)

ĂS'iv

assuasive

dissuasive
evasive
invasive
persuasive
pervasive
suasive

ĂS'iv

impassive
massive
passive

ĂS'ka

Alaska
Athabaska
Nebraska

ĂS'kal

mascle
paschal
rascal
(cf. Haskell,
etc.)

ĂS'kar

Lascar
Madagascar

ĂS'kest

askest
baskest
bemaskest
maskest
taskest
unmaskest

ĂS'ket

basket
bread-basket
casket
flasket

gasket
lasket

ĂS'keth

asketh
basketh
bemasketh
masketh
tasketh
unmasketh

ĂS'king

asking
basking
bemasking
masking
overtasking
tasking
unmasking

ĂS'ko

Belasco
fiasco
tabasco
tasco

ĂS'kur

asker
basker
casquer
masker

ĂS'kus

Damascus

ĂSK'with

Asquith

ĂS' 'l

castle
entassel

envassal
tassel
vassal
wrastle

ĂS'les

aceless
baseless
caseless
faceless
graceless
laceless
maceless
paceless
placeless
raceless
spaceless
traceless

ĂS'let

bracelet

ĂS'let

haslet
taslet

ĂS'li

basely
commonplacely

ĂS'man

baseman
first baseman
laceman
paceman
placeman
raceman
second baseman
third baseman

ĂS'man

classman

ōld, ôr, ŏdd, oil, fŏŏt, out; ūse, ûrn, ŭp; THis. thĭ⁻

gasman	ÅS'nur	ÅS'peth	short-waisted
glassman	chastener	*claspeth*	tasted
	hastener	*enclaspeth*	untasted
ÅS'ment		*gaspeth*	unwasted
abasement	ÅS'nes	*graspeth*	war-wasted
basement	crassness	*raspeth*	wasted
begracement		*unclaspeth*	
belacement	ÅS'o		ÅS'ted
casement	say-so	ÅS'pik	blasted
debasement		aspic	contrasted
defacement	ÅS'o, ÅS'o		fasted
displacement	basso	ÅS'ping	flabbergasted
effacement	lasso	clasping	lasted
embracement	Sargasso	enclasping	masted
encasement	Tasso	engrasping	outlasted
enlacement		gasping	unblasted
erasement	ÅS'ok	grasping	undermasted
interlacement	cassock	rasping	
misplacement	hassock	unclasping	ÅS'tel
placement			pastel
replacement	ÅS'on	ÅS'pur	
retracement	caisson	asper	ÅST'est
self-abasement	Grayson	Caspar	*bastest*
	Jason	Casper	chastest
ÅS'ment	mason	clasper	*foretastest*
amassment	(cf. ÅS'n)	gasper	*hastest*
		grasper	*pastest*
ÅS'min or	ÅS'on	jasper	*tastest*
ÅZ'min	casson	rasper	*wastest*
jasmine	(cf. fasten)		*wastest*
		ÅS'ta	
ÅS' 'n	ÅS'pēn	Shasta	ÅST'est
chasten	aspen		*castest*
enchasten		Å'star	*contrastest*
hasten	ÅS'pest	day-star	fastest
(cf. ÅS'in,	*claspest*		*lastest*
Ås'on)	*enclaspest*	ÅS'ted	*outlastest*
	gaspest	basted	*vastest*
ÅS' 'n	*graspest*	hasted	
fasten	*raspest*	long-waisted	ÅST'eth
(cf. casson)	*unclaspest*	pasted	*basteth*

foretasteth
hasteth
pasteth
tasteth
wasteth

ĂST'eth
casteth
contrasteth
fasteth
lasteth
outlasteth

ĂST'ful
distasteful
tasteful
wasteful

ĂS'ti
hasty
pasty
tasty

ĂS'ti
blasty
epinasty
genioplasty
masty
nasty
vasty

ĂS'tif
mastiff

ĂS'tij
wastage

ĂS'tik
amphiblastic
anaclastic
antiphrastic

antonomastic
bioplastic
bombastic
ceroplastic
chiliastic
clastic
deutoplastic
dichastic
docimastic
drastic
dynastic
ecclesiastic
elastic
emplastic
encomiastic
enthusiastic
esemplastic
fantastic
galvanoplastic
gelastic
gymnastic
Hudibrastic
iconoclastic
inelastic
mastic
metaphrastic
monastic
neoplastic
onomastic
orgiastic
paraphrastic
parasceuastic
paronomastic
peirastic
periphrastic
phelloplastic
plagioclastic
plastic
pleonastic
proplastic
protoplastic

sarcastic
scholastic
scholiastic
spastic
tetrastich

ĂS'tiks
ecclesiastics
elastics
fantastics
gymnastics
phelloplastics

ĂS'tim
pastime

ĂST'ing
basting
foretasting
hasting
pasting
tasting
unwasting
wasting

ĂST'ing
blasting
casting
contrasting
everlasting
fasting
flabbergasting
forecasting
lasting
recasting

ĂS'tingz
Hastings
bastings, etc.

ĂST'les
basteless

hasteless
pasteless
tasteless
waistless
wasteless

ĂST'li
ghastly
lastly
steadfastly
vastly

ĂST'ment
blastment
contrastment

ĂST'nes
fastness
vastness

ĂST'ning
fastening

ĂS'ton
Aston
Gaston

ĂS'tral
astral
cadastral
subastral

ĂS'tri
pastry

ĂS'trik
cacogastric
digastric
gastric
hypogastric
perigastric

ōld, ôr, ŏdd, oil, fŏŏt, out; ūse, ûrn, ŭp; THis, thin

ĂS'tron
apastron
plastron

ĂS'trus
disastrous

ĂS'tur
baster
chaster
foretaster
paster
taster
waster

ĂS'tūr
pasture

ĂS'tŭr, AS'tur
alabaster
aster
Astor
band-master
barrack-master
beplaster
blaster
burgomaster
bushmaster
cadastre
canaster
caster
castor
china-aster
contraster
courtplaster
criticaster
disaster
faster
flabbergaster
forecaster
Goniaster

grammaticaster
grand-master
interpilaster
Latinitaster
master
medicaster
oleaster
overmaster
pastor
piaster
pilaster
plaster
poetaster
postmaster
quarter-master
schoolmaster
shin-plaster
sticking-plaster
taskmaster
vaster

ĂS'tur
shaster

ĂS'turd,
   AS'turd
bastard
beplastered
dastard
mastered
overmastered
pilastered
plastered
unmastered

ĂS'tus
Erastus
Rastus

ĂS'tyun
bastion
(cf. Erastian)

ĀS'ur
abaser
ambulance-
   chaser
baser
begracer
belacer
bracer
chaser
debaser
defacer
disgracer
displacer
effacer
embracer
encaser
eraser
facer
footracer
gracer
grimacer
horse-racer
interlacer
lacer
macer
misplacer
outpacer
pacer
placer
racer
replacer
retracer
spacer
steeple-chaser
tracer
unlacer

ĂS'ur
amasser
antimacassar
masser

passer
placer
surpasser

ĂS'ur
kirsh-wasser

Ā'ta
albata
data
dentata
errata
Invertebrata
postulata
pro rata
strata
ultimata
Vertebrata

ĂT'a
matamata
regatta
strata
(cf. yerba-
   mata)

Ä'ta
a ballata
batata
cantata
data
imbrocata
inamorata
Mahratta
pro rata
reata
serenata
sonata
(cf. yerba-
   mata)

ĀT'al

fatal
natal
prenatal
post-natal
Statal

ĀT'an

Satan
(cf. ĀT'on)

ĀT'ant

blatant
latent
natant
patent
statant

ĀT'ed

abated
abbreviated
abdicated
ablocated
abnegated
abominated
abrogated
accelerated
accentuated
accommodated
accumulated
acidulated
actuated
addle-pated
adjudicated
adulterated
advocated
aërated
affiliated
agglomerated
aggravated
aggregated

agitated
alienated
alleviated
allocated
alternated
amalgamated
ameliorated
ampliated
amputated
annihilated
annotated
annulated
annumerated
annunciated
antedated
anticipated
antiquated
appreciated
approbated
appropriated
approximated
arbitrated
armillated
armor-plated
arrogated
articulated
asphyxiated
aspirated
assassinated
asseverated
assimilated
assimulated
associated
asteriated
attenuated
augurated
aurated
authenticated
awaited
baited
bated

belated
berated
bifurcated
calculated
calumniated
camphorated
capacitated
capitulated
captivated
carbonated
castellated
castigated
celebrated
certificated
circulated
circumstanti-
    ated
coagulated
cogitated
collated
collocated
commemo-
    rated
comminated
commiserated
communicated
compensated
complicated
concentrated
conciliated
confabulated
confederated
confiscated
conglomerated
congratulated
congregated
conjugated
consecrated
consolidated
consummated
contaminated

contemplated
co-operated
co-ordinated
copper-plated
copulated
coronated
correlated
corroborated
corrugated
created
cremated
crenellated
crepitated
culminated
cultivated
dated
debated
debilitated
decapitated
decimated
decorated
dedicated
degenerated
delegated
deliberated
delineated
demonstrated
denominated
depopulated
deprecated
depreciated
derogated
desecrated
desiderated
designated
desolated
deteriorated
detonated
devastated
deviated
dictated

---

differentiated	excommuni-	hated	interrogated
dilapidated	cated	heavy-gaited	intimated
dilated	excoriated	heavy-	intimidated
discriminated	execrated	weighted	intoxicated
disintegrated	exhilarated	hesitated	inundated
dislocated	exonerated	humiliated	invalidated
disseminated	exorbitated	idle-pated	investigated
dissimulated	expatiated	ill-fated	invigorated
dissipated	expatriated	illuminated	invocated
dissociated	expectorated	illustrated	irradiated
domesticated	expiated	imitated	irrigated
dominated	expostulated	immigrated	irritated
dunder-pated	extenuated	immolated	isolated
duplicated	exterminated	impersonated	iterated
educated	extricated	implicated	jasperated
effectuated	fabricated	imprecated	legislated
efflated	facilitated	impropriated	levigated
ejaculated	fascinated	inaugurated	liberated
elaborated	fated	incapacitated	liquidated
elated	federated	incarcerated	located
electro-plated	felicitated	incastellated	lubricated
elevated	fêted	incinerated	luxuriated
eliminated	flagellated	incorporated	macerated
elucidated	fluctuated	incriminated	manipulated
emaciated	foreordinated	incubated	marinated
emanated	formulated	indicated	masticated
emancipated	freighted	indoctrinated	mated
emasculated	frustrated	indurated	matriculated
emigrated	fulminated	inebriated	medicated
emulated	fumigated	infatuated	meditated
enumerated	gaited	inflated	methylated
enunciated	gated	infuriated	migrated
equivocated	generated	ingratiated	militated
eradicated	germinated	initiated	mitigated
estimated	gesticulated	innovated	moderated
evacuated	graduated	inoculated	modulated
evaporated	granulated	insinuated	mutilated
eventuated	grated	instated	narrated
exaggerated	gratulated	instigated	navigated
exasperated	gravitated	insulated	necessitated
excavated	habituated	interpolated	negotiated

āle, câre, ădd, ärm, åsk; mē, hẹre, ĕnd; īce, ĭll;

nickle-plated
nominated
nucleolated
obligated
obliterated
obviated
officiated
operated
opinionated
originated
oscillated
osculated
overrated
overstated
palliated
palpitated
participated
penetrated
perambulated
percolated
peregrinated
perforated
permeated
perpetrated
perpetuated
personated
placated
plaited
plated
plicated
populated
postulated
prated
precipitated
predestinated
predicated
predominated
premeditated
prevaricated
procrastinated
prognosticated

propagated
propitiated
punctuated
radiated
rated
rattle-pated
recapitulated
reciprocated
recreated
recriminated
recuperated
refrigerated
regenerated
regulated
rehabilitated
reinstated
reiterated
rejuvenated
related
relegated
remunerated
renovated
Reno-vated
repatriated
repudiated
resuscitated
retaliated
reverberated
ruminated
rusticated
salivated
sated
satiated
saturated
scintillated
segregated
separated
shallow-pated
sibilated
silicated
silver-plated

simulated
situated
skated
slated
sophisticated
speculated
spifflicated
stated
stimulated
stipulated
subjugated
sublimated
subordinated
substantiated
suffocated
superannuated
supplicated
syncopated
syndicated
tabulated
tergiversated
terminated
tessellated
titillated
tittivated
tolerated
translated
triangulated
triturated
ululated
unabated
unappropri-
    ated
unauthenti-
    cated
uncreated
undecorated
underrated
understated
undulated
unilluminated

unmitigated
unpremedi-
    tated
unrelated
unsophisti-
    cated
unstated
vacated
vaccinated
vacillated
validated
variated
variegated
vegetated
venerated
ventilated
vindicated
violated
vitiated
vituperated
vociferated
waited
weighted

ĂT′ed

battēd
chatted
dratted
fatted
hatted
matted
patted
plaited
platted
(cf. caryatid)

ĂT′en

batten
fatten
flatten

ōld, ôr, ŏdd, oil, fŏŏt, out; ūse, ûrn, ŭp; THis, thin

paten	decoratest	ĂT′est	debateth
ratten	deprecatest	battest	decorateth
	devastatest	chattest	dedicateth
ĂT′ent or	dictatest	fattest	depopulateth
ĂT′ent	dilatest	flattest	devastateth
patent	ejaculatest	pattest	dictateth
	elevatest		dilateth
ĂT′est	emulatest	ĂT′eth	dissipateth
abatest	exaggeratest	abateth	dominateth
abdicatest	fascinatest	abdicateth	educateth
accommodatest	frustratest	accelerateth	ejaculateth
accumulatest	graduatest	accommodateth	elevateth
adulteratest	greatest	accumulateth	emulateth
advocatest	hatest	adulterateth	estimateth
aggravatest	hesitatest	advocateth	exaggerateth
agitatest	imitatest	agitateth	excavateth
alleviatest	indicatest	alleviateth	excommuni-
animatest	irritatest	ameliorateth	cateth
annihilatest	latest	animateth	exhilarateth
anticipatest	liberatest	annihilateth	expiateth
appreciatest	matest	anticipateth	extenuateth
articulatest	narratest	appropriateth	extricateth
assimilatest	necessitatest	arbitrateth	fabricateth
associatest	overratest	articulateth	fascinateth
awaitest	plaitest	associateth	frustrateth
baitest	pratest	awaiteth	hateth
beratest	radiatest	baiteth	hesitateth
calculatest	ratest	calculateth	imitateth
captivatest	regulatest	cancellateth	indicateth
celebratest	relatest	captivateth	irritateth
cogitatest	repudiatest	celebrateth	liberateth
commemoratest	skatest	circulateth	locateth
communicatest	slatest	conciliateth	luxuriateth
conjugatest	statest	confiscateth	mateth
consecratest	toleratest	congratulateth	meditateth
contaminatest	translatest	consecrateth	narrateth
contemplatest	underratest	contaminateth	operateth
createst	vacatest	contemplateth	overrateth
cultivatest	violatest	createth	prateth
debatest	waitest	cremateth	rateth
		cultivateth	regulateth

āle, câre, ădd, ärm, åsk; mē, hēre, ĕnd; īce, ĭll;

relateth	Ăth'en	Ăth'ing	rather
separateth	lathen	bathing	(cf. bother,
skateth		lathing	etc.)
stateth	Ăth'ful		
suffocateth	faithful	Ăth'les	ĂTH'urz
underrateth		faithless	slathers
vaccinateth	Ăth'ful, Ăth'ful	scatheless	gathers, etc.
violateth	wrathful		
waiteth		Ăth'les	ĂT'į
	Ăth'ik	bathless	Ate
ĂT'eth	allopathic	pathless	eighty
batteth	antipathic	wrathless	ex necessitate
chatteth	chrestomathic		Haiti
fatteth	electropathic	ĂTH'om	Jubilate
patteth	felspathic	fathom	maty
	heteropathic		platy
ĂT'ez	homeopathic	ĂTH'omd	slaty
penates	hydropathic	unfathomed	weighty
	idiopathic		
ĂT'foot	kinemato-	Ăth'os	ĂT'ī
flatfoot	graphic	bathos	antenati
	neuropathic	pathos	illuminati
ĂT'form	orthognathic		literati
platform	osteopathic	Ăth'u	
ĂT'ful	philomathic	Matthew	ĂT'į
fateful	polymathic		batty
grateful	prognathic	ĂTH'ur	catty
hateful	psycopathic	bather	chatty
ungrateful	spathic	swather	Cincinnati
	telepathic		fatty
ĂT'ha	theopathic	ĂTH'ur	Hattie
Jagannatha		blather	Mattie
(cf. marana-	ĂTH'ing	forgather	matty
tha)	bathing	gather	natty
Ăth'an	swathing	lather	patty
Elnathan	unswathing	ungather	Pattie
Nathan		upgather	ratty
ĂT'hed	Ā'thing	ĂTH'ur,	ĂT'īd
fathead	plaything	ĂTH'ur	bat-eyed
flathead	(cf. scathing)	father	cat-eyed

ōld, ôr, ŏdd, oil, fŏŏt, out; ūse, ûrn, ŭp; THis, thin

ĂT'ĭd	commatic	magistratic	protatic
caryatid	dalmatic	*majestatic*	quadratic
(cf. batted, etc.)	democratic	mathematic	rhematic
	diagrammatic	melodramatic	rheumatic
ĂT'ĭf	diaphragmatic	miasmatic	sabbatic
caitiff	dichromatic	mobocratic	Sarmatic
	dilemmatic	monochro-	schematic
ĂT'ĭk	diplomatic	matic	schismatic
achromatic	dogmatic	monogram-	sciatic
acousmatic	dramatic	matic	smegmatic
acroatic	*ecbatic*	morganatic	Socratic
acrobatic	ecstatic	muriatic	somatic
acromono-	Eleatic	*noematic*	static
grammatic	emblematic	numismatic	stigmatic
adiabatic	emphatic	ochlocratic	stromatic
Adriatic	endermatic	operatic	subaquatic
aerostatic	enigmatic	palatic	sulphatic
agnatic	epigrammatic	pancratic	sylvatic
anagram-	erratic	pancreatic	symptomatic
matic	fanatic	pantisocratic	systematic
anastatic	fluviatic	paradigmatic	thematic
aphorismatic	geostatic	parallelo-	theocratic
aplanatic	grammatic	grammatic	theorematic
apophtheg-	hallelujatic	pathematic	thermostatic
matic	Hanseatic	phantomatic	timocratic
aquatic	hepatic	phlegmatic	traumatic
aristocratic	hieratic	phosphatic	trigrammatic
arithmocratic	hierogram-	piratic	truismatic
aromatic	matic	platic	vatic
Asiatic	hydrostatic	pleochromatic	viatic
astatic	hyperbatic	plutocratic	villatic
asthmatic	hypostatic	pneumatic	zeugmatic
attic	idiocratic	poematic	zygomatic
autocratic	idiomatic	polychromatic	
automatic	idiosyncratic	pragmatic	**ĂT'ĭk**
axiomatic	isochromatic	prelatic	aquatic
bureaucratic	isodiabatic	prismatic	(see chaotic,
caryatic	kinematic	problematic	etc.)
categorematic	lavatic	proceleus-	
chromatic	lipogrammatic	matic	**ĂT'ĭks**
climatic	lymphatic	prostatic	aerostatics

āle,   câre,   ădd,   ärm,   ăsk;   mē,   hẹre,   ĕnd;   īce,   ĭll;

electro-statics	alleviating	conciliating	determinating
hydrostatics	alternating	confabulating	detonating
hygrostatics	amalgamating	confederating	devastating
mathematics	ameliorating	confiscating	deviating
pneumatics	amputating	congratulating	dictating
statics	animating	congregating	differentiating
attics, etc.	annihilating	conjugating	dilapidating
	annumerating	consecrating	dilating
Ā'tim	anticipating	consolidating	discriminating
daytime	appreciating	consummating	disintegrating
playtime	appropriating	contaminating	dislocating
	approximating	contemplating	disseminating
ĀT'im	arbitrating	co-operating	dissimulating
literatim	armor-plating	corroborating	dissipating
seriatim	articulating	corrugating	dissociating
verbatim	assassinating	creating	dominating
	assimilating	cremating	duplicating
ĀT'in	associating	criminating	educating
Latin	attenuating	culminating	ejaculating
matin	augurating	cultivating	elaborating
patine	authenticating	dating	electro-plating
platen	awaiting	debating	elevating
satin	baiting	debilitating	eliminating
	bating	decapitating	elucidating
ĀT'ing	berating	decimating	emaciating
abating	calculating	decorating	emanating
abbreviating	calumniating	dedicating	emancipating
abdicating	capitulating	degenerating	emigrating
abnegating	castigating	delegating	emulating
abominating	celebrating	deliberating	enumerating
accelerating	circulating	delineating	equivocating
accentuating	coagulating	demonstrating	eradicating
accommodating	cogitating	denominating	estimating
accumulating	collocating	depopulating	evacuating
adulterating	commemorat-	deprecating	evaporating
advocating	ing	depreciating	exaggerating
aërating	commiserating	derivating	exasperating
aggravating	communicating	derogating	excavating
aggregating	compensating	desecrating	excommunica-
agitating	complicating	designating	ting
alienating	concentrating	deteriorating	excruciating

---

execrating
exhilarating
exonerating
expatiating
expectorating
expiating
expostulating
extenuating
extricating
fabricating
facilitating
fascinating
federating
felicitating
fêting
flagellating
fluctuating
formulating
fornicating
freighting
frustrating
fulminating
fumigating
generating
germinating
gesticulating
graduating
granulating
grating
gratulating
gravitating
hating
hesitating
humiliating
illuminating
illustrating
imitating
immigrating
immolating
impersonating
implicating

imprecating
inaugurating
incapacitating
incarcerating
incriminating
incubating
indicating
indiscrimi-
   nating
inebriating
infanticipating
infatuating
inflating
infuriating
ingratiating
initiating
innovating
inoculating
insinuating
instigating
insulating
interpolating
interrogating
intimating
intimidating
intoxicating
inundating
invalidating
investigating
invigorating
invocating
irradiating
irrigating
irritating
isolating
iterating
legislating
liberating
liquidating
locating
lubricating

luxuriating
manipulating
masticating
mating
matriculating
mediating
meditating
migrating
militating
mitigating
moderating
modulating
mutilating
narrating
navigating
necessitating
negotiating
nickle-plating
nominating
obliterating
obviating
operating
originating
oscillating
osculating
overrating
overstating
palliating
palpitating
participating
penetrating
perambulating
percolating
peregrinating
perforating
permeating
perpetrating
perpetuating
personating
plaiting
plating

populating
postulating
prating
precipitating
predominating
premeditating
prevaricating
prognosticat-
   ing
promulgating
propagating
propitiating
punctuating
quadrupli-
   cating
radiating
rating
rebating
recapitulating
reciprocating
recreating
recriminating
recuperating
refrigerating
regulating
reinstating
reiterating
rejuvenating
relating
relegating
remunerating
renovating
repudiating
resuscitating
retaliating
reverberating
ruminating
rusticating
satiating
saturating
scintillating

---

separating
simulating
skating
slating
sophisticating
speculating
stating
stimulating
stipulating
subjugating
suffocating
supplicating
syncopating
tabulating
terminating
titillating
tittivating
tolerating
translating
unabating
unaccommo-
    dating
underrating
understating
undeviating
undiscrimi-
    nating
undulating
vacating
vaccinating
vacillating
validating
variegating
vegetating
venerating
ventilating
verberating
vindicating
violating
vitiating
vituperating

vociferating
waiting
weighting

ĀT'ing

batting
chatting
fatting
matting
patting
platting
ratting
tatting
vatting

ĀT'ir

satire

ĀT'is

gratis

ĀT'is

brattice
lattice

ĀT'ish

cattish
fattish
flattish

ĀT'iv

abrogative
accelerative
accumulative
administrative
agglomerative
agglutinative
aggregative
agitative
alleviative
alliterative

alterative
ameliorative
animative
anticipative
annunciative
appreciative
approbative
appropriative
approximative
assimilative
associative
authoritative
coagulative
cogitative
collative
commemora-
    tive
commiserative
communica-
    tive
confederative
consolidative
contaminative
continuative
co-operative
co-ordinative
copulative
corroborative
creative
criminative
cumulative
dative
decorative
degenerative
deliberative
denominative
denunciative
deprecative
depreciative
desiderative
designative

determinative
dilative
discriminative
disseminative
dominative
duplicative
edulcorative
elaborative
elucidative
emanative
emulative
enumerative
enunciative
eradicative
estimative
evaporative
exaggerative
execrative
exonerative
explicative
federative
generative
germinative
glutinative
gravitative
hesitative
illuminative
imaginative
imbricative
imitative
implicative
incogitative
incommunica-
    tive
incorporative
incriminative
incubative
indiscrimina-
    tive
initiative
innovative

inoperative
insinuative
interpenetra-
   tive
interpretative
investigative
irritative
iterative
justificative
lacerative
legislative
manipulative
meditative
ministrative
mitigative
modificative
native
operative
opinionative
originative
oscillative
palliative
participative
penetrative
perforative
predestinative
procreative
prognostica-
   tive
pronunciative
propagative
purificative
qualificative
qualitative
quantitative
radiative
ratiocinative
recreative
recriminative
recuperative
refrigerative

regenerative
reiterative
remunerative
replicative
reprobative
resuscitative
retaliative
reverberative
sative
separative
significative
speculative
stative
stimulative
subordinative
suffocative
supplicative
suppurative
terminative
translative
undulative
vegetative
velicative
ventilative
verificative
vindicative
violative
vituperative
vivificative

ĂT'kins

Atkins
Batkins
(cf. Watkins)

ĂT' 'l

battel
battle
cattle
chattel
death-rattle

embattle
prattle
rattle
Seattle
tattle
tittle-tattle

ĂT'las, ĂT'les

atlas
cravatless
hatless
(see ĂT + less)

ĂT'les

baitless
dateless
estateless
freightless
gaitless
gateless
grateless
hateless
mateless
rateless
stateless
weightless

ĂT'li (ĬT'li)

accurately
adequately
affectionately
alternately
appropriately
approximately
compassion-
   ately
consummately
delicately
desolately
desperately
disconsolately

effeminately
elaborately
extortionately
fortunately
greatly
illiterately
immaculately
immoderately
inarticulately
inconsider-
   ately
intemperately
intimately
irately
lately
legitimately
moderately
sedately
stately
straitly
ultimately

ĂT'li

fatly
flatly
patly
rattly

ĂT'ling

battling
catling
fatling
gatling
prattling
rattling
tattling

ĂT'lur

battler
prattler
rattler

āle, câre, ădd, ärm, ăsk; mē, hĕre, ĕnd; īce, ĭll:

Statler
tattler

ĀT'ment
abatement
affreightment
instatement
overstatement
reinstatement
statement
understate-
  ment

ĀT'nes
appropriate-
  ness
considerate-
  ness
greatness
innateness
lateness
ornateness
sedateness
straightness

ĂT'nes
fatness
flatness
patness

ĂT'o
literato
Plato
pomato
potato
tomato

ĂT'o
chateau
mulatto
plateau

Ă'to
annatto
chateau
enamorato
legato
obbligato
pizzicato
pomato
staccato
tomato

ĂT'om
atom

ĂT'on
Clayton
Dayton
Leighton
peyton
Satan

ĂT'on
baton
Hatton

ĂT'ra
Cleopatra

Ā'tre
baytree
maytree

ĀT'red
hatred

ĀT'res
dictatress
imitatress
spectatress
traitress
waitress

ĂT'res
mattress
mulattress

ĂT'rik
hippiatric
iatric
kinesiatric
matric
Patrick
theatric

ĂT'riks
administratrix
aviatrix
cicatrix
generatrix
imitatrix
impropriatrix
matrix
mediatrix
spectatrix
testatrix

ĂT'ris, ĂT'ris
matrice

ĂT'ron
matron
natron
patron

ĀTS'man
statesman

ĂTS'man
batsman

ĂT'son
Batson
Matson

ĂT'u
statue

ĀT'um
datum
desideratum
erratum
pomatum
postulatum
stratum
substratum
superstratum
ultimatum

ĂT'um
stratum

ĂT'um
datum
pomatum

ĀT'ūr
good-nature
ill-nature
legislature
nature
nomenclature
plicature
unnature

ĀT'ŭr
abator
abbreviator
abdicator
abnegator
abrogater
accelerator
accumulator
adjudicator
administrator

adulator	confiscator	eliminator	grater
affreighter	conjugator	elucidator	greater
aggravator	consecrator	emanator	hater
agitator	conservator	emancipator	hesitater
alienator	consolidator	emendator	humilater
alleviator	contaminator	emulator	hypothecator
alligator	contemplator	enumerator	illuminator
alma mater	co-operator	enunciator	illustrator
amalgamator	corroborator	equator	imitator
ameliorator	crater	equivocator	imperator
annihilator	creator	eradicator	impersonator
annotator	cremator	evaporator	imprimatur
annunciator	criminator	exaggerator	incarcerator
appropriator	cultivator	excavator	incorporator
arbitrator	dater	execrator	incriminator
arch-traitor	debater	exhilarator	incubator
aspirater	decapitator	exonerator	indicator
asseverator	decorator	expatiator	inflater
assimilator	dedicator	expectorator	initiator
authenticator	deliberator	expiator	innovator
aviator	delineator	extenuator	inoculator
awaiter	demonstrator	exterminator	insinuator
baiter	denominator	extricator	instigator
berater	denunciator	fabricator	insulator
calculator	depopulator	facilitator	interpolator
calumniator	depreciator	fascinator	interrogator
captivator	depredator	federator	intimidator
castigator	designator	felicitator	investigator
cater	devastator	first-rater	invigorator
cogitator	deviator	flagellator	invocator
collaborator	dictater	formulator	irrigator
commemo-	dictator	fornicator	irritator
rator	disintegrator	frater	later
commentator	disseminator	freighter	laudator
comminator	dissimulator	frustrator	legislator
commiserator	duplicator	fumigator	liberator
compotator	dura mater	gaiter	liquidator
compurgator	educater	generator	litigator
computator	ejaculator	germinator	locater
concentrator	elaborator	gesticulator	lubricator
conciliator	elevator	gladiator	manipulator

āle, câre, ădd, ärm, ȧsk; mē, hẹre, ĕnd; īce, ĭll;

masticator	promulgator	supplicator	patter
mater	propagator	tabulator	platter
mediator	propitiator	"tater"	ratter
meditator	radiator	tergiversator	satyr
migrater	rater	testator	scatter
mitigator	reciprocator	third-rater	shatter
moderator	refrigerator	titillator	smatter
modulator	regenerator	tittivator	spatter
mutilator	regrater	traitor	splatter
narrator	regulator	translator	subject-matter
navigator	reinstater	vaccinator	tatter
negotiator	reiterator	vacillator	
nominator	relater	vaticinator	**ĂT'ur**
obliterator	remonstrator	venerator	alma mater
officiator	renovator	ventilator	mater
operator	repudiator	versificator	pater
originator	respirator	vindicator	Stabat Mater
oscillator	resuscitator	violator	
pacificator	retaliator	vituperator	**ĂT'urn**
palliator	ruminator	vociferator	pattern
palpitator	rusticator	waiter	Saturn
pater	satyr		slattern
perambulator	scintillator	**ĂT'ūr**	willow-pattern
percolator	scrutator	stature	
peregrinator	second-rater		**ĂT'us**
perforator	sedater	**ĂT'ŭr**	afflatus
permeator	separator	attar	apparatus
perpetrator	simulator	batter	hiatus
personator	skater	beflatter	literatus
pia mater	slater	bepatter	saleratus
piscator	sophisticator	bescatter	senatus
plaiter	spectator	bespatter	status
plater	speculator	blatter	stratous
prater	Stabat Mater	chatter	stratus
precipitator	stater	clatter	
predominator	stimulator	clitter-clatter	**ĂT'us**
prestidigitator	stipulator	fatter	apparatus
prevaricator	straighter	flatter	
procrastinator	straiter	hatter	**ĂT'ut**
procurator	subjugator	latter	statute
prognosticator	supererogator	matter	

ōld, ôr, ŏdd, oil, fŏŏt, out; ūse, ûrn, ŭp; THis, thin

ĀT′wa	player	**ĂV′el**	**ĂV′eth**
gateway	portrayer	gavel	*behaveth*
straitway	prayer	gravel	*beslaveth*
	preyer	ravel	*braveth*
Ā′ur	prepayer	travel	*craveth*
affrayer	purveyor	unravel	*depraveth*
allayer	relayer	(cf. cavil)	*engraveth*
arrayer	repayer		*enslaveth*
assayer	slayer	**ĂV′eld**	*forgaveth*
belayer	soothsayer	gravelled	*gaveth*
betrayer	sprayer	ravelled	*laveth*
brayer	stayer	travelled	*paveth*
conveyer	strayer	untravelled	*raveth*
defrayer	surveyer		*saveth*
delayer	swayer	**ĂV′en**	*shaveth*
disarrayer	underpayer	craven	*slaveth*
dismayer	underplayer	*engraven*	*waiveth*
disobeyer	viséer	graven	*waveth*
displayer	waylayer	haven	
essayer	weigher	shaven	**ĂV′ez**
flayer			Davies
gainsayer	**Ă′va**	**ĂV′est**	
gayer	brava	*behavest*	**ĂV′i**
grayer	cassava	*beslavest*	affidavy
greyer	guava	bravest	cavy
hoorayer	Java	*cravest*	Davie
inlayer	lava	*depravest*	Davy
interlayer		*engravest*	gravy
inveigher	**ĂV′al**	*enslavest*	navy
layer	travail	*forgavest*	peccavi
matineer		*gavest*	ravy
mayor	**ĂV′e**	*gravest*	slavey
mislayer	agave	*lavest*	wavy
missayer	ave	*pavest*	
neigher	**Ă′ve**	*ravest*	**ĀV′id**
obeyer	ave	*savest*	David
outlayer		*shavest*	*engraved*, etc.
outstayer	**ĀV′el**	*slavest*	
outweigher	gavel	suavest	**ĂV′id**
overlayer	naval	*waivest*	avid
payer	navel	*wavest*	gravid

āle, câre, ădd, ärm, ȧsk; mē, hĕre, ĕnd; īce, ĭll;

impavid	waving	staveless	cadaver
pavid	wood-engrav-	waveless	claver
	ing		craver
ĂV´ij		**ĂV´li**	demiquaver
ravage	**ĂV´ing**	bravely	depraver
savage	having	gravely	disfavor
scavage	salving	knavely	engraver
		suavely	enslaver
ĂV´ik	**ĂV´ing**		favor
gravic	calving	**ĂV´lin**	flavor
Pan-Slavic	halving	javelin	graver
Slavic	salving	ravelin	laver
			marriage-
ĂV´in	**ĂV´is**	**ĂV´ling**	favor
savin	clavis	shaveling	Papaver
spavin	Davis		paver
	mavis	**ĂV´ment**	quaver
ĂV´ing	rara avis	depravement	raver
behaving		engravement	saver
belaving	**ĂV´ish**	enslavement	savor
beslaving	bravish	lavement	semiquaver
braving	knavish	pavement	shaver
caving	slavish		slaver
craving		**ĀV´nes**	suaver
depraving	**ĂV´ish**	braveness	waiver
engraving	enravish	graveness	waver
enslaving	lavish	suaveness	wood-engraver
graving	McTavish		
labor-saving	ravish	**ĀV´o**	**ĀV´ur**
laving		bravo	beslaver
misbehaving	**ĂV´it**	octavo	cadaver
outbraving	affidavit		palaver
paving	indicavit	**ĂV´o**	haver
raving		bravo	
saving	**ĂV´it**	octavo	**ĂV´ur**
shaving	davit		palaver
slaving		**ĂV´ok**	suaver
staving	**ĀV´les**	havoc	
steel-engrav-	caveless		**ĂV´urd**
ing	graveless	**ĂV´ur**	favored
waiving	slaveless	braver	flavored

ōld, ôr, ŏdd, oil, fŏŏt, out; ūse, ûrn, ŭp; THis, thin

ill-favored	Ā'yan	ĀZ'est	dazes
quavered	Altaian	*amazest*	gazes
savored	Cataian	*braisest*	glazes
wavered	Himalayan	*bepraisest*	grazes
well-favored	Malayan	*blazest*	hazes
		dazest	mayonnaises
ĀV'urn	Ā'yan	*gazest*	mazes
cavern	Himalayan	*hazest*	paraphrases
tavern		*glazest*	phases
	Ā'yard	*paraphrasest*	phrases
ĀV'us	Bayard	*phrasest*	praises
Gustavus		*praisest*	raises
	Ā'yo	*raisest*	razes
ĀV'yur	K.O.	*razest*	
behavior	kayo	*upraisest*	Ā'zhun
havior	Mayo		abrasion
misbehavior		ĀZ'eth	dissuasion
Pavier	Ā'yu	*amazeth*	erasion
pavior	gay-you	*bepraiseth*	evasion
savior	Vayu	*blazeth*	invasion
Xavier		*braiseth*	occasion
	ĀZ'a	*dazeth*	persuasion
Ā'ward	Gaza	*gazeth*	suasion
wayward		*glazeth*	(cf. Caucasian,
	ĂZ'a	*hazeth*	and Ā'zhi-an
Ă'ward	cazazza	*paraphraseth*	words)
vaward	piazza	*phraseth*	
	plaza	*praiseth*	Ā'zhur
Ā'wir		*raiseth*	azure
haywire	ĀZ'al	*razeth*	brazier
	appraisal	*upraiseth*	embrasure
Ā'worn	hazel		erasure
sprayworn	nasal	ĀZ'ez	Frazier
wayworn	witch-hazel	amazes	glazier
		bemazes	grazier
Ā'ya	ĂZ'ard	blazes	razure
Aglaia	haphazard	braises	
ayah	hazard	brazes	ĂZH'ur
calisaya	hazard	chaises	åzure
Isaiah	*mazard*	crazes	ĀZ'i
naia	mazzard	daisies	blazy

---

crazy	brazing	**ĂZ'ling**	**ĂZ'mus**
daisy	dazing	dazzling	Erasmus
hazy	gazing	frazzling	
jasey	glazing		**ĂZ'on**
lackadaisy	grazing	**ĂZ'ma**	blazon
lazy	hazing	asthma	brazen
mazy	lazing	miasma	diapason
phrasey	outblazing	phantasma	emblazon
paraphrasey	outgazing	Phasma	glazen
	paraphrasing	plasma	scazon
ĂZ'i	phrasing	protoplasma	**ĂZ'ur**
ghawazi	praising		appraiser
ghazi	raising	**ĂZ'mal**	blazer
	self-praising	miasmal	dispraiser
ĂZ'il	star-gazing	phantasmal	Eleazer
Basil	upblazing	protoplasmal	Fraser
(cf. ĂZ''l)	upraising		gazer
		ĂZ'ment	geyser
ĂZ'in		amazement	lazar
raisin	**ĂZ''l**	appraisement	paraphraser
	Basil	praisement	phraser
ĂZ'ing	bedazzle		praiser
ʌblazing	dazzle	**ĂZ'mi**	raiser
amazing	frazzle	chasmy	razer
bemazing	razzle-dazzle		razor
bepraising		**ĂZ'mik**	self-praiser
blazing	**ĂZ'les**	bioplasmic	star-gazer
braising	praiseless	miasmic	upgazer
		protoplasmic	upraiser

E

For a discussion of words included under the accented vowels following, see the beginning of E rhymes in Section I.

Ē'a	cavalleria	dyspnea	Lucia
Althæa	Crimea	Hosea	Maria
Astræa	Cypræa	Hygeia	Medea
Ave Maria	dahabeah	idea	melopœia
Cassiopea	Dorothea	Latakia	obeah

ōld, ôr, ŏdd, oil, fŏŏt, out; ūse. ûrn, ŭp; THis. thin

onomatopœia
panacea
pathopœia
pharmacopœia
ratafia
Rhea
spiræa
Zea

Ē′al
Arctogaeal
beau ideal
empyreal
hymeneal
ideal
laryngeal
real
unideal
unreal

Ē′an
Achean
adamantean
Adonean
Ægean
amœbean
amphigean
Andean
Anomoean
antipodean
apogean
Archimedean
Argean
Assidean
astraean
Atlantean
Augean
Berean
Cadmean
Caribbean
Chaldean

Circean
colossean
Crimean
cyclopean
Cytherean
ditrochean
empyrean
epicurean
Etnean
European
Galilean
gigantean
Hasmonaean
Hyblæan
hymenean
Indo-European
Judean
Laodicean
laryngean
lethean
Linnaean
lyncean
Maccabean
Manichaean
mausolean
Medicean
Melibean
Nemean
Niobean
nymphean
Orphean
pæan
Palæogæan
pampean
Pandean
perigean
phalangean
Pharisean
plebeian
protean
Pyrenean

Pythagorean
Sabæan
Sadducean
Sisyphean
terpsichorean
theodicean
Vendean
Zoilean

Ē′as
Aeneas
Zaccheus

Ē′ba
amœba
Reba
Seba
Sheba
zareba

Ē′be
Hebe
Phoebe
T.B.

ĔB′en
Eben

ĔB′ing
ebbing
unebbing
webbing

ĔB″l
enfeeble
feeble

ĔB″l
arch-rebel
djebel
pebble

rebel
treble

Ē′bo
gazeebo
Nebo
placebo

ĔB′on
ebon

Ē′bord
free-board
key-board
seaboard

Ē′born
free-born
sea-born

ĔB′ra
zebra

ĔB′rok
pibroch

ĔB′ru
Hebrew

ĔB′ur
Gheber

ĔB′ur
ebber
webber
Weber

Ē′bus
glebous
Phoebus
rebus

āle,   câre,   ădd,   ärm,   åsk;   mē,   hĕre,   ĕnd;   īce,   ĭll:

ĔCH'ed
wretched
(see ĔCH+ed)

ĔCH'est
beseechest
bleachest
foreachest
impeachest
overreachest
preachest
reachest
screechest
sea-chest
tea-chest
teachest

ĔCH'eth
beseecheth
bleacheth
forereacheth
impeacheth
overreacheth
preacheth
reacheth
screecheth
teacheth

ĔCH'ez
beaches
beeches
beseeches
bleaches
breaches
breeches
forereaches
impeaches
leeches
overreaches
peaches
preaches

reaches
screeches
sea-reaches
speeches
teaches

ĔCH'ĭ
beachy
Beatrice
beechy
bleachy
breachy
campeachy
peachy
preachy
reachy
qucachy
reechy
screechy
speechy

ĔCH'ĭ
fetchy
sketchy
stretchy
tetchy
vetchy

ĔCH'ing
beaching
beseeching
bleaching
breaching
breeching
forereaching
foreteaching
impeaching
leaching
leeching
overreaching
peaching

preaching
reaching
screeching
teaching

ĔCH'ing
etching
fetching
sketching
stretching

ĔCH'les
beachless
beechless
breachless
peachless
reachless
speechless
teachless

ĔCH'ment
beseechment
impeachment
preachment

ĔCH'up
catchup
ketchup

ĔCH'ur
Beecher
beseecher
bleacher
breacher
breecher
forereacher
impeacher
leacher
leecher
overreacher
peacher

preacher
reacher
screecher
teacher
(cf. Ē'tūr)

ĔCH'ur
etcher
fetcher
fletcher
lecher
retcher
sketcher
stretcher
treacher

Ē'da
Leda
olla podrida
Theda
Veda
Vida

ĔD'a
Edda
Nedda

ĔD'ant
pedant

ĔD'bed
reedbed
seedbed
weedbed

ĔD'bet
deadbeat

ĔD'breast
redbreast

ōld, ôr, ŏdd, oil, fŏŏt, out; ūse, ûrn, ŭp; THis, thin

ĔD'bug
bedbug
redbug

ĔD'ed
acceded
anteceded
beaded
ceded
conceded
deeded
exceeded
heeded
impeded
interceded
kneaded
needed
pleaded
preceded
proceeded
receded
reeded
retroceded
seceded
seeded
stampeded
succeeded
superseded
unheeded
unweeded
weeded

ĔD'ed
addle-headed
arrow-headed
bare-headed
bedded
beetle-headed
beheaded
blunderheaded
bullheaded

chuckle-
   headed
clear-headed
dreaded
dunder-headed
embedded
fat-headed
feather-headed
fiddle-headed
flat-headed
giddy-headed
gross-headed
headed
heavy-headed
hoary-headed
hot-headed
hydra-headed
idle-headed
Janus-headed
leaded
light-headed
longheaded
many-headed
muddle-
   headed
pig-headed
pudding-
   headed
puzzle-headed
rattle-headed
shock-headed
shredded
sleek-headed
soft-headed
thick-headed
threaded
trundle-
   headed
unbedded
undreaded
unthreaded

unwedded
warm-headed
weak-headed
wedded
wrong-headed

ĔD'en
Eden
reeden
Sweden

ĔD'ĕn
deaden
leaden
redden
threaden

ĔD'ens
antecedence
credence
intercedence
precedence
(cf. antece-
   dents)

ĔD'ent
antecedent
credent
decedent
intercedent
needn't
precedent
retrocedent
sedent

Ē'dep
knee-deep
sea-deep
three-deep

ĒD'est
accedest

bleedest
breedest
cedest
concedest
exceedest
feedest
heedest
impedest
intercedest
kneadest
leadest
misleadest
needest
overfeedest
pleadest
precedest
proceedest
readest
recedest
secedest
seedest
speedest
stampedest
succeedest
supersedest
weedest

ĔD'est
beheadest
dreadest
outspreadest
reddest
sheddest
spreadest
threadest
treadest
weddest

ĒD'eth
accedeth
bleedeth

breedeth	**ĒD'ful**	**ĔD'i**	interceding
cedeth	deedful	already	interpleading
concedeth	heedful	Eddie	kneading
exceedeth	meedful	eddy	leading
feedeth	needful	Freddie	love-lies-
heedeth	speedful	heady	bleeding
impedeth	unheedful	leady	misleading
intercedeth	unneedful	ready	misreading
kneadeth		reddy	needing
leadeth	**ĔD'ful**	shreddy	outspeeding
misleadeth	dreadful	steady	over-feeding
needeth		thready	pleading
overfeedeth	**ĒD'gron**	unready	preceding
pleadeth	reed-grown	unsteady	proceeding
precedeth	seed-grown		reading
proceedeth	weed-grown	**ĔD'ik**	receding
readeth		comedic	reeding
recedeth	**ĔD'hed**	cyclopædic	retroceding
secedeth	deadhead	encyclopædic	seceding
seedeth	redhead	Vedic	seeding
speedeth			speeding
stampedeth	**ĔD'het**	**ĔD'ik**	stampeding
succeedeth	dead-heat	Eddic	succeeding
supersedeth	red-heat	Samoyedic	superseding
weedeth			unbleeding
	ĒD'i	**ĔD'ikt**	underfeeding
ĔD'eth	beady	edict	unheeding
beheadeth	creedy		weeding
dreadeth	deedy	**ĒD'ing**	
headeth	encyclopedy	acceding	**ĔD'ing**
outspreadeth	greedy	beading	bedding
overspreadeth	heedy	bleeding	beheading
sheddeth	indeedy	breeding	bespreading
shreddeth	Leedy	ceding	dreading
spreadeth	needy	conceding	embedding
threadeth	*predy*	exceeding	heading
treadeth	reedy	feeding	leading
weddeth	seedy	God-speeding	outspreading
	speedy	heeding	overspreading
ĔD'fast	unheedy	impeding	redding
steadfast	weedy	interbreeding	shedding

shredding
sledding
spreading
steading
tedding
threading
treading
wedding

ĔD'ish
deadish
eddish
reddish

ĔD'it
accredit
credit
discredit
edit
miscredit
subedit
you said it

ĒD'ith
Edith
(cf. needeth,
etc.)

ĔD'iz
teddies
(see ĔD'i+s)

ĔD''l
beadle
bi-pedal
centipedal
dædal
needle
pedal
semipedal
tweedle
wheeled

ĔD''l
bi-pedal
heddle
intermeddle
medal
meddle
pedal
peddle
reddle
treadle
tripedal

ĔD'lam
Bedlam

ĔD'land
headland

ĔD'les
breedless
creedless
deedless
heedless
needless
seedless
speedless
steedless
weedless

ĔD'les
bedless
breadless
dreadless
headless
leadless

ĔD'li
chance-medley
deadly
medley
redly

ĔD'lin
breadline
dead-line
head-line

ĒD'ling
needling
reedling
seedling
wheedling

ĔD'ling
intermeddling
meddling
peddling

ĔD'lit
dead-light
red-light

ĔD'lok
deadlock
wedlock

ĒD'lur
needler
wheedler

ĔD'lur
intermeddler
meddler
medlar
peddler
treadler

ĔD'man
Friedman

ĔD'man
dead-man
Edman

headman
red-man

ĔD'na
Edna

ĔD'nes
deadness
redness

Ē'do
credo
Lido
stampedo
teredo
Toledo
torpedo

ĔD'o
meadow

ĔD'ra
ex cathedra
exedra

ĔD'ral
cathedral
decahedral
didecahedral
diedral
dihedral
pro-cathedral

ĔD'rest
bed-rest
head-rest

ĔD'ston
headstone

ĔD'tim
feed-time
seed-time

āle, câre, ădd, ärm, åsk; mē, hęre, ĕnd; īce, ĭll;

Ē'dum	succeeder	ĔDZ'man	leafy
freedom	superseder	headsman	reefy
(cf. sedum)	weeder	leadsman	sheafy
ĒD'ūr	ĔD'ur	ĔD'zo	ĒF'ij
procedure	bedder	intermezzo	leafage
supersedure	beheader	mezzo	
	bespreader		ĔF'ik
ĒD ŭr	Cheddar	Ē'est	malefic
acceder	deader	*agreest*	peristrephic
anteceder	double-header	*feest*	
breeder	dreader	*fleest*	ĒF'les
cedar	edder	*foreseest*	briefless
ceder	embedder	freest	chiefless
conceder	header	*overseest*	griefless
exceeder	leader	*refereest*	leafless
feeder	redder	*seest*	sheafless
heeder	shedder	weest	
impeder	shredder		ĔF'nes
impleader	spreader	Ē'eth	deafness
interceder	tedder	*agreeth*	
interpleader	threader	*feeth*	Ē'fom
kneader	treader	*fleeth*	sea-foam
leader	unthreader	*foreseeth*	
misleader		*freeth*	Ē'foul
needer	ĔD'wa	*overseeth*	pea-fowl
overfeeder	headway	*seeth*	sea-fowl
pleader			
preceder	ĔD'ward	ĒF'as	ĔFT'nes
proceeder	bedward	Cephas	deftness
reader	Edward	(cf. Josephus)	
receder			ĔF'ri
retroceder	ĔD'wood	ĒF'dom	Geoffrey
ring-leader	dead-wood	chiefdom	Jeffrey
scripture-	redwood	ĒF'en	
reader		deafen	ĒF'stak
seceder	ĔDZ'man	(cf. Strephon)	beefsteak
seeder	beadsman		
speeder	bedesman	ĒF'i	ĒF'tin
stampeder	seedsman	beefy	chieftain

ĔF′uj	**ĒG′ ′l**	**ĒG′ur**	foreseeing
refuge	bald eagle	beleaguer	freeing
	beagle	eager	guaranteeing
Ē′ful	eagle	eagre	inbeing
gleeful	gregal	fatiguer	overseeing
	illegal	intriguer	refereeing
ĔF′ur	inveigle	leaguer	seeing
beefer	kleagle	meagre	spreeing
briefer	legal	overeager	teeing
chiefer	regal		unforeseeing
liefer	vice-regal	**ĔG′ur**	unseeing
reefer	(cf. sea-gull)	beggar	well-being
		booklegger	
ĔF′ur	**ĒG′lur**	bootlegger	**Ē′ist**
deafer	beagler	egger	antitheist
feoffor	inveigler	legger	deist
heifer		pegger	hylotheist
zephyr	**ĔG′ment**	seggar	manicheist
	segment		monotheist
Ē′ga		**Ē′gurt**	polytheist
omega	**ĔG′nant**	sea-girt	theist
Riga	impregnant		
Talladega	pregnant	**Ē′ik**	**Ē′it**
Vega	queen-regnant	caffeic	albeit
	regnant	mythopœic	sobeit
ĔG′i		rheic	
dreggy	**Ē′go**	xanthoproteic	**Ē′izm**
eggy	ego		absenteeism
leggy	Oswego	**Ē′in**	antitheism
Peggy	Otsego	caffeine	autotheism
		codeine	cosmotheism
ĔG′ing	**Ē′gren**	zein	deism
fatiguing	pea-green		henotheism
intriguing	sea-green	**Ē′ing**	hylotheism
leaguing		agreeing	manicheism
	ĒG′res	being	monotheism
ĔG′ing	egress	clear-seeing	Parseeism
begging	negress	decreeing	Phariseeism
egging	regress	disagreeing	polytheism
legging		feeing	Sadduceeism
pegging	**ĒG′ro**	fleeing	sciotheism
unpegging	negro		

Sutteeism
theism
weism

Ē'jance
allegiance

ĔJ'burd
hedge-bird
sedge-bird

ĔJ'end
legend

ĔJ'ent
regent

ĔJ'est
allegest
dredgest
fledgest
hedgest
impledgest
⊕ledgest
⊕edgest

ĔJ'eth
allegeth
dredgeth
fledgeth
hedgeth
impledgeth
pledgeth
wedgeth

ĔJ'ez
alleges
dredges
edges
hedges
kedges

ledges
pledges
sledges
wedges

ĔJ'i
cledgy
edgy
hedgy
ledgy
sedgy
wedgy

ĔJ'ing
alleging
dredging
edging
enhedging
fledging
hedging
kedging
impledging
interpledging
pledging
sledging
wedging

ĔJ'ling
fledgeling

ĔJ'man
liegeman

ĔJ'ment
besiegement

ĔJ'un
legion
region
under-region
(cf. collegian

and Ē'ji-an
words)

ĔJ'ur
alleger
dredger
edger
hedger
ledger
leger
pledger
sledger

ĔJ'us
egregious
sacrilegious

ĔJ'wood
Edgewood
Wedgewood

Ē'ka
bibliotheca
chica
Costa Rica
Dominica
eureka
Frederica
Fredrika
glyptotheca
Meeka
Tanganyika
Topeka
Ulrica
zotheca

ĔK'a
Rebecca
Mecca

ĔK'ad
decade

ĔK'al
bibliothecal
cæcal
fæcal
thecal
treacle

ĔK'ant
piquant
precant
secant

ĔK'ant
impeccant
peccant

ĔK'en
weaken
(see ĔK'on)

ĔK'est
bespeakest
bleakest
meekest
leakest
reekest
seekest
shriekest
sneakest
speakest
squeakest
streakest
uniquest
weakest
wreakest

ĔK'est
bedeckest
checkest
deckest
reckest
wreckest

ōld, ôr, ŏdd, oil, fŏŏt, out; ūse, ûrn, ŭp; THis, thin

ĒK'eth
bespeaketh
leaketh
reeketh
seeketh
shrieketh
sneaketh
speaketh
squeaketh
streaketh
wreaketh

ĔK'eth
bedecketh
checketh
decketh
recketh
wrecketh

ĒK'i
bleaky
Bolsheviki
cheeky
cliquey
cockaleekie
creaky
leaky
Mensheviki
peeky
reeky
sheiky
sleeky
sneaky
squeaky
streaky

ĒK'id
meek-eyed
oblique-eyed
weak-eyed

ĒK'ing
bespeaking
cheeking
creaking
eking
forespeaking
leaking
reeking
seeking
self-seeking
sheiking
shrieking
sneaking
speaking
squeaking
tweaking
wreaking

ĔK'ing
bedecking
bewrecking
checking
decking
flecking
henpecking
pecking
recking
trekking
wrecking

ĒK'ish
bleakish
cliquish
freakish
Greekish
meekish
peakish
sneakish
weakish

ĔK'ish
peckish

ĒK"l
treacle
(see ĒK'al)

ĔK"l
befreckle
bespeckle
deckle
freckle
heckle
Jeckyll
keckle
Seckel
shekel
speckle

ĔK'les
feckless
fleckless
necklace
reckless
speckless

ĔK'li
bleakly
meekly
obliquely
sleekly
treacly
uniquely
weakly
weekly

ĔK'li
freckly
speckly

ĒK'ling
weakling

ĔK'ling
freckling

heckling
keckling
speckling

ĔK'lur
heckler
freckler, etc.

ĔK'mat
checkmate
deck-mate

ĒK'nes
antiqueness
bleakness
meekness
obliqueness
sleekness
uniqueness
weakness

ĔK'nik
philotechnic
polytechnic
pyrotechnic
technic
theotechnic

ĔK'ning
beckoning
reckoning
unreckoning

Ē'ko
beccafico
fico

ĔK'o
echo
gecko
re-echo
secco

Ē′kok	*flexeth*	insection	prexy
Leacock	*perplexeth*	inspection	pyrexy
meacock	*unsexeth*	insubjection	
peacock	*vexeth*	insurrection	**ĔK′sil**
		intellection	exile
ĔK′on	**ĔK′shun**	interjection	flexile
archdeacon	abjection	intersection	
beacon	adjection	introspection	**ĔK′sing**
deacon	affection	irreflection	annexing
meeken	bisection	lection	flexing
weaken	by-election	misdirection	inflexing
	circumspection	objection	perplexing
ĔK′on	circumvection	perfection	unsexing
beckon	collection	predilection	vexing
reckon	complexion	prelection	
	confection	projection	**ĔK′sis**
ĔK′ond	connection	prospection	Alexis
second	convection	protection	
unreckoned,	correction	provection	**ĔK′sit**
etc.	defection	recollection	exit
	deflection	rection	
Ē′krab	dejection	re-election	**ĔK′stant**
pea-crab	detection	reflection	extant
sea-crab	dilection	rejection	sextant
tree-crab	direction	resurrection	
	disaffection	retrospection	**ĔK′stil**
ĔK′ret	disinfection	section	bissextile
secret	dissection	selection	sextile
	effection	subjection	textile
ĔK′sas	ejection	trajection	
Texas	election	trisection	**ĔK′ston**
	erection	venesection	sexton
ĔK′sest	evection	vivisection	
annexest	flection		**ĔK′strin**
flexest	genuflexion	**ĔK′shus**	dextrin
perplexest	imperfection	infectious	textrine
unsexest	incorrection		
vexest	indirection	**ĔK′si**	**ĔK′strus**
	infection	apoplexy	ambidextrous
ĔK′seth	inflection	kexy	ambisextrous
annexeth	injection	kyriolexy	dextrous

ōld, ôr, ŏdd, oil, fŏŏt, out; ūse, ûrn, ŭp; THis, thin

ĔK'stūr	bisected	resurrected	*subjectest*
intertexture	collected	selected	*suspectest*
texture	complected	subjected	
	confected	suspected	**ĔK'teth**
ĔK'stŭr	connected	unaffected	*affecteth*
ambidexter	corrected	unconnected	*bisecteth*
dexter	defected	unexpected	*collecteth*
	deflected	unprotected	*connecteth*
ĔK'sūr	dejected	unsuspected	*detecteth*
deflexure	detected		*directeth*
flexure	directed	**ĔK'test**	*disinfecteth*
inflexure	disaffected	abjectest	*dissecteth*
plexure	disconnected	*affectest*	*effecteth*
	disinfected	*bisectest*	*ejecteth*
ĔK'sŭr	dissected	*collectest*	*electeth*
annexer	effected	*connectest*	*erecteth*
flexor	ejected	*detectest*	*expecteth*
perplexer	elected	directest	*infecteth*
unsexer	erected	*disinfectest*	*injecteth*
vexer	expected	*dissectest*	*inspecteth*
	flected	*effectest*	*interjecteth*
ĔK'sus	ill-affected	*ejectest*	*misdirecteth*
nexus	infected	*electest*	*neglecteth*
plexus	inflected	*erectest*	*objecteth*
(cf. Texas)	injected	*expectest*	*projecteth*
	inspected	*infectest*	*protecteth*
ĔK'tant	interjected	*injectest*	*recollecteth*
amplectant	intersected	*inspectest*	*reflecteth*
annectent	invected	*interjectest*	*rejecteth*
aspectant	misdirected	*neglectest*	*respecteth*
disinfectant	neglected	*objectest*	*resurrecteth*
expectant	objected	*projectest*	*selecteth*
humectant	obtected	*protectest*	*subjecteth*
inexpectant	perfected	*recollectest*	*suspecteth*
reflectant	prelected	*reflectest*	*trisecteth*
respectant	projected	*rejectest*	
suspectant	protected	*respectest*	**ĔKT'ful**
unexpectant	recollected	*resurrectest*	disrespectful
	reflected	*resurrectest*	neglectful
ĔK'ted	rejected	selectest	respectful
affected	respected		

ĔK'tik
acatalectic
analectic
apoplectic
brachycatalec-
  tic
cachectic
catalectic
dialectic
eclectic
hectic
hypercatalectic
pectic

ĔK'tiks
dialectics

ĔK'til
insectile
projectile
sectile

ĔK'ting
affecting
bisecting
collecting
connecting
deflecting
detecting
directing
disconnecting
disinfecting
dissecting
effecting
ejecting
electing
erecting
expecting
infecting
injecting
inspecting

interjecting
misdirecting
neglecting
objecting
projecting
protecting
recollecting
reflecting
rejecting
respecting
resurrecting
selecting
self-respecting
subjecting
suspecting
trisecting
unsuspecting

ĔK'tiv
affective
circumspective
collective
connective
corrective
defective
deflective
detective
directive
effective
elective
erective
humective
ineffective
infective
inflective
injective
inspective
introspective
invective
irreflective
irrespective

neglective
objective
perfective
perspective
prospective
protective
recollective
refective
reflective
rejective
respective
retrospective
sective
selective
subjective

ĔK'tizm
eclectism
sectism

ĔKT'ment
ejectment
projectment
rejectment

ĔKT'nes
abjectness
correctness
directness
erectness
incorrectness
indirectness
selectness

ĔK'tor
Hector
nectar
rector
sector
vector

vivisector
(cf. ĔK'tur)

ĔK'tord
hectored
nectared
rectored

ĔK'tral
spectral

ĔK'tres
directress
electress
inspectress
protectress
rectress

ĔK'tric
anelectric
dielectric
electric
idioelectric

ĔK'tron
electron

ĔK'trum
electrum
plectrum
spectrum

ĔK'tūr
architecture
belecture
confecture
conjecture
lecture
projecture

ĔK'tur
bisecter
collector

connector	pectous	pecker	Bella
corrector	prospectus	three-decker	capella
deflector		trekker	Della
detector	**ĒK'um**	woodpecker	Ella
director	cæcum	wrecker	fellah
disrespector	vade-mecum		fenestella
dissector		**ĒK'urz**	gentianella
ejector	**ĒK'und**	sneakers	Isabella
elector	fecund	beakers, etc.	lamella
erecter	infecund		lirella
expecter		**ĔK'urz**	Littorella
flector	**ĒK'ur**	checkers	Marcella
hector	beaker	henpeckers, etc.	patella
infecter	bespeaker		Pimpinella
injecter	bleaker	**ĔK'wal**	prunella
inspector	Bleecker	coequal	Rosabella
interjecter	cheeker	equal	scutella
lector	creaker	inequal	stella
misdirecter	meeker	sequel	tarantella
nectar	peeker		umbella
neglecter	reeker	**ĔK'wence**	umbrella
objector	seeker	frequence	
prelector	self-seeker	infrequence	**ĔL'an**
projector	shrieker	sequence	Atellan
prospector	sleeker		Magellan
protector	sneaker	**ĔK'went**	McClellan
recollecter	speaker	frequent	
rector	squeaker	infrequent	**ĔL'ant**
reflector	stump-speaker	sequent	appellant
rejecter	tweaker		divellent
respecter	weaker	**Ē'la**	impellent
resurrecter		gila	interpellant
sector	**ĔK'ur**	philomela	propellent
selector	bedecker	sequela	repellent
spectre	brekker	stele	revellent
subjecter	checker	seguidilla	
suspecter	chequer	Venezuela	**ĔL'arz**
trisecter	decker		Sellars
	exchequer	**ĔL'a**	(cf. Sellers)
ĔK'tus	flecker	a capella	**ĔL'at**
conspectus	henpecker	Adela	appellate

constellate
debellate
flabellate
interpellate
ocellate
prelate
stellate

ĔL'ba
Elba
Melba

ĔL'born
hell-born
well-born

ĔL'bound
hell-bound
spell-bound

ĔL'burt
Elbert

ĔL'chest
belchest, etc.

ĔL'cheth
belcheth, etc.

ĔL'ching
belching
squelching
welching

ĔL'chur
belcher
squelcher
welsher

ĔL'da
Griselda

Nelda
Zelda

ĔL'dans
yieldance

ĔL'ded
fielded
shielded
unshielded
wielded
yielded

ĔL'dest
eldest
heldest
weldest

ĔL'dur
elder
Gelder
Melder
Van Gelder
welder

ELD'far
fieldfare

ĔL'di
unwieldy

ĔL'ding
enshielding
fielding
shielding
unshielding
unyielding
wielding
yielding

ĔL'ding
gelding
welding

ĔL'dom
seldom
swelldom

ĔL'en
Ellen
Helen
Llewellyn
Mellen
(cf. Mellon)

ĔL'est
annealest
appealest
concealest
congealest
dealest
feelest
genteelest
healest
kneelest
lealest
pealest
peelest
reelest
repealest
revealest
sealest
squealest
stealest
steelest
wheelest

ĔL'est
compellest
dispellest
dwellest
excellest
expellest
fellest
foretellest

impellest
knellest
propellest
quellest
rebellest
repellest
sellest
shellest
smellest
spellest
swellest
tellest
undersellest
yellest

ĔL'eth
annealeth
appealeth
concealeth
congealeth
dealeth
feeleth
healeth
kneeleth
pealeth
peeleth
reeleth
repealeth
revealeth
sealeth
squealeth
stealeth
steeleth
wheeleth

ĔL'eth
compelleth
dispelleth
dwelleth
excelleth
expelleth

felleth	ĔL'ful	ĔL'ij	healing
foretelleth	seelful	pellage	heeling
impelleth	wealful		interdealing
knelleth	zealful	ĔL'ik	keeling
propelleth		parhelic	kneeling
quelleth	Ē'lī		misdealing
rebelleth	Eli	ĔL'ik	pealing
repelleth		angelic	peeling
selleth	Ĕl'ĭ	archangelic	reeling
shelleth	Ealey	Aristotelic	repealing
smelleth	freely	bellic	revealing
spelleth	Healey	evangelic	sealing
swelleth	Keeley	melic	self-healing
telleth	mealy	nickelic	shealing
underselleth	seely	parhelic	squealing
yelleth	steely	Pentelic	stealing
	wheely	pimelic	steeling
ĔL'far	(cf. genteelly)	relic	uncongealing
welfare		superangelic	underdealing
	Ē'li	telic	unfeeling
ĔL'fik	belly		unsealing
	cancelli	ĔL'iks	wheeling
Delphic	Donatelli	Felix	
Guelphic	felly	helix	**ĔL'ing**
	helly		belling
ĔL'fin	jelly	Ē'lin	cloud-
delphin	Kelly	bee-line	compelling
delphine	O'Delly	feline	compelling
elfin	rakehelly	sea-line	dispelling
	Shelley		dwelling
ĔL'fir	shelly	ĔL'ing	excelling
hellfire	Skelly	annealing	expelling
	smelly	appealing	felling
ĔL'fish	vermicelli	automobiling	foretelling
elfish		ceiling	fortune-telling
pelfish	**ĔL'id**	concealing	impelling
selfish	bellied	congealing	knelling
shellfish	gelid	dealing	misspelling
unselfish	jellied	double-dealing	paralleling
		feeling	propelling
ĔL'fri	ĔL'ij	fellow-feeling	quelling
belfry	keelage		
pelfry	wheelage		

rebelling
repelling
selling
sentinelling
shelling
smelling
spelling
swelling
telling
underselling
welling
yelling

ĔL'is
Ellis
trellis

ĔL'ish
disrelish
embellish
hellish
relish
swellish

ĔL'kom
welcome

ĔL'ma
Elma
Selma
Thelma
Velma

ĔL'man
bellman
Elman
Wellman

ĔL'ment
concealment
congealment

repealment
revealment

ĔL'met
helmet

ĔL'ming
dishelming
helming
overwhelming
unhelming
whelming

ĔL'mur
Elmer

ĔL'nes
genteelness
lealness

ĔL'nes
fellness
wellness

ĔL'o
bellow
brocatello
cobra-de-
    capello
cello
duello
felloe
fellow
good-fellow
mellow
morello
niello
play-fellow
prunello
punchinello
saltarello

scrivello
violoncello
yellow

ĔL'od
unmellowed
bellowed, etc.

ĔL'on
enfelon
felon
melon
water-melon

ĔL'op
develop
envelop

ĔL'ot
helot
zealot

ĔL'oz
bellows
fellows, etc.

ĔLP'ful
helpful
self-helpful
unhelpful

ĔL'pi
kelpie

ĔL'ping
helping
yelping

ĔLP'les
helpless
whelpless
yelpless

ĔL'pur
helper
self-helper
yelper

ĔL'sa
Elsa

ĔL'skin
eel-skin
seal-skin

ĔL'son
kelson
Nelson

ĔL'ta
delta
pelta

ĔL'ted
belted
felted
melted
pelted
smelted
unbelted
welted

ĔL'test
beltest, etc.

ĔL'teth
belteth, etc.

ĔL'thi
healthy
stealthy
wealthy

ĔL'tik
Celtic
Keltic

ĔL'ting	ĔL'ug	cloud-com-	procellous
belting	deluge	peller	vitellus
felting		compeller	zealous
melting	ĔL'um	dispeller	
pelting	cerebellum	dweller	ĔL'vet
smelting	flabellum	exceller	velvet
unbelting	flagellum	expeller	
welting	vellum	feller	ĔL'ving
		foreteller	delving
ĔLT'les	ĔL'ur	fortune-teller	helving
beltless	annealer	Geller	shelving
Celtless	appealer	impeller	
feltless	concealer	interstellar	ĔL'vish
peltless	congealer	Keller	elvish
weltless	dealer	lamellar	
	double-dealer	"meller"	ĔL'vur
ĔL'tri	feeler	propeller	delver
peltry	four-wheeler	queller	helver
sweltry	healer	rebeller	shelver
	heeler	repeller	
ĔL'tur	interdealer	screw propeller	ĔL'ya
belter	keeler	Sellar	Amelia
felter	kneeler	seller	Aurelia
helter-skelter	misdealer	sheller	Bedelia
inshelter	pealer	smeller	camellia
kelter	peeler	speller	Cecelia
melter	reeler	stellar	Celia
pelter	repealer	sweller	Cordelia
shelter	revealer	tale-teller	Cornelia
smelter	sealer	teller	Delia
spelter	squealer	twin propeller	Lelia
swelter	stealer	underseller	lobelia
welter	steeler	Weller	
	ward heeler	wine-cellar	ĔL'yal
ĔL'turd	wheeler	yeller	Belial
unsheltered			
sheltered, etc.	ĔL'ur	ĔL'us	ĔL'yon
	appellor	apellous	chameleon
ĔL'ud	cave-dweller	entellus	(see Ē'li+on)
prelude	cellar	jealous	
		overzealous	ĔL'yon
			rebellion

āle, câre, ădd, ärm, åsk; mē, hẹre, ĕnd; īce, ĭll;

(cf. rhymes on
 ĔL'+on)

ĔL'yus
rebellious

ĔL'za
Elsa

ĔM'a
bema
blastema
eczema
edema
empyema
erythema
Fatima
Lima
myxedema
schema
seriema
terza-rima

ĔM'a
analemma
dilemma
Emma
gemma
lemma
maremma
neurilemma
stemma
trilemma

Ē'māl
female
she-male

ĒM'ăl
blastemal
hemal

Ē'man
able-seaman
beeman
freeman
G-man
gleeman
he-man
leman
merchant-sea-
 man
seaman
teaman
(cf. Bremen)

ĔM'b'l
assemble
dissemble
resemble
semble
tremble

ĔM'blans
assemblance
dissemblance
resemblance
semblance

ĔM'blant
resemblant
semblant

ĔM'b'ld
undissembled
assembled, etc.

ĔM'blem
emblem

ĔM'bli
assembly
trembly

ĔM'blij
assemblage

ĔM'bling
assembling
dissembling
resembling
trembling

ĔM'blur
assembler
dissembler
resembler
trembler

ĔM'bral
bimembral
trimembral

ĔM'brans
remembrance

ĔM'bur
December
dismember
disremember
ember
member
November
remember
September

ĔM'burd
dismembered
unremembered,
 etc.

ĔM'ens
Clemens

Ē'ment
agreement

decreement
disagreement

ĔM'ent
clement
inclement

ĒM'est
beamest
blasphemest
deemest
dreamest
esteemest
extremest
gleamest
misdeemest
reedemest
schemest
screamest
seemest
steamest
streamest
supremest

ĔM'est
begemmest
condemnest
hemmest
stemmest

ĔM'et
Emmett

ĒM'eth
beameth
blasphemeth
deemeth
dreameth
esteemeth
gleameth
redeemeth

schemeth
screameth
seemeth
steameth
streameth

ĔM'eth
begemmeth
condemneth
contemneth
hemmeth
stemmeth

ĒM'ful
beamful
dreamful
schemeful
teemful

ĒM'i
beamy
creamy
daydreamy
dreamy
gleamy
screamy
seamy
steamy
streamy
teemy
(cf. Mimi)

ĔM'i
demi
gemmy
jemmy
semi

ĒM'ik
anemic
racemic
systemic

ĔM'ik
academic
alchemic
chemic
endemic
epidemic
pandemic
polemic
stratagemic
systemic
theoremic
totemic

ĒM'ing
beaming
beseeming
blaspheming
creaming
daydreaming
deeming
dreaming
esteeming
gleaming
overstreaming
redeeming
scheming
screaming
seeming
steaming
streaming
summer-
  seeming
teeming
unbeseeming

ĔM'ing
begemming
condemning
contemning
Fleming
gemming

hemming
leming
self-condemn-
  ing
stemming

ĔM'ish
blemish
Flemish
unblemish

ĔM'isht
blemished
unblemished

ĔM'ist
extremist
schemist

ĔM'ist
chemist

ĔM'it, ĔM'it
Semite

ĔM'land
dreamland

ĔM'less
beamless
creamless
dreamless
schemeless
seamless
streamless

ĔM'let
streamlet

ĔM'li
extremely

seemly
supremely
unseemly

ĔM'non
Agamemnon
Memnon

ĒM'o
a tempo primo
Cremo
primo

ĔM'o
memo

ĔM'on
agathodæmon
cacodemon
demon
eudæmon

ĔM'on
lemon
(cf. "gem-
  man")

ĔM'pest
tempest

ĔM'pir
empire

ĔM'p'l
Semple
stemple
temple

ĔM'plar
exemplar
templar

ĔM′plat	pre-empting	**ĒM′ur**	concertina
contemplate	tempting	beamer	Czarina
template		blasphemer	farina
	ĔMP′tiv	daydreamer	Faustina
ĔMP′shun	pre-emptive	dreamer	galena
ademption	redemptive	femur	gena
coemption		lemur	Georgina
diremption	**ĔMP′tres**	reamer	Helena
emption	temptress	redeemer	hyena
exemption		schemer	Justina
pre-emption	**ĔMP′tur**	screamer	Lena
redemption	attempter	seamer	Magdalena
	exempter	seemer	maizena
ĔMP′stur	pre-emptor	steamer	Medina
dempster	tempter	streamer	Messina
sempster	unkempter	teemer	Modena
			Paulina
ĔMP′ted	**ĔM′pur**	**ĔM′ur**	philopena
attempted	attemper	begemmer	scarlatina
exempted	distemper	condemner	scena
pre-empted	Semper	contemner	Selena
tempted	temper	hemmer	semolina
unattempted	untemper	stemmer	Serena
untempted			signorina
	ĔM′purd	**ĔM′us**	subpœna
ĔMP′test	ill-tempered	Nicodemus	Tsarina
attemptest	tempered	Remus	verbena
exemptest	untempered		Wilhelmina
temptest		**ĔM′yer**	
	ĔM′son	premier	**ĔN′a**
ĔMP′teth	Clemson		antenna
attempteth	Empson	**ĒN′a**	duenna
exempteth		arena	Gehenna
tempteth	**ĔM′song**	Alexandrina	henna
	theme-song	Argentina	Ravenna
ĔMP′ti		Athena	senna
empty	**ĔM′stur**	catena	Sienna
	deemster	cavatina	Vienna
ĔMP′ting	seamster	Celestina	
attempting	teamster	Christina	**ĒN′al**
exempting		Clementina	machinal

penal
plenal
renal
venal
weanel

ĔN'al
antennal

ĔN'ant
lieutenant
pennant
sub-lieutenant
tenant

ĔN'ard
Leonard

Ē'nas
Enas
Zenas

ĔN'as
menace
tenace
(cf. tennis)

ĔN'at
brevipennate
impennate
longipennate
pennate
tripennate

ĔN'chant
trenchant

ĔN'chest
bedrenchest
blenchest
clenchest

drenchest
flenchest
intrenchest
quenchest
retrenchest
trenchest
unclenchest
wrenchest

ĔN'cheth
bedrencheth
blencheth
clencheth
drencheth
flencheth
intrencheth
quencheth
retrencheth
trencheth
unclencheth
wrencheth

ĔN'ching
bedrenching
benching
blenching
clenching
drenching
flenching
intrenching
quenching
retrenching
trenching
unclenching
unquenching
wrenching

ĔNCH'les
quenchless
(see ĔNCH +
less)

ĔNCH'man
Frenchman
henchman

ĔNCH'ment
intrenchment
retrenchment

ĔN'chur
bedrencher
bencher
blencher
clencher
drencher
intrencher
quencher
retrencher
trencher
unclencher
wrencher

ĔN'da
agenda
Benda
Brenda
corrigenda
delenda
hacienda
Zenda

ĔN'dal
prebendal
sendal
trendle

ĔN'dans
ascendance
attendance
condescendence
dependence
descendance

impendence
independence
interdepend-
ence

pendence
resplendence
superintend-
ence
tendance
transcendence
(cf. attendant
+ s)

**ĔN'dant,
ĔN'dent**
appendant
ascendant
attendant
contendant
defendant
dependant
dependent
descendant
descendent
equipendent
impendent
independent
intendant
interdependent
pendant
pendent
resplendent
splendent
superintendent
transcendent
transplendent

ĔN'ded
amended
appended
apprehended

āle,   câre,   ădd,   ärm,   ăsk;   mē,   hĕre,   ĕnd;   īce,   ĭll;

ascended	undefended	*tendest*	*subtendeth*
attended	unextended	*unbendest*	*suspendeth*
befriended	unfriended	*vendest*	*tendeth*
bended	wended	*wendest*	*transcendeth*
blended	(cf. splendid)		*vendeth*
commended		**ĔN'deth**	*wendeth*
comprehended	**ĔN'dest**	*amendeth*	
condescended	*amendest*	*appendeth*	**ĔN'di**
contended	*appendest*	*apprehendeth*	bendy
defended	*apprehendest*	*ascendeth*	Effendi
depended	*ascendest*	*attendeth*	
descended	*attendest*	*befriendeth*	**ĔN'dik**
distended	*befriendest*	*bendeth*	Wendic
emended	*bendest*	*blendeth*	zendik
ended	*blendest*	*commendeth*	
expended	*commendest*	*comprehendeth*	**ĔN'ding**
extended	*comprehendest*	*condescendeth*	amending
fended	*condescendest*	*contendeth*	appending
friended	*contendest*	*defendeth*	apprehending
impended	*defendest*	*dependeth*	ascending
inextended	*dependest*	*descendeth*	attending
intended	*descendest*	*emendeth*	befriending
interblended	*emendest*	*endeth*	bending
mended	*endest*	*expendeth*	blending
misappre-	*expendest*	*extendeth*	commending
hended	*extendest*	*fendeth*	comprehending
offended	*fendest*	*impendeth*	condescending
portended	*intendest*	*intendeth*	contending
pretended	*interblendest*	*interblendeth*	defending
reascended	*lendest*	*lendeth*	depending
recommended	*mendest*	*mendeth*	descending
reprehended	*offendest*	*misapprehendeth*	distending
subtended	*pretendest*	*offendeth*	emending
superintended	*recommendest*	*portendeth*	ending
suspended	*rendest*	*pretendeth*	expending
tended	*reprehendest*	*reascendeth*	extending
transcended	*sendest*	*recommendeth*	*forfending*
trended	*spendest*	*rendeth*	*forelending*
unattended	*subtendest*	*reprehendeth*	*forespending*
unbefriended	*superintendest*	*sendeth*	heart-rending
unblended	*suspendest*	*spendeth*	impending

ōld, ôr, ŏdd, oil, fŏŏt, out; ūse, ûrn, ŭp; THis, thin

intending
interblending
lending
mending
misspending
offending
pending
perpending
portending
pretending
recommending
rending
reprehending
sending
spending
subtending
superintending
suspending
tending
transcending
trending
unattending
unbending
unending
unfriending
unoffending
unpretending
vending
wending

ĒN'dish

fiendish

ĔND'les

endless
friendless

ĔND'li

friendly
unfriendly

ĔND'ment

amendment
befriendment
intendment

ĔN'do

cresendo
decrescendo
diminuendo
innuendo

ĔN'dron

liriodendron
lithodendron
rhododendron

ĔND'ship

friendship

ĔN'dum

addendum
agendum
corrigendum
credendum
referendum

ĔN'dur

amender
apprehender
ascender
attender
befriender
bender
blender
commender
comprehender
contender
defender
depender
descender
emender

ender
engender
entender
expender
extender
fender
gender
intender
interblender
lender
mender
money-lender
offender
perpender
pretender
recommender
render
reprehender
sender
slender
spender
splendor
surrender
suspender
tailender
tender
vendor
week-ender
wender

ĔN'durd

unsurrendered
tendered, etc.

ĔN'dus, not
  ĔN'jus

stupendous
tremendous

ĔND'waz

endways

ĔN'el

fennel
Fennell
kennel
unkennel

ĔN'elm

Kenelm

ĒN'est

bescreenest
cleanest
contravenest
convenest
demeanest
gleanest
greenest
intervenest
keenest
leanest
meanest
screenest
serenest
supervenest
weanest
weenest

ĔN'et

Bennett
jennet
rennet
senate
tenet

ĔN'eth

bescreeneth
cleaneth
contraveneth
conveneth
demeaneth
gleaneth

interveneth
keeneth
leaneth
meaneth
screeneth
superveneth
weaneth
weeneth

ĔN'eth
Kenneth
penneth, etc.

ĔNG'then
lengthen
strengthen

ĔNG'thi
lengthy

ĒN'horn
greenhorn

ĒN'ĭ
Cheney
Cheyney
fantoccini
genie
greeny
Hippocrene
meany
Selene
sheeny
spleeny
Sweeney
teeny
visne
weeny

ĔN'ĭ
any

Benny
fenny
Jenny
Kilkenny
Penney
many
penny
Rennie
spinning-jenny
tenney
true-penny
wenny

ĒN'ĭd
green-eyed
keen-eyed

ĒN'ij
careenage
greenage
teenage

ĒN'ĭk
phenic
scenic

ĔN'ĭk
alphenic
anthropogenic
asthenic
callisthenic
chromogenic
crystallogenic
Demosthenic
deuterogenic
Diogenic
diplogenic
ecumenic
Edenic
embryogenic
eugenic

galenic
geoselenic
glycogenic
Hellenic
hygienic
hysterogenic
irenic
lichenic
metagenic
neurasthenic
nitrogenic
organogenic
oxygenic
Panhellenic
paragenic
parthenic
parthenogenic
pathogenic
phenic
Philhellenic
phosphorogenic
photogenic
phrenic
protogenic
Prutenic
pyrogenic
pythogenic
Saracenic
scenic
selenic
splenic
sthenic
thermogenic
tungstenic
zoogenic

ĔN'im
denim

ĔN'in
Lenin

ĒN'ing
advening
bemeaning
cleaning
contravening
convening
demeaning
double-mean-
  ing
eaning
gleaning
greening
intervening
keening
leaning
machining
meaning
overweening
preening
queening
screening
shebeening
subvening
supervening
unmeaning
upleaning
weaning
weening
well-meaning
yeaning

ĒN'ingz
screenings
cleanings, etc.

ĔN'ingz
Jennings
pennings, etc.

ĔN'is
Dennis

tennis
(cf. menace,
    tenace)

ĒN'ish
cleanish
greenish
keenish
leanish
meanish
queenish
spleenish

ĔN'ish
plenish
replenish
Rhenish
wennish

ĒN'ist
machinist
magazinist
plenist
routinist

ĔN'iz
bennies
pennies
spinning-jen-
    nies

ĔN'jans
vengeance

ĔN'jin
engine

ĔN'jing
avenging
revenging
venging

ĔN'jur
avenger

ĔN'li
cleanly
greenly
keenly
leanly
meanly
obscenely
queenly
serenely

ĔN'li
cleanly
Henley
Schenley
Senley
uncleanly

ĔN'ling
weanling
yeanling

ĔN'man
fenman
penman

ĔN'nes
cleanness
greenness
keenness
leanness
meanness
obsceneness
sereneness
uncleanness

ĔN'o
andantino
baldachino

bambino
casino
festino
Filipino
keno
maraschino
merino
peacherino
peperino
pianino
Reno
San Marino
Sereno
tondino
Valentino
vetturino

ĒN'ok
Enoch

ĒN'old
Reynold

ĔN'olz
Reynolds

ĔN'om
envenom
venom

ĔN'on
pennon
tenon

ĒN'os
Enos

ĔN'ri
Denry
Henry

ĔN'sal
bimensal
commensal
forensal
mensal

ĔN'sat
compensate
condensate
insensate
intensate

ĔN'sest
commencest
condensest
densest
dispensest
fencest
incensest
intensest
recompensest

ĔN'seth
commenceth
condenseth
dispenseth
fenceth
incenseth
recompenseth

ĔN'sez
Albigenses
amanuenses
menses

ĔNS'forth
henceforth
thenceforth
whenceforth

ĔN'shal
agential

bigential
coessential
conferential
confidential
consequential
credential
deferential
differential
equipotential
essential
evidential
existential
expediential
experiential
exponential
inconsequential
indulgential
inessential
inferential
influential
intelligential
irreverential
jurisprudential
nonessential
obediential
omnipresential
penitential
pestilential
potential
precedential
preferential
presidential
Provencial
providential
prudential
querulential
quintessential
referential
reminiscential
residential
reverential

rodential
sapiential
sciential
sentential
sequential
superessential
tangential
torrential
transferential
unessential

ĒN'ship

deanship
queenship

ĚN'shun

abstention
accension
apprehension
ascension
attention
circumvention
coextension
comprehension
condescension
contention
contravention
convention
declension
deprehension
descension
detention
dimension
dissension
distention
extension
inapprehension
inattention
incomprehen-
    sion
inextension

intension
intention
intervention
invention
mention
misapprehen-
    sion
obtention
obvention
ostension
pension
portention
preapprehen-
    sion
prehension
presention
pretension
prevention
propension
recension
reprehension
retention
subvention
supervention
suspension
tension
thermo-tension

ĚN'shund

unmentioned
unpensioned
well-inten-
    tioned

ĚN'shus

conscientious
contentious
dissentious
licentious
pestilentious
pretentious

sententious
silentious

ĚN'sil

extensile
pencil
pensile
prehensile
stencil
tensile
utensil

ĚN'sild

pencilled
stencilled

ĚN'sing

commencing
condensing
dispensing
fencing
incensing
recompensing

ĚN'siv

apprehensive
ascensive
comprehensive
condensive
condescensive
defensive
descensive
distensive
expensive
extensive
inapprehensive
incensive
incomprehen-
    sive
indefensive
inexpensive

influencive
inoffensive
intensive
offensive
ostensive
pensive
protensive
recompensive
reprehensive
self-defensive
suspensive
tensive
unapprehen-
   sive

ĔNS'les
defenceless
expenseless
fenceless
offenceless
senseless

ĔNS'ment
commencement
incensement

ĔNS'nes
denseness
immenseness
intenseness
propenseness
tenseness

ĔN'son
Benson
Henson

ĔN'sūr
censure

ĔN'sŭr
censer

censor
commencer
condenser
denser
dispenser
extensor
fencer
incensor
intenser
prehensor
recompenser
spencer
Spenser
tensor

ĔN'sus
census

ĔN'ta
magenta
Pimenta
polenta

ĔN'tal
accidental
alimental
antecedental
argental
argumental
atramental
bidental
cental
coincidental
complemental
complimental
continental
dental
dentil
dentile
departmental
detrimental

developmental
documental
elemental
experimental
falcon-gentle
firmamental
fragmental
fundamental
gentle
governmental
impedimental
incidental
instrumental
intercontin-
   ental
kentle
labiodental
Lental
ligamental
linguadental
medicamental
mental
monumental
nutrimental
occidental
oriental
ornamental
parental
parliamental
pedimental
pigmental
placental
predicamental
recremental
regimental
rental
rudimental
sacramental
segmental
sentimental
supplemental

temperamental
tenemental
testamental
transcendental
trental
tridental
ungentle
(cf. ĔN'til)

ĔN'tans
repentance
sentence
unrepentance

ĔN'tant
repentant
representant
unrepentant

ĔN'tat
bidentate
commentate
dementate
dentate
edentate
quadridentate
tridentate

ĔN'te
aguardiente
cognoscente
diapente

ĔN'ted
absented
accented
assented
augmented
battlemented
cemented
circumvented

āle, câre, ădd, ärm, åsk; mē, hĕre, ĕnd; īce, ĭll;

commented
complimented
consented
contented
demented
dented
discontented
dissented
fermented
frequented
fomented
ill-contented
indented
invented
lamented
misrepresented
ornamented
presented
prevented
relented
rented
repented
represented
resented
scented
supplemented
sweet-scented
tented
tormented
unlamented
unornamented
unprecedented
unprevented
unrepented
untented
untormented
vented
well-contented

ĔN'test
absentest

accentest
assentest
augmentest
cementest
circumventest
commentest
complimentest
consentest
contentest
dissentest
fermentest
fomentest
frequentest
indentest
inventest
lamentest
misrepresentest
ornamentest
presentest
preventest
relentest
rentest
repentest
representest
resentest
sentest
scentest
supplementest
tormentest
ventest

ĔN'teth
absenteth
accenteth
assenteth
augmenteth
cementeth
circumventeth
commenteth
complimenteth
consenteth

contenteth
dissenteth
fermenteth
fomenteth
frequenteth
indenteth
inventeth
lamenteth
misrepreseneth
ornamenteth
presenteth
preventeth
relenteth
renteth
repenteth
representeth
resenteth
scenteth
supplementeth
tormenteth
venteth

ĔNT'ful
eventful
resentful
uneventful

ĔNT'hous
penthouse

ĔN'ti
dolce far niente
Henty
plenty
presidente
tormenty
twenty

ĔN'tij
percentage
ventage

ĔN'tik
argentic
authentic
identic

ĔN'tīl
Gentile

ĔN'tĭl
lentil
(cf. ĔN'tal)

ĔN'tin
dentine
Quentin
San Quentin
torrentine
tridentine

ĔN'ting
absenting
accenting
assenting
augmenting
cementing
circumventing
commenting
complimenting
consenting
contenting
denting
dementing
dissenting
fermenting
fomenting
frequenting
indenting
inventing
lamenting
misrepresent-
  ing

ornamenting
presenting
preventing
relenting
renting
repenting
representing
resenting
scenting
self-tormenting
suppplement-
  ing
tenting
tormenting
unconsenting
unrelenting
unrepenting
venting

ĔN'tis

appentice
apprentice
non compos
  mentis
pentice
prentice

ĔN'tist

apprenticed
dentist
preventist

ĔN'tiv

adventive
assentive
attentive
circumventive
inattentive
incentive
inventive
irretentive

pendentive
presentive
preventive
resentive
retentive

ĔNT'les

cementless
centless
dentless
lamentless
relentless
rentless
scentless
tentless, etc.

ĔNT'li

eminently
evidently
gently
impotently
innocently
insolently
intently
(see ĔNT+ly)

ĔNT'ment

contentment
discontentment
presentment
relentment
representment
resentment

ĔNT'nes

intentness

ĔN'to

cento
cinque-cento
divertimento

lento
memento
pimento
polento
portamento
pronuncia-
  mento
quattrocento
rifacimento
Sacramento

ĔN'ton

Benton
Denton
Fenton
Trenton

ĔN'tor

bucentaur
centaur
mentor
stentor
succentor
(cf. ĔN'tur)

ĔN'tral

central
ventral

ĔN'trans

entrance

ĔN'trat

concentrate

ĔNT'res

inventress
tormentress

ĔN'tri

entry

gentry
sentry

ĔN'trik

acentric
anthropocen-
  tric
barycentric
centric
concentric
eccentric
geocentric
gynecocentric
heliocentric
paracentric
selenocentric

ĔN'tum

momentum
sarmentum

ĔN'tūr

adventure
debenture
indenture
misadventure
peradventure
tenture
venture

ĔN'tŭr

assenter
augmenter
cementer
center
circumventor
commenter
concenter
consenter
contenter
dead-center

āle, câre, ădd, ärm, åsk; mē, hẹre, ĕnd; īce, ĭll;

denter
dissenter
enter
experimenter
fermenter
fomenter
frequenter
indenter
inventor
lamenter
lentor
misrepresenter
ornamenter
precentor
presenter
preventer
re-enter
relenter
renter
repenter
representer
resenter
supplementer
tenter
tormenter
venter
(cf. centaur,
  etc.)

ĔN'turd

entered
self-centered
centered, etc.

ĔN'tus

immomentous
ligamentous
momentous
pedetentous
pigmentous
portentous

sarmentous
unguentous

ĔN'um

frenum
plenum

ĔN'ur

cleaner
contravener
convener
demeanor
gleaner
greener
intervener
keener
leaner
machiner
magaziner
meaner
misdemeanor
obscener
screener
seiner
serener
shebeener
supervener
weaner
wiener

ĔN'ur

Fenner
penner
tenner
tenor
Venner

ĔN'us

genus
Silenus

venous
Venus

ĔN'vi

envy

ĔN'vil

Bienville
Glenville
Grenville

ĔN'yal

congenial
(see ĒN'i-al)

ĔN'yan

Armenian
(see ĒN'i-an)

ĔN'yens

lenience
(see ĒN'i-ens)

ĔN'yent

convenient
(see ĒN'i-ent)

ĔN'yor

monsignor
seignior
senior
signor

ĔN'yus

genius
(see ĒN'i-us)

ĔN'za

cadenza
influenza

ĔNZ'da

Wednesday

ĔN'zes

cleanses
lenses

ĔN'zi

frenzy
McKenzie

ĔN'zo

Lorenzo

ĔN'zon

tenzon
venison

Ē'o

Cleo
Leo
Theo
trio

Ē'on

æon
Creon
Leon
neon
odeon
pæon
pantheon
peon
pheon

ĔP'ard

jeopard
leopard
peppered
shepherd

ōld, ôr, ŏdd, oil, fŏŏt, out; ūse, ûrn, ŭp; THis, thin

ĒP'en	heapy	sweeping	intussusception
cheapen	kepi	unsleeping	misconception
deepen	seepy	unweeping	obreption
steepen	sleepy	weeping	perception
	steepy		preconception
ĒP'est	sweepy	**ĒP'ish**	preperception
cheapest	tepee	deepish	reception
cheepest	weepy	sheepish	self-deception
creepest		steepish	subreption
deepest	**ĔP'i**		surreption
heapest	tepee	**ĒP' 'l**	
keepest		*empeople*	**ĔP'si**
leapest	**ĔP'id**	people	apepsy
outsleepest	intrepid	steeple	catalepsy
overleapest	lepid	unpeople	dyspepsy
oversleepest	tepid		epilepsy
peepest	trepid	**ĒP'les**	eupepsy
reapest		sleepless	
sleepest	**ĔP'ij**	weepless	**ĔP'sis**
steepest	seepage		asepsis
sweepest	sweepage	**ĒP'nes**	analepsis
weepest		cheapness	epanalepsis
	ĔP'ik	deepness	metalepsis
ĒP'eth	epic	sleepness	paralepsis
cheepeth	orthoepic		prolepsis
creepeth		**ĔP'on**	scepsis
heapeth	**ĔP'ing**	weapon	syllepsis
keepeth	cheeping		
leapeth	creeping	**ĔP'shun**	**ĒP'skin**
outsleepeth	heaping	*abreption*	sheepskin
overleapeth	house-keeping	apperception	
oversleepeth	keeping	*arreption*	**ĔP'tans**
peepeth	leaping	conception	acceptance
reapeth	outsleeping	contraception	
sleepeth	overleaping	deception	**ĔP'tant**
sweepeth	oversleeping	ereption	acceptant
weepeth	peeping	exception	exceptant
	reaping	imperception	reptant
ĔP'i	safe-keeping	inception	
cheepy	sleeping	interception	**ĔP'ted**
creepy	steeping	introsusception	accepted

excepted
intercepted

ĔP'test
acceptest
adeptest
exceptest
interceptest

ĔP'teth
accepteth
excepteth
intercepteth

ĔP'tik
acataleptic
analeptic
antiseptic
aseptic
bradypeptic
cataleptic
dyspeptic
epileptic
eupeptic
metaleptic
nympholeptic
organoleptic
peptic
proleptic
sceptic
septic
sylleptic

ĔP'ting
accepting
excepting
incepting
intercepting

ĔP'tiv
acceptive

conceptive
deceptive
exceptive
imperceptive
inceptive
insusceptive
interceptive
intussusceptive
irreceptive
perceptive
preceptive
receptive
susceptive

ĔPT'nes
ineptness

ĔP'tun
Neptune

ĔP'tur
accepter
adepter
excepter
inceptor
intercepter
preceptor
sceptre
susceptor

ĔP'ur
cheaper
cheeper
creeper
deeper
heaper
hedge-keeper
housekeeper
keeper
leaper
peeper

reaper
shopkeeper
sleeper
steeper
sweeper
wall-creeper
weeper
wicket-keeper

ĔP'ur
hepper
high-stepper
leper
overstepper
pepper
stepper

ĔP'wôk
sheep-walk
sleep-walk

Ē'ra
Ça ira
chimera
era
gerah
Hera
lira
Madeira
Vera

ĔR'af
seraph
teraph

ĘR'al
feral
spheral

ĔR'ald
Gerald

herald
Herrold

ĔR'ans
aberrance

ĔR'ant
aberrant

ĔR'as
terrace
(cf. ĔR'is)

ĔR'at
serrate

ĘR'ded
bearded

ĘRD'li
weirdly

ĘR'ens
adherence
appearance
arrearance
clearance
coherence
disappearance
incoherence
inherence
interference
perseverance
reappearance

ĘR'ent
adherent
coherent
inadherent
incoherent
inherent
perseverant

ōld, ôr, ŏdd, oil, fŏŏt, out; ūse, ûrn, ŭp; THis, thin

querent	spearest	**ĘR'ful**	cemetery
vicegerent	steerest	cheerful	cherry
	unrearest	earful	Derry
ĘR'est	veerest	fearful	ferry
adherest		sneerful	Gerry
appearest	**ĔR'et**	tearful	Kerry
austerest	ferret	uncheerful	lamasery
besmearest	terret	unfearful	merry
careerest			millinery
cheerest	**ĘR'eth**	**Ę'ri, Ē'ri**	monastery
clearest	adhereth	ærie	perry
coherest	appeareth	aweary	Pondicherry
dearest	besmeareth	beery	presbytery
disappearest	careereth	bleary	sherry
drearest	cheereth	cheery	skerry
endearest	cleareth	deary	stationery
fearest	disappeareth	dreary	very
gearest	endeareth	eerie	wherry
hearest	feareth	Erie	(cf. ĀR'i)
insincerest	geareth	forweary	
interferest	heareth	hara-kiri	**ĘR'īd**
jeerest	interfereth	jeery	blear-eyed
leerest	jeereth	leary	clear-eyed
merest	leereth	life-weary	tear-eyed
nearest	overheareth	miserere	
overhearest	peereth	overweary	**ĘR'ĭd**
peerest	persevereth	peri	queried
perseverest	reappeareth	quære	unwearied
queerest	reareth	query	war-wearied
reappearest	revereth	smeary	wearied
rearest	seareth	sneery	world-wearied
reverest	sheareth	sphery	(cf. virid)
searest	smeareth	teary	
serest	sneereth	uncheery	**ĔR'id**
severest	speareth	veery	berried
uprearest	steereth	weary	buried
shearest	upreareth		cherried
sheerest	veereth	**ĔR'i**	ferried
sincerest		beriberi	serried
smearest	**ĘR'fon**	berry	unburied
sneerest	earphone	bury	

ĔR'if
sheriff
(cf. ĔR'af)

ĘR'ij
arrearage
clearage
peerage
pierage
steerage

ĔR'ĭk
alexiteric
amphoteric
anisomeric
atmospheric
chimeric
chromospheric
cleric
climacteric
derrick
enteric
Eric
esoteric
exoteric
ferric
generic
helispheric
hemispheric
Herrick
Homeric
hysteric
icteric
isomeric
masseteric
mesmeric
neoteric
numeric
peripheric
perispheric
phylacteric

piperic
spheric
suberic
valeric

ĔR'iks
esoterics
hysterics
clerics, etc.

ĔR'il
beryl
chrysoberyl
peril
sterile

ĘR'in
Erin

ĘR'ing
adhering
appearing
auctioneering
Bering
besmearing
blearing
cannoneering
careering
cashiering
cheering
clearing
cohering
Dearing
disappearing
domineering
earing
electioneering
endearing
engineering
fearing
gearing

gondoliering
hearing
interfering
immerit
jeering
leering
mountaineering
nearing
overhearing
peering
persevering
pioneering
privateering
queering
reappearing
rearing
rehearing
revering
searing
shearing
skeering
sneering
spearing
steering
ungearing
upcheering
uprearing
veering
venecring
volunteering
(cf. earring)

ĔR'is
ferris
terrace
Terris

ĔR'ish
cherish
perish

ĔR'it
demerit

disherit
disinherit
immerit
inherit
merit

ĘR'iz
dearies
overwearies
queries
series
wearies

ĔR'iz
berries
buries
cherries
ferries
sherries
wherries

ĘR'les
cheerless
earless
fearless
gearless
peerless
spearless
tearless
yearless

ĘR'li
austerely
cavalierly
cheerly
clearly
dearly
merely
nearly
queerly
severely

sincerely	ẸR'sur	peerer	ĔS'chund
yearly	fiercer	perseverer	questioned
	piercer	queerer	unquestioned
ẸR'ling		rearer	
shearling	ẸR'sing	reverer	ĔS'ed
steerling	ear-piercing	severer	blessed
yearling	piercing	shearer	(see ĔS+ed)
	transpiercing	sneerer	
ẸR'ment		spearer	ĔS'el
cerement	ẸR'son	steerer	Diesel
endearment	Grierson	teerer	
	Pearson	ungearer	ĔS'en
ẸR'nes		veerer	lessen
austereness	ĔR'ub	(cf. mirror)	
clearness	cherub		ĔS'ens
dearness		ẸR'us	indecence
nearness	ĔR'ul	sclerous	
queerness	ferrule	serous	ĔS'ens
severeness	ferule		accrescence
sincereness	perule	ĔR'us	acquiescence
	spherule	ferrous	adolescence
ẸR'o, Ē'ro			arborescence
hero	ẸR'ur	ẸRZ'man	calescence
lillibullero	adherer	privateersman	calorescence
zero	appearer	steersman	candescence
	austerer		coalescence
ĔR'on	besmearer	Ē'sa	concrescence
heron	cheerer	Felica	contabescence
	clearer	mesa	convalescence
Ē'room	dearer	Theresa	defervescence
sea-room	disappearer		deliquescence
tea-room	electioneerer	Ē'saj	delitescence
	endearer	presage	effervescence
ĔR'or	fearer		efflorescence
error	fleerer	ĔS'chun	emollescence
terror	hearer	congestion	erubescence
	interferer	digestion	essence
ẸR'os, ĔR'os	jeerer	indigestion	evanescence
Eros	leerer	ingestion	*exacerbescence*
	nearer	question	excrescence
ẸRS'nes	overhearer	suggestion	florescence
fierceness			

āle, câre, ădd, ärm, ȧsk; mē, hĕre, ĕnd; īce, ĭll;

fluorescence
fremescence
frondescence
fructescence
frutescence
glaucescence
hyalescence
incalescence
incandescence
incoalescence
ineffervescence
inflorescence
intumescence
iridescence
juvenescence
lactescence
lapidescence
latescence
obsolescence
opalescence
petrescence
phosphor-
 escence
pubescence
putrescence
quiescence
quintessence
recrudescence
reflorescence
rejuvenescence
revalescence
revirescence
rubescence
senescence
spumescence
supercrescence
torpescence
tumescence
turgescence
viridescence

virilescence
vitrescence

ĒS'ent

decent
indecent
recent

ĔS'ent

accrescent
acquiescent
adolescent
albescent
alkalescent
arborescent
cessant
coalescent
convalescent
crescent
decrescent
deliquescent
delitescent
depressant
effervescent
efflorescent
erubescent
evanescent
excrescent
fervescent
flavescent
florescent
fluorescent
fremescent
fructescent
frutescent
gangrenescent
glaucescent
herbescent
ignescent
incalescent
incandescent

incessant
increscent
ineffervescent
iridescent
jessant
juvenescent
lactescent
languescent
lapidescent
latescent
liquescent
lutescent
marcescent
maturescent
nigrescent
obsolescent
opalescent
petrescent
phosphorescent
pubescent
putrescent
quiescent
rancescent
recrudescent
rejuvenescent
revalescent
rubescent
rufescent
senescent
spinescent
spinulescent
spumescent
suffrutescent
sugescent
supercrescent
torpescent
turgescent
violescent
virescent
viridescent
vitrescent

ĒS'ept

precept

ĒS'est

ceasest
creasest
decreasest
fleecest
greasest
increasest
leasest
releasest

ĔS'est

acquiescest
addressest
assessest
blessest
caressest
compressest
confessest
depressest
digressest
distressest
dressest
expressest
guessest
impressest
oppressest
possessest
pressest
professest
progressest
redressest
repressest
suppressest
trangressest
undressest

ĒS'eth

ceaseth

ōld, ôr, ŏdd, oil, fŏŏt, out; ūse, ûrn, ŭp; THis, thin

creaseth
decreaseth
fleeceth
greaseth
increaseth
leaseth
releaseth

ĔS'eth

acquiesceth
addresseth
assesseth
blesseth
caresseth
compresseth
confesseth
depresseth
digresseth
distresseth
dresseth
expresseth
guesseth
impresseth
oppresseth
possesseth
presseth
professeth
progresseth
redresseth
represseth
suppresseth
transgresseth
undresseth

ĒS'ez

battlepieces
caprices
ceases
creases
decreases
fleeces

greases
increases
leases
mantel-pieces
master-pieces
nieces
peaces
pelisses
pieces
releases

ĔS'ez

dresses
presses, etc.

ĒS'ful

capriceful
peaceful
unpeaceful

ĔS'ful

successful
(see ĔS+ful)

ĔSH'al

especial
special

ĒSH'an

Grecian
(see ĒSH'un)

ĔSH'est

enmeshest
freshest
immeshest
refreshest
threshest

ĔSH'eth

enmesheth

immesheth
mesheth
refresheth
thresheth

ĔSH'ez

species

ĔSH'i

fleshy
meshy

ĔSH'ing

meshing
refreshing
threshing

ĔSH'ingz

fleshings
meshings, etc.

ĔSH'les

fleshless
meshless

ĔSH'li

fleshly
freshly
unfleshly

ĔSH'man

freshman

ĔSH'ment

refreshment

ĔSH'nes

freshness

Ē'shor

sea-shore

Ē'shun

accretion
completion
concretion
deletion
depletion
Grecian
impletion
incompletion
internecion
repletion
secretion
(cf. Ē'shi-an,
    etc.)

ĔSH'un

accession
aggression
cession
compression
concession
confession
depression
digression
discretion
dispossession
egression
expression
freshen
impression
indiscretion
ingression
insession
intercession
introgression
intropression
obsession
oppression
possession
precession
prepossession

procession
profession
progression
recession
regression
repossession
reimpression
repossession
repression
retrocession
retrogression
secession
self-possession
session
succession
supersession
suppression
transgression
(cf. Hessian,
etc.)

ĔSH'unz
quarter-ses-
sions, acces-
sions, etc.

ĔSH'ur
flesher
fresher
mesher
pressure
refresher
thresher
tressure

Ē'shus
facetious
specious

ĔSH'us
precious

ĔS'ĭ
creasy
fleecy

ĔS'ĭ
Bessie
Cressy
dressy
Jesse
Jessie
messy
Tessie
tressy
(cf. in esse)

Ē'sid
lee-side
sea-side

ĔS'ij
expressage
message
pesage
presage

ĔS'ik
eugenesic
geodesic

**Ē'sil, ĔS'il or
ĬS'il**
Cecil

ĔS'ing
ceasing
creasing
decreasing
fleecing
greasing
increasing
leasing

piecing
policing
releasing
surceasing
unceasing

ĔS'ing
acquiescing
addressing
assessing
blessing
caressing
coalescing
compressing
confessing
convalescing
depressing
digressing
dispossessing
distressing
dressing
excessing
expressing
guessing
impressing
messing
oppressing
possessing
prepossessing
pressing
professing
progressing
redressing
repressing
retrogressing
suppressing
undressing
unprepos-
sessing
water-dressing

ĔS'is
anamnesis
anesthesis
anthesis
aposiopesis
catachresis
deesis
diaphoresis
diesis
erotesis
exegesis
hyperesthesis
mathesis
mimesis
ochlesis
paracentesis
perichoresis
schesis
synteresis
thesis
tmesis

ĔS'iv
adhesive
cohesive

ĔS'iv
accessive
aggressive
compressive
concessive
concrescive
congressive
crescive
depressive
digressive
excessive
expressive
impressive
inexpressive
oppressive

ōld, ôr, ŏdd, oil, fŏŏt, out; ūse, ûrn, ŭp; THis, thin

possessive
progressive
recessive
redressive
regressive
repressive
retrogressive
successive
suppressive
transgressive
unexpressive

ĔS'ki
de Reszke
pesky

ĔSK'nes
grotesqueness
picturesqueness
statuesqueness

ĔS'ko
al fresco
fresco
tedesco

ĔS'ku
fescue
rescue

Ē'skwar
T-square

ĔS"l
Cecil
chessel
nestle
pestle
redressal
trestle
unnestle

vessel
wrestle

ĔS'les
capriceless
ceaseless
creaseless
fleeceless
leaseless
peaceless

ĔS'ling
nestling
pestling
wrestling

ĔS'lur
nestler
wrestler

ĔS'man
policeman

ĔS'man
pressman
yes man

ĔS'mat
mess-mate

ĔS'mel
piecemeal

ĔS'ment
assessment
impressment
redressment

ĔS'nes
obeseness

ĔS'on
Gleason
Leisen

ĔS'on
lessen
lesson

ĔS'pit
respite

ĔS'pur
Hesper
vesper

ĔS'ta
podesta
siesta
Vesta
Zend-Avesta

ĔS'tal
festal
vestal

ĔS'tan
Avestan
sebesten

ĔS'tant
contestant
gestant

ĔS'tat
intestate
testate

ĔS'ted
arrested
attested
bested

breasted
castle-crested
chested
chicken-
  breasted
congested
contested
crested
detested
digested
disinterested
divested
double-breasted
foam-crested
indigested
infested
ingested
interested
invested
jested
manifested
marble-
  breasted
molested
nested
pigeon-
  breasted
predigested
protested
redigested
requested
rested
sable-vested
single-breasted
suggested
tested
unbreasted
undigested
unmolested
unrested

āle, câre, ădd, ärm, ăsk; mē, hĕre, ĕnd; īce, ĭll;

vested
wrested

ĔS'test
arrestest
attestest
bestest
breastest
contestest
crestest
detestest
digestest
divestest
infestest
interestest
investest
jestest
manifestest
molestest
protestest
requestest
restest
suggestest
testest
wrestest

ĔS'teth
arresteth
attesteth
breasteth
contesteth
cresteth
detesteth
digesteth
divesteth
infesteth
interesteth
investeth
jesteth
manifesteth
molesteth

nesteth
protesteth
requesteth
resteth
suggesteth
testeth
wresteth

ĔS'tez
Estes

ĔST'ful
blestful
jestful
restful
unrestful

ĔS'ti
beastie
bheesty
yeasty

ĔS'ti
chesty
cresty
resty
testy
yesty

ĔS'tij
prestige
vestige

ĔS'tik
agrestic
alkahestic
anamnestic
anapestic
aposiopestic
asbestic
catachrestic

domestic
gestic
majestic
telestic
telestich

ĔS'tin
asbestine
clandestine
destine
intestine
predestine
sestine

ĔS'tind
destined
predestined
undestined

ĔS'ting
easting
feasting
unpriesting
yeasting

ĔS'ting
arresting
attesting
besting
breasting
congesting
contesting
cresting
detesting
digesting
disinteresting
divesting
infesting
ingesting
interesting
investing
jesting

manifesting
molesting
nesting
protesting
questing
reinvesting
requesting
resting
suggesting
testing
uninteresting
unresting
vesting
westing
wresting

ĔS'tiv
attestive
congestive
digestive
festive
infestive
restive
suggestive
tempestive

ĔST'les
breastless
crestless
guestless
jestless
questless
restless

ĔST'li
beastly
priestly

ĔST'ling
nestling
westling

ōld, ôr, ŏdd, oil, fŏŏt, out: ūse, ûrn, ŭp; THis, thin

ĔST'ment	**ĔS'tus**	nor'-wester	piecer
arrestment	asbestus	pester	releaser
divestment	cestus	*prester*	
investment		protester	**ĔS'ŭr**
vestment	**ĔST'ward**	requester	acquiescer
	eastward	rester	addresser
ĔS'to		semester	aggressor
manifesto	**ĔST'ward**	sequester	antecessor
presto	westward	sou'-wester	assessor
		suggester	blesser
Ē'ston	**ĔS'ter**	Sylvester	caresser
freestone		tester	cesser
keystone	Dniester	trimester	compressor
	down-easter	vester	confessor
ĔS'ton	Easter	wrester	depressor
Weston	feaster	*yester*	digresser
	north-easter		distresser
ĔS'tral	south-easter	**ĔS'turd**	dresser
ancestral	**ĔS'tur**	sequestered	excesser
campestral	arrester	unsequestered	guesser
fenestral	attester	festered, etc.	impresser
kestrel	Bester		intercessor
orchestral	Bestor	**ĔS'turn**	lesser
trimestral	breaster	eastern	messer
	Chester		oppressor
ĔS'trat	contester	**ĔS'turn**	possessor
fenestrate	digester	*hestern*	predecessor
sequestrate	divester	north-western	presser
	Dnestr	south-western	professor
ĔS'trik	Esther	western	progressor
orchestric	fester	*yestern*	redresser
palaestric	Hester		represser
	infester		successor
ĔS'tur	investor	**ĒS'ur**	suppressor
divesture	jester	creaser	transgressor
gesture	Leicester	decreaser	
investure	Lester	fleecer	**ĒT'a**
purpresture	mid-sementer	greaser	cheetah
revesture	molester	increaser	Chiquita
vesture	nester	leaser	Juanita

Rita	reheated	eaten	*receiptest*
zeta	repeated	moth-eaten	*repeatest*
	retreated	overeaten	*repletest*
ĔT'a	seated	storm-beaten	*retreatest*
animetta	secreted	sweeten	*seatest*
arietta	self-conceited	tempest-beaten	sweetest
biretta	sheeted	unbeaten	*treatest*
burletta	sleeted	weather-beaten	(cf. defeatist,
codetta	treated	wheaten	etc.)
comedietta	unmeeted	worm-eaten	
Etta	unseated	(cf. ĔT'on)	**ĔT'est**
Henrietta	wine-heated		*abettest*
lametta	(cf. fetid)	**ĔT'en**	*backsettest*
mozetta		*fretten*	*bayonettest*
operetta	**ĔT'ed**	threaten	*begettest*
Retta	abetted	(cf. Bretton)	*benettest*
Rosetta	benetted		*besettest*
vendetta	betted	**ĔT'est**	*bettest*
Yetta	brevetted	*beatest*	*coquettest*
	coquetted	*bleatest*	*forgettest*
ĔT'ed	coroneted	*cheatest*	*frettest*
accreted	curvetted	*competest*	*gettest*
bleated	fretted	completest	*lettest*
cheated	gazetted	*defeatest*	*nettest*
competed	indebted	*deletest*	*oversettest*
completed	interfretted	*depletest*	*pettest*
conceited	jetted	discreetest	*regrettest*
defeated	netted	*eatest*	*settest*
deleted	petted	effetest	*upsettest*
depleted	pirouetted	elitest	wettest
entreated	regretted	*entreatest*	*whettest*
escheated	sweated	fleetest	
evil-treated	unfretted	*greetest*	**ĔT'eth**
excreted	unnetted	*heatest*	*beateth*
greeted	wetted	*ill-treatest*	*bleateth*
heated	whetted	incompletest	*cheateth*
ill-treated	(cf. fetid)	*maltreatest*	*competeth*
incompleted		*meetest*	*completeth*
maltreated	**ĔT'en**	neatest	*defeateth*
meted	beaten	*overeatest*	*deleteth*
receipted	Cretan	*pleatest*	*depleteth*

ōld, ôr, ŏdd, oil, fŏŏt, out; ūse, ûrn, ŭp; THis, thin

eateth	Ēth'al	ſeething	Ēth'ur
entreateth	ethal	terror-	ether
greeteth	lethal	breathing	
heateth		unsheathing	ĔTH'ur
maltreateth	Ēth'an	wreathing	altogether
meeteth	Ethan		aweather
overeateth		Ēth'les	blether
pleateth	Ĕth'el	sheathless	feather
receipteth	Bethel	wreathless	heather
repeateth	ethal		leather
retreateth	Ethel	Ĕth'les	nether
seateth	(cf. Ĕth'il)	breathless	patent-leather
treateth		deathless	pinfeather
	ĔTH'en		tether
ĔT'eth	heathen	Ĕth'li	together
abetteth	wreathen	deathly	weather
begetteth			wether
benetteth	Ĕth'i	ĔTH'ment	white-feather
betteth	heathy	bequeathment	whitleather
bewetteth	Lethe	ensheathment	whether
coquetteth	lethy	enwreathment	
forgetteth			ĔTH'urd
fretteth	Ĕth'i	Ĕth'nik	unfeathered
getteth	deathy	ethnic	weathered
letteth		holethnic	feathered, etc.
netteth	Ĕth'il		
petteth	ethyl	Ĕth'od	ĔT'i
regretteth	methyl	method	entreaty
setteth			meaty
whetteth	ĔTH'ing	ĔTH'ren	peaty
	bequeathing	brethren	sleety
ĔT'ful	breathing		spermaceti
deceitful	ensheathing	ĔTH'ur	sweetie
	enwreathing	bequeather	sweety
ĔT'ful	inbreathing	breather	treaty
forgetful	incense-	either	
fretful	breathing	enwreather	ĔT'i
regretful	interwreathing	neither	Alligretti
	inwreathing	seether	Bettie
ĔTH'al	seething	sheather	betty
bequeathal	sheathing	wreather	confetti

āle, câre, ădd, ārm, ȧsk; mē, hẹre, ĕnd; īce, ĭll;

fretty
Hettie
Hetty
Irish confetti
jetty
Lettie
Letty
libretti
netty
Nettie
petit
petty
Rossetti
spaghetti
spermaceti
Vanizetti
sweaty

ĔT'id, ĔT'id
fetid
(cf. ĒT'ed,
  ĔT'ed)

ĔT'ij
cheatage
cleatage
eatage
escheatage
metage

ĔT'ik
acetic
cetic
Cretic
Rhætic

ĔT'ik
abietic
abiogenetic
æsthetic
agamogenetic

alexipyretic
allopathetic
aloetic
alphabetic
amuletic
anesthetic
anchoretic
antipathetic
antithetic
apathetic
apologetic
arithmetic
ascetic
athletic
auletic
Baphometic
bathetic
biogenetic
biomagnetic
catechetic
colletic
cometic
cosmetic
diamagnetic
dianoetic
diaphoretic
dietetic
docetic
electro-
  magnetic
emetic
emporetic
energetic
epigenetic
epithetic
erotetic
eugenetic
exegetic
frenetic
galactopoietic
Gangetic

genetic
geodetic
Helvetic
hermetic
histogenetic
homiletic
homogenetic
hypothetic
idiopathetic
inergetic
Japhetic
kinetic
Lettic
logarithmetic
magnetic
Masoretic
metic
mimetic
mythopoetic
noetic
nomothetic
ochletic
onomatopoetic
ontogenetic
palingenetic
pangenetic
parathetic
parenthetic
paretic
partheno-
  genetic
pathetic
pathogenetic
peripatetic
phonetic
phrenetic
phylogenetic
plethoretic
poetic
polygenetic
polysynthetic

prophetic
quercetic
quodlibetic
splenetic
strategetic
sympathetic
syncretic
synthetic
tabetic
theopathetic
theoretic
threnetic
zetetic

ĔT'iks
apologetics
dietetics
exegetics
homiletics
poetics
aesthetics, etc.

ĒT'ing
beating
bitter-
  sweeting
bleating
cheating
competing
completing
concreting
defeating
eating
entreating
fleeting
flesh-eating
greeting
heating
ill-treating
maltreating
meeting

ōld, ôr, ŏdd, oil, fŏŏt. out: ūse. ûrn. ŭp; THis, thin

meting	wetting	decretal	sweetly
overeating	whetting	fetal	unmeetly
receipting			
repeating	**ĒT'is**	**ĒT"l**	**ĔT'ling**
retreating	Thetis	abettal	nettling
seating		Babbitt metal	settling
secreting	**ĔT'is**	Chettle	unsettling
sheeting	lettuce	fettle	
sweeting		kettle	**ĒT'ment**
toad-eating	**ĔT'ish**	metal	entreatment
treating	coquettish	mettle	ill-treatment
unseating	fetish	Monel metal	maltreatment
	Lettish	nettle	treatment
ĔT'ing	pettish	petal	
abetting	wettish	Popocatapetl	**ĔT'ment**
backsetting		resettle	abetment
begetting	**ĒT'ist**	settle	besetment
benetting	defeatist, etc.	type-metal	indebtment
besetting		white-metal	revetment
betting	**ĒT'it**		
brevetting	beat it	**ĔT"ld**	**ĒT'nes**
coquetting		high-mettled	completeness
curvetting	**ĒT'iv**	nettled	concreteness
forgetting	accretive	petalled	discreetness
fretting	completive	unsettled	effeteness
gazetting	concretive	mettled, etc.	featness
getting	decretive		fleetness
intersetting	depletive	**ĔT'les**	incompleteness
jetting	discretive	debtless	meetness
letting	repletive	threatless	neatness
minuetting	secretive		obsoleteness
netting		**ĒT'li**	repleteness
oversetting	**ĔT'iz**	completely	sweetness
petting	entreaties	concretely	
regretting	sweeties	discreetly	**ĔT'nes**
retting	treaties	*featly*	setness
setting	treatise	fleetly	wetness
somersetting		indiscreetly	
sweating	**ĒT"l**	meetly	**ĒT'o**
undersetting	beetle	neatly	bonito
upsetting	betel	obsoletely	mosquito

āle, câre, ădd, ärm, åsk; mē, hēre, ĕnd; īce, ĭll;

san-benito	audiometric	**ĒT'rus, ĔT'rus**	kilometer
veto	barometric	petrous	liter
	bathymetric	saltpetrous	lotus-eater
ĔT'o	calorimetric	triquetrous	meeter
allegreto	clinometric		meter
amoretto	chlorometric	**ĒT'um**	metre
falsetto	chronometric	arboretum	neater
ghetto	diametric	fretum	overeater
lazaretto	dimetric	pinetum	Peter
libretto	electrometric	zibetum	prætor
palmetto	endosmometric		receipter
stiletto	eudiometric	**ĒT'ūr**	repeater
terzetto	gasometric	creature	retreater
zucchetto	geometric	feature	saltpeter
	goniometric	(cf. ĒCH'ur)	seater
ĒT'on	gravimetric		secreter
Beaton	hexametric	**ĒT'ur**	skeeter
Eaton	hydrometric	beater	smoke-eater
Eton	hygrometric	beefeater	superheater
Keaton	hypsometric	bleater	sweeter
Keyton	isobarometric	cake-eater	teeter
Seaton	isometric	cheater	toad-eater
Seyton	logometric	centimeter	treater
Zyzzogeton	magnetometric	competer	unseater
(cf. ĒT'en)	metric	completer	water-meter
	micrometric	decaliter	
ĔT'on	monometric	defeater	**ĔT'ur**
Bretton	obstetric	Demeter	abettor
	ozonometric	depleter	begetter
ĒT'ral, ĒT'rel	pedometric	eater	besetter
diametral	photometric	entreater	better
petrel	stereometric	escheator	carburetor
	symmetric	fire-eater	coquetter
ĒT'ri	tasimetric	fleeter	curvetter
Petrie	thermometric	frog-eater	dead-letter
	trigonometric	gas-meter	debtor
ĔT'rik	trimetric	goldbeater	enfetter
actinometric	volumetric	greeter	fetter
alkalimetric		heater	forgetter
anemometric	**ĒT'rok**	hectoliter	fretter
anisometric	sheetrock	ill-treater	getter

go-getter	colosseum	upheaval	leaven
jetter	lyceum	(cf. weevil)	seven
letter	mausoleum		
netter	museum	ĔV'an	ĔV'end
petter	peritoneum	Evan	leavened
red-letter	prytaneum	Devon	unleavened
regretter	Te Deum	(cf. Ĕv'en)	
resetter			ĔV'enth
setter	Ē'ur	ĒV'ans	eleventh
somersetter	agreer	achievance	seventh
sweater	feer	grievance	
type-setter	fleer	perceivance	ĒV'enz
wetter	freer	retrievance	Stevens
whetter	over-seer		
	seer	ĔV'el, ĔV'l	ĒV'est
ĔT'urd	sight-seer	bedevil	achievest
featured		bevel	believest
	Ē'us	devil	bereavest
ĔT'urd	choreus	dishevel	cleavest
fettered	corypheus	Greville	conceivest
unfettered	gluteus	kevel	deceivest
unlettered	onomatopœous	level	disbelievest
bettered, etc.	plumbeous	Neville	grievest
	scarabæus	revel	heavest
ĔT'urz		sea-level	inweavest
Peters	Ē'va	spirit-level	leavest
	diva	water-level	perceivest
ĔT'us	Eva		receivest
acetous	Geneva	ĒV'en	relievest
Cetus	Kamadeva	even	reprievest
fetus	Kivah	good-even	retrievest
quietus	Mahadeva	Hallow-even	thievest
	viva	Stephen	upheavest
ĔT'wurk		Steven	weavest
fretwork	ĒV'al	unbereaven	
network	coeval	uneven	ĒV'eth
	longeval	yester-even	achieveth
Ē'um	medieval		believeth
amœbæum	primeval	ĔV'en	bereaveth
athenæum	retrieval	eleven	cleaveth
bronteum	shrieval	heaven	conceiveth

āle, câre, ădd, ärm, ȧsk; mē, hēre, ĕnd; īce, ĭll;

deceiveth
disbelieveth
grieveth
heaveth
inweaveth
leaveth
perceiveth
receiveth
relieveth
reprieveth
retrieveth
thieveth
upheaveth
weaveth

Ē'vī
Levi

Ē'vĭ
Levy

ĔV'ĭ
bevy
chevy
clevy
heart-heavy
heavy
levee
levy
nevvy
top-heavy

ĔV'ij
cleavage
leavage

ĔV'ĭl
evil
king's-evil
weevil

ĔV'il
devil
Neville
(see ĔV'el)

ĔV'ilz
blue-devils
devils, etc.

ĔV'in
levin
replevin

ĔV'ing
achieving
aggrieving
believing
bereaving
cleaving
conceiving
deceiving
disbelieving
grieving
heaving
interweaving
inweaving
leaving
misconceiving
perceiving
preconceiving
receiving
relieving
reprieving
retrieving
sheaving
steeving
thieving
unbelieving
undeceiving
unweaving

upheaving
weaving

ĔV'ingz
leavings, etc.

ĔV'ish
peevish
thievish

ĔV'les
leaveless
sheaveless
sleeveless

ĔV'ment
achievement
bereavement
retrievement

ĔV'ning
evening

ĔV'ri
every

ĔV'ur
achiever
aggriever
ballast-heaver
beaver
believer
bereaver
brever
cantilever
cleaver
coal heaver
conceiver
deceiver
Deever
disbeliever

enfever
fever
griever
Guadalquivir
heaver
interleaver
interweaver
jungle-fever
keever
leaver
lever
liever
livre
makebeliever
misconceiver
naïver
perceiver
preconceiver
reaver
reever
receiver
reiver
reliever
repriever
retriever
sheaver
unbeliever
undeceiver
upheaver
weaver
weever
yellow-fever

ĔV'ur
assever
cantilever
clever
dissever
endeavor
ever
forever

---

however

howsoever

lever

never

sever

unsever

whatever

whatsoever

whencesoever

whenever

whensoever

wheresoever

wherever

whichever

whichsoever

whithersoever

whoever

whomsoever

whosesoever

whosoever

ĔV′urd

unsevered

dissevered, etc.

ĔV′us

grievous

longevous

primevous

Ē′wa

leeway

seaway

Ē′ward

leeward

seaward

Ē′wit

peewit

Ē′ya

Cassiopeia

(cf. Ē′a)

Ē′yan

Tarpeian

(cf. Ē′an)

ĔZ′a

Liza

Louisa

Pisa

ĔZ′ans

defeasance

easance

malfeasance

misfeasance

ĔZ′ans, ĔZ′ens

omnipresence

pleasance

presence

peasants, etc.

ĔZ′ant, ĔZ′ent

displeasant

omnipresent

peasant

pheasant

pleasant

present

unpleasant

ĔZ′dal

Teasdale

ĔZ′dal

Esdale

ĔZ′el

easel

teasel

Teazle

weasel

ĔZ′el

bezel

(cf. ĔZ″l)

ĔZ′els

easels

measles, etc.

Ē′zha

magnesia

(see Ĕz′i-a)

Ē′zhan

Milesian

(see ĔZ′i-an)

Ē′zhun

adhesion

cohesion

inadhesion

inhesion

lesion

Silesian

trapezian

(cf. ĔZ′i-on)

Ē′zhur

leisure

seizure

ĔZH′ur

admeasure

displeasure

entreasure

leisure

measure

outmeasure

pleasure

treasure

Ē′zhurd

unleisured

Ē′zhurd

immeasured

unleisured

unmeasured

untreasured

measured, etc.

ĔZ′i

breezy

cheesy

easy

free-and-easy

freezy

greasy

queasy

sleazy

sneezy

speakeasy

uneasy

wheezy

Zambezi

ĔZ′iks

skeeziks

ĔZ′in

seizin

ĔZ′ing

appeasing

breezing

displeasing

easing

foreseizing

freezing

greasing

āle, câre, ădd, ärm, ȧsk; mē, hẹre, ĕnd; īce, ĭll;

pleasing	ĔZ'lur	ĔZ'ra	sneezer
seizing	embezzler	Ezra	squeezer
self-pleasing			teaser
sneezing	ĒZ'ment	ĒZ'ur	tweezer
squeezing	appeasement	appeaser	wheezer
teasing	easement	Cæsar	
unpleasing		easer	ĔZ'urt
wheezing	ĒZ'on	Ebenezer	desert
ĒZ'it		freezer	
cheese it	reason	friezer	ĒZ'urz
	season	geezer	tweezers, etc.
ĔZ"l	treason	greaser	
embezzle	unreason	leaser	ĒZ'us
(cf. ĔZ'el)	unseason	pleaser	Jesus

I

For a discussion of words included under the accented vowels
following, see the beginning of I rhymes in Section I.

Ī'a	Sophia	Ī'adz	retrial
Amariah	stria	Hyads	*rial*
asthenia	Thalia	dryads, etc.	self-denial
Ave Maria	Tobiah		supplial
Azariah	Uriah	Ī'ak	trial
Beniah	via	elegiac	vial
Beriah	Zachariah	guiac	viol
Black Maria	Zebediah	kayak	
gorgoneia	Zedekiah	phrenesiac	Ī'am
Hezekiah	Zephaniah		Priam
Isaiah		Ī'al, Ī'ol	Siam
Jedediah	Ī'ad	basihyal	
Jeremiah		bass-viol	Ī'amb
Josiah	dryad	decrial	iamb
Keziah	dyad	denial	
latria	hamadryad	dial	Ī'an
Maria	Jeremiad	espial	Altaian
messiah	Pleiad	genial	Brian
Obadiah	triad	phial	Bryan

ōld, ôr, ŏdd, oil, fŏŏt, out; ūse, ûrn, ŭp; THis, thin

Chian	scient	*inscribest*	Libby
genian	self-reliant	*prescribest*	Tibbie
Orion		*proscribest*	
O'Ryan	**Ī'as**	*subscribest*	**ĪB'ing**
Ryan	Ananias	*superscribest*	ascribing
styan	bias	*transcribest*	bribing
thalian	Elias		circumscribing
(cf. Ī'on)	eyas	**ĬB'esť**	describing
	Jeremias	*fibbest*	gibing
Ī'and	Josias	glibbest	imbibing
viand	Lias	*jibbest*	inscribing
	Matthias		prescribing
Ī'andz	Messias	**ĬB'et**	proscribing
viands	Tobias, etc.	flibbertigibbet	subscribing
	unbias	gibbet	transcribing
Ī'ans	(see Ī'us)	Tibbett	
affiance		zibet	**ĬB'ing**
alliance	**Ī'at**	(cf. ĬB'it)	fibbing
appliance	fiat		jibbing
compliance		**ĬB'eth**	ribbing
defiance	**Ī'azm**	*ascribeth*	squibbing
incompliance	miasm	*bribeth*	
misalliance		*circumscribeth*	**ĬB'it**
reliance	**Ī'ba**	*describeth*	adhibit
science	capaiba	*gibeth*	cohibit
self-reliance	Ziba	*imbibeth*	exhibit
suppliance		*inscribeth*	inhibit
(cf. giants,	**ĬB'ald**	*prescribeth*	prohibit
etc.)	ribald	*proscribeth*	
	Theobald	*subscribeth*	**Ī'b'l**
Ī'ant		*superscribeth*	Bible
affiant	**ĬB'dis**	*transcribeth*	libel
alliant	Charybdis		tribal
calorifient		**ĬB'eth**	
client	**ĬB'est**	*fibbeth*	**ĬB"l**
compliant	*ascribest*	*jibbeth*	cribble
defiant	*bribest*		dibble
giant	*circumscribest*	**ĬB'ī**	dribble
pliant	*describest*	Kibbee	fribble
reliant	*gibest*	Libbey	gribble
	imbibest	Libbey	ish ka bibble

---

kibble
nibble
quibble
scribble
sibyl
thribble

ĬB″ld
cribbled
ribald
dibbled, etc.

ĬB′lest
dribblest
scribblest, etc.

ĬB′let
driblet
giblet
triblet

ĬB′leth
dribbleth
scribbleth, etc.

ĬB′li
dribbly
glibly
nibbly
quibbly
scribbly
thribbly
tribbly

ĬB′lik
niblick

ĬB′ling
cribbling
dibbling
dribbling

fribbling
kibbling
nibbling
quibbling
scribbling
tribbling

Ī′blo
by-blow
fly-blow

ĬB′lur
cribbler
dibbler
dribbler
fribbler
kibbler
nibbler
quibbler
scribbler
transcribbler

Ī′bôl
eye-ball
high-ball
sky-ball

Ī′bôld
piebald

ĬB′on
gibbon
ribbon

ĬB′onz
Gibbons
ribbons, etc.

Ī′born
high-born
sky-born

ĬB′rant
vibrant

ĬB′rat
equilibrate
librate
vibrate

Ī′brou
eyebrow
high-brow

ĬB′sen
Ibsen

ĬB′son
Ibson
Gibson

ĬB′un
tribune

ĬB′ur
ascriber
briber
circumscriber
describer
fiber
giber
imbiber
inscriber
Leiber
liber
prescriber
proscriber
scriber
subscriber
Tiber
transcriber

ĬB′ur
bibber

cribber
dibber
fibber
flibbergibber
gibber
glibber
jibber
nibber
quibber
squibber
wine-bibber

ĬB′ut
attribute
contribute
distribute
redistribute
retribute
tribute

ĬCH′ard
Pritchard
Richard

ĬCH′el
Kitchell
Mitchell
Turchell
switchel

ĬCH′en
kitchen
lichen

ĬCH′est
bewitchest
enrichest
hitchest
pitchest
richest
stitchest

ōld, ôr, ŏdd, oil, fŏŏt, out; ūse, ûrn, ŭp; THis, thin

switchest
twitchest

ĬCH'et

fitchet
Fitchett
Pritchett
Twichett
witchet

ĬCH'eth

bewitcheth
enricheth
hitcheth
pitcheth
stitcheth
switcheth
twitcheth

ĬCH'ez

bewitches
bitches
breeches
ditches
enriches
flitches
hitches
itches
niches
pitches
riches
scritches
stitches
switches
twitches
witches

ĬCH'ĭ

fitchy
itchy
pitchy

Richie
stitchy
witchy

ĬCH'ing

bewitching
ditching
enriching
hitching
itching
miching
pitching
stitching
switching
twitching
witching

ĬCH'les

hitchless
itchless
stitchless
switchless
witchless

ĬCH'ment

bewitchment
enrichment

ĬCH'nes

richness

ĬCH'ur

bewitcher
ditcher
enricher
hitcher
itcher
pitcher
richer
stitcher
switcher
twitcher

ĬCH'us

righteous

Ī'da

Ida
Lida
Oneida

ĪD'ans

abidance
guidance
misguidance
subsidence

ĪD'ans

forbiddance
riddance

ĪD'ant

dividant
guidant

ĪD'ed

backslided
betided
bided
chided
coincided
collided
confided
decided
derided
divided
elided
glided
guided
lopsided
many-sided
misguided
one-sided
presided

prided
provided
resided
sided
slab-sided
subdivided
subsided
tided
undecided
undivided
unguided
unprovided
(cf. tidied)

ĬD'ed

kidded
lidded, etc.

ĪD'en

Dryden
widen
(cf. ĪD'on)

ĬD'en

bidden
chidden
forbidden
hag-ridden
hidden
kitchen-midden
midden
overridden
priest-ridden
ridden
slidden
stridden
unbidden
unforbidden
wife-ridden

ĪD'ent

bident

āle, câre, ădd, ārm, ăsk; mē, hĕre, ĕnd; īce, ĭll;

rident
strident
trident

ĪD'est
abidest
backslidest
bidest
chidest
coincidest
collidest
confidest
decidest
deridest
dividest
elidest
glidest
guidest
hidest
overridest
presidest
pridest
providest
residest
ridest
sidest
slidest
stridest
subdividest
subsidest
tidest
widest

ĬD'est
biddest
forbiddest, etc.

ĬD'eth
abideth
betideth
bideth

chideth
coincideth
collideth
confideth
decideth
derideth
divideth
elideth
glideth
guideth
hideth
overrideth
presideth
prideth
provideth
resideth
rideth
sideth
slideth
strideth
subdivideth
subsideth
tideth

ĬD'eth
biddeth
forbiddeth, etc.

ĬD'i
bonafide
Friday
sidy
tidy
untidy
vide

ĬD'i
biddy
chickabiddy
giddy
kiddy

middy
stiddy
"widdy"

ĪD'id
tidied
(cf. ĪD'ed)

ĪD'ij
guidage
hidage

ĬD'ik
druidic
fatidic
juridic
pyramidic

ĬD'il or ĪD'il
idyll

ĪD'ing
abiding
backsliding
bestriding
betiding
biding
chiding
coinciding
colliding
confiding
deciding
deriding
dividing
eliding
gliding
guiding
hiding
law-abiding
misguiding
niding

outriding
outstriding
overriding
presiding
priding
providing
residing
riding
siding
sliding
striding
subsiding

ĬD'ing
bidding
forbidding
kidding
lidding
outbidding
overbidding
ridding
skidding
unforbidding

ĬD'ingz
tidings
backslidings,
     etc.

ĪD"l
bridal
bridle
fratricidal
homicidal
idle
idol
infanticidal
matricidal
parricidal
patricidal
regicidal

ōld, ôr, ŏdd, oil, fŏŏt, out; ūse, ûrn, ŭp; THis, thin

sidle
suicidal
tidal
tyrannicidal

ĪD″l
Biddle
fiddle
diddle
flumadiddle
griddle
Liddle
middle
quiddle
riddle
rum-tum-tiddle
tiddle
twiddle
unriddle

ĪD″ld
unbridled
bridled, etc.

ĬD′ld
fiddled, etc.

ĬD′lest
idlest, etc.

ĬD′lest
fiddlest, etc.

ĬD′leth
idleth, etc.

ĬD′leth
fiddleth, etc.

ĬD′li
bridely
widely

ĪD′ling
bridling
idling
sidling

ĬD′ling
diddling
fiddling
kidling
middling
riddling
twiddling

ĬD′lings
middlings
kidlings, etc.

ĪD′lit
guide-light
side-light

ĪD′lur
bridler
idler

ĬD′lur
fiddler
quiddler
riddler
tiddler
twiddler

ĬD′nes
piedness
wideness

ĬD′ni
kidney
Sidney
Sydney

ĪD′o
Dido
Fido

ĬD′o
kiddo
widow

ĪD′on
guidon
Poseidon
Sidon
(cf. widen)

ĬD′or
nidor
stridor
(cf. ĪD′ur)

ĪD′rule
slide rule

ĪD′ur
backslider
bestrider
chider
cider
coincider
collider
confider
decider
derider
divider
eider
elider
Fulenwider
glider
guider
hider
insider
misguider

one-sider
outrider
outsider
presider
provider
resider
rider
rough-rider
Schneider
sider
slider
Snider
Snyder
spider
strider
subdivider
subsider
wider

ĬD′ur
bidder
consider
forbidder
kidder
outbidder
overbidder
ridder
skidder

ĬD′urd
considered
ill-considered
unconsidered

Ī′ens
science
(see Ī′ans)

Ī′ent
calorifient
client

āle,   câre,   ădd,   ärm,   ăsk;   mē,   hẹre,   ĕnd;   īce,   ĭll;

inscient
scient
(see affiant,
  etc.)

Ī'est
alliest
amplifiest
appliest
awryest
beautifiest
bedyest
beliest
bespyest
brutifiest
buyest
certifiest
clarifiest
classifiest
compliest
criest
crucifiest
decriest
defiest
deifiest
deniest
descriest
diest
dignifiest
diversifiest
driest
dyest
edifiest
electrifiest
espiest
eyest
falsifiest
fliest
fortifiest
friest
glorifiest

gratifiest
hiest
highest
horrifiest
identifiest
impliest
justifiest
liest
liquefiest
magnifiest
modifiest
mollifiest
mortifiest
multipliest
mystifiest
nighest
notifiest
nullifiest
occupiest
ossifiest
outviest
pacifiest
personifiest
pliest
prophesiest
pryest
purifiest
qualifiest
ratifiest
rectifiest
reliest
repliest
sanctifiest
satisfiest
shyest
sighest
signifiest
simplifiest
slyest
specifiest
spryest

spyest
stupefiest
suppliest
terrifiest
testifiest
tiest
tryest
typifiest
untiest
verifiest
versifiest
viest
vilifiest
vitrifiest
wryest

Ī'et
diet
inquiet
piet
quiet
(cf. riot)

Ī'eth
allieth
amplifieth
applieth
bedyeth
belieth
bespyeth
buyeth
certifieth
clarifieth
classifieth
complieth
crieth
crucifieth
decrieth
defieth
deifeth
denieth

descrieth
dieth
dignifieth
diversifieth
drieth
dyeth
edifieth
electrifieth
espieth
eyeth
falsifieth
flieth
fortifieth
frieth
glorifieth
gratifieth
hieth
horrifieth
identifieth
implieth
justifieth
lieth
liquefieth
magnifieth
modifieth
mollifieth
mortifieth
multiplieth
mystifieth
notifieth
nullifieth
occupieth
outvieth
pacifieth
personifieth
plieth
prophesieth
purifieth
qualifieth
ratifieth
rectifieth

---

relieth	**ĬF'eth**	mucific	tiffing
replieth	*sniffeth,* etc.	omnific	whiffing
sanctifieth		ossific	
satisfieth	**ĬF'i**	pacific	**ĬF'ish**
sigheth	cliffy	petrific	miffish
signifieth	jiffy	petroglyphic	sniffish
simplifieth	sniffy	photoglyphic	stiffish
specifieth	spiffy	phytoglyphic	tiffish
spyeth	squiffy	pontific	
stupefieth		prolific	**Ī'f'l**
supplieth	**ĬF'ik**	pulsific	Eiffel
terrifieth	acidific	rubific	rifle
testifieth	algific	sacrific	stifle
tieth	anaglyphic	salvific	trifle
trieth	aurific	saporific	
typifieth	beatific	scientific	**ĬF"l**
untieth	calorific	sensific	piffle
verifieth	classific	siccific	riffle
versifieth	colorific	somnific	sniffle
vieth	cornific	sonorific	whiffle
vilifieth	damnific	soporific	
vitrifieth	deific	specific	**ĬF'les**
vivifieth	diaglyphic	sudorific	fifeless
	dolorific	tabific	knifeless
ĬF'en, ĬF'on	finific	tenebrific	lifeless
hyphen	frigorific	terrific	strifeless
siphon	glyphic	torporific	wifeless
Typhon	grandific	triglyphic	
	hieroglyphic	vaporific	**ĬF'li**
ĬF'en, ĬF'on	honorific	vivific	rifely
griffon	horrific	vulnific	wifely
stiffen	humorific		
	incoherentific	**ĬF'in**	**ĬF'lik**
ĬF'est	lactific	biffin	lifelike
sniffest	lapidific	griffin	wifelike
stiffest	lithoglyphic	tiffin	
whiffest	lucific	(cf. stiffen,	**ĬF'ling**
	magnific	etc.)	rifling
	mellific		stifling
ĬF'et	mirific	**ĬF'ing**	trifling
whiffet	morbific	sniffing	

ĬF'ling
piffling
riffling
sniffling
whiffling

ĬF'lur
rifler, etc.

ĬF'lur
piffler
riffler
sniffler
whiffler

ĬF'on, ĬF'en
hyphen
siphon
Typhon

ĬF'ted
drifted
gifted
lifted
rifted
shifted
sifted
ungifted
uplifted

ĬF'test
driftest
liftest
riftest
shiftest
siftest
swiftest
upliftest

ĬF'teth
drifteth

lifteth
rifteth
shifteth
sifteth
uplifteth

ĬF'ti
clifty
drifty
fifty
fifty-fifty
nifty
rifty
shifty
thrifty

ĬF'ting
drifting
lifting
rifting
shifting
shop-lifting
sifting
uplifting

ĬFT'les
driftless
riftless
shiftless
thriftless

ĬFT'nes
swiftness

ĬF'ton
Clifton

ĬF'thong
diphthong
triphthong

ĬFT'ur
drifter
lifter
scene-shifter
shifter
shop-lifter
sifter
swifter
uplifter

ĬF'ur
cipher
decipher
fifer
lifer
knifer
rifer

ĬF'ur
differ
sniffer
stiffer

Ī'ga
saiga

ĬG'and
`brigand

ĬG'at
frigate
(cf. bigot)

ĬG'bi
Digby

ĬG'est
biggest
diggest
riggest
triggest

ĬG'eth
diggeth, etc.

ĬG'i
biggy
piggy
piggy-wiggy
spriggy
twiggy

ĬG'ing
digging
gigging
jigging
rigging
sprigging
swigging
thimblerigging
trigging
twigging
unrigging
wigging

ĬG'inz
Dwiggins
Higgins
Wiggins

ĬG'ish
piggish
priggish
whiggish

ĬG''l
giggle
higgle
jiggle
niggle
sniggle
squiggle
wiggle
wriggle

ōld, ôr, ŏdd, oil, fŏŏt, out; ūse, ûrn, ŭp; THis, thin

Ī'glas
eye-glass
spy-glass

ĬG''ld
giggled, etc.

ĬG'lest
gigglest, etc.

ĬG'leth
giggleth, etc.

ĬG'li
Piggly-Wiggly
giggly, etc.

ĬG'lif
diglyph
monotriglyph
triglyph

ĬG'ling
giggling
higgling, etc.

ĬG'lur
giggler
higgler, etc.

ĬG'ma
enigma
sigma
stigma

ĬG'ment
figment
pigment

ĬG'mi
pygmy

ĬG'nal
signal

ĬG'nans
malignance

ĬG'nant
benignant
indignant
malignant

ĬG'net
cygnet
signet

ĬG'nit
lignite

ĬG'num
ecce signum
lignum

Ī'go
caligo
fuligo
impetigo
Loligo
vertigo

Ī'gon
bygone
trigone

ĬG'on
big 'un
Ligon

Ī'gor
rigor
vigor
(cf. ĬG'ur)

Ī'got
bigot
gigot
spigot
(cf. frigate)

ĬG'res
tigress

Ī'gur
Niger
tiger

ĬG'ūr
configure
disfigure
figure
ligure
prefigure
transfigure

ĬG'ur
bigger
chigger
digger
"figger"
gold-digger
grave-digger
gigger
jigger
ligger
market-rigger
nigger
outrigger
prigger
rigger
snigger
sprigger
swigger
thimblerigger
trigger
twigger

(cf. rigor
and vigor)

ĬG'urd
"figgered"
jiggered
niggard
sniggered
unniggard

Ī'ing
acidifying
adrying
alibing
allying
amplifying
applying
beatifying
beautifying
bedying
belying
bespying
brutifying
butterflying
buying
candifying
certifying
clarifying
classifying
codifying
complying
countrifying
crucifying
crying
damnifying
dandifying
decrying
defying
deifying
denying
descrying

dignifying
disqualifying
dissatisfying
diversifying
drying
dulcifying
dyeing
dying
edifying
electrifying
emulsifying
espying
exemplifying
eyeing
falsifying
fying
fortifying
Frenchifying
fructifying
frying
glorifying
gratifying
guying
hieing
horrifying
humanifying
hushabying
identifying
implying
indemnifying
intensifying
justifying
kite-flying
labifying
liquefying
lying
magnifying
modifying
mollifying
mortifying
multiplying

mystifying
notifying
nullifying
occupying
ossifying
outcrying
outflying
outlying
outvying
pacifying
personifying
petrifying
piing
plying
preachifying
preoccupying
prophesying
prying
purifying
putrefying
qualifying
ramifying
rarefying
ratifying
rectifying
relying
replying
revivifying
sanctifying
satisfying
scarifying
scorifying
self-denying
self-relying
self-satisfying
shying
sighing
signifying
simplifying
skying
solidifying

specifying
spying
stultifying
stupefying
supplying
terrifying
testifying
torpifying
torrefying
trying
typifying
uncomplying
under-buying
underlying
undying
unifying
unsatisfying
untying
verifying
versifying
vieing
vilifying
vitrifying
vivifying

Ĭ'ja

Abijah
Elijah

Ĭ'jak

highjack

ĬJ'est

digest
disobligest
obligest

ĬJ'id

frigid
rigid

ĬJ'il

sigil
strigil
vigil

ĬJ'ing

disobliging
obliging

ĬJ'ing

abridging
bridging
ridging

ĬJ'it

Bridget
Brigit
digit
fidget
"ijjit"
midget

ĬJ'on

irreligion
pigeon
religion
widgeon

ĬJ'ur

abridger
bridger

ĬJ'us

irreligious
litigious
prodigious
religious
sacrilegious

ĪK'a

balalaika

ōld, ôr, ŏdd, oil, fŏŏt, out; ūse, ûrn, ŭp; THis, thin

lorica
mica
Micah
pica
pika

Ĭ'kal
Michael

ĬK'ard
Pickard
Rickard

ĬK'at
exsiccate
siccate

Ĭk'ed
wicked
(see ĬK+ed)

ĬK'en
lichen
liken
unliken

ĬK'en
chicken
horror-stricken
quicken
sicken
stricken
terror-stricken
thicken
wicken
wonder-
 stricken

ĬK'enz
chickens
slickens
the dickens

ĬK'est
dislikest
likest
obliquest
spikest
strikest

ĬK'est
clickest
flickest
kickest
lickest
pickest
prickest
slickest
stickest
thickest
tickest
trickest

Ĭk'et
clicket
cricket
midwicket
picket
Pickett
pricket
Prickett
Rickett
thicket
ticket
walking-ticket
wicket

ĬK'eth
disliketh
liketh
spiketh
striketh

ĬK'eth
clicketh

flicketh
kicketh
licketh
picketh
pricketh
sticketh
ticketh
tricketh

ĬK'ets
rickets
crickets, etc.

ĬK'i
spiky
(cf. Psyche)

ĬK'i
bricky
dickey
do-hickey
Ficke
gin-rickey
quickie
rickey
sticky
tricky

ĬK'ik
psychic

ĬK'iks
psychics

ĬK'ing
biking
disliking
dyking
misliking
piking
spiking

striking
viking
well-liking

ĬK'ing
besticking
bricking
clicking
cricking
flicking
kicking
licking
picking
pocket-picking
pricking
snicking
sticking
thicking
ticking
tricking
wicking

ĬK'ish
brickish
sickish
slickish
thickish

ĬK"l
cycle
epyicycle
psychal

ĬK"l
fickle
mickle
nickel
pickle
prickle
sickle
stickle

āle, câre, ădd, ärm, ăsk; mē, hĕre, ĕnd; īce. ĭll:

strickle
tickle
trickle

ĬK′lest
ficklest
picklest
ticklest
tricklest

ĬK′leth
pickleth
prickleth
tickleth
trickleth

ĬK′li
belikely
likely
obliquely
unlikely

ĬK′li
prickly
quickly
sickly
slickly
stickly
thickly
trickly

ĬK′lik
bicyclic
cyclic
encyclic
epicyclic
geocyclic

ĬK′ling
cycling

ĬK′ling
chickling
pickling
prickling
tickling
trickling

ĬK′lish
pricklish
ticklish

ĬK′list
cyclist

ĬK′lon
cyclone

ĬK′lur
fickler
prickler
stickler
strickler
tickler

ĬK′nes
likeness
obliqueness
unlikeness

ĬK′nes
love-sickness
quickness
sickness
slickness
thickness

ĬK′nik
picnic
strychnic

ĬK′nin
strychnine

ĬK′ning
quickening
sickening
thickening

ĬK′on
icon

ĬK′or
ichor

Ī′kount
viscount

ĬK′sen
mixen
vixen

ĬK′sest
affixest
fixest
intermixest
mixest
prefixest
transfixest

ĬK′set
quickset
thick-set

ĬK′seth
affixeth
fixeth
intermixeth
mixeth
prefixeth
transfixeth

ĬK′shun
abstriction
addiction

affixion
affliction
affriction
benediction
confliction
constriction
contradiction
conviction
crucifixion
depiction
dereliction
diction
eviction
fiction
friction
indiction
infliction
interdiction
jurisdiction
malediction
obstriction
prediction
prefixion
reliction
restriction
suffixion
transfixion
valediction

ĬK′shus
contradictious
fictious

ĬK′si
Dixey
Dixie
nixie
pixie
tricksy
Trixie
water-nixie

ōld, ôr, ŏdd, oil, fŏŏt, out; ūse, ûrn, ŭp; THis, thin

ĬK'sing

admixing
affixing
fixing
intermixing
mixing
prefixing
transfixing

ĬK'son

Dickson
Dixon
Hickson
Hixon

ĬK'sti

sixty

ĬK'stūr

admixture
affixture
fixture
immixture
incommixture
intermixture
mixture

ĬK'stŭr

trickster

ĬK'sur

affixer
elixir
fixer
intermixer
mixer
prefixer
transfixer

ĬK'tat

dictate
ɔictate

ĬK'ted

addicted
afflicted
conflicted
constricted
contradicted
convicted
depicted
evicted
inflicted
interdicted
predicted
relicted
restricted
self-inflicted
unrestricted

ĬK'test

addictest
afflictest
conflictest
contradictest
convictest
depictest
evictest
inflictest
predictest
restrictest
strictest

ĬK'teth

addicteth
afflicteth
conflicteth
contradicteth
convicteth
depicteth
evicteth
inflicteth
predicteth
restricteth

ĬK'tik

apodictic
deictic
endeictic
epideictic
ictic

ĬK'tim

victim

ĬK'ting

addicting
afflicting
conflicting
constricting
contradicting
convicting
depicting
evicting
inflicting
interdicting
predicting
restricting

ĬK'tiv

addictive
afflictive
benedictive
conflictive
constrictive
contradictive
convictive
depictive
fictive
indictive
inflictive
interdictive
jurisdictive
predictive
restrictive
vindictive

ĬKT'li

derelictly
strictly

ĬKT'nes

strictness

ĬK'tor

(see ĬK'tur)

ĬK'tum

dictum

ĬK'tūr

depicture
impicture
picture
stricture
word-picture

ĬK'tŭr

afflicter
boa-constrictor
conflicter
constrictor
contradicter
depicter
fictor
inflicter
lictor
Pictor
predicter
restricter
stricter
victor

ĬK'tus

acronyctous
Benedictus
ictus

ĬK'ur

biker

āle, câre, ădd, ärm, åsk; mē, hẹre, ĕnd; īce, ĭll;

Diker	**ĬL'a**	**ĬL'an**	**ĬL'dest**
hiker	Hyla	arch-villain	mildest
liker	Lila	villain	wildest
obliquer		villein	
piker	**ĬL'a**		**ĬL'dest**
Riker	anilla	**Ĭ'land**	*begildest*
spiker	armilla	highland	*buildest*
striker	barilla	island	*gildest*
	bismillah	Rhode Island	
ĬK'ur	camarilla		**ĬL'deth**
bicker	Camilla	**Ĭ'lark**	*begildeth*
clicker	cascarilla	phylarch	*buildeth*
dicker	cedilla	sky-lark	*gildeth*
flicker	chinchilla		
kicker	codilla	**ĬL'as**	**ĬLD'hood**
knicker	Drusilla	Silas	childhood
licker	flotilla	Vilas	
liquor	gorilla		**ĬL'ding**
nicker	granadilla	**Ĭ'lash**	childing
picker	granilla	eyelash	wilding
pricker	guerrilla		
quicker	Lilla	**ĬL'at**	**ĬL'ding**
sicker	Manila	distillate	begilding
slicker	manilla	penicillate	building
snicker	mantilla		castle-building
sticker	maxilla	**ĬL'burt**	gilding
thicker	Priscilla	filbert	rebuilding
ticker	sabadilla	Gilbert	unbuilding
tricker	sapodilla	Wilbert	ungilding
vicar	sarsaparilla		
wicker	seguidilla	**ĬL'da**	**ĬL'dish**
	Sybilla	Hilda	childish
ĬK'urz	vanilla	Mathilda	mildish
knickers	villa	Matilda	wildish
bickers, etc.			
	ĬL'ak		**ĬLD'les**
ĬK'us	lilac	**ĬL'ded**	childless
Picus		begilded	mildless
spicous	**ĬL'aks**	builded	
	lilacs	gilded	**ĬLD'li**
ĬK'wid	smilax	ungilded	childly
liquid			

ōld, ôr, ŏdd, oil, fŏŏt, out; ūse, ûrn, ŭp; THis, thin

mildly	ĪL'est	pilot	*tilleth*
wildly	*beguilest*	sky-pilot	*trilleth*
	compilest	stylet	*willeth*
ĪLD'lik	*defilest*		
childlike	*filest*	**ĬL'et**	**ĪL'ful**
	pilest	billet	guileful
ĪLD'nes	*reconcilest*	fillet	smileful
mildness	*revilest*	millet	wileful
riledness	*rilest*	rillet	
unmildness	*smilest*	skillet	**ĬL'ful**
wildness	*stylest*	willet	skilful
	vilest		wilful
ĬL'dred	*whilest*	**ĬL'eth**	unskilful
Mildred	*wilest*	*beguileth*	
ILL BRED		*compileth*	**ĬL'fur**
ĪLD'ren	**ĬL'est**	*defileth*	pilfer
children	*befrillest*	*fileth*	
	chillest	*pileth*	**ĬL'grim**
ĬL'dur	*distillest*	*reconcileth*	pilgrim
milder	*drillest*	*revileth*	
wilder	*enthrillest*	*rileth*	**Ī'li**
	fillest	*smileth*	ancile
ĬL'dur	*frillest*	*styleth*	drily
begilder	*fulfillest*	*tileth*	highly
bewilder	*grillest*	*up-pileth*	O'Reilly
builder	illest	*whileth*	Reilly
castle-builder	*instillest*	*wileth*	Riley
gilder	*killest*		shyly
guilder	*millest*	**ĬL'eth**	slily
rebuilder	shrillest	*chilleth*	wily
wilder	*spillest*	*distilleth*	wryly
	stillest	*drilleth*	
ĪLD'wood	*swillest*	*enthrilleth*	**ĬL'i**
wildwood	*thrillest*	*filleth*	Billee
	tillest	*fulfilleth*	Billie
ĪL'ens	*trillest*	*instilleth*	billy
silence	*willest*	*killeth*	Chile
		milleth	chili
ĬL'ent	**Ī'let, Ī'lot**	*spilleth*	chilly
silent	eyelet	*stilleth*	daffy-down-
si'lent	islet	*thrilleth*	dilly

āle, câre, ădd, ärm, ăsk; mē, hēre, ĕnd; īce, ĭll;

filly
frilly
gillie
grilly
hilly
illy
lily
Millie
Milly
Piccadilly
piccalilli
silly
shrilly
skilly
stilly
tiger-lily
Tillie
Tilly
water-lily
Willie
Willy
willy-nilly

Ī′lid
eyelid

ĪL′id
lilied

ĪL′ij
grillage
pillage
tillage
village
thrillage, etc.

ĪL′ik
amylic
basilic
Cyrillic
dactylic

idyllic
macrodactylic
methylic
odylic
salicylic
zygodactylic

Ī′lin
sky-line
styline

ĪL′in
MacMillin
McQuillin
(cf. McMillan,
     Dillon, etc.)

ĪL′ing
beguiling
compiling
defiling
filing
piling
reconciling
reviling
riling
smiling
styling
tiling
time-beguiling
up-piling
whiling
wiling

ĬL′ing
befrilling
billing
chilling
distilling
drilling
enthrilling

filling
frilling
fulfilling
grilling
instilling
killing
milling
shilling
shrilling
skilling
spilling
stilling
swilling
thrilling
tilling
trilling
unwilling
upfilling
willing

ĬL′ingz
Billings
drillings, etc.

ĬL′ip
Philip

ĬL′ips
Philips

ĬL′is
Amaryllis
Myrtillis
Phyllis
Willis
Wyllis

ĬL′ish
stylish

Ī′lit
dry-light

high-light
skylight
stylite
twilight
xylite

ĪL′iz
chilies
fillies
gillies
lilies
sillies
the Willies

ĬL′izm
Carlylism
hylism

ĬL′joy
killjoy

ĬL′ken
milken
silken

ĬL′ki
milky
silky

ĬL′king
bilking
milking

ĬL′koks
Philcox
Silcox
Wilcox

ĪL′les
guileless
smileless
wileless

ōld, ôr, ŏdd, oil, fŏŏt, out; ūse, ûrn, ŭp; THis, thin

ĬL'man	**ĪL'o**	sky-pilot	*kilteth*
billman	high-low	(cf. islet)	*lilteth*
Gilman	milo		*quilteth*
grillman	silo	**ĬL'pin**	*tilteth*
hill-man		Gilpin	*wilteth*
mill-man	**ĬL'o**		
Stillman	armadillo	**ĬL'room**	**ĬL'thi**
	billow	grill-room	filthy
ĬL'ment	embillow	still-room	
	grenadillo		**ĬL'ti**
beguilment	*killow*	**ĬL'sid**	guilty
defilement	kilo	hillside	silty
exilement	negrillo	rill-side	stilty
irreconcilement	peccadillo		
reconcilement	pillow	**ĬL'son**	**ĬL'ting**
revilement	*pulvillo*	Gilson	jilting
	weeping-	Stillson	kilting
ĬL'ment	willow	Wilson	lilting
distilment	willow		quilting
fulfilment		**ĬL'ted**	silting
instilment	**ĬL'od**	hilted	tilting
	unpillowed	jilted	wilting
ĬL'mi	billowed, etc.	kilted	
filmy		lilted	**ĬL'ton**
	ĬL'oid	overtilted	Chilton
ĬL'mor	styloid	quilted	Hilton
Filmore	xyloid	silted	Milton
Gilmore		stilted	Stilton
	Ĩ'lok	tilted	Tilton
ĬL'nes	Shylock	tip-tilted	
juvenileness		wilted	**ĬL'tur**
vileness	**ĬL'ok**		filter
	hillock	**ĬL'test**	infilter
ĬL'nes		*jiltest*	jilter
chillness	**ĬL'om**	*kiltest*	kilter
illness	whilom	*liltest*	philter
shrillness		*quiltest*	quilter
stillness	**ĬL'on**	*tiltest*	tilter
	Dillon	*wiltest*	wilter
ĬL'nur	**ĬL'ot**	**ĬL'teth**	**ĪL'um**
Milner	pilot	*jilteth*	asylum

āle, câre, ădd, ärm, ăsk; mē, hẹre, ĕnd; īce, ĭll;

phylum
Wylam

ĪL'ur
beguiler
bifilar
compiler
defiler
filar
filer
Huyler
piler
reconciler
reviler
riler
Schuyler
smiler
stylar
tiler
Tyler
up-piler
viler
wiler
Zuyler

ĪL'ur
befriller
biller
caterpillar
chiller
distiller
driller
filler
friller
fulfiller
griller
iller
ill-willer
instiller
Joe-Miller
killer

lady-killer
man-killer
maxillar
miller
pillar
Schiller
shriller
siller
spiller
stiller
swiller
thiller
thriller
tiller
willer

ĪL'us
aspergillus
bacillus
favillous
fibrillous
orgillous
villus

ĪL'van
sylvan

ĪL'vur
silver

ĪL'yam
Gilliam
William

ĪL'yans
brilliance
(cf. ĪL'i-ans,
   ĪL'i-ens)

ĪL'yant
brilliant

(cf. ĪL'i-ant,
   ĪL'i-ent)

ĪL'yar
atrabiliar
auxiliar
conciliar
domiciliar
familiar
(cf. ĪL'i-ur)

ĪL'yardz
billiards
milliards

ĪL'yun
billion
carillon
cotillion
decillion
mandillon
million
modillion
nonillion
octillion
pavilion
pillion
postillion
quadrillion
quintillion
sextillion
stillion
trillion
tourbillion
vermilion
(cf. ĪL'i-an)

ĪL'yunth
billionth
millionth
trillionth, etc.

ĪM'a
cyma
Jemima
Lima

ĪM'aks
anti-climax
climax

ĪM'al
isocheimal
isocrymal
primal

Ī'man
Hymen
picman
Simon
Wyman

ĪM'at
acclimate
climate
primate

ĪM'bal
cymbal
fimble
gimbal
nimble
symbol
thimble
tymbal
wimble

ĪM'bo
akimbo
bimbo
kimbo
limbo

ōld, ôr, ŏdd, oil, fŏŏt, out; ūsc, ûrn, ŭp; THis, thin

ĬM'brel
timbrel
whimbrel

ĬM'bur
imber
limber
timber
timbre
unlimber

ĬM'burd
untimbered
limbered, etc.

ĬM'bus
limbus
nimbus

ĬM'el
Friml
gimmal
Grimmell
Himmel
kümmel

Ī'men
Hymen
(see Ī'man)

ĬM'en
women
(cf. persim-
mon)

ĬM'est
begrimest
berhymest
beslimest
chimest
climbest

primest
rhymest
sublimest

ĬM'est
brimmest
dimmest
grimmest
primmest
skimmest
slimmest
swimmest
trimmest

ĪM'eth
begrimeth
berhymeth
beslimeth
chimeth
climbeth
rhymeth

ĬM'eth
brimmeth
dimmeth
skimmeth
swimmeth
trimmeth

ĬM'flam
flimflam

ĪM'i
beslimy
blimy
grimy
limy
rimy
rhymy
slimy

stymie
thymy

ĬM'i
gimme
jimmy
shimmy
whimmy

ĬM'id
timid

ĬM'ij
image
scrimmage

ĬM'ik
alchimic
cacochymic
cherubimic
eponymic
etymic
homonymic
lipothymic
metonymic
metronymic
mimic
pantomimic
patronymic
synonymic
zymic (also
    ĪM'ik)

ĪM'ing
begriming
beliming
berhyming
besliming
chiming
climbing
griming

liming
priming
rhyming
sliming
timing

ĬM'ing
bedimming
betrimming
brimming
dimming
grimming
skimming
slimming
swimming
trimming

ĬM'ist
rhymist
timist

ĬM'it
limit

ĬM'jams
jimjams

ĬM'krak
gimcrack

ĬM'les
chimeless
crimeless
grimeless
limeless
rhymeless
rimeless
slimeless
thymeless
timeless
overtimeless

ĬM'les
brimless
hymnless
limbless
rimless
swimless
vimless
whimless

ĬM'li
primely
sublimely
timely
untimely

ĬM'li
dimly
grimly
primly
slimly
trimly

ĬM'nal, ĬM'nel
hymnal
simnel

ĬM'nes
primeness
sublimeness

ĬM'nes
dimness
grimness
primness
slimness
trimness

ĬM'ni
chimney

Ī'mon
Simon

Timon
(see Ī'man)

ĬM'on
persimmon
Rimmon
(cf. women)

ĬM'onz
Simmons
persimmons

ĬM'pet
limpet

ĬM'pi
crimpy
impi
impy
skimpy

ĬM'ping
blimping
crimping
imping
limping
primping
scrimping
shrimping
skimping

ĬM'pish
impish

ĬM'pit
lime-pit
slime-pit

ĬM'p'l
bewimple
crimple
dimple

pimple
rimple
simple
wimple

ĬM'plest
crimplest
dimplest
pimplest
rimplest
simplest
wimplest

ĬM'pleth
crimpleth, etc.

ĬM'pli
crimply
dimply
limply
pimply
simply

ĬM'pling
crimpling
dimpling
impling
pimpling
rimpling
shrimpling
wimpling

ĬM'plur
crimpler
dimpler
rimpler
simpler
wimpler

ĬM'pur
crimper

limper
scrimper
shrimper
simper
skimper
whimper

ĬM'ros
primrose

ĬM'shi
imshi

ĬM'son
jimson

ĬM'stur
rhymester

ĬM'ur
begrimer
chimer
climber
Hergesheimer
old-timer
primer
rhymer
timer
sublimer

ĬM'ur
brimmer
dimmer
gimmer
glimmer
grimmer
primer
primmer
shimmer
simmer
skimmer

slimmer
swimmer
trimmer
Zimmer

ĬM′us
primus
rimous
simous
timeous
untimeous

ĬM′zi
flimsy
slimsy
whimsey

ĬM′zon
crimson
encrimson

Ī′na
Adelina
Angelina
Carolina
Catalina
China
Dinah
Evelina
farina
Jaina
Lucina
Meleagrina
Messalina
Platyrhina
Regina
Sabina
Sabrina
salina
semolina

Shekinah
trichina

Ĭn′a
Corinna
Erinna
Minna

ĬN′al
acclinal
anticlinal
binal
caninal
cerebro-spinal
crinal
declinal
endocrinal
equinal
final
isoclinal
matutinal
officinal
periclinal
piscinal
rhinal
spinal
synclinal
trinal
Vinal

ĬN′as
pinnace

ĬN′at
binate
quinate

ĬN′chest
clinchest
flinchest

lynchest
pinchest

ĬN′cheth
clincheth
flincheth
lyncheth
pincheth

ĬN′ching
clinching
flinching
lynching
pinching
unflinching

ĬN′chur
clincher
flincher
lyncher
pincher

ĬN′churz
pinchers, etc.

ĬN′da
Belinda
Chlorinda
Dorinda
Ethelinda
Lucinda

ĬN′ded
alike-minded
blinded
bloody-minded
carnal-minded
double-minded
even-minded
earthly-minded
evil-minded

fair-minded
feeble-minded
fleshly-minded
free-minded
high-minded
light-minded
like-minded
low-minded
minded
narrow-minded
public-minded
reminded
rinded
self-blinded
simple-minded
single-minded
snow-blinded
soberminded
strongminded
winded
worldly-minded

ĬN′ded
abscinded
brinded
broken-winded
exscinded
interscinded
long-winded
rescinded
short-winded
winded

ĬN′den
linden
Lindon
Minden

ĬN′dest
bindest
blindest

 āle,   câre,   ădd,   ärm,   ăsk;   mē,   hęre,   ĕnd;   īce,   ĭll;

findest   unbinding   kindler   ĬN'en
grindest   unwinding   swindler, etc.   linen
kindest   upbinding
remindest   upwinding   ĪND'nes   Ī'nes
windest   winding   blindness   dryness
                                 color-blindness highness
ĬN'deth   ĬN'd'l   kindness   nighness
bindeth   brindle   loving-kindness shyness
blindeth   dwindle   slyness
findeth   enkindle   ĬN'do   spryness
grindeth   kindle   window   wryness
mindeth   rekindle
remindeth   spindle   ĬN'drans   ĬN'es
windeth   swindle   hindrance   Inness
                                                  Guinness
ĪND'ful   ĬN'd'ld   ĬN'dred   (cf. pinnace)
mindful   brindled, etc.   kindred
remindful   ĬN'est
unmindful   ĬN'dlest   ĬN'dur   *assignest*
                brindlest, etc. binder   *benignest*
ĬN'di   ĬN'dleth   blinder   *combinest*
Lindy   *brindleth,* etc. faultfinder   condignest
Lucindy   finder   *confinest*
shindy   ĪND'li   grinder   *consignest*
windy   blindly   hinder   *countersignest*
                kindly   kinder   *declinest*
ĬN'dig   unkindly   minder   *definest*
shindig   ĪND'li   pathfinder   *designest*
                                 reminder   *dinest*
ĬN'dik   Hindley   spellbinder   divinest
indic   spindly   stem-winder   *enshrinest*
syndic   water-finder   *entwinest*
                ĪND'ling   winder   finest
ĬN'ding   brindling   *inclinest*
binding   dwindling   ĬN'dur   *intertwinest*
blinding   enkindling   cinder   malignest
finding   kindling   flinder   *minest*
grinding   rekindling   hinder   *outlinest*
inbinding   swindling   pinder   *outshinest*
minding   rescinder   *overtwinest*
reminding   ĪND'lur   tinder   *pinest*
                dwindler

reassignest
reclinest
refinest
resignest
shinest
signest
superfinest
supinest
twinest
underlinest
underminest
undersignest
untwinest
whinest
winest

ĬN'est
beginnest
dinnest
grinnest
pinnest
sinnest
skinnest
spinnest
thinnest
winnest

ĬN'et
linnet
minute
spinet

ĬN'eth
assigneth
combineth
confineth
consigneth
countersigneth
declineth
defineth
designeth

dineth
divineth
enshrineth
entwineth
inclineth
intertwineth
maligneth
mineth
outlineth
outshineth
overtwineth
pineth
reassigneth
reclineth
refineth
resigneth
shineth
signeth
twineth
underlineth
undermineth
undersigneth
untwineth
whineth
wineth

ĬN'eth
beginneth
dinneth
ginneth
grinneth
pinneth
sinneth
skinneth
spinneth
winneth

ĬN'fant
infant

ĬN'ful
sinful

ĬNG'am
Bingham

ĬNG'bolt
king-bolt
ring-bolt
wring-bolt

ĬNG'dom
kingdom

ĬNG'duv
ring-dove

ĬNG'ed
winged
(see ĭng + ed)

ĬNG'est
bringest
clingest
flingest
outwingest
ringest
singest
slingest
springest
stingest
stringest
swingest
wingest
wringest

ĬNG'eth
bringeth
clingeth
flingeth
outwingeth
ringeth
singeth
slingeth

springeth
stingeth
stringeth
swingeth
unslingeth
wingeth
wringeth

ĬNG'ga
anhinga

ĬNG'gi
dinghy
(cf. Feringhee)

ĬNG'g'l
commingle
cringle
dingle
immingle
intermingle
jingal
jingle
Kriss Kringle
mingle
shingle
single
springal
surcingle
swingle
tingle
tringle

ĬNG'g'ld
unmingled
commingled,
etc.

ĬNG'glest
jinglest
minglest
tinglest

ĬNG′gleth
jingleth
mingleth
tingleth

ĬNG′gli
jingly
mingly
shingly
singly
tingly

ĬNG′gling
intermingling
jingling
kingling
mingling
singling
tingling
wingling

ĬNG′glish
English
tinglish

ĬNG′glur
intermingler
jingler
mingler
shingler
tingler

ĬNG′go
dingo
flamingo
gringo
jingo
lingo
stingo

ĬNG′gur
finger

forefinger
index-finger
linger
malinger

ĬNG′gurd
light-fingered
rosy-fingered
web-fingered
fingered, etc.

ĬNG′gus
dingus

ĬNG′gwal
bilingual
lingual

ĬNG′gwish
contradistin-
   guish
distinguish
extinguish

ĬNG′i
clingy
springy
stingy
stringy
swingy
wingy

ĬNG′ing
bringing
clinging
dinging
enringing
flinging
outwinging
plainsinging
ringing

singing
slinging
springing
stinging
stringing
swinging
unslinging
unstringing
upbringing
upstringing
winging
wringing

ĬNGK′est
bethinkest
blinkest
chinkest
clinkest
drinkest
hoodwinkest
inkest
linkest
pinkest
shrinkest
sinkest
slinkest
stinkest
thinkest
winkest

ĬNGK′et
trinket

ĬNGK′eth
bethinketh
blinketh
chinketh
clinketh
drinketh
hoodwinketh
inketh

linketh
pinketh
shrinketh
sinketh
slinketh
stinketh
thinketh
winketh

ĬNGK′go
ginkgo

ĬNGK′i
blinky
inky
kinky
pinky
zincky

ĬNGK′id
blink-eyed
pink-eyed

ĬNGK′ing
bethinking
blinking
chinking
clinking
drinking
enlinking
free-thinking
hoodwinking
inking
interlinking
linking
pinking
rinking
shrinking
sinking
slinking
stinking

ōld, ôr, ŏdd, oil, fŏŏt, out; ūse, ûrn, ŭp; THis, thin

thinking
unblinking
unlinking
unshrinking
unthinking
unwinking
winking

ĬNGK"l

besprinkle
crinkle
inkle
periwinkle
sprinkle
tinkle
twinkle
winkle
wrinkle

ĬNGK"ld

unwrinkled
besprinkled,
  etc.

ĬNGK'lest

crinklest
sprinklest
tinklest
twinklest
wrinklest

ĬNGK'leth

crinkleth
sprinkleth
tinkleth
twinkleth
wrinkleth

ĬNGK'li

crinkly
pinkly

tinkly
twinkly
wrinkly

ĬNGK'ling

besprinkling
crinkling
inkling
sprinkling
tinkling
twinkling
wrinkling

ĬNGK'lur

sprinkler
tinkler
twinkler
wrinkler

ĬNGK'o

stinko

ĬNGK'on

Lincoln
pink 'un

ĬNGK'shun

contradistinc-
  tion
distinction
extinction
indistinction
intinction

ĬNGK'tiv

contradistinc-
  tive
distinctive
instinctive

ĬNGK'tnes

distinctness

indistinctness
succinctness

ĬNGK'tur

cincture
encincture
tincture

ĬNGK'turd

cinctured
encinctured
uncinctured
untinctured

ĬNGK'ur

bethinker
blinker
clinker
drinker
enlinker
free-thinker
hoodwinker
inker
linker
pinker
prinker
rinker
shrinker
sinker
slinker
stinker
thinker
tiddledewinker
tinker
winker

ĬNGK'us

ornithorhyn-
  chus
oxyrhynchus
scincus
zincous

ĬNG'les

kingless
ringless
springless
stingless
wingless

ĬNG'let

kinglet
ringlet
springlet
winglet

ĬNG'lik

kinglike
springlike
winglike

ĬN'gram

Ingram

ĬNG'song

singsong
spring-song

ĬNG'tim

ring-time
spring-time

ĬNG'ur

ballad-singer
bringer
clinger
dinger
flinger
humdinger
master-singer
Meistersinger
minnesinger
ringer
singer

āle. câre, ădd, ärm, åsk; mē, hĕre, ĕnd; īce, ĭll;

slinger
springer
stinger
stringer
swinger
unslinger
unstringer
whinger
winger
wringer

ĬN'i
briny
Heine
liney
miny
moonshiny
outliney
piney
shiny
spiny
sunshiny
tiny
twiney
viny
whiney
winy

ĬN'i
finny
guinea
hinny
ignominy
jinny
Minnie
ninny
pickaninny
pinny
Pliny
shinney
skinny

spinney
squinny
tinny
vinny
whinny

ĬN'ik
kinic
pinic
vinic

ĬN'ik
aclinic
actinic
adiactinic
Brahminic
clinic
cynic
delphinic
diactinic
finic
Franklinic
fulminic
isoclinic
Jacobinic
mandarinic
monoclinic
narcotinic
Odinic
pinic
platinic
polygynic
quinic
rabbinic
vinic

ĬN'im
minim
(cf.
   houyhnhmn)

ĬN'ing
aligning
assigning
beshining
combining
confining
consigning
countermining
countersigning
declining
defining
designing
dining
divining
enshrining
entwining
fining
inclining
interlining
intermining
intertwining
lining
maligning
mining
moonshining
opining
outlining
outshining
overtwining
pining
reclining
refining
repining
resigning
shining
signing
subsigning
trephining
twining
underlining
undermining

untwining
whining
wining

ĬN'ing
beginning
chinning
dinning
grinning
inning
pinning
shinning
sinning
skinning
spinning
thinning
tinning
underpinning
unpinning
unsinning
winning

ĬN'ingz
innings
beginnings, etc.

ĬN'ish
diminish
finish
Finnish
thinnish
tinnish

ĬN'ist
violinist

ĬN'it
crinite
finite

ĬN'jens
contingence

(cf. astringents, etc.)

ĬN'jent
astringent
constringent
contingent
fingent
impingent
refringent
restringent
ringent
stringent
tingent

ĬN'jest
befringest
cringest
fringest
hingest
imfringest
infringest
singest
swingest
tingest
twingest
unhingest

ĬN'jeth
befringeth
cringeth
fringeth
hingeth
impingeth
infringeth
singeth
swingeth
tingeth
twingeth
unhingeth

ĬN'jez
befringes
constringes
cringes
fringes
hinges
impinges
infringes
perstringes
scringes
singes
springes
swinges
tinges
twinges
unhinges

ĬN'ji
cringy
dingy
fringy
stingy
swingy
twingy

ĬN'jing
cringing
fringing
hinging
infringing
singeing
swingeing
tingeing
twingeing

ĬNJ'les
fringeless
hingeless
swingeless
tingeless
twingeless

ĬNJ'ment
impingement
infringement
unhingement

ĬNJ'ur
cringer
fringer
ginger
hinger
infringer
injure
singer
swinger
twinger

ĬN'ka
Inca
Katinka

ĬN'klad
pine-clad
vine-clad

ĬN'kom
income

ĬN'kres
increase

ĬN'kround
pine-crowned
vine-crowned

ĬN'kwent
delinquent
relinquent

ĬN'kwish
relinquish
vinquish

ĬN'les
dinless
finless
ginless
kinless
pinless
sinless
skinless
tinless
winless

ĬN'li
aquilinely
benignly
caninely
condignly
divinely
finely
malignly
saturninely
superfinely
supinely

ĬN'li
Finley
inly
McGinley
McKinley
thinly

ĬN'ment
alignment
assignment
confinement
consignment
designment
entwinement
inclinement
interlinement
refinement
resignment

ĬN'nes
condignness
divineness
fineness
salineness
superfineness
supineness

ĬN'nes
thinness
(cf. ĬN'es)

ĬN'o
Aino
albino
jure divino
rhino

ĬN'o
minnow
winnow

ĬN'of
sign-off

ĬN'sel
tinsel
(cf. Insull)

ĬN'sens
incense

ĬN'sent
St. Vincent
vincent

ĬN'ses
princess

ĬN'sest
convincest

evincest
mincest
rinsest
wincest
(cf. incest)

ĬN'ceth
convinceth
evinceth
minceth
rinseth
winceth

ĬN'shal
provincial

ĬN'si
Quincy
rinsey

ĬN'sing
convincing
evincing
mincing
rinsing
unconvincing
wincing

ĬN'siv
evincive

ĬNS'li
princely

ĬNS'ment
convincement
evincement

ĬN'som
winsome

ĬN'strel
minstrel

ĬN'stur
minster
spinster

ĬN'sur
convincer
mincer
rinser
wincer

ĬN'surz
pincers
convincers, etc.

ĬN'ted
dinted
glinted
hinted
imprinted
minted
misprinted
printed
rainbow-tinted
rosy-tinted
sprinted
squinted
stinted
tinted
vinted

ĬN'test
glintest
hintest
imprintest
mintest
printest
sprintest
squintest
stintest
tintest

ĬN'teth
glinteth
hinteth
imprinteth
minteth
printeth
sprinteth
squinteth
stinteth
tinteth

ĬN'ti
ninety

ĬN'ti
Dinty
flinty
glinty
linty
McGinty
squinty

ĬNT'id
flint-eyed
squint-eyed

ĬN'tij
mintage
vintage

ĬN'thick
absinthic
labyrinthic

ĬN'thin
hyacinthine
labyrinthine
terebinthine

ĬN'ting
aquatinting

ōld, ôr, ŏdd, oil, fŏŏt, out; ūse, ûrn, ŭp; THis, thin

dinting
glinting
hinting
imprinting
minting
misprinting
printing
sprinting
squinting
stinting
tinting

ĬN't'l
lintel
pintle
quintal

ĬN'to
mezzotinto
Shinto
ĬN'trest
interest
self-interest
winterest

ĬN'tri
splintry
vintry
wintry

ĬN'tur
aquatinter
dinter
hinter
imprinter
minter
printer
splinter
sprinter
squinter

stinter
tinter
winter

ĬN'u
continue
discontinue
retinue
sinew
unsinew
venue

ĬN'ud
continued
discontinued
sinewed
unsinewed

ĬN'ur
arch-designer
assigner
benigner
calciner
combiner
confiner
consigner
decliner
definer
designer
diner
diviner
enshriner
entwiner
finer
incliner
intertwiner
liner
maligner
miner
minor
penny-a-liner
decliner

refiner
repiner
shiner
signer
Steiner
supiner
twiner
underliner
underminer
whiner

ĬN'ur
beginner
bread-winner
Bynner
dinner
finner
grinner
inner
pinner
shinner
sinner
skinner
spinner
thinner
tinner
twinner
winner

ĬN'us
binous
echinus
linous
Linus
Lupinus
minus
Pinus
salinous
sinus
spinous
vinous

ĬN'ward
inward

ĬN'yon
dominion
minion
opinion
pinion
(cf. ĬN'i-an)

ĬN'yond
dominioned
opinioned
pinioned
self-opinioned

ĬN'zi
Lindsay
Lindsey
linsey
quinsey
thinsey

ĬN'zik
extrinsic
intrinsic

ĬN'zman
kinsman

ĬN'zor
Windsor

Ī'o
Clio
Io
trio

Ī'ol
bass-viol
(see Ī'al)

Ī'on

dandelion
ion
Ixion
lion
Orion
scion
sea-lion
Zion

Ī'or

prior
(see Ī'ur)

Ī'ot

eyot
piot
riot
Sciot
(cf. quiet)

ĬP'a

Philippa

Ī'pal, Ī'p'l

disciple
ectypal

ĬP'ant

flippant
trippant

ĬP'en

enripen
ripen

ĬP'end

ripened
stipend

ĬP'est

pipest

---

ripest
typest
wipest
(cf. typist)

ĬP'est

chippest
clippest
dippest
drippest
equippest
flippest
grippest
gyppest
horsewhippest
nippest
outstrippest
rippest
shippest
sippest
skippest
slippest
snippest
strippest
tippest
trippest
whippest

ĬP'et

sippet
skippet
snippet
tippet
(cf. skip it)

ĬP'eth

gripeth
pipeth
typeth
wipeth

ĬP'eth

chippeth
clippeth
dippeth
drippeth
equippeth
flippeth
grippeth
gyppeth
horsewhippeth
nippeth
outstrippeth
rippeth
shippeth
sippeth
skippeth
slippeth
snippeth
strippeth
tippeth
trippeth
whippeth

ĬP'i

pipy
swipey
(cf. I.P.)

ĬP'i

chippy
dippy
grippy
Lippo Lippi
lippy
Mississippi
nippy
shippy
snippy
zippy

ĬP'id

insipid

ĬP'ij

kippage
scrippage
strippage

ĬP'ik

daguerreotypic
electrotypic
hippic
homotypic
idiotypic
monotypic
philippic
phonotypic
stereotypic
typic

ĬP'in

pippin

ĬP'ing

griping
Peiping
piping
stereotyping
striping
swiping
typing
wiping

ĬP'ing

atripping
chipping
clipping
dipping
dripping
equipping
flipping
gripping
nipping
outstripping

---

overtripping
quipping
ripping
shipping
sipping
skipping
slipping
snipping
stripping
tipping
transhipping
tripping
whipping

ĬP'ish

grippish
hippish
hyppish
snippish

ĬP''l

becripple
cripple
grippal
nipple
ripple
sipple
stipple
swiple
tipple
triple

ĬP'let

liplet
ripplet
siplet
triplet

ĬP'li

cripply
ripply

stipply
triply

ĬP'ling

crippling
Kipling
rippling
stippling
stripling
tippling

ĬP'lur

crippler
tippler

ĬP'ment

equipment
shipment
transhipment

ĬP'nes

dead-ripeness
overripeness
ripeness

ĬP'o

hippo
gippo

ĬP'res

cypress

ĬP'shun

ascription
circumscription
conniption
conscription
description
Egyptian
inscription
prescription

proscription
rescription
subscription
superscription
transcription

ĬP'si

gypsy
Poughkeepsie
Skipsey
tipsy

ĬP'sis

ellipsis
tripsis

ĬP'tik

anaglyptic
apocalyptic
cryptic
diptych
ecliptic
elliptic
glyptic
holocryptic
iatraliptic
styptic
triptych

ĬP'tiv

adscriptive
ascriptive
circumscriptive
descriptive
indescriptive
inscriptive
prescriptive
proscriptive
rescriptive
transcriptive

ĬP'tur

scripture

ĪP'ur

bag-piper
daguerreotyper
electrotyper
griper
linotyper
monotyper
piper
riper
stereotyper
sniper
striper
swiper
typer
viper
wiper

ĬP'ur

chipper
clipper
dipper
dripper
flipper
fripper
gallinipper
gripper
kipper
lady's-slipper
nipper
outstripper
ripper
shipper
sipper
skipper
slipper
snipper
stripper
swipper

āle,   câre,   ădd,   ärm,   ȧsk;   mē,   hĕre,   ĕnd;   īce,   ĭll;

tipper	ĬR'āt	*bemirest*	*tireth*
tripper	circumgyrate	*conspirest*	*transpireth*
whipper	dextro-gyrate	*desirest*	*umpireth*
	gyrate	*direst*	*wireth*
ĬP'urd	irate	*enquirest*	
kippered	lyrate	*expirest*	**ĬR'fli**
skippered		*firest*	firefly
slippered	**ĬR'ăt**	*hirest*	
	pirate	*inquirest*	**ĬR'ful**
Ĭ'ra		*inspirest*	direful
Almira	**ĬR'e**	*mirest*	ireful
Elmira	Dies Irae	*perspirest*	
Elvira	præmunire	*requirest*	**ĬR'ĭ**
Ira	(cf. ĬR'ĭ)	*respirest*	*acquiry*
Lyra		*retirest*	dairi
Myra	**ĬR'el**	*suspirest*	enquiry
Palmyra	squirrel	*tirest*	inquiry
Thyra		*transpirest*	miry
	Ĭ'rem	*umpirest*	spiry
ĬR'ah	bireme	*wirest*	squiry
sirrah	trireme		wiry
		ĬR'eth	(cf. ĬR'e)
ĬR'al	**Ĭ'rēn**	*acquireth*	
gyral	pyrene	*admireth*	**ĬR'ĭ**
retiral	squireen	*aspireth*	eyrie
spiral		*attireth*	
	Ĭ'rĕn	*bemireth*	**ĬR'id**
ĬR'am	lepidosiren	*conspireth*	irid
Hiram	siren	*desireth*	
		enquireth	**ĬR'ïk**
ĬR'ant	**ĬR'ent**	*expireth*	butyric
arch-tyrant	inquirent	*fireth*	empiric
aspirant	sempervirent	*hireth*	lyric
conspirant	virent	*inquireth*	panegyric
expirant	(cf. tyrant, etc.)	*inspireth*	Pyrrhic
gyrant		*mireth*	satiric
spirant	**ĬR'est**	*perspireth*	satyric
tyrant	*acquirest*	*requireth*	
(cf. inquirent,	*admirest*	*respireth*	**ĬR'il**
etc.)	*aspirest*	*retireth*	Cyril
	attirest	*suspireth*	virile

ōld, ôr, ŏdd, oil, fŏŏt, out; ūse, ûrn, ŭp; THis, thin

ĪR'ing
acquiring
admiring
aspiring
attiring
bemiring
conspiring
desiring
enquiring
expiring
firing
hiring
inquiring
inspiring
miring
perspiring
requiring
respiring
retiring
squiring
suspiring
tiring
transpiring
unaspiring
undesiring
untiring
wiring

ĪR'is
iris
Osiris

ĪR'ish
Irish

ĪR'ist
irised
lyrist

ĪR'ist
lyrist
panegyrist

ĬR'it
dispirit
inspirit
master-spirit
party-spirit
spirit

ĬR'ling
hireling
squireling

ĪR'man
fireman

ĬR'ment
acquirement
aspirement
bemirement
requirement
retirement

ĪR'nes
direness
entireness

ĪR'o
Cairo
tyro

Ī'rod
byroad
highroad

ĪR'on
Byron
Chiron
environ
gyron

ĪR'os
gyrose
virose

ĪR'sid
fireside

ĪR'som
iresome
tiresome

ĪR'up
chirrup
stirrup
syrup

ĪR'ur
acquirer
admirer
aspirer
attirer
bemirer
conspirer
desirer
direr
enquirer
expirer
firer
hirer
inquirer
inspirer
mirer
perspirer
requirer
respirer
retirer
suspirer
tirer
wirer

ĪR'us
apyrous
Cyrus
desirous
Epirus

papyrus
virus

ĪR'wurks
fire-works
wire-works

ĬS'a
Clarissa
Lissa
Melissa
Nerissa

Ī'sal
sky-sail
try-sail

ĪS'al
paradisal

ĬS'chif
mischief

ĬS'chan
anti-Christian
Christian

ĬS'ens
license

ĬS'ens
dehiscence
fatiscence
indehiscence
reminiscence
resipiscence
reviviscence

ĬS'ent
dehiscent
indehiscent

āle, câre, ădd, ärm, åsk; mē, hẹre, ĕnd; īce, ĭll;

reminiscent
reviviscent

ĬS'est

bespicest
concisest
enticest
nicest
precisest
pricest
sacrificest
slicest
spicest
splicest
sufficest

ĬS'est

dismissest
hissest
kissest
missest

ĬS'eth

bespiceth
enticeth
priceth
sacrificeth
sliceth
spiceth
spliceth
sufficeth

ĬS'eth

dismisseth
hisseth
kisseth
misseth

ĬS'ēz

Ulysses

ĬS'ēz

abysses
artifices
benefices
blisses
cockatrices
dismisses
edifices
hisses
kisses
misses
precipices
prejudices
Swisses

ĬS'ful

blissful
remissful
unblissful

ĬSH'a

Elisha

ĬSH'a

Delicia
Letitia

ĬSH'al

accrementitial
artificial
beneficial
comitial
edificial
exitial
extrajudicial
gentilitial
inartificial
initial
interstitial
judicial
natalitial

official
policial
prejudicial
recrementitial
rusticial
sacrificial
solstitial
superficial
tribunitial
veneficial

ĬSH'an

academician
logician
magician
optician, etc.
(see ĬSH'un)

ĬSH'ens

deficience
efficience
insufficience
maleficience
omniscience
perspicience
proficience
prospicience
self-sufficience

ĬSH'ent

beneficient
calorificient
co-efficient
deficient
efficient
indeficient
inefficient
insufficient
maleficient
objicient
omniscient

official
perficient
proficient
self-sufficient
sufficient
volitient

ĬSH'est

dishest
fishest
swishest
wishest

ĬSH'eth

dishetk
fisheth
swisheth
wisheth

ĬSH'ful

dishful
wishful

ĬSH'i

fishy
swishy

ĬSH'ing

dishing
fishing
ill-wishing
swishing
well-wishing
wishing

ĬSH'op

bishop

ĬSH'un

abannition
abligurition
abolition

academician
accrementition
acoustician
acquisition
addition
adhibition
admission
admonition
affinition
aglutition
ambition
ammunition
Apician
apparition
apposition
arithmetician
atomician
attrition
audition
bipartition
circuition
coalition
cognition
commission
competition
composition
condition
contraposition
contrition
decomposition
definition
deglutition
demission
demolition
dentition
departition
deperdition
deposition
detrition
dialectician
dismission

disposition
disquisition
ebullition
edition
electrician
emission
epinician
erudition
exhibition
expedition
exposition
extradition
fission
fruition
futurition
Galician
geometrician
Hebrician
hydrostatician
ignition
illinition
imbibition
immission
imposition
inanition
indisposition
inhibition
inition
inquisition
insition
insubmission
intermission
interposition
intromission
intuition
irremission
juxtaposition
logician
magician
magnetician
manumission

mathematician
mechanician
metaphysician
metrician
mission
monition
munition
musician
Neoplatonician
nolition
nutrition
obdormition
obstetrician
omission
opposition
optician
partition
parturition
patrician
Paulician
perdition
permission
perquisition
petition
Phenician
physician
politician
position
practician
precognition
precondition
predisposition
premonition
preposition
presupposition
preterition
prohibition
proposition
punition
pyrotechnician
readmission

recognition
recomposition
reddition
redition
remission
rendition
repetition
reposition
requisition
resilition
reunition
rhetorician
rubrician
sedition
simplician
sortition
statistician
submission
submonition
superaddition
superposition
superstition
supposition
suspicion
tactician
tradition
tralatition
transition
transmission
transposition
tribunitian
tripartition
tuition
vendition
volition
vomition

ĬSH'und

ill-conditioned
uncommis-
  sioned

āle, câre, ădd, ärm, åsk; mē, hēre, ĕnd; īce, ĭll;

conditioned,
etc.

ĬSH'ur

disher
Fischer
fisher
fissure
ill-wisher
kingfisher
swisher
well-wisher
wisher

ĬSH'us

addititious
adjectitious
adscititious
advectitious
adventitious
ambitious
arreptitious
ascititious
ascriptitious
auspicious
avaricious
capricious
cilicious
deglutitious
delicious
exitious
expeditious
factitious
fictitious
flagitious
gentilitious
inauspicious
injudicious
inofficious
judicious
lateritious

malicious
meretricious
multiplicious
natalitious
nutritious
obreptitious
obstetricious
officious
pernicious
piceous
profectitious
propitious
pumiceous
puniceous
satellitious
secretitious
seditious
sericeous
silicious
stillatitious
superstitious
supposititious
surreptitious
suspicious
tralatitious
veneficious
vermicious
vicious

ĬS'i

Datisi
icy
nisi
spicy

ĬS'i

missy
sissy

ĬS'ik

masticic
silicic

ĬS'il

fissile
missile
scissile
(cf. abyssal,
  scissel, etc.)

ĬS'id

viscid

ĬS'in

datiscin
viscin

ĬS'ing

bespicing
dicing
enticing
icing
pricing
sacrificing
self-sacrificing
self-sufficing
slicing
spicing
splicing
sufficing

ĬS'ing

dehiscing
dismissing
hissing
kissing
missing

ĬS'is

crisis
Isis
phthisis

ĬS'ish

missish

ĬS'it

elicit
explicit
illicit
implicit
licit
solicit

ĬS'iv

cicatrisive
collisive
decisive
derisive
divisive
incisive
indecisive
precisive

ĬS'iv

admissive
commissive
demissive
emissive
intermissive
irremissive
missive
nonsubmissive
omissive
permissive
promissive
remissive
submissive
transmissive

ĬS'ka

Mariska

ĬS'kal

discal
fiscal
obeliscal

ĬS'kat
confiscate
inviscate

ĬS'kest
briskest
friskest
riskest
whiskest

ĬS'ket
brisket
frisket

ĬS'keth
frisketh
risketh
whisketh

ĬSK'ful
friskful
riskful

ĬS'ki
frisky
risky
whiskey

ĬS'kin
griskin
siskin

ĬS'king
brisking
frisking
risking
whisking

ĬS'kit
biscuit

ĬS'ko
Crisco
Francisco
San Francisco

ĬS'kur
bewhisker
brisker
frisker
risker
whisker

ĬS'kus
abaciscus
discous
discus
hibiscus
lemniscus
lentiscus
meniscus
trochiscus
viscous

ĬS''l
abyssal
bristle
dismissal
epistle
gristle
missal
scissel
thistle
whistle
(cf. missile,
etc.)

ĬS'les
adviceless
diceless
iceless
miceless

priceless
spiceless
spliceless
viceless, etc.

ĬS'li
Cicely
concisely
nicely
precisely

ĬS'li
bristly
gristly
thistly

ĬS'ling
bristling
whistling

ĪS'ment
enticement
sufficement

ĬS'mus
isthmus
(see Christmas)

ĬS''n
christen
glisten
listen
relisten

ĬS'nes
conciseness
niceness
overniceness
preciseness

ĬS'nes
remissness
thisness

ĬS'ning
Christening
glistening
listening

ĬS'om
lissome

ĪS'on
bison
Dyson
grison
hyson
Tyson
vison

ĬS'pest
crispest
lispest

ĬS'peth
crispeth
lispeth

ĬS'pi
crispy

ĬS'pin
Crispin
St. Crispin

ĬS'ping
crisping
lisping

ĬS'pur
crisper
lisper
stage-whisper
whisper

āle, câre, ădd, ärm, åsk; mē, hĕre, ĕnd; īce, ĭll;

ĬS'ta
ballista
genista
vista

ĬS'tal, ĬS't'l
crystal
listel
pistol
pocket-pistol

ĬS'tan
Tristan

ĬS'tans
assistance
coexistence
consistence
desistance
distance
equidistance
existence
inconsistence
inexistence
insistence
nonexistence
persistence
pre-existence
resistance
subsistence
(cf. assitants,
etc.)

ĬS'tant, ĬS'tent
assistant
coexistent
consistent
distant
equidistant
existent
inconsistent

inexistent
insistent
nonexistent
nonresistant
persistent
pre-existent
resistant
subsistent

ĪST'dom
Christdom

ĬS'ted
assisted
black-listed
close-fisted
consisted
cysted
desisted
encysted
enlisted
entwisted
existed
fisted
hard-fisted
insisted
intertwisted
iron-fisted
listed
misted
persisted
resisted
subsisted
twisted
unassisted
unresisted
untwisted
white-listed

ĬS'tem
system

ĬS'test
assistest
consistest
desistest
enlistest
existest
insistest
listest
persistest
resistest
subsistest
twistest

ĬS'teth
assisteth
consisteth
desisteth
enlisteth
existeth
insisteth
listeth
misteth
persisteth
resisteth
resisteth
subsisteth
twisteth

ĪST'ful
mistful
wistful

ĬS'tik
absolutistic
adiaphoristic
agonistic
alchemistic
altruistic
anabaptistic
anachronistic
animistic

annalistic
anomalistic
antagonistic
anarchistic
aoristic
aphlogistic
aphoristic
artistic
atheistic
ballistic
baptistic
belletristic
bibliopegistic
bibliopolistic
Buddhistic
cabalistic
Calvinistic
cameralistic
canonistic
casuistic
catechistic
characteristic
Chauvinistic
communalistic
communistic
curialistic
cystic
deistic
dialogistic
dualistic
egoistic
egotistic
eleetro-
    ballistic
Elohistic
epilogistic
eristic
Eucharistic
eudemonistic
euhemeristic
eulogistic

euphemistic
euphuistic
evangelistic
familistic
fatalistic
fetichistic
fistic
formularistic
Hebraistic
Hellenistic
humanistic
humoristic
idealistic
illuministic
individualistic
interimistic
Jehovistic
journalistic
Judaistic
juristic
Latinistic
liberalistic
linguistic
logistic
materialistic
methodistic
monistic
monotheistic
mystic
naturalistic
neologistic
nihilistic
nominalistic
optimistic
palæocrystic
pantheistic
papistic
parallelistic
patristic
pessimistic

philanthropis-
    tic
philosophistic
phlogistic
pietistic
polaristic
polytheistic
pugilistic
puristic
quietistic
rationalistic
realistic
ritualistic
schistic
sciolistic
sensualistic
simplistic
socialistic
solecistic
somnambu-
    listic
sophistic
spiritualistic
stylistic
syllogistic
synchronistic
talmudistic
theistic
touristic
tritheistic
unionistic
universalistic

ĬS'tiks
agonistics
mystics
sphragistics
statistics

ĬS'til
pistil

ĬS'tin
amethystine
Philistine
pristine
Sistine

ĬS'ting
assisting
consisting
desisting
enlisting
entwisting
existing
insisting
intertwisting
listing
misting
pre-existing
persisting
resisting
subsisting
twisting
unresisting
untwisting

ĬS'tiv
persistive
resistive

ĬST'les
listless
resistless
twistless

ĬST'mus
Christmas
cf. isthmus

ĬST'ment
agistment
enlistment

ĬS'tral
mistral

ĬS'tram
Tristram

ĬS'tres
mistress

ĬS'tur
agistor
assister
bister
blister
enlister
exister
foster-sister
glister
insister
intertwister
lister
magister
mister
passive-resister
persister
resister
sister
subsister
twister

ĬS'turn
cistern

ĬS'tus
acathistus
schistous

ĬS'u
issue
tissue

ĪS′ur	ĬT′an, ĬT′en	frighted	benefited
conciser	Britain	ignited	bitted
dicer	Britten	incited	blunt-witted
enticer	(cf. Briton)	indicted	committed
geyser		indited	counterfeited
nicer	ĬT′ans	invited	emitted
preciser	acquittance	knighted	fat-witted
sacrificer	admittance	lighted	fitted
slicer	omittance	long-sighted	flitted
spicer	permittance	near-sighted	gritted
splicer	pittance	nighted	half-witted
	quittance	oversighted	interknitted
ĬS′ŭr	remittance	plighted	intermitted
dehiscer	transmittance	quick-sighted	knitted
dismisser		recited	lean-witted
hisser	ĪT′e	requited	manumitted
kisser	Amphitrite	reunited	nimble-witted
misser	Aphrodite	righted	omitted
remisser	arbor-vitæ	second-sighted	outwitted
	lignum-vitæ	sharp-sighted	permitted
ĬS′us	(cf. ĪT′i)	short-sighted	pitted
byssus		sighted	quick-witted
Issus	ĪT′ed	sited	quitted
"missus"	affrighted	slighted	ready-witted
narcissus	alighted	spited	recommitted
	attrited	troth-plighted	refitted
ĬT′al	bedighted	unaffrighted	remitted
cital	beknighted	unbenighted	sharp-witted
detrital	benighted	*undighted*	short-witted
entitle	blighted	unfrighted	slitted
parasital	cited	united	spitted
recital	clear-sighted	unplighted	submitted
requital	delighted	unrequited	subtle-witted
title	despited	unrighted	transmitted
vital	detrited	unsighted	twitted
	dighted		unbenefited
ĬT′alz	eagle-flighted	ĬT′ed	unbitted
vitals	eagle-sighted	acquitted	underwitted
recitals, etc.	excited	admitted	unfitted
	far-sighted	after-witted	unremitted
ĪT′an	foresighted	befitted	witted
Titan			

writted
(cf. pitịed, etc.)

ĬT'em
item

ĬT'en
brighten
enlighten
frighten
heighten
lighten
tighten
Titan
whiten
(cf. Ī'ton)

ĬT'en
bitten
Briton
conscience-
   smitten
flea-bitten
fly-bitten
hunger-bitten
kitten
mitten
smitten
sun-smitten
terror-smitten
underwritten
unsmitten
unwritten
weather-bitten
written

ĬT'ent
emittent
intermittent
intromittent
remittent

ĪT'est
affrightest
alightest
beknightest
bitest
blightest
brightest
citest
delightest
excitest
fightest
impolitest
incitest
inditest
invitest
knightest
lightest
mightest
plightest
politest
recitest
requitest
reunitest
rightest
sightest
sleightest
slightest
smitest
spitest
tightest
tritest
unitest
uprightest
whitest
writest

ĬT'est
acquittest
admittest
benefitest

committest
fittest
flittest
hittest
knittest
omittest
outwittest
permittest
pittest
quittest
refittest
remittest
sittest
slittest
spittest
splittest
submittest
twittest

ĪT'eth
affrighteth
alighteth
beknighteth
biteth
blighteth
citeth
delighteth
exciteth
fighteth
igniteth
inciteth
inditeth
inviteth
plighteth
reciteth
requiteth
righteth
sighteth
sleighteth
smiteth

spiteth
uniteth
writeth

ĬT'eth
acquitteth
admitteth
befitteth
benefiteth
committeth
fitteth
flitteth
hitteth
knitteth
omitteth
out-witteth
permitteth
pitteth
quitteth
refitteth
remitteth
sitteth
slitteth
spitteth
splitteth
submitteth
twitteth

ĬT'ez
pyrites
sorites

ĪT'ful
delightful
despiteful
frightful
mightful
rightful
spiteful
sprightful

āle, câre, ădd, ärm, ȧsk; mē, hēre, ĕnd; īce, ĭll;

ĬT′ful	palæolithic	hither	ĬT′id
fitful	trilithic	nowhither	citied
witful		slither	pitied
	ĬTH′ing	somewhither	unpitied
ĬTH′ee	*nithing*	swither	(cf. acquitted,
prithee	scything	thither	etc.)
	tithing	whither	
ĬTH′en	trithing	wither	ĬT′ik
battle-writhen	writhing		aconitic
writhen		ĬTH′urd	actinolitic
	ĬTH″m	withered	Adamitic
ĬTH′est	rhythm	unwithered	aerolitic
blithest			analytic
lithest	ĬTH′mik	ĬTH′urz	anthracitic
writhest	logarithmic	withers	anthropomor-
	polyrhythmic		phitic
ĬTH′eth	rhythmic	ĬT′i	arthritic
writheth		almighty	biolytic
	ĬTH′nes	blighty	Cabiritic
ĬTH′ful	blitheness	flighty	catalytic
blitheful	litheness	highty-tighty	cenobitic
litheful		mighty	conchitic
	Ī′thon	mity.	critic
ĬTH′i	python	whity	dendritic
blithy		(cf. Aphrodite,	diacritic
lithy	ĬTH′som	etc.)	dialytic
Ĭth′i	blithesome		diphtheritic
pithy	lithesome	ĬT′i	dolomitic
smithy		banditti	electrolytic
stithy	ĬTH′ur	city	enclitic
withy	blither	committee	eophytic
	either	ditty	epiphytic
Ĭth′ik	neither	flitty	eremitic
eolithic	tither	Giovanitti	gingitic
lithic	writher	gritty	granitic
megalithic		kitty	Hamitic
microlithic	ĬTH′ur	pity	hematitic
monolithic	anywhither	pretty	hermaphro-
mythic	*behither*	self-pity	ditic
neolithic	blither	witty	heteroclitic
ornithic	dither		hypercritic

ōld, ôr, ŏdd, oil, fŏŏt, out; ūs͞e ûrn, ŭp; THis, thin

hypocritic
Islamitic
Israelitic
Jacobitic
Jesuitic
Levitic
lignitic
margaritic
mephitic
Nazaritic
nummulitic
oneirocritic
oolitic
palmitic
paralytic
parasitic
phosphoritic
pleuritic
porphyritic
preadamitic
proclitic
rachitic
sagenitic
selenitic
Semitic
Shemitic
Sinaitic
stalactitic
stalagmitic
steatitic
strontitic
sybaritic
syenitic
theodolitic
Titanitic
tonsilitic
toxophilitic
trilobitic
trogodytic
tympanitic
uranitic

variolitic
zeolitic
zoophytic

ĬT′iks

analytics
critics, etc.

ĪT′in

chitin
(cf. ĪT′en,
   ĪT′on)

ĪT′ing

affrighting
alighting
back-biting
beknighting
biting
blighting
citing
copyrighting
delighting
disuniting
dynamiting
exciting
expediting
fighting
frighting
hand-writing
igniting
inciting
indicting
inditing
inviting
kiting
knighting
lighting
plighting
reciting
requiting

reuniting
righting
sighting
slighting
smiting
spiting
underwriting
uniting
whiting
writing

ĬT′ing

acquitting
admitting
befitting
benefiting
bitting
committing
counterfeiting
emitting
fitting
flitting
gritting
hair-splitting
hitting
knitting
manumitting
misfitting
omitting
outsitting
outwitting
permitting
pitting
pretermitting
quitting
recommitting
refitting
remitting
sitting
skitting

slitting
spitting
splitting
submitting
transmitting
twitting
unbefitting
unfitting
unremitting
unsubmitting
unwitting
witting

ĬT′is

appendicitis
arthritis
bronchitis
carditis
colitis
endocarditis
gastritis
hyalitis
laryngitis
meningitis
neuritis
pericarditis
pharyngitis
rachitis
tonsillitis
trachitis

ĬT′ish

anchoritish
Canaanitish
eremitish
Ishmaelitish
Israelitish
lightish
tightish
whitish

ĬT'ish
British
skittish

ĬT'iv
appetitive
expeditive

ĬT"l
entitle
title
(cf. ĬT'al)

ĬT"l
acquittal
belittle
brittle
committal
knittle
lickspittle
little
non-committal
remittal
skittle
spital
spittle
tittle
transmittal
victual
whittle

ĬT'les
delightless
fightless
frightless
heightless
knightless
lightless
nightless
riteless
sightless

spiteless
sprightless

ĬT'les
witless
(see ĬT+less)

ĬT'lest
brittlest
littlest
belittlest, etc.

ĬT'leth
belittleth, etc.

ĬT'li
brightly
impolitely
Kneightly
knightly
lightly
nightly
politely
rightly
sightly
slightly
sprightly
tightly
tritely
unknightly
unsightly
uprightly
whiteley
whitely

ĬT'li
fitly
unfitly

ĬT'ling
entitling
titling

ĬT'ling
kitling
titling
witling
whittling

ĬT'lur
brittler
littler
victualler
whittler

ĬT"lz
skittles
victuals
belittles, etc.

ĬT'ment
affrightment
excitement
frightment
incitement
indictment
invitement

ĬT'ment
acquitment
commitment
fitment
refitment
remitment

ĬT'nes
brightness
impoliteness
lightness
politeness
rightness
slightness

tightness
triteness
uprightness
whiteness

ĬT'nes
eye-witness
fitness
unfitness
witness

ĬT'ni
jitney
Mt. Whitney
Whitney

ĬT'ning
brightening
frightening
heightening
lightening
lightning
sheet-lightning
tightening
whitening

ĬT'nur
brightener
frightener
heightener
lightener
whitener

ĪT'on
chiton
triton
(cf. whiten,
 chitin, etc.)

ĪT'rat
nitrate
titrate

ĬT′ri
mitry
nitry

ĬT′rik
nitric

ĬT′rik
citric
vitric

ĬT′ur

alighter
arbeiter
back-biter
bemitre
biter
blighter
brighter
citer
delighter
dynamiter
exciter
fighter
flighter
igniter
impoliter
inciter
indicter
inditer
inviter
lamplighter
lighter
miter
moonlighter
niter
plighter
politer
reciter
requiter
righter

sighter
slighter
smiter
tighter
triter
typewriter
underwriter
uniter
unmiter
whiter
writer

ĬT′ur

acquitter
admitter
befitter
benefitter
bitter
committer
counterfeiter
critter
embitter
emitter
fitter
flitter
fritter
glitter
gritter
hitter
intermitter
intromitter
knitter
litter
manumitter
misfitter
omitter
outsitter
outwitter
permitter
pitter
pretermitter

quitter
recommitter
refitter
remitter
sitter
slitter
spitter
splitter
submitter
titter
transmitter
twitter
unfitter
Witter

ĬT′urd
unembittered
frittered, etc.

ĬT′urn
bittern
flittern
gittern

ĬT′urz
bitters
glitters, etc.

ĬT′us
St. Vitus
Titus
Vitus

ĬT′wat
lightweight

ĬT′wit
nitwit

ĬT′zi
Fritzy

itsy-bitsy
Ritzy

Ĭ′umf
triumph

Ĭ′un
triune

Ĭ′ur
amplifier
applier
Bayer
beautifier
Biedermeier
briar
brier
buyer
certifier
clarifier
classifier
codifier
complier
crier
crucifier
cryer
decryer
defier
defyer
deifier
denier
descrier
dignifier
disqualifier
diversifier
drier
dyer
edifier
electrifier
exemplifier
eyer

falsifier	pryer	vilifier	rival
flier	purifier	vivifier	salival
fortifier	putrifier	white-friar	survival
friar	qualifier	wryer	
frier	ramifier	(cf. tiar)	**ĪV'an**
fructifier	ratifier	(cf. fire, etc.)	Ivan
glorifier	rectifier		(cf. ĪV'en)
gratifier	relier	**Ī'urn**	
hier	replier	grappling-iron	**ĪV'ans**
higher	revivifier	iron	arrivance
horrifier	sanctifier	lofting-iron	connivance
identifier	satisfier		contrivance
implier	scarifier	**Ī'urz**	survivance
indemnifier	scorifier	Meyers	
intensifier	shyer	Myers	**ĪV'ant**
justifier	sigher	pliers	trivant
kite-flier	signifier	briers, etc.	
lammergeier	simplifier		**ĪV'at**
liar	skyer	**Ī'us**	private
lier	slyer	bacchius	
liquefier	specifier	Darius	**ĪV'en**
magnifier	speechifier	nisi prius	enliven
Mayer	spryer	pious	
Meier	spyer	Pius	**ĪV'en**
Meyer	stultifier	(see Ī'as)	driven
modifier	stupefier		forgiven
mollifier	supplier	**ĪV'a**	given
mortifier	sweet-briar	Saiva	overdriven
multiplier	terrifier	saliva	riven
Myer	testifier	Siva	scriven
mystifier	tier		shriven
nigher	town-crier	**ĪV'al**	stormdriven
notifier	trier	adjectival	thriven
nullifier	trior	archival	undriven
occupier	tyer	arrival	unforgiven
pacifier	typifier	conjunctival	unshriven
personifier	Untermyer	estival	weather-
petrifier	untier	imperatival	driven
plyer	verifier	nominatival	
prior	versifier	outrival	**ĪV'ent**
prophesier	vier	revival	connivent

ōld, ôr, ŏdd, oil, fŏŏt, out; ūse, ûrn, ŭp; THis, thin

ĬV'est
arrivest
connivest
contrivest
deprivest
derivest
divest
drivest
livest
revivest
rivest
shrivest
strivest
survivest
thrivest

ĬV'est
forgivest
givest
livest
misgivest
outlivest

ĬV'et
civet
grivet
privet
rivet
trivet
unrivet

ĬV'eth
arriveth
conniveth
contriveth
depriveth
deriveth
diveth
driveth
reviveth
shriveth

striveth
surviveth
thriveth

ĬV'eth
forgiveth
giveth
liveth
misgiveth
outliveth

ĬV'i
ivy

ĬV'i
chivvy
divi-divi
divvy
Livy
privy
tantivy
tivy

ĬV'id
ivied

ĬV'id
livid
vivid

ĬV'ik
civic

ĬV'il, ĬV'el
civil
drivel
rivel
shrivel
snivel
swivel
uncivil

ĬV'ing
arriving
conniving
contriving
depriving
deriving
diving
driving
hiving
reviving
shriving
striving
surviving
thriving
uncontriving
wiving

ĬV'ing
ever-living
forgiving
giving
lawgiving
life-giving
living
misgiving
outliving
thanksgiving
unforgiving

ĬV'li
lively

ĬV'li
absotively
positively

ĬV'ling
shrivelling
snivelling

ĬV'ment
deprivement
revivement

ĬV'nes
forgiveness

ĬV'ot
divot
pivot

ĬV'ring
delivering
quivering
shivering
slivering

ĬV'ur
arriver
conniver
contriver
depriver
deriver
diver
driver
fiver
hiver
liver
pearl-diver
reviver
river
shriver
skiver
slave-driver
sliver
stiver
striver
surviver
thriver

ĬV'ur
cantaliver

deliver
flivver
forgiver
freeliver
giver
Indian giver
liver
misgiver
outliver
quiver
river
shiver
skiver
sliver
Spoon River
stiver
tiver

ĬV'urd
delivered
lily-livered
pigeon-livered
quivered
shivered
slivered
unshivered
white-livered

ĬV'us
acclivous
declivous
proclivous
salivous

ĬV'yal
trivial
(see ĬV'i-al)

Ī'wa
byway

highway
skyway

Ī'za
Eliza
Isa

ĪZ'ak
Isaac

ĪZ'al
comprisal
revisal
surprisal

ĬZ'ard
blizzard
gizzard
izzard
lizard
lounge-lizard
scissored
visored
vizard
wizard

ĬZ'dal
Grisdale

ĬZ'dom
wisdom

ĪZ'en
bedizen
dizen

ĬZ'en, ĬZ'on
arisen
bedizen
dizen
imprison

mizzen
prison
risen
ptisan
wizen

ĪZ'est
advertisest
advisest
agonizest
apologizest
arisest
baptizest
catechizest
chastisest
civilizest
comprisest
compromisest
criticizest
despisest
devisest
disguisest
dramatizest
emphasizest
eulogizest
excisest
exercisest
exorcisest
improvisest
merchandisest
mobilizest
monopolizest
organizest
patronizest
premisest
prizest
realizest
recognizest
revisest
risest
sizest

solemnizest
supervisest
surmisest
surprisest
sympathizest
theorizest
tyrannizest
uprisest
wisest

ĬZ'est
fizzest, etc.

ĪZ'eth
advertiseth
adviseth
agonizeth
apologizeth
ariseth
baptizeth
catechizeth
chastiseth
civilizeth
compriseth
compromiseth
criticizeth
despiseth
deviseth
disguiseth
dramatizeth
emphasizeth
eulogizeth
exerciseth
exorciseth
improviseth
merchandiseth
mobilizeth
monopolizeth
organizeth
patronizeth
premiseth

ōld, ôr, ŏdd, oil, fŏŏt, out; ūse, ûrn, ŭp; THis, thin

prizeth
realizeth
recognizeth
reviseth
riseth
sizeth
solemnizeth
superviseth
surmiseth
surpriseth
sympathizeth
theorizeth
tyrannizeth
upriseth

ĬZ′eth
fizzeth, etc.

ĬZH′un
abscission
allision
collision
concision
decision
derision
division
elision
envision
excision
illision
imprecision
incision
indecision
irrision
misprision
precision
prevision
provision
recision
rescission
revision

scission
subdivision
supervision
television
transition
vision
(cf. ĬZ′i-an)

ĬZH′und
provisioned
visioned

ĬZH′ur
scissure

ĬZ′i
sizy

ĬZ′i
busy
dizzy
frizzy
jizzy
Lizzy
tin-lizzie
tizzy

ĬZ′id
busied
dizzied
unbusied

ĬZ′ij
visage

ĬZ′ik
metaphysic
paradisic
phthisic
physic

ĬZ′iks
physics

ĪZ′ing
advertising
advising
aggrandizing
agonizing
analyzing
anglicizing
antagonizing
apologizing
apostatizing
appetizing
apprising
arising
authorizing
baptizing
brutalizing
canonizing
capitalizing
capsizing
catechizing
Catholicizing
cauterizing
centralizing
characterizing
chastising
civilizing
colonizing
comprising
compromising
criticizing
crystallizing
demising
demoralizing
deodorizing
despising
devising
disguising
disorganizing

dramatizing
economizing
emphasizing
enterprising
equalizing
eternalizing
eulogizing
evangelizing
exercising
exorcising
familiarizing
fertilizing
galvanizing
generalizing
gormandizing
harmonizing
Hebraizing
humanizing
hybridizing
hypnotizing
idealizing
idolizing
immortalizing
improvising
italicizing
jeopardizing
journalizing
localizing
macadamizing
magnetizing
materializing
mesmerizing
methodizing
minimizing
mobilizing
modernizing
monopolizing
moralizing
neutralizing
organizing
paralyzing

---

patronizing
pauperizing
plagiarizing
premising
prizing
pulverizing
rationalizing
realizing
recognizing
revising
revolution-
  izing
rising
ruralizing
scandalizing
scrutinizing
secularizing
sermonizing
signalizing
sizing
solemnizing
soliloquizing
specializing
standardizing
sterilizing
stigmatizing
subsidizing
summarizing
supervising
surmising
surprising
symbolizing
sympathizing
systematizing
tantalizing
temporizing
terrorizing
theorizing
totalizing
tranquillizing
tyrannizing

uncompromis-
  ing
underprizing
uprising
utilizing
vaporizing
visualizing
vitalizing
vocalizing
volatilizing
vulgarizing

ĬZ'ing
befrizzing
fizzing
frizzing
phizzing
quizzing
whizzing

ĬZ'it
visit
what-is-it

ĪZ'krak
wisecrack

ĬZ"l
drizzle
chisel
crizzle
enchisel
fizzle
frizzle
grizzle
mizzle
sizzle
swizzle
twizzle

ĬZ"ld
grizzled
drizzled, etc.

ĬZ'li
chiselly
drizzly
frizzly
grisly
grizzly

ĬZ'ling
chiseling
drizzling
fizzling
frizzling
grizzling
mizzling
sizzling
swizzling

ĬZ"m
izzum-wizzum

ĬZ'mal
abysmal
aneurismal
baptismal
cataclysmal
catechismal
chrismal
dismal
embolismal
paroxysmal
rheumatismal

ĬZ'man
exciseman
prizeman

ĬZ'ment
aggrandize-
  ment

apprizement
assizement
baptizement

ĬZ'met
kismet

ĬZ'mi
prismy

ĬZ'mik
aphorismic
cataclysmic
clysmic
embolismic
paroxysmic

ĬZ'mus
accismus
strabismus
tarantismus
trismus

ĪZ'nes
wiseness

ĬZ'nes
business

ĬZ'om
chrisom
(cf. schism)

ĪZ'on
horizon
Kyrie eleison

ĪZ'ord
visored

ĬZ'ord
(see ĬZ'ard)

ĬZ'ur

advertiser	disguiser	Keyser	synchronizer
adviser	disorganizer	Kyser	tantalizer
aggrandizer	divisor	lionizer	temporizer
agonizer	dogmatizer	magnetizer	terrorizer
analyzer	economizer	miser	theorizer
apologizer	elisor	moralizer	tranquillizer
appetizer	epitomizer	organizer	tyrannizer
apprizer	equalizer	pauperizer	upriser
assizer	eulogizer	polarizer	vaporizer
atomizer	exerciser	prizer	victimizer
authorizer	exorciser	proselytizer	vitalizer
baptizer	extemporizer	pulverizer	vocalizer
canonizer	fertilizer	realizer	vulgarizer
capsizer	galvanizer	reviser	vulcanizer
catechizer	generalizer	riser	wiser
cauterizer	geyser	scandalizer	
chastiser	gormandizer	scrutinizer	**ĬZ'ur**
civilizer	guiser	sermonizer	befrizzer
colonizer	harmonizer	sizer	frizzer
deodorizer	humanizer	solemnizer	quizzer
despiser	hybridizer	sterilizer	scissor
deviser	idolizer	stigmatizer	vizor
devisor	improviser	supervisor	
dialyser	incisor	surmiser	**ĬZ'urz**
	itemizer	surpriser	scissors, etc.
	Kaiser	sympathizer	

O

For a discussion of words included under the accented vowels following, see the beginning of O rhymes in Section I.

Ō'a	moa	**Ō'ab**	**Ō'ba**
boa	Noah	Joab	arroba
entozoa	proa	Moab	*bona-roba*
epizoa	protozoa	**Ō'al**	dagoba
Genoa	quinoa	bestowal	
Gilboa	Samoa		**Ŏ'ba**
jerboa	spermatazoa	**Ô'al**	Cahaba
metazoa	(cf. aloha)	withdrawal	Catawba

āle,   câre,   ădd,   ärm,   åsk;   mē,   hẹre,   ĕnd;   īce,   ĭll;

Ō'ball
no-ball
snow-ball

Ō'bat
globate
lobate
probate

ŎB'est
disrobest
enrobest
probest
robest
unrobest

ŎB'est
daubest, etc.

ŎB'est
robbest
sobbest
throbbest

ŎB'eth
disrobeth
enrobeth
probeth
robeth
unrobeth

ŎB'et
Cobbett

ŎB'eth
daubeth, etc.

ŎB'eth
robbeth
sobbeth
throbbeth

Ō'bī
go-by

ŌB'ī, ŌB'e
adobe
globy
Gobi
hydrophoby
Kobe
obi

ŎB'i
bobby
cobby
hobby
knobby
lobby
mobby
nobby
scobby
snobby
squabby

ŌB'il, ŌB'ēl
automobile
immobile
mobile

ŎB'in
bobbin
dobbin
ragged-robin
robbin
robin
round robin

ŌB'ing
disrobing
enrobing
globing
probing

robing
unrobing

ŎB'ing
blobbing
bobbing
cobbing
hobnobbing
jobbing
knobbing
lobbing
mobbing
robbing
snobbing
sobbing
swabbing
throbbing

ŎB'inz
Jobbins
Robbins
bobbins, etc.

ŎB'ish
bobbish
mobbish
nobbish
snobbish
squabbish

ŎB'jekt
object

ŎB"l
ennoble
ignoble
noble
unnoble

ŎB"l
bauble

ŎB"l
cobble
coble
gobble
hobble
nobble
squabble
wabble

ŎB'li
cobbly
squabbly
wabbly
Wobbly

ŎB'lin
goblin

ŎB'ling
cobbling
gobbling
hobbling
nobbling
snobling
squabbling
wabbling

ŎB'lur
cobbler
gobbler
hobbler
knobbler
nobbler
sherry-cobbler
squabbler
wabbler

ŌB'o
hobo
lobo
zobo

Ō'boi	ŏB'ur	*broacheth*	scotching
doughboy	beslobber	*encroacheth*	splotching
	blobber	*poacheth*	watching
Ó'bonz	clobber	*reproacheth*	
jawbones	cobber		ŏCH'man
sawbones	jobber	ŏCH'eth	Scotchman
	knobber	*blotcheth, etc.*	watchman
ōB'ra	lobber		
cobra	robber	ōCH'ez	ōCH'ment
	slobber	approaches	approachment
Ō'brou	snobber	broaches	encroachment
lowbrow	sobber	brooches	
	swabber	coaches	ōCH'ur
ŏB'son	throbber	encroaches	approacher
Jobson		loaches	broacher
Robeson	ŏB'urn	poaches	encroacher
Robson	auburn	reproaches	poacher
		roaches	reproacher
ŏB'son	ōB'us	self-reproaches	self-reproacher
dobson	globus		
Jobson	jacobus	ōCH'ful	ŏCH'ur
Robson	obus	reproachful	blotcher
			botcher
ŏB'stur	ŏB'web	ŏCH'i	notcher
lobster	cobweb	blotchy	splotcher
		botchy	watcher
ŏB'ul	ōCH'est	notchy	
globule	*approachest*	splotchy	ŏCH'wurd
lobule	*broachest*		watchword
	encroachest	ōCH'ing	
ōB'ur	*poachest*	approaching	ōD'a
disrober	*reproachest*	broaching	coda
enrober		coaching	pagoda
October	ŏCH'est	encroaching	Rhoda
prober	*blotchest, etc.*	poaching	soda
rober		reproaching	trinoda
sober	ŏCH'et		
	crotchet	ŏCH'ing	ōD'al
ŏB'ur	*rotchet*	blotching	internodal
bedauber	ōCH'eth	botching	modal
dauber	*approacheth*	notching	nodal

trinodal
yodel

ŌD'al

bicaudal
caudal
caudle
dawdle

ŌD'ard

Goddard
Stoddard
(cf. foddered)

ŌD'ed

boded
coded
corroded
eroded
exploded
foreboded
goaded
loaded
outmoded
overloaded
unloaded
woaded

ŎD'ed

nodded
plodded
podded
prodded
sodded
wadded
(cf. bodied,
   etc.)

ŌD'el

yodel
(cf. ŌD'al)

ŌD'en

foreboden
Woden

ŎD'en

broaden

ŎD'en

hodden
sodden
trodden
untrodden
water-sodden
(cf. ÄD'en)

ŎD'ent

corrodent
erodent
explodent
rodent

ŎD'es

goddess
(cf. bodice)

ŎD'est

*bodest
corrodest
explodest
forebodest
goadest
loadest
unloadest*

ŌD'est

*applaudest
belaudest
broadest
defraudest
laudest
maraudest*

ŎD'est

immodest
modest
noddest
oddest
*ploddest
proddest*

ŌD'eth

*bodeth
corrodeth
explodeth
forebodeth
goadeth
loadeth
unloadeth*

ŌD'eth

*applaudeth
belaudeth
defraudeth
laudeth
maraudeth*

ŎD'eth

noddeth, etc.

ŌD'i

toady

ÔD'i

bawdy
dawdy
gaudy

ŎD'i

body
busy-body
cloddy
embody
hoddy

noddy
roddy
shoddy
soddy
somebody
squaddy
toddy
waddy
(cf. ÄD'i)

ŎD'id

ablebodied
bodied
disembodied
unbodied
unembodied
(cf. ŎD'ed)

ŎD'ik

odic

ŎD'ik

anodic
episodic
exodic
hellanodic
hydriodic
iodic
kinesodic
melodic
methodic
odic
parodic
periodic
rhapsodic
sarcodic
spasmodic
synodic

ŎD'in

Odin
Wodin

ōld, ôr, ŏdd, oil, fŏŏt, out; ūse, ûrn, ŭp; THis. thin

ŎD'ing
boding
corroding
exploding
foreboding
goading
loading
outmoding
overloading
unloading

ŎD'ing
applauding
belauding
defrauding
lauding
marauding

ŎD'ing
codding
nodding
plodding
podding
prodding
wadding

ŎD'is
bodice
(cf. goddess)

ŎD'ish
cloddish
goddish

ŎD'ist
codist
modist
palinodist

ŎD'it
audit
plaudit

ŎD'kast
broadcast

ŎD''l
coddle
model
mollycoddle
noddle
remodel
swaddle
toddle
twaddle
waddle

ŎD'li
godly
twaddly
ungodly
waddly

ŎD'lin
maudlin

ŎD'ling
coddling
codling
godling
modelling
remodelling
swaddling
toddling
twaddling
waddling

ŎD'lur
coddler
modeller
mollycoddler
swaddler
toddler

twaddler
waddler

ŎD'nes
oddness

Ō'do
dodo
quasimodo

ŎD'om
Sodom

ŎD'ri
bawdry
tawdry

ŎD'ron
squadron

ŎD'son
Dodson
Hodson

ŎD'ston
loadstone
lodestone
toad-stone

ŎD'stur
goadster
roadster

ŎD'ukt
product

ŎD'ul
module
nodule

ŌD'ur
corroder

exploder
foreboder
goader
loader
malodor
muzzle-loader
Oder
odor
unloader

ŎD'ur
applauder
belauder
broader
defrauder
lauder
marauder
sawder
soft-sawder

ŎD'ur
codder
dodder
fodder
nodder
odder
plodder
podder
prodder
solder

ŎD'urn
modern

ŌD'us
modus
nodous

Ō'ed
coed

Ō'el
Crowell
Joel
Lowell
Noel

Ō'em
poem
proem

Ō'en
Bowen
Cohen
Owen

Ō'est
bestowest
blowest
crowest
flowest
foregoest
foreknowest
foreshowest
glowest
goest
growest
hoest
knowest
lowest
mowest
outgoest
overflowest
overgrowest
overthrowest
owest
rowest
sewest
showest
slowest
snowest
sowest

stowest
throwest
towest
undergoest
undertowest
upthrowest

Ō'est
awest
drawest
overawest
rawest
withdrawest

Ō'et
poet

Ō'eth
bestoweth
bloweth
croweth
floweth
foregoeth
foreknoweth
foreshoweth
gloweth
goeth
groweth
hoeth
knoweth
loweth
moweth
outgoeth
overfloweth
overgroweth
overthroweth
oweth
roweth
seweth
showeth
snoweth

soweth
stoweth
throweth
toweth
undergoeth

Ō'eth
aweth, etc.

Ō'fa
sofa

Ō'fet
Tophet

ŎF'et, ŎF'it
archprophet
profit
prophet
soffit
weather-
    prophet

ŌF'i
Sophie
strophe
trophy

ŎF'i
coffee
spoffy
toffy

ŎF'ĭk
antistrophic
apostrophic
catastrophic
hypertrophic
philosophic
theosophic
theophilosophic

ŎF'il
profile

ŎF'in
coffin
encoffin

ŎF'ing
coughing
doffing
golfing
offing
scoffing

ŎF'is
office

ŎF'ish
crawfish
standoffish

ŎF'ish
offish
spoffish

ŎF"l
offal
waffle

ŎF"n
often
soften

ŎF'ted
lofted

ŎF'test
softest

ŎF'ti
lofty
softy

ōld, ôr, ŏdd, oil, fŏŏt, out; ūse, ûrn, ŭp; THis, thin

ŎFT′li
softly

ŎF′tur
crofter
lofter
softer

Ō′ful
woeful

Ô′ful
awful
lawful
unlawful

ŌF′ur
chauffeur
gopher
loafer
Ophir

ŎF′er
coffer
cougher
doffer
goffer
golfer
offer
proffer
scoffer

ŌG′a
Saratoga
snoga
Ticonderoga
toga
yoga

ŎG′a
Chicamauga
Sylacauga

ŌG′al
dogal

ŎG′al
synagogal

ŌG′an
brogan
Hogan
slogan

ŎG′an
toboggan

ŌG′i
bogey
bogie
dogie
fogey
stogie
yogi

ŎG′i
boggy
cloggy
doggy
foggy
froggy
groggy
joggy
soggy

ŎG′in
noggin

ŌG′ing
befogging
bogging
clogging
cogging
dogging

flogging
fogging
jogging
nogging
slogging
togging
unclogging

ŎG′ish
doggish
hoggish

ŌG′ish
roguish

ŌG″l
bogle
fogle
ogle

ŎG″l
boondoggle
boggle
coggle
goggle
joggle
toggle

ŎG′ling
boondoggling
boggling
goggling
joggling

ŌG′lur
ogler

ŎG′lur
boondoggler
boggler
goggler
joggler

ŎG′mir
quagmire

ŌG′ram
programme

ŌG′res
ogress
progress

ŎG′res
progress

ŎG′trot
dog-trot
jog-trot

ŌG′ur
ogre

ŌG′ur
auger
augur
inaugur
mauger

ŎG′ur
befogger
clogger
cogger
dogger
flogger
hogger
jogger
logger
pettifogger
slogger
togger
wholehogger

ŌG′us
bogus

āle,   câre,   ădd,   ärm,   åsk;   mē,   hĕre,   ĕnd;   īce,   ĭll;

ÔG′ust	**OI′ans**	rhomboidal	**OI′eth**
August	annoyance	saccharoidal	*annoyeth*
	buoyance	sigmoidal	*buoyeth*
ŎG′wood	clairvoyance	spheroidal	*cloyeth*
bog-wood	joyance	trochoidal	*convoyeth*
dog-wood		typhoidal	*decoyeth*
logwood	**OI′ant**		*destroyeth*
	annoyant	**OID′ans**	*employeth*
Ō′hen	buoyant	avoidance	*enjoyeth*
Cohen	chatoyant		*joyeth*
	clairvoyant	**OID′ed**	*toyeth*
Ō′hunk	flamboyant	avoided	
Bohunk	prevoyant	voided	**OI′ful**
			joyful
Ō′i	**OI′b'l**	**OID′en**	
blowy	foible	hoyden	**OI′ij**
Bowie			alloyage
Chloe	**OID′al**	**OID′ur**	buoyage
doughy	asteroidal	avoider	voyage
Floey	colloidal	broider	
glowy	conchoidal	embroider	**OI′ing**
Joey	conoidal	moider	annoying
showy	coralloidal	voider	buoying
snowy	crinoidal		cloying
towy	cycloidal		convoying
Zoe	dendroidal	**OI′e**	decoying
	discoidal	employee	deploying
Ŏ′i	elephantoidal		destroying
flawy	ellipsoidal	**OI′est**	employing
jawy	ethnoidal	*annoyest*	enjoying
strawy	ganoidal	*buoyest*	joying
thawy	hemispheroidal	*cloyest*	toying
(cf. Ä′i̦)	lithoidal	*convoyest*	
	metalloidal	coyest	**OI′ish**
OI′al	negroidal	*decoyest*	boyish
chapel-royal	ooidal	*deployest*	coyish
disloyal	ovoidal	*destroyest*	toyish
loyal	paraboloidal	*employest*	
pennyroyal	planetoidal	*enjoyest*	**Ō′ij**
royal	prismatoidal	*joyest*	flowage
sur-royal	prismoidal	*toyest*	stowage
			towage

ōld, ôr, ŏdd, oil, fŏŏt, out; ūse, ûrn, ŭp; THis, thin

Ō'ik	*broileth*	broiler	going
azoic	*coileth*	coiler	growing
benzoic	*despoileth*	despoiler	helloing
Cenozoic	*embroileth*	embroiler	hoeing
dichroic	*foileth*	foiler	inflowing
dyspnoic	*recoileth*	oiler	knowing
Eozoic	*roileth*	recoiler	lowing
heroic	*soileth*	soiler	mowing
hylozoic	*spoileth*	spoiler	oboeing
hypozoic	*toileth*	toiler	outflowing
melanochroic	*uncoileth*	uncoiler	outgoing
Mesozoic			outgrowing
mock-heroic	**OIL'i**	**OI'man**	overcrowing
Neozoic	coyly	decoy-man	overflowing
Palæozoic	doily	hoyman	overgrowing
pleochroic	oily	toyman	overthrowing
protozoic	roily		owing
Stoic		**OI'ment**	rowing
Troic	**OIL'ing**	deployment	sea-going
xanthochroic	assoiling	employment	self-knowing
	boiling	enjoyment	sewing
OIL'est	broiling		showing
boilest	coiling	**OIN'dur**	slowing
broilest	despoiling	rejoinder	snowing
coilest	embroiling		sowing
despoilest	foiling	**OI'nes**	stowing
embroilest	moiling	coyness	*strowing*
foilest	oiling		thorough-going
recoilest	recoiling	**Ō'ing**	throwing
roilest	soiling	bestowing	toeing
soilest	spoiling	blowing	towing
spoilest	toiling	bowing	undergoing
toilest	uncoiling	cock-crowing	undertowing
uncoilest		crowing	unknowing
	OIL'ment	easy-going	unflowing
OIL'et	despoilment	flowing	upgrowing
oillet	embroilment	foregoing	
toilet	recoilment	foreknowing	**Ô'ing**
		foreshowing	awing
OIL'eth	**OIL'ur**	glass-blowing	begnawing
boileth	boiler	glowing	cawing

āle,   câre,   ădd,   ärm,   åsk: mē,   hĕre,   ĕnd;   īce,   ĭll;

chawing
clawing
drawing
gnawing
guffawing
heehawing
jawing
lawing
outlawing
overawing
overdrawing
pawing
pshawing
sawing
thawing
wiredrawing
withdrawing
yawing

OIN'ij

coinage

OIN'ing

adjoining
coining
conjoining
disjoining
enjoining
groining
joining
purloining
rejoining
subjoining

OIN'ted

anointed
appointed
conjointed
disappointed
disjointed
jointed

pointed
unanointed
unpointed
unjointed

OIN'ting

anointing
appointing
disappointing
disjointing
jointing
pointing

OINT'les

jointless
pointless

OINT'ment

anointment
appointment
disappointment
disjointment
ointment

OIN'tur

anointer
appointer
disappointer
disjointer
jointer
pointer

OIN'ur

coiner
conjoiner
enjoiner
joiner
purloiner
rejoiner

OI'ride

joyride

Ō'is

Lois

Ō'ish

showish
snowish

OIS'ing

rejoicing
voicing
unrejoicing

OIS'les

choiceless
voiceless

OI'som

noisome
toysome

OIS'ti

foisty
moisty

OI'stik

joystick

OIS'ting

foisting
hoisting
joisting

OIS'tral

cloistral
coystrel

OIS'tur

cloister
encloister
foister
hoister

moister
oyster
pearl-oyster
royster
uncloister

OIT'ed

doited
exploited

OIT'i

dacoity
hoity-toity

OIT'ring

loitering
reconnoitring

OIT'ūr

exploiture
voiture

OIT'ŭr

adroiter
exploiter
goiter
loiter
reconnoiter

OI'ur

annoyer
Boyar
Boyer
coyer
decoyer
deployer
destroyer
employer
enjoyer
self-destroyer
toyer

ōld, ôr, ŏdd, oil, fŏŏt, out; ūse, ûrn, ŭp; THis, thin

OI'us
joyous

OIZ'ez
boyses
noises
poises

OIZ'i
noisy

OIZ'ing
noising
poising

OIZ'on
empoison
foison
poison
toison

OIZ'onz
foisons
poisons, etc.

Ō'jan
Trojan

ŎJ'ez
Hodges
dodges, etc.

ŎJ'e
anagoge
apagoge
èpagoge
paragoge

ŎJ'i
pedagogy
podgy
stodgy

ŎJ'ik
aerologic
anagogic
anthropologic
archæologic
astrologic
biologic
chronologic
curiologic
demagogic
demonologic
dialogic
entomologic
epagogic
epilogic
ethnologic
ethologic
etymologic
eulogic
geologic
gnomologic
hierologic
histologic
horologic
ichthyologic
idealogic
isagogic
lithologic
logic
martyrologic
meteorologic
mineralogic
morphologic
mycologic
myologic
mystagogic
mythologic
necrologic
neologic
ontologic
ophiologic

paragogic
pathologic
pedagogic
philologic
phonologic
photologic
phraseologic
physiologic
psychologic
sarcologic
sociologic
tautologic
theologic
tropologic
zymologic

ŎJ'iks
pedagogics

ŎJ'ing
dislodging
dodging
lodging

ŎJ'ur
codger
dislodger
dodger
lodger
Roger

ŌJ'urn
sojourn

Ō'kā
croquet
roquet

ŌK'ă
coca
tapioca

ŌK'al
bocal
focal
local
phocal
socle
vocal
yokel

ŌK'e
troche
trochee
(cf. choky, etc.)

ŌK'en
bespoken
betoken
broken
fair-spoken
fine-spoken
forespoken
foretoken
freespoken
heart-broken
Hoboken
oaken
outspoken
soft-spoken
spoken
token
unbroken
unspoken

ŎK'en
Brocken

ŌK'est
chokest
cloakest
convokest
croakest

evokest
invokest
jokest
provokest
revokest
smokest
soakest
spokest
unyokest
yokest

ŎK'est

balkest
stalkest
talkest
walkest

ŎK'est

bemockest
blockest
dockest
flockest
knockest
lockest
mockest
rockest
sockest
shockest
smockest
stockest
unfrockest
unlockest

ŎK'et

air-pocket
brocket
cocket
crocket
Crockett
docket
impocket

locket
Lockett
pickpocket
pocket
rocket
sky-rocket
socket
sprocket

ŌK'eth

choketh
cloaketh
convoketh
croaketh
evoketh
invoketh
joketh
poketh
provoketh
revoketh
smoketh
soaketh
spoketh
unyoketh
yoketh

ŎK'eth

balketh
stalketh
talketh
walketh

ŎK'eth

bemocketh
blocketh
docketh
flocketh
knocketh
locketh
mocketh
rocketh

shocketh
smocketh
stocketh
unlocketh

ŎK'hed

blockhead
shock-head

ŌK'i

choky
cokey
croaky
hokey
joky
Loki
moky
oaky
okey-dokey
poky
roky
slow-poky
smoky
soaky
yoky
(cf. troche and trochee)

ŎK'i

balky
chalky
gawky
Milwaukee
pawky
squawky
stalky
talkie
talky
walkie

ŎK'i

cocky

crocky
flocky
hockey
jockey
locky
rocky
stocky

ŎK'id

cockeyed

ŌK'ij

brokage
cloakage
soakage

ŎK'ij

dockage
lockage
soccage

ŌK'ing

besmoking
choking
cloaking
convoking
croaking
evoking
invoking
joking
poking
provoking
revoking
smoking
soaking
stoking
stroking
troching
uncloaking
yoking

ōld, ôr, ŏdd, oil, fŏŏt, out; ūse, ûrn, ŭp; THis, thin

ŎK'ing
balking
calking
hawking
jaywalking
squawking
stalking
talking
walking

ŎK'ing
bemocking
blocking
clocking
cocking
docking
flocking
hocking
interlocking
knocking
locking
mocking
rocking
shocking
smocking
stocking
unlocking

ŎK'inz
Dawkins
Hawkins

ŎK'ish
hawkish
mawkish

ŎK'ish
blockish
cockish
mockish
stockish

ŎK''l
cockle
hockle
socle
strockle

ŎK'les
cloakless
jokeless
smokeless
yokeless
yolkless

ŎK'ling
cockling
flockling
rockling

ŎK'lor
folklore

ŎK'man
Brockman
lockman
socman

ŌK'ment
invokement
provokement
revokement

ŎK'ni
cockney

Ō'ko
baroco
coco
cocoa
koko
loco
locofoco

rococo
troco

ŎK'o
Morocco
sirocco

ŎK'port
Brockport
Lockport
Stockport

ŌK'ra
okra

ŎK'sen, ŎK's'n
cockswain
oxen

ŎK'shal
equinoctial
trinoctial

ŎK'shun
auction

ŎK'shun
concoction
decoction

ŎK'shus
innoxious
noxious
obnoxious

ŎK'si
cacodoxy
Coxey
doxy
foxy
heterodoxy

orthodoxy
paradoxy
proxy

ŎK'sid
fox-eyed
ox-eyed
oxide

ŎK'sin
tocsin

ŌK'sing
coaxing
hoaxing

ŎK'sing
boxing
foxing

ŌKS'man
spokesman
strokesman

ŌK'smith
jokesmith

ŌK'sur
coaxer
hoaxer

ŎK'sur
boxer
oxer

ŎK'til
coctile
trioctile

ŎK'tiv
concoctive
decoctive

ŎK'ton
Blockton
Brockton
Stockton

ŎK'trin
doctrine

ŎK'tur
concocter
doctor
proctor

ŎK'turn
nocturne

Ō'kum
hokum
oakum

Ō'kund
jocund

ŎK'ur
broker
choker
cloaker
convoker
croaker
evoker
invoker
joker
mediocre
ocher
poker
provoker
revoker
smoker
soaker
stoker
stroker

uncloaker
yoker

ŎK'ur
balker
calker
deer-stalker
gawker
hawker
jaywalker
shop-walker
sleep-walker
squawker
stalker
street-walker
talker
tomahawker
walker

ŎK'ur
blocker
cocker
docker
Fokker
hougher
Knickerbocker
knocker
locker
mocker
rocker
shocker
soccer
socker
stocker

ŎK'urz
knickerbockers
dockers, etc.

Ō'kus
crocus

focus
hocus
hocus-pocus
Hohokus
locus

ŎK'us
caucus
Daucus
glaucous
raucous

Ō'kust
locust
focussed, etc.

ŎK'ward
awkward

Ō'la
Angola
Appalachicola
carambola
coca-cola
gola
gondola
Gorgonzola
kola
Leola
Maizola
Pensacola
Ramola
scagliola
stola
Viola
Zola

ŎL'a
Eufaula
Guatamala
Paula

ŌL'a
corolla
holla
mollah

ŌL'ak
Polack

ŌL'an
Dolan
Nolan

Ō'land
Boland
Bowland
lowland
Noland
Roland
Rowland

ŌL'ar
(see ŌL'ur)

ŌL'ard
bollard
collard
collared
dollared
Lollard
pollard
scollard

ŌL'as
solace

ŌL'chun
falchion

ŌL'da
Alda

ŌL'ded
blindfolded

ōld, ôr, ŏdd, oil, fŏŏt, out; ūse, ûrn, ŭp; THis, thin

enfolded
infolded
manifolded
molded
refolded
scolded
unfolded

ŌL'den
beholden
embolden
golden
holden
misbeholden
olden
withholden

ŎL'den
Alden

ŌL'dest
beholdest
boldest
coldest
enfoldest
foldest
holdest
infoldest
interfoldest
moldest
oldest
refoldest
scoldest
unfoldest
upholdest
withholdest

ŎL'dest
baldest
scaldest

ŌL'deth
beholdeth
enfoldeth
foldeth
holdeth
infoldeth
interfoldeth
moldeth
refoldeth
scoldeth
unfoldeth
upholdeth
withholdeth

ŎL'deth
scaldeth

ŌLD'ham
Oldham

ŌL'di
foldy
moldy

ŌL'ding
beholding
enfolding
folding
holding
infolding
interfolding
molding
refolding
scolding
slave-holding
unfolding
upholding
weather-
  molding
withholding

ŌL'ding
Balding
Paulding
scalding
Spaulding

ŌL'dish
coldish
oldish

ŌLD'li
boldly
coldly
manifoldly

ŌLD'man
Goldman
Oldman

ŌLD'ment
enfoldment
withholdment

ŌLD'nes
boldness
coldness
oldness

ŌLD'ron
caldron
pauldron

ŌL'drumz
doldrums

ŌLD'smith
Goldsmith

ŌL'dur
beholder
bolder
bottleholder

boulder
colder
enfolder
freeholder
holder
householder
infolder
interfolder
landholder
leaseholder
molder
older
pattern-
  molder
polder
refolder
scolder
shareholder
shoulder
slave-holder
smolder
unfolder
upholder
withholder

ŎL'dur
alder
balder
Baldur
scalder

ŌL'durd
bouldered
broad-
  shouldered
moldered
shouldered
smoldered

ŌLD'win
Baldwin

ŏL'eg
colleague

ŏL'ej
acknowledge
college
foreknowledge
knowledge
self-knowledge

ŏL'ejd
acknowledged
unacknowl-
 edged

ŏL'em, ŏL'um
column
solemn

ŏL'en
stolen
swollen

ŏL'en
chop-fallen
fallen
wind-fallen

ŏL'ent
equipollent
prepollent

ōL'er
(see ŏL'ur)

Ŏ'les
clawless
flawless
jawless
lawless
mawless
sawless

ōL'est
bowlest
cajolest
condolest
consolest
controllest
dolest
drollest
enrollest
patrollest
pollest
rollest
strollest
tollest
trollest
unrollest
uprollest

ŏL'est
bawlest
bemawlest
brawlest
callest
crawlest
drawlest
enthrallest
forestallest
maulest
scrawlest
smallest
sprawlest
squallest
tallest

ŏL'et
collet
La Follette
wallet

ōL'eth
bowleth

cajoleth
condoleth
consoleth
controlleth
doleth
enrolleth
patrolleth
polleth
rolleth
strolleth
tolleth
trolleth
unrolleth
uprolleth

ŏL'eth
bawleth
bemawleth
brawleth
calleth
crawleth
drawleth
enthralleth
forestalleth
mauleth
scrawleth
sprawleth
squalleth

ŏL'fin
dolphin

ŏL'fing
golfiing

ŏL'ful
bowlful
doleful
soulful

ŏL'fur
golfer

ŏL'fus
Adolphus
Rodolphus
Rudolphus

ōL'hous
poll-house
toll-house

ōL'i
coaly
holy
lowly
moly
roly-poly
shoaly
slowly
unholy
(cf. ōL'li)

ŏL'i
Macaulay
Macauley
sprawly
squally
whally

ŏL'i
Bali
collie
dolly
folly
golly
Holley
holly
jolly
loblolly
melancholy
Molly
Polly
rolley

Tolley
trolley
volley

ŎL'ĭd
jollied
olid
solid
squalid
stolid
A2: vollēyed

Ō'lĭf
lowlife

ŎL'ĭj
hallage
haulage
stallage

ŎL'ĭk
aulic
Gallic
hydraulic
interaulic

ŎL'ĭk
Aeolic
alcoholic
apostolic
bibliopolic
bucolic
carbolic
colic
diabolic
diastolic
embolic
epipolic
epistolic
frolic
hyperbolic

melancholic
metabolic
parabolic
petrolic
rollick
symbolic
systolic
variolic
vicar-apostolic
vitriolic

ŎL'ĭn
tarpaulin

ŎL'ĭng
bolling
bowling
cajoling
caracoling
coaling
condoling
consoling
controlling
doling
drolling
enrolling
extolling
foaling
holing
inscrolling
parolling
patrolling
poling
rolling
shoaling
strolling
tolling
trolling
unrolling
uprolling

ŎL'ĭng
appalling
balling
bawling
befalling
bemawling
blackballing
brawling
calling
caterwauling
crawling
drawling
enthralling
falling
footballing
forestalling
galling
hauling
installing
mauling
miscalling
overhauling
palling
Pawling
recalling
scrawling
snow-balling
sprawling
squalling
thralling
trawling
walling

ŎL'ĭng
caracolling
extolling
lolling

ŎL'ĭnz
Collins

Hollins
Rollins

ŎL'ĭs
Collis
Cornwallis
Hollis
Wallace
Wallis

ŎL'ĭsh
drollish
Polish

ŎL'ĭsh
Gaulish
smallish
squallish
tallish

ŎL'ĭsh
abolish
demolish
polish

ŎL'ĭsht
abolished
demolished
polished
unpolished

ŎL'ĭv
olive

ŎL'jur
soldier

ŎL'ka
polka

ŎL'kon
falcon

gerfalcon	ÔL'nes	ÔLS'hood	jolted
soar-falcon	allness	falsehood	molted
sorefalcon	smallness		revolted
BALKAN	tallness	ÔL'sid	unbolted
ÔLK'nur		palsied	
falconer	Ô'lo		ÔL'ted
	polo	ÔLS'nes	assaulted
ÔL'li	solo	falseness	defaulted
drolly			exalted
solely	ÔL'o	ÔL'so	faulted
wholly	Apollo	also	halted
(cf. ÔL'i)	follow		malted
	hollo	ÔL'som	salted
ÔL'man	hollow	dolesome	vaulted
coal-man	swallow	wholesome	
Coleman	wallow		ÔL'ten
Colman		ÔL'son	molten
Holman	Ô'lok	Jolson	
toll-man	Moloch	Olsen	ÔL'test
	rowlock	Olson	*boltest, etc*
ÔL'ment		Tolson	
cajolement	ÔL'on	Toulson	ÔL'test
condolement	colon		*assaultest*
controlment	eidolon	ÔL'star	*defaultest*
enrollment	semicolon	pole-star	*exaltest*
	Solon		*haltest*
ÔL'ment	stolon	ÔL'ston	*vaultest*
appallment	(cf. ÔL'an,	gallstone	
disenthrallment	ÔL'en)		ÔL'teth
enthrallment		ÔL'ston	*bolteth, etc.*
epaulement	ÔL'op	Alston	
instalment	collop	Balston	ÔL'teth
installment	dollop	Ralston	*assaulteth*
	escalop		*defaulteth*
ÔL'most	lollop	ÔL'stur	*exalteth*
almost	scallop	bolster	*halteth*
	trollop	holster	*vaulteth*
ÔL'nes	wallop	upholster	
drollness			ÔL'ti
soleness	ÔL'or	ÔL'ted	faulty
wholeness	dolor	bolted	malty

ōld, ôr, ŏdd, oil, fŏŏt, out; ūse, ûrn, ŭp; THis, thin

salty	ŌL'ton	ŌLT'sur	bemawler
vaulty	Bolton	waltzer	brawler
	Colton	(cf. falser)	caller
ŌL'tij	Moulton		crawler
voltage		ŌL'ūm	drawler
	ŌL'ton	colyum	enthraller
ŌL'tij	Dalton	volume	faller
maltage	Walton		footballer
vaultage		ŌL'um	forestaller
	ŌL'tri	column	hauler
ŌL'tik	poultry	solemn	mauler
asphaltic			scrawler
Baltic		ŌL'ur	smaller
basaltic	ŌL'tur	bowler	sprawler
cobaltic	bolter	cajoler	squaller
peristaltic	colter	circumpolar	taller
	jolter	coaler	trawler
ŌL'ting	revolter	condoler	
bolting	unbolter	consoler	ŌL'ur
jolting		controller	choler
molting	ŌL'tur	doler	collar
revolting	altar	dolor	dollar
unbolting	alter	droller	extoller
	assaulter	enroller	loller
ŌL'ting	defaulter	molar	scholar
assaulting	exalter	patroller	sollar
defaulting	falter	polar	squalor
exalting	Gibraltar	poler	
faulting	halter	poller	ŌL'us
halting	malter	roller	bolus
malting	McWalter	scroller	holus-bolus
salting	palter	shoaler	solus
vaulting	psalter	solar	
	Salter	stroller	ŌL'usk
ŌL'tish	unalter	toller	mollusk
coltish	vaulter	troller	
doltish	Walter	unipolar	ŌL'vent
		unroller	dissolvent
ŌLT'les	ŌL'turn	uproller	evolvent
faultless	saltern		insolvent
maltless	subaltern	ŌL'ur	resolvent
saltless		bawler	solvent

ŎL'vest
absolvest
devolvest
dissolvest
evolvest
involvest
resolvest
revolvest
solvest

ŎL'veth
absolveth
devolveth
dissolveth
evolveth
involveth
resolveth
revolveth
solveth

ŎL'ving
absolving
devolving
dissolving
evolving
involving
resolving
revolving
solving

ŎLV'ment
devolvement
evolvement
involvement

ŎL'vur
absolver
dissolver
evolver
involver
resolver

revolver
solver

ŎL'wart
stalwart

ŎL'waz
always
HALLWAYS

Ō'ma
aboma   AZ¿
aroma
coma
diploma
Natoma
sarcoma
Roma
Sonoma
Tacoma
theobroma
zygoma

ŎM'a
comma
momma

Ō'mad
nomad
ohmad

Ō'man
bowman
foeman
Roman
showman
yeoman

ŎM'as
Thomas

ŎM'bat
combat
wombat

ŎM'bi
Abercrombie
Dombey
zombie

ŎM'brus
sombrous

ŎM'bur
hombre
omber
Scomber
somber

ŌM'en, Ō'men
abdomen
agnomen
bowmen
cognomen
foemen
omen   *showmen*
prænomen
yeomen
(cf. gnomon)
DOMEN

ŎM'end
ill-omened
omened

Ō'ment
bestowment
moment

ŎM'et
comet
domett
grommet

ŎM'i
foamy

homy
loamy

ŎM'i
mommy
Tommie

ŎM'ij
homage

ŎM'ik
bromic
chromic
gnomic
hydrobromic
polychromic

ŎM'ik
agronomic
anatomic
astronomic
atomic
autonomic
cinnamomic
comic
diatomic
dystomic
economic
entomic
gastronomic
heliochromic
isonomic
metronomic
microtomic
monatomic
nomic
orthodromic
palindromic
phantomic
physiognomic
serio-comic

ōld,   ôr,   ŏdd,   oil,   fŏŏt,   out;   ūse,   ûrn,   ŭp;   THis,   thin

stereochromic
stereotomic
taxonomic
tragi-comic
triatomic
vomic

ŏM'iks
economics
phoronomics

ŏM'in
bromine
theobromine

ŏM'ing
befoaming
coaming
combing
foaming
gloaming
homing
roaming

ŏM'is
promise

ŏM'ish
Romish

ŏM'les
foamless
combless
homeless

ŏM'let
homelet
tomelet

ŏM'let
omelet

ŏM'li
homely

ō'mo
chromo
Como
Ecce Homo
major-domo

ŏM'on
common

ŏM'pi
Pompey

ŏMP'ish
rompish
swampish

ŏM'plish
accomplish

ŏMP'ted
prompted
unprompted

ŏMP'ton
Brompton
Compton
Lecompton

ŏMP'us
pompous

ŏM'spun
homespun

ŏM'sted
homestead

ŏM'ur
beachcomber

comber
gomer
homer
Homer
misnomer
omer
roamer
vomer
wool-comber

ŏM'ur
bomber

ŏM'urs
commerce

ŏM'ward
homeward

ō'na
annona
Arizona
Barcelona
Bellona
Bologna
cinchona
corona
Cremona
Desdemona
Iona
Jonah
mona
Nona
Pomona
Ramona
Zona

ŏN'a
Mauna

ŏN'a
belladonna

donna
Madonna
prima donna

ŏN'al
coronal
subumbonal
tonal
zonal

ŏN'ald
Donald
McDonald
Ronald

ŏN'ant
intersonant
sonant
(cf. deponent, etc.)

ŏN'ark
monarch

ŏN'as
Jonas

ŏN'at
donate
zonate

ŏN'da
anaconda

ŏN'de
arrondi

ŏN'de
dispondee
spondee

āle, câre, ădd, ärm, ăsk; mē, hẹre, ĕnd; īce, ĭll;

ŎN'ded
absconded
bonded
corresponded
desponded
responded

ŌN'def
stone-deaf
tone-deaf

ŎN'del
rondel

ŎN'dens
correspondence
despondence
respondence

ŎN'dent
co-respondent
correspondent
despondent
frondent
respondent

ŎN'dest
abscondest
bondest
correspondest
fondest
respondest

ŎN'deth
abscondeth
bondeth
correspondeth
respondeth

ŎN'dij
bondage

frondage
vagabondage

ŎN'ding
absconding
corresponding
desponding
responding

ŎN'd'l
fondle
rondle

ŎND'li
fondly

ŎND'ling
bondling
fondling

ŎND'nes
blondness
fondness

ŎN'dur
absconder
bonder
corresponder
desponder
fonder
hypochonder
ponder
responder
squander
wander
yonder
(cf. condor)

ŎN'durz
Saunders

ŎN'e
Pawnee
Punxatawnee
Sewanee
Shawnee
Swanee
(cf. ŎN'i)

ŌN'ent
component
deponent
exponent
interponent
opponent
proponent
(cf. sonant)

Ō'nes
lowness
slowness

ŌN'est
atonest
bemoanest
condonest
dethronest
disownest
dronest
enthronest
groanest
intonest
honest
loanest
lonest
moanest
ownest
postponest
stonest
thronest
tonest

ŎN'est
connest
dishonest
donnest
honest
non-est
wannest

ŎN'et
bonnet
sonnet
unbonnet

ŌN'eth
atoneth
begroaneth
bemoaneth
condoneth
dethroneth
disowneth
droneth
enthroneth
groaneth
honeth
intoneth
loaneth
moaneth
owneth
postponeth
stoneth
throneth
toneth

ŎNG'est
longest
strongest

ŎNG'ful
songful
throngful
wrongful

ōld, ôr, ŏdd, oil, fŏŏt, out; ūse, ûrn, ŭp; THis, thin

ŎNG'go

Bongo
Congo

ŎNG'gur

conger
longer

ŎNG'ing

belonging
longing
prolonging
thronging
wronging

ŎNG'ish

longish
prongish
songish
strongish

ŎNG'ki

donkey

ŎNG'kur

conker
conquer

ŎNG'kurz

conquers
Yonkers

ŎNG'li

longly
wrongly

ŎNG'nes

longness
wrongness

ŎNG'stur

songster

ŎNG'ur

prolonger
wronger

ŎNG'wav

long-wave

ŎN'hed

bonehead

Ō'ni

alimony
aloney
antimony
baloney
bologney
bony
Coney
cony
crony
drony
lazzaroni
macaroni
Mahoney
Maloney
matrimony
parsimony
patrimony
phony
pony
sanctimony
stony
testimony
tony
(cf. cicerone)

ŌN'i

brawny
lawny
mulligatawny
orange-tawny

sawney
scrawny
tawny
yawny

ŎN'i

bonnie
bonny
Connie
Lonnie
Renee
Ronnie

ŎN'ik

phonic
zonic

ŎN'ik

Aaronic
acronyc
Adonic
agonic
Amphictyonic
anharmonic
antiphonic
architectonic
atonic
Babylonic
cacophonic
canonic
carbonic
cataphonic
Chalcedonic
chronic
colophonic
conic
crotonic
cyclonic
dæmonic
demonic
diaphonic

diatonic
draconic
embryonic
euphonic
ganglionic
geogonic
geoponic
gnominic
harmonic
hedonic
hegemonic
histrionic
homophonic
Housatonic
intergan-
    glionic
Ionic
ironic
isotonic
jargonic
laconic
macaronic
masonic
Metonic
Miltonic
mnemonic
monochronic
monophonic
monotonic
neoplatonic
Olympionic
paratonic
parsonic
pathogno-
    monic
Pharaonic
philharmonic
phonic
photophonic
Platonic
Plutonic

āle, câre, ădd, ärm, åsk; mē, hĕre, ĕnd; īce, ĭll;

pneumonic
polyphonic
pulmonic
Pyrrhonic
pythonic
sardonic
semitonic
sermonic
siphonic
Slavonic
Solomonic
stentoronic
stratonic
symphonic
tectonic
telephonic
Teutonic
theogonic
tonic
Tychonic
zoonic

ŏN'iks

geoponics
hedonics
histrionics
Megalonyx
mnemonics
onyx

ōN'ing

atoning
bemoaning
boning
dethroning
disowning
droning
enthroning
groaning
intoning
moaning

owning
postponing
stoning
throning
toning

ŌN'ing

awning
dawning
fawning
pawning
spawning
undawning
yawning

ŏN'ing

conning
donning

ŌN'is

Adonis
Coronis

ŌN'ish

Babylonish
dronish

ŏN'ish

admonish
astonish
tonnish
wannish

ŏN'je

congee
pongee

ŌN'les

boneless
throneless
toneless
zoneless

ŌN'li

lonely
only

ŌN'ment

atonement
condonement
dethronement
disownment
enthronement
postponement

ŌN'nes

loneness
proneness
unknownness

ŌN'or

donor
(cf. ŌN'ur)

ŏN'rad

Conrad

ŏN'shens

conscience

ŏN'shus

conscious
self-conscious
sub-conscious

ŏN'siv

corresponsive
irresponsive
responsive

ŌN'som

lonesome

ŏN'son

Johnson

Jonson
(cf. Wiscon-
sin)

ŏN'sor

sponsor
tonsor

ŏN'stant

constant
inconstant

ŏN'ston

Johnston

ŏN'strans

monstrance
remonstrance

ŏN'strat

demonstrate
remonstrate

ŏN'strous

monstrous

ŏN'stur

monster

ŏN'tal

fontal
frontal
horizontal
peridontal

ŏN'tan

cismontane
tramontane
ultramontane

ŏN'ted

daunted

ōld, ôr, ŏdd, oil, fŏŏt, out; ūse, ûrn, ŭp; THis, thin

flaunted
haunted
taunted
undaunted
vaunted
wanted

ŎN'ted
wanted

ŎN'test
dauntest
flauntest
hauntest
tauntest
vauntest
wantest

ŎN'teth
daunteth
flaunteth
haunteth
taunteth
vaunteth
wanteth

ŎN'ti
flaunty
jaunty

ŎN'tif
pontiff

ŎN'tij
wantage

ŎN'tij
pontage
wantage

ŎN'tik
Anacreontic

archontic
mastodontic
pontic
quantic

ŎN'tin
dracontine
Hellespontine
pontine
(cf. tontine)

ŎN'ting
daunting
flaunting
haunting
jaunting
taunting
vaunting
wanting

ŎN'ting
wanting

ŎNT'les
dauntless
tauntless
vauntless

ŎNT'let
gantlet
gauntlet

ŎN'ton
wanton
(cf. fronton)

ŎN'trit
contrite
uncontrite

ŎN'tum
quantum

ŌN'tur
daunter
flaunter
gaunter
haunter
saunter
taunter
vaunter

ŌN'ur
atoner
bemoaner
boner
condoner
dethroner
droner
groaner
honer
intoner
moaner
owner
phoner
postponer
telephoner
stoner
(cf. donor)

ŎN'ur
awner
barley-awner
brawner
fawner
pawner
spawner
yawner

ŎN'ur
Bonner
conner
Connor
dishonor

goner
honor
O'Conner
O'Connor
wanner

ŎN'urd
dishonored
honored
timehonored
unhonored

ŎN'urz
Conners
Connors
O'Connors
honors, etc.

Ō'nus
bonus
onus
tonous

ŎN'yard
poniard

ŎN'zo
Alonzo
Alphonso
Alphonzo

Ō'on
entozoon
epizoon
phytozoon
zoon

O͞OD'ed
hooded
wooded

ŎOD′en
wooden

ŎOD′i
goody
goody-goody
woody

ŎOD′ing
gooding
hooding
pudding

ŎOD′ish
goodish

ŎOD′li
goodly

ŎOD′man
goodman
hoodman
woodman

ŎOD′nes
goodness

ŎOG′ur
sugar

ŎOK′ed
crooked
(see ŎOK +
  ed)

ŎOK′i
bookie
cooky
hookey

hooky
rooky

ŎOK′ing
booking
brooking
cooking
crooking
hooking
ill-looking
looking
over-looking
rooking
unhooking
well-looking

ŎOK′let
booklet
brooklet

ŎOK′up
hook-up

ŎOK′ur
cooker
hooker
looker
overlooker
stooker

ŎOL′bul
bulbul

ŎOL′en
woollen

ŎOL′et
bullet
pullet

ŎOL′i
bully
fully
pulley
woolly

ŎOL′id
bullied, etc.

ŎOL′ing
bulling
pulling

ŎOL′ish
bullish
fullish

ŎOL′man
Pullman
Woolman

ŎOL′nes
fullness

ŎOL′ur
buller
fuller
puller
wire-puller

ŎOM′an
woman

ŎO′si
pussy

ŎOT′ed
footed
nimble-footed

ŎOT′ing
footing
putting

ŎOT′ur
footer
putter

ō′pa
Europa

ō′pal, ō′p′l
Adrianople
Bhopal
Constantinople
nopal
opal

ō′paz
topaz

ō′pen
open

ŌP′est
copest
elopest
gropest
hopest
interlopest
mopest
ropest
soapest

ŏP′est
choppest
droppest
hoppest
loppest
moppest

overtoppest
poppest
proppest
shoppest
stoppest
toppest

ŏP′et

moppet
poppet

ŏP′eth

copeth
elopeth
gropeth
hopeth
interlopeth
mopeth
ropeth
soapeth

ŏP′eth

choppeth
droppeth
hoppeth
loppeth
moppeth
poppeth
proppeth
shoppeth
stoppeth
toppeth

ŏP′ful

hopeful
unhopeful

ŏP′hed

hophead

ŏP′i

dopey

mopy
ropy
slopy
soapy

ŏP′ī

Pop-eye

ŏP′ĭ

choppy
copy
croppy
droppy
floppy
hoppy
loppy
moppy
poppy
shoppy
sloppy
soppy

ŏP′ij

proppage
stoppage

ŏP′ik

acopic
allotropic
anthropic
canopic
Cyclopic
dichroscopic
eletroscopic
Ethiopic
galvanoscopic
geotropic
helioscopic
heliotropic
horoscopic
hydroscopic

hygroscopic
isotropic
kaleidoscopic
laryngoscopic
metopic
metoscopic
microscopic
misanthropic
myopic
necroscopic
pantascopic
periscopic
philanthropic
presbyopic
psilanthropic
spectroscopic
stereoscopic
stethoscopic
telescopic
theanthropic
theophilan-
　　thropic
topic
tropic

ŏP′iks

topics
tropics

ŏP′ing

coping
doping
eloping
groping
hoping
interloping
loping
moping
roping
sloping
soaping

stoping
toping

ŏP′ing

bedropping
chopping
clip-clopping
copping
cropping
dropping
eavesdropping
flopping
hopping
lopping
mopping
overtopping
plopping
popping
propping
shopping
slopping
sopping
stopping
stropping
swapping
topping
Wapping
whopping

ŏP′ish

mopish
popish

ŏP′ish

foppish
shoppish

ŏP″l

estoppel
hopple
popple

stopple
topple

ŎP'les
hopeless
popeless
soapless

ŎP'ling
fopling
toppling

ŎP'ment
elopement

Ŏ'pô
pawpaw

Ŏ'pok
slowpoke

ŎP'shun
adoption
option

ŎP'si
copsy
dropsy
Mopsy
Topsy

ŎP'sis
ampelopsis
lycopsis
synopsis
thanatopsis

ŎP'stur
dopester

ŎP'ted
adopted
co-opted

ŎP'tik
autoptic
Coptic
optic
synoptic

ŎP'trik
catadioptric
catoptric
dioptric

ŎP'ur
coper
doper
eloper
groper
interloper
moper
roper
sloper
soaper
toper

ŎP'ur
pauper
scauper

ŎP'ur
chopper
clodhopper
copper
cropper
dropper
eaves-dropper
finale-hopper
grasshopper
hopper
improper
lopper
mopper
overtopper

plopper
popper
proper
propper
shopper
sopper
stopper
swapper
tiptopper
topper
whopper

Ŏ'pus
Canopus
lagopous
Lagopus
opus

Ō'ra
Angora
aurora
Cora
Dora
dumb Dora
Eldora
Endora
flora
Floradora
Leonora
Marmora
Masora
Nora
Pandora
passiflora
signora
Theodora
Torah

ŎR'a
aura
Chamæsaura

Laura
Maura

ŎR'ā
foray

ŎR'ă
Andorra
Gomorrah

Ō'raks
borax
corax
storax
thorax

Ō'ral
auroral
chloral
choral
floral
horal
oral
sororal
thoral
trifloral

ŎR'al
aural
binaural
(cf. laurel)

ŎR'al
coral
immoral
moral
quarrel
sorrel
(cf. laurel)

ŎR'anj
orange

ŌR'ant
soarant
vorant

Ō'rat
chlorate
deflorate
perchlorate

ŌR'at
inaurate
instaurate

ŌR'bi
corbie
orby

ŌR'bid
morbid

ŌR'bing
absorbing
orbing
resorbing

ŌR'b'l
corbel
warble

ŌR'blur
warbler

**ŌR'chard, ŌR'-
churd**
orchard
tortured

ŌR'chur
scorcher
torcher

ŌR'dan
Jordan
(cf. ŌR'don)

ŌR'dans
accordance
concordance
discordance

ŌR'dant
accordant
concordant
disaccordant
discordant
inaccordant
mordant

ŌR'ded
afforded
boarded
forded
hoarded
sworded
unforded
unhoarded
uphoarded

ŌR'ded
accorded
awarded
belorded
chorded
corded
lorded
recorded
rewarded
swarded
unlorded
unrecorded
unrewarded
warded
(cf. sordid)

ŌR'den
warden
way-warden

ŌR'dest
boardest
fordest
hoardest

ŌR'dest
accordest
awardest
belordest
lordest
recordest
rewardest
wardest

ŌR'deth
boardeth
fordeth
hoardeth

ŌR'deth
accordeth
awardeth
belordeth
cordeth
lordeth
recordeth
rewardeth
wardeth

ŌRD'ful
discordful
rewardful

ŌR'did
sordid
(cf. accorded,
etc.)

ŌR'dij
boardage
bordage

ŌR'dij
cordage

ŌR'ding
affording
boarding
fording
hoarding
unhoarding
uphoarding
weather-board-
ing

ŌR'ding
according
awarding
belording
cording
lording
recording
rewarding
unrecording
unrewarding
warding

ŌRD'li
lordly
unlordly

ŌR'don
cordon
Gordon

ŌRD'ship
lordship
wardship

ŌR'dur
boarder
forder
hoarder

āle, câre, ădd, ärm, åsk; mē, hĕre, ĕnd; īce, ĭll;

parlor-
 boarder

ŌR'dur
accorder
awarder
border
corder
disorder
emborder
money-order
order
recorder
reorder
rewarder
unorder
warder

ŌR'durd
bordered
disordered
ordered
reordered
well-ordered

ŌRDZ'man
swordsman

ŌR'ed
forehead

ŌR'el, ŌR'el
laurel
(cf. ŌR'al,
 ŌR'al)

ŌR'en, ŌR'an
sporran
warren

ŌR'ens
abhorrence

Lawrence
St. Lawrence

ŌR'ens
Dorrance
Florence
(cf. torrents,
 etc.)

ŌR'ent, ŌR'ant
death-warrant
horrent
torrent
warrant
(cf. abhôrrent)

ŌR'est
adorest
borest
deplorest
encorest
explorest
floorest
gorest
hoarest
ignorest
implorest
outsoarest
porest
pourest
restorest
roarest
scorest
snorest
soarest
sorest
storest

ŌR'est
abhorrest
warrest

ŌR'est
afforest
disafforest
enforest
forest

ŌR'eth
adoreth
boreth
deploreth
encoreth
exploreth
flooreth
goreth
ignoreth
imploreth
outsoareth
poreth
poureth
restoreth
roareth
scoreth
snoreth
soareth
storeth

ŌR'eth
abhorreth
warreth

ŌR'fan
orphan

ŌR'fik
allomorphic
anthropo-
 morphic
automorphic
dimorphic
endomorphic
heteromorphic
ichthyomor-
 phic
idiomorphic
isomorphic
metamorphic
morphic
ophiomorphic
Orphic
pantamorphic
polymorphic
protomorphic
pseudomor-
 phic
theormorphic
trimorphic
zoomorphic

ŌR'fing
dwarfing
wharfing

ŌR'fist
anthropomor-
 phist
metamorphist
wharfist

ŌR'fit
forfeit

ŌR'fizm
allomorphism
amorphism
anamorphism
anthropomor-
 phism
automorphism
dimorphism
isodimorphism
isomeromor-
 phism

ōld, ôr, ŏdd, oil, fŏŏt, out; ūse, ûrn, ŭp; THis, thin

isomorphism
isotrimor-
　phism
metamorphism
monomor-
　phism
pleomorphism
polymorphism
trimorphism
zoomorphism

ŌR'fūs

Morpheus
Orpheus

ŌR'fŭs

amorphous
anthropomor-
　phous
dimorphous
isodimor-
　phous
isomorphous
isotrimorphous
ophiomorphous
paramor-
　phous
polymor-
　phous
trimorphous

ŌR'gan

barrel-organ
Dorgan
Morgan
morgen
organ

ŌR'hand

aforehand
beforehand
forehand

ŌR'hous

storehouse
whorehouse

Ō'ri

abbreviatory
abjuratory
absolutory
acceleratory
acclamatory
accusatory
additory
adhortatory
adjuratory
admonitory
adulatory
a fortiori
allegory
amatory
ambagitory
ambulatory
amendatory
annotatory
annunciatory
a posteriori
appellatory
applicatory
appreciatory
approbatory
a priori
aratory
aspiratory
asseveratory
assimilatory
auditory
auxiliatory
basement-story
bibitory
cachinnatory
calculatory
calumniatory

castigatory
category
circulatory
commandatory
commemora-
　tory
commendatory
comminatory
communicatory
compellatory
compensatory
conciliatory
condemnatory
confabulatory
confirmatory
confiscatory
congratulatory
conservatory
consolatory
contributory
corroboratory
crematory
criminatory
damnatory
declamatory
declaratory
dedicatory
defamatory
delineatory
demonstratory
denunciatory
depilatory
depository
deprecatory
depreciatory
depredatory
derogatory
designatory
desultory
dictatory
dilatory

disapprobatory
discriminatory
dispensatory
dormitory
dory
edificatory
ejaculatory
emendatory
emulatory
exaggeratory
exclamatory
exculpatory
execratory
executory
exhortatory
expiatory
expiratory
explanatory
expostulatory
expurgatory
extenuatory
exterminatory
extirpatory
feudatory
flory
frigeratory
funambulatory
gesticulatory
gladiatory
glory
gory
gradatory
grallatory
gratulatory
gustatory
gyratory
habilatory
hallucinatory
hoary
hortatory
hunky-dory

āle, câre, ădd, ärm, åsk; mē, hẹre, ĕnd; īce, ĭll;

imperatory	osculatory	restoratory	**ŌR'i**
imprecatory	pacificatory	retaliatory	Laurie
improvisatory	palliatory	retardatory	Maury
incantatory	peremptory	retributory	
incriminatory	perfumatory	reverberatory	**ŎR'i**
incubatory	perspiratory	revocatory	Corrie
inculpatory	piscatory	rogatory	Florrie
indicatory	plauditory	rotatory	lorry
inflammatory	postulatory	sacrificatory	quarry
initiatory	potatory	saltatory	sorry
inspiratory	predatory	salutatory	(cf. ÄR'ĭ)
interlocutory	predicatory	sanatory	
interrogatory	prefatory	sanitory	**ŌR'id**
inventory	premonitory	shory	gloried
investigatory	preparatory	sibilatory	storied
invitatory	probatory	signatory	
invocatory	procrastinatory	significatory	**ŎR'id**
jaculatory	procuratory	simulatory	florid
judicatory	profanatory	snory	horrid
laboratory	prohibitory	speculatory	torrid
laudatory	promissory	sternutatory	
libatory	promontory	stillatory	**ŌR'ij**
liberatory	pronunciatory	story	shorage
lory	propitiatory	stridulatory	storage
Maggiore	punitory	sublimatory	
mandatory	purgatory	sudatory	**ŎR'ij**
masticatory	purificatory	supplicatory	borage
migratory	recommenda-	terminatory	forage
monitory	tory	territory	
narratory	recriminatory	tory	**Ō'rik**
natatory	reformatory	transitory	chloric
negatory	refrigeratory	transpiratory	choric
negotiatory	refutatory	undulatory	euchloric
nugatory	regeneratory	usurpatory	hydrochloric
oary	remuneratory	vacillatory	perchloric
objurgatory	repertory	vain-glory	roric
obligatory	repository	vehiculatory	
observatory	reprobatory	vibratory	**ŎR'ĭk**
offertory	reptatory	vindicatory	allegoric
oratory	requisitory	vomitory	amphigoric
oscillatory	respiratory	whory	amphoric

armoric
caloric
camphoric
Doric
elydoric
historic
lithophosphoric
metaphoric
meteoric
paregoric
peloric
phantasmagoric
phosphoric
pictoric
plethoric
prehistoric
prophoric
pyloric
Pythagoric
semaphoric
sophomoric
theoric
zoophoric
zoosporic

Ō'rin
florin

ŌR'ing
adoring
boring
choring
deploring
encoring
exploring
flooring
goring
ignoring
imploring
Loring
outsoaring

poring
pouring
restoring
roaring
scoring
shoring
snoring
soaring
storing
upsoaring

ŌR'ing
abhorring
warring

ŌR'is
Doris
loris

ŌR'is
Doris

ŌR'is
doch-an-dorris
Doris
Horace
loris
morris
orris

ŌR'ja
Borgia
Georgia

ŌR'jal,
   ŌRD'yal
cordial

ŌR'ji
orgy

porgy
storge

ŌR'jing
forging

ŌR'jiz
Georges
George's
orgies, etc.

ŌR'jur
forger

ŌR'jus
gorgeous

ŌR'kas
Dorcas

ŌR'ki
corky
forky

ŌR'kid
orchid

ŌR'king
corking
Dorking
forking
uncorking

ŌR'les
coreless
oarless
oreless
shoreless

ŌR'li
schorly
warly

ŌR'ling
shoreling

ŌR'lok
forelock
oarlock

ŌR'lok
warlock

ŌR'mal
abnormal
anormal
cormal
formal
informal
normal
uniformal
(cf. cormel)

ŌR'man
doorman
floorman
foreman
longshoreman
shoreman

ŌR'man,
   ŌR'mon
Gorman
Mormon
Norman
O'Gorman

ŌR'mans
conformance
dormance
performance

ŌR'mant
conformant
dormant
informant

āle, câre, ădd, ärm, åsk; mē, hĕre, ĕnd; īce, ĭll;

ŌR'ment
adorement
deplorement
explorement
ignorement
implorement
restorement

ŌR'ment
torment

ŌR'mest
conformest
deformest
formest
informest
performest
reformest
stormest
swarmest
transformest
warmest

ŌR'meth
conformeth
deformeth
formeth
informeth
performeth
reformeth
stormeth
swarmeth
transformeth
warmeth

ŌR'mi
dormy
stormy
swarmy

ŌR'ming
bestorming

conforming
deforming
forming
informing
nonconforming
performing
reforming
storming
swarming
transforming
warming

ŌR'mist
conformist
nonconformist
reformist

ŌRM'les
formless
stormless

ŌRM'li
warmly
uniformly

ŌR'most
foremost
head-foremost

ŌR'mur
barn-stormer
conformer
deformer
dormer
foot-warmer
former
informer
performer
reformer
stormer
swarmer

transformer
warmer

ŌR'mus
abnormous
cormous
cormus
enormous
multiformous

ŌR'na
cromorna
Lorna
Norna

ŌR'nat
ornate

ŌR'nes
soreness

ŌR'nest
adornest
bescornest
forewarnest
scornest
subornest
warnest

ŌR'net
cornet
hornet

ŌR'neth
adorneth
bescorneth
forewarneth
scorneth
suborneth
warneth

ŌRN'ful
mournful

ŌRN'ful
scornful

ŌR'ni
corny
Hornie
horny
thorny

ŌR'ning
mourning

ŌR'ning
adorning
bescorning
dehorning
dishorning
forewarning
good-morning
horning
morning
scorning
suborning
yester-morning
warning

ŌR'nis
Aepyornis
cornice
Dinornis
Gastornis
Heliornis
Ichthyornis

ŌR'nish
Cornish
hornish

ŌRN'les
hornless

---

scornless
thornless

ÔRN'ment
adornment

ÔR'nun
forenoon

ÔR'nur
mourner

ÔR'nur
adorner
bescorner
chimney-corner
corner
forewarner
horner
scorner
suborner
warner

Ô'ro
Moro
toro

ÔR'o
amorrow
borrow
good-morrow
morrow
sorrow
to-morrow

ÔR'od
borrowed
sorrowed
unsorrowed

ÔR'old
Thorold
(cf. quarrelled)

ÔR'or
horror

ÔR'pid
torpid

ÔR'por
torpor

ÔR'sal
dextrorsal
dorsal
dorsel
morsel
torsel

ÔR'sen
coarsen
hoarsen

ÔR'sest
coarsest
coursest
discoursest
divorcest
enforcest
forcest
hoarsest
reinforcest

ÔR'sest
endorsest, etc.

ÔR'seth
courseth
discourseth
divorceth
enforceth
forceth
reinforceth

ÔR'seth
endorseth, etc.

ÔRS'ful
forceful
resourceful

ÔRS'ful
remorseful

ÔR'shun
apportion
disproportion
portion
proportion

ÔR'shun
abortion
consortion
contortion
detortion
distortion
extorsion
intorsion
retortion
torsion

ÔR'shund
apportioned
disproportioned
portioned
proportioned
unportioned

ÔR'si
gorsy
horsy

ÔR'sing
coursing
discoursing
divorcing
enforcing
forcing
reinforcing

ÔR'siv
discoursive
divorcive
enforcive

ÔRS'les
forceless
resourceless
sourceless

ÔRS'les
horseless
remorseless

ÔRS'man
horseman
lighthorseman
Norseman

ÔRS'ment
deforcement
divorcement
enforcement
forcement
reinforcement

ÔRS'ment
endorsement

ÔRS'nes
coarseness
hoarseness

ÔR'som
foursome

ÔR'son
Orson

ÔR'song
warsong

āle, câre, ădd, ärm, åsk; mē, hĕre, ĕnd; īce, ĭll;

ŌR'sur

coarser
courser
discourser
divorcer
enforcer
forcer
hoarser
reinforcer

ŌR'sur

endorser

ŌR'tal

portal
transportal

ŌR'tal

aortal
immortal
mortal
(cf. ŌRT"l)

ŌR'tans

supportance
transportance

ŌR'tans

importance

ŌR'tant

important

ŌR'ted

courted
disported
exported
imported
reported
sported
supported
transported

ÔR'ted

aborted
assorted
consorted
contorted
detorted
distorted
escorted
exhorted
extorted
resorted
retorted
snorted
sorted
thwarted
unsorted

ÔR'teks

cortex
vortex

ŌR'tem

post-mortem

ŌR'ten

shorten

ŌR'tent

portent

ŌR'test

courtest
disportest
exportest
importest
reportest
sportest
supportest
transportest

ÔR'test

assortest
consortest
contortest
detortest
distortest
escortest
exhortest
extortest
resortest
retortest
shortest
snortest
sortest
swartest
thwartest

ŌR'teth

courteth
disporteth
exporteth
importeth
reporteth
sporteth
supporteth
transporteth

ÔR'teth

assorteth
consorteth
contorteth
detorteth
distorteth
escorteth
exhorteth
extorteth
resorteth
retorteth
snorteth
sorteth
thwarteth

ŌRT'gid

court-guide
port-guide

ÔR'thi

swarthy

ŌR'ti

forty
pianoforte
snorty
sortie
swarty
warty

ŌR'tij

shortage

ŌR'tim

aforetime
beforetime

ŌR'ting

courting
deporting
disporting
exporting
importing
reporting
sporting
supporting
transporting

ÔR'ting

aborting
assorting
consorting
contorting
detorting
distorting
escorting

exhorting
extorting
resorting
retorting
snorting
sorting
thwarting

ŌR'tiv

sportive
transportive

ÔR'tiv

abortive
contortive
distortive
ortive
retortive
tortive

ÔRT"l

chortle
whortle
(cf. ÔR'tal)

ÔRT'land

Courtland
Portland

ÔRT'li

courtly
portly
uncourtly

ÔRT'li

shortly

ÔRT'ment

comportment
deportment

disportment
transportment

ÔRT'ment

assortment

ÔRT'nes

swartness
thwartness

ÔRT'nit

fortnight

ÔR'ton

Horton
Morton
Norton

ÔR'trat

portrait

ÔR'tres

fortress

ÔRT'ship

courtship

ÔRTS'man

sportsman

ÔR'tun

befortune
enfortune
fortune
importune
misfortune

ÔR'tur

courter
disporter
exporter
importer

porter
reporter
sporter
supporter
transporter

ÔR'tūr

torture

ÔR'tŭr

assorter
consorter
contorter
detorter
distorter
escorter
exhorter
extorter
mortar
quarter
resorter
retorter
shorter
snorter
sorter
thwarter
weather-
    quarter
woolsorter

**ÔR'turd,
    ÔR'chard**

orchard
tortured

ÔR'turz

winter-quarters
assorters, etc.

ÔRT'wav

short-wave

Ō'rum

decorum
forum
indecorum
jorum
quorum
variorum
cf. ad valorem

ŌR'ur

adorer
borer
corer
decorer
deplorer
encorer
explorer
floorer
gorer
ignorer
implorer
outpourer
outsoarer
porer
pourer
restorer
roarer
scorer
snorer
soarer
sorer
storer

Ō'rus

canorous
chorus
decorous
Horus
imporous
indecorous
porous

āle, câre, ădd, ärm, åsk; mē, hĕre, ĕnd; īce, ĭll;

pylorus	Formosa	swashy	**ŎSH'un**
sonorous	mimosa	toshy	caution
torous		washy	incaution
torus	**ŎS'chun**	wishy-washy	precaution
	exhaustion		
ŌR'us		**ŎSH'ing**	**ŌSH'us**
brontosaurus	**ŌS'est**	sloshing	atrocious
dolichosaurus	closest, etc.	squashing	ferocious
hadrosaurus	grossest	swashing	nepotious
ichthyosaurus	*dosest,* etc.	washing	precocious
megalosaurus			
mososaurus	**ŎS'est**	**ŌSH'ur**	**ŎSH'us**
nanosaurus	*crossest*	gaucher	cautious
pleiosaurus	*embossest*	kosher	incautious
plesiosaurus	*glossest*		precautious
protosaurus	*tossest*	**ŎSH'ur**	
regnosaurus		cosher	**ŎS'i**
Taurus	**ŎS'et**	josher	saucy
teleosaurus	faucet	squasher	
thesaurus		swasher	**ŎS'i**
tyranosaurus	**ŎS'et**	washer	bossy
	bosset		drossy
ŌR'ward	cosset	**Ō'shun**	Flossie
foreward	posset	Bœotian	flossy
shoreward	sack-posset	commotion	glossy
		devotion	mossy
ŎR'ward	**ŎS'eth**	emotion	posse
forward	*crosseth*	groschen	tossy
henceforward	*embosseth*	indevotion	
norward	*glosseth*	locomotion	**ŎS'ij**
straightforward	*tosseth*	lotion	sausage
thenceforward		motion	
	Ō'shal	nicotian	**ŎS'ik**
ŎR'worn	antisocial	notion	fossick
war-worn	intersocial	ocean	glossic
	social	potion	
ŌRZ'man		prenotion	**ŎS'il**
oarsman	**ŎSH'i**	promotion	docile
	boshy	promotion	indocile
Ō'sa	sloshy	remotion	
amorosa	squashy	self-devotion	**ŎS'il**
			docile

dossil
fossil
(see ŎS"l)

ŎS'ing

dosing
engrossing

ŎS'ing

bossing
crossing
dossing
embossing
glossing
railway-
  crossing
tossing

ŎS'ip

gossip

Ō'sis

anadiplosis
anamorphosis
ankylosis
apotheosis
carcinosis
chlorosis
cirrhosis
diagnosis
enantiosis
endosmosis
epanadiplosis
epanorthosis
exosmosis
geognosis
heliosis
heterosis
hypnosis
hypotyposis
ichthyosis

meiosis
metasomatosis
metem-
  psychosis
metemptosis
metensomatosis
morosis
morphosis
narcosis
necrosis
neurosis
osmosis
proemptosis
prognosis
psychosis
ptosis
pyrosis
sarcosis
scirrhosis
sorosis
tuberculosis
zygosis
zymosis

ŎS'is

proboscis

ŎS'iv

corrosive
erosive
explosive
inexplosive

ŎS'kar

Oscar

ŎS'ki

bosky

ŎS"l

apostle

colossal
dosel
dossil
fossil
hypoglossal
jostle
throstle
tossel
wassail

ŎS'lur

hostler
jostler
Rossler

ŎS'li

crossly

ŎS'nes

closeness
grossness
jocoseness
moroseness
verboseness

Ō'so

amoroso
arioso
doloroso
gracioso
so-so
virtuoso

ŎS'om

blossom
odontoglossum
opossum
orangeblossom
possum

ŎS'on

Dawson

Lawson
Rawson

ŎS'pel

gospel

ŎS'pish

waspish

ŎS'pur

prosper

ŎS'tal

coastal
postal

ŎS'tal

costal
infracostal
intercostal
Pentecostal
supra-costal

ŎS'tat

apostate
laticostate
quadricostate

ŎS'ted

boasted
coasted
posted
roasted
toasted
unposted

ŎS'ted

exhausted

ŎS'ted

accosted
frosted

āle, câre, ădd, ärm, åsk; mē, hĕre, ĕnd; īce, ĭll;

ŎS'tel, ŎS″l
hostel

ÔS'ten
Austen

ŎS'tes
hostess

ŎS'test
boastest
coastest
postest
roastest
toastest

ŌS'teth
boasteth
coasteth
posteth
roasteth
toasteth

ŌST'hous
oasthouse
post-house

ŎS'ti
frosty

ŎS'tij
postage

ŎS'tij
hostage

ÔS'tik
catacaustic
caustic
diacaustic
encaustic

ŎS'tik
acrostic
agnostic
diagnostic
eteostic
geognostic
gnostic
paracrostic
pentacostic
prognostic

ŎS'til
hostile

ÔS'tin
Austin

ŌS'ting
boasting
coasting
posting
roasting
toasting

ŎS'ting
exhausting

ŎS'ting
accosting
costing
frosting

ŎS'tiv
exhaustive
inexhaustive

ŎS'tiv
costive

ŌST'li
ghostly
mostly

ŎST'li
costly

ŌST'man
postman

ŌST'mark
postmark

ŎS'ton
Boston

Ô'storm
snow-storm

ŎS'tral
austral
claustral

ŎS'tral, ŎS'trel
costrel
lamellirostral
longirostral
rostral
(cf. nostril)

ŎS'trat
prostrate
rostrate

ŎS'trich
ostrich

ŎS'trum
nostrum
rostrum

ŎS'tum
costume

ŌS'tur
boaster

coaster
four-poster
poster
roaster
throwster
toaster

ŎS'tur
auster
exhauster

ŎS'tūr
imposture
posture

ŎS'tŭr
accoster
coster
foster
Gloucester
imposter
Paternoster
pentecoster
roster

ŎS'turn
postern

ŎS'tus
Faustus

ŌS'ur
closer
doser
engrosser
grocer
grosser
jocoser
moroser

ÔS'ur
Chaucer

ōld, ôr, ŏdd, oil, fŏŏt, out; ūse, ûrn, ŭp; THis, thin

Naw sir	**ŌT'at**	jotted	*denotest*
saucer	*denotate*	knotted	*devotest*
	notate	lotted	*dotest*
ŎS'ur	rotate	plotted	*floatest*
bosser		potted	*gloatest*
crosser	**ŎT'ash**	rotted	*misquotest*
dosser	potash	shotted	*notest*
embosser		slotted	*promotest*
glosser	**ŌT'ed**	sotted	*quotest*
josser	bloated	spotted	*votest*
tosser	boated	squatted	
	coated	totted	**ŎT'est**
ŎS'us	demoted	trotted	*clottest, etc.*
colossus	denoted	unblotted	
molossus	devoted	underplotted	**ŌT'eth**
	doted	unknotted	*demoteth*
Ō'ta	floated	unspotted	*denoteth*
Dakota	gloated	wainscotted	*devoteth*
flota	misquoted	(cf. carotid	*doteth*
iota	moated	and parotid)	*floateth*
Minnesota	noted		*gloateth*
quota	parti-coated	**ŎT'en**	*noteth*
rota	petticoated	oaten	*misquoteth*
	promoted		*promoteth*
ŌT'al	quoted	**ŎT'en, ŎT'on**	*quoteth*
anecdotal	refloated	begotten	*voteth*
antidotal	self-devoted	cotton	
dotal	throated	first-begotten	**ŎT'eth**
extradotal	unnoted	forgotten	*clotteth, etc.*
notal	voted	gotten	
rotal		hard-gotten	**ŎT'ful**
sacerdotal	**ŎT'ed**	ill-gotten	thoughtful
sclerotal	allotted	misbegotten	
teetotal	besotted	misgotten	**Ōth'a**
total	bespotted	rotten	quotha
	blood-bespotted	unbegotten	
ŌT'ant, ŌT'ent	blotted	unforgotten	**Ōth'al**
flotant	cheviotted	ungotten	betrothal
potent	clotted		
prepotent	dotted	**ŎT'est**	**Ōth'am**
	garotted	*demotest*	Gotham
			Jotham

āle, câre, ădd, ärm, åsk; mē, hĕre, ĕnd; īce, ĭll:

ŎTH'am	**Ŏ'thorn**	parotid	erotic
Gotham	Cawthorn	(cf. ŎT+ed)	escharotic
	hawthorn		exotic
ŌTH'est		**ŌT'ij**	glottic
clothest	**ŌTH'som**	anecdotage	henotic
loathest	loathsome	dotage	hidrotic
		floatage	hypnotic
ŌTH'eth	**Ŏth'ur**	flotage	idiotic
clotheth	author		macrobiotic
loatheth		**ŎT'ij**	narcotic
	ŎTH'ur	cottage	nepotic
ŌTH'ful	bother	pottage	neurotic
loathful	fother	wattage	Nilotic
	pother		osmotic
Ōth'ful	(cf. father,	**ŌT'ik**	otic
slothful	rather)	otic	patriotic
			pyrotic
Ŏth'ful	**ŌT'i**	**ŎT'ik**	quixotic
wrathful	bloaty	aeronautic	san-culottic
	coyote	argonautic	sarcotic
Ŏth'i	dhoty	nautic	sclerotic
frothy	Doty		semeiotic
mothy	Doughty	**ŎT'ik**	zootic
	floaty	acrotic	zymotic
Ŏth'ik	goaty	agrypnotic	
Gothic	throaty	anaptotic	**ŌT'ing**
Mœso-gothic		anecdotic	bloating
Ostrogothic	**ÔT'i**	ankylotic	boating
Visigothic	haughty	anti-patriotic	coating
	naughty	aptotic	demoting
ŌTH'ing		aquatic	denoting
clothing	**ŎT'i**	carotic	devoting
loathing	clotty	chaotic	doting
	dotty	chlorotic	floating
Ōth'ment	knotty	cirrhotic	gloating
betrothment	spotty	culottic	misquoting
	totty	demotic	noting
ŌT'hook		despotic	promoting
boathook	**ŎT'id**	endosmotic	quoting
coathook	carotid	epiglottic	throating
		epizootic	voting

ŎT′ing

allotting
besotting
blotting
clotting
dotting
garotting
jotting
knotting
plotting
potting
rotting
sotting
spotting
squatting
totting
trotting
underplotting
unknotting
yatching

ŎT′is

epiglottis
glottis

ŎT′ish

dotish
goatish

ŎT′ish

Scottish
sottish

ŎT′ist

anecdotist
noticed
Scotist
unnoticed

ŎT′ist

sans-culottist

ŎT′iv

emotive
locomotive
motive
promotive
votive

ŎT′kinz

Otkins
Watkins

ŎT″l

bottle
dottle
glottal
mottle
pottle
throttle
tottle
twattle
wattle

ŎT′les

thoughtless

ŎT′les

blotless
clotless
cotless
dotless
jotless
knotless
lotless
potless
rotless
sotless
spotless
totless
trotless

ŎT′li

hotly
motley

ŎT′ling

bottling, etc.

ŎT′man

boatman

ŎT′man

Cotman
Ottman

ŎT′ment

demotement
denotement
devotement

ŎT′ment

allotment
besotment

ŎT′nes

hotness
whatness

Ō′to

De Soto
divoto
ex voto
fagotto
in toto
Kioto
photo

ŎT′o

blotto
grotto
lotto
motto

otto
ridotto
risotto
(cf. staccato)

ŎT′om

bottom

Ō′ton

Croton
proton
(cf. oaten)

Ŏ′ton

Lawton

ŎT′on

cotton
Groton
(see ŎT′en)

ŎT′rel

Cottrell
dottrel

ŎT′si

hotsy-totsy

ŎTS′man

Scotsman
yachtsman

ŎT′son

Watson

Ō′tum

quotum
tee-totum

ŎT′um

autumn

āle, câre, ădd, ärm, ȧsk; mē, hęre, ĕnd; īce, ĭll;

ŌT'ur
bloater
boater
demoter
denoter
devoter
doter
fagot-voter
floater
gloater
locomotor
magnetomotor
motor
noter
promoter
quoter
rotomotor
rotor
scoter
toter
vaso-motor
voter

ŎT'ur
backwater
daughter
fire-water
fizz-water
giggle-water
milk-and-
  water
slaughter
soda-water
water

ŎT'ur
blotter
bogtrotter
clotter
complotter
cotter

dotter
garotter
globe-trotter
hotter
jotter
knotter
ottar
otter
plotter
potter
rotter
spotter
squatter
totter
trotter
underplotter
unknotter
yachter

Ō'tus
Gymnotus
lotus
macrotous

OU'al
avowal
disavowal
(cf. OU″el)

OU'an
gowan
McGowan
rowan
rowen

OU'ans
allowance
avowance
disallowance
disavowance

OU'ard
coward
Howard
(cf. OU'urd)

OUCH'est
avouchest, etc.

OUCH'eth
avoucheth, etc.

OUCH'ing
avouching
couching
crouching
grouching
pouching
slouching
vouching

OUCH'ur
avoucher
coucher
croucher
Goucher
groucher
poucher
sloucher
voucher

OU'da
howdah

OUD'ed
beclouded
clouded
crowded
enshrouded
overclouded
overcrowded
shrouded

unbeclouded
unclouded
unshrouded

OUD'est
becloudest
beshroudest
cloudest
crowdest
enshroudest
loudest
overcloudest
overcrowdest
proudest
shroudest

OUD'eth
becloudeth
beshroudeth
cloudeth
crowdeth
enshroudeth
overcloudeth
overcrowdeth
shroudeth

OUD'ĭ
cloudy
crowdy
dowdy
Gowdy
howdie
howdy
pandowdy
proudy
rowdy
shroudy
uncloudy
(cf. summa
  cum laude)

ōld, ôr, ŏdd, oil, fŏŏt, out; ūse, ûrn, ŭp; THis, thin

OUD'ing
beclouding
beshrouding
clouding
crowding
enshrouding
overclouding
overcrowding
shrouding
unshrouding

OUD'ish
loudish
proudish

OUD'li
loudly
proudly

OUD'nes
loudness
proudness

OUD'ur
baking powder
clam chowder
bepowder
chowder
crowder
louder
powder
prouder
seidlitz-powder

OU'el
bowel
dowel
embowel
Howell
Powell
Prowell

rowel
towel
trowel
vowel
(cf. OU'al)

OU'es
prowess

OU'est
allowest
avowest
bowest
cowest
disallowest
endowest
ploughest
vowest

OU'et
Howett
Jowett

OU'eth
alloweth
avoweth
boweth
coweth
disalloweth
endoweth
plougheth
voweth

OU'i
Dowie
zowie

OU'ing
allowing
avowing
bowing

cowing
disallowing
endowing
ploughing
plowing
rowing
vowing

OUL'est
foulest
growlest
howlest
prowlest
scowlest

OUL'et
owlet

OUL'eth
growleth
howleth
prowleth
scowleth

OU'li
Cowley
Powley
Rowley

OUL'ing
fouling
fowling
growling
howling
prowling
scowling

OUL'ish
foulish
owlish

OUL'ur
fouler
fowler
growler
howler
prowler
scowler
yowler

OU'ment
avowment
endowment

OUN'ded
abounded
astounded
bounded
compounded
confounded
dumfounded
expounded
founded
grounded
hounded
impounded
mounded
pounded
propounded
rebounded
redounded
resounded
rounded
sounded
superabound-
  ed
surrounded
unbounded
unfounded
ungrounded
unsounded

well-founded
wounded

OUN'del
roundel

OUN'den
bounden

OUN'dest
aboundest
astoundest
boundest
compoundest
confoundest
expoundest
foundest
groundest
houndest
impoundest
poundest
profoundest
propoundest
reboundest
resoundest
roundest
soundest
*superabound-
est*
surroundest

OUN'deth
aboundeth
astoundeth
boundeth
compoundeth
confoundeth
dumfoundeth
expoundeth
foundeth
groundeth

houndeth
impoundeth
poundeth
propoundeth
reboundeth
redoundeth
resoundeth
roundeth
soundeth
surroundeth

OUN'dij
groundage
poundage
soundage

OUN'ding
abounding
astounding
big-sounding
bounding
compounding
confounding
dumfounding
expounding
founding
grounding
high-sounding
hounding
impounding
pounding
propounding
rebounding
redounding
resounding
rounding
sounding
superabound-
ing
surrounding

unbounding
wounding

OUND'les
boundless
groundless
soundless

OUND'li
profoundly
roundly
soundly
unsoundly

OUND'ling
foundling
groundling

OUND'nes
profoundness
roundness
soundness
unsoundness

OUN'drel
scoundrel

OUN'dri
foundry

OUN'dur
bounder
compounder
confounder
dumfounder
expounder
flounder
founder
four-pounder
impounder
iron-founder

pounder
profounder
propounder
rebounder
resounder
rounder
sounder
surrounder
type-founder

OUN'est
brownest
crownest
drownest
frownest

OUN'eth
browneth
crowneth
drowneth
frowneth

OUN'i
brownie
browny
downy
frowny
towny

OUN'ing
browning
clowning
crowning
discrowning
downing
drowning
frowning
gowning
intowning
uncrowning

ōld, ôr, ŏdd, oil, fŏŏt, out; ūse, ûrn, ŭp; THis, thin

OUN'ish	denouncement	*recountest*	counter
brownish	pronounce-	*remountest*	discounter
clownish	ment	*surmountest*	encounter
frownish	renouncement		mounter
		OUN'teth	recounter
OUN'jing	**OUN'sur**	*accounteth*	remounter
lounging	announcer	*amounteth*	reencounter
	bouncer	*counteth*	surmounter
OUN'les	denouncer	*discounteth*	
crownless	flouncer	*dismounteth*	**OUN'ur**
frownless	pouncer	*miscounteth*	browner
gownless	pronouncer	*mounteth*	crowner
	renouncer	*recounteth*	drowner
OUN'sest	trouncer	*remounteth*	frowner
announcest, etc.		*surmounteth*	
	OUN'ted		**OUN'ward**
OUN'seth	accounted	**OUN'ti**	downward
announceth, etc.	amounted	bounty	townward
	counted	county	
OUN'sez	discounted	mounty	**OUN'zman**
announces	dismounted	viscounty	gownsman
bounces	miscounted		townsman
denounces	mounted	**OUN'tin**	
flounces	recounted	catamountain	**Ō'ur**
ounces	remounted	fountain	bestower
pounces	surmounted	mountain	blower
pronounces	uncounted		flower
renounces	unmounted	**OUN'ting**	foregoer
trounces	unrecounted	accounting	foreknower
		amounting	foreshower
OUN'sing	**OUN'tes**	counting	glass-blower
announcing	countess	discounting	goer
bouncing		dismounting	glower
denouncing	**OUN'test**	miscounting	grower
flouncing	*accountest*	mounting	hoer
pouncing	*amountest*	recounting	knower
pronouncing	*countest*	remounting	lower
renouncing	*discountest*	surmounting	mower
trouncing	*dismountest*		outgoer
	miscountest	**OUN'tur**	overthrower
OUNS'ment	*mountest*	accounter	ower
announcement			

rower	*devoureth*	doubted	louty
sewer	*scoureth*	flouted	moughty
shower	*soureth*	gouted	pouty
slower		grouted	snouty
sower	**OUR'i**	misdoubted	touty
stower	avowry	pouted	
thrower	cowrie	redoubted	**OUT'ing**
tower	dowry	routed	beshouting
undergoer	floury	scouted	bespouting
wine-grower	houri	shouted	besprouting
	(cf. OU'ur-i)	spouted	clouting
Ō'ur		sprouted	doubting
cawer	**OUR'ing**	undoubted	flouting
clawer	bescouring		grouting
drawer	deflowering	**OUT'est**	louting
gnawer	devouring	*cloutest*	outing
guffawer	flouring	devoutest	pouting
"jawer"	off-scouring	*doubtest*	routing
overawer	scouring	*floutest*	scouting
pawer	souring	*poutest*	shouting
rawer	(cf. OU'ur-	*scoutest*	spouting
sawer	ing)	*shoutest*	sprouting
tawer		*spoutest*	touting
wiredrawer	**OUR'li**	*sproutest*	undoubting
withdrawer	hourly	stoutest	
	sourly		**OUT'let**
Ō'urd, Ō'ard		**OUT'eth**	outlet
lowered	**OUR'nes**	*clouteth*	troutlet
toward	sourness	*doubteth*	
untoward		*flouteth*	**OUT'li**
	OUR'ur	*pouteth*	devoutly
OUR'est	deflowerer	*scouteth*	stoutly
bescourest	devourer	*shouteth*	
deflowerest	scourer	*spouteth*	**OUT'nes**
devourest	sourer	*sprouteth*	devoutness
scourest			stoutness
sourest	**OU'son**	**OUT'i**	
	Dowson	doughty	**OUT'ur**
OUR'eth		droughty	devouter
bescoureth	**OUT'ed**	gouty	doubter
deflowereth	clouted	grouty	

ōld, ôr, ŏdd, oil, fŏŏt, out; ūse, ûrn, ŭp; THis, thin

down-and-
  outer
flouter
jowter
out-and-outer
pouter
router
scouter
shouter
spouter
sprouter
stouter
touter

OU'ur

allower
avower
beacon-tower
beflower
bower
Brower
candle-power
cauliflower
cower
deflower
dower
embower
empower
endower
enflower
flower
glower
horse-power
imbower
lower
overpower
overtower
passion-flower
plougher
plower
power

rower
shower
thunder-show-
  er
tower
vower
water-power
(cf. OUR)

OU'urd

unshowered
untowered
bowered, etc.
(cf. OU'ard)

OU'urz

Powers
avowers, etc.

OU'wou

bow-wow
pow-wow
wow-wow

OU'zal

arousal
carousal
espousal
housel
ousel
spousal
tousle

OU'zand

thousand

OUZ'est

arousest, etc.

OUZ'eth

arouseth, etc.

OUZ'ez

arouses
blouses
browses
carouses
espouses
houses
rouses
spouses

OUZ'i

bowsie
drowzy
frowzy
lousy
mousy

OUZ'ij

espousage
housage
spousage

OUZ'ing

arousing
blowzing
browzing
carousing
housing
rousing

OUZ'ur

arouser
browser
carouser
espouser
mouser
rouser
Towser
trouser

OUZ'urz

trousers
carousers, etc.

Ō'va

Jehovah

Ō'val

oval

ŎV'el

grovel
hovel
novel

ŌV'en

cloven
hoven
interwoven
inwoven
uncloven
woven

ŌV'i

anchovy
covy
grovy

ŌV'in

bovine
ovine

ŌV'ing

roving
shroving

ŌV'o

ab ovo
de novo

ŌV'ur

clover

āle,   câre,   ădd,   ärm,   ăsk;   mē,   hẹre,   ĕnd;   īce,   ĭll;

Dover	ŌZ'al	*imposest*	ŌZ'ez
drover	*desposal*	*inclosest*	Moses
flopover	disposal	*interposest*	roses, etc.
half-seas-over	interposal	*juxtaposest*	
moreover	opposal	*opposest*	ŌZ'ez
over	presupposal	*posest*	causes
plover	proposal	*presupposest*	clauses
pushover	reposal	*proposest*	gauzes
rover	rosal	*recomposest*	pauses
sea-rover	supposal	*reimposest*	vases
stover	transposal	*reposest*	
trover		*superimposest*	ŌZ'ga
walkover	ŌZ'bud	*supposest*	nosegay
	rosebud	*transposest*	
ŎV'urb			Ō'zhan
proverb	ŌZ'div	ŌZ'eth	ambrosian
	nose-dive	*closeth*	(cf. Ō'zi-an,
ŌV'urz		*composeth*	Ō'zi-on)
estovers	ŌZ'en	*decomposeth*	
drovers, etc.	chosen	*deposeth*	Ō'zhun
	forechosen	*discloseth*	corrosion
Ō'ward	frozen	*discomposeth*	erosion
froward	*hosen*	*disposeth*	explosion
	Posen	*dozeth*	implosion
Ō'whar	*rosen*	*encloseth*	(cf. Ō'zi-an,
nowhere	squozen	*exposeth*	etc.)
		imposeth	
Ō'yez	ŎZ'enj	*incloseth*	Ō'zhur
oyez	lozenge	*intercloseth*	crosier
		interposeth	Dozier
Ō'yur	ŌZ'est	*juxtaposeth*	hosier
bowyer	*closest*	*opposeth*	osier
oyer	*composest*	*poseth*	
	decomposest	*presupposeth*	ŌZ'ĭ
Ŏ'yur	*deposest*	*proposeth*	
lawyer	*disclosest*	*recomposeth*	cozy
sawyer	*discomposest*	*reimposeth*	dozy
topsawyer	*disposest*	*reposeth*	nosy
	dozest	*superimposeth*	posy
ŌZ'a	*enclosest*	*supposeth*	prosy
Rosa	*exposest*	*transposeth*	rosy
Spinoza			

ōld, ôr, ŏdd, oil, fŏŏt, out; ūse, ûrn, ŭp; THis, thin

ŎZ'i
gauzy
causey

ŌZ'id
posied
rosied

ŎZ'ing
closing
composing
decomposing
deposing
disclosing
discomposing
disposing
dozing
enclosing
exposing
imposing
inclosing
interposing
juxtaposing
nosing
opposing
posing
predisposing
presupposing
proposing

prosing
recomposing
reposing
supposing
transposing
unclosing
unimposing

ŎZ'ing
causing
pausing

ŎZ'it
closet
deposit
interposit
juxtaposit
posit
reposit

ŎZ'iv
applausive
plausive
unapplausive

ŎZ"l
nozzle
schnozzle
sozzle

ŎZ'mik
cosmic
endosmic
microcosmic

ŌZ'o
bozo

ŌZ'on
ozone

ŌZ'ūr
closure
composure
disclosure
discomposure
disposure
exposure
foreclosure
inclosure
reposure

ŌZ'ŭr
bulldozer
closer
composer
deposer
discloser

disposer
dozer
encloser
exposer
forecloser
glozer
imposer
incloser
interposer
juxtaposer
opposer
poser
predisposer
presupposer
proposer
roser
reimposer
reposer
superimposer
supposer
transposer
uncloser

ŎZ'ur
causer
hawser
pauser

āle, câre, ădd, ärm, åsk; mē, hẹre, ĕnd; īce, ĭll;

U

For a discussion of words included under the accented vowels following, see the beginning of U rhymes in Section I.

Ū'al
dual
eschewal
pursual
renewal
reviewal
subdual
(cf. Ū'el)

Ū'an
Chouan
duan
Peguan

Ū'ans
eschewance
pursuance
renewance

Ū'ant
pursuant
truant

Ū'ard
leeward
steward
(see Ū'urd)

Ū'ba
Cuba
juba
tuba

Ū'ben
Reuben

Steuben
(cf. Lubin)

ŪB'i
booby
looby
ruby

ŬB'i
bubby
chubby
cubby
fubby
grubby
hubby
nubby
rabi
rubby
scrubby
shrubby
stubby
tubby

ŪB'id
rubied

ŬB'ik
cherubic
cubic
pubic

ŪB'ing
cubing
tubing

ŬB'ing
blubbing
clubbing
drubbing
dubbing
grubbing
nubbing
rubbing
scrubbing
snubbing
stubbing
subbing
tubbing

ŬB'ish
clubbish
cubbish
grubbish
rubbish
tubbish

ŬB'it
cubit

ŬB'jekt
subject

Ū'b'l
ruble

ŬB''l
bubble
double
grubble
Hubbell

hubble-bubble
nubble
redouble
rubble
stubble
trouble

ŬB''ld
bubbled
doubled
redoubled
stubbled
troubled
untroubled

ŬB'lest
bubblest, etc.

ŬB'let
doublet

ŬB'leth
bubbleth, etc.

ŬB'li
bubbly
doubly
knubbly
nubbly
rubbly
stubbly

ŬB'lik
public
republic

ŬB'ling
bubbling
doubling
troubling

ŬB'lish
publish

ŬB'lur
bubbler
doubler
troubler

ŬB'lus
troublous

ŬB'orn
stubborn

ŪB'rik
lubric
rubric

ŬB'stak
grubstake

ŬB'stans
substance

ŬB'ur
goober
Huber
tuber

ŬB'ur
blubber
clubber
drubber
dubber
grubber
india-rubber

landlubber
lubber
money-grub-
    ber
rubber
scrubber
slubber
snubber
stubber
tubber
tub-drubber

ŬB'urd
blubbered
cupboard
Hubbard
mother hub-
    bard
rubbered

ŪB'urt
Hubert

ŬCH'es
archduchess
duchess
Dutchess

ŬCH'est
clutchest, etc.

ŬCH'eth
clutcheth, etc.

ŬCH'ez
clutches
crutches
hutches
retouches
scutches
smutches
touches

ŬCH'i
coochy
hoochy-coochy

ŬCH'i
archduchy
clutchy
duchy
smutchy
touchy

ŬCH'ing
clutching
retouching
scutching
smutching
touching

ŬCH'on
escutcheon

ŬCH'ur
retoucher
scutcher
smutcher
toucher

Ū'da
Barbuda
barracuda
Bermuda
Buddha
Ishkooda
Judah

Ū'dad
doodad

ŪD'al
feudal

paludal
udal

ŪD'ed
alluded
brooded
colluded
concluded
deluded
denuded
detruded
duded
eluded
excluded
extruded
exuded
illuded
included
interluded
intruded
obtruded
occluded
precluded
preluded
protruded
recluded
retruded
secluded
snooded
subtruded
transuded
undeluded

ŬD'ed
bestudded
blooded
budded
flooded
scudded
spudded
studded

thudded
(cf. muddied,
    etc.)

ŬD'en

sudden

ŬD'ens

jurisprudence
prudence

ŬD'ent

concludent
imprudent
jurisprudent
occludent
prudent
student

ŬD'est

alludest
broodest
concludest
crudest
deludest
denudest
detrudest
eludest
excludest
extrudest
exudest
illudest
includest
intrudest
nudest
obtrudest
precludest
preludest
protrudest
recludest
retrudest

rudest
secludest
shrewdest
subtrudest

ŬD'eth

alludeth
broodeth
colludeth
concludeth
deludeth
denudeth
detrudeth
eludeth
excludeth
extrudeth
exudeth
illudeth
includeth
intrudeth
obtrudeth
occludeth
preludeth
protrudeth
retrudeth
recludeth
secludeth
subtrudeth
transudeth

ŬD'i

broody
moody
scudi

ŬD'i

bloody
buddy
cuddy
muddy
puddy

ruddy
studdy
study

ŬD'id

bloodied
muddied
ruddied
studied
unstudied
(cf. studded,
    etc.)

ŬD'ing

abrooding
alluding
brooding
concluding
deluding
denuding
detruding
eluding
excluding
extruding
exuding
illuding
including
intruding
obtruding
occluding
precluding
preluding
protruding
recluding
retruding
secluding
snooding
subtruding
transuding

ŬD'ing

bestudding

budding
flooding
scudding
spudding
studding

ŬD'ish

prudish
rudish
shrewdish

ŬD'ith

Judith

ŬD''l

boodle
caboodle
canoodle
flapdoodle
kiyoodle
noodle
poodle
Yankee-doodle

ŬD''l

bemuddle
buddle
cuddle
fuddle
huddle
muddle
nuddle
puddle
ruddle
scuddle

ŬD'lest

bemuddlest, etc.

ŬD'leth

bemuddleth, etc.

ŪD′li
crudely
lewdly
nudely
rudely
shrewdly

ŬD′li
Dudley

ŬD′ling
bemuddling
cuddling
fuddling
huddling
muddling
puddling
scuddling

ŬD′lum
hoodlum

ŬD′lur
cuddler
fuddler
huddler
muddler
puddler

ŪD′nes
lewdness
nudeness
crudeness
rudeness
shrewdness

ŬD′ok
puddock
ruddock

ŪD′os
kudos

ŬD′son
Hudson
Judson

ŪD′ur
alluder
brooder
concluder
cruder
deluder
denuder
detruder
eluder
excluder
extruder
exuder
illuder
includer
intruder
obtruder
occluder
precluder
preluder
protruder
recluder
retruder
ruder
secluder
shrewder
subtruder
transuder
Tudor

ŬD′ur
dudder
flooder
mudder
pudder
rudder
scudder

shudder
udder

ŬD′zi
sudsy

Ū′e
cooee
(see Ū′i)

Ū′el
bejewel
crewel
cruel
duel
fuel
gruel
Hewell
jewel
newel
Reuel
Sewell
tewel
(cf. Ū′al)

Ū′es
Jewess

Ū′est
accruest
bedewest
beshrewest
bluest
brewest
chewest
cooest
doest
drewest
enduest
ensuest

eschewest
fewest
flewest
gluest
grewest
hallooest
hewest
imbrewest
imbuest
interviewest
knewest
mewest
newest
pursuest
renewest
reviewest
ruest
screwest
shampooest
shoest
shooest
spuest
stewest
strewest
subduest
suest
tattooest
threwest
truest
undoest
unscrewest
untruest
ungluest
viewest
withdrewest
wooest

Ū′et
cruet
suet

Ŭ'eth

accrueth
bedeweth
beshreweth
breweth
cheweth
cooeth
doeth
dreweth
endueth
ensueth
escheweth
glueth
greweth
hallooeth
heweth
imbreweth
imbueth
intervieweth
kneweth
meweth
pursueth
reneweth
revieweth
rueth
screweth
shampooeth
shoeth
shooeth
speweth
steweth
subdueth
sueth
streweth
tabooeth
tattooeth
threweth
undoeth
unglueth
unscreweth
vieweth

withdreweth
wooeth

Ū'fa

chufa
stufa
tufa
Ufa

Ū'feld

Bluefield
Newfield

ŬF'en

roughen
toughen

ŬF'est

bepuffest
bluffest
cuffest
gruffest
luffest
muffest
puffest
rebuffest
roughest
sloughest
snuffest
stuffest
toughest

ŬF'et

buffet

ŬF'eth

bluffeth, etc.

ŬF'hous

roughhouse

ŬF'i

goofy
roofy
spoofy
woofy

ŬF'i

bluffy
buffy
chuffy
fluffy
huffy
pluffy
puffy
sloughy
snuffy
stuffy

ŬF'in

muffin
puffin
ragamuffin

ŬF'ing

roofing
waterproofing
woofing

ŬF'ing

bluffing
cuffing
fluffing
huffing
luffing
puffing
roughing
sloughing
stuffing

ŬF'ish

gruffish

huffish
roughish
toughish

ŬF"l

bemuffle
buffle
double- shuffle
duffel
muffle
ruffle
scuffle
shuffle
snuffle
truffle
unmuffle
unruffle

ŬF"ld

bemuffled, etc.

ŬF'lest

bemufflest, etc.

ŬF'leth

bemuffleth, etc.

ŬF'li

bluffly
gruffly
muffly
roughly
ruffly
scuffly
sluffly
snuffly
toughly
truffly

ŬF'ling

bemuffling

ōld, ôr, ŏdd, oil, fŏŏt, out; ūse, ûrn, ŭp; THis, thin

muffling
ruffling
scuffling
shuffling
snuffling
unmuffling
unruffling

ŬF'lur

muffler
ruffler
scuffler
shuffler
snuffler
unmuffler

ŬF'nes

bluffness
gruffness
roughness
toughness

ŬF'ted

tufted

ŬF'ti

mufti
tufty

ŬF'ur

aloofer
hoofer
roofer
spoofer

ŬF'ur

bluffer
buffer
cuffer
duffer
gruffer

huffer
luffer
puffer
rougher
snuffer
stuffer
suffer
tougher

Ŭ'fus

goofus
rufous
Rufus

ŬG'a

meshuggah

Ŭ'gar

cougar

ŬG'ard

sluggard

ŬG'ed

rugged
(see ŬG + ed)

ŬG'est

drugges†
huggest
juggest
luggest
muggest
pluggest
shruggest
sluggest
smuggest
snuggest
tuggest
(cf. druggist)

ŬG'et

drugget
nugget

ŬG'eth

druggeth
huggeth
juggeth
luggeth
muggeth
pluggeth
shruggeth
sluggeth
tuggeth

ŬG'hous

bughouse

ŬG'i

buggy
muggy
puggi
puggy
sluggy

ŬG'ij

luggage

ŬG'ing

drugging
hugging
jugging
lugging
mugging
plugging
shrugging
slugging
tugging

ŬG'ish

muggish

sluggish
smugish
snuggish

ŬG'ist

druggist

ŬG''l

bugle
febrifugal
frugal
fugal
infrugal
jugal
McDougall
vermifugal

ŬG''l

death-struggle
guggle
juggle
smuggle
snuggle
struggle

ŬG'lest

jugglest, etc.

ŬG'leth

juggleth, etc.

ŬG'li

guggly
juggly
plug-ugly
smugly
snuggly
struggly
ugly

ŬG'ling

guggling

juggling
smuggling
struggling

ŬG'lur
bugler
fugler

ŬG'lur
juggler
smuggler
snuggler
struggler

ŬG'nes
smugness
snugness

Ū'go
Hugo

ŬG'ur
drugger
hugger
hugger-
  mugger
lugger
mugger
plugger
rugger
shrugger
snugger
tugger

ŬG'wump
mugwump

Ū'i
bedewy
bluey
Bowie

buoy
chop suey
coo-ee
coue
dewy
fluey
gluey
Louis
screwy
thewy
viewy

Ū'ĭd
blue-eyed
true-eyed

Ū'ĭd
druid
fluid

Ū'ij
brewage
sewage

Ū'ik
catechuic
toluic

Ū'in
blue-ruin
bruin
ruin
sewen

Ū'ing
accruing
barbecuing
bedewing
bestrewing
blueing
brewing
canoeing

chewing
clewing
cooing
cueing
doing
enduing
ensuing
eschewing
eweing
gluing
hallooing
hewing
imbruing
imbuing
interviewing
mewing
mildewing
misconstruing
misdoing
mooing
outdoing
overdoing
poohpoohing
pursuing
renewing
reviewing
screwing
shampooing
shoeing
spewing
stewing
strewing
subduing
suing
tattooing
undoing
unscrewing
viewing
well-doing
wooing
wrong-doing

Ū'ingz
doings
misdoings, etc.

Ū'is
Lewis
Louis
(cf. Jewess)

Ū'ish
blueish
glueish
Jewish
newish
shrewish
truish

ŬJ'el
cudgel

ŬJ'est
begrudgest, etc.

ŬJ'et
budget

ŬJ'eth
begrudgeth, etc.

ŬJ'ez
adjudges
begrudges
budges
drudges
forejudges
fudges
grudges
judges
misjudges
nudges
prejudges

ōld, ôr, ŏdd, oil, fŏŏt, out; ūse, ûrn, ŭp; TIIis, thin

rejudges
sludges
smudges
trudges

ŬJ'i
pudgy
sludgy
smudgy

ŬJ'ing
adjudging
begrudging
budging
drudging
forejudging
fudging
grudging
judging
misjudging
nudging
prejudging
rejudging
sludging
smudging
trudging
ungrudging

ŬJ'ment
judgment

ŬJ'on
bludgeon
curmudgeon
dudgeon
gudgeon

ŬJ'ur
adjudger
begrudger
budger

drudger
forejudger
fudger
grudger
judger
misjudger
nudger
prejudger
rejudger
sludger
smudger
trudger

Ū'ka
bucca
felucca
festuca
fistuca
garookuh
palooka
sambouka
yucca

Ū'kal
archducal
ducal
noctilucal
nuchal
Pentateuchal

Ū'kan
antelucan
toucan

Ū'kas
ukase

ŪK'ăs
Clucas
Lucas

ŬK'est
rebukest, etc.

ŬK'est
pluckest, etc.

ŬK'et
bucket
Luckett
Nantucket
Pawtucket
Puckett
sucket
tucket

ŬK'eth
rebuketh, etc.

ŬK'eth
plucketh, etc.

ŪK'i
fluky
snooky
spooky

ŬK'i
ducky
Kentucky
lucky
mucky
plucky
unlucky

ŪK'ing
puking
rebuking

ŬK'ing
bucking
chucking

clucking
ducking
mucking
plucking
shucking
sucking
trucking
tucking

ŬK'ish
buckish
muckish
puckish

ŬK''l
bruckle
buckle
chuckle
honeysuckle
huckle
knuckle
muckle
parbuckle
suckle
truckle
unbuckle

ŬK''ld
buckled
chuckled
knuckled
suckled
truckled
unbuckled
(cf. cuckold)

ŬK'les
luckless

ŬK'lest
bucklest, etc.

ŬK'leth
buckleth, etc.

ŬK'ling
buckling
chuckling
duckling
knuckling
suckling
truckling
unbuckling

ŬK'lur
buckler
chuckler
knuckler
swash-buckler
truckler

Ū'ko
Duco
Pernambuco

ŬK'old
cuckold
(cf. ŬK"ld)

ŬK'rak
muckrake

ŬK'shot
buck-shot
duck-shot

ŬK'siv
influxive

ŬK'som
buxom
lucksome

ŬK'stur
huckster

ŬK'shun
abduction
adduction
affluxion
conduction
construction
deduction
defluxion
destruction
diduction
duction
eduction
effluxion
fluxion
induction
influxion
instruction
introduction
manuduction
misconstruc-
    tion
non-conduc-
    tion
obduction
obstruction
over-produc-
    tion
production
reduction
reproduction
ruction
seduction
self-destruction
subduction
substruction
suction
superinduction

superstruction
traduction

ŬK'tans
reluctance

ŬK'tant
reluctant

ŬK'ted
abducted
conducted
constructed
deducted
fructed
inducted
instructed
miconstructed
obstructed
superstructed
unobstructed

ŬK'test
abductest
conductest
constructest
deductest
inductest
instructest
misconstructest
obstructest

ŬK'teth
abducteth
conducteth
constructeth
deducteth
inducteth
instructeth
misconstructeth
obstructeth

ŬK'til
ductile
inductile
productile

ŬK'ting
abducting
conducting
constructing
deducting
inducting
instructing
misconducting
non-conducting
non-obstruct-
    ing
obstructing

ŬK'tiv
adductive
conductive
constructive
deductive
destructive
inductive
instructive
introductive
obstructive
productive
reconductive
reconstructive
reductive
reproductive
seductive
self-destructive
superinductive
superstructive
traductive

ŬK'tres
conductress

instructress
introductress
seductress

pucker
sap-sucker
seer-sucker
shucker

Ū'lep
julep
(cf. tulip)

ŬL'fur
sulphur
(cf. Gulfer)

ŬK'tūr
structure
substructure
superstructure

succor
sucker
trucker
tucker

Ū'les
clueless
cueless
dewless
Jewless
mewless
pewless
screwless
viewless

ŬL'gar
vulgar

ŬL'gat
promulgate
vulgate

ŬK'tŭr
abductor
adductor
conductor
constructor
destructor
ductor
eductor
inductor
instructor
introductor
manuductor
non-conductor
obstructor

Ū'kus
caducous
fucus
leucous
mucous
noctilucous
rukus

ŬL'est
befoolest
coolest
foolest
pulest
rulest

Ū'li
bluely
Cooley
coolie
coolly
Dooley
duly
Gilhooley
Gillooley
Gilluley
guly
newly
patchouli
Thule
truly
tule
Ultima Thule
unduly
unruly

Ū'la
Ashtabula
Beulah
Boola Boola
Eula
hula-hula
Loula
Missoula
Wallula

ŬK'u, ŎŌ'ku
cuckoo

ŬL'est
annullest
cullest
dullest
lullest
scullest

Ū'kur
euchre
fluker
lucre
puker
rebuker

ŬL'a
ampulla
medulla
mullah
nullah

ŬL'et
cullet
gullet
mullet

ŬL'i
cully
dully
gully
hully
sully

ŬL'eth
befooleth, etc.

ŬK'ur
bucker
chucker
chukker
clucker
ducker
mucker

ŬL'da
Hulda

ŬL'en
Cullen
sullen
(cf. ŬL'in)

ŬL'eth
annulleth
gulleth
lulleth
sculleth

ŬL'id
gullied
sullied
unsullied

ŪL′ij	ŬL′is	divulges	ŬL′nes
Coolidge	portcullis	effulges	coolness
		indulges	
ŬL′ij	ŬL′ish		ŬL′nes
gullage	coolish	ŬL′jing	dullness
sullage	foolish	bulging	
ullage	mulish	divulging	ŬL′ok
	pound-foolish	effulging	hullock
ŬL′in	tom-foolish	indulging	rowlock
McMullin		promulging	
mullein	ŬL′ish		ŬL′pat
	dullish	ŬLJ′ment	disculpate
ŪL′ing	gullish	divulgement	exculpate
befooling		indulgement	inculpate
cooling	Ŭ′liks		
drooling	spondulix	ŬL′jur	ŬL′pest
fooling		divulger	gulpest, etc.
mewling	ŬL′jens	indulger	
misruling	effulgence	promulger	ŬL′peth
overruling	indulgence		gulpeth, etc.
puling	refulgence	ŬL′kat	
ruling	self-indulgence	inculcate	ŬL′pi
schooling		sulcate	gulpy
spooling	ŬL′jent	trisulcate	pulpy
tooling	circumfulgent	ŬLK′ing	
	effulgent	bulking	ŬL′pin
ŬL′ing	emulgent	hulking	vulpine
annulling	fulgent	skulking	
culling	indulgent	sulking	ŬL′prit
dulling	interfulgent		culprit
gulling	profulgent	ŬLK′i	
hulling	refulgent	bulky	ŬLP′tor
lulling	self-indulgent	hulky	sculptor
mulling		sulky	
sculling	ŬL′jest		ŬLP′tur
	indulgest, etc.	ŬLK′ur	sculpture
ŬL′inz		bulker	
Mullins	ŬL′jeth	skulker	ŬL′sest
	indulgeth, etc.	sulker	repulsest, etc.
Ū′lip			
tulip	ŬL′jez	ŬL′man	ŬL′set
(cf. julep)	bulges	Ullman	dulcet

ōld, ôr, ŏdd, oil, fŏŏt, out; ūse, ûrn, ŭp; THis, thin

ŬL'seth	ŬL'tan	ŬL'tūr	cruller
repulseth, etc.	sultan	agriculture	culler
		apiculture	discolor
ŬL'shun	ŬL'tans	arboriculture	duller
appulsion	exultance	aviculture	guller
avulsion	resultance	culture	huller
compulsion		floriculture	luller
convulsion	ŬL'tant	horticulture	medullar
demulsion	exultant	inculture	miscolor
divulsion	resultant	multure	Muller
emulsion		pisciculture	multicolor
evulsion	ŬL'ted	self-culture	rose-color
expulsion	consulted	sylviculture	sculler
impulsion	exulted	terra-culture	technicolor
propulsion	insulted	viticulture	tricolor
pulsion	occulted	vulture	water-color
repulsion	resulted		
revulsion		ŬL'tur	ŬL'urd
	ŬL'test	consulter	colored
ŬL'sing	*consultest*, etc.	exulter	discolored
convulsing		insulter	dullard
pulsing	ŬL'teth	resulter	high-colored
repulsing	*consulteth*, etc.		over-colored
		Ū'lu	party-colored
ŬL'siv	ŬL'ting	Honolulu	peach-colored
appulsive	consulting	Lulu	rosy-colored
compulsive	exulting	Zulu	sky-colored
convulsive	insulting		wine-colored
divulsive	occulting	Ū'lur	
emulsive	resulting	cooler	Ū'lus
expulsive		drooler	screw-loose
impulsive	ŬL'tiv	mewler	
propulsive	consultive	puler	ŬL'yar
pulsive	resultive	ridiculer	peculiar
repulsive		ruler	
revulsive	ŬLT'nes	spooler	ŬL'yun
	adultness	wine-cooler	cullion
ŬL'sur	occultness		mullion
repulser		Ū'lur	scullion
ulcer	ŬL'tri	annulier	
	sultry	color	Ū'ma
			duma

āle, câre, ădd, ärm, åsk; mē, hęre, ĕnd; īce, ĭll;

mazuma	ŬM′b′l	ŬM′bli	ŬM′bril
Montezuma	bejumble	crumbly	tumbril
puma	bumble	humbly	
Yuma	crumble	stumbly	ŬM′brus
	fumble	tumbly	cumbrous
Ū′man	grumble		penumbrous
human	humble	ŬM′bling	slumbrous
inhuman	jumble	crumbling	unslumbrous
Newman	mumble	fumbling	
superhuman	rumble	grumbling	ŬM′bug
Truman	scumble	humbling	humbug
	stumble	jumbling	
ŪM′at	tumble	mumbling	ŬM′bul
despumate	umbel	rumbling	Trumbull
exhumate		stumbling	
inhumate	ŬM′b′ld	tumbling	ŬM′bur
	unhumbled		cumber
ŬM′at	crumbled, etc.	ŬM′blur	disencumber
consummate		crumbler	encumber
	ŬM′blest	drumbler	Humber
ŬM′ba, ŪM′ba	*crumblest*	fumbler	lumbar
rumba	*fumblest*	grumbler	lumber
	grumblest	humbler	number
ŬM′bat	humblest	jumbler	outnumber
combat	*jumblest*	mumbler	slumber
(cf. wombat)	*mumblest*	rumbler	number
	rumblest	stumbler	
ŬM′bel	*stumblest*	tumbler	ŬM′burd
dumbbell	*tumblest*		unnumbered
		ŬM′bo	cumbered, etc.
ŬM′bent	ŬM′bleth	gumbo	
accumbent	*crumbleth*	Jumbo	ŬM′drum
decumbent	*fumbleth*	Mumbo-Jumbo	humdrum
incumbent	*grumbleth*		
procumbent	*humbleth*	ŬM′brat	ŬM′el
recumbent	*jumbleth*	adumbrate	bepummel
superincum-	*mumbleth*	inumbrate	hummel
bent	*rumbleth*	obumbrate	pommel
ŬM′bik	*stumbleth*		
columbic	*tumbleth*	ŬM′brij	Ū′men
plumbic		umbrage	acumen

ōld, ôr, ŏdd, oil, fŏŏt, out; ūse, ûrn, ŭp; THis, thin

albumen	numbest	**ŬM'fit**	**ŪM'id**
bitumen	rummest	comfit	humid
catechumen	*strummest*		tumid
legumen	*succumbest*	**ŬM'fort**	
rumen		comfort	**ŪM'ij**
(cf. illumine,	**ŬM'et**		fumage
etc.)	grummet	**ŬM'fri**	plumage
	plummet	Humphrey	
Ū'ment	(cf. summit)		**ŬM'ij**
accrument		**ŬM'friz**	chummage
eschewment	**ŪM'eth**	Humphreys	rummage
imbruement	*assumeth*		scrummage
imbuement	*bloometh*	**ŪM'ful**	
induement	*boometh*	bloomful	**ŪM'in**
subduement	*consumeth*	doomful	illumine
	costumeth		relumine
ŪM'est	*doometh*	**ŪM'i**	(cf. acumen,
assumest	*entombeth*	bloomy	etc.)
bloomest	*exhumeth*	broomy	
boomest	*fumeth*	Fiume	**ŬM'ing**
consumest	*groometh*	fumy	assuming
costumest	*illumeth*	gloomy	blooming
doomest	*perfumeth*	plumy	booming
entombest	*plumeth*	rheumy	consuming
exhumest	*presumeth*	roomy	disentombing
fumest	*resumeth*	spumy	dooming
groomest			entombing
illumest	**ŬM'eth**	**ŬM'i**	exhuming
perfumest	*becometh*	crumby	fuming
plumest	*cometh*	crummie	glooming
presumest	*drummeth*	dummy	grooming
resumest	*gummeth*	gummy	illuming
	hummeth	lummy	looming
ŬM'est	*strummeth*	mummy	perfuming
becomest	*succumbeth*	plummy	pluming
comest		rummy	predooming
drummest	**ŬM'fal**	scrummy	presuming
dumbest	triumphal	scummy	resuming
glummest		thrummy	unassuming
gummest	**ŬM'fant**	tummy	unpresuming
hummest	triumphant	yummy	

ŬM'ing
becoming
benumbing
chumming
coming
drumming
forthcoming
gumming
humming
mumming
numbing
overcoming
plumbing
plumming
scrumming
shortcoming
slumming
strumming
succumbing
summing
thumbing
unbecoming

ŬM'is
pumice

ŬM'it
summit
(cf. grummet,
etc.)

ŬM'les
bloomless
broomless
doomless
fumeless
groomless
loomless
plumeless
roomless
tombless

ŬM'let
boomlet
groomlet
plumelet

ŬM'li
Cholmondesley
Chumley
comely
cumbersomely
dumbly
frolicsomely
glumly
humorsomely
numbly
rumly
troublesomely,
etc.

ŬM'nal
autumnal
columnal

ŬM'nes
dumbness
glumness
numbness

ŬM'nur
Sumner

ŬM'ok
hummock
stomach

ŬM'oks
lummox
(cf. stomachs)

ŬM'on
come-on
summon

ŬM'ond
Drummond

ŬM'pas
compass
encompass
rumpus

ŬM'pest
bethumpest
bumpest
dumpest
humpest
jumpest
lumpest
plumpest
pumpest
stumpest
thumpest
trumpest

ŬM'pet
crumpet
strumpet
trumpet

ŬM'peth
bethumpeth
bumpeth
dumpeth
humpeth
jumpeth
lumpeth
pumpeth
stumpeth
thumpeth
trumpeth

ŬM'pi
bumpy
chumpy

clumpy
crumpy
dumpy
frumpy
grumpy
humpy
jumpy
lumpy
mumpy
plumpy
slumpy
stumpy
thumpy

ŬMP'ing
bethumping
bumping
dumping
bumping
jumping
lumping
mumping
plumping
pumping
slumping
stumping
thumping
trumping

ŬMP'ir
umpire

ŬMP'ish
bumpish
dumpish
frumpish
grumpish
humpish
jumpish
lumpish
mumpish

ōld, ôr, ŏdd, oil, foŏt, out; ūse, ûrn, ŭp; THis, thin

plumpish
slumpish

ŬMP′kin
bumpkin
pumpkin
(cf. Lumkin)

ŬM′p′l
crumple
rumple
unrumple

ŬM′plest
crumplest, etc.

ŬM′pleth
crumpleth, etc.

ŬM′pling
crumpling
dumpling
rumpling

ŬMP′nes
plumpness

ŬM′po
Bumpo

ŬMP′shun
assumption
consumption
gumption
presumption
resumption
subsumption

ŬMP′shus
bumptious
scrumptious

ŬMP′tiv
assumptive
consumptive
presumptive
resumptive
subsumptive

ŬM′pur
bethumper
bumper
counter-jumper
dumper
jumper
lumper
mumper
plumper
pumper
stumper
thumper
trumper
tub-thumper

ŬM′pus
rumpus
(see ŬM′pas)

ŬM′ston
tombstone

ŬM′tur
Sumter

ŪM′ur
assumer
bloomer
boomer
consumer
doomer
entomber
fumer
humor

ill-humor
illumer
perfumer
plumer
presumer
resumer
roomer
rumor
tumor

ŪM′ur
comer
Cummer
drummer
dumber
glummer
grummer
gummer
hummer
incomer
midsummer
mummer
newcomer
number
plumber
rummer
scrummer
scummer
strummer
summer

ŪM′urd
good-humored
humored
ill-humored
rumored

ŪM′urz
bloomers
rumors, etc.

ŬM′urz
Somers

ŪM′us
brumous
dumous
fumous
grumous
humous
humus
implumous
plumous
spumous

ŪMZ′da
doomsday

ŬM′zi
clumsy
mumsie

ŬMZ′man
doomsman
groomsman

Ū′na
Acuna
fortuna
lacuna
luna
Peruna
Una
vicuna

Ū′nal
lacunal
tribunal

ŬN′chest
bunchest, etc.

āle,   câre,   ădd,   ärm,   åsk;   mē,   hẹre,   ĕnd;   īce,   ĭll;

ǓN′cheth
buncheth, etc.

ǓN′chez
brunches
bunches
crunches
hunches
lunches
munches
punches
scrunches

ǓN′chi
bunchy
crunchy
hunchy
punchy

ǓN′ching
bunching
crunching
hunching
lunching
munching
punching
scrunching

ǓN′chun
bruncheon
luncheon
nuncheon
puncheon
scuncheon
truncheon

ǓN′chur
bruncher
buncher
cruncher
huncher

luncher
muncher
puncher
scruncher

ǓN′dan
antemundane
extramundane
infra-mundane
intermundane
intramundane
mundane
supermundane
supramundane
ultramundane

ǓN′dans
abundance
redundance
sun dance
superabun-
  dance

ǓN′dant
abundant
redundant
superabundant

ǓN′dat
fecundate
secundate

ǓN′ded
unwounded
wounded

ǓN′ded
funded
refunded
retunded

ǓN′dest
woundest, etc.

ǓN′dest
fundest, etc.

ǓN′deth
woundeth, etc.

ǓN′deth
fundeth, etc.

ǓN′di
Bundy
fundi
Fundy
Grundy
Lundy
Monday
salmagundi
Sunday

ǓN′din
hirundine

ǓN′ding
funding
refunding

ǓN′dit
conduit
pundit

ǓN′d′l
bundle
trundle
unbundle

ǓN′dlest
bundlest, etc.

ǓN′dleth
bundleth, etc.

ǓN′dling
bundling
trundling, etc.

ǓN′don
London
(cf. undone)

ǓN′dred
hundred

ǓN′dri
sundry
thund′ry

ǓN′drus
wondrous

ǓN′dur
asunder
blunder
dissunder
dunder
down-under
enthunder
Gunder
plunder
refunder
rotunder
sunder
thereunder
thunder
under
wonder

ǓN′el
funnel
gunwale

ōld, ôr, ŏdd, oil, fŏŏt, out; ūse, ûrn, ŭp; THis, thin

runnel	*oppugneth*	**ŬNGK'at**	conjunction
trunnel	*pruneth*	averruncate	defunction
tunnel	*spooneth*	detruncate	disjunction
	swooneth	truncate	expunction
ŬN'et	*tuneth*		function
punnet		**ŬNGK'en**	injunction
runnet	**ŬN'eth**	drunken	interjunction
	runneth, etc.	shrunken	interpunction
Ū'nes		sunken	inunction
blueness	**ŬN'ful**		junction
fewnesss	tuneful	**ŬNGK'et**	punction
newness	runeful	junket	*sejunction*
trueness	spoonful	Plunkett	subjunction
			unction
ŪN'est	**UNG'g'l**	**ŬNGK'i**	
attunest	bungle	chunky	**ŬNGK'shus**
communest	jungle	flunkey	compunctious
croonest		funky	rambunctious
entunest	**ŬNG'gling**	hunky	unctious
harpoonest	bungling	monkey	
importunest		powder-	**ŬNGK'tiv**
impugnest	**ŬNG'gur**	monkey	abjunctive
moonest	ballad-monger	punkie	adjunctive
oppugnest	borough-	spunky	compunctive
prunest	monger		conjunctive
soonest	costermonger	**ŬNG'kin**	disjunctive
spoonest	enhunger	punkin	subjunctive
swoonest	fishmonger	(cf. ŬN'kan)	
tunest	hunger		**ŬNGK'tur**
	ironmonger	**ŬNGK'ish**	acupuncture
ŬN'est	monger	funkish	conjuncture
runnest, etc.	Munger	monkish	juncture
	younger	skunkish	puncture
ŪN'eth			
attuneth	**ŬNGK'al**	**ŬNGK'o**	**ŬNGK'um**
communeth	carbuncle	bunco	Buncombe
crooneth	caruncle	junco	bunkum
entuneth	peduncle		
harpooneth	truncal	**ŬNGK'shun**	**ŬNGK'ur**
impugneth	uncle	adjunction	bunker
mooneth		compunction	drunker

dunker	**ŬN′i**	mooning	**ŬN′izm**
flunker	acrimony	nooning	buffoonism
funker	agrimony	oppugning	opportunism
hunker	alimony	pruning	poltroonism
junker	antimony	spooning	
punker	bunny	swooning	**ŬN′jent**
tunker	funny	tuning	pungent
	gunny		
ŬNGK′urd	honey	**ŬN′ing**	**ŬN′jest**
bunkered	matrimony	cunning	*expungest,* etc
drunkard	money	dunning	
Dunkard	parsimony	funning	**ŬN′jeth**
	patrimony	gunning	*expungeth,* etc.
ŬNGK′us	sanctimony	outrunning	
aduncous	sonny	overrunning	**ŬN′jez**
dohunkus	sunny	punning	expunges
juncous	Tunney	running	lunges
	tunny	shunning	plunges
ŬNG′ling	unsunny	stunning	sponges
youngling		sunning	
	ŬN′ij		**ŬN′ji**
ŬN′gri	dunnage	**Ū′nis**	plungy
hungry	gunnage	Eunice	spongy
	tonnage	Tunis	
ŬNG′stur			**ŬN′jing**
tonguester	**ŬN′ik**	**ŪN′ish**	expunging
youngster	Munich	buffoonish	lunging
	Punic	poltroonish	plunging
ŬNG′ur	runic		sponging
lunger	tunic	**ŬN′ish**	
		punish	**ŬN′jun**
ŪN′i	**ŬN′in**	Hunnish	dungeon
Dooney	run-in		*plungeon*
loony		**ŪN′ist**	
Mooney	**ŪN′ing**	balloonist	**ŬN′jur**
moony	ballooning	bassoonist	blunger
Mulrooney	communing	harpoonist	expunger
Muni	crooning	opportunist	lunger
puisne	expugning		plunger
puny	harpooning	**Ū′nit**	sponger
spoony	impugning	unit	

ōld, ôr, ŏdd, oil, fŏŏt, out; ūse, ûrn, ŭp; THis, thin

ŬN'kan
Duncan
(cf. ŬNG'kin)

ŬN'les
moonless
runeless
tuneless

ŬN'les
runless
sonless
sunless

ŬN'lit
moonlight
noon-light

ŬN'man
gunman

ŬN'nes
inopportune-
   ness
jejuneness
opportuneness

Ū'no
Bruno
Juno

ŬN'riz
moonrise

ŬN'si
Munsey

ŬN'stan,
   ŬN'ston
Dunstan
Funston

ŬN'stur
gunster
punster

ŬN'tal
contrapuntal
frontal
gruntle

ŬN'ted
affronted
blunted
bunted
confronted
fronted
grunted
hunted
punted
shunted
stunted
unblunted
unwonted
wonted

ŬN'test
affrontest
bluntest
buntest
confrontest
gruntest
huntest
puntest
shuntest
stuntest

ŬN'teth
affronteth
blunteth
bunteth
confronteth
grunteth

hunteth
punteth
shunteth
stunteth

ŬN'ti
punty
runty
stunty

ŬN'ting
affronting
bunting
confronting
fronting
grunting
head-hunting
hunting
punting
reed-bunting
shunting
stunting
yellow-bunting

ŬNT'les
frontless
wontless

ŬNT'nes
bluntness
stuntness

ŬN'to
junto

ŬN'tri
country

ŬN'tu
unto

ŬN'tur
affronter
blunter
bunter
confronter
fortune-hunter
grunter
Gunter
head-hunter
hunter
legacy-hunter
punter
shunter
stunter

ŬNTS'vil
Blountsville
Huntsville

Ū'nuk
eunuch

ŬN'ur
attuner
ballooner
communer
crooner
dragooner
harpooner
importuner
impugner
interlunar
lacunar
lampooner
lunar
mooner
novilunar
oppugner
piano-tuner
plenilunar
pruner

āle, câre, ădd, ärm, ȧsk; mē, hĕre, ĕnd; īce, ĭll;

schooner	ŬP'ans	ŪP'i	ŬP''l
semilunar	come-uppance	croupy	octuple
sooner	thruppence	droopy	quadruple
spooner		soupy	quintuple
sublunar	ŪP'e	(cf. whoopee)	septuple
swooner	whoopee		sextuple
translunar	(cf. ŪP'i)	ŬP'i	scruple
tuner		cuppy	subduple
	ŪP'est	guppy	(cf. pupil)
ŬN'ur	*coopest*	puppy	
dunner	*droopest*		ŬP''l
forerunner	*dupest*	Ū'pid	couple
gunner	*groupest*	Cupid	supple
overrunner	*loopest*	stupid	
punner	*recoupest*		ŪP'lest
runner	*scoopest*	Ū'pil	*scruplest*, etc.
stunner	*stoopest*	pupil	
	swoopest	(cf. Ū'p'l)	ŬP'lest
ŪN'yon	*troopest*		*couplest*, etc.
communion	*whoopest*	ŪP'ing	
disunion		cooping	ŬP'let
excommunion	ŬP'est	drooping	octuplet
intercom-	*suppest*, etc.	duping	quintuplet, etc.
munion		grouping	
reunion	ŬP'et	hooping	ŪP'leth
trades-union	puppet	looping	*scrupleth*, etc
union		recouping	
	ŪP'eth	scooping	ŬP'leth
ŬN'yon	*coopeth*	stooping	*coupleth*, etc.
bunion	*droopeth*	swooping	
munnion	*dupeth*	trooping	ŬP'lur
onion	*groupeth*	whooping	coupler
ronyon	*loopeth*		suppler
trunnion	*recoupeth*	ŬP'ing	
	scoopeth	cupping	ŪP'ment
ŪN'yor	*stoopeth*	supping	aggroupment
junior	*swoopeth*	tupping	recoupment
	troopeth		
Ū'pa	*whoopeth*	ŬP'ish	Ū'pon
pupa	ŬP'eth	puppish	coupon
supa	*suppeth*, etc.	uppish	jupon

ōld, ôr, ŏdd, oil, fŏŏt, out; ūse, ûrn, ŭp; THis, thin

ŬP'or

stupor
(see ŬP'ur)

ŬP'shal

antenuptial
nuptial
post-nuptial

ŬP'shun

abruption
corruption
disruption
eruption
incorruption
interruption
irruption
ruption

ŬP'ted

abrupted
corrupted
disrupted
interrupted
irrupted

ŬP'test

abruptest
corruptest
interruptest

ŬP'teth

corrupteth, etc.

ŬP'ting

corrupting
erupting
interrupting

ŬP'tiv

corruptive

disruptive
eruptive
incorruptive
interruptive
irruptive

ŬPT'li

abruptly
corruptly, etc.

ŬPT'nes

abruptness
corruptness
incorruptness

ŬP'ur

cooper
drooper
duper
grouper
hooper
looper
recouper
scooper
snooper
stooper
stupor
super
swooper
trooper
whooper

ŬP'ur

crupper
cupper
scupper
supper
upper

ŬP'urt

Rupert
(cf. Newport)

ŬP'ward

upward

Ū'ra

Angostura
appoggiatura
bravura
caesura
coloratura
Cuticura
datura
fissura
flexura
Keturah
pietra-dura
pleura
purpura
sura
velatura
vettura

Ū'ral

antemural
caesural
commissural
crural
extramural
intermural
interneural
intramural
jural
mural
neural
pleural
plural
rural
sinecural
sural
tellural
Ural

ŬR'ans

allurance
assurance
durance
endurance
insurance
perdurance
reassurance

ŬR'āt

curate

ŬR'ăt

jurat

ŬR'bal

herbal
verbal

ŬR'ban

suburban
turban
urban

ŬR'bans

disturbance

ŬR'bar

durbar

ŬR'bat

acerbate
perturbate

ŬR'best

blurbest
curbest
disturbest
perturbest

ŬR'bet

sherbet

ŬR'beth
blurbeth
curbeth
disturbeth
perturbeth

ŬR'bi
Derby
herby
Iturbi
Kirby

ŬR'bid
herbid
turbid

ŬR'bin
turbine

ŬR'bing
curbing
disturbing
perturbing

ŬR'bot
burbot
turbot

ŬR'bur
Berber
blurber
curber
disturber
Ferber
Gerber
perturber
superber

ŬR'burt
Herbert

ŬR'chant
merchant
perchant

ŬR'chas
purchase

ŬR'chast
purchased

ŬR'chen
birchen
(cf. urchin)

ŬR'chest
birchest
lurchest
perchest
searchest
smirchest
(cf. purchased)

ŬR'cheth
bircheth
lurcheth
percheth
searcheth
smircheth

ŬR'chez
besmirches
birches
churches
lurches
perches
researches
searches
smirches

ŬR'chif
kerchief

ŬR'ching
besmirching
birching
churching
lurching
perching
searching
smirching

ŬRCH'les
churchless
smirchless

ŬR'chur
besmircher
bircher
lurcher
percher
researcher
searcher
smircher
(cf. nurture)

ŬRD'book
herdbook
word-book

ŬR'ded
begirded
curded
engirded
girded
herded
sherded
worded

ŬR'den
burden
disburden
overburden

unburden
(cf. ŬR'don)

ŬR'dest
absurdest
begirdest
engirdest
girdest
heardest

ŬR'deth
begirdeth, etc.

ŬR'di
birdie
curdy
hurdy-gurdy
sturdy
wordy

ŬR'dikt
verdict

ŬR'ding
begirding
engirding
girding
herding
ungirding
wording

ŬR'd'l
begirdle
curdle
engirdle
girdle
hurdle

ŬR'don
Burdon
guerdon
(cf. ŬR'den)

ōld, ôr, ŏdd, oil, fŏŏt, out; ūse, ûrn, ŭp; THis, thin

ÛR'dŭr	ÛR'est	*stirrest*	*recurreth*
verdure	*abjurest*	*transferrest*	*referreth*
(cf. perjure)	*adjurest*		*spurreth*
	allurest	ÛR'et	*stirreth*
ÛR'dŭr	*assurest*	turret	*transferreth*
absurder	*conjurest*		
Burder	*curest*	ÛR'eth	ÛR'fas
engirder	demurest	*abjureth*	surface
girder	*endurest*	*adjureth*	
herder	*ensurest*	*allureth*	ÛR'fekt
murder	*immurest*	*conjureth*	perfect
self-murder	impurest	*cureth*	
thirder	*insurest*	*endureth*	ÛR'fi
worder	*lurest*	*immureth*	Durfey
ÛRDZ'man	*maturest*	*lureth*	Murphy
herdsman	*moorest*	*matureth*	scurfy
wordsman	obscurest	*obscureth*	surfy
	poorest	*procureth*	turfy
ÛR'el	*procurest*	*secureth*	
squirrel	purest	*assureth*	ÛR'fit
Burrell	*reassurest*	*ensureth*	surfeit
	securest	*insureth*	
ÛR'ens	surest	*mooreth*	ÛR'for
concurrence	*tourest*	*reassureth*	therefore
deterrence	*unmoorest*	*toureth*	(cf. wherefore)
incurrence		*unmooreth*	
intercurrence	ÛR'est		ÛR'fum
occurrence	*bestirrest*	ÛR'eth	perfume
recurrence	*blurrest*	*bestirreth*	
transference	*concurrest*	*blurreth*	ÛR'gat
	conferrest	*concurreth*	expurgate
ÛR'ent, ÛR'ant	*deferrest*	*conferreth*	objurgate
concurrent	*demurrest*	*deferreth*	virgate
currant	*errest*	*erreth*	
current	*incurrest*	*demurreth*	ÛR'g'l
decurrent	*inferrest*	*incurreth*	burgle
deterrent	*interrest*	*inferreth*	gurgle
intercurrent	*preferrest*	*interreth*	
recurrent	*purrest*	*occurreth*	ÛR'glar
susurrant	*referrest*	*preferreth*	burglar
undercurrent	*spurrest*	*purreth*	gurgler

ŬR'go
a tergo
ergo
Virgo

ŬR'gur
burgher
jerguer

ŬR'gus
demiurgus
Mergus
thaumaturgus

ŬR'i
de jure
Drury
ewry
fury
houri
Jewry
jury
Missouri

ŬR'i
burry
curry
firry
flurry
furry
hurry
hurry-scurry
lurry
Murray
scurry
Surrey
slurry
whirry
worry

ŬR'id
lurid

ŬR'id
curried
flurried
hurried
scurried
worried

ŬR'ij
moorage
murage

ŬR'ij
courage
demurrage
discourage
encourage

ŬR'ik
hydrosulphuric
hydrotelluric
purpuric
sulphuric
telluric

ŬR'ik
myrrhic

ŬR'im
purim
urim

ŬR'in
burin
daturin
neurin
neurine

ŬR'ing
abjuring
adjuring
alluring

assuring
conjuring
curing
during
enduring
ensuring
everduring
immuring
insuring
inuring
juring
luring
manuring
maturing
mooring
non-juring
obscuring
procuring
reassuring
securing
touring
unmooring

ŬR'ing
astirring
bestirring
blurring
concurring
conferring
deferring
demurring
erring
incurring
inferring
interring
non-concurring
occurring
preferring
purring
recurring
referring

shirring
slurring
spurring
stirring
transferring
unerring
whirring
(cf. herring)

ŬR'ish
amateurish
boorish
Moorish
poorish

ŬR'ish
burrish
currish
flourish
nourish

ŬR'ist
caricaturist
jurist
purist
tourist

ŬR'iz
curries
flurries
hurries
scurries
worries

ŬR'izm
purism
tourism

ŬR'jens
convergence
deturgence

ōld, ôr, ŏdd, oil, fŏŏt, out; ūse, ûrn, ŭp; THis, thin

divergence
emergence
resurgence
submergence

ÛR'jent

abstergent
assurgent
convergent
detergent
divergent
emergent
insurgent
resurgent
splurgent
turgent
urgent
vergent

ÛR'jest

convergest
dirgest
divergest
emergest
mergest
purgest
scourgest
splurgest
submergest
surgest
urgest

ÛR'jeth

convergeth
dirgeth
divergeth
emergeth
mergeth
purgeth
scourgeth
splurgeth

submergeth
surgeth
urgeth

ÛR'jez

asperges
Boanerges
converges
dirges
diverges
emerges
merges
purges
scourges
serges
submerges
surges
urges
verges

ÛR'ji

aciurgy
clergy
dirgie
dramaturgy
metallurgy
periergy
surgy
thaumaturgy

ÛR'jid

turgid

ÛR'jik

chirurgic
demiurgic
dramaturgic
energic
liturgic
metallurgic

thaumaturgic
theurgic

ÛR'jin

virgin

ÛR'jing

converging
dirging
diverging
emerging
immerging
merging
purging
scourging
splurging
submerging
surging
urging
verging

ÛR'jist

dramaturgist
metallurgist
thaumaturgist

ÛR'jun

burgeon
Spurgeon
sturgeon
surgeon

ÛR'jûr

perjure
(cf. verdure)

ÛR'jŭr

converger
dirger
diverger
emerger

merger
purger
scourger
submerger
urger
verger

ÛR'jus

verjuice

ÛR'kal

Lupercal
novercal
(cf. circle)

ÛR'kest

clerkest, etc.

ÛR'keth

clerketh, etc.

ÛR'ki

jerky
lurky
mirky
murky
perky
quirky
shirky
smirky
talk turkey
turkey

ÛR'kin

firkin
gherkin
jerkin
merkin

ÛR'kins

Firkins

āle, câre, ădd, ärm, åsk; mē, hẹre, ĕnd; īce, ĭll;

Perkins
gherkins, etc.

ÛR'king
aworking
clerking
hard-working
jerking
lurking
perking
shirking
smirking
working

ÛR'kish
quirkish
Turkish

ÛR'kit
circuit

ÛR'k'l
circle
encircle
Merkle
semicircle
turkle

ÛR'klet
circlet

ÛR'kli
circly
clerkly

ÛR'kling
circling

ÛRK'man
Turkman
workman

ÛRK'som
irksome
mirksome

ÛR'kur
burker
jerker
jerquer
lurker
shirker
smirker
wonder-worker
worker

ÛR'kus
bifurcous
circus
Quercus
(cf. work-
 house)

ÛR'kwoiz
turquoise

ÛRLD'li
worldly

ÛRLD'ling
worldling

ÛR'lest
curlest
furlest
hurlest
swirlest
twirlest
unfurlest
whirlest

ÛR'leth
curleth

furleth
hurleth
purleth
swirleth
twirleth
unfurleth
whirleth

ÛRL'hood
girlhood

ÛR'li
demurely
maturely
obscurely
poorly
purely
securely

ÛR'li
burly
churly
curly
early
girlie
girly
hurly-burly
knurly
pearly
Shirley
surly
swirly
whirly

ÛR'lin
merlin
pearlin

ÛR'ling
curling
furling
herling

hurling
pearling
purling
Sperling
sterling
Stirling
swirling
twirling
uncurling
unfurling
upcurling
upwhirling

ÛR'lish
churlish
girlish
pearlish

ÛR'loin
purloin
sirloin

ÛR'lu
curlew
purlieu

ÛR'lur
burler
curler
furler
hurler
pearler
purler
skirler
twirler
whirler

ÛR'ma
Burma
derma
Irma
syrma

ōld. ôr. ŏdd, oil, fōot. out; ūse, ûrn, ŭp; THis, thin

ŬR'mad
mermaid

ŬR'mal
dermal
diathermal
epidermal
geothermal
hydrothermal
hypodermal
isogeothermal
isothermal
pachydermal
synthermal
taxidermal
thermal

ŬR'man
cousin-german
firman
German
merman
(cf. sermon)

ŬR'mans
affirmance
confirmance
disaffirmance

ŬR'ment
abjurement
allurement
conjurement
immurement
obscurement
procurement

ŬR'ment,
  ŬR'mant
affirmant

averment
deferment
determent
disinterment
ferment
interment
preferment
referment

ŬR'mest
confirmest
firmest
infirmest
squirmest
termest
wormest

ŬR'meth
confirmeth, etc.

ŬR'mez
Hermes
kermes

ŬR'mi
germy
taxidermy
wormy

ŬR'mik
adiathermic
dermic
diathermic
endermic
epidermic
geothermic
hydrodermic
hypodermic
isogeothermic
pachydermic
sclerodermic

taxidermic
thermic

ŬR'min
determine
ermine
vermin

ŬR'mind
determined
ermined
undetermined

ŬR'ming
affirming
confirming
squirming
worming

ŬR'mis
dermis
epidermis

ŬR'mish
skirmish

ŬR'mīt
termite

ŬR'mĭt
hermit
permit

ŬRM'li
firmly
termly

ŬR'moil
turmoil

ŬR'mur
affirmer

bemurmur
confirmer
firmer
infirmer
murmur
squirmer
termer
termoı
wormer

ŬR'na
Myrna
Verna

ŬR'nal
cavernal
coeternal
colonel
diurnal
diuternal
eternal
external
fraternal
hesternal
hibernal
hodiernal
infernal
internal
journal
kernel
lucernal
maternal
nocturnal
paraphernal
paternal
semi-diurnal
sempiternal
sternal
supernal
urnal
vernal

ŬR'nant,
ŬR'nent
alternant
secernent
vernant

ŬR'nard
Bernard

ŬR'nas
furnace

ŬR'nat
alternate
cothurnate
subalternate
ternate

ŬR'ned
learned
(see ŬRN +
ed)

ŬR'nes
demureness
immatureness
impureness
insecureness
matureness
obscureness
poorness
pureness
secureness
sureness

ŬR'nes
Furness
(cf. furnace)

ŬR'nest
adjournest

burnest
churnest
concernest
discernest
earnest
Ernest
learnest
over-earnest
overturnest
returnest
sojournest
spurnest
sternest
turnest
yearnest

ŬR'neth
adjourneth
burneth
churneth
concerneth
discerneth
learneth
overturneth
returneth
sojourneth
spurneth
turneth
yearneth

ŬR'ni
attorney
Berney
Birney
burny-burny
ferny
Gurney
journey
Turney
tourney

ŬR'ning
adjourning
booklearning
burning
churning
concerning
discerning
earning
heart-burning
learning
overburning
overturning
returning
sojourning
spurning
table-turning
turning
undiscerning
unlearning
upturning
urning
yearning

ŬR'nish
burnish
furnish

ŬR'nisht
burnished
furnished
unburnished
unfurnished

ŬRN'ment
adjournment
attornment
concernment
discernment
secernment
sojournment

ŬRN'nes
sternness

ŬR'no
inferno
Sterno

ŬR'num
laburnum

ŬR'nur
adjourner
burner
discerner
earner
learner
overturner
returner
sojourner
spurner
sterner
turner
yearner

ŬR'nus
cothurnus

ŬR'o
bureau
chiaroscuro
maduro

ŬR'o
borough
burrow
furrow
thorough

ŬR'od
burrowed
furrowed
unfurrowed

ōld, ôr, ŏdd, oil, fŏŏt, out; ūse, ûrn, ŭp; THis, thin

ŬR'or
furor
juror
(cf. ŬR'ur)

ŬR'pent
serpent

ŬR'pest
chirpest, etc.

ŬR'peth
chirpeth
turpeth
usurpeth

ŬR'ping
burping
chirping
usurping

ŬR'p'l
empurple
purple

ŬR'pos
purpose

ŬR'pur
burper
chirper
usurper

ŬR'sa
ursa
vice versa

ŬR'sal
controversal
rehearsal
reversal

tercel
transversal
universal
ursal
versal

ŬR'sant
aversant
recursant
versant

ŬR'sed
accursed
(see ŬRS+ed)

ŬR'sest
accursest
becursest
coercest
conversest
cursest
disbursest
dispersest
immersest
interspersest
nursest
rehearsest
reimbursest
reversest
traversest

ŬR'set
tercet

ŬR'seth
accurseth
becurseth
coerceth
converseth
curseth
disburseth

disperseth
immerseth
intersperseth
nurseth
rehearseth
reimburseth
reverseth
traverseth

ŬR'sez
accurses
amerces
becurses
coerces
converses
curses
disburses
disperses
hearses
immerses
intersperses
nurses
purses
rehearses
reimburses
reverses
submerses
traverses
verses

ŬR'shal
commercial
controversial
tertial
uncommercial

ŬR'ship
worship

ŬR'shum
nasturtium

ŬR'shun
abstersion
animadversion
apertion
aspersion
assertion
aversion
circumversion
coercion
concertion
contraversion
controversion
conversion
demersion
desertion
disconcertion
discursion
dispersion
diversion
emersion
eversion
excursion
exertion
extersion
immersion
incursion
insertion
inspersion
intersertion
interspersion
introversion
inversion
mersion
nasturtion
obversion
perversion
recursion
retroversion
reversion
self-assertion
submersion

āle, câre, ădd, ärm, åsk; mē, hĕre, ĕnd; īce, ĭll;

subversion
tertian
version
(cf. ŬR'si-an)

ŬR'si
Circe
controversy
gramercy
mercy
Mersey
Percy
pursy
Searcy

ŬR'sing
accursing
becursing
coercing
conversing
cursing
disbursing
dispersing
immersing
nursing
rehearsing
reimbursing
reversing
transversing
traversing
versing

ŬR'siv
abstersive
animadversive
aspersive
aversive
coercive
conversive
cursive
decursive

detersive
discursive
dispersive
eversive
excursive
incursive
perversive
precursive
subversive

ŬRS'ment
amercement
disbursement
imbursement
reimburse-
    ment

ŬRS'nes
adverseness
averseness
perverseness
terseness

ŬR'son
Gerson
McPherson
person

ŬR'sted
bursted
thirsted
worsted

ŬR'stest
burstest, etc.

ŬR'steth
bursteth, etc.

ŬR'sti
thirsty

ŬR'sting
bursting
thirsting
worsting

ŬR'stur
burster
thirster

ŬR'sur
accurser
amercer
ante-cursor
bursar
coercer
commercer
converser
curser
cursor
disburser
disperser
hearser
immerser
mercer
nurser
perverser
precursor
purser
rehearser
reimburser
reverser
traverser
verser
worser

ŬR'sus
excursus
thyrsus
ursus
versus

ŬR'ta
Alberta
Elberta

ŬR'tan
certain
curtain
encurtain
incertain
uncertain

ŬR'ted
adverted
asserted
averted
blurted
concerted
converted
deserted
disconcerted
diverted
exerted
flirted
inserted
interserted
inverted
perverted
preconcerted
reverted
spurted
squirted
subverted
undiverted
unperverted

ŬR'ten
thirteen

ŬR'tens
advertence
inadvertence
misadvertence

ōld, ôr, ŏdd, oil, fŏŏt, out; ūse, ûrn, ŭp; THis, thin

ŬR′test	ŬR′tha	flirty	ŬR′tis
advertest	Bertha	Gertie	Curtis
assertest	Hertha	thirty	
avertest			ŬR′t′l
blurtest	ŬR′THen	ŬR′ting	fertile
concertest	burthen	adverting	hurtle
controvertest	disburthen	asserting	kirtle
convertest	unburthen	averting	myrtle
curtest		blurting	spurtle
disconcertest	ŬR′then	concerting	turtle
divertest	earthen	controverting	whortle
exertest		converting	
hurtest	ŬR′THur	deserting	ŬRT′les
insertest	further	disconcerting	shirtless
invertest		diverting	skirtless
pertest	ŬR′THest	exerting	
pervertest	furthest	flirting	ŬRT′li
revertest		hurting	alertly
skirtest	ŬRth′ful	inserting	curtly
spurtest	mirthful	interserting	expertly
subvertest	worthful	interverting	inertly
		inverting	inexpertly
ŬR′teth	ŬRth′les	perverting	pertly
averteth	birthless	preconcerting	
asserteth	mirthless	retroverting	ŬRT′nes
averteth	worthless	reverting	alertness
blurteth		self-asserting	curtness
concerteth	ŬR′THi	shirting	expertness
controverteth	noteworthy	skirting	inertness
converteth	sea-worthy	spurting	inexpertness
disconcerteth	trust-worthy	squirting	pertness
diverteth	worthy	subverting	
exerteth	unworthy		ŬR′ton
hurteth		ŬR′tiv	Berton
inserteth		assertive	(cf. ŬR′tan)
inverteth	ŬR′thi	divertive	
perverteth	earthy	exertive	ŬR′trud
reverteth		furtive	Gertrude
skirteth	ŬR′ti	revertive	
spurteth	cherty	self-assertive	ŬRT′si
subverteth	dirty		curtsey

ŬR'tu

virtue

ŬR'tŭr

nurture

(cf. ŬR'chur)

ŬR'tŭr

adverter
animadverter
asserter
averter
converter
curter
disconcerter
diverter
exerter
hurter
inserter
inverter
perter
perverter
preconcerter
spurter
squirter
subverter

ŬR'up

stirrup

(cf. ĬR'up)

ŬR'ur

abjurer
adjurer
allurer
assurer
conjurer
curer
demurer
endurer
ensurer

immurer
impurer
insurer
inurer
juror
lurer
manurer
maturer
moorer
nonjuror
obscurer
poorer
procurer
purer
reassurer
securer
surer
tourer
unmoorer

(cf. ŬR'or)

ŬR'ur

averrer
bestirrer
blurrer
concurrer
conferrer
deferrer
demurrer
incurrer
inferrer
interrer
preferrer
spurrer
stirrer
transferrer

ŬR'us

anurous
Arcturus
dolichurus

Eurus
urus

ŬR'us

susurrous
wurrus

ŬR'uz

Burroughs
Burrows

(cf. ŬR'o + s)

ŬR'va

Minerva

ŬR'val

acerval
curval

ŬR'vans,
    ŬR'vens

fervence
inobservance
observance
unobservance

ŬR'vant,
    ŬR'vent

conservant
curvant
fervent
inobservant
observant
recurvant
servant
unobservant

ŬR'vat

acervate
curvate
enervate

incurvate
recurvate
trinervate

ŬR'ven

nervine

ŬR'vest

conservest
curvest
deservest
observest
preservest
reservest
servest
swervest
unnervest

ŬR'veth

conserveth
curveth
deserveth
observeth
preserveth
reserveth
serveth
swerveth
unnerveth

ŬR'vi

nervy
scurvy
topsy-turvy

ŬR'vid

fervid
perfervid
topsy-turvied

ŬR'vĭl

servile

ÛR'vĭl	game-preserver	reversion	interlucent
chervil	life-preserver	subversion	lucent
servile	nerver	version	producent
	observer		reducent
ÛR'vim	preserver	**ÛR'zi**	relucent
cervine	reserver	furzy	traducent
nervine	server	jersey	*tralucent*
	swerver	kersey	translucent
ÛR'ving	time-server		unlucent
conserving	unnerver	**Ū'sa**	
curving		Arethusa	**ŪS'est**
deserving	**ÛR'vus**	Coosa	abstrusest̄
Irving	nervous	Medusa	*adducest*
nerving	recurvous	Sousa	*conducest*
observing		Susa	*deducest*
preserving	**ÛR'win**	Tallapoosa	*inducest*
reserving	Erwin	Tuscaloosa	*introducest*
serving	Irwin		loosest
swerving	Merwin	**ŪS'al**	*producest*
time-serving		hypotenusal	*profusest*
undeserving	**ÛRZ'da**		*reducest*
unnerving	Thursday	**ŪS'chun**	*reproducest*
unobserving		*adustion*	*seducest*
unswerving	**ÛR'zha**	combustion	sprucest
	Persia	fustian	*traducest*
ÛR'vis			*unloosest*
lip-service	**ÛR'zhun**	**ŪS'ed**	
merchant-serv-	animadver-	deuced	**ŪS'est**
ice	sion	(see ŪS+ed)	*fussest,* etc.
Purvis	aspersion		
sea-service	aversion	**ŪS'en**	**ŪS'et**
service	conversion	loosen	gusset
unservice	demersion	unloosen	russet
	discursion		
ÛRV'les	dispersion	**ŪS'ens**	**ŪS'eth**
nerveless	diversion	translucence	*adduceth*
	excursion		*conduceth*
ÛR'vur	incursion	**ŪS'ent**	*deduceth*
conserver	introversion	abducent	*educeth*
deserver	inversion	adducent	*induceth*
fervor	perversion	conducent	*introduceth*

		ŬSH'ez	absolution
looseth	discusses	blushes	allocution
produceth	fusses	brushes	attribution
reduceth	Gus's	crushes	circumlocution
reproduceth	musses	flushes	circumvolu-
seduceth	trusses	gushes	tion
spruceth	**ŪS'ful**	hushes	collocution
traduceth	juiceful	lushes	comminution
unlooseth	useful	mushes	constitution
ŬS'eth		onrushes	contribution
fusseth, etc.	**ŪSH'a**	plushes	convolution
	Jerusha	rushes	destitution
ŬS'ez	**ŪSH'a**	thrushes	devolution
abuses	Prussia	tushes	dilution
adduces	Russia	uprushes	diminution
burnooses			dissolution
cabooses	**ŪSH'al**	**ŬSH'i**	distribution
conduces	crucial	blushy	electrocution
deduces	fiducial	brushy	elocution
Druses		gushy	evolution
excuses	**ŬSH'an**	lushy	execution
induces	Prussian	rushy	immination
introduces	Russian	slushy	*insecution*
juices			institution
looses	**ŬSH'est**	**ŪSH'ing**	interlocution
nooses	*blushest*	douching	involution
produces	*brushest*	ruching	irresolution
reduces	*crushest*		Lilliputian
reproduces	*flushest*	**ŬSH'ing**	locution
seduces	*gushest*	blushing	obvolution
sluices	*hushest*	brushing	persecution
spruces	*rushest*	crushing	pollution
traduces		flushing	prosecution
truces	**ŬSH'eth**	gushing	prostitution
unlooses	*blusheth*	hushing	redargution
uses	*brusheth*	lushing	resolution
	crusheth	rushing	restitution
ŬS'ez	*flusheth*	unblushing	retribution
buses	*gusheth*		revolution
busses	*husheth*	**Ū'shun**	solution
cusses	*rusheth*	ablution	substitution

ōld, ôr, ŏdd, oil, fŏŏt, out; ūse, ûrn, ŭp; THis, thin

ventrilocution   **ŬS'id**   conclusive   **ŬS'kest**
volution   lucid   conducive   *duskest,* etc.
                     mucid   confusive
ŬSH'un   pellucid   contusive   **ŬS'ket**
concussion   translucid   deducive   busket
discussion   delusive   musket
incussion   **ŬS'ij**   diffusive
percussion   *abusage*   effusive   **ŬS'keth**
Prussian   usage   elusive   *dusketh,* etc.
recussion   exclusive
repercussion   **ŬS'il**   illusive   **ŬSki**
Russian   protrusile   inclusive   dusky
succussion   inconclusive   husky
                     ŬS'ing   infusive   musky
ŬSH'ur   adducing   inobtrusive   tusky
blusher   conducing   intrusive
brusher   deducing   obtrusive   **ŬS'kin**
crusher   educing   perfusive   buskin
flusher   inducing   reclusive   Ruskin
gusher   introducing   seclusive
husher   loosing   seducive   **ŬS'king**
plusher   producing   transfusive   dusking
rusher   reducing   husking
usher   reproducing   **ŬS'iv**   tusking
                     seducing   concussive
ŬSH'us   sprucing   discussive   **ŬS'kul**
Lucius   traducing   percussive   crepuscule
                     unloosing   repercussive   majuscule
ŬSH'us   succussive   minuscule
luscious   **ŬS'ing**   opuscule
                     bussing   **ŬS'kan**
ŬS'i   cussing   Della-Cruscan   **ŬS'kur**
goosy   discussing   dusken   husker
juicy   fussing   Etruscan   tusker
Lucy   mussing   molluscan
sluicy   trussing   Tuscan   **ŬS'l**
                                                          bustle
ŬS'ĭ   **ŬS'iv**   **ŬS'kat**   corpuscle
fussy   abusive   coruscate   hustle
hussy   allusive   infuscate   justle
mussy   collusive   obfuscate   muscle

---

mussel
opuscle
rustle
tussle

ŪS'les
juiceless
useless

ŬS'lest
bustlest, etc.

ŬS'leth
bustleth, etc.

ŬS'ling
bustling
hustling
muscling
rustling
tussling

ŬS'lur
bustler
hustler
rustler
tussler

ŬS"lz
Brussels
bustles, etc.

ŪS'ment
conducement
deducement
inducement
reducement
seducement
superinduce-
    ment
traducement

ŪS'nes
abstruseness
diffuseness
looseness
obtuseness
profuseness
recluseness
spruceness

Ū'so
Crusoe
trousseau
whoso

Ū'som
gruesome
twosome

ŬS'ta
Augusta

ŬS'tas
Eustace

ŬS'tat
incrustate

ŬS'ted
adjusted
bedusted
betrusted
busted
combusted
crusted
disgusted
distrusted
dusted
encrusted
entrusted
fusted
lusted

mistrusted
rusted
trusted

ŬS'test
adjustest
disgustest
distrustest
dustest
encrustest
entrustest
justest
lustest
mistrustest
robustest
rustest
thrustest
trustest

ŬS'teth
adjusteth
disgusteth
distrusteth
dusteth
encrusteth
entrusteth
lusteth
mistrusteth
thrusteth
trusteth

ŬST'ful
distrustful
lustful
mistrustful
overtrustful
trustful
untrustful

ŬS'ti
crusty

dusty
fustie
fusty
gusty
lusty
musty
rusty
trusty

ŬS'tik
fustic
rustic

ŬS'tin
Dustin
Justin

ŬS'ting
adjusting
bedusting
betrusting
busting
coadjusting
crusting
disgusting
distrusting
dusting
encrusting
entrusting
lusting
mistrusting
overtrusting
rusting
self-adjusting
thrusting
trusting
unmistrusting

ŬS'tingz
dustings
hustings
thrustings

ŬS'tis	ŬS'trum	clustered	immutate
Custis	flustrum	custard	scutate
justice	lustrum	flustered	
		lustered	ŪT'ed
ŬS'tiv	ŬS'trus	mustard	allocuted
adjustive	blustrous	mustered	bebooted
combustive	lustrous		booted
		ŬS'tus	bruited
ŬST'li	ŪS'tur	Augustus	comminuted
augustly	booster	Justus	commuted
justly	brewster		computed
robustly	Fewster	ŪS'ur	confuted
	jouster	abstruser	constituted
ŬST'ment	rooster	adducer	convoluted
adjustment	Worcester	conducer	deputed
encrustment		deducer	diluted
maladjustment	ŬS'tur	inducer	disputed
	adjuster	introducer	elocuted
ŬST'nes	bluster	looser	electrocuted
augustness	buster	producer	executed
justness	coadjuster	reducer	fluted
robustness	cluster	reproducer	fruited
	Custer	seducer	hooted
ŬS'to	distruster	sprucer	immuted
gusto	duster	traducer	imputed
	filibuster		instituted
ŬS'tom	fluster	ŬS'ur	involuted
custom	juster	cusser	looted
(cf. Rustum)	knuckle-duster	discusser	mooted
	lack-lustre	fusser	persecuted
ŬS'tral	luster	musser	polluted
lacustral	lustre	trusser	prosecuted
lustral	muster		prostituted
palustral	robuster	ŪT'al	recruited
	thruster	brutal	refuted
ŬS'trat	trust-buster	footle	reputed
frustrate	truster	tootle	rooted
illustrate		(cf. ŪT'il)	saluted
			self-constituted
ŬS'trin	ŬS'turd	ŪT'at	substituted
lacustrine	blustered	circumnutate	suited
palustrine	bustard		

tooted	*substitutest*	**ŪTH′est**	**Ŭth′ur**
transmuted	*suitest*	smoothest	Luther
unbooted	*transmutest*	soothest	uncouther
unconfuted	*uprootest*		
undisputed		**Ŭth′ful**	**Ŭth′ur**
unpersecuted	**ŬT′est**	ruthful	another
unpolluted	*buttest*	toothful	brother
unrooted	*ruttest*, etc.	truthful	Charter
unsuited		untruthful	brother
uprooted	**ŪT′eth**	youthful	foremother
voluted	*commuteth*		foster-brother
(cf. bootied,	*confuteth*	**ŪTH′ing**	foster-mother
putid)	*constituteth*	smoothing	half-brother
	deputeth	soothing	mother
ŬT′ed	*diluteth*		other
butted	*disputeth*	**Ŭth′ing**	smother
rutted, etc.	*executeth*	toothing	t′other
	hooteth		
ŪT′est	*imputeth*	**Ŭth′ing**	**ŪTH′urn**
acutest	*instituteth*	*doth*-ing	Sothern
astutest	*looteth*	nothing	southern
commutest	*overshooteth*		
confutest	*persecuteth*	**Ŭth′les**	**ŪT′i**
constitutest	*polluteth*	ruthless	agouti
cutest	*prosecuteth*	toothless	booty
deputest	*recruiteth*	truthless	beauty
dilutest	*refuteth*		cootie
disputest	*rooteth*	**ŪTH′nes**	cutie
executest	*saluteth*	smoothness	Djibouti
hootest	*shooteth*		duty
imputest	*suiteth*	**Ŭth′nes**	fluty
institutest	*transmuteth*	uncouthness	freebooty
lootest	*unbooteth*		fruity
minutest	*uprooteth*	**Ŭth′som**	Jibuti
mutest		toothsome	looty
persecutest	**ŬT′eth**	youthsome	rooty
recruitest	*butteth*		snooty
refutest	*rutteth*, etc.	**ŪTH′ur**	sooty
resolutest		smoother	tutti-frutti
salutest	**ŪT′ful**	soother	
shootest	fruitful		

ŬT'i

butty
gutty
jutty
nutty
putty
rutty
smutty
tutty

ŬT'ij

fruitage
mutage
scutage

ŬT'ik

diazeutic
emphyteutic
hermeneutic
maieutic
pharmaceutic
propædeutic
scorbutic
therapeutic
toreutic

ŬT'il

futile
inutile
rutile
sutile
(cf. ŬT'al)

ŬT'ing

booting
comminuting
commuting
computing
confuting
constituting
darned tooting

deputing
diluting
disputing
executing
fluting
fruiting
high-faluting
hooting
imputing
instituting
looting
mooting
offshooting
outshooting
overshooting
permuting
persecuting
polluting
prosecuting
prostituting
reconstituting
recruiting
refuting
rooting
saluting
scooting
shooting
substituting
suiting
tooting
transmuting
unbooting
unrooting
uprooting

ŬT'ing

abutting
butting
crosscutting
cutting
glass-cutting

glutting
gutting
jutting
nutting
putting
rebutting
rutting
shutting
strutting

ŬT'ish

brutish
sootish

ŬT'ish

ruttish
sluttish

ŬT'ist

flutist
hermeneutist
lutist
pharmaceutist
therapeutist

ŬT'iv

coadjutive
constitutive
indutive
persecutive
resolutive

ŬT'izm

brutism
mutism

ŬT''l

abuttal
cuttle
guttle
rebuttal

ruttle
scuttle
shuttle
subtle
suttle
Tuttle

ŬT'las

cutlass

ŬT'les

bootless
fruitless

ŬT'lest

scuttlest, etc.

ŬT'let

cutlet

ŬT'leth

scuttleth, etc.

ŬT'li

absolutely
posilutely

ŬT'ling

footling
tootling

ŬT'ling

gutling
scuttling
sutling

ŬT'lur

butler
cutler
scuttler
subtler
sutler

ŬT'ment	**ŬT'rid**	luter	pilot-cutter
confutement	putrid	minuter	putter
imbrutement		mooter	rebutter
recruitment	**ŬT'riks**	muter	scutter
	persecutrix	neuter	shutter
ŬT'nes	tutrix	parachuter	splutter
absoluteness		pea-shooter	sputter
acuteness	**ŬT'ron**	permuter	strutter
astuteness	neutron	persecutor	stutter
cuteness		pewter	utter
hirsuteness	**ŬT'si**	polluter	wood-cutter
minuteness	tootsie-wootsie	prosecutor	
muteness		prostitutor	**ŬT'urd**
	ŬT'ūr	recruiter	unuttered
Ū'to	future	refuter	fluttered, etc.
Pluto	puture	restitutor	
	suture	ringtailed	**Ū'ur**
Ū'ton		tooter	bedewer
Brewton	**ŬT'ŭr**	rooter	bestrewer
Newton	accoutre	saluter	bluer
Teuton	acuter	sharp-shooter	brewer
	astuter	shooter	canoer
ŬT'on	booter	substitutor	chewer
bachelor-	chuter	suitor	cooer
button	coadjutor	tooter	derring-doer
button	commuter	transmuter	doer
Dutton	computer	tutor	enduer
glutton	confuter	uprooter	eschewer
Hutton	constitutor		evildoer
mutton	cuter	**ŬT'ur**	ewer
Sutton	deputer	abutter	fewer
	diluter	bread-and-	gluer
ŬT'or	disputer	butter	hallooer
suitor	executor	butter	hewer
tutor, etc.	fluter	clutter	imbuer
(see ŬT'ur)	fouter	cutter	interviewer
	freebooter	flutter	mewer
ŬT'ral	hooter	glutter	misconstruer
neutral	imputer	gutter	misdoer
	institutor	mutter	newer
ŬT'res	looter	nutter	outdoer
buttress			

ōld, ôr, ŏdd, oil, fŏŏt, out; ūse, ûrn, ŭp; THis, thin

overdoer
pursuer
renewer
reviewer
ruer
sewer
screwer
shampooer
shoer
skewer
stewer
subduer
tattooer
truer
undoer
unscrewer
viewer
well-doer
wooer
wrong-doer

Ū'urd
leeward
sewered
skewered
steward

ŪV'al
approval
disapproval
disproval
removal
reproval

ŪV'ed
beloved

ŬL'el
scovel
shovel

ŬV'en
hooven
proven

ŬV'en
coven
oven
sloven

ŪV'est
approvest
disapprovest
disprovest
improvest
movest
provest
removest
reprovest

ŬV'eth
approveth
disapproveth
disproveth
improveth
moveth
proveth
removeth
reproveth

ŬV'i
movie

ŬV'i
covey
dovey
lovey

ŬV'ing
approving
disapproving
disproving
grooving

improving
moving
proving
removing
reproving
unmoving

ŬV'ing
gloving
loving
self-loving
shoving
ungloving
unloving

ŬV'les
gloveless
loveless

ŬV'ment
approvement
improvement
movement

ŬV'ur
approver
disapprover
disprover
groover
Hoover
improver
maneuver
mover
prover
remover
reprover
Vancouver
(cf. Louvre)

ŬV'ur
cover
discover

glover
lover
plover
recover
rediscover
shover
table-cover
uncover

ŬV'urn
govern

Ū'ya
alleluia

Ū'yans
buoyance

Ū'yant
buoyant

ŪZ'a
lallapalooza

ŪZ'al
musal
refusal
(cf. fusil)

ŪZ'an
Susan

ŬZ'ard
buzzard

ŬZ'band
husband

ŪZ'di
Tuesday

ŪZ'est
abusest

āle, câre, ădd. ārm, åsk; mē, hĕre, ĕnd; īce, ĭll;

accusest

amusest

boozest

bruisest

choosest

confusest

cruisest

diffusest

excusest

fusest

infusest

losest

musest

oozest

perusest

refusest

snoozest

suffusest

transfusest

usest

ŬZ'est

buzzest, etc.

ŪZ'eth

abuseth

accuseth

amuseth

boozeth

bruiseth

chooseth

confuseth

cruiseth

diffuseth

excuseth

fuseth

infuseth

loseth

museth

oozeth

peruseth

refuseth

snoozeth

suffuseth

transfuseth

useth

ŬZ'eth

buzzeth, etc.

ŪZ'ez

abuses

accuses

amuses

bemuses

bruises

chooses

circumfuses

confuses

contuses

cruises

diffuses

disabuses

disuses

druses

excuses

fuses

infuses

interfuses

loses

misuses

muses

nooses

oozes

peruses

refuses

snoozes

suffuses

transfuses

uses

ŬZ'ez

buzzes

fuzzes

Ū'zhun

abstrusion

abusion

affusion

allusion

circumfusion

collusion

conclusion

confusion

contusion

delusion

detrusion

diffusion

dissillusion

effusion

elusion

exclusion

extrusion

fusion

illusion

inclusion

infusion

interclusion

interfusion

intrusion

Malthusian

obtrusion

occlusion

perfusion

pertusion

preclusion

profusion

prolusion

protrusion

reclusion

refusion

retrusion

seclusion

self-delusion

suffusion

transfusion

trusion

(cf. ŪZ'i-an)

ŪZ'i

boozy

fluzie

oozy

woozy

ŬZ'i

fuzzy

hussy

ŪZ'ik

music

ŬZ'in

cousin

cozen

dozen

ŪZ'ing

abusing

accusing

amusing

boozing

bruising

choosing

confusing

contusing

cruising

diffusing

disusing

excusing

fusing

infusing

interfusing

losing
musing
oozing
perusing
refusing
self-accusing
snoozing
suffusing
transfusing
using

ŬZ'ing
buzzing
fuzzing

ŬZ'inz
cousins
cozens
couzens
dozens

ŪZ'iv
amusive
unamusive

ŬZ″l, ŪZ'al
bamboozle

foozle
gumfoozle
perusal
refusal

ŬZ″l
bemuzzle
fuzzle
guzzle
muzzle
nuzzle
puzzle
unmuzzle

ŬZ'lest
bemuzzlest, etc.

ŬZ'leth
bemuzzleth, etc.

ŬZ'lin
muslin

ŬZ'ling
bemuzzling
guzzling
muzzling

nuzzling
puzzling

ŪZ'lur
bamboozler
foozler

ŬZ'lur
guzzler
muzzler
puzzler

ŬZ'm
izzum-wuzzum

ŪZ'man
newsman
trewsman

ŪZ'ment
amusement

ŪZ'om
bosom

Ŭz'rel
newsreel

ŪZ'ur
abuser
accuser
amuser
boozer
bruiser
chooser
confuser
cruiser
diffuser
excuser
fuser
infuser
interfuser
lallapaloozer
loser
muser
non-user
oozer
peruser
refuser
snoozer
suffuser
transfuser
user

āle, câre, ădd, ärm, åsk; mē, hẹre, ĕnd; īce, ĭll;

WORDS ACCENTED ON THE THIRD SYLLABLE FROM THE END: ANTEPENULTS; TRIPLE RHYMES

A

For a discussion of words included under the accented vowels following, see the beginning of A rhymes in Section I.

(Note on Archaic Verb-forms among Triple Rhymes.—The archaic verb forms ending in-*est* and -*eth* have not as a rule been listed among the triple rhymes, to avoid needlessly expanding the book. When desired, they can be found by locating the present participles of triple-rhymed verbs, the -*ing* form: such forms as *laboring, bracketing, fracturing, dallying, hampering, clamoring, meandering,* and the rest. These can be turned without difficulty into the desired archaic forms: as, *laborest, laboreth; bracketest, bracketeth;* and so with all of them.)

Ă'a-b'l
conveyable
defrayable
impayable
payable
portrayable
repayable
unpayable
unprayable
unswayable

ĂB'a-sis
anabasis
catabasis
metabasis

ĂB'el-ur
gabeler
labeller

ĂB'i-a
Arabia
labia
Suabia

ĂB'i-an
Arabian
Fabian
Sabian
Sorabian
Suabian

ĂB'id-nes
rabidness
tabidness

ĂB'i-est
flabbiest
shabbiest

ĂB'i-ez
rabies
scabies

ĂB'i-fi
dissyllabify
labefy
syllabify
tabefy

ĂB'i-kal
Arabical
monosyllabical
polysyllabical

ĂB'i-li
flabbily
shabbily

ĂB'i-nes
flabbiness
scabbiness
shabbiness
slabbiness

ĂB'i-net
cabinet
tabinet

ĂB'i-tud
habitude
tabitude

ĂB'i-ur
flabbier
gabbier
shabbier

ĂB'la-tiv	**ĂB'u-lus**	**ĂD'e-us**	autographical
ablative	fabulous	Amadeus	bibliographical
bablative	pabulous		biographical
	sabulous	**ĂD'e-us**	calligraphical
ĂB″l-ment	tintinnabulous	Thaddeus	cartographical
babblement			cosmographical
brabblement	**ĂB'ur-ing**	**ĂD'i-an**	diagraphical
dabblement	belaboring	Acadian	ethnographical
gabblement	laboring	Arcadian	geographical
rabblement	neighboring	Barbadian	glossographical
	unlaboring	Canadian	graphical
ĂB″l-nes		nomadian	lexicographical
sableness	**ĂB'ur-ur**	Orcadian	lexigraphical
stableness	laborer	Palladian	orthographical
unstableness	taborer		palæonto-
		ĂD'i-ant	graphical
ĂB'o-la	**ĂCH'a-b'l**	irradiant	photographical
Metabola	attachable	radiant	physiograph-
parabola	catchable		ical
	detachable	**ĂD'i-ent**	phytographical
ĂB'ri-el	immatchable	gradient	pterylograph-
Gabriel	matchable		ical
	scratchable	**ĂD'i-tiv**	seraphical
ĂB'u-lar	unmatchable	additive	topographical
confabular		traditive	typographical
pabular	**ĂD'a-b'l,**		
tabular	**ĂD'i-b'l**	**ĂD'i-um**	**ĂF'ti-li**
tintinnabular	evadible	palladium	craftily
	persuadable	radium	draughtily
ĂB'u-lat	shadable	stadium	
confabulate	tradable	vanadium	**ĂG'ed-li**
tabulate	wadable		jaggedly
		ĂD'o-ing	raggedly
ĂB'u-list	**ĂD'ed-nes**	foreshadowing	
fabulist	bejadedness	overshadowing	**ĂG'ed-nes**
vocabulist	degradedness	shadowing	craggedness
	fadedness		jaggedness
ĂB'u-lum	jadedness	**ĂF'a-nus**	raggedness
acetabulum	persuadedness	diaphanous	
pabulum	shadedness	**ĂF'i-kal**	**ĂG'i-nes**
tintinnabulum		autobiographi-	bagginess
		cal	

āle, câre, ădd, ärm, ăsk; mē, hẹre, ĕnd; īce, ĭll;

cragginess
knagginess
scragginess
shagginess

ĂG′on-ist
agonist
antagonist
protagonist

ĂG′on-iz
agonize
antagonize

ĂG′on-izm
agonism
antagonism

ĂG′ran-si
flagrancy
fragrancy
vagrancy

ĂG′ur-i
faggery
jaggery
raggery
waggery
zigzaggery

ĂG′ur-ing
staggering
swaggering

ĂG′ur-ur
staggerer
swaggerer

Ā′ïk-al
algebraical
archaical
Hebraical

laical
paradisaical
pharisaical

Ā′it-i
gaiety
laity

ĂJ′a-b'l
assuageable
gaugeable

ĂJ′i-an
Brobdignagian
magian
pelagian
(cf. contagion)

ĂJ′i-kal
magical
tragical

ĂJ′il-nes
agileness
fragileness

ĂJ′in-al
imaginal
paginal
vaginal

ĂJ′in-us
cartilaginous
farraginous
lumbaginous
mucilaginous
oleaginous
voraginous

ĂJ′us-nes
advantageous-
    ness

courageous-
    ness
disadvan-
    tageousness
outrageous-
    ness
rampageous-
    ness
umbrageous-
    ness

ĂK′a-b'l
breakable
impacable
implacable
mistakable
pacable
placable
undertakable
unshakable

ĂK′et-ed
bracketed
jacketed
racketed

ĂK′et-ing
bracketing
jacketing
racketing

ĂK′i-an
batrachian
eustachian
Noachian

ĂK′i-nes
flakiness
quakiness
shakiness
snakiness

ĂK′ish-nes
brackishness
knackishnes
slackishness

ĂK′ri-ti
acrity
alacrity

ĂK′ron-izm
anachronism
metachronism

ĂK′sa-b'l
relaxable
taxable

ĂK′shun-al
factional
fractional
pactional

ĂK′shus-nes
factiousness
fractiousness

ĂK′ta-b'l,
    ĂK′ti-b'l
attractable
compactible
contractible
detractible
distractible
extractible
infractible
intactable
intractable
refractable
retractable
tactable
tractable

ĂK'ted-nes
abstractedness
contractedness
distractedness
protractedness

ĂK'ti-kal
didactical
practical

ĂK'ti-lus
didactylous
hexadactylous
leptodactylous
pachydacty-
   lous
pterodacty-
   lous

ĂK'tiv-nes
abstractive-
   ness
activeness
attractiveness
contractive-
   ness
detractiveness
distractiveness
protractiveness
putrefactive-
   ness
refractiveness

ĂK'to-ri
detractory
dissatisfactory
factory
lactary
manufactory
olfactory
phylactery

refractory
satisfactory
tractory

ĂK'tu-al
actual
factual
tactual

ĂK'tur-ing
fracturing
manufacturing

ĂK'u-lar
oracular
piacular
spectacular
supernacular
tabernacular
tentacular
vernacular

ĂK'u-lat
bimaculate
ejaculate
immaculate
jaculate
maculate

ĂK'u-lus
abaculus
miraculous
oraculous
piaculous
vernaculous

ĂK'ur-i
bakery
fakery
fakiry
rakery

ĂK'ur-i
hackery
hijackery
knick-knackery
quackery
Thackeray
Zachary

ĂK'ur-izm
fakirism
Quakerism
Shakerism

ĂK'we-us
aqueous
subaqueous
terraqueous

ĂL'a-b'l
assailable
available
bailable
exhalable
mailable
retailable
sailable
saleable
unassailable
unavailable
unsailable

ĀL'e-a
azalea
(cf. regalia)

ĀL'e-at, ĂL'i-at
malleate
palliate

ĂL'en-tin
Ballantine
Valentine

Ā'li-a
Adalia
Attalia
Australia
Centralia
echolalia
Eulalia
Fidelia
regalia
Rosalia
Sedalia
Thalia
(cf. azalea, and
   ĀL'ya)

ĂL'i-bur
caliber
Excalibur

ĂL'id-nes
impallidness
invalidness
pallidness
validness

ĂL'i-fi
alkaify
calefy
salify

ĂL'i-ing
dallying
rallying
sallying
tallying

ĂL'i-nes
dailiness
scaliness

ĂL'i-sis
analysis

catalysis
dialysis
paralysis

curiality
dextrality
duality
egality

inimicality
instrumen-
  tality
integrality

personality
plurality
potentiality
practicality

ĂL'i-son
Alison
Callison

elementality
ephemerality
essentiality
ethereality

intellectuality
intentionality
intrinsicality
irrationality

preternatur-
  ality
principality
prodigality

ĂL'i-ti
abnormality
accidentality
actuality
alamodality
animality
artificiality
banality
bestiality
Biblicality
brutality
carnality
causality
centrality
circumstan-
  tiality
classicality
comicality
confidentiality
congeniality
conjecturality
conjugality
connubiality
constitution-
  ality
consubstan-
  tiality
conventionality
conviviality
cordiality
corporality
corporeality
criminality

eventuality
externality
exterritorial-
  ity
fantasticality
fatality
feminality
feudality
finality
finicality
formality
frugality
fundamen-
  tality
generality
geniality
graduality
gutturality
horozontality
hospitality
ideality
illegality
immateriality
immorality
immortality
impartiality
imperiality
impersonality
inconsequen-
  tialty
individuality
ineffectuality
informality

joviality
laicality
laterality
legality
liberality
lineality
literality
locality
logicality
magistrality
materiality
mentality
meridionality
mesnality
modality
morality
mortality
municipality
mutuality
nasality
nationality
naturality
neutrality
notionality
occidentality
officiality
orientality
originality
orthodoxality
parochiality
partiality
pedality
penality

proportion-
  ality
provinciality
prudentiality
punctuality
radicality
rascality
rationality
reality
reciprocality
regality
rivality
rurality
sectionality
sensuality
sentimentality
septentrion-
  ality
seriality
sesquiped-
  ality
severality
sexuality
signality
sociality
sodality
speciality
spectrality
spirality
spirituality
substantiality
superficiality
supernaturality

ōld, ôr, ŏdd, oil, fŏŏt, out; ūse, ûrn, ŭp; THis, thin

technicality
temporality
theatricality
tonality
totality
traditionality
transcenden-
  tality
triality
triviality
universality
unusuality
vegetality
venality
veniality
verbality
verticality
visuality
vitality
vocality
whimsicality

ĂL'i-um
pallium
thallium

ĂL'i-ur
dallier
rallier
sallier
tallier

ĂL'ji-a
neuralgia
nostalgia

ĂL'o-est
callowest
hallowest
sallowest
shallowest

ĂL'o-gi
analogy
crustalogy
genealogy
genethlialogy
mammalogy
mineralogy
paralogy
petralogy
pyroballogy
tetralogy

ĂL'o-gist
analogist
decalogist
dialogist
genealogist
mammalogist
mineralogist
penalogist

ĂL'o-giz
analogize
dialogize
genealogize
paralogize

ĂL'o-gizm
analogism
dialogism
paralogism

ĂL'o-ish
sallowish
shallowish
tallowish

ĂL'o-nes
callowness
fallownes

sallowness
shallowness

ĂL'o-ur
callower
hallower
sallower
shallower
tallower

ĂL'ur-i
nailery
raillery

ĂL'ur-i
gallery
raillery
salary

ĀL'yen-izm,
  ĀL'yan-izm
alienism
bacchanalian-
  ism
episcopalian-
  ism
saturnalianism
sesquipeda-
  lianism
universalian-
  ism

ĂM'a-b'l
blamable
claimable
framable
irreclaimable
namable
reclaimable
tamable
unblamable
untamable

ĂM'a-ri
gramarye
mammary

ĂM'a-tist
dramatist
epigrammatist
grammatist
hierogram-
  matist
lipogrammatist
melodramatist

ĂM'a-tiv
amative
exclamative

ĂM'a-tiz
anagramma-
  tize
diagramma-
  tize
dramatize
epigramma-
  tize

ĂM'bu-lat
ambulate
deambulate
funambulate
perambulate
somnambu-
  late

ĂM'bu-list
funambulist
noctambulist
somnambulist

ĂM'bu-lizm
funambulism

noctambulism
somnambulism

ĂM'et-er
diameter
dynameter
hexameter
octameter
parameter
pentameter
peirameter
pluviameter
tetrameter
viameter
voltameter

ĂM'ful-nes
blamefulness
shamefulness

Ā'mi-a
lamia
Mesoptomania

ĂM'i-kal
amical
balsamical
dynamical

ĂM'in-a
lamina
stamina

ĂM'i-nat
contaminate
laminate

ĂM'is-tri
palmistry
psalmistry

ĂM'i-ti
amity
calamity

ĂM'les-nes
aimlessness
blamelessness
damelessness
famelessness
namelessness
shamelessness
tamelessness

ĂM'on-it
Ammonite
Mammonite

ĂM'on-izm
Mammonism
Shamanism

ĂM'or-us
amorous
clamorous
glamorous

ĂM'pi-on
campion
champion
tampion

ĂM'pur-ing
hampering
pampering
scampering
tampering

ĂM'pur-ur
hamperer
pamperer
scamperer
tamperer

ĂM'ul-us
famulus
hamulus
ramulous

ĂM'ur-ing
clamoring
hammering
stammering
yammering

ĂM'ur-on
Decameron
Heptameron

ĂM'ur-ur
clamorer
hammerer
stammerer

ĂN'a-b'l
ascertainable
attainable
chainable
constrainable
containable
detainable
distrainable
drainable
explainable
gainable
maintainable
obtainable
ordainable
overstrainable
restrainable
retainable
sprainable
strainable
sustainable

trainable
unattainable

ĂN'a-b'l
insanable
sanable
tannable
(cf. cannibal)

ĂN'ar-i
chicanery
lanary
planary

ĂN'a-ri
granary
panary
(see ĂN'ur-i)

ĂN'ches-tur
Granchester
Manchester

ĂND'a-b'l
commandable
countermand-
    able
demandable
reprimandable
sandable
understandable

ĂN'di-fi
candify
dandify

ĂN'di-nes
dandiness
handiness
sandiness

ĂN'dri-an
Alexandrian
meandrian
Menandrian

ĂN'dur-ing
meandering
pandering
philandering
slandering

ĂN'dur-ing
wandering
(see ŎN-dur-
ing)

ĂN'dur-son
Anderson
Sanderson

ĂN'dur-ur
meanderer
panderer
philanderer
slanderer

ĂN'dur-ur
launderer
wanderer
(see ŎN'dur-
ur)

ĂN'dur-us
panderous
slanderous

ĂN'el-ing
channelling
panelling

ĂN'e-us
antecedaneous

araneous
circumforane-
 ous
coëtaneous
contemporane-
 ous
cutaneous
dissentaneous
extemporane-
 ous
exterraneous
extraneous
instantaneous
mediterra-
 neous
membraneous
miscellaneous
momentaneous
porcelaneous
simultaneous
spontaneous
subcutaneous
subterraneous
succedaneous
temporaneous
terraneous

ĀN'ful'i
banefully
disdainfully
painfully

ĀN'ful-nes
disdainfulness
gainfulness
painfulness

ĂNGK'ur-ing,
ĂNGK'or-ing
anchoring
cankering

encankering
hankering

ĂNGKur-us
cankerous
cantankerous

ĂNG"lsom
anglesome
tanglesome
wranglesome

ĂNG'u-lar
angular
octangular
pentangular
quadrangular
rectangular
slangular
triangular

Ā-ni-a
Albania
Anglo-mania
Aquitania
bibliomania
decalcomania
demonomania
dipsomania
eleuthero-
 mania
erotomania
Gallomania
kleptomania
Lithuania
logomania
Lusitania
mania
Mauretania
megalomania
metromania

miscellanea
monomania
nymphomania
Pennsylvania
pyromania
Rumania
succedanea
Tasmania
Titania
Transylvania
Tripolitania
Ukrainia
Urania

Ā'ni-ak
bibliomaniac
dipsomaniac
eleutheroman-
 iac
kleptomaniac
maniac
megalomaniac
monomaniac
nymphomaniac

Ā'ni-al
cranial
domanial
subterraneal

Ā-ni-an
Albanian
Alcmanian
Aquitanian
circumforanean
cyanean
extemporanean
Iranian
Lithuanian
Mauretanian
Mediterranean

Pennsylvani-
an
Rumanian
Sandemanian
subterranean
Tasmanian
Transylvanian
Tripolitanian
Turanian
Ukrainian
Uranian
volcanian

ĂN'i-bal
cannibal
Hannibal
(cf. sanable)

ĂN'i-el
Daniel
Nathaniel
(cf. spaniel)

ĂN'i-gan
Brannigan
Flannigan
Mullanigan

ĂN'i-kal
botanical
Brahmanical
charlatanical
galvanical
mechanical
panicle
tyrannical

ĂN'i-fi
humanify
insanify
sanify

ĂN'i-mus
animus
magnanimous
multanimous
pusillanimous
unanimous

ĂN'i-shing
banishing
planishing
vanishing

ĂN'ish-ment
banishment
evanishment
vanishment

ĂN'is-tur
banister
canister
ganister

ĂN'i-ti
aldermanity
Christianity
gigmanity
humanity
immanity
inanity
inhumanity
inorganity
insanity
inurbanity
mundanity
paganity
profanity
sanity
subterranity
urbanity
vanity
volcanity

Ā'ni-um
cranium
geranium
pericranium
succedaneum
titanium
uranium

ĂN'jen-si
plangency
tangency

ĂN'ji-b'l
frangible
infrangible
intangible
refrangible
tangible

ĂN'i-kin
manikin
pannikin

ĂN'o-graf
galvanograph
pianograph

ĂN'o-skop
diaphanoscope
galvanoscope

ĂN'shi-an
Byzantian
(cf. ĂN'shun)

ĂN'shi-at
circumstantiate
substantiate
transubstanti-
ate

ĂN'siv-nes
advanciveness
expansiveness

ĂN'som-est
handsomest
ransomest

ĂN'som-ur
handsomer
ransomer

ĂNT'a-b'l
grantable
plantable

ĂN'tur-ing
bantering
cantering

ĂNT'ur-ur
banterer
canterer

ĂN'thro-pi
apanthropy
aphilanthropy
lycanthropy
misanthropy
philanthropy
physianthropy
psilanthropy
theanthropy
theophilan-
thropy
zoanthropy

ĂN'thro-pist
misanthropist
philanthropist

ōld, ôr, ŏdd, oil, fŏŏt, out; ūse, ûrn, ŭp; THis, thin

psilanthropist
theophilan-
  thropist

ĂN'thro-pizm
psilanthropism
theanthropism
theophilanthro-
  pism

ĂN'ti-sid
giganticide
infanticide

ĂN'tik-nes
franticness
giganticness
romanticness

ĂN'u-al
annual
manual

ĂN'u-la
cannula
granula

ĂN'u-lar
annular
cannular
penannular

ĂN'u-lat
annulate
campanulate
granulate

ĂN'ur-et
banneret
lanneret

ĂN'ur-i
cannery

charlatanery
granary
panary
stannary
tannery

ĂP'a-b'l
capable
drapable
escapable
incapable
inescapable
papable
shapeable

ĂP'id-li
rapidly
sapidly
vapidly

ĂP'id-nes
rapidness
sapidness
vapidness

ĂP'i-est
happiest
sappiest
snappiest

ĂP'i-li
happily
snappily

ĂP'i-nes
happiness
sappiness
snappiness

ĂP'i-ur
happier

sappier
snappier

ĂP'o-lis
Annapolis
Indianapolis
Minneapolis

ĂP'ur-i
apery
drapery
grapery
napery
papery
vapory

ĂP'ur-ing
capering
papering
tapering
vaporing

ĂP'ur-ur
caperer
paperer
vaporer

ĂR'a-b'l
airable
bearable
dareable
declarable
pairable
repairable
swearable
tearable
unbearable
unwearable
wearable

ĂR'a-b'l
arable
parable

ĂR'a-dis
imparadise
paradise

ĂR'as-ing
embarrassing
harassing

ĂR'as-ment
embarrassment
harassment

ĂR'a-tiv
comparative
declarative
narrative
preparative
reparative

ĂR'bur-ing
barbering
harboring

ĂR'di-an
guardian
pericardian

ĂR'di-nes
fool-hardiness
hardiness
tardiness

Â're-a
area
(see Â'ri-a)

ĂR'ful-i
carefully
prayerfully
uncarefully

āle,   câre,   ădd,   ärm,   ăsk;   mē,   hẹre,   ĕnd;   īce,   ĭll;

ÄR'ful-nes
carefulness
prayerfulness
sparefulness
uncarefulness
warefulness

A'ri-a
adversaria
area
Bulgaria
caballeria
Calceolaria
Cineraria
dataria
digitaria
Hilaria
malaria
wistaria
(cf. pariah)

ÄR'i-al
actuarial
areal
calendarial
commissarial
diarial
glossarial
malarial
nectarial
notarial
ovarial
puparial
secretarial
vicarial

ÄR'i-an
abecedarian
Adessenarian
agrarian
alphabetarian

altitudinarian
anecdotarian
antiquarian
antisabbatarian
antitrinitarian
apiarian
Apollinarian
aquarian
Arian
Aryan
atrabilarian
attitudinarian
barbarian
Bavarian
Briarean
Bulgarian
Cæsarian
centenarian
diarian
dietarian
disciplinarian
doctrinarian
equalitarian
estuarian
experimenta-
  rian
futilitarian
grammarian
humanitarian
Hungarian
Icarian
Janizarian
lapidarian
latitudinarian
libertarian
librarian
limitarian
lunarian
Megarian
millenarian
miscellanarian

necessarian
necessitarian
nectarian
nonagenarian
octagenarian
ovarian
Parian
parliamenta-
  rian
platitudinarian
plenitudinarian
predestinarian
proletarian
riparian
sabbatarian
sacramentarian
sanitarian
sectarian
sententiarian
septuagenarian
sexagenarian
societarian
stipendarian
sublapsarian
supralapsarian
Tartarean
tractarian
trinitarian
ubiquarian
ubiquitarian
unitarian
utilitarian
valetudinarian
vegetarian
veterinarian
vulgarian

ÄR'i-ant
contrariant
omniparient
variant

ÄR'i-at
variate
vicariate

ÄR'i-at
commissariat
lariat
proletariat
prothonotariat
secretariat

ÄR'i-est
chariest
variest
wariest

ÄR'i-et, ÄR'i-ot
Harriet
Iscariot
Marryatt
Marriott

A'ri-ez
Aries
caries

ÄR'i-fi
clarify
saccharify
scarify

ÄR'i-form
peariform
scalariform

ÄR'i-gan
Garrigan
Harrigan

ÄR'i-ing
carrying
harrying

ōld, ôr, ŏdd, oil, fŏŏt, out; ūse, ûrn, ŭp; THis, thin

marrying

tarrying

ĂR'i-nes

airiness

arbitrariness

chariness

contrariness

glariness

hairiness

salutariness

sanguinariness

sedentariness

solitariness

temporariness

tumultuariness

ubiquitariness

voluntariness

wariness

ĂR'i-nes

starriness

tarriness

ĂR'ing-li

blaringly

daringly

flaringly

glaringly

sparingly

tearingly

ĂR'ing-ton

Barrington

Carrington

Farrington

Harrington

ĂR'i-o

impresario

(cf. Lothario)

ĂR'i-on

clarion

Marion

(cf. Marian)

ĂR'i-son

garrison

Harrison

ĂR'i-ti

debonairity

rarity

ĂR'i-ti

angularity

barbarity

charity

circularity

clarity

disparity

dissimilarity

exemplarity

familiarity

fissiparity

gemmiparity

globularity

hilarity

imparity

insularity

irregularity

jocularity

molecularity

muscularity

omniparity

parity

particularity

peculiarity

perpendicu-

  larity

piacularity

polarity

popularity

pupilarity

rectangularity

rectilinearity

regularity

secularity

similarity

singularity

solidarity

titularity

triangularity

uncharity

vascularity

viviparity

vulgarity

ĂR'i-tud

amaritude

claritude

ĂR'i-um

aquarium

aqua-vivarium

barium

columbarium

glaciarium

honorarium

sacrarium

sanitarium

tepidarium

termitarium

vivarium

ĂR'i-ur

charier

warier

ĂR'i-ur

barrier

carrier

farrier

harrier

marrier

tarrier

ĂR'i-us

arbitrarious

arenarious

Aquarius

atrabilarious

calcareous

contrarious

denarius

frumentarious

gregarious

hilarious

horarious

malarious

multifarious

nectareous

nefarious

omnifarious

precarious

quadragena-

  rious

Sagittarius

tartareous

temerarious

testudinarious

vagarious

valetudinarious

various

vicarious

viparious

ĂR'ki-kal

archical

hierarchical

hylarchical

monarchical

tetrarchical

āle. câre, ădd, ärm, ăsk; mē, hĕre, ĕnd; īce, ĭll;

ÄR′la-tan
charlatan
tarlatan

ÄR′ming-li
alarmingly
charmingly
farmingly
harmingly

ÄR′nish-ing
garnishing
tarnishing
varnishing

ÄR′nish-ur
garnisher
tarnisher
varnisher

ÄR′o-est
harrowest
narrowest

ÄR′o-i
arrowy
marrowy
sparrowy
yarrowy

ÄR′o-ing
harrowing
narrowing

Ä′ron-it
Aaronite
Maronite

ÄR′o-ur
harrower
narrower

ÄR′sen-i
coparceny
larceny

ÄR′sen-ur
coparcener
larcener
parcener

ÄR′shal-izm
martialism
partialism

ÄR′ted-nes
departedness
false-
    heartedness
frank-
    heartedness
free-
    heartedness
hard-
    heartedness
kind-
    heartedness
light-
    heartedness
open-
    heartedness
soft-
    heartedness
tender-
    heartedness
true-
    heartedness
warm-
    heartedness

ÄR′ti-k′l
article
particle

ÄR′ti-zan
artizan
bartizan
partisan

ÄRT′les-li
artlessly
heartlessly

ÄRT′les-nes
artlessness
heartlessness

ÄRT′ur-ing
bartering
chartering
martyring

ÄRT′ur-ur
barterer
charterer

ĂS′a-b′l
chasable
effaceable
erasible
evasible
ineffaceable
retraceable
traceable

ĂS′en-si
adjacency
complacency
interjacency

ĂS′ful-nes
disgracefulness

gracefulness
ungracefulness

A′shi-a
acacia
Asia
Aspasia
(cf. Ä′zhi-a,
    Ä′zi-a, Ä′sha,
    Ä′zha. So in
    all similar
    cases)

ĂSH′i-a
cassia
Parnassia
quassia

Ä′shi-al
basial
(cf. spatial)

A′shi-an
Alsatian
Asian
Athanasian
Australasian
Galatian
Haytian
Hieracian
Horatian
Latian
Pancratian
Thracian
(cf. Ä′shun,
    Ä′zhun)

ĂSH′i-an
Circassian
Parnassian
(cf. ĂSH′un)

Ā′shi-at
emaciate
expatiate
glaciate
ingratiate
insatiate
satiate

Ā′shi-ent
calefacient
delirefacient
facient
liquefacient
parturifacient
rubefacient
sensifacient
sorbefacient
stupefacient
tumefacient
(cf. Ā′shent)

ĂSH′i-nes
ashiness
flashiness
trashiness

Ā′shun-al
associational
congregational
conservational
conversational
creational
denominational
derivational
dissertational
educational
emigrational
gradational
gyrational
ideational
imitational

inspirational
observational
probational
relational
representational
respirational
rotational
sensational
stational
terminational

ĂSH′un-al
international
irrational
national
rational

ĂSH′un-at
compassionate
dispassionate
impassionate
incompassion-
  ate
passionate

ĂSH′un-ing
compassioning
fashioning
passioning

Ā′shun-ist
annexationist
annihilationist
annotationist
causationist
conversationist
convocationist
cremationist
degenerationist
educationist
emancipationist

emigrationist
imitationist
inflationist
innovationist
inspirationist
repudiationist
restorationist
transmutation-
  ist

Ā′shun-les
conversation-
  less
educationless
emigrationless
foundationless
immigration-
  less
imitationless
inspirationless
temptationless

Ā′shun-ur
foundationer
oblationer
probationer
reprobationer
restorationer
stationer

ĂSH′ur-i
fashery
haberdashery
sashery

Ā′shus-nes
audaciousness
capaciousness
contumacious-
  ness

disputatious-
  ness
edaciousness
efficaciousness
fallaciousness
fugaciousness
graciousness
incapacious-
  ness
ineffacious-
  ness
loquaciousness
mendaciousness
ostentatious-
  ness
perspicacious-
  ness
pertinacious-
  ness
pugnaciousness
rapaciousness
sagaciousness
salaciousness
sequaciousness
spaciousness
tenaciousness
ungraciousness
veraciousness
vexatiousness
vivaciousness
voraciousness

ĂS′i-b'l
impassible
irascible
passable
passible
renascible
surpassable

ĂS′i-nat
abbacinate

assassinate
deracinate
exacinate
fascinate

ĂS′i-nes
laciness
raciness

ĂS′i-nes
brassiness
classiness
glassiness
grassiness
massiness
sassiness

ĂS′i-ti
audacity
bellacity
bibacity
capacity
contumacity
dicacity
edacity
feracity
fugacity
incapacity
loquacity
mendacity
minacity
mordacity
opacity
perspicacity
pertinacity
pervicacity
procacity
pugnacity
rapacity
sagacity
salacity

saponacity
sequacity
tenacity
veracity
vivacity
voracity

ĂS′iv-li
impassively
massively
passively

Ā′siv′nes
dissuasiveness
evasiveness
persuasiveness
pervasiveness
suasiveness

ĂS′iv-nes
impassiveness
massiveness
passiveness

ĂSP′ing-li
gaspingly
raspingly

ĂS′tar-di
bastardy
dastardy

ĂST′ful-i
tastefully
wastefully
distastefully

ĂS′ti-kal
ecclesiastical
elastical
encomiastical

enthusiastical
fantastical
gymnastical

ĂS′ti-li
hastily
pastily
tastily

ĂS′ti-sizm
ecclesiasticism
fantasticism
monasticism
scholasticism

ĂS′tri-an
alabastrian
Lancastrian
Zoroastrian

ĂS′tro-fe
catastrophe
epanastrophe

ĂS′tur-ship
mastership
pastorship

ĂS′tur-i
dicastery
mastery
plastery
self-mastery

ĂS′tur-ing
beplastering
mastering
overmastering
plastering

ĂS′ur-at
emacerate

lacerate
macerate

ĂS′ur-i
bracery
embracery
tracery

ĂT′a-b'l
abatable
beratable
collatable
creatable
debatable
dilatable
gratable
hatable
matable
ratable
regulatable
statable
translatable
untranslatable

ĂT′a-b'l
combatable
(see ĂT′i-b'l)

ĂT′e-lit
patellite
satellite

Ā′ten-si
latency
patency

ĂT′ful-i
fatefully
gratefully
hatefully

ĂT′ful-nes
fatefulness

gratefulness
hatefulness

Ā'thi-an
Carpathian
Sabbathian

Ăth'e-sis
diathesis
parathesis

Ăth'i-kal
anthropopath-
  ical
chrestomath-
  ical

ĂTH'ur-ing
blathering
foregathering
gathering
lathering
upgathering
wool-gathering

ĂTH'ur-ur
foregatherer
gatherer
latherer
tax-gatherer
toll-gatherer
upgatherer

ĂT'i-b'l
combatable
come-atable
compatible
impatible
incompatible
patible

ĂT'i-fi
beatify
gratify
ratify
stratify

ĂT'ik-a
Attica
dalmatica
hepatica
sciatica

ĂT'ik-al
abbatical
acroamatical
aerostatical
anathematical
anidiomatical
apophthegmat-
  ical
apostatical
aristocratical
asthmatical
autocratical
automatical
axiomatical
bureaucratical
climatical
democratical
diplomatical
dogmatical
dramatical
ecstatical
emblematical
emphatical
enigmatical
epigrammat-
  ical
fanatical
grammatical
hebdomatical

idiomatical
leviratical
mathematical
phantasmatical
piratical
pragmatical
primatical
sabbatical
schismatical
separatical
Socratical
spasmatical
statical
vatical

ĂT'in-at
gelatinate
Palatinate

ĂT'i-nes
slatiness
weightiness

ĂT'i-nes
chattiness
fattiness
nattiness

ĂT'in-iz
gelatinize
Latinize
platinize

ĂT'i-nus
gelatinous
platinous

ĂT'i-siz
emblematicize
fanaticize
grammaticize

ĂT'i-sizm
Asiaticism

fanaticism
grammaticism

ĂT'i-tud
attitude
beatitude
gratitude
ingratitude
latitude
platitude

Ā'tiv-nes
alliterativeness
imitativeness
nativeness
penetrative-
  ness

ĂT"l-ment
battlement
embattlement
prattlement
tattlement

ĂT'om-i
anatomy
atomy

ĂT'om-ist
anatomist
atomist

ĂT'om-iz
anatomize
atomize

ĂT'om-izm
anatomism
atomism

ĂT'om-us
diatomous
paratomous

āle,   câre.   ădd,   ärm,   ăsk;   mē,   hẹre,   ĕnd;   īce,   ĭll;

ĂT'or-i	quadrilateral	flatterer	Batavian
obsecratory	unilateral	patterer	Belgravian
ratiocinatory		scatterer	Moravian
recapitulatory	**ĂT'ur-an**	shatterer	Scandinavian
	cateran	smatterer	Shavian
ĂT'ri-kal	Lateran	splatterer	
idolatrical			**ĂV'ij-ing**
theatrical	**ĂT'ur-at**	**Ā'ur-i**	ravaging
	maturate	aëry	scavaging
ĂT'ri-sid	saturate	*faërie*	
fratricide	supersaturate		**ĂV'ij-ur**
matricide		**ĂV'an-ez**	ravager
patricide	**ĂT'ur-i**	Havanese	savager
	battery	Javanese	scavager
Ā'tron-al	flattery		
matronal	shattery	**ĂV'el-ing**	**ĂV'ish-ing**
patronal	slattery	gravelling	enravishing
	tattery	ravelling	lavishing
Ā'tron-ij		travelling	ravishing
matronage	**ĂT'ur-ing**	unravelling	**ĂV'ish-ment**
patronage	battering		enravishment
	beflattering	**ĂV'el-ur**	lavishment
Ā'tron-iz	bepattering	raveller	ravishment
matronize	bescattering	traveller	
patronize	bespattering	unraveller	**ĂV'ish-nes**
	blattering		knavishness
ĂT'u-lat	chattering	**ĂV'en-dur**	slavishness
congratulate	clattering	chavender	
gratulate	flattering	lavender	**ĂV'ish-ur**
spatulate	pattering		lavisher
	scattering	**Ā'vi-a**	ravisher
ĂT'ūr-al	shattering	Batavia	**ĂV'i-ti**
natural	smattering	Belgravia	cavity
preternatural	spattering	Jugo-slavia	concavity
supernatural	splattering	Moravia	depravity
		Octavia	gravity
ĂT'ŭr-al	**ĂT'ur-ur**	Pavia	pravity
bilateral	batterer	Scandinavia	suavity
collateral	blatterer		
equilateral	chatterer	**Ā'vi-an**	**ĂV'ur-i**
lateral	clatterer	avian	bravery

gravery	**ĀV′ur-ur**	**Ā′zi-a**	Rabelaisian
savory	favorer	Aspasia	(cf. Ā′zhun)
slavery	flavorer	athanasia	
unsavory	quaverer	aphasia	**ĀZ′i-b′l**
	waverer	euthanasia	persuasible
		paronomasia	praisable
ĀV′ur-ing	**ĀV′ur-us**		raisable
favoring	flavorous	**A′zi-an**	suasible
flavoring	savorous	Asian	
quavering		Athanasian	**ĀZ′i-nes**
savoring	**ĂV′ur-us**	Australasian	craziness
unwavering	cadaverous	Caucasian	haziness
wavering	papaverous	Eurasian	laziness
			maziness

E

For a discussion of words included under the accented vowels following, see the beginning of E rhymes in Section I.

Ē′a-b′l	**Ē′al-ti**	impeachable	impedible
agreeable	fealty	reachable	obedible
creable	realty	teachable	pleadable
decreeable		unimpeachable	readable
disagreeable	**Ē′an-izm**	unteachable	
feeable	epicureanism		**ĔD′a-b′l**
irremeable	Laodiceanism	**ĔCH′i-nes**	dreadable
	peanism	sketchiness	(see ĔD′i-b′l)
Ē′al′ist	plebeianism	tetchiness	
idealist	Pythagorean-		**ĒD′ful-nes**
realist	ism	**ĔCH′ur-i**	heedfulness
	Sabæanism	lechery	needfulness
Ē′al-iz	**ĒB′ri-us**	treachery	unheedfulness
idealise	ebrious		unneedfulness
realise	funebrious	**ĔCH′ur-us**	**Ē′di-al**
	inebrious	lecherous	bimedial
Ē′al-izm	tenebrious	treacherous	intermedial
idealism			medial
realism	**ĔCH′a-b′l**	**ĒD′a-b′l**	pedial
	bleachable	exceedable	remedial

āle, câre, ădd, ärm, åsk; mē, hęre, ĕnd, Ice, ĭll;

Ē′di-an	readiest	readiness	needier
comedian	steadiest	steadiness	reedier
encyclopedian	unsteadiest	threadiness	seedier
median		unreadiness	speedier
tragedian	**ĔD′i-kal**	unsteadiness	weedier
	medical		
Ē′di-at	pedicle	**ĔD′i-nus**	**ĔD′i-ur**
immediate		mucedinous	headier
intermediate	**ĔD′i-kant**	putredinous	readier
mediate	medicant	rubedinous	steadier
	predicant		unsteadier
ĔD′i-b'l		**ĔD′i-ted**	
credible	**ĔD′i-kat**	accredited	**Ē′di-us**
dreadable	dedicate	credited	intermedious
edible	medicate	discredited	tedious
incredible	predicate	edited	
		miscredited	**ĔD′les-li**
Ē′di-ens	**ĔD′i-li**	unaccredited	heedlessly
disobedience	greedily		needlessly
expedience	needily	**ĔD′i-ting**	
inexpedience	speedily	accrediting	**ĔD′les-nes**
obedience		crediting	heedlessness
	ĔD′i-li	discrediting	needlessness
Ē′di-ent	headily	editing	
disobedient	readily	miscrediting	**ĔD′u-lus**
expedient	steadily		credulous
inexpedient	unsteadily	**ĔD′i-tiv**	incredulous
ingredient		redditive	sedulous
obedient	**ĔD′i-ment**	sedative	
	impediment		**ĔD′ur-al**
ĔD′i-est	pediment	**ĔD′i-tor**	federal
beadiest	sediment	creditor	hederal
greediest		editor	
neediest	**ĔD′i-nes**		**ĔD′ur-ship**
reediest	greediness	**Ē′di-um**	leadership
seediest	neediness	medium	readership
speediest	seediness	tedium	
weediest	speediness		**ĒF′i-nes**
	weediness	**ĔD′i-ur**	beefiness
ĔD′i-est	**ĔD′i-nes**	beadier	leafiness
headiest	headiness	greedier	

ōld, ôr, ŏdd, oil, foŏt, out; ūse, ûrn, ŭp; THis, thin

ĔF′i-sens
beneficence
maleficence

ĔF′i-sent
beneficent
maleficent

ĔF′ur-ens
cross-reference
deference
preference
reference

ĔF′ur-ent
deferent
efferent

ĔG′a-b'l
beggable
legable

Ē′gal-izm
legalism
regalism

Ē′gal-nes
illegalness
legalness
regalness

ĔG′i-nes
dregginess
legginess

ĔG′nan-si
pregnancy
regnancy

ĔG′ur-i
beggary

eggery
(cf. Gregory)

Ē′gur-li
eagerly
meagrely
overeagerly

Ē′gur-nes
eagerness
meagreness
overeagerness

Ē′i-ti
aseity
contempora-
  neity
corporeity
deity
diathermaneity
extraneity
femineity
gaseity
hæcceity
hermaphro-
  deity
heterogeneity
homogeneity
incorporeity
instantaneity
multeity
omneity
personeity
plebeity
seity
simultaneity
spontaneity
terreity
velleity

Ē′ji-an
collegian

Fuegian
Norwegian
(cf. ĒJ′un)

ĔJ′i-b'l
allegeable
illegible
legible

Ē′jus-nes
egregiousness
sacrilegious-
  ness

ĔK′a-b'l
speakable
unspeakable

ĔK′a-b'l
impeccable
insecable
peccable

ĔK′i-li
cheekily
creakily
leakily
sleekily
sneakily
squeakily

ĔK′i-nes
cheekiness
creakiness
leakiness
sneakiness
squeakiness

ĔK′ish-nes
cliquishness
freakishness
sneakishness

ĔK′on-ing
beckoning
dead-reckoning
reckoning

ĔK′re-ment
decrement
recrement

ĔK′shun-al
affectional
complexional
correctional
inflectional
insurrectional
interjectional
intersectional
protectional
sectional

ĔK′shun-ist
insurrectionist
perfectionist
protectionist
resurrectionist

ĔK′shun-iz
resurrectionize
sectionize

ĔK′si-b'l
flexible
inflexible
nexible
reflexible

ĔK′si-ti
complexity
convexity
intercom-
  plexity

āle,   câre,   ădd,   ärm,   åsk;   mē,   hĕre,   ĕnd;   īce,   ĭll;

perplexity
reflexity

ĔK′siv-nes
perplexiveness
reflexiveness

ĔK′ta-b'l
respectable
(see ĔK′ti-b'l)

ĔK′tar-i
nectary
(see ĔK′to-ri)

ĔK′ted-nes
abjectedness
affectedness
dejectedness
disaffectedness
infectedness
suspectedness
unsuspected-
    ness

ĔK′ti-b'l
affectible
collectible
correctible
defectible
delectable
detectible
dissectible
effectible
erectable
expectable
indefectible
indelectable
objectable
prefectible
reflectible

rejectable
respectable
suspectable

ĔK′ti-fi
objectify
rectify

ĔK′ti-kal
apoplectical
dialectical

ĔK′ti-tud
rectitude
senectitude

ĔK′tiv-li
collectively
defectively
effectively, etc.

ĔK′tiv-nes
collectiveness
defectiveness
effectiveness
ineffectiveness
objectiveness
prospectiveness
protectiveness
reflectiveness
subjectiveness

ĔK′to-ral
electoral
pectoral
protectoral
rectoral
sectoral

ĔK′to-rat
directorate

electorate
expectorate
protectorate
rectorate

ĔK′to-ri
correctory
directory
nectary
rectory
refectory
sectary

ĔK′tu-al
effectual
ineffectual
intellectual
lectual

ĔK′tur-al
architectural
conjectural

ĔK′tur-ur
conjecturer
lecturer

ĔK′u-lar
molecular
secular
specular

ĔK′u-lat
peculate
speculate

ĔK′u-tiv
consecutive
executive
subsecutive

ĔL′a-b'l
concealable
congealable
healable
inconcealable
repealable
revealable

ĔL′a-tiv
compellative
correlative
relative

ĔL′e-gat
delegate
relegate

ĔL′fish-nes
elfishness
selfishness

Ē′li-a
Amelia
Aurelia
Bedelia
Cecelia
Celia
Cordelia
Cornelia
Fidelia
Lelia
Ophelia
(also ĒL′ya)

Ē′li-an
Aristotelian
carnelian
Delian
Hegelian
Ismaelian
Machiavelian

ōld, ôr, ŏdd, oil, fŏŏt, out; ūse, ûrn, ŭp; THis, thin

Mephisto-
  phelian
Mingrelian
(also ĒL′yan)

ĔL′i-an
Boswellian
Cromwellian
evangelian
selion
(also ĔL′yan,
  ĔL′yun,
  which see)

ĔL′i-b′l,
  ĔL′a-b′l
compellable
delible
expellable
fellable
gelable
indelible
ingelable
spellable
tellable

ĔL′i-kal
angelical
bellical
evangelical
helical
pellicle

Ē′li-on
anthelion
aphelion
chameleon

ĔL′ish-ing
embellishing
relishing

ĔL′ish-ment
embellishment
relishment

Ē′li-us
Aurelius
Cornelius
(also ĒL′yus)

ĔL′o-est
bellowest
mellowest
yellowest

ĔL′o-ing
bellowing
mellowing
yellowing

ĔL′on-i
felony
melony

ĔL′o-ur
bellower
mellower
yellower

ĔL′thi-est
healthiest
stealthiest
wealthiest

ĔL′thi-li
healthily
stealthily
wealthily

ĔL′thi-ur
healthier
stealthier
wealthier

ĔL′tur-i
sheltery
smeltery

ĔL′tur-ing
sheltering
weltering

ĔL′tur-ur
shelterer
welterer

ĔL′u-lar
cellular
intercellular
stellular
unicellular

ĔL′ur-i
celery
stellary

ĔL′us-li
jealously
overzealously
zealously

ĒM′a-b′l
esteemable
redeemable

Ē′ma-tist
schematist
thematist

ĔM′a-tist
emblematist
theorematist

ĔM′bur-ing
Decembering

dismembering
membering
Novembering
remembering
unremembering

Ē′mi-a
Bohemia
Euphemia

Ē′mi-al
academial
endemial
gremial
vindemial

Ē′mi-an
academian
Bohemian

ĔM′i-kal
academical
alchemical
chemical
electro-chem-
  ical
endemical
epidemical
polemical

ĔM′i-li
beamily
creamily
dreamily
steamily

ĔM′i-nal
feminal
geminal
seminal

ĔM′i-nat
effeminate

geminate
ingeminate

ĔM'i-nes
creaminess
dreaminess
steaminess

Ē'mi-on
anthemion
procemion

ĔM'i-ur
beamier
creamier
dreamier
premier

ĔM'ni-ti
indemnity
solemnity

ĔM'on-e
Agapemone
anemone
(cf. Gethsem-
ane)

ĔM'or-al
femoral
nemoral
(cf. ephemeral)

ĔM'o-ri
Emery
Emory
memory

**ĔM'por-ur,
ĔM'pur-ur**
emperor
temperer

ĔM'u-lent
temulent
tremulent

ĔM'u-lus
emulous
tremulous

Ĕm'ur-ald
emerald
ephemeralled

ĔM'ur-i
creamery
dreamery

ĔM'ur-i
gemmery
(cf. ĔM'o-ri)

ĔM'ur-ist
ephemerist
euhemerist

Ē'na-b'l
amenable
convenable

ĔN'a-ri
centenary
denary
decennary
hennery

ĔN'a-tor
senator
progenitor

ĔND'i-b'l
accendible

amendable
commendable
comprehendible
defendable
dependable
descendable
endable
extendible
invendible
lendable
mendable
recommendable
rendible
unascendable
vendible

ĔN'den-si
ascendancy
attendancy
dependency
equipendency
impendency
independency
intendancy
interdepend-
ency
resplendency
superintend-
ency
tendency
transcendency
transplendency

ĔN'di-us
compendious
incendious

ĔND'les-li
endlessly
friendlessly

ĔND'les-nes
endlessness
friendlessness

ĔN'dur-est
engenderest
renderest
slenderest
surrenderest
tenderest

ĔN'dur-ing
engendering
gendering
rendering
surrendering
tendering

ĔN'dur-li
slenderly
tenderly

ĔN'dur-nes
slenderness
tenderness

ĔN'dur-ur
engenderer
renderer
slenderer
surrendered
tenderer

ĔN'dus-li
(not ĔN'jus-li)
stupendously
tremendously

ĔN'e-sis
abiogenesis
biogenesis

ōld, ôr, ŏdd, oil, fŏŏt, out; ūse, ûrn, ŭp; THis, thin

ectogenesis
eugenesis
genesis
heterogenesis
homogenesis
ontogenesis
organogenesis
palingenesis
pangenesis
paragenesis
parenesis
partheno-
   genesis
phylogenesis
phytogenesis
polygenesis
psychogenesis
xenogenesis

ĔN'et-ing
jenneting
renneting

Ē'ni-a
Armenia
Eugenia
gardenia
neurosthenia
Parthenia
Xenia

Ē'ni-al
congenial
demesnial
genial
menial
primigenial
uncongenial
venial
(cf. ĒN'yal)

ĔN'i-al
biennial
centennial
decennial
duodecennial
millennial
novennial
octennial
perennial
quadrennial
quinquennial
septennial
triennial
vicennial

Ē'ni-an
Armenian
Athenian
Cyrenian
Estremenian
Fenian
Hellenian
Madrilenian
Ruthenian

Ē'ni-ens
convenience
inconvenience
lenience
(cf. ĔN'yens)

Ē'ni-ent
advenient
convenient
inconvenient
intervenient
introvenient
lenient
supervenient
(cf. ĒN'yent)

ĔN'i-form
antenniform
penniform

ĔN'i-kal
arsenical
cathechumen-
   ical
ecumenical
scenical
sirenical

ĔN'i-ti
amenity
lenity
obscenity
serenity
terrenity

ĔN'i-tiv
genitive
lenitive
primogenitive
splenitive

ĔN'i-tud
lenitude
plenitude
serenitude

Ē'ni-um
proscenium
selenium
xenium

Ē'ni-us
arsenious
extrageneous
genius
heterogeneous
homogeneous

ingenious
nitrogeneous
pergameneous
primigenious
selenious

ĔN'i-zon
benison
denizen
endenizen
venison

ĔN'sa-b'l
condensable
(see ĔN'si-b'l)

ĔN'sa-ri
dispensary
(see ĔN'so-ri)

ĔN'sa-tiv
compensative
condensative
defensative
dispensative
insensitive
intensitive
pensative
sensitive

ĔN'sha-ri
penitentiary
residentiary

ĔN'shi-at
essentiate
licentiate
potentiate

ĔN'shi-ent
assentient

---

consentient
dissentient
insentient
presentient
sentient

ĔN'shun-al

ascensional
conventional
descensional
extensional
intentional
preventional

ĔN'shun-ist

ascentionist
extensionist
recensionist

ĔN'shus-nes

conscientious-
  ness
contentiousness
licentiousness
pretentious-
  ness

ĔN'si-b'l

comprehensible
condensable
defensible
deprehensible
dispensable
distensible
extensible
incomprehen-
  sible
incondensable
indefensible
indispensable
insensible

ostensible
reprehensible
sensible
subsensible
suspensible
tensible

ĔN'si-kal

forensical
nonsensical

ĔN'si-ti

condensity
density
immensity
intensity
propensity
tensity

ĔN'siv-nes

comprehensive-
  ness
expensiveness
extensiveness
inoffensive-
  ness
intensiveness
offensiveness
pensiveness

ĔNS'les-li

defencelessly
senselessly

ĔNS'les-nes

defencelessness
senselessness

ĔN'so-ri

defensory
dispensary

incensory
ostensory
prehensory
reprehensory
sensory
suspensory

ĔN'ta-b'l

fermentable
frequentable
inventible
presentable
preventable
rentable
representable

ĔN'ta-k'l

pentacle
tentacle

ĔN'tal-i

accidentally
experimentally
fundamentally
incidentally
instrumentally
sentimentally
transcendent-
  ally

ĔN'tal-ist

experimentalist
fundamentalist
instrumentalist
Orientalist
sentimentalist
transcendenta-
  list

ĔN'tal-iz

experimental-
  ize

Orientalize
sentimentalize

ĔN'tal-izm

accidentalism
elementalism
Orientalism
sentimentalism
transcendental-
  ism

ĔN'tal-nes

accidentalness
fundamental-
  ness
gentleness
incidentalness
instrumental-
  ness
sentimental-
  ness
ungentleness

ĔN'ta-ri

accidentary
alimentary
complementary
complimentary
dentary
elementary
filamentary
instrumentary
integumentary
parliamentary
pigmentary
placentary
rudimentary
sacramentary
sedimentary
tegumentary
tenementary

ōld, ôr, ŏdd, oil, fŏŏt, out; ūse, ûrn, ŭp; THis, thin

testamentary
unparliamen-
tary

ĔN'ta-tiv
argumentative
augmentative
commentative
complimenta-
tive
alimentative
experimenta-
tive
fermentative
frequentative
misrepresenta-
tive
presentative
pretentative
preventative
representative
tentative

ĔN'ti-kal
authentical
conventical
conventicle
denticle
identical

ĔN'ti-kul
denticule
lenticule

ĔN'ti-ment
presentiment
sentiment

ĔN'ti-nal
dentinal
sentinel

ĔN'ti-ti
entity
identity
nonentity

ĔN'tiv-nes
alimentiveness
attentiveness
inattentiveness
inventiveness
retentiveness

ĔN'tu-al
accentual
adventual
conventual
eventual

ĔN'tu-at
accentuate
eventuate

ĔN'tus-li
momentously
portentously

ĔN'tus-nes
momentous-
ness
portentousness

ĔN'u-ant
attenuant
genuant

ĔN'u-at
attenuate
extenuate
tenuate

ĔN'ur-at
degenerate

generate
ingenerate
intenerate
progenerate
regenerate
venerate

ĔN'ur-i
deanery
greenery
machinery
plenary
scenery

ĔN'ū-ri
penury

ĔN'ŭr-i
denary
decennary
hennery
senary
venery

ĔN'u-us
disingenuous
ingenuous
strenuous
tenuous

ĔN'yen-si
conveniency
inconveniency
leniency

ĔP'i-li
creepily
sleepily

ĔP'i-nes
creepiness

sleepiness
steepiness
weepiness

ĔP'ta-b'l
acceptable
deceptible
imperceptible
insusceptible
perceptible
receptible
susceptible

ĔP'ti-kal
antiseptical
protreptical
receptacle
sceptical

ĔP'tiv-nes
deceptiveness
receptiveness
susceptiveness

ĔP'ur-us
leperous
obstreperous
perstreperous
streperous

ĔR'an-si
aberrancy
errancy
inerrancy

ĔR'a-pi
balneotherapy
hydrotherapy
kinesitherapy
phototherapy
radiotherapy

āle,   câre,   ădd,   ärm,   åsk;   mē,   hęre,   ĕnd;   īce,   ĭll;

ĔR′ful-i
cheerfully
fearfully
tearfully

ĔR′ful-nes
cheerfulness
fearfulness
tearfulness

ĔR′i-a, Ē′ri-a
Algeria
diphtheria
Egeria
eleutheria
Etheria
hesperia
hysteria
icteria
Liberia
Nigeria
Valkyria

ĔR′i-al, Ē′ri-al
aerial
arterial
cereal
ethereal
ferial
funereal
immaterial
imperial
magisterial
managerial
manerial
material
ministerial
monasterial
presbyterial
rhinocerial
serial

siderial
vizierial

ĔR′i-an
Abderian
aerian
Algerian
Celtiberian
Cimmerian
Hanoverian
Hesperian
Iberian
Keplerian
Luciferian
phalansterian
Pierian
Presbyterian
Shakespearean
Shakesperian
Siberian
Spenserian
Valerian
Valkyrian
Wertherian
(cf. ĔR′i-on
　and ĪR′i-an)

ĔR′i-dez
Anterides
Hesperides
Pierides

ĔR′i-est
beeriest
bleariest
cheeriest
dreariest
eeriest
weariest

ĔR′i-est
buriest

ferriest, etc.
merriest

ĔR′i-ez
congeries
series

ĔR′-ing
berrying
burying
ferrying
wherrying

ĔR′i-kal
alexiterical
atmospherical
chimerical
clerical
climacterical
esoterical
exoterical
heliospherical
helispherical
hysterical
numerical
phylacterical
rhinocerical
spherical
sphericle

ĔR′i-li
cheerily
drearily
eerily
wearily

ĔR′i-li
merrily
verily

ĔR′i-man
ferryman

Merriman
wherryman

ĔR′i-ment
merriment
(cf. ŬR′i-ment)

ĔR′i-nes
beeriness
bleariness
cheeriness
dreariness
eeriness
weariness

ĔR′i-on
allerion
criterion
Hyperion
(cf. ĔR′i-an)

ĔR′i-or
anterior
exterior
inferior
interior
posterior
superior
ulterior
(cf. ĔR′i-ur)

ĔR′ish-ing
cherishing
perishing
unperishing

ĔR′i-ted
disherited
disinherited
emerited
ferreted

inherited
merited
(cf. turreted)

ĔR'i-ti
ambidexterity
asperity
austerity
celerity
dexterity
indexterity
insincerity
legerity
posterity
procerity
prosperity
severity
sincerity
temerity
verity

ĔR'it-ing
ferreting
inheriting
meriting

Ē'ri-um
acroterium
apodyterium
dinotherium
megatherium
palæotherium
titanotherium

ĔR'i-ur
beerier
blearier
bleerier
cheerier
drearier
eerier

wearier
(cf. ĔR'i-or)

ĔR'i-ur
burier
merrier
terrier

Ē'ri-us, ĔR'i-us
cereous
cereus
deleterious
ethereous
imperious
mysterious
serious
sidereous

ĔR'les-nes
cheerlessness
fearlessness
peerlessness

ĔR'o-gat
interrogate
(cf. ŬR'o-gat)

ĔR'yal-ist
immaterialist
imperialist
materialist

ĔR'yal-izm
immaterialism
imperialism
materialism

ĔS'a-b'l
creasable
releasable

ĔS'a-ri
confessary

intercessory
pessary
professory
successary

Ē'sen-si
decency
indecency
recency

ĔS'en-si
acescency
acquiescency
adolescency
alkalescency
convalescency
defervescency
delitescency
effervescency
efflorescency
erubescency
excrescency
incalescency
incandescency
liquescency
pubescency
quiescency
recrudescency
rejuvenescency
turgescency

Ē'sent-li
decently
indecently
recently

Ē'shi-an
Capetian
Epictetian
Grecian
Venetian

geodesian
gynæcian
Megalesian
Melanesian
Peloponnesian
Silesian
(cf. ĔSH'an,
ĔSH'un)

ĔSH'i-ens
nescience
prescience

ĔSH'i-nes
fleshiness
meshiness

ĔSH'li-nes
fleshliness
freshliness
unfleshliness

ĔSH'un-al
accessional
confessional
congressional
digressional
discretional
expressional
intercessional
possessional
processional
professional
progressional
recessional
retrocessional
sessional
successional
transgressional

ĔSH'un-ist
impressionist

āle, câre, ădd, ärm, àsk; mē, hĕre, ĕnd; īce, ĭll;

progressionist
secessionist
successionist

ĔSH′un-ur
possessioner
processioner
secessioner

Ē′shus-nes
facetiousness
speciousness

ĔS′ĭ-b'l
accessible
compressible
concessible
concrescible
effervescible
expressible
fermentescible
impressible
imputrescible
inaccessible
incessable
incompressible
ineffervescible
inexpressible
insuppressible
irrepressible
marcescible
putrescible
redressible
repressible
suppressible
transgressible
vitrescible

ĔS′ĭ-mal
centesimal
decimal

infinitesimal
millesimal
nonagesimal
quadragesimal
septuagesimal
sexagesimal

ĔS′ĭ-ti
obesity

ĔS′ĭ-ti
necessity
obesity

ĔS′iv-nes
aggressiveness
depressiveness
excessiveness
expressiveness
impressiveness
inexpressive-
ness
oppressiveness
progressiveness

ĔS′ti-al
agrestial
bestial
celestial
supercelestial

ĔS′ti-b'l
comestible
congestible
contestable
detestable
digestible
divestible
incontestable
indigestible

intestable
testable

ĔS′tin-al
destinal
intestinal

ĔS′tin-at
destinate
festinate
predestinate

ĒS′ti-nes
reastiness
yeastiness

ĔS′ti-nes
restiness
testiness

ĔS′tiv-nes
festiveness
restiveness
suggestiveness

ĒST′li-nes
beastliness
priestliness

ĔS′tri-al
pedestrial
superterrestrial
terrestrial
trimestrial

ĔS′tri-an
campestrian
equestrian
palestrian
pedestrian
sylvestrian

ĔS′tri-us
pedestrious
terestrious

ĔS′tu-ral
gestural
vestural

ĔS′tur-ing
festering
pestering
westering

ĔS′tu-us
incestuous
tempestuous

ĔT′a-b'l
cheatable
eatable
entreatable
escheatable
uneatable

ĔT′a-b'l
forgetable
getable
regretable
setable
unforgetable

ĔT′al-en
acetylene

ĔT′a-lin
metalline
petaline

ĔT′al-izm
bimetallism

---

monometallism
petalism

ĔT′ful-i
forgetfully
fretfully
regretfully

ĔT′ful-nes
forgetfulness
fretfulness
regretfulness

Ĕth′les-li
breathlessly
deathlessly

Ĕth′les-nes
breathlessness
deathlessness

ĔTH′ur-i
feathery
heathery
leathery
weathery

ĔTH′ur-ing
feathering
leathering
tethering
weathering

ĔT′i-kal
æsthetical
aloetical
alphabetical
anchoretical
antipathetical
antithetical
apathetical

apologetical
arithmetical
catechetical
cosmetical
dietetical
emporetical
energetical
epithetical
exegetical
heretical
hermetical
homiletical
hypothetical
noetical
planetical
poetical
theoretical

ĔT′i-kul
poeticule
reticule

ĔT′i-nes
meatiness
peatiness
sleetiness

ĔT′i-nes
jettiness
pettiness
sweatiness

ĔT′in-u
detinue
retinue

ĔT′ish-li
coquettishly
pettishly

ĔT′ish′nes
coquettishness
pettishness

ĔT′i-sizm
æstheticism
asceticism
athleticism
peripateticism

ĔT′o-ri
completory
depletory
repletory
secretory

ĔT′ri-kal
alkalimetrical
asymmetrical
barometrical
craniometrical
diametrical
geometrical
gnomiometrical
graphometrical
horometrical
isoperimetrical
metrical
obstetrical
perimetrical
planimetrical
pluviometrical
stichometrical
symmetrical
trigonometrical

ĔT′ri-ment
detriment
retriment

ĔT′ur-ing
bettering
fettering
lettering

ĔV′a-b′l
achievable
believable
cleavable
conceivable
deceivable
grievable
imperceivable
inconceivable
irretrievable
perceivable
receivable
relievable
retrievable
unbelievable
undeceivable

ĔV′el-est
bevellest
dishevellest
levellest
revellest

ĔV′el-ing
bedevilling
bevelling
dishevelling
levelling
revelling

ĔV′el-izm
devilism
levelism

ĔV′el-ur
beveller
bedeviller
disheveller
leveller
reveller

Ē'vi-at
abbreviate
alleviate
deviate

ĔV'il-ment
bedevilment
devilment
revelment

ĔV'il-ry
devilry
revelry

Ē'vish-li
· peevishly
thievishly

Ē'vish-nes
peevishness
thievishness

ĔV'i-ti
brevity
levity
longevity

Ē'vi-us
devious
previous

ĔV'ol-ens
benevolence
malevolence

ĔV'ol-ent
benevolent
malevolent

ĔV'ol-us
benevolous
malevolous

ĔV'ol-ut
evolute
revolute

ĔV'ur-est
cleverest
endeavourest
Everest
severest

ĔV'ur-mor
evermore
nevermore

ĔV'ur-ur
cleverer
endeavorer
severer

Ē'za-b'l
appeasable
cohesible
defeasible
feasible
freezable
inappeasable
indefeasible
infeasible

seizable
squeezable
unappeasable

ĔZ'an-tri
peasantry
pheasantry
pleasantry

Ē'zhi-a, Ē'zi-a
amnesia
anæsthesia
ecclesia
esthesia
magnesia
parrhesia
Rhodesia
Silesia
Zambesia

Ē'zi-an
artesian
cartesian
ecclesian
Ephesian
etesian
magnesian
Milesian
Polynesian
trapezian
(cf. ĒZH'yan)

ĔZ'i-dent
president
resident

ĔZ'i-li
breezily
easily
greasily
uneasily
wheezily

ĔZ'i-nes
breezines
cheesiness
easiness
greasiness
queasiness
sleaziness
uneasiness
wheeziness

ĔZ'ing-li
appeasingly
freezingly
pleasingly
teasingly
wheezingly

Ē'zon-ing
reasoning
seasoning
unreasoning

ĔZ'ur-ing
measuring
pleasuring
treasuring

ĔZ'ur-ur
measurer
pleasurer
treasurer

ōld, ôr, ŏdd, oil, fŏŏt, out; ūse, ûrn, ŭp; THis, thin

I

For a discussion of words included under the accented voweĺs following, see the beginning of I rhymes in Section I.

Ī'a-b'l
acidifiable
appliable
classifiable
compliable
deniable
diversifiable
electrifiable
exemplifiable
falsifiable
fortifiable
friable
impliable
justifiable
liable
liquefiable
magnifiable
modifiable
pacifiable
petrifiable
pliable
qualifiable
rarefiable
rectifiable
reliable
saponifiable
satisfiable
solidifiable
triable
undeniable
verifiable
viable
vitrifiable

Ī'a-bli
deniably

justifiably
reliably
undeniably, etc.

Ī'a-dez
hamadryades
Hyades
Pleiades

Ī'a-kal
bibliomaniacal
cardiacal
demoniacal
elegiacal
encyclopediacal
heliacal
hypochondria-
cal
maniacal
monomaniacal
paradisiacal
prosodiacal
simoniacal
zodiacal

Ī'an-si, Ī'en-si
cliency
compliancy
pliancy
riancy

Ī'ant-li
compliantly
defiantly
pliantly
reliantly

Ī'ar-i
friary
(see Ī'ur-i)

Ī'ar-ist
diarist
Piarist

Ī'ar-ki
diarchy
triarchy

Ī'a-sis
elephantiasis
hypochondria-
sis

Ī'a-sizm
demoniacism
hypochondriac-
ism

Ī'a-tur
psychiater
(cf. archiater)

ĬB'a-b'l
bribable
describable
indescribable
inscribable
scribable
subscribable
undescribable

ĬB'i-a
amphibia

Libya
tibia

ĬB'i-al
amphibial
stibial
tibial

ĬB'i-an
amphibian
Libyan

ĬB'i-tiv
exhibitive
prohibitive

ĬB'i-us
amphibious
bathybius
stibious

ĬB'u-lar
fibular
infundibular
mandibular
vestibular

ĬCH'i-nes
itchiness
pitchiness

ĬCH'ur-i
bewitchery
michery
stitchery
witchery

āle,   câre,   ădd,   ärm,   åsk;   mē,   hĕre,   ĕnd;   īce,   ĭll;

ĬD′a-b'l

decidable
dividable
ridable
bestridable, etc.

ĬD′en-nes

forbiddenness
hiddenness

ĬD′e-us

hideous
(see ĬD′i-us)

ĬD′i-al

noctidial
presidial

ĬD′i-an

antemeridian
Gideon
Lydian
meridian
Midian
nullifidian
Numidian
obsidian
ophidian
Ovidian
postmeridian
quotidian
rachidian

ĬD′i-at

dimidiate
insidate

ĬD′i-fi

acidify
lapidify
solidify

ĬD′i-kal

druidical
juridical
pyramidical
veridical

ĬD′i-nus

libidinous
(cf. pingue-
    dinous)

ĬD′i-ti

acidity
acridity
aridity
avidity
cupidity
frigidity
insipidity
insolidity
intrepidity
invalidity
gelidity
gravidity
hispidity
humidity
hybridity
limpidity
liquidity
lividity
lucidity
marcidity
morbidity
pallidity
pavidity
pellucidity
putidity
putridity
quiddity
rabidity

rancidity
rapidity
rigidity
sapidity
solidity
squalidity
stolidity
stupidity
timidity
torpidity
torridity
trepidity
tumidity
turbidity
turgidity
validity
vapidity
viridity
viscidity
vividity

**ĬD′i-om,
    ĬD′i-um**

idiom
iridium
peridium

ĬD′i-us

avidious
fastidious
hideous
insidious
invidious
lapideous
ophidious
parricidious
perfidious
Phidias
splendidious
stillicidious

ĬD′u-al

individual
residual

ĬD′u-at

assiduate
individuate

ĬD′u-lat

acidulate
stridulate

ĬD′u-lus

acidulous
stridulous

ĬD′u-us

assiduous
deciduous
prociduous
residuous
succiduous
viduous

Ī′en-si

cliency
(see Ī′an-si)

Ī′et-al

dietal
hyetal
parietal
varietal

Ī′et-ed

dieted
disquieted
quieted
rioted

Ī′et-est

dietest

ōld, ôr, ŏdd, oil, fŏŏt, out; ūse, ûrn, ŭp; THis, thin

quietest
riotest

Ĭ'et-i

anxiety
contrariety
dubiety
ebriety
filiety
impiety
impropriety
inebriety
insobriety
luxuriety
mediety
nimiety
notoriety
nullibiety
omniety
piety
propriety
satiety
sobriety
society
ubiety
variety

Ĭ'et-ing

dieting
disquieting
quieting
rioting

Ĭ'et-ist

anxietist
dietist
pietist
proprietist
quietist
varietiest

Ĭ'et-izm

pietism
quietism
varietism

Ĭ'et-ur, Ĭ'et-or

dieter
proprietor
quieter
rioter

ĬF'i-kal

beatifical
dolorifical
lanifical
pontifical
specifical

ĬF'i-kant

insignificant
mundificant
sacrificant
significant

ĬF'i-kat

certificate
pontificate
significate

ĬF'i-sens

magnificence
munificence

ĬF'i-sent

magnificent
mirificent
munificent

ĬF'i-sur

artificer
opificer

ĬF'lu-us

dulcifluous
fellifluous
ignifluous
mellifluous
sanguifluous

ĬF'on-i

antiphony
oxyphony
polyphony

ĬF'ra-gus

fedrifragous
ossifragous
saxifragous

ĬF'ta-b'l

liftable
shiftable

ĬF'ti-li

shiftily
thriftily

ĬF'ti-nes

shiftiness
thriftiness

ĬFT'les-nes

shiftlessness
thriftlessness

ĬF'u-gal

centrifugal
febrifugal
vermifugal

ĬF'ur-us

acidiferous
aliferous

aluminiferous
ammonitiferous
antenniferous
argentiferous
armiferous
astriferous
auriferous
balaniferous
balsamiferous
bulbiferous
calcariferous
calciferous
carboniferous
cheliferous
cirriferous
conchiferous
coniferous
coralliferous
cruciferous
diamantiferous
diamondiferous
doloriferous
ensiferous
fatiferous
ferriferous
filiferous
flammiferous
floriferous
fluctiferous
foliferous
foraminiferous
fossiliferous
frondiferous
frugiferous
fumiferous
furciferous
gemmiferous
geodiferous
glandiferous
glanduliferous

graniferous
granuliferous
guttiferous
gypsiferous
hederiferous
herbiferous
igniferous
lactiferous
lamelliferous
laminiferous
lanciferous
laniferous
laticiferous
lauriferous
lethiferous
ligniferous
lignitiferous
luciferous
lucriferous
luminiferous
magnetiferous
maliferous
mammaliferous
mammiferous
margaritiferous
melliferous
membrani-
   ferous
metalliferous
monstriferous
mortiferous
multiferous
nectariferous
nickeliferous
nimbiferous
nitriferous
noctiferous
nubiferous
nuciferous
odoriferous
oleiferous

omniferous
oolitiferous
ossiferous
ostriferous
ozoniferous
palmiferous
pestiferous
pistilliferous
platiniferous
plumbiferous
polypiferous
proliferous
pruniferous
pulmoniferous
quartiziferous
racemiferous
resiniferous
roriferous
sacchariferous
sacciferous
saliferous
saliniferous
salutiferous
sanguiferous
scopiferous
scutiferous
sebiferous
sensiferous
setiferous
siliciferous
somniferous
soniferous
soporiferous
spiciferous
spiniferous
spumiferous
stameniferous
stanniferous
stelliferous
stoloniferous
succiferous

sudoriferous
tentaculiferous
tergiferous
thuriferous
tuberiferous
umbelliferous
umbraculifer-
   ous
umbriferous
vaporiferous
vasculiferous
vociferous
zinciferous

ĬG'am-i

bigamy
digamy
polygamy
trigamy

ĬG'am-ist

bigamist
polygamist
trigamist

ĬG'am-us

bigamous
digamous
polygamous
trigamous

ĬG'ma-tist

enigmatist
stigmatist

ĬG'ma-tiz

enigmatize
paradigmatize
stigmatize

ĬG'nan-si

indignancy
malignancy

ĬG'ne-us

igneous
ligneous

ĬG'ni-fi

dignify
ignify
lignify
malignify
signify
undignify

ĬG'ni-ti

benignity
dignity
indignity
malignity

ĬG'or-us

rigorous
vigorous

ĬG'ra-fi

calligraphy
epigraphy
lexigraphy
pasigraphy
poligraphy
pseudepigrahy
stratigraphy
tachygraphy

ĬG'u-lat

figulate
ligulate

ĬG'ur-i

piggery
Whiggery
wiggery

ōld, ôr, ŏdd, oil, fŏŏt, out; ūse, ûrn, ŭp; THis, thin

ĬG′u-us
ambiguous
contiguous
exiguous
irriguous

ĬJ′en-us
alkaligenous
coralligenous
epigenous
fuliginous
gelatigenous
ignigenous
indigenous
marigenous
melligenous
montigenous
nubigenous
omnigenous
oxygenous
polygenous
pruriginous
sanguigenous
terrigenous
uliginous
unigenous
vertiginous
vortiginous

ĬJ′i-an
Cantabrigian
Phrygian
Stygian

ĬJ′id-li
frigidly
rigidly

ĬJ′id-nes
frigidness
rigidness

ĬJ′i-ti
digity
fidgety

ĬJ′ur-at
belligerate
frigerate
refrigerate

ĬJ′ur-ent
belligerent
refrigerant

ĬJ′ur-us
aligerous
armigerous
belligerous
cirrigerous
coralligerous
cornigerous
crucigerous
dentigerous
immorigerous
lanigerous
linigerous
morigerous
navigerous
ovigerous
palpigerous
pedigerous
pennigerous
piligerous
plumigerous
proligerous
setigerous
spinigerous

ĬJ′us-nes
litigiousness
prodigiousness
religiousness

ĬK′a-ment
medicament
predicament

ĬK′a-tiv
abdicative
desiccative
exsiccative
fricative
indicative
predicative
siccative

ĬK′en-ing
quickening
sickening
thickening

ĬK′et-i
pernicketty
rickety
thicketty

ĬK′et-ing
cricketing
picketing
ticketing

ĬK′et-ur
cricketer
picketer

ĬK′i-li
stickily
trickily

ĬK′i-nes
stickiness
trickiness

ĬK′li-nes
prickliness
sickliness

ĬK′o-list
agricolist
ignicolist
plebicolist

ĬK′o-lus
agricolous
sepicolous
terricolous

ĬK′o-mus
auricomous
flavicomous

ĬK′sa-b'l
fixable
mixable

ĬK′shun-al
contradictional
fictional
frictional
jurisdictional

ĬK′si-ti
fixity
prolixity
siccity

ĬK′tiv-li
restrictively
vindictively

ĬK′tiv-nes
restrictiveness
vindictiveness

ĬK′to-ri
benedictory
contradictory
interdictory

āle, câre, ădd, ärm, ȧsk; mē, hĕre, ĕnd; īce, ĭll;

valedictory
victory

ĬK'u-la
Canicula
fidicula
zeticula

ĬK'u-lar
acicular
adminicular
articular
auricular
calycular
canicular
clavicular
cubicular
cuticular
fascicular
follicular
funicular
lenticular
navicular
orbicular
ovicular
particular
pellicular
perpendicular
quinquarticular
radicular
reticular
spicular
subcuticular
vehicular
ventricular
vermicular
versicular
vesicular

ĬK'u-lat
articulate

canaliculate
denticulate
fasciculate
funiculate
geniculate
gesticulate
matriculate
monticulate
paniculate
particulate
reticulate
spiculate
vehiculate
vermiculate
vesiculate

ĬK'u-lum
curriculum
geniculum

ĬK'u-lus
dendiculus
denticulus
fasciculus
folliculous
meticulous
ridiculous
urbiculous
ventriculous
vermiculous
vesiculous

ĬK'wi-ti
antiquity
iniquity
obliquity
ubiquity

ĬK'wi-tus
iniquitous
ubiquitous

ĬL'a-b'l
distillable
fillable
refillable
syllable
tillable
unrefillable

Ĭ'lan-dur
highlander
islander

ĬL'a-ri
Hilary
(see ĬL'ur-i)

ĬL'et-ed
billeted
filleted
unfilleted

ĬL'et-ing
billeting
filleting

ĬL'ful-i
guilefully
wilefully

ĬL'ful-i
skilfully
wilfully
unskilfully

ĬL'ful-nes
guilefulness
wilefulness

ĬL'ful-nes
skilfulness

wilfulness
unskilfulness

ĬL'i-a
memorabilia
notabilia
sedilia

ĬL'i-ad
chiliad
Iliad
(cf. Gilead)

ĬL'i-an
Brazilian
Castilian
Cecilian
crocodilian
Kurilian
lacertilian
Lilian
Maximilian
perfectibilian
reptilian
Virgilian
(cf. ĬL'yun)

ĬL'i-ar
atrabiliar
auxiliar
conciliar
domiciliar
(see ĬL'yar)

ĬL'i-at
affiliate
conciliate
domiciliate
filiate
humiliate

ĬL′i-ens
consilience
dissilience
resilience
transilience
(cf. brilliance)

ĬL′i-ent
dissilient
resilient
transilient
(cf. brilliant)

ĬL′i-est
chilliest
hilliest
silliest
stilliest

ĬL′i-fi
fossilify
nobilify
stabilify
vilify

ĬL′i-form
filiform
plumiliform

ĬL′i-gan
Gilligan
McMilligan

ĬL′ij-ur
pillager
villager

ĬL′i-ka
basilica
silica

ĬL′i-kal
basilical

filical
silicle
umbilical

ĬL′i-nes
chilliness
hilliness
silliness

ĬL′ing-li
killingly
thrillingly
trillingly
willingly

ĬL′i-o
pulvillio
punctilio

ĬL′i-tat
abilitate
debilitate
facilitate
habilitate
impossibilitate
militate
nobilitate
rehabilitate
stabilitate

ĬL′i-ti
ability
absorbability
accendibility
acceptability
accessibility
accountability
acquirability
adaptability
addibility
admirability

admissibility
adoptability
adorability
advisability
affability
affectibility
agility
agreeability
alienability
alterability
amenability
amiability
amicability
amissibility
anility
appetibility
applicability
assimilability
associability
attainability
attemptability
attractability
audibility
availability
capability
changeability
civility
cognoscibility
cohesibility
combustibility
communicabil-
   ity
commutability
compatibility
comprehensibil-
   ity
compressibility
computability
conceivability
condensability
conducibility

conductability
conformability
confusability
contemptibility
contractibility
contractility
convertibility
corrigibility
corrodibility
corrosibility
credibility
creditability
crocodility
culpability
curability
damnability
debility
deceptibility
deducibility
defectibility
demisability
demonstrabil-
   ity
deplorability
descendibility
desirability
despicability
destructibility
determinability
detestability
diffusibility
digestibility
dilatability
disability
dissolubility
dissolvability
distensibility
divisibility
docibility
docility
ductility

āle, câre, ădd, ärm, åsk; mē, hẹre, ĕnd; īce, ĭll;

durability
edibility
educability
eligibility
equability
exchangeability
excitability
exhaustibility
expansibility
extensibility
facility
fallibility
feasibility
fermentability
fertility
fictility
flexibility
fluctuability
fluxibility
formidability
fossility
fragility
frangibility
friability
fusibility
futility
generability
gentility
gracility
gullibility
habitability
hostility
humility
ignobility
illability
imbecility
imitability
immeability
immeasura-
    bility
immiscibility

immovability
immutability
impalpability
impartibility
impassibility
impeccability
impenetrability
impercepti-
    bility
imperdibility
impermeability
imperturba-
    bility
imperviability
implacability
impossibility
impregnability
imprescripti-
    bility
impressibility
impressiona-
    bility
improbability
imputability
inability
inaccessibility
incivility
incogitability
incognoscibility
incombusti-
    bility
incommensura-
    bility
incommunica-
    bility
incommuta-
    bility
incompatibility
incomprehensi-
    bility

incompressi-
    bility
inconceiva-
    bility
incondensa-
    bility
incontroverti-
    bility
inconvertibility
incorrigibility
incorruptibility
incredibility
incurability
indefatigability
indefeasibility
indefectibility
indelibility
indemonstra-
    bility
indestructi-
    bility
indigestibility
indiscernibility
indiscerpti-
    bility
indispensability
indisputability
indissolubility
indivisibility
indocibility
indocility
inductility
ineffability
ineffervesci-
    bility
ineligibility
inevitability
inexhaustibility
inexorability
inexplicability
infallibility

infeasibility
infertility
inflammability
inflexibility
infrangibility
infusibility
inhability
inhabitability
inheritability
inimitability
innumbera-
    bility
insanability
insatiability
insensibility
inseparability
insociability
insolubility
instability
insuperability
insurmounta-
    bility
insusceptibility
intangibility
intelligibility
interchange-
    ability
intractability
inutility
invendibility
invincibility
inviolability
invisibility
invulnerability
irascibility
irreconcilability
irreductibility
irremovability
irreparability
irresistibility
irresponsibility

ōld, ôr, ŏdd, oil, fŏŏt, out; ūse, ûrn, ŭp; THis, thin

irritability
juvenility
lability
laminability
laudability
legibility
liability
malleability
manageability
memorability
mensurability
miscibility
mobility
modifiability
modificability
motility
movability
mutability
navigability
negotiability
neurility
nihility
nobility
notability
opposability
organizability
ostensibility
palpability
partibility
passibility
peccability
penetrability
pensility
perceptibility
perdurability
perfectibility
permissibility
persuasibility
perturbability
placability
plausibility

pliability
ponderability
portability
possibility
practicability
precipitability
preferability
prescriptibility
preventability
probability
producibility
puerility
quotability
ratability
readability
receivability
receptibility
redeemability
reductibility
reflexibility
refragability
refrangibility
refutability
reliability
remissibility
removability
remunerability
renewability
reparability
repealability
resistibility
resolvability
respectability
responsibility
reversibility
revocability
risibility
saleability
salvability
sanability
satiability

scurrility
senility
sensibility
separability
servility
sociability
solubility
solvability
sportability
squeezability
stability
sterility
suability
subtility
suitability
susceptibility
suspensibility
tactility
tamability
tangibility
taxability
temptability
tenability
tensibility
tensility
tolerability
torsibility
tortility
tractability
tractility
tranquillity
transferability
transmissibility
transmutability
transportability
unaccount-
  ability
unbelievability
unutterability
utility
vaporability

variability
vegetability
vendibility
venerability
verisimility
vernility
versability
versatility·
viability
vibratility
vindicability
virility
visibility
volatility
volubility
vulnerability
writability

ĬL′ĭ-us

atrabilious
bilious
punctilious
supercilious
(cf. as ĬL′yus)'

ĬL′ki-est

milkiest
silkiest

ĬL′ki-ur

milkier
silkier

Ī′lo-bat

stylobate
trilobate

ĬL′o-i

billowy
pillowy
willowy

ĬL′o-ing
billowing
pillowing

ĬL′o-ji
antilogy
brachylogy
dilogy
fossilogy
palilogy
trilogy

ĬL′o-jiz
epilogize
syllogize

ĬL′o-jizm
epilogism
episyllogism
syllogism

ĬL′o-ri
pillory
(see ĬL′ur-i)

ĬL′o-kwens
blandiloquence
breviloquence
grandiloquence
magniloquence
somniloquence
stultiloquence

ĬL′o-kwent
flexiloquent
grandiloquent
magniloquent
melliloquent
pauciloquent
sanctiloquent
stultiloquent

suaviloquent
veriloquent

ĬL′o-kwi
dentiloquy
gastriloquy
pauciloquy
pectoriloquy
soliloquy
somniloquy
stultiloquy
suaviloquy
ventriloquy

ĬL′o-kwist
dentiloquist
gastriloquist
somniloquist
ventriloquist

ĬL′o-kwiz
soliloquize
ventriloquize

ĬL′o-kwizm
gastriloquism
pectoriloquism
somniloquism
ventriloquism

ĬL′o-kwus
grandiloquous
magniloquous
pectoriloquous
somniloquous
ventriloquous

ĬL′ur-i
artillery
capillary
cilery

codicillary
distillery
Hilary
phyllary
pillory
Sillery

ĬL′yan-si
brilliancy
resiliency
transiliency

ĬL′yar-i
atrabiliary
auxiliary

ĬM′a-nus
longimanous
pedimanous

ĬM′a-tur
climature
limature

ĬM′bri-kat
fimbricate
imbricate

Ĭ′mer-i
primary
rhymery

ĬM′et-ri
alkalimetry
asymmetry
bathymetry
calorimetry
isoperimetry
longimetry
planimetry
polarimetry

saccharimetry
symmetry

ĬM′et-ur
alkalimeter
altimeter
calorimeter
dasymeter
dimeter
focimeter
gravimeter
limiter
lucimeter
pelvimeter
perimeter
planimeter
polarimeter
pulsimeter
rhysimeter
saccharimeter
salimeter
scimiter
tasimeter
trimeter
velocimeter
zymosimeter
(cf. scimitar)

ĬM′i-an,
  ĬM′i-on
Endymion
simian
Simeon

ĬM′i-kal
alchymical
homonymical
inimical
metonymical
mimical

ōld,   ôr,   ŏdd,   oil,   fŏŏt,   out;   ūse,   ûrn,   ŭp;   THis,   thin

ĬM′i-nal
criminal
regiminal
subliminal
viminal

ĬM′i-nat
accriminate
criminate
discriminate
eliminate
incriminate
indiscriminate
recriminate

ĬM′i-nes
griminess
sliminess

ĬM′i-ni
Bimini
jiminy
nimini-pimini
postliminy

ĬM′i-nus
criminous
moliminous

ĬM′i-ti
anonymity
dimity
equanimity
magnanimity
parvanimity
proximity
pseudonymity
pusillanimity
sanctanimity
sublimity
unanimity

ĬM′pur-ing
simpering
whimpering

ĬM′pur-ur
simperer
whimperer

ĬM′u-lat
assimulate
dissimulate
simulate
stimulate

ĬM′u-lus
limulus
stimulus

ĬM′ur-us
dimerous
polymerous

ĬN′a-b'l
assignable
combinable
declinable
definable
designable
finable
inclinable
indeclinable
indefinable
signable

ĬN′ar-i
binary
(see ĬN′ur-i)

ĬN′a-tiv
combinative
finative

ĬN′di-kat
indicate
syndicate
vindicate

ĬN′dur-i
bindery
grindery

ĬN′dur-i
cindery
tindery

ĬN′e-al, ĬN′i-al
consanguineal
finial
gramineal
interlineal
lineal
pectineal
pineal
stamineal

ĬN′e-ma
cinema
kinema

ĬN′e-us
cartilagineous
consanguine-
  ous
flamineous
fulmineous
gramineous
ignominious
sanguineous
stamineous
stramineous
testudineous
vimineous

ĬNG′gur-ing
fingering
lingering
malingering

ĬNG′gur-ur
fingerer
lingerer
malingerer

ĬNG′i-nes
ringiness
springiness
stringiness

ĬNGK′a-b'l
drinkable
shrinkable
thinkable
undrinkable
unshrinkable
unsinkable
unthinkable

ĬNGK′i-nes
inkiness
kinkiness
pinkiness
slinkiness

ĬNGK′wi-ti
longinquity
propinquity

ĬN′i-al
finial
(see ĬN′e-al)

ĬN′i-a
Abyssinia
Lavinia

āle,   câre,   ădd,   ärm,   åsk;   mē,   hĕre,   ĕnd;   īce,   ĭll;

Sardinia
Virginia
zinnia

ĬN′i-an
Abyssinian
anthropopha-
  ginian
Arminian
Augustinian
Carolinian
Carthaginian
czarinian
Darwinian
Delphinian
Eleusinian
Hercynian
Justinian
Palestinean
Sardinian
serpentinian
Socinian
viraginian
Virginian
(cf. ĬN′yon)

ĬN′i-at, ĬN′e-at
delineate
laciniate
lineate
miniate

ĬN′i-est
briniest
shiniest
spiniest
tiniest

ĬN′i-form
actiniform

aluminiform
laciniform

ĬN′i-kin
finikin
minikin

ĬN′i-k′l
adminicle
binnacle
binocle
Brahminical
clinical
cynical
dominical
finical
flaminical
pinnacle
Sinical
synclinical

ĬN′i-ment
liniment
miniment

ĬN′ish-ing
diminishing
finishing

ĬN′is-tral
ministral
sinistral

ĬN′is-tur
administer
minister
sinister

ĬN′i-ti
affinity
alkalinity
asininity

consanguinity
divinity
felinity
femininity
infinity
Latinity
masculinity
patavinity
peregrinity
salinity
sanguinity
satinity
trinity
vicinity
viraginity
virginity

ĬN′i-tiv
combinative
finitive
infinitive

ĬN′i-ur
brinier
shinier
spinier
tinier

ĬN′jen-si
astringency
contingency
refringency
stringency

ĬN′ji-an
Carlovingian
Merovingian
Thuringian

ĬN′ji-li
dingily
stingily

ĬN′ji-nes
dinginess
stinginess

ĬN′lan-dur
Finlander
inlander

ĬN′o-lin
crinoline
quinoline

ĬN′thi-an
absinthian
Corinthian
hyacinthian
labyrinthian

ĬN′tur-est
interest
splinterest
winterest

ĬN′tur-i
printery
splintery
wintery

ĬN′ur-i
alpinery
binary
finary
finery
pinery
quinary
refinery
swinery
vinery

ĬN′u-at
continuate

ōld, ôr, ŏdd, oil, fŏŏt, out; ūse, ûrn, ŭp; THis, thin

insinuate
sinuate

ĬN′u-us
continuous
sinuous

Ĭ′ol-a
variola
viola

Ĭ′o-let
triolet
violet

Ĭ′o-list
sciolist
violist

Ĭ′o-lus
gladiolus
sciolous
variolous

Ĭ′o-pe
Calliope
myopy
presbyopy

Ĭ′o-tur
rioter
(see Ĭ′et-ur)

Ĭ′o-sen
Miocene
Pliocene
post-Pliocene

ĬP′ar-us
biparous
criniparous

deiparous
fissiparous
floriparous
foliiparous
frondiparous
fructiparous
gemelliparous
gemmiparous
larviparous
multiparous
omniparous
opiparous
oviparous
ovoviviparous
polyparous
polypiparous
sebiparous
sudoriparous
tomiparous
uniparous
vermiparous
viviparous

ĬP′a-thi
antipathy
kinesipathy
somnipathy

ĬP′a-thist
antipathist
somnipathist

ĬP′ed-al
equipedal
solipedal
(cf. ĒD′al)

ĬP′li-kat
sesquiplicate
triplicate

ĬP′o-li
Gallipoli
Tripoli

ĬP′o-tens
armipotence
ignipotence
omnipotence
plenipotence

ĬP′o-tent
armipotent
bellipotent
ignipotent
multipotent
omnipotent
plenipotent

ĬP′ti-kal
apocalyptical
cryptical
elliptical

ĬP′tur-us
dipterous
peripterous
tripterous

ĬP′u-lat
astipulate
manipulate
stipulate

ĬP′ur-i
frippery
slippery

ĬR′a-b′l
acquirable
desirable
expirable

perspirable
requirable
respirable
transpirable
untirable

ĪR′as-i
piracy
retiracy

ĪR′as-i
conspiracy
deliracy

ĪR′ful-nes
direfulness
irefulness

ĬR′i-an
Assyrian
Styrian
Syrian
Tyrian
(cf. ᴇ̆R′i-an)

ĬR′i-kal
empirical
lyrical
miracle
panegyrical
satirical

ĬR′i-sizm
empiricism
lyricism

ĬR′i-us
delirious
Sirius
(cf. ᴇ̆R′i-us)

ĬR'on-i
gyronny
irony

ĬS'en-ing
christening
glistening
listening
unlistening

ĬS'en-si
reminiscency
reviviscency

ĬS'en-ur
christener
listener

ĬSH'al-i
judicially
officially
prejudicially
superficially

ĬSH'al-izm
judicialism
officialism

ĬSH'en-sĭ
alliciency
beneficiency
deficiency
efficiency
inefficiency
insitiency
insufficiency
proficiency
self-sufficiency
sufficiency

ĬSH'i-a
Alicia

Delicia
Felicia

ĬSH'i-at
initiate
maleficiate
novitiate
officiate
patriciate
propitiate
vitiate

ĬSH'i-ens
omniscience
(cf. ĬSH'ens)

ĬSH'i-ent
omniscient
(cf. ĬSH'ent)

ĬSH'on-al
additional
commissional
conditional
definitional
dispositional
disquisitional
inquisitional
intuitional
positional
prepositional
propositional
repetitional
suppositional
traditional
transitional
transpositional
volitional

ĬSH'on-ist
abolitionist
coalitionist

exhibitionist
expeditionist
oppositionist
prohibitionist
requisitionist
traditionist

ĬSH'on-ur
admonitioner
coalitioner
commissioner
exhibitioner
missioner
practitioner
traditioner

ĬSH'us-nes
adventitious-
  ness
auspiciousness
avariciousness
capriciousness
deliciousness
expeditiousness
fictitiousness
flagitiousness
inauspicious-
  ness
judiciousness
maliciousness
meretricious-
  ness
perniciousness
propitiousness
seditiousness
superstitious-
  ness
supposititious-
  ness
suspiciousness
viciousness

ĬS'i-b'l
admissible
amissible
dismissible
immiscible
incommiscible
irremissable
miscible
omissible
permiscible
permissible
remissible
scissible
transmissible

ĬS'i-est
iciest
spiciest

Ĭ'si-k'l
bicycle
icicle
tricycle

ĬS'i-li
icily
spicily

ĬS'i-mo
bravissimo
fortissimo
generalissimo
pianissimo
prestissimo

ĬS'i-nal
fidicinal
medicinal
officinal
vaticinal
vicinal

ĬS'i-nes
iciness
spiciness

ĬS'i-ti
accomplicity
achromaticity
authenticity
benedicite
caloricity
canonicity
catholicity
causticity
centricity
clericity
complicity
conicity
domesticity
duplicity
eccentricity
elasticity
electricity
electrotonicity
ellipticity
endemicity
evangelicity
felicity
historicity
hygroscopicity
immundicity
impudicity
inelasticity
infelicity
lubricity
mendicity
multiplicity
pepticity
periodicity
plasticity
publicity
pudicity

rubricity
rusticity
simplicity
spasticity
sphericity
spheroidicity
stoicity
stypticity
tonicity
triplicity
unicity
verticity
volcanicity
vulcanicity

ĬS'it-nes
explicitness
illicitness
implicitness
licitness

ĬS'i-tud
solicitude
spissitude
vicissitude

Ī'si-us
Dionysius
(cf. Lycias)

ĬS'iv-li
decisively
derisively
incisively
indecisively

ĬS'iv-nes
decisiveness
derisiveness
incisiveness
indecisivenes

ĬS'ki-est
friskiest
riskiest

ĬS'on-us
fluctisonous
unisonous

ĬS'or-i, ĬS'ur-i
decisory
derisory
incisory
spicery

ĬS'or-i
admissory
dismissory
emissory
remisory
rescissory

ĬS'ten-si
consistency
distancy
existency
inconsistency
persistency
pre-existency
subsistency

ĬS'ti-kal
agonistical
alchemistical
anarchistical
anomalistical
antagonistical
antarchistical
aoristical
apathistical
aphoristical
artistical

atheistical
cabalistical
Calvanistical
casuistical
cathechistical
characteristical
chemistical
deistical
dialogistical
egostical
egotistical
eucharistical
eulogistical
euphemistical
hemistichal
linguistical
methodistical
mystical
paragraphisti-
cal
pietistical
puristical
sophistical
statistical
theistical
theosophistical

ĬS'ti-kat
dephlogisticate
sophisticate

ĬST'les-nes
listlessness
resistlessness

ĬS'to-ri
consistory
history
mystery

ĪT'a-b'l
citable

excitable | ĬTH′som-nes | ĬT′i-nes | obliterate
ignitible | blithesomeness | almightiness | reiterate
incitable | lithesomeness | flightiness | transliterate
indictable | | mightiness |
lightable | ĬTH′ur-ward | | ĬT′ur-est
requitable | hitherward | ĬT′i-nes | bitterest
unitable | thitherward | flittiness | embitterest
writable | whitherward | grittiness | fritterest
| | prettiness | glitterest
ĬT′a-b′l | ĬT′i-gant | wittiness |
admittable | litigant | | ĬT′ur-ing
fittable | mitigant | ĬT′i-sizm | bittering
irremittable | | Britticism | embittering
knittable | ĬT′i-gat | witticism | frittering
quittable | litigate | | glittering
transmittible | mitigate | ĬT′li-nes | tittering
| | knightliness | twittering
ĬT′an-i | ĬT′i-kal | spriteliness |
dittany | Abrahamitical | unsightliness | Ĭ′ur-i
kitteny | acritical | | briery
litany | analytical | ĬT″l-nes | fiery
| anchoritical | brittleness | friary
ĬT′a-tiv | cosmopolitical | littleness | (cf. diary)
excitative | critical | |
incitative | diacritical | ĬT′u-al | ĬV′a-b′l
writative | electrolytical | habitual | contrivable
| hermitical | obitual | deprivable
ĬT′ful-i | hypercritical | ritual | derivable
delightfully | hypocritical | | revivable
frightfully | Jesuitical | ĬT′u-at |
rightfully | Levitical | habituate | ĬV′a-b′l
spitefully | political | situate | forgivable
| pulpitical | | givable
Ĭth′e-sis | soritical | ĬT′u-lar | livable
antithesis | thersitical | capitular | unforgivable
epithesis | | titular |
| ĬT′i-li | | ĬV′a-lent
ĬTH′som-li | grittily | ĬT′ur-at | equivalent
blithesomely | prettily | illiterate | multivalent
lithesomely | wittily | iterate | omnivalent
| | literate | quinquivalent

trivalent
univalent

ĬV′an-si

connivancy
survivancy

ĬV′a-tiv

derivative
privative

ĬV′el-ur,
  ĬV′il-ur

civiller
driveller
sniveller

ĬV′i-a

Bolivia
Livia
Olivia
trivia

ĬV′i-al

convivial
lixivial
oblivial
quadrivial
trivial

ĬV′i-an

Bolivian
Vivian
(cf. Vivien)

ĬV′id-nes

lividness
vividness

ĬV′i-ti

absorptivity

acclivity
activity
captivity
causativity
cogitativity
collectivity
conductivity
declivity
festivity
impassivity
incogitativity
instinctivity
motivity
nativity
negativity
objectivity
passivity
perceptivity
positivity
privity
proclivity
productivity
receptivity
relativity
sensitivity
subjectivity

ĬV′i-us

bivious
lascivious
lixivious
multivious
oblivious

ĬV′o-kal

equivocal
univocal

ĬV′o-li

Rivoli
Tivoli

ĬV′o-ri, ĬV′ar-i

ivory
vivary

ĬV′or-us

carnivorous
equivorous
frugivorous
fucivorous
graminivorous
granivorous
herbivorous
insectivorous
omnivorous
ossivorous
panivorous
phytivorous
piscivorous
sanguinivorous
vermivorous

ĬV′ur-i

delivery
gaol-delivery
jail-delivery
livery
rivery
shivery

ĬV′ur-ing

delivering
quivering
shivering

ĬV′ur-ur

deliverer
quiverer
shiverer

ĬZ′a-b′l

advisable

analysable
crystallizable
demisable
despisable
devisable
electrolysable
excisable
exercisable
magnetizable
organizable
oxidizable
prizable
realizable
recognizable
sizable
vaporizable

ĬZ′a-b′l

acquisible
divisible
indivisible
invisible
risible
visible

ĬZH′on-al

divisional
provisional
revisional
transitional
visional

ĬZ′i-an

Elysian
Frisian
Paradisean
Parisian
precisian
(cf. ĬZH′un)

āle,   câre,   ădd,   ärm,   åsk;   mē,   hęre,   ĕnd;   īce,   ĭll;

ĬZ'i-est
busiest
dizziest

ĬZ'i-kal
metaphysical
paradisical
phthisical

physical
psychophysical

ĬZ'i-li
busily
dizzily

ĬZ'i-tor
acquisitor

inquisitor
requisitor
visitor

ĬZ'i-ur
busier
dizzier
frizzier

ĪZ'or-i
advisory
irrisory
provisory
revisory
supervisory

O

For a discussion of words included under the accented vowels following, see the beginning of O rhymes in Section I.

Ō'bi-a
hydrophobia,
  etc.
phobia
Zenobia

ŎB'i-net
bobbinet
robinet

ŎB'u-lar
globular
lobular

ŎB'ur-ĭ
daubery
(cf. straw-
  berry)

ŎB'ur-i
bobbery
jobbery
robbery
slobbery

snobbery
stockjobbery

ŎB'ur-ing
clobbering
slobbering

ŌD'i-al
allodial
custodial
episodial
palinodial
prosodial
threnodial

ŌD'i-an
custodian
Herodian
prosodian
Rhodian
(cf. ŌD'i-on)

ŎD'el-ur
modeller
(cf. ŎD'lur)

ŎD'i-fi
codify
modify

ŎD'i-kal
codical
episcodical
methodical
monodical
nodical
periodical
prosodical
rhapsodical
spasmodical
synodical

ŎD'i-nes
bawdiness
gaudiness

ŎD'i-ti
commodity
incommodity
oddity

ŎD'i-um
odium
rhodium
sodium

ŎD'i-us
commodious
incommodious
melodious
odious

ŎD'ri-nes
bawdriness
tawdriness

ŎD'u-lar
modular
nodular

ŎD'ur-ik
Roderick
Theoderic

ŎD'ur-ing
doddering
foddering

ōld, ôr, ŏdd, oil, fŏŏt, out; ūse, ûrn, ŭp; THis, thin

ŎF′a-gan
saprophagan
sarcophagan
theophagan
zoophagan

ŎF′a-gī
androphagi
anthropophagi
cardophagi
heterophagi
hippophagi
lithophagi
Lotophagi
sarcophagi

ŎF′a-gĭ
anthropophagy
chthonophagy
hippiphagy
ichthyophagy
pantophagy
phytophagy
theophagy
xerophagy

ŎF′a-gist
galactophagist
geophagist
hippophagist
ichthyophagist
pantophagist

ŎF′a-gus
androphagous
batrachopha-
  gous
esophagus
galactophagous
geophagous
hippophagous

hylophagous
lithophagous
necrophagous
ophiophagous
pantophagous
phytophagous
saprophagous
sarcophagus
theophagous
xylophagous
zoophagous

ŎF′i-kal
philosophical
theosophical
trophical

ŎF′i-list
bibliophilist
Russophilist
zoophilist

ŎF′i-lizm
bibliophilism
necrophilism
Russophilism

ŎF′il-us
acidophilus
anemophilous
Theophilus
xylophilous

ŎF′o-ni
cacophony
homophony
laryngophony
microphony
orthophony
photophony
Satanophany

tautophony
theophany

ŎF′on-us
cacophonous
homophonous
hydrophanous
hygrophanous
megalophonous
monophanous
pyrophanous

ŎF′or-us
actinophorous
adenophorous
electrophorus
galactophorous
isophorus
mastigo-
  phorous
phyllophorous
pyrophorous
zoophorous

Ŏ′ful-i
awfully
lawfully
unlawfully

Ŏ′ful-nes
awfulness
lawfulness
unlawfulness

ŎF′ur-ing
coffering
offering
peace-offering
proffering

ŎG′am-i
cœnogamy

deuterogamy
endogamy
exogamy
misogamy
monogamy

ŎG′am-ist
deuterogamist
misogamist
monogamist
neogamist

ŎG′am-us
endogamus
exogamous
heterogamous
monogamous
phænogamous
phanerog-
  amous

ŎG′a-tiv
derogative
interrogative
prerogative

Ŏ′gi-ism
bogeyism
fogeyism

ŎG′no-mi
craniognomy
pathognomy
physiognomy

ŎG′ra-fi
anthography
anthropog-
  raphy
autobiography
autography

āle,   câre,   ădd,   ärm,   ȧsk;   mē,   hẹre,   ĕnd;   īce,   ĭll;

balneography
bibliography
biography
cacography
calcography
chartography
chirography
chorography
Christianog-
　raphy
chromatog-
　raphy
chromophotog-
　raphy
chromotypog-
　raphy
chromoxylog-
　raphy
climatography
cosmography
cryptography
crystalography
dactyliography
demography
dendrography
epistolography
ethnography
galvanography
geography
glossography
glyphography
glyptography
gypsography
hagiography
haliography
heliography
heliotypog-
　raphy
hematography
heresiography
heterography

hierography
histography
historiography
horography
horologi-
　ography
hyalography
hydrography
hyetography
hymnography
ichnography
ichthyography
iconography
ideography
isography
lexicography
lichenography
lithography
logography
mechanog-
　raphy
metallography
microcosmog-
　raphy
monography
neography
neurography
nomography
nosography
numismatog-
　raphy
odontography
ophiography
oreography
organography
orography
orthography
osteography
palæography
palæontog-
　raphy

paneiconog-
　raphy
pantography
perspectog-
　raphy
petrography
phantasma-
　tography
pharmacog-
　raphy
phonography
photography
phycography
physiography
phytography
plastography
pneumography
pornography
potamography
psalmography
pseudography
psychography
pterylography
rhyparography
scenography
sciography
seismography
selenography
semeiography
siderography
sphenography
steganography
stelography
stenography
stereography
steoreotypog-
　raphy
stratography
stylography
symbolæog-
　raphy

tacheography
thermography
topography
toreumatog-
　raphy
typography
uranography
xylography
xylopyrography
zincograyhy
zoography

ŎG′ra-fist
chirographist
lichenographist
mechano-
　graphist
metallo-
　graphist
monographist
museographist
organogra-
　phist
orthographist
palæographist
phonographist
photographist
psalmographist
selenographist
siderographist
sphenographist
steganogra-
　phist
stenographist
topographist
uranographist
zoographist

ŎG′ra-fur
autobiographer
bibliographer

ōld, ôr, ŏdd, oil, fo͞ot, out; ūse, ûrn, ŭp; ·THis, thin

biographer
calcographer
cartographer
chartographer
chorographer
chronographer
cosmographer
cryptographer
crystallogra-
  pher
ethnographer
geographer
glossographer
glyphographer
glyptographer
haliographer
heresiographer
hierographer
historiographer
horologiogra-
  pher
hydrographer
hymnographer
iambographer
lexicographer
lichenographer
lithographer
logographer
mimographer
monographer
mythographer
nomographer
orthographer
osteographer
palæographer
petrographer
phonographer
photographer
psalmographer
selenographer
sphenographer

stenographer
topographer
typographer
xylographer
zincographer
zoographer

OI′a-b'l

employable
enjoyable

OI′al-i

loyally
royally

OI′al-ist

loyalist
royalist

OI′al-izm

loyalism
royalism

OI′al-ti

loyalty
royalty
viceroyalty

Ŏ′i-kal

egoical
heroical
stoical

OIN′ted-li

disjointedly
pointedly

OIS′tur-ing

cloistering
roistering

ŎJ′en-i

abiogeny
anthropogeny
biogeny
embryogeny
ethnogeny
geogeny
heterogeny
histogeny
homogeny
hymenogeny
misogyny
monogeny
odontogeny
ontogeny
osteogeny
pathogeny
philogyny
photogeny
phylogeny
progeny
protogyny
zoogeny

ŎJ′en-ist

abiogenist
biogenist
heterogenist
misogynist
monogenist
philogynist

ŎJ′en-us

endogenous
exogenous
hydrogenous
hypogynous
lithogenous
nitrogenous
pyrogenous
thermogenous

Ŏ′ji-an

archæologian
astrologian
gambogian
geologian
mythologian
neologian
philologian
theologian

ŎJ′i-kal

aërological
amphibiological
amphibological
analogical
anthological
anthropological
archæological
astrological
bibliological
biological
bryological
chronological
climatological
conchological
cosmological
craniological
demagogical
demonological
deontological
dialogical
doxological
Egpytological
etiological
etymological
genealogical
geological
glossological
glottological
homological
hydrological

---

ichnological	tautological	ŎK'en-li	pantisocracy
ideological	technicological	brokenly	pedantocracy
illogical	technological	outspokenly	plantocracy
lithological	teleological		plousiocracy
logical	teratological	ŎK'i-li	plutocracy
mazological	terminological	chalkily	shopocracy
metalogical	theological	gawkily	slavocracy
meteorological	toxicological	pawkily	snobocracy
mythological	tropological		stratocracy
necrological	universological	ŎK'i-nes	theocracy
neological	zoological	chalkiness	theocrasy
neurological	zoophytological	gawkiness	timocracy
nosological	zymological	pawkiness	
odontological		squawkiness	ŎK'ra-tizm
organological	ŎJ'on-i	talkiness	democratism
ornithological	autogony		Socratism
orological	cosmogony	ŎK'i-nes	
osteological	geogony	cockiness	ŎK'ro-mi
palæontolog-	pathogony	rockiness	heliochromy
ical	physiogony	stockiness	metallochromy
pantological	theogony		monochromy
paralogical	zoogony	ŎK'ra-si	stereochromy
penological		aristocracy	
perissological	ŎJ'o-nist	arithmocracy	ŎK'ron-us
petrological	cosmogonist	autocracy	isochronous
philological	theogonist	cottonocracy	tautochronous
phraseological		democracy	
phrenological	ŎK'a-liz	demonocracy	ŎK'si-kal
physiological	focalize	despotocracy	orthodoxical
phytological	localize	gerontocracy	paradoxical
pneumatologi-	vocalize	gynæcocracy	toxical
cal		hagiocracy	
pomological	ŎK'al-izm	hierocracy	ŎK'tor-ship
psychological	localism	hypocrisy	doctorship
selenological	vocalism	idiocrasy	proctorship
semeiological		logocracy	
Sinological	ŎK'a-tiv	mobocracy	ŎK'u-lar
sociological	locative	monocracy	binocular
spectrological	invocative	neocracy	jocular
symbological	provocative	nomocracy	locular
synagogical	vocative	ochlocracy	monocular

ōld, ôr. ŏdd, oil, fŏŏt, out; ūse, ûrn, ŭp; THis, thin

ocular
vocular

ŌK'ur-i
crockery
mockery
rockery

ŌL'a-b'l
consolable
controllable
rollable
tollable

ŌL'a-b'l
enthrallable
recallable

ŌL'a-ri
bolary
cajolery
polary
solary
volary

ŌL'ar-iz
polarize
solarize

ŌL'a-tri
anthropolatry
astrolatry
bibliolatry
cosmolatry
demonolatry
geolatry
gyneolatry
heliolatry
hierolatry
ichthyolatry
idiolatry

idolatry
litholatry
lordolatry
Mariolatry
necrolatry
ophiolatry
physiolatry
pyrolatry
symbolatry
thaumatolatry
topolatry
zoolatry

ŌL'a-trus
idolatrous
symbolatrous

ŌL'a-tur
bibliolater
heliolater
iconolater
idolater
Mariolater
pyrolater

ŌL'e-um
linoleum
petroleum
(cf. ŌL'i-um)

ŌL'ful-nes
dolefulness
soulfulness

Ō'li-a
Aetolia
magnolia
melancholia
Mongolia

Ō'li-an
Æolian

capitolian
Creolean
melancholian
metabolian
Mongolian
Pactolian
(cf. Napoleon)

ŌL'i-at
foliate
infoliate
spoliate

ŌL'id-li
solidly
squalidly
stolidly

ŌL'id-nes
solidness
squalidness
stolidness

Ō'li-est
holiest
lowliest

ŌL'i-fi
idolify
mollify
qualify

ŌL'i-fid
mollified
qualified
unqualified

ŌL'i-kal
apostolical
bibliopolical
catholical

diabolical
hyperbolical
parabolical
symbolical

ŌL'ik-som
frolicsome
rollicksome

Ō'li-nes
holiness
lowliness
shoaliness
unholiness

Ō'li-o
folio
olio
portfolio
Sapolio

ŌL'ish-ing
abolishing
demolishing
polishing

ŌL'ish-ur
abolisher
demolisher
polisher

ŌL'i-ti
equality
frivolity
inequality
interpolity
isopolity
jollity
polity
quality

āle, câre, ădd, ärm, åsk; mē, hęre, ĕnd; īce, ĭll;

ŎL'i-um
scholium
trifolium

Ŏ'li-ur
Grolier
holier
lowlier
olier
unholier

ŎL'ĭ-vur
Oliver
Taliaferro
Tolliver

ŎL'o-gus
heterologous
homologous
isologous
tautologous

ŎL'o-ing
following
holloing
hollowing
swallowing
wallowing

ŎL'o-ji
actinology
adenochirapsol-
　ogy
aerology
æsthematology
æsthesiology
agmatology
agriology
alethiology
amphibiology
amphibology

angelology
anthology
anthropology
aphnology
apology
arachnology
archæology
aretology
aristology
arteriology
asthenology
astrology
astrometeorol-
　ogy
astro-theology
atomology
balneology
barology
battology
bibliology
biology
botanology
bromatology
brontology
bryology
bugology
cacology
campanology
cephalology
Christology
chromatology
chronology
climatology
conchology
conchyliology
cosmology
craniology
cryptology
dactyliology
dactylology
demonology

dendrology
deontology
dermatology
desmology
dialectology
dicæology
dittology
dosology
doxology
ecclesiology
eccrinology
Egyptology
electro-biology
electrology
electro-physi-
　ology
embryology
emetology
emmenology
endemiology
enteradenology
enterology
entomology
entozoology
epidemiology
epistemology
eschatology
ethnology
ethology
etiology
etymology
filicology
fossilology
fungology
galvanology
gastrology
genesiology
geology
gigantology
glossology
glottology

gnomology
gnomonology
gynæcology
gypsology
hagiology
heterology
hierology
histology
historiology
homology
horology
hydrology
hyetology
hygiology
hygrology
hylology
hymenology
hymnology
hypnology
hysterology
ichnolithnology
ichnology
ichorology
ichthyology
iconology
ideology
insectology
kinology
laryngology
leptology
lexicology
lichenology
lithology
liturgiology
macrology
malacology
mantology
martyrology
mastology
mazology
membranologу

ōld, ôr, ŏdd, oil, fŏŏt, out; ūse, ûrn, ŭp; THis, thin

menology
meteorology
methodology
metrology
miasmology
microgeology
micrology
misology
monadology
monology
morphology
muscology
mycology
myology
mythology
necrology
neology
nephrology
neurology
neurypnology
nomology
noölogy
nosology
numismatology
oceanology
odontology
ology
onĕirology
onology
onomatology
ontology
oology
ophiology
ophthalmology
orchidology
organology
orismology
ornithichnol-
ogy
ornithology
orology

osmonosolgy
osteology
otology
ovology
palæoëthnology
palæology
palæontology
palæophy-
tology
palæozoology
palætiology
pantheology
pantology
paradoxology
parasitology
parisology
paromology
parthenology
pathology
patronomatol-
ogy
penology
periodology
perissology
petrology
pharmacology
pharology
pharyngology
phenomenol-
ogy
philology
phlebology
phonology
photology
phraseolgy
phrenology
phycology
physiology
phytolithology
phytology

phytopathol-
ogy
phyto-
physiology
pneumatology
pneumology
pomology
ponerology
posology
potamology
protophytology
psilology
psychology
psychonosol-
ogy
pteridology
punnology
pyretology
pyritology
pyrology
quinology
runology
sarcology
seismology
selenology
sematology
semeiology
sinology
sitology
skeletology
sociology
somatology
soteriology
spasmology
speciology
spectrology
spermatology
spermology
splanchnology
splenology
statistology

stoichiology
stromatology
symbology
symptomatol-
ogy
synchronology
syndesmology
systematology
tautology
taxology
technology
teleology
teratology
terminology
termonology
testaceology
thanatology
theology
thereology
thermology
therology
threpsology
tidology
topology
toreumatology
toxicology
tropology
typology
universology
uranology
urology
uronology
vulcanology
zoology
zoophytology
zymology

ŏL'o-jist
aërologisť
agriologist
anthropologisť

āle, câre, ădd, ārm, ăsk; mē, hĕre, ĕnd; īce, ĭll;

apologist
archæologist
Assyriologist
battologist
biologist
campanologist
chronologist
conchologist
cosmologist
craniologist
crustaceologist
demonologist
dendrologist
deontologist
dermatologist
ecclesiologist
Egyptologist
electro-
  biologist
embryologist
entomologist
ethnologist
ethologist
etymologist
galvanologist
geologist
glossologist
glottologist
gypsologist
hagiologist
hierologist
histologist
horologist
hydrologist
hymnologist
hypnologist
ichthyologist
ideologist
lexicologist
lithologist
mantologist

martyrologist
mazologist
meteorologist
monologist
morphologist
mycologist
myologist
mythologist
necrologist
neologist
neurologist
noölogist
nosologist
numismatolo-
  gist
oneirologist
onomatologist
ontologist
oologist
ophiologist
orchidologist
ornithologist
orologist
osteologist
palæoethnolo-
  gist
palæologist
palæontologist
palætiologist
pantheologist
pantologist
pathologist
petrologist
pharmacologist
philologist
phonologist
photologist
phraseologist
phrenologist
physiologist

phytolitholo-
  gist
phytologist
phytopatholo-
  gist
pneumatologist
pomologist
pseudologist
psychologist
pteridologist
pyrologist
quinologist
runologist
saintologist
sarcologist
seismologist
sinologist
sociologist
symbologist
tautologist
technologist
teleologist
teratologist
theologist
thereologist
therologist
toxicologist
universologist
vulcanologist
zoologist
zymologist, etc.

ŎL'o-jiz

apologize
astrologize
battologize
doxologize
entomologize
etymologize
geologize
mythologize

neologize
philologize
sociologize
tautologize
theologize
zoologize, etc.

ŎL'o-jur

acknowledger
astrologer
botanologer
etymologer
geologer
horologer
mythologer
osteologer
philologer
phonologer
phrenologer
physiologer
sockdolager
theologer

ŎL'o-ur

follower
hollower
swallower
wallower

ŎL'ti-est

faultiest
saltiest

ŎL'ti-nes

faultiness
maltiness
saltiness

ŎL'tur-ing

altering
faltering

paltering
unaltering
unfaltering

ŎL'tur-ur
alterer
falterer
palterer

ŎL'u-b'l
insoluble
soluble
voluble

ŎL'u-tiv
solutive
supervolutive
(cf. evolutive,
  revolutive)

ŎL'va-b'l
absolvable
dissolvable
indissolvable
insolvable
resolvable
solvable

ŎL'ven-si
insolvency
revolvency
solvency

ŎM'ak-i
alectryomachy
gigantomachy
iconomachy
logomachy
monomachy
psychomachy

sciomachy
theomachy

ŎM'ath-i
chrestomathy
philomathy

Ō'ma-tizm
achromatism
chromatism
diplomatism

ŎM'en-a
antilegomena
paralipomena
phenomena
prolegomena

ŎM'en-on
phenomenon
prolegomenon

ŎM'e-tri
barometry
biometry
chronometry
craniometry
eudiometry
galvanometry
gasometry
geometry
goniometry
helicometry
horometry
hydrometry
hygrometry
hypsometry
Mahometry
micrometry
odometry
orthometry

ozonometry
pathometry
photometry
planometry
pneumometry
polygonometry
pyrometry
rheometry
saccharometry
seismometry
stereometry
stichometry
stoichiometry
trigonometry

ŎM'e-tur
absorptiometer
actinometer
altometer
astrometer
audiometer
barometer
bathometer
cephalometer
chartometer
chromatometer
chronometer
clinometer
craniometer
declinometer
dendrometer
drosometer
dynamometer
echometer
electrometer
endosmometer
eudiometer
galvanometer
geometer
geothermo-
  meter

goniometer
graphometer
heliometer
horometer
hydrometer
hygrometer
hypsometer
lactometer
logometer
macrometer
magnetometer
micrometer
micronometer
monometer
nauropometer
odometer
oleometer
ombrometer
optometer
ozonometer
pantometer
pedometer
phonometer
photometer
piezometer
planometer
platometer
pluviometer
pneumatometer
pulsometer
pyrometer
radiometer
refractometer
rheometer
saccharometer
salinometer
seismometer
sonometer
spectrometer
speedometer
spherometer

---

stereometer	prominent	**ŎN´dur-ur**	*oxygonial*
stethometer	subdominant	ponderer	patrimonial
stratometer	superdominant	squanderer	sanctimonial
tachometer		wanderer	testimonial
tannometer	**ŎM´i-nat**		
thermometer	abominate	**ŎN´el-i**	**Ō´ni-an**
tribometer	agnominate	Connolly	Aberdonian
trochometer	comminate	Donnelly	Amazonian
udometer	denominate		Ammonian
vinometer	dominate	**Ō´ni-a**	Aonian
volumenometer	nominate	Adonia	Ausonion
zymometer	*ominate*	ammonia	Babylonian
	predominate	Ansonia	Baconian
ŎM´ik-al	prenominate	Antonia	bezonian
anatomical		aphonia	Caledonian
agronomical	**ŎM´in-i**	begonia	Cameronian
astronomical	Chickahomini	bryonia	Catonian
atomical	dominie	Donia	Chelonian
comical	hominy	Fredonia	Chthonian
coxcombical	(cf. Romany)	Ionia	Ciceronian
domical		Laconia	colophonian
economical	**ŎM´in-us**	Latonia	Cottonian
iconomachal	abdominous	Patagonia	Daltonian
tragi-comical	dominus	pneumonia	demonian
zootomical	ominous	Slavonia	Devonian
	prolegomenous	Sonia	Draconian
ŎM´in-al		Sophronia	Etonian
abdominal	**ŎM´ur-us**	valonia	Favonian
cognominal	*glomerous*		Gorgonean
nominal	isomerous	**Ō´ni-ak**	Grandisonian
prenominal		demoniac	halcyonian
surnominal	**ŌN´a-b'l**	simoniac	Heliconian
	loanable		Ionian
ŎM´in-ans	tonable	**Ō´ni-al**	Johnsonian
dominance	unatonable	baronial	Laconian
predominance		ceremonial	Lapponian
prominence	**ŎN´dur-ing**	colonial	Livonian
	pondering	demonial	Macedonian
ŎM´in-ant	squandering	intercolonial	Miltonian
dominant	unwandering	matrimonial	Myrmidonian
predominant	wandering	monial	Neronian

ōld, ôr, ŏdd, oil, fŏŏt, out; ūse, ûrn, ŭp; THis, thin

Newtonian
Oxonian
Patagonian
Plutonian
Pyrrhonian
Sardonian
Serbonian
Simonian
Slavonian
Thessalonian

ŎN′i-est
brawnies
tawniest

ŎN′i-fi
personify
saponify
(cf. ozonify)

ŎN′i-ka
harmonica
veronica

ŎN′i-kal
acronycal
antichronical
antiphonical
architectonical
Babylonical
canonical
chronicle
conical
diaphonical
euphonical
geoponical
harmonical
iconical
ironical
Sorbonical
synchronical

tautophonical
thrasonical
tonical
uncanonical

ŎN′i-kon
chronicon
harmonicon

ŎN′i-mi
homonymy
metonymy
paronymy
polyonymy
synonymy
(cf. ŎN′o-mi)

ŎN′i-mus
anonymous
autonomous
eponymous
heteronymous
homonymous
paronymous
polyonymous
pseudnymous
synonymous

ŎN′ish-ing
admonishing
astonishing
monishing

ŎN′ish-ment
admonishment
astonishment
premonishment

ŎN′i-sizm
histrionicism

laconicism
Teutonicism

Ŏ′ni-um
harmonium
pandemonium
pelargonium
stramonium
zirconium

Ŏ′ni-us
acrimonious
alimonious
Antonius
ceremonious
erroneous
euphonious
felonious
harmonious
inharmonious
matrimonious
parsimonious
querimonious
sanctimonious
simonious
symphonious
Trebonius
ultroneous

ŎN′o-graf
chronograph
monograph
(cf. phono-
graph)

ŎN′o-mi
agronomy
astronomy
autonomy
dactylonomy
Deuteronomy

economy
gastronomy
heteronomy
isonomy
morphonomy
taxonomy

ŎN′o-mist
agronomist
autonomist
economist
eponymist
gastronomist
synonymist

ŎN′o-miz
astronomize
economize
gastronomize

ŎN′o-mur
astronomer
gastronomer

ŎŎD′i-nes
woodiness
(cf. ŪD′i-nes)

ŎŎK′ur-i
bookery
cookery
rookery

Ŏ′o-lit
oolite
zoolite

ŎŎM′an-li
womanly
(cf. Ū′man-li)

ŎP'ath-i
allopathy
enantiopathy
heteropathy
homœopathy
hydropathy
ideopathy
isopathy
neuropathy
psychopathy
somnopathy
theopathy

ŎP'ath-ist
allopathist
homœopathist
hydropathist
hylopathist
osteopathist
somnopathist

Ō'pi-a
Ethiopia
myopia
presbyopia
Utopia

Ō'pi-an,
Ō'pe-an
Aesopian
Esopian
Ethiopian
Fallopian
Utopian

ŎP'i-kal
allotropical
metoposcopical
microscopical
misanthropical
sub-tropical

topical
tropical

ŎP'i-nes
dopiness
ropiness
slopiness
soapiness

ŎP'i-nes
choppiness
sloppiness
soppiness

ŎP'ish-nes
dopishness
mopishness
popishness

ŎP'o-lis
acropolis
cosmopolis
Heliopolis
metropolis
necropolis

ŎP'o-list
bibliopolist
monopolist
pharmacopolist

ŎP'o-lit
cosmopolite
metropolite

ŎP'si-kal
dropsical
mopsical
Popsicle

ŎP'ti-kal
autoptical
optical

ŎP'tur-us
lepidopterous
macropterous
orthopterous

ŎP'u-lat
copulate
populate

ŌP'ur-i
dopery
popery
ropery

ŎP'ur-i
coppery
foppery

ŌR'a-b'l
adorable
deplorable
explorable
restorable

ŌR'a-tiv
explorative
restorative

ŌR'di-al
cordial
exordial
primordial

ŌR'di-nat
co-ordinate
foreordinate
insubordinate
ordinate
subordinate

ŌR'di-on,
ŌR'di-an
accordion
Gordian

ŌR'dur-ing
bordering
ordering

ŌR'e-at
aureate
baccalaureate
laureate
poet-laureate

ŌR'e-ol
aureole
laureole

ŌR'gon-iz,
ŌR'gan-iz
gorgonize
organize

Ō'ri-a
aporia
Astoria
Castoria
dysphoria
euphoria
Gloria
Honoria
infusoria
littoria
Peoria
phantasma-
    goria
Pretoria
scoria
victoria

Ō'ri-al
accessorial
accusatorial
adaptorial
admonitorial

amatorial	infusorial	territorial	**Ō′ri-fi**
ambassadorial	inquisitorial	textorial	glorify
ancestorial	insessorial	tinctorial	scorify
arboreal	intercessorial	tonsorial	
armorial	inventorial	tutorial	**ŎR′i-fi**
accessorial	legislatorial	uxorial	historify
auditorial	manorial	victorial	horrify
authorial	marmoreal	visitatorial	torrefy
boreal	mediatorial		
censorial	memorial	**Ō′ri-an**	**ŎR′i-kal**
commentatorial	mentorial	amatorian	allegorical
compromis-	monitorial	Bosphorian	categorical
sorial	motorial	censorian	coracle
compurgatorial	oratorial	consistorian	historical
consistorial	phantasma-	dictatorian	metaphorical
corporeal	gorial	Dorian	oracle
cursorial	pictorial	gladiatorian	oratorical
dedicatorial	piscatorial	Gregorian	pictorical
dictatorial	preceptorial	Hectorean	rhetorical
directorial	prefatorial	historian	tautegorical
disquisitorial	proctorial	hyperborean	
editorial	procuratorial	marmorean	**ŎR′i-nes**
electorial	professorial	mid-Victorian	desultoriness
emporial	proprietorial	Nestorian	dilatoriness
equatoreal	protectorial	oratorian	goriness
escritorial	purgatorial	prætorian	hoariness
executorial	raptorial	purgatorian	peremptoriness
expurgatorial	rasorial	salutatorian	
exterritorial	rectorial	senatorian	**Ō′ri-ol**
extraterritorial	reportorial	stentorian	gloriole
factorial	risorial	valedictorian	gloryhole
fossorial	sartorial	Victorian	oriole
gladiatorial	scansorial		
grallatorial	sectorial	**Ō′ri-at**	**ŎR′i-ti**
gressorial	seigniorial	excoriate	anteriority
gubernatorial	senatorial	professoriate	authority
historial	sensorial		deteriority
immemorial	spectatorial	**ŎR′id-li**	exteriority
imperatorial	speculatorial	floridly	inferiority
improvisatorial	sponsorial	horridly	interiority
incorporeal	suctorial	torridly	juniority

āle, câre, ădd, ärm, ȧsk; mē, hĕre, ĕnd; īce, ĭll;

majority
meliority
minority
posteriority
priority
seniority
sorority
superiority

Ō′ri-um

aspersorium
auditorium
ciborium
corium
crematorium
digitorium
emporium
fumatorium
haustorium
inclinatorium
moratorium
prætorium
prospectorium
sanatorium
scriptorium
sensorium
sudatorium
suspensorium
thorium
triforium

Ō′ri-us

amatorious
arboreous
censorious
circulatorious
desultorious
expiatorious
expurgatorious
glorious
hippicanorious

inglorious
inquisitorious
laborious
lusorious
meritorious
notorious
oratorious
purgatorious
raptorious
saltatorious
scorious
senatorious
stentorious
stertorious
suctorious
uproarious
ustorious
uxorious
vainglorious
victorious

ŎR′ma-tiv

afformative
dormitive
formative
informative
reformative
transformative

ŎR′mi-ti

abnormity
conformity
deformity
enormity
inconformity
multiformity
noncomformity
uniformity

ŎR′o-ing

borrowing
sorrowing

ŎR′o-ur

borrower
sorrower

ŎRS′a-b′l,
  ŎRS′i-b′l

divorceable
enforceable
forcible

ŎR′ti-fī

fortify
mortify

ŎRT′i-kal

cortical
vortical

ŎRT′i-nes

swartiness
wartiness

ŎRT′li-nes

courtliness
portliness
uncourtliness

ŎR′tu-nat

fortunate
importunate

Ō′rus-li

decorously
porously
sonorously

ŎR′yus-li

gloriously
ingloriously
laboriously
meritoriously

notoriously
stentoriously
uproariously
uxoriously
vaingloriously
victoriously

ŎS′for-us

Bosphorus
phosphorus

Ō′shi-an

Bœotian
Nicotian
(cf. Ō′shun)

Ō′shun-al

devotional
emotional
notional

Ō′shus-nes

atrociousness
ferociousness
precociousness

ŎS′i-nat

patrocinate
ratiocinate

ŎS′i-nes

drossiness
glossiness
mossiness

ŎS′i-ti

paucity
raucity

ŎS′i-ti

actuosity

anfractuosity
angulosity
animosity
anonymosity
aquosity
atrocity
caliginosity
callosity
carnosity
curiosity
docity
dubiosity
ebriosity
fabulosity
ferocity
foliosity
fuliginosity
fumosity
fungosity
furiosity
gemmosity
generosity
gibbosity
glandulosity
glebosity
globosity
glutinosity
grandiosity
gulosity
gummosity
hideosity
impecuniosity
impetuosity
ingeniosity
inunctuosity
libidinosity
litigiosity
lugubriosity
luminosity
monstrosity
muscosity

musculosity
nebulosity
negotiosity
nervosity
nodosity
oleosity
otiosity
pilosity
plumosity
pomposity
ponderosity
porosity
preciosity
precocity
pretiosity
reciprocity
religiosity
ridiculosity
rimosity
rugosity
sabulosity
saporosity
scirrhosity
scrupulosity
sensuosity
serosity
sinuosity
speciosity
spicosity
spinosity
tenebrosity
torosity
tortuosity
tuberosity
tumulosity
unctuosity
varicosity
velocity
verbosity
viciosity
villosity

vinosity
virtuosity
viscosity
vitiosity
vociferosity

Ō′siv-nes

corrosiveness
explosiveness

ŏS′ko-pi

cranioscopy
geloscopy
geoscopy
hieroscopy
horoscopy
meteoroscopy
metoposcopy
omoplatoscopy
oneiroscopy
organoscopy
ornithoscopy
retinoscopy
stereoscopy
stethoscopy
uranoscopy

ŏS′ko-pist

metoposcopist
microscopist
oneiroscopist
ornithoscopist
stereoscopist
stethoscopist

ŏS′of-i

gymnosophy
philosophy
psilosophy
theosophy

ŏS′o-fist

chirosophist
deipnosophist
gymnosophist
philosophist
theosophist

ŏS′o-fiz

philosophize
theosophize

ŏS′o-fur

philosopher
psilosopher
theosopher

Ō′ta-b'l

floatable
notable
potable
quotable
votable

Ō′tal-izm

sacerdotalism
teetotalism

ŏT′an-i

botany
botonee
cottony
monotony

Ō′ta-ri

notary
rotary
votary

Ō′ta-tiv

connotative

denotative
rotative

ŌT'ed-lĭ
bloatedly
devotedly
notedly

ŌT'ĭ-est
haughtiest
naughtiest

ŎT'ĭ-kal
anecdotical
bigotical
despotical
erotical
exotical
zealotical

ŎT'ĭ-lĭ
haughtily
naughtily

ŎT'ĭ-nes
haughtiness
naughtiness

ŎT'ĭ-nes
dottiness
knottiness
spottiness

ŎT'ĭ-ur
haughtier
naughtier

ŎT'om-ĭ
apotome
bottomy
bronchotomy

dermotomy
dichotomy
encephalotomy
ichthyotomy
phlebotomy
phytotomy
scotomy
stereotomy
tracheotomy
zootomy

ŎT'o-mist
ichthyotomist
phlebotomist
phytotomist
zootomist

ŎT'ur-ĭ
cautery
watery

ŎT'ur-ĭ
lottery
pottery
tottery
trottery

ŎT'ur-ing
slaughtering
watering

ŎT'ur-ur
slaughterer
waterer

OU'a-b'l
allowable
avowable
endowable

OUD'ed-nes
cloudedness

crowdedness
overcrowded-
  ness
uncloudedness

OUD'ĭ-izm
dowdyism
rowdyism

OUD'ĭ-nes
cloudiness
dowdiness
rowdiness

OUL'ur-ĭ
owlery
prowlery

OUND'a-b'l
compoundable
soundable
unsoundable

OUND'ed-nes
astoundedness
confounded-
  ness
dumfounded-
  ness
unboundedness
ungrounded-
  ness

OUND'les-lĭ
boundlessly
groundlessly
soundlessly

OUND'les-nes
boundlessness

groundlessness
soundlessness

OUNT'a-b'l
countable
discountable
insurmountable
mountable
surmountable
unaccountable

OUT'ĭ-nes
doughtiness
droughtiness
goutiness

OU'ur-ĭ
bowery
dowery
flowery
glowery
lowery
showery
towery
(cf. OUR'ĭ)

OU'ur-ing
cowering
dowering
empowering
flowering
glowering
lowering
overpowering
overtowering
showering
towering
(cf. OUR'ing)

OUZ'ĭ-nes
drowsiness
frowziness

ŎV′el-ing	**Ō′zhi-al, Ō′zi-al**	**Ō′zi-li**	crosier
grovelling	ambrosial	cozily	Dozier
hovelling	roseal	nosily	hosier
Ō′vi-al		prosily	nosier
jovial	**O′zhi-an,**	rosily	osier
synovial	**Ō′zi-an**		prosier
	ambrosian	**Ō′zi-nes**	rosier
Ō′vi-an	(cf. Ō′zhun)	coziness	
Cracovian		doziness	**Ō′zur-i**
Jovian	**Ō′zi-est**	nosiness	composery
	coziest	prosiness	dozery
Ō′zhi-a, Ō′zi-a	nosiest	rosiness	rosary
ambrosia	prosiest	**Ō′zi-ur**	(*not* hosiery)
symposia	rosiest	cozier	
(cf. Theodosia)			

U

For a discussion of words included under the accented vowels following, see the beginning of U rhymes in Section I.

Ū′a-b′l	jubilate	**Ū′bri-us**	pudency
doable	nubilate	insalubrious	recrudency
pursuable	obnubilate	lugubrious	
renewable	*volubilate*	salubrious	**ŬD′i-b′l**
reviewable			eludible
suable	**ŬB′i-nes**	**Ū′bur-us**	includible
subduable	chubbiness	protuberous	
	grubbiness	suberous	**ŬD′i-li**
Ū′bi-an	scrubbiness	tuberous	bloodily
Danubian	shrubbiness		muddily
Nubian	stubbiness	**ŬD′a-b′l**	ruddily
rubian		alludable	
	Ū′bi-us	deludable	**Ū′di-nal**
Ū′bi-kal	dubious	includable	aptitudinal
cubical	rubious	protrudable	attitudinal
cherubical			consuetudinal
	Ū′bri-kat		longitudinal
Ū′bi-lat	lubricate	**ŬD′en-si**	testudinal
enubilate	rubricate	concludency	

āle, câre, ădd, ärm, ȧsk; mē, hẽre, ĕnd; īce, ĭll;

ŪD'i-nes
moodiness
(cf. ŎŎD'i-nes)

ŬD'i-nes
bloodiness
muddiness
ruddiness

Ū'di-niz
attitudinize
platitudinize

Ū'di-nus
fortitudinous
latitudinous
multitudinous
paludinous
platitudinous
solicitudinous
vicissitudinous

Ū'di-ti
crudity
nudity
rudity

Ū'di-us
preludious
studious

ŬD'ur-i
duddery
shuddery
studdery

Ū'el-ing
bejewelling
duelling
fueling
gruelling

Ū'el-ur
crueller
dueller
fueller
jeweller

ŬF'i-nes
fluffiness
huffiness
puffiness
stuffiness

ŬG'ur-i
pugaree
snuggery
thuggery

Ū'i-nes
dewiness
glueyness

Ū'in-us
pruinous
ruinous

Ū'ish-nes
Jewishness
shrewishness

Ū'i-ti
acuity
ambiguity
annuity
assiduity
circuity
conspicuity
contiguity
continuity
discontinuity
exiguity
fatuity

gratuity
ingenuity
innocuity
perpetuity
perspicuity
promiscuity
strenuity
suety
superfluity
tenuity
vacuity

Ū'i-tus
circuitous
fatuitous
fortuitous
gratuitous
pituitous

ŪJ'i-nus
æruginous
ferruginous
lanuginous
salsuginous

ŬK'i-li
luckily
pluckily

ŬK'shun-al
constructional
fluxional
inductional
instructional

ŬK'shun-ist
constructionist
destructionist
fluxionist

ŬK'ti-b'l
conductible

destructible
indestructible
instructible

ŬK'tiv-li
constructively
destructively
instructively
productively

ŬK'tiv-nes
constructive-
    ness
destructiveness
instructiveness
productiveness

ŬK'to-ri
conductory
introductory
reproductory

Ū'ku-lent
luculent
muculent
(cf. succulent)

ŬK'ur-ing
puckering
succoring

Ū'le-an
cerulean
herculean
Julian

ŪL'ish-nes
foolishness
mulishness

Ū'li-ti
credulity

ōld, ôr, ŏdd, oil, fŏŏt, out; ūse, ûrn, ŭp; THis, thin

garrulity
incredulity
sedulity

ŬL'ki-nes
bulkiness
sulkiness

ŬL'mi-nant
culminant
fulminant

ŬL'mi-nat
culminate
fulminate

ŬL'siv-li
convulsively
impulsively
repulsively

ŬL'siv-nes
compulsiveness
convulsiveness
impulsiveness
repulsiveness
revulsiveness

ŬL'tur-i
adultery
consultary

ŬL'tur-ism
agriculturism,
   etc.
vulturism

ŬL'ur-i
gullery
medullary
scullery

ŬL'vur-in
culverin
pulverin

ŪM'a-b'l
assumable
consumable
presumable
resumable

Ū'man-li
humanly
(cf. womanly)

ŬM'bur-i
slumbery
umbery

ŬM'bur-ing
cumbering
encumbering
lumbering
numbering
outnumbering
slumbering
unslumbering

ŬM'bur-ur
cumberer
encumberer
lumberer
numberer
slumberer

Ū'mi-nant
illuminant
luminant
ruminant

Ū'mi-nat
acuminate

catechumenate
ferruminate
illuminate
luminate
ruminate

ŪM'i-nes
gloominess
roominess
spuminess

ŬM'ing-li
becomingly
benumbingly
hummingly
numbingly
unbecomingly

Ū'mi-nus
aluminous
bituminous
fluminous
leguminous
luminous
voluminous

ŬM'pish-nes
dumpishness
frumpishness
grumpishness
lumpishness
mumpishness

ŬMP'shus-li
bumptiously
scrumptiously

ŬMP'tu-us
presumptuous
sumptuous

Ū'mu-lat
accumulate
tumulate

Ū'mu-lus
cumulus
tumulous

Ū'mur-al
humeral
numeral

ŪM'ur-i
perfumery
plumery
rumory
(cf. roomery)

ŬM'ur-i
flummery
mummery
nummary
plumbery
summary
summery

Ū'mur-us
humerus
humorous
numerous
rumorous

ŪN'a-b'l
expugnable
tunable

Ū'na-ri
lunary
(cf. Ū'nur-i)

ŬN'di-ti
fecundity

---

jocundity
jucundity
moribundity
profundity
rotundity
rubicundity

ŬN'dur-ing
blundering
plundering
sundering
thundering
wondering

ŬN'dur-song
undersong
wonder-song

ŬN'dur-ur
blunderer
plunderer
sunderer
thunderer
wonderer

ŬN'dur-us
blunderous
thunderous
wonderous

ŬN'dur-world
under-world
wonder-world

ŬNG'gur-ing
hungering
mongering

ŬNGK'shun-al
conjunctional
functional

ŬNGK'u-lar
avuncular
carbuncular
caruncular
peduncular
uncular

Ū'ni-kat
communicate
excommunicate
tunicate

Ū'ni-form
cuniform
luniform
uniform

ŬN'i-li
funnily
sunnily

Ū'ni-ti
community
immunity
importunity
impunity
inopportunity
intercommu-
   nity
jejunity
opportunity
triunity
unity

Ū'ni-tiv
punitive
unitive

ŬNT'ed-li
affrontedly

stuntedly
unwontedly
wontedly

ŬN'ur-i
buffoonery
cocoonery
pantaloonery
poltroonery

ŬN'ur-i
gunnery
nunnery

Ū'pur-at
recuperate
vituperate

Ū'ra-b'l
assurable
curable
durable
endurable
incurable
insurable
procurable
securable

ŬR'a-b'l
conferrable
demurrable
inferable
referable
transferable

Ū'ral-ist
ruralist
(cf. pluralist)

Ū'ral-ism
ruralism
(cf. pluralism)

Ū'ra-tiv
curative
depurative
indurative
maturative

ŬR'bal-ist
herbalist
verbalist

ŬR'bal-izm
herbalism
verbalism

ŬRB'i-al
adverbial
proverbial
suburbial

ŬR'bu-lent
herbulent
turbulent

ŬR'di-li
sturdily
wordily

ŬRD'ur-ur
murderer
verderer

ŬR'en-si
concurrency
currency
recurrency

ŬR'et-ed
turreted
(cf. ĔR'i-ted)

ŬR'flu-us
subterfluous
superfluous

Ū'ri-a
Lemuria
Manchuria

Ū'ri-al
augurial
figurial
mercurial
purpureal
seigneurial

ŪR'i-an
Ū'ri-an
centurian
Etrurian
Missourian
scripturian
Silurian

Ū'ri-ans
luxuriance

Ū'ri-ant
luxuriant

Ū'ri-at
infuriate
luxuriate
muriate
parturiate

Ū'ri-ens
prurience

Ū'ri-ent
esurient
parturient
prurient
scripturient

ŪR'i-est
furriest

hurriest
worriest

Ū'ri-fi
purify
thurify

ŬR'i-ing
currying
flurrying
hurrying
scurrying
worrying

ŬR'i-ment
worriment
(cf. ĔR'i-ment)

ŬR'ish-ing
flourishing
nourishing

Ū'ri-ti
demurity
immaturity
impurity
insecurity
maturity
obscurity
prematurity
purity
security

ŬR'i-ur
currier
flurrier
furrier
hurrier
scurrier
worrier

Ū'ri-us
curious

furious
incurious
injurious
luxurious
penurious
perjurious
spurious
strangurious
sulphureous
usurious

ŬR'jen-si
assurgency
convergency
detergency
divergency
emergency
insurgency
urgency
vergency

ŬR'ji-kal
chirurgical
clergical
demiurgical
energical
liturgical
surgical
thaumaturgical
theurgical

ŬR'jur-i
chirurgery
perjury
purgery
surgery

ŬR'ku-lar
circular
furcular
tubercular

ŬR'ku-lat
circulate
tuberculate

ŬR'ku-lus
surculus
surculous
tuberculous

ŬR'li-est
burliest
churliest
curliest
earliest
pearliest
surliest

ŬR'li-nes
burliness
curliness
earliness
pearliness
surliness

ŬR'lish-li
churlishly
girlishly

ŬR'lish-nes
churlishness
girlishness

ŬR'mi-nal
germinal
terminal

ŬR'mi-nant
determinant
germinant
terminant

ŬR'mi-nat
determinate

exterminate
germinate
indeterminate
interminate
terminate

ŬR'mi-nus
coterminous
terminus
verminous

ŬR'na-b'l
burnable
discernible
indiscernible
learnable
overturnable
returnable

ŬR'nal-ist
eternalist
journalist

ŬR'nal-iz
eternalize
externalize
journalize

ŬR'nal-izm
externalism
infernalism
journalism

ŬR'ni-an
Avernian
Falernian
Hibernian
Saturnian

ŬR'nish-ing
burnishing
furnishing

ŬR'nish-ur
burnisher
furnisher

ŬR'ni-ti
alternity
diuternity
eternity
fraternity
maternity
modernity
paternity
sempiternity
taciturnity

ŬR'nur-i
fernery
turnery

ŬR'o-gat
surrogate
(cf. ĔR'o-gat)

ŬR'pen-tin
serpentine
turpentine

ŬR'sa-ri
anniversary
aspersory
bursary
controversary
cursory
nursery
percursory

ŬR'shi-al
controversial
(cf. ŬR'shal)

ŬR'shi-an
Cistercian

lacertian
Persian
(also as
ŬR'shan,
ŬR'zhan)

**ŬR'si-b'l,
ŬR'sa-b'l**
amerceable
conversable
conversible
coercible
immersible
incoercible
irreversible
reimbursable
reversible

ŬR'si-form
diversiform
ursiform
versiform

ŬR'siv-nes
coerciveness
detersiveness
discursiveness
excursiveness

ŬRth'les-nes
mirthlessness
worthlessness

ŬR'ti-tud
certitude
incertitude
inertitude

ŬR'van-si
conservancy
fervency

ŬR'va-tiv
conservative
curvative
enervative
observative
preservative
reservative

ŬR'zhun-ist
excursionist
immersionist
versionist

Ū'se-an, Ū'si-an
caducean
Confucian
Rosicrucian

Ū'sed'li
deucedly
lucidly
mucidly
pellucidly

Ū'sen-si
lucency
tralucency
translucency

Ū'shi-al
crucial
fiducial

Ū'shun-al
circumlocu-
    tional
constitutional
elocutional
evolutional
institutional
substitutional

ōld, ôr, ŏdd, oil, fŏŏt, out; ūse, ûrn, ŭp⁄ ΓHis, thin

Ū'shun-ist
circumlocution-
    ist
constitutionist
elocutionist
evolutionist
resolutionist
revolutionist

Ū'shun-ur
ablutioner
executioner
resolutioner
revolutioner

Ū'si-b'l
adducible
conducible
crucible
deducible
educible
inducible
irreducible
producible
reducible
seducible
traducible

Ū'siv-nes
abusiveness
allusiveness
conclusiveness
conduciveness
delusiveness
diffusiveness
effusiveness
exclusiveness
illusiveness
inconclusive-
    ness
inobtrusiveness

intrusiveness
obtrusiveness

ŬS'ki-li
duskily
huskily
muskily

ŬS'ku-lar
bimuscular
corpuscular
crepuscular
muscular

ŬS'ku-lus
corpusculous
crepusculous
musculous

Ū'so-ri
collusory
conclusory
delusory
elusory
exclusory
extrusory
illusory
lusory
prelusory
reclusory

ŬST'ful-i
distrustfully
lustfully
mistrustfully
trustfully

ŬST'i-b'l
adjustible
combustible
dustible

incombustible
(cf. bustable,
    etc.)

ŬS'ti-est
crustiest
dustiest
fustiest
gustiest
lustiest
mustiest
rustiest
trustiest

ŬS'ti-li
crustily
dustily
fustily
gustily
lustily
mustily
rustily
thrustily

ŬS'ti-nes
crustiness
dustiness
fustiness
gustiness
lustiness
mustiness
rustiness
trustiness

ŬS'tri-us
illustrious
industrious

ŬS'tur-ing
blustering
clustering

flustering
mustering

Ū'ta-b'l
commutable
computable
confutable
disputable
executable
immutable
imputable
incommutable
inscrutable
mootable
mutable
permutable
refutable
scrutable
suitable
transmutable

Ū'ta-tiv
commutative
confutative
disputative
imputative
putative
sputative
sternutative

Ū'te-us
beauteous
duteous
luteous

Ūth'ful-i
ruthfully
truthfully
youthfully

Ūth'ful-nes
truthfulness
youthfulness

Ūth'les-li
ruthlessly
truthlessly
youthlessly

ŬTH'ur-hood
brotherhood
motherhood

ŬTH'ur-i
brothery
mothery
smothery

ŬTH'ur-ing
brothering
mothering
smothering

ŬTH'ur-li
brotherly
motherly
southerly
unbrotherly
unmotherly

ŬTH'ur-lik
brotherlike
motherlike

Ū'ti-fi
beautify
brutify

Ū'ti-ful
beautiful
dutiful

Ū'ti-k'l, Ū'ti-kal
cuticle
latreutical
pharmaceutical
scorbutical
therapeutical

Ū'ti-ner
mutineer
scrutineer

Ū'ti-ni
mutiny
scrutiny

Ū'ti-nus
glutinous
mutinous
velutinous
scrutinous

ŬT'lur-i
cutlery
sutlery

ŬT'on-i
buttony
gluttony
muttony

Ū'tur-i
freebootery
fruitery
pewtery
rootery

ŬT'ur-ing
buttering
fluttering
guttering
muttering
spluttering
sputtering
stuttering
uttering

ŬT'ur-ur
butterer
flutterer
mutterer
splutterer
sputterer
stutterer
utterer

ŪV'a-b'l
approvable
immovable
improvable
irremovable
movable
provable
removable
reprovable

Ū'vi-al
alluvial
antediluvial
diluvial
effluvial
exuvial

fluvial
postdiluvial
pluvial

Ū'vi-an
antediluvian
diluvian
Peruvian
postdiluvian
Vesuvian

Ū'vi-us
Jupiter Pluvius
Vesuvius

Ū'za-b'l
amusable
confusable
diffusible
excusable
fusible
inexcusable
infusible
losable
transfusible
usable

Ū'zi-an
Carthusian
(cf. Ū'zhun)

ŬZ'ĭ-nes
fuzziness
muzziness
wuzziness

ōld, ôr, ŏdd, oil, fŏŏt, out; ūse, ûrn, ŭp; THis, thir